volume two

Understanding the American Experience

Recent Interpretations

VOLUME TWO

Understanding the American Experience

Recent Interpretations

edited by

James M. Banner, Jr.   *Princeton University*

Sheldon Hackney   *Princeton University*

Barton J. Bernstein   *Stanford University*

Under the General Editorship of
John Morton Blum, Yale University

Harcourt Brace Jovanovich, Inc.

New York   Chicago   San Francisco   Atlanta

ISBN: 0-15-592881-3

Library of Congress Catalog Card Number: 73-75178

Printed in the United States of America

Preface

These volumes present a selection of recent interpretations of major issues in American history from the colonial period to the present. They contain some of the most readable and provocative essays of many of the most thoughtful historians writing today. They also introduce recently developed historical methodologies that have uncovered neglected facts and generated significant interpretations, along with selections on subjects that have increasingly attracted historical concern, such as "inarticulate" classes, women, racial minorities, violence, and war.

We have grouped the readings into topical sections, many of which illustrate controversies among historians. We have provided an introduction for each essay that offers readers factual and historiographical information to assist them in understanding the argument. We have also in some cases raised criticisms that students will wish to consider. A short annotated bibliography of the most important related works follows each group of essays.

We wish to thank Dan T. Carter of the University of Maryland, Robert D. Cuff of York University, George M. Fredrickson of Northwestern University, James M. McPherson of Princeton University, Gary B. Nash of the University of California at Los Angeles, and Gordon S. Wood of Brown University for their advice in the preparation of the manuscript.

James M. Banner, Jr.
Sheldon Hackney
Barton J. Bernstein

Table of Contents

To Heal New Wounds

Reconstruction: Ultraconservative Revolution

Eric L. McKitrick

As Eric L. McKitrick of Columbia University states at the outset of the following essay, the Civil War and Reconstruction were "about" the status of blacks in American life. This is to say that slavery was a necessary cause of secession and the war, that emancipation became an important mechanism for winning the war and a symbol of one of its purposes, and that the fate of the freedmen depended on the outcome of Reconstruction. Even though there were many other motives that were irrelevant to, or inconsistent with, the racial equalitarianism of northern war aims, it is possible to think of the Civil War as a revolution launched by the North. The South, when it seceded, was striking out in a bold, preemptive counterrevolution.

Most historians now think of the Civil War and Reconstruction as a tragedy, although not because they still believe the myth of Black Reconstruction, according to which venal carpetbaggers and viciously ignorant ex-slaves ruled the South together and made a mockery of honest government and democracy during "the tragic era." The current view of this period emphasizes the positive achievements of radical governments, especially in the areas of constitutional

3

Richmond, Virginia, April 1865 (Library of Congress)

reform and the public education, and balances the
prevalence of corruption in the South against the
scandals of the Grant Administration, Boss Tweed in
New York, and the Great Barbecue of private greed
at public expense that characterized the early years of
the last third of the nineteenth century, which was
the Gilded Age in the North. Reconstruction was a
tragic chapter in American history because, despite
all the pain and suffering, it failed to achieve a new
position of dignity and equality for blacks. When the
Republican Party in Congress gave up its attempt to
force on the South a new balance of political power
based on a coalition of freedmen, poor whites,
carpetbaggers, and a few members of the antebellum
elite, it in effect decided that its political and
economic interests were better served through
cooperating with the native white elite and leaving
to them the task of finding a solution to the problem
of race relations. The result is still with us. This is one
more instance of betrayal in Afro-American history.

Perhaps the crucial question to ask about
Reconstruction is how it could have succeeded.
There have been several answers to this question in
the past. One, associated with William A. Dunning
(*Reconstruction, Political and Economic, 1865–1877**
[1907]), stresses the futility of trying to change by
coercion such deep-seated social attitudes as those
regarding race relations. The attempt of the North to
use military occupation and black political power to
alter permanently the relationships between races and
classes in the South was bound to fail because it only
induced hostility in the minds of those it was supposed
to change. Gradual amelioration through education
and economic improvement was the only sure way to
progress. This, in a much more sophisticated form, is
also the view expressed by Eric McKitrick in his
study *Andrew Johnson and Reconstruction* (1960)
and in the short comparative essay reprinted here. It is
a view that is favorable to Andrew Johnson and that
emphasizes the need to keep social change within the
existing framework of society.

The second answer is that the only thing wrong
with Congressional Reconstruction was that it did
not go far enough and that it stopped too soon. Had
the South been compelled to act equitably toward the

Reconstruction: Ultraconservative Revolution. From Chapter 11, "Reconstruction:
Ultraconservative Revolution," by Eric McKitrick in *The Comparative Approach to
American History* edited by C. Vann Woodward, pp. 146–59. Copyright © 1968 by
C. Vann Woodward.

freedmen for long enough, white southerners would eventually have accepted the new values. Unfortunately, the North, and particularly the Republican Party, was influenced from the beginning by ulterior motives, both political and economic, rather than by idealism. When Republican leaders Thaddeus Stevens and Charles Sumner died and the panic of 1873 provided a distraction, they quickly abandoned their radical policies and came to terms with the old ruling class in the South. John Hope Franklin (*Reconstruction: After the Civil War** [1951]) and Kenneth Stampp (*The Era of Reconstruction, 1865–1877** [1965]) are among the distinguished historians who lean toward this view.

There is a third answer, which is perhaps a variant of the second, and is argued most vigorously by LaWanda Cox in "The Promise of Land for the Freedmen" (*Mississippi Valley Historical Review*, XLV [December 1958]). According to her the major flaw of Reconstruction strategy was that the federal government did not give the freedman land. Actually, though plantation land was not confiscated and distributed to freedmen, the government did make some generally less desirable public land available to freedmen through homesteading procedures. Relatively little such land was taken up, and little of that which was claimed was kept, because freedmen lacked the capital and the education to make farming profitable. Without land, the freedman was easy prey to his old master who controlled land and credit; thus, his ballot was useless. The debates of the time, invoking as they did past revolutionary experience, show that the radicals were aware of the importance of giving the freedmen an economic base. But despite promises, efforts, and some Congressional action, land was not effectively made available to blacks, and they came out of Reconstruction as they went in, landless, poverty-stricken, and trapped into the new institution of debt peonage and tenantry.

Had the radicals succeeded in transferring usable land to the freedmen, blacks certainly would have been better off, at least for a while. It is difficult to believe, however, that land ownership and suffrage would have been enough to enable blacks to change the course of history in the South. To make blacks full participating citizens in 1865 probably would have taken a massive and long-term federal commitment. The federal government would have had to offer education, social services, and legal protection to the freedmen for more than a generation in order to try to prevent southern whites from capturing black land as they captured black votes. Solid evidence of the odds against which freedmen fought is provided by the fact that southern whites in the years following the end of Reconstruction were also increasingly forced into tenantry and the crop lien system and were eventually subjected to a curtailment of their suffrage.

Why was a massive effort by the government not undertaken? McKitrick theorizes that it was not so much that the southern counterrevolution eventually succeeded as that the northern revolution was from the first so timid. Preservation of the Union was the first war aim, and emancipation was dragged in only as a means to that end. During Presidential Reconstruction, getting the states readmitted to the Union took first priority, and the order of the day was to change as little as possible. The few radical Republicans in Congress with a revolutionary social policy for the South got control of Reconstruction policy only because of conflicting political ambitions within Congress, and perhaps because of the public's need for some sort of ritual capitulation or self-abasement on the part of the South. Even then, as McKitrick shows through a careful comparative technique, the measures taken were unprecedentedly mild.

At the conclusion of his essay, McKitrick, without elaborating his idea fully, suggests that the federal system was not adequate to cope with a social problem of the dimensions of the racial dilemma. One crucial difference between the 1860s and the 1960s, he says, was that in the earlier period race was never a national problem. We might ask to what degree that distinction is valid, and what explains the inability of the federal system in mid-nineteenth century America to deal more satisfactorily with the race question.

I

*I*t has been understood for some time that the American Civil War was a revolution. But more than a hundred years have had to pass before Americans can finally begin to understand what sort of revolution it actually was. Not so many years ago our historians were still arguing that the Civil War—"the Second American Revolution," as the late Charles Beard called it—represented the final victory of Northern capitalism in its relentless aggressions against the agrarian economy of the South, and that slavery was in no true sense the central issue. Such a point of view was first encouraged by Marx and Engels, who observed the war and followed its course with great interest, and arguments based on some version of that same viewpoint have not entirely disappeared from the discussions of historians even today. Other writers in turn have argued that the Civil War should not be considered as a Marxian revolution of North against South, but rather as a revolution of the South against the United States—that slavery *was* indeed the central issue, and that in order to preserve slavery the Southern states were willing to undertake a war of liberation. The true revolutionary act, then, was the South's effort to achieve separation from the Federal Union. And yet by viewing the Reconstruction that followed the Civil War, and by considering it and the war together as parts of the same process, we begin to see that perhaps the North was, in a larger sense, the revolutionary aggressor after all. Moreover, by connecting these events with the events of today as part of an even larger pattern, we may see at last what sort of revolution it really was. We may see that its deepest, most pressing, most fundamental issue was, and still is, the proper place of the American Negro in American life. And we may even wonder, as we consider the experience of Reconstruction, whether the American political and constitutional structure itself provides a truly adequate framework within which the revolution may be brought to a satisfactory as well as peaceful close.

It has been very difficult for historians or anyone else to view all this as a single revolutionary cycle. One reason is that the cycle has been so long: it began at least a generation before the Civil War and has not yet ended. But the more important reason is that its central problem—the Negro's place in American life—was one which Americans were never willing to confront directly, even at the most critical phases of the revolution, those of the Civil War and Reconstruction. This confusion, this ambiguity, this reluctance to face the implications of a problem of such magnitude, have had curious effects on Americans' very habits of historical thought. Despite the enormous and persistent interest in the Civil War, and despite the lesser but still considerable interest in Reconstruction, the latter period has become intellectually encapsulated. It has been isolated within the national consciousness and the national memory in a very unusual way, considering the things that a revolution does to a nation's life. With regard to the objectives of the Reconstruction, even of the Civil War, the quality of our writing, our thought, and our public discourse has been very diffuse and has shown a remarkable lack of precision. Nevertheless, the demands of the 1960's have made it clear that the revolution is not yet finished, that it has not gone nearly far enough, and that the original character of the revolution must be considered all over again.

The problem, indeed, was systematically quarantined from the very first, even while society was beginning to concede its urgency. In a way this is understandable. In almost every ordinary sense the United States on the eve of the Civil War was politically, socially, and economically one of the most stable countries in the world. A political and constitutional system had been established which was acceptable to virtually the entire population. It was characterized by universal white manhood suffrage and a level of citizen participation not seen since the days of the Greek republics. Its electoral practices may have included strong elements of demagoguery and vulgar carnival appeal, but the result was a system of party government which was in many respects the most sophisticated in the world. And whereas most European countries at mid-century were permeated with the ferment of social revolution, the United States was perhaps the one nation in the Western world where the overwhelming bulk of the population was profoundly committed to laissez-faire capitalism. It had no tory class, no tory socialism, no aristocracy with traditions of noblesse oblige or a sense of responsibility for checking the excesses of laissez faire. American society, as Tocqueville had discovered a generation earlier, had become intensely egalitarian and intensely committed to the ideal of equal opportunity and careers open to talent. It would be difficult for most Europeans to understand that those values normally regarded elsewhere as "bourgeois" were in 1860 the values of the American farmer, the American workingman, and the American entrepreneur.

All of these values were embodied in the career and person of Abraham Lincoln, who was to be the leader of the "revolutionary" party of 1860. Lincoln, rising from the poorest possible origins, largely self-educated, a leader in politics while still a young man, becoming a successful railroad lawyer, and emerging from state politics in Illinois to become the Republican nominee for the Presidency, insisted again and again that there was no real gulf between capital and labor. "There is no permanent class of hired laborers amongst us," he announced in one of several speeches he made on this subject in 1859. "Twenty-five years ago, I was a hired laborer. The hired laborer of yesterday, labors on his own account today; and will hire others to labor for him to-morrow. Advancement—improvement in condition—is the order of things in a society of equals." Probably few men of any class who heard these words would have thought of doubting their essential truth. For most Americans living in the North, this highly satisfactory state of affairs had come to be directly connected with the continued stability of the Federal Union. The one great flaw in it, as Lincoln reminded his audiences in each of these speeches, was the continued existence of a very rigid system of chattel slavery.

Americans had inevitably been brought to confront this problem. But they did so reluctantly, despite the steady growth of antislavery feeling which had already begun to force itself into national politics by the 1840's. This feeling could only be admitted into the realm of political discourse and contention by placing all stress upon the Union and virtually none upon the Negro, in order to maintain some sort of unity even in the North. It was done not by a direct assault upon slavery, but through the formula of "Free Soil": not by challenging slavery where it was, but by declaring that it should not be carried into new places where it did not yet exist. In short, men did face the issue, but they deliberately avoided facing it directly as long as they possibly could.

Even after the war broke out, they continued to avoid it. In order to prevent the alienation of a sizable portion of the Northern people, to say nothing of the border states which had not seceded, the administration felt it necessary to declare that its sole purpose in waging war was to restore the

Federal Union. Lincoln announced this on many occasions in the most solemn tones. "I would save the Union," he insisted;

> I would save it the shortest way under the Constitution. The sooner the national authority can be restored, the nearer the Union will be 'the Union as it was.' . . . My paramount object in this struggle is to save the Union, and is *not* either to save or to destroy slavery.

And yet the man to whom this was written—Horace Greeley, editor of the influential New York *Tribune*—himself represented a growing sector of public opinion which was insisting that emancipation should be made one of the objects of the war. It had already become obvious to Lincoln by the summer of 1862 that without the support of this sector the continued vigor of the war effort might itself be undermined; and although he had told Greeley, "If I could save the Union without freeing any slave, I would do it," he also conceded that if he "could do it by freeing all the slaves," he would do that. But if he conceded this much, he was hardly prepared to go the whole way, because he too understood public opinion, probably better than Greeley. The Emancipation Proclamation (which, according to one of our historians, "had all the moral grandeur of a bill of lading") was presented not as a statement of high purpose but as a measure of military necessity.

It was the same with regard to the use of Negro troops in the Union Army. Two objectives might be served by accepting Negro enlistments. One of them directly concerned the Negro himself: "Once let the black man get upon his person the brass letters, U.S.," as the Negro abolitionist Frederick Douglass expressed it, ". . . and there is no power on earth which can deny that he has earned the right to citizenship in the United States." The other was that Negro soldiers might augment the declining strength of the army and thus assist in suppressing the rebellion. Of the two objectives, the Northern public would accept only the second. Even this could occur only after the war was well under way, and after many discouraging military reverses. Few concessions were made to the Negro's representing any more than a matter of military policy. Negro regiments could have no Negro officers, and the United States Congress refused to grant them equal pay with white troops until the war was nearly over. The Negro's proper role, even in the society of wartime, could not be considered on its own terms, but only in the interest of some other objective. Even the President, despite his "oft-expressed personal wish that all men everywhere could be free," could still think of no more satisfactory way of dealing with slaves who had been freed than to encourage them to leave the country. His "first impulse," he had stated in 1854, "would be to free all the slaves and send them to Liberia"; eight years later, on the very eve of emancipation, he was earnestly urging a committee of Negro leaders to colonize themselves and their families in Central America, as the best example that could be offered to American Negroes everywhere.

II

Once the war was over, the problem of dealing both with the Negro and with the readmission of Southern states to the Federal Union dominated all else. But all emphasis was placed upon the latter. And again, the first instinct was to change as little as possible. By constitutional amendment the Negro had been given his freedom, but few steps were taken to adjust him to his new status. At the same time elaborate efforts were made by the administration of Lincoln's successor, Andrew Johnson, to reestablish state governments in the South which would be more or less identical with those in existence before the war. Certain things were rejected almost out of hand. There was to be no redistribution of land, either with or without compensation. There was no insistence that Negroes be accorded rights of citizenship. Federal responsibility for education and welfare was regarded as being only of the most temporary and limited kind. Legislation to expand even the minimal services of this sort that did exist—those performed by the wartime Freedmen's Bureau—was opposed by the President, and there were not enough votes in the national Congress to enact it over his veto. It is certainly true that the President's position on these questions lagged behind that of the Republican majority in Congress, and perhaps even somewhat behind the center position in public opinion. But the differences, in 1865 and 1866, were hardly more than differences in degree.

The revolution was destined to go considerably further than anything Andrew Johnson had in mind. But its conservative nature would still be such, even at its height, as to make it hardly comparable to any other revolutionary or counterrevolutionary movement known to modern Western history. Not one political prisoner, for example, was ever put to death. The political head of the rebellion was kept in prison for two years and then set free, while the rebellion's military chief was never molested at all. The President of the United States spent much of his time during the first year of peace over matters of amnesty and pardon; and a few years later, while Congressional Reconstruction was still in full force, an act of general amnesty in effect removed that problem from further contention altogether. The government of Soviet Russia was executing enemies of the Revolution years after the Revolution itself was over. Even in England, whose revolution was one of the earliest and mildest, the revolutionary party felt it expedient to execute the head of the state, after having done away with his two chief advisors, and to massacre priests, women, and children in Ireland. With the Restoration, only the genial disposition of the king himself prevented a blood bath of vengeance and limited the number of executions to a dozen regicides.

The political, constitutional, legal, and administrative changes effected in the United States through the Civil War and Reconstruction were almost invisible compared with those that remained in France from the French Revolution, even after the restoration of the Bourbon monarchy. There, the provincial boundaries of the Old Regime were eliminated forever (in the America of 1865 and 1866, the very thought of such a thing made men turn pale with consternation); while the new geographical boundaries were designed in such a way that the resulting "departments" could be uniformly administered through the central government in Paris. (In the American South, even today, mere "interference" by the central government is the issue most likely to unite the entire population.) The most sweeping changes in property, class, fiscal, and jurisdictional relationships throughout French society, effected by the Revolution and codified by Bonaparte, were never reversed despite all efforts by the Bourbons to turn back the clock. The American "Bourbons," as the South's post-Reconstruction leaders were called, hardly needed to turn back the clock at all. No changes on this scale had been effected in the first place. As for the emancipated slaves, far less was done for them by the United States government in the way of land redistribution and social planning than was done during that very same period for the emancipated serfs of autocratic imperial Russia.

By 1867 the extraordinary refusal of President Andrew Johnson to co-operate with Northern leadership on any of the problems of readjustment, plus the determination of the South to resist even the minimal implications of change, had brought the North—still reluctantly—to see the need for stronger measures. The result was called "Radical Reconstruction." These measures, designed to protect Negroes and those Southern whites who had supported the Union, represented the high point of revolutionary action. The military occupation, followed by the enfranchisement of the entire Negro male population, the temporary disqualification of former Confederate leaders from suffrage and officeholding, and the establishment and support of state governments heavily dependent upon Negro votes and operated by pro-Union whites and Negroes constituted the closest thing to a revolutionary situation that was reached.

This situation, which began deteriorating almost at once, lasted no more than a few years. By 1877 all of the so-called "Radical" state governments had been expelled, mostly through the force of local pressure. Two general criticisms of this experiment may be made, not counting the traditional one that the Southern white people had been forced for a time to accept regimes which they did not want. One is that this relatively radical political program was not accompanied by anything systematic in the way of social and economic welfare. Much of what was accomplished in matters of education, for example, had to be undertaken through private efforts by Northern philanthropic groups, and in the face of enormous local resistance. There was no confiscation of estates, and no systematic effort to aid the freedmen in acquiring holdings of their own. Thus it might be said that the true priorities were reversed: that the Negro was given the vote before he had either the education or the economic power that would enable him to make effective use of it. The other criticism is that, even if it were granted that political rights ought to have come first after all, the federal government was still unprepared to undertake the massive commitment of long-term supervision, combined with continuing force, that would have been needed to preserve those rights.

Thus in the face of corruption, inefficiency, and chronic local aggression and unrest, the federal government gradually withdrew its support and allowed the white community in each state to re-establish full control. By 1877 the political, social, and economic systems of the South had become remarkably similar to what they had been in 1860, except that now the Negro was a landless laborer rather than a legally bound slave. A final stage of reaction remained. In the general effort to reconstitute the structure which had been disrupted by the Civil War and Reconstruction, even the Negro's small political gains—to say nothing of the minimal social rights he had acquired, in no way commensurate with the total effort and sacrifices implied in that war—were systematically removed. One by one, and with no interference whatever, the Southern states now began by law to impose systems of social segregation and disfranchisement which set the Negro entirely outside the mainstream of Southern civic life. By 1900 the process was virtually complete.

III

Without a clear center of gravity, historical discussion of this entire problem has had a somewhat erratic character. For the most part, it has been considered well within the context of the American constitutional system, and with very cautious assumptions, quite orthodox and traditional, as to where the boundaries of that system are located. One line of thought, probably more persistent than any other, regards the whole episode of Reconstruction with the most profound distaste, because it prolonged into peacetime the internal conflicts and alienations which had driven the American people into fratricidal war. The Civil War and Reconstruction thus represented a breach that must above all be healed, smoothed over, reknit. Perhaps the definitive statement of this position was made by Paul Buck in his *Road to Reunion, 1865–1900*. Yet it may also be significant that the terminal date of Professor Buck's study coincides with that very point in time at which the Negro's own exclusion from American society had been made all but complete.

My own study of Andrew Johnson's role in Reconstruction, published seven years ago, also assumes reunion to be a primary value, without questioning the limits of the system as it then existed. I argued, perhaps somewhat conservatively, that within those limits, and without violating the basic assumptions and values of the most enlightened men of the time, far more might have been done toward solving the problems of reconstruction, as well as of reunion, than was in fact done. And yet these assumptions might themselves be questioned. An English historian of great perception and intelligence, William R. Brock, has recently looked at the subject of Reconstruction through the eyes of an outsider. He concludes that the very system of federalism, as established by the Constitution and construed by two generations of pre-Civil War Americans, was simply not adequate for the containment of a problem of such dimensions and magnitude.

As the problem confronts us all over again in the 1960's, we might well consider the bare possibility, at least, of Brock's being right. It could be argued that the decision to commit federal power to reconstruction would not have been taken at all but for the abnormal stimulus of a crisis between the executive and legislative branches of the federal government. Then, as the will to maintain that commitment began to wane, there remained to the states—thanks to the federal "balance"—all the power they needed to expel with relative ease those features of Reconstruction they found not to their liking. By the turn of the century the states, using the authority of their state governments to render federal law inoperative, could place restrictions on the political and social rights of Negroes which the judicial branch of the federal government could overlook only by allowing the law to be construed in a highly strained and dubious way. These restrictions—virtual disfranchisement and complete social segregation—remained until World War II almost wholly unchallenged. As late as 1964 the Assistant Attorney General in charge of civil rights, Burke Marshall, was not optimistic about the future of federal law enforcement. At that time Mr. Marshall devoted two public lectures at a major university to the inherent restrictions imposed by the very structure of the federal system. Even the guarantee of voting rights, despite a series of federal laws beginning in 1957 which simply attempted to enforce the Fifteenth Amendment, had been for practical purposes frustrated in innumerable Southern communities.

Thus in view of what is minimally indispensable to complete the revolution begun with emancipation and Reconstruction, the restrictions of the federal structure do indeed seem formidable. The minimum obligations go well beyond political rights. They include full employment and whatever is necessary to guarantee it: special programs of training, the full opening of union membership, and the elimination of job discrimination. They include massive support for education, recognizing that the need for special compensatory instruction enormously complicates a problem complex enough already. They include a vast expansion of municipal recreation facilities, and automatic government responsibility in all cases of major social disturbance. They include adequate housing, which means not simply a great deal more low-cost public housing but open access to all housing, even to the point of public guarantees of property values. Whatever the present restrictions of the federal structure, it seems imperative that any real movement toward realizing these aims requires a national government with the power to act.

And yet this is hardly as utopian as may now appear, nor need one be so quick to assume that the governmental structure of federalism is the truly critical factor. History itself shows us otherwise. It is rather a question of the community's will to use what powers its federal government already has. Mr. Marshall's pessimism in 1964 over Negro voter registration, for example, was rendered to a considerable extent out of date after two more years of focused federal legislation and effort, and resistance to Negro registration is no longer the major issue it was then. Or, to go back a full century: although there was not the remotest constitutional precedent for the Reconstruction legislation of 1867, the majority found a constitutional sanction for it anyway, strained though it may have been, in the obligation of Congress to guarantee to each state a republican form of government. During the New Deal period of the 1930's, federal intervention in state affairs went beyond anything most men would have thought possible a few years before. And this was nothing to the vast scope which federal power allowed itself for the purposes of fighting World War II. Controlling and directing the entire national economy, and in effect regulating the lives of millions of people, both military and civilian, the federal government impinged itself on the rights of the citizenry to a degree vastly exceeding anything that would be required to fulfill every demand of the Negro revolution. The difference was that in its objectives the government had the overwhelming support of the entire society.

It is a matter not so much of the government's defining its powers as the community's defining its needs. Even the "revolutionary" terminology I have been using up to now may be more confusing than enlightening. The problem of the Negro's place in American life was one which, despite the upheavals of emancipation and Reconstruction, had by 1900 been solved in a way that a majority of Americans found satisfactory. A majority today is finding that same "solution" not only unsatisfactory but intolerable. Times have changed, and it is not simply the moral weather that has changed; the very conditions of community life have changed.

The "revolution," if we wish to go on calling it that, has shifted to the Northern cities, and thinking on federal civil rights policy has shifted from voting rights to matters of much broader social and economic significance. The problem of race relations is now of such a nature that it can no longer be encapsulated as it could be in post-Reconstruction times. Moreover, the problem is inexorable; its dynamic element is an increasing concentration of Negroes in urban areas, and the lives of a majority of Americans are coming to be tied in more and more ways to the condition of the Negro community. Whatever the immediate vicissitudes of the question—the "backlash" vote in the 1966 elections, the continued preference of Southern communities for segregationist candidates, the failure of the 1966 civil rights bill— the problem will not go away. It is there, and there it remains; no one living in an American city can escape it.

The situation contains elements today which it did not have in Reconstruction, and broadening the battleground to include the Northern cities has perhaps for the first time provided a base upon which the problem can be—as indeed it must be—truly nationalized. In such a setting there is no longer any way to avoid dealing with the Negro as a functioning part of the community's economic, social, and political life. It is here that the pressure and energy needed to sustain a high level of federal concern are most likely to be generated, and as a more and more substantial portion of the decision-making community accustoms itself to acting systematically and conceiving policy in massive terms, the sooner a base will be built upon which permanent national standards may be formed.

The complexities of the federal system have often functioned in an inhibitive way, and pockets of regional resistance have traditionally operated to undermine the national will. And yet whenever standards of national necessity have had majority support, and where majority will has been present for insisting upon such standards, the abstract rigidities of the federal system have had a way of becoming surprisingly fluid. History does provide us tests for this. They are, as I have said, such as may be found in the depression years of the 1930's, in World War II, in the Civil War, and even— though in a form we can now see as much too temporary—in Reconstruction.

The Strange Career of a Historical Controversy

C. Vann Woodward

In 1955, on the eve of the massive assault on the system of racial segregation in the South, C. Vann Woodward, now the Sterling Professor of History at Yale University, published a pathbreaking study of race relations in the South which struck a heavy blow against the myth that racial segregation was an age-old institution. The thesis of his book *The Strange Career of Jim Crow* was that following Reconstruction there was a period of some years in which the socially prescribed roles of blacks were not clearly defined and were not established by law. It was an era "of experiment and variety in race relations of the South in which segregation was not the invariable rule." This period of flux was brought to a close between 1890 and 1910 by the passage of laws throughout the South that made rigid and formal and uniform a policy of physical separation of the races in almost all areas of life.

The fresh aspect of Woodward's findings was that the establishment of Jim Crow was not the immediate and automatic reaction of whites at the end of slavery, but that it was a delayed reaction that did not occur until thirty or forty years later. It is important to note that Woodward was not arguing that racial prejudice in the South was unknown before the onset of Jim Crow laws, but that legal segregation as an expression of the dominant group's attitude toward the minority was only one of many possible expressions of white racism and that it arrived on the scene relatively late. By implication, the late nineteenth century was a period of missed opportunities and alternative roads not taken.

As Woodward notes in the following essay, others have challenged but not overturned his original thesis. While many previous examples of the legal separation of the races, in both North and South, can be found, the problem is not really to locate the first occurrence of segregation but to locate the time and place at which the entire pattern of race relations changed in form and segregation became standard. Woodward's answer to that problem is the best we have.

In the essay reprinted here, Woodward goes on to address the question of why segregation appeared. In a brilliantly underplayed use of the comparative method and of concepts borrowed from the social sciences, the author argues that physical separation is an aspect of the competitive style of race relations that replaced the paternalistic style characteristic of societies based on human bondage. In the slave system, the social distance between the races is so clear and so well understood that no other emblem of superiority and inferiority is necessary. According to Woodward, the United States since the Civil War has been in a period in which the paternalistic and competitive styles of race relations overlap. Aspects of paternalism persist here and there even while physical and legal separation, insisted on by members of the dominant group who are coming into competition with the subordinate group, begin to dominate the pattern of race relations.

One needs also to explain why in the years around 1900 informal paternalism suddenly gave way to legal codes of segregation. Woodward argues forcefully that this was the result not of any great change in economic relationships, but that it was a political necessity. Upper-class whites who had previously acquiesced in the demands of militant blacks during Reconstruction years for open access to public accommodations and job opportunities were frightened in the 1890s by the insurgency of lower-class whites. In order to maintain their own

The Strange Career of a Historical Controversy. From *American Counterpoint: Slavery and Race in the North-South Dialogue* by C. Vann Woodward (Boston: Little, Brown, 1971), pp. 234–60. Copyright © 1971 by C. Vann Woodward. Reprinted by permission of Little, Brown and Co.

political position, the patricians abandoned racial paternalism in favor of legal segregation as demanded by whites who felt themselves to be increasingly in competition with blacks.

There were undoubtedly other forces making for change in race relations in the period from the end of Reconstruction to the First World War. It is instructive to try to identify all the pressures for change and to wonder if it could have happened differently. Given Woodward's model of paternalism and competition as styles of race relations, one is also left to ponder the style of race relations in the North and how the northern pattern at any particular time compares with the southern.

One traditional way we have of arriving at historical truth—or more accurately groping for it—might be described as adversary procedure. The term, like the method, suggests the court of law, with its assumption of opposing if not antagonistic claims and its presumptions that any litigant deserves a hearing for the best case that can be made for his cause. This tradition thrusts historians rather arbitrarily and awkwardly into the role of advocates. Their adjustment has not always been a happy one. In response to Shakespeare's admonition, "Do as adversaries do in law,/Strive mightily, but eat and drink as friends," historians have unfortunately been more likely to follow the first rather than the second part. Too often they have tended to think of the adversary in the manner of Milton when he capitalized the word and left no doubt to Whom he was referring. Rejecting the more genial convention of barristers, historians have too readily fallen in with the lawyer's less fortunate habit of being more concerned about winning the suit than about pursuing the truth.

Examples of adversary procedure abound in our historical literature. So numerous are they and so cooperative the historians in providing examples, that teachers have seized upon them as the meat of history and a method of pedagogy. Publishers have obligingly packaged them in reprint combinations, organizing whole series of books along the adversary-procedure line. So taught and obliged so to read, students have come to perceive history in this manner, and to think and speak in either-or terms of such complicated aspects of American history as priority in the origins of slavery or race prejudice, democratic-or-aristocratic colonial government, motives of the Constitution framers, and the causes of the War of 1812. Students and professors fall readily into making simplistic dichotomies in treating the origins and character of abolitionists, Jacksonian Democrats, Radical Republicans, Scalawags and Carpetbaggers, Mugwumps, Populists, Progressives, New Dealers, and Cold Warriors. The students are not to blame, and it is difficult to say whether the teachers, the publishers, or the historians bear the greatest share of responsibility.

Historians are sometimes trapped unawares in the role of advocate in an adversary procedure. Typically, one of them will hit upon a new way of looking at an old question, or a new answer, a new interpretation, or a new question to ask of old data. Since it *is* new, he will emphasize it, perhaps overemphasize it in his publication simply to overcome the weight of presumption against any challenge of accepted views. In time, allies will rally to his support with reviews, articles, and books that sustain his new findings, facts, interpretations, and strengthen his conviction that he is right. The challenge is on the way to becoming the Accepted View. Should the new view sustain hope for public policies and support for views in public controversy which the author shares, his sympathies may become involved with his vanity as investments in his thesis. Faced eventually with adverse criticism and evidence that contradicts his thesis, he is tempted to assume a defensive posture. He may well become more resentful on seeing his meaning misconstrued or distorted for polemical advantage. And even more so on seeing the young, thoroughly indoctrinated with the notion that adversarial notoriety is the approved ladder to advancement in the guild, join the pack in hot pursuit. In these circumstances, historians of stature have been known to stoop to vituperative exchanges with their opponents in public print. Along with the pursuit of truth, the Shakespearean ideal of genial adversaries is likely to be abandoned, and in its place there comes to prevail something more resembling the concept of the Apostle Peter: "Your adversary, the devil, as a roaring lion, walketh about, seeking whom he may devour."

The instance of adversarial historiography under scrutiny here—the literature on the origins and development of racial segregation in the American South—is a minor and not altogether typical one. The literature of the subject illustrates some, but fortunately not all—and particularly not the recriminatory and vituperative—aspects of the model described above. In fact, the present writer was able to say in summing up the criticisms of his thesis in 1966 that, "Without exception, they have been offered in a spirit of detachment, generosity, and courtesy that I shall try to emulate in making use of their findings and dealing with their criticisms in revising my own work."[1] There is no guarantee, of course, of such continued good fortune in the maintenance of decorum and the attraction of Shakespearean adversaries. Since no end to the controversy yet seems in sight, it might be well to survey its course and if possible lay it to rest before any serious breach in good manners occurs. One purpose in so doing is to see if there is any mutually agreeable reformulation of the problem that will get at its essence better than previous formulations. If so, it might release the historians from their adversarial involvement and obligations and permit them all to retire from the contest with honor. It might also serve to redirect energies for the pursuit of truth that might otherwise be spent in the winning of a suit.

[1] C. Vann Woodward, *The Strange Career of Jim Crow*, second revised ed. (New York, 1966), vii. Subsequent references will be to this edition, but there have been two others, the original in 1955 and a first revision in 1957.

It began in a mild way with a series of lectures in the fall of 1954 that were published the following year. The thesis was relatively simple, though it was guardedly advanced and elaborately qualified, and the implications were *not* simple. Briefly stated, the thesis was, first, that racial segregation in the South in the rigid and universal form it had taken did not appear with the end of slavery, but toward the latter years of the century and later; and second, that before it appeared in this form there transpired an era of experiment and variety in race relations of the South in which segregation was not the invariable rule.

The initial response had little to do with scholarly scruple and research. In this respect the origins-of-segregation question bears a resemblance to another and older example of adversarial historiography, the origins-of-slavery problem. In his account of the latter controversy, Winthrop D. Jordan points out that passions were stirred because if race prejudice were a consequence of slavery, the hope for eliminating prejudice was better than if slavery were a consequence of prejudice.[2] Similarly the thesis about the development of segregation in the South had immediate implications both for the embattled defenders and the crusading opponents of racial segregation. If the thesis were sound, then the traditional defenses of segregation were breached and weakened because they pictured the system as entrenched in immemorial and unbroken usage and quite beyond the reach of legal action. And again, if the system were of relatively recent origin and was itself the result of political and legal action, then reformers might take hope that segregation was not all that invulnerable and that the law might be used effectively to bring about change. Usefulness to reformers or embarrassment to conservatives should, of course, never be regarded as an admissible test of the validity of any historical thesis. Yet the time and attention of the author were initially (and for a long time) preoccupied, not with answering historical criticism, but with attempting to correct misreadings, distortions, and misuses of his work by partisans in a raging debate over public policy. No, he had not said that segregation was superficially rooted or easily eradicated; it was rooted in prejudices older than slavery and might be as difficult to uproot. No, he had never suggested that the period after reconstruction was a golden age of race relations. Yes, he was quite aware that *de facto* segregation normally antedated *de jure* segregation and that it was widely practiced in several areas before the 1890's. And so forth and so on.

Scholarly response was slower in coming. In publishing his thesis, the author had observed that his subject was relatively new and inadequately explored, that he would inevitably make mistakes, and that he would "expect and hope to be corrected." In this he was not to be disappointed. Initially, however, the corrective scholarship took the form of extending the investigation backward in time and arriving at findings not incompatible with the original thesis. The author had confined his study to the South. In 1961, Leon F. Litwack published a path-breaking study of race relations in the North before the Civil War which demonstrated that Negroes of the free

2 Winthrop D. Jordan, "Modern Tensions and the Origins of American Slavery," *Journal of Southern History*, XXVII (1962), 18–30.

states were segregated "in virtually every phase of existence" and that the Jim Crow system had been thoroughly established in the North before moving South.[3] Subsequent studies of the Northwestern states supported these findings and sustained Tocqueville's observation that "The prejudice of race appears to be stronger in the states that have abolished slavery than in those where it still exists; and nowhere is it so intolerant as in those states where servitude has never been known."[4]

While these findings required no alteration of the thesis as applied to the South, other findings did. Richard C. Wade in 1964 discovered a rudimentary but unmistakable pattern of segregation in some of the larger cities of the antebellum slave states. It was not uniform, never complete, and enforcement was not rigid, but it was undoubtedly present. Since less than 2 percent of the total slave population lived in the cities, however, and since urban life was so uncharacteristic of the Old South, this evidence did not disturb the validity of the thesis in the rural and typical South. Moreover, Wade's evidence of physical proximity and intimacy of the races in residential, social, and sexual relations in cities—far greater than in the North—gave more emphasis to close contact and association than to separation of black and white.[5] But in South Carolina, according to a study of the Negro during Reconstruction in that state by Joel Williamson published the following year, the slave experience of "constant, physical intimacy between the races" came to an abrupt end with slavery. "Well before the end of Reconstruction," he writes, "separation had crystallized into a comprehensive pattern which, in its essence, remained unaltered until the middle of the twentieth century." In fact, he goes so far as to say that "the pattern of separation was fixed in the minds of the whites almost simultaneously with the emancipation of the Negro."[6] Of course this seemed irreconcilable with the disputed thesis. If Williamson were right about South Carolina, and if that state were not wholly untypical of others, little remained to be said in defense of the thesis.

In the meantime, however, quite opposite conclusions were announced in studies of the other Southern states. A monograph on Virginia by Charles E. Wynes concluded that "the Woodward thesis is essentially sound. Of course certain qualifications must be made, but they do not destroy or greatly impair its essential validity."[7] A book on North Carolina by Frenise A. Logan contained similar endorsement of the thesis and the assurance "that segregation and white supremacy, certainly as they pertain to North Carolina, are products of twentieth-century Southern-White mentality," that "between 1865 and 1898 North Carolina witnessed only a few of 'the policies of proscription, segregation, and disfranchisement' which were later to

[3] Leon F. Litwack, *North of Slavery: The Negro in the Free States, 1790–1860* (Chicago, 1961).

[4] Eugene H. Berwanger, *The Frontier Against Slavery: Western Anti-Negro Prejudice and the Slavery Extension Controversy* (Urbana, 1967); V. Jacque Voegeli, *Free but Not Equal: The Midwest and the Negro During the Civil War* (Chicago, 1967).

[5] Richard C. Wade, *Slavery in the Cities: The South 1820–1860* (New York, 1964).

[6] Joel Williamson, *After Slavery: The Negro in South Carolina During Reconstruction, 1861–1877* (Chapel Hill, 1965), 274, 275, 298.

[7] Charles E. Wynes, *Race Relations in Virginia, 1870–1902* (Charlottesville, Va., 1961), 148–150.

characterize Negro-White relations in that state."[8] A more recent monograph by Margaret Law Callcott concludes that "Maryland's experience seems to fit readily into this pattern," that the extension of segregation "into public transportation, residential housing, and public accommodations grew out of the purposefully generated racism that marked the return of the Democratic party to power in 1900," and that this was "a new and startling development" with which Maryland Negroes "were frankly unfamiliar."[9] Other works under way or already published supported the thesis in various ways.[10]

In 1968 Joel Williamson compiled and edited briefs of the long adversary procedure up to that date—pro and con, old and new—under the title, *The Origins of Segregation.*[11] One could not hope for fairer or more scrupulous treatment from an editor, nor could one find in the entire roster of contemporary American historians one who combined more naturally a devotion to the pursuit of truth with an adherence to the Shakespearean tradition of adversarial ethic. He placed all parties to the controversy in his debt. That debt would have increased had he been able thereby to put an end to the whole controversy, but unfortunately this lay beyond his power—perhaps beyond the power of anyone. The adversary procedure appears to be endowed with autonomous powers of self-perpetuation.

It surfaced next in the learned journals, in one of which appeared an article elaborating for New Orleans the investigations of Richard Wade on antebellum race relations in Southern cities and coming to much the same conclusions. It was a picture of whites "mixing freely with Negroes in colored taverns, bawdy houses, and dance halls," a scene where Negroes enjoyed "an unusual scope of freedom," where "Negroes, free and slave, made a mockery of the 'Sambo' stereotype," and where "control over the Negro population was, in short, virtually nonexistent." Antebellum segregation laws are presented as evidence of frantic white efforts to curb mixing and separate the races. Unlike Wade, however, this author identifies his picture of antebellum urban experiments in segregation with the twentieth-century system, holding that "both systems effected a thoroughgoing separation of the races . . . in nearly every area of public activity."[12] Unfortunately the author overlooked a previously published study of race relations in the same state which assembled massive evidence that "the Woodward thesis is basically sound for Louisiana between 1877 and 1898. . . . Clearly segregation in Louisiana did not exist before 1898 as a permanent and thorough system of race relations."[13] Called to account for his oversight, the author of the New Orleans study admitted that this city presented "a

[8] Frenise A. Logan, *The Negro in North Carolina, 1876–1894* (Chapel Hill, N.C., 1964), vii–viii, 180.

[9] Margaret Law Callcott, *The Negro in Maryland Politics, 1870–1912* (Baltimore, 1969), ix–x, 134–135.

[10] Vernon L. Wharton, *The Negro in Mississippi, 1865–1890* (Chapel Hill, 1967); George B. Tindall, *The South Carolina Negroes, 1877–1900* (Columbia, S.C., 1952).

[11] Joel Williamson (ed.), *The Origins of Segregation* (New York, 1968).

[12] Roger A. Fischer, "Racial Segregation in Ante Bellum New Orleans," *American Historical Review*, LXXIV (February 1969), 926–37.

[13] Henry C. Dethloff and Robert P. Jones, "Race Relations in Louisiana, 1877–1898," *Louisiana History*, IX (Fall, 1968), 322.

decidedly unique situation," that his article was "not so much an attack on the 'Woodward thesis' as it was a rejection of certain dogmatic Woodwardian disciples," and that his departure from the former represented only a "delicate difference."[14]

The latest efforts of reconciliation are those of August Meier and Elliott Rudwick, two prominent historians of American race relations. "It is our belief," they write, "that the views of Woodward on the one hand, and Williamson and Wade, on the other, are both correct."[15] The substantive suggestions and findings of these two scholars deserve and will receive full consideration. In passing, however, one is reminded of the efforts of historians at the crest of American nationalism to reconcile North and South on the occasion of the semicentennial anniversary of the Civil War. "Both sides were right!" declared one of them. "Neither could have given in and remained true to itself."[16] One would like to believe that the latest effort of conciliation might be more successful than the earlier one, but the prospect was not very reassuring. In spite of the relatively bloodless and decorous character of the segregation controversy and the civilized deference with which most of the disputants have treated opponents, escalation seemed to be more indicated than abatement—the disposition to "remain true" more prevalent than the impulse to "give in." Investments of time, defenses of vanity, and the loyalties of allies all made their demands. More additions to the already formidable shelf of monographs, pro and con, were on the way, and as the shelf lengthened the patience of readers shortened. One collector of historical fallacies inadvertently contributed one of his own making by impatiently dismissing one side of the argument as "wrong in all major parts."[17] Even if the preponderance of new studies continued to sustain the disputed thesis, as in the past, they would not resolve the controversy. The prospect of continued proliferation of monographs, pro and con, may well be viewed with dismay.

What is needed is a theory, a model, perhaps a typology of race relations that would conceive of the historical problem of segregation not as one of dating origins at a point in linear time but of accounting for the phenomenon in whatever degree it appears. Such a model might accommodate pieces of evidence that seem contradictory when arrayed in the present formulation of the problem. Several suggestions have been made, to two of which the present writer has been invited to subscribe but finds himself unable to accept. One is "an evolutionary concept of segregation."[18] This suggests a gradual and organic growth over a prolonged span of time, which does not accommodate the evidence of long periods of dormance and sudden bursts of proliferation. A second proposal is that segregation be

[14] Letter to the Editor from Dethloff and Jones and reply from Fischer, *American Historical Review*, LXXV (October 1969), 326–27.

[15] August Meier and Elliott Rudwick, "A Strange Chapter in the Career of 'Jim Crow,'" in a collection edited by the same authors, *The Making of Black America: Essays in Negro Life and History* (2 vols., New York, 1969), II, 15.

[16] Emerson D. Fite, *The Presidential Campaign of 1860* (New York, 1911), 195–96.

[17] David Hackett Fischer, *Historian's Fallacies: Toward a Logic of Historical Thought* (New York, 1970), 148–49.

[18] Roger A. Fischer, Letter to the Editor, *American Historical Review*, LXXV (October 1969), 327.

viewed as "a cyclical development."[19] But this suggests a pattern of regularity and predictability without a causal explanation and without sufficient examples from history to provide a test. A third idea would have it "that industrialization is a master agent of social transformation" in race relations. The most persuasive critique of this theory, however, concludes that "available evidence everywhere sustains the thesis that when introduced into a racially ordered society industrialization conforms to the alignment and code of the racial order." Changes in the racial pattern arise mainly from political, not industrial pressures.[20] No clearer instance of this can be found than in the industrialization of the South. None of the three proposed theories seems very helpful.

More promising are theories derived from comparative history and sociology. Pierre L. van den Berghe works out a typology of race relations based on a comparison of the history of Mexico, Brazil, the United States, and South Africa. The "two ideal types" of race relations that he proposes are the "paternalistic" and its opposite, the "competitive," which he thinks of as parallel with the distinction between *Gemeinschaft* and *Gesellschaft*. The first relies on social distance, the second on physical distance to define status. In the paternalistic system race relations follow a master-servant model, in which a dominant minority rationalizes its rule as a benevolent despotism that regards the subordinates as childish, irresponsible, but lovable in "their place." The subordinate group accommodates to or "accepts" inferior status and sometimes "internalizes" inferiority feelings. Role and status are sharply defined on racial lines and social distance is symbolized by elaborate etiquette and "nonreciprocal terms of address." The system accepts miscegenation and concubinage, and the "great degree of social distance allows close symbiosis and even intimacy, without any threat to status inequalities. Consequently, physical segregation is not prominently used as a mechanism of social control and may, in fact, be totally absent between masters and servants living together in a state of 'distant intimacy.' " Racial prejudice often takes the form of "pseudotolerance," with professions of love for the subordinated. Typical relations are "unequal but intimate." In the opposite or *competitive* type of race relations, role and job are no longer sharply defined by race, and class lines begin to cut across race lines as the gap narrows between races in education, occupation, income, and life style. The master-servant model that established social distance with etiquette gives way to sharp competition between the subordinate race and the working class of the dominant race. The latter joins the upper class to form a "*Herrenvolk* democracy" to put the excluded race down. "To the extent that social distance diminishes, physical segregation is introduced as a second line of defense for the preservation of the dominant group's position." Contact declines, miscegenation decreases, racial ghettos appear. Instead of the jolly, irresponsible child-race of paternalistic days, the lower caste of the competitive era appears "uppity," insolent, and aggressive. In place of the condescending tolerancce and *noblesse oblige* benevolence of the old days,

[19] Meier and Rudwick, "A Strange Chapter," 19.
[20] Herbert Blumer in Guy Hunter (ed.), *Industrialisation and Race Relations: A Symposium* (London, 1965), 220, 245.

race hatred and virulent bigotry appear and conflict erupts in lynchings and riots. The shift to the competitive type of race relations is identified by van den Berghe with industrialization, but as we have seen, there are reasons to doubt the necessity of this identification. This author also fails to note anticipations of the competitive type in the paternalistic phase of race relations.[21]

Philip Mason more informally suggests a typology of "three main stages" based on his personal experience in England, India, and the West Indies, plus a sophisticated reading of Shakespeare's *Othello* and *The Tempest*. Although Mason arrives at his analysis quite independently and includes English class relations as well as colonial race relations, the first two stages of his typology resemble those of van den Berghe. The first he calls "a stage of certainty; a slave is a slave and can be sold, but you can eat with him, talk with him, travel with him." He finds "this same certainty of status and freedom of personal relationship" characteristic of class relations of the old England emerging slowly from the Middle Ages as well as of race relations of old colonial days in India; even in South Africa there was a time when white men could eat with a free black. "The key to this stage," he writes, "is that the relationship is accepted on both sides." The second stage is one of "challenge and rivalry, of growing bitterness, of personal estrangement and aloofness, of insistence on barriers. This means that the top people are frightened." In this stage neither dominance on the one hand nor dependence and acquiescence on the other can be taken for granted, and status is uncertain. The third stage, a "stage of crisis," contains many contradictions and ambiguities and is more hesitantly defined. Here the dominant group, recognizing the inevitable, makes concessions that it finds unwelcome, but may be greeted by a "proud refusal to accept what has long been withheld." Symptoms of the third stage will be familiar enough to observers of the contemporary racial scene in America, but we are not concerned with it here. It does not necessarily follow from the other two, but the first stage "will almost always be succeeded by the second." It is with Mason's first two stages, and especially with their overlapping—as with van den Berghe's two types and their overlapping—that we are mainly concerned in reexamining the disputed origins of segregation in the South.[22]

These and other writers provide numerous examples of race relations in other cultures that illustrate the typologies outlined. We might start, however, with one closer home offered by Philip Mason: "Tom Sawyer and Huckleberry Finn thought it wicked to help a runaway slave to escape but were not at all embarrassed at eating with him; sixty years later, their judgements would have been reversed." In far-off India, he offers a picture of the future Governor of Bombay in 1830 sitting cross-legged on the floor with an old Indian clerk who was instructing him in treasury accounts and whom he addressed by an Indian term of respect meaning "uncle." Then eighty years later the picture of a venerable Brahmin lawyer being pushed rudely from his pony by British subalterns because no Indian was permitted

[21] Pierre L. van den Berghe, *Race and Racism: A Comparative Perspective* (New York, 1967), 25–37.

[22] Philip Mason, *Prospero's Magic: Some Thoughts on Class and Race* (London, 1962), 27–33.

to ride a horse in the presence of his white masters. The explanation, says Mason, is that

> so long as there is a formal, and in extreme cases a legal, distinction between the status of persons who consider themselves to belong to different groups— whether they are divided by class or by race—they can often mix on a personal level with easy relaxation. But as the formal nature of the difference diminishes, so the dominant group tends to put up barriers and personal relationships deteriorate.[23]

Both Mason and van den Berghe point out overlappings of their archetypes. Thus the latter writes that "in the process of a society's evolution from a paternalistic to a competitive situation a number of 'survivals' of the paternalistic type can linger on for long periods, even though the society as a whole clearly moves toward a closer approximation to competitive conditions."[24] And in India, Mason observes that "the stage of fixed status and friendly personal relations based on paternalism and dependence lingered on in remote country districts long after it had come to an end in the towns, and in the Indian army never really came to an end until the British went."[25]

The history of race relations in Brazil presents differences from that of Anglo-America and the colonies of Northern Europe, differences that are instructive in ways other than the conventional uses of this popular comparison. The sources of the difference are cultural and arise out of a Catholic society that skipped the Protestant Reformation and much of the Enlightenment. Missing in large measure from its history are the egalitarian, Protestant, achievement-oriented, aggressive-competitive traditions of the Northern societies. In place of the Northern sociological pattern of aggression-withdrawal, Brazil maintained a tradition of dominance-submission. Slaves of Brazil were only the most degraded of several dependent classes that were "embedded in a broad, diversified system of personal domination which pervaded the economy, polity and society of nineteenth-century Brazil."[26]

Florestan Fernandes, the distinguished Brazilian social historian, has spelled out the ironic consequences of this tradition for race relations in his country after the decline and abolition of slavery. Since white men did not entertain "any fear of the probable economic, social, and political consequences of social equality and open competition with Negroes" and therefore felt "no kind of anxiety or restlessness and no sort of intolerance or racial hatred," they erected no "barriers designed to block the vertical mobility of the Negro," no measures "to avert the risks which competition with this racial group might have incurred for the white"—no segregation and no Jim Crow. Instead, they relied tacitly, unconsciously, upon "factors of sociocultural inertia" and "the survival *en masse* of patterns of social behavior that were often archaic," including "the old pattern of race relations, as well as certain

---

[23] *Ibid.*, 27.
[24] Van den Berghe, *Race and Racism*, 34.
[25] Mason, *Prospero's Magic*, 33.
[26] I am indebted to unpublished papers of Richard Morse for these insights, especially his "Comments on Professor Carl N. Degler's Paper," read at a meeting of the Organization of American Historians at Philadelphia, April 17, 1969.

social distinctions and prerogatives." This was the old paternalistic heritage of slavery combined with the dominance-submission order of Brazilian society. It was not imposed by threatened lower-class whites, but by the elites, who "tended to maintain rigid, incomprehensible and authoritarian attitudes" toward blacks and "acted as if they still lived in the past and exaggerated the potential risks of an open liberalization of the social guarantees for Negroes." While the common white "did not feel he had to compete, contend, and struggle against the Negro, the latter tended passively to accept the continuation of old patterns of racial adjustment." What then of the famed "racial democracy" of Brazil? The elites continued to protest benevolence and maintain social distance. They reproved racial prejudice should it appear among new white immigrants, but kept the Negro at arm's length. "He was not openly rejected, but neither was he openly accepted without restrictions," an ambivalence coupling rejection "with apparent acceptance of the exigencies of the new democratic order." This might encourage friendliness and intimacy between races, but as Fernandes says, "The existence, intensity, and closeness of the contact between whites and Negroes were not, in themselves, indisputable evidence of racial equality. All such contact developed within the most thorough, rigid, and unsurmountable racial inequality." Continued protestation of loyalty to democratic ideals and social justice of the new order were combined with preservation of white supremacy. "In the name of a perfect equality of the future," writes Fernandes, "the black man was chained to the invisible fetters of the past, a subhuman existence and disguised form of perpetual enslavement. . . . And thus was born one of the great myths of our times: the myth of Brazilian racial equality."[27]

Neither Fernandes nor Richard Morse can conceive of anything quite comparable happening in the competitive, aggressive society of the United States.[28] They are certainly right about the Northern or "free" states. Slavery had never struck deep roots in the North, nor had slaves or free blacks concentrated in large numbers, and there had been no soil in which a paternalistic order could really become established. The paternalistic type of race relations existed only rudimentarily and in the main as a fashionable imitation of a romanticized South. Northern slaves were emancipated piecemeal and entered free society as slaves without masters, terribly handicapped but potential competitors of lower class and immigrant whites and threats to their status. Free blacks met immediate measures of segregation and proscription and passed into the rigors of the competitive stage of race relations with little if any cushioning from a paternalistic experience. Race relations in the North and West as described by Leon Litwack, Eugene Berwanger, and Jacque Voegeli fully bear out Tocqueville's observation that the intensity of race feeling was highest in states where slavery had never been established at all. Most of the anti-Negro legislation and rhetoric of the Northwest, however, was inspired not so much by the presence of blacks, which was usually minimal, as by the threat of a black invasion either as bondsmen of an expanding slave society of the South or as a massive migration of black

[27] Florestan Fernandes, *The Negro in Brazilian Society* (New York, 1969), 134–37, 164, 178.
[28] *Ibid.*, 135, and Morse, "Comments on Professor Carl Degler's Paper."

freedmen after the abolition of slavery. It was in this area of the United States that the competitive type of race relations arrived at its first expression and that the sociological model of aggression-withdrawal thrived unchecked by any dependence-submission heritage of paternalism.[29]

The slave society of the South *was* a paternalistic order, perhaps the most paternalistic of the slave societies in the New World.[30] This implies no invidious judgment of comparative benevolence. There is no necessary correlation between benevolence and the patriarchal family, and severity is quite as compatible with paternalism in master-slave relations as in father-child relations. But whatever paternalism implied in race relations, the South might be expected to provide in full measure. The master-servant model was with rare exceptions supreme. Role and status were defined not only by race but by law. Social distance was so wide and so clearly symbolized by punctilious etiquette, by terms of address, by gestures and rituals and manners manifesting subservience and dominance that precautions of physical distance, segregation, were rendered superfluous in all but exceptional circumstances. Certainty of status permitted "distant intimacy" and affective bonds between the races and encouraged "pseudotolerance" in the master class. This was what W. E. B. DuBois described "before and directly after the [Civil] war" as "bonds of intimacy, affection, and sometimes blood relationship, between the races," particularly with "domestic servants in the best of the white families."[31]

Even in slavery times, however, not all elements in the Southern population came equally under the ambiance of the patriarchy. Some people simply did not "fit in" conveniently or they responded skeptically or rebelliously to paternalistic authority. These were the free black people, scarcely more than a quarter of a million at most; yet they occupied a disproportionate share of white concern and anxiety in spite of their overwhelming dependency and submissiveness. While nonslaveholding whites generally looked to planters for leadership on the slave issue, there were some who were never happy with upperclass casualness about "distant intimacy" with blacks. And there was an underclass of whites whose social distance from them was not all that secure. These elements tended to concentrate in the antebellum cities of the South. There free blacks and underclass whites were thrown together with slaves under conditions hostile to both the discipline of slavery and certainty of racial status. As Richard Wade observes of the two races in urban setting, "they encountered each other at every corner, they rubbed elbows at every turn," and they lived together on virtually every city block. In most situations, as Wade says, they were "placed in such a way that social distance between the races was maintained even under conditions of close physical proximity." But social distance was not enough to define caste status in the larger cities. This was especially true in New Orleans, where for a time free people of color, largely French-speaking, were almost as numerous as slaves. Among them were families of wealth and

[29] See footnote 4 above.

[30] This is obviously a disputable position, depending much on one's conception of paternalism. See Eugene D. Genovese, *The World the Slaveholders Made* (New York, 1969), 96, 101, 131, 199.

[31] W. E. B. DuBois, *The Souls of Black Folk* (Chicago, 1903), 183–85.

education. Class lines crossed race and caste lines at both ends of the social spectrum. At the lower end, working-class whites competed with and drove Negroes out of many trades, and at both ends of the social scale, the races mixed promiscuously for pleasures and amusements on a more or less clandestine basis.[32]

Under these circumstances, the paternalistic type of race relations began to tip over into the competitive type, and as soon as this happened, physical distance began to supplement or reinforce social distance with various forms of segregation, legal and extralegal. It is true that urban life was rare in the slave South, and that five of the Southern states did not boast a town with as much as 10,000 population. It is also true that the degree and kind of segregation differed from city to city, was rarely rigid and never uniform, and that in no antebellum city of the South did segregation approximate the rigidity and completeness the system was to attain throughout the South in the twentieth century and had already attained in parts of the North by the mid-nineteenth century. Nevertheless it is perfectly clear that segregation in the South made its first appearance in the cities of the slave regime. If the problem is simply that of locating the first appearance of segregation in linear time, this is the answer and there is nothing more to add. But that is not a very significant or challenging problem. More important, it would seem, is the fact that the old paternalistic order of race relations continued to prevail in the rest of the South and that the urban experiments with the competitive order and segregation solutions touched the lives of few Southerners, black or white, during the Old Regime.

The first great crisis[33] in race relations of the South occurred in two parts: first, over the abolition of slavery, and second, over the earlier part of Reconstruction. Both added physical distance between races, but the distances produced by the two experiences were of different origins and permanency. The first kind was a more or less automatic and simultaneous withdrawal of both master and slave from the enforced and more onerous intimacies and the more burdensome obligations of the old allegiance: duties on the one side, responsibilities on the other. On these, there occurred a general walkout on both sides, and even the master was often disposed to say "good riddance" to this aspect of separation. Bereft of the benefits, he could at least shake off the obligations. The other type of separation sprang from different causes and was generated entirely on the white side. The cause was mainly fright—fear of the known, and real apprehension of a menacing unknown. Not only were the slaves liberated, but many were armed, and there was talk of making them full citizens, giving them the franchise, endowing them with equal political and civil rights, and even distributing the plantation estates among them. This was not only competition, it looked to many whites like a takeover. Racial hegemony itself appeared to be in jeopardy. Temporarily, at least, the immediate postwar years fully qualified for Philip Mason's stage of race relations in which "the top people are frightened." They responded in numerous ways, some of which were to erect barriers

---

[32] Wade, *Slavery in the Cities*, 55, 277; Fischer, "Racial Segregation in Ante Bellum New Orleans," 926–37.

[33] Certainly greater than the crises over slave rebellions and threats of rebellion in the first third of the nineteenth century.

and add physical distance between the races. The Black Codes of 1865–66 were mainly concerned with forced labor and police laws to get the freedmen back to the fields and under control.[34] But some of the statutes were segregationist. Three states adopted laws discriminating against Negroes on trains, mainly excluding them from first-class cars. Only one required a Jim Crow car. Public facilities that housed members of both races continued to quarter them separately, most often without statutory requirement as they had before the war, and the new schools followed suit. Such segregation laws and practices as Southern cities had adopted before the war were continued and a few more were added in the immediate postwar years.

It is in connection with the urban situation that the suggestions of Meier and Rudwick, mentioned above, have particular significance for the disputed thesis about segregation. They have called attention to the segregation of Negroes on streetcars in New Orleans, Richmond, Charleston, Louisville, and Savannah in the early postwar years. In some cities this was a continuation of prewar practices, in some the result of new laws. In each city the black freedmen organized protests, demonstrations, or boycotts against the segregated streetcar system, and in each case the whites backed down and abolished it. This occurred in 1867 in New Orleans, Charleston, and Richmond, and three years later in Savannah and Louisville. This leads Meier and Rudwick to suggest "that because of Negro opposition segregation did indeed decline markedly for a period, at least in public transportation." There were no more Jim Crow cars in those cities until after 1900 and the era of full segregation. "Between these two eras," they write, "southern white practices, at least in the cities under consideration, had been less rigid and less harsh toward the Negroes, and there had been acceptance of integrated streetcars."[35] Two forces were at work here, and neither can be neglected in explaining the history of segregation and race relations in Reconstruction and the period following. There was not only the militancy of the blacks, but also the acquiescence of the dominant Southern whites between the early 1870's and the late 1890's. Neither of these attitudes was to survive that period, and black militancy quickly subsided, but the presence of both at some point is required in accounting for the strange character of race relations while the period lasted.

It has been suggested that economic developments are the main clues to changes in style and type of race relations. The rise of racial antipathy and segregation have been variously associated with commercialization, the growth of the bourgeois, the ascendancy of capitalist and industrialization over precapitalist forms.[36] These correlations doubtless have validity in the long run and in more "normal" circumstances. But circumstances were not "normal" in the postwar South, and race relations did not respond "normally" to economic imperatives, at least not for some time. Slavery collapsed, the old planter regime crumbled, industrialization got underway, and a bourgeois regime of the "New South" took charge. But except for an ini-

[34] Theodore B. Wilson, *The Black Codes of the South* (University, Ala., 1965).

[35] Meier and Rudwick, "A Strange Chapter in the Career of Jim Crow," 15–19; see also Woodward, *Strange Career of Jim Crow*, 27–28.

[36] Genovese, *The World the Slaveholders Made, 109–13;* can den Berghe, *Race and Racism,* 29–37.

tial shock and hysteria, race relations responded mainly to political and sociological rather than to economic determinants.

Among the political determinants was a temporarily radical Congress and later radical state administrations that adopted civil rights and antidiscrimination statutes to protect freedmen and for a time showed some disposition toward enforcing them. With their franchise in hand, their brothers in office, and some protection for their civil rights, Negroes were emboldened to try new roles, enter strange places, and experiment with race relations in ways that had been unthinkable before and would become so again.[37] The radical phase of the new freedom passed soon, but while it lasted freedmen were capable of rising to such actions as smashing the incipient Jim Crow streetcar systems in five of the largest Southern cities. But what explains white acquiescence? The presence of radical power helps to explain the initial capitulation, but what explains the degree of white acquiescence until the end of the century? That is more complicated.

For one thing, Southern whites of the ruling class realized very early, usually by 1870, that their initial fright and hysteria were unwarranted. Reconstruction was not going to jeopardize racial hegemony. The North quickly backed away from radicalism. There would be no black takeover, no real competitive stage of race relations, not even a serious disruption of racial hegemony. By and large, the blacks still "knew their place"; with a few exceptions, mainly political, roles were still defined by race and so was status; social distance prevailed over physical propinquity. The ancient racial etiquette persisted with few breaches, and so did personal relationships, and so did the dominance-submission pattern. There was restiveness among the white working class over competition with free blacks, but that could be contained for the time being. It was true that blacks continued to vote in large numbers and to hold minor offices and a few seats in Congress, but this could be turned to account by the conservative white rulers who had trouble with white lower-class rebellion. Black votes could be used to overcome white working-class majorities, and upper-class white protection was needed by blacks under threat of white lower-class aggression. Many reciprocal accommodations between upper-class whites and blacks were possible under the paternalistic order.[38]

For all the differences between the two countries in the history of their racial relations, one is reminded of the South of this era in Roger Bastide's description of Brazil in the postabolition period:

> Slavery had disappeared, but the consequence was not that the mass of Negroes rose into the global community; the Negroes remained just where they were before, not forming a competitive group. It is precisely because they did not constitute a danger to the traditional social structure, because they did not threaten the whites' status, that the latter did not feel fear, resentment or frustration toward colored people. Personal, emotional relationships could thus come about between whites and blacks. . . .

[37] Wynes, *Race Relations in Virginia* (cited in note 7), 68–83; Logan, *Negro in North Carolina* (cited in note 8), 25–41, 180; Callcott, *Negro in Maryland Politics* (cited in note 9), ix, 134–35.

[38] C. Vann Woodward, *Origins of the New South, 1877–1912* (Baton Rouge, 1951), 103–106.

Paternalism prevented tensions and softened the relations between races. But, at the same time, it . . . institutionalized the subordination of the Negroes, who could only benefit from the protection of the whites, or from a certain familiarity in the whites' treatment of them, on condition that they 'knew their place' and proved their deference, gratitude and respect. It was therefore an instrument of political and economic control, which, by avoiding the competitive relations . . . by preventing a struggle, and by rendering useless any wish for collective mobility on the part of the Negroes, assured supremacy and security to the white class. Under these circumstances, one can understand why prejudices are at a minimum in a paternalist society, or, at least, why they remain latent rather than finding external expression. The reason is that they are unnecessary.[39]

Of course there was more white racism and incipient segregation in Southern paternalism, both during slavery and after, than in Brazil, and the South did not make the distinctions in shades of color that Brazilians made. Among other differences, the Brazilian Negro did not enjoy even such experience of political power and participation as their Southern cousins precariously enjoyed during and after Reconstruction. Even so, a good deal of similarity exists between the Southern and the Brazilian extension of white paternalism under bourgeois auspices after the end of slavery. There is also similarity in the bourgeois curtailment of paternalistic benefits under the two regimes. The Southern extension ended earlier, but it served many of the same purposes.

The distinctiveness of the Southern style required the heritage of Reconstruction as well as the heritage of slavery, the political as well as the sociological ingredients to subordinate for a time the economic imperatives of the competitive order in race relations. While the radical promise of black equality and the threat to white racial hegemony quickly faded, the black franchise lingered on for thirty years, and the civil rights statutes remained on the books—honored mainly in the breach though they were. Black members, reduced in number but still a conspicuous presence, continued to sit in Southern state legislatures, and black voters sent as many congressmen to Washington in the last quarter of the century as they had during Reconstruction. They could not be ignored politically as they could be after disfranchisement, and they had something to offer as well as something to beg of their paternalistic patrons. Together the oddly paired combination held at bay the worst of the fanatics and for a while stemmed the tide of proscription, segregation, and disfranchisement. In the patrician style, white conservatives sometimes denounced Jim Crow laws as "unnecessary and uncalled for" and "a needless affront to our respectable and well-behaved colored people." They ridiculed Jim Crow measures as preposterous and snobbishly identified the demand for them as lower class. One declared that he would rather "travel with respectable and well-behaved colored people than with unmannerly and ruffianly white men," and that if a Jim Crow car were needed it was for the latter. They made concessions, but when the first state Jim Crow law for trains was passed in 1887, a conservative paper rather shamefacedly admitted it was done "to please the crackers."

[39] Roger Bastide, "The Development of Race Relations in Brazil," in Hunter (ed.), *Industrialisation and Race Relations* (cited in note 20), 14–15.

In the years 1900–1906 the Jim Crow movement swept the cities of the South, and one city after another passed municipal ordinances or applied new state laws requiring segregation of the streetcars throughout the former Confederacy. Messrs. Meier and Rudwick, who investigated the Negro protest that ended the abortive Jim Crow streetcar system in the 1860's have also done a revealing study of its recrudescence in the 1900's. "For Negroes the new order was startling, even shocking," they report. The Negroes' response was an attempt to repeat the triumph of the 1860's. Between 1900 and 1906, they staged boycotts lasting from a few weeks to two or three years in more than twenty-five Southern cities. The protests were "almost entirely led by conservative business and professional men," who were "known as impeccably respectable men rather than as radicals or firebrands," and the movement is described as "conservative in the sense that it was seeking to preserve the status quo—to prevent a change from an older and well-established pattern." Black protest leaders naturally looked to their conservative white allies for support. "Universally the effect [of the boycotts] was startling to the white population." A few conservatives responded with appeals to maintenance of the "traditional harmony," and respect for "old Mammy," but the needed support was not forthcoming. After a few temporary successes, "in the end, the boycott movements against Jim Crow trolleys failed in all of the cities where they were initiated."[40]

The paternalistic order under bourgeois custody had been insecure for some years, and by this time the collapse of the "traditional harmony" and the political alliance that sustained it was almost complete. Its collapse was but one of several reasons for the rise of as harsh, as rigid, and as brutal and universally segregated a system as any example of the competitive order of race relations on record, surpassing that of the North in completeness and in the opinion of a South African white in 1915, as thorough as that of his native land. The forces that combined to bring about the change have been sketched elsewhere by the writer and there is no reason for repeating them here.[41] They are complex and numerous and some of them, important ones, were neither regional nor national in origin. One factor requires further comment, however, in view of the earlier reference to typologies and models of race relations. "Models" are always suspect by historians, for they know that however suggestive models and typologies may be for hypotheses, concrete history never fits into them. Historians have somewhat the same reservations about comparative history. One model suggested that the tipping point between the paternalistic and the competitive order of race relations came when "the top people are frightened." The top people of the South *were* in this instance frightened to some degree, all right, but they were frightened by the white lower class, not by the blacks. Some of them may have sounded like it at times, but they were usually "talking for the crackers." The ratio of whites to blacks has always set the South off as distinctive from other societies of "Plantation America," and not enough has been made of this white preponderance in comparing slavery systems and race rela-

[40]August Meier and Elliott Rudwick, "The Boycott Movement Against Jim Crow Streetcars in the South, 1900–1906," *Journal of American History*, LV (March 1969), 756–75.

[41] Woodward, *Strange Career of Jim Crow*, 69–109.

tions. A great proportion of Southern whites had never been slaveholders or come personally within the paternalist system. They had been economically distressed and politically rebellious since Reconstruction. The pinch of depression in the 1890's undoubtedly intensified their unhappiness, but no momentous shift in the means of production or its ownership intervened to account for the rush into a new era of race relations, "competitive" or otherwise. The upper class desertion of the blacks and capitulation to racist demagogues and their ruthless program of proscription, disfranchisement, and segregation stemmed from political not economic pressures. The new order of race relations was shaped and defined by political means and measures, and they came not to meet the needs of commerce or industry but the needs of politicians.

For all that, the Manichean categories of the "paternalistic" versus "competitive" typology do not do full justice to historical realities. It remains to admit that segregation of itself might be regarded as in some measure a modification or extension rather than an end of the paternalistic order. The escalation of lynching, disfranchisement, and proscription reflected concessions to the white lower class. So did legal segregation. But while segregation diminished the range of "distant intimacy" and "pseudo-tolerance," it was not inconsistent with a modified paternalism of the upper class whites.[42] It provided a legal definition of role and status that formalized social distance sufficiently for the older personal and paternalistic black-white relationships to be carried on. Only in this way can the differences that were still observable between Southern and Northern styles of racial relations in the mid-twentieth century be accounted for. Viewed in this way the first half of the twentieth century may be seen as an extension of the overlap between paternalistic and competitive systems. Not until the Civil Rights Movement knocked out the institutional foundations of the modified paternalism, already undermined by competitive encroachments, did the South finally join the North in the fully competitive phase.

To return finally to the question of adversary procedure, the writer has confessions of fault and responsibility bred of further thought. While he did take pains to say in so many words when he originally advanced his thesis that the "new era of race relations was really a heritage of slavery times,"[43] he probably did not sufficiently emphasize the paternalistic character of those relations. In neglecting to do this, he (unconsciously?) permitted the hopeful but unwary modern reader to identify such casualness and permissiveness as graced that remote Southern interlude of paternalism with the type of open, color-blind egalitarianism to which the modern liberal aspires. That was a mistake. It was also a mistake not to warn the unsuspecting that although the permissiveness of that era allowed such precocious Southern liberals as George W. Cable and Lewis H. Blair to speak their minds on race relations, they did not speak for the South of their day, but against it. And in his sympathy for the Populists, he probably neglected to point out that their egalitarian approach to Negro voters was itself mixed with a good deal

[42] I am unable, however, to go so far as Guion Griffis Johnson goes in identifying segregation with paternalism. See her article, "Southern Paternalism toward Negroes after Emancipation," *Journal of Southern History*, XXIII (1957), 483–509.

[43] Woodward, *Strange Career of Jim Crow*, 43.

of paternalism. Sensing these shortcomings without precisely spotting them, but realizing something was wrong, critics were lured into an adversary posture. If it would help to sidetrack the controversy, the writer would gladly concede that paternalism was never a way out for the Negro. It helped to temper race relations and postpone the worst rigors of segregation, not so much as Fernandes and Bastide describe it doing in Brazil, but with much the same effect and at the same cost. It bound the black man to the past, to dependence and withdrawal, to "his place." It avoided much competition and some overt tension, but it closed the door to independence and the future.

Where does this leave the adversary procedure? If it leaves the writer as advocate for the plaintiff, he would enter a plea of *nolle prosequi*. If spokesman for the defendant, a plea of *nolo contendere*. If neither plea be granted and the procedure be involuntarily protracted, he will persist as adversary only in conformity with the Shakespearean admonition.

Suggested Reading

The best one-volume history of the Confederacy is Clement Eaton's *A History of the Southern Confederacy** (1954), though Frank Vandiver's book *Their Tattered Flags* (1970) is more adventurous and written with more verve than Eaton's. E. Merton Coulter's *The Confederate States of America, 1861–1865* (1950) is longer than either. The war itself is the subject of a huge literature, as one can see from the useful guide by Allan Nevins, James I. Robertson, Jr., and Bell J. Wiley, eds., *Civil War Books: A Critical Bibliography* (2 vols., 1967–69). The course of the war can be followed engrossingly in Bruce Catton's trilogy, *Mr. Lincoln's Army** (1951), *Glory Road** (1952), and *A Stillness at Appomattox** (1953), or in his study, *The Centennial History of the Civil War* (3 vols., 1961–65). The list of shorter works on the war is also led by Catton's *This Hallowed Ground** (1956), but Fletcher Pratt's *A Short History of the Civil War** (1935), and T. Harry Williams' *Lincoln and His Generals* (1952) are well worth reading. David Donald has brought together a stimulating set of essays in *Why the North Won the Civil War** (1960).

The most authoritative text on the Civil War era is still James G. Randall and David Donald's *The Civil War and Reconstruction*, 2nd ed. (1961), which includes an exhaustive bibliography. A more recent survey is Thomas H. O'Connor, *The Disunited States: The Era of Civil War and Reconstruction** (1972). New studies have shed light on the domestic, political, and social movements in the North: James M. McPherson's *The Struggle for Equality: Abolitionists and the Negro in the Civil War and Reconstruction* (1964), George M. Fredrickson's *The Inner Civil War: Northern Intellectuals and the Crisis of the Union* (1965), David Montgomery's *Beyond Equality: Labor and the Radical Republicans, 1862–1872* (1967), and Jacque Voegeli's *Free But Not Equal: The Midwest and the Negro During the Civil War* (1967).

The Lincoln literature is enormous. The best one-volume introduction is Benjamin P. Thomas's *Abraham Lincoln: A Biography* (1952). The most thorough scholarly study is James G. Randall's *Lincoln: The President** (4 vols., 1945–1955); his one-volume interpretive work *Lincoln: The Liberal Statesman** (1947) is judicious. Richard N. Current's *The Lincoln Nobody Knows** (1958) and

David Donald's collection of essays *Lincoln Reconsidered** (1956) are excellent. T. Harry Williams assesses Lincoln's performance as commander-in-chief in *Lincoln and his Generals* (1952).

The pro-Southern and antiblack sentiments of William A. Dunning's students dominated reconstruction historiography throughout the first half of the twentieth century. Dunning himself was generally more balanced than his students, as can best be seen in *Reconstruction: Political and Economic, 1865–1877** (1907). W. E. B. DuBois challenged the idea that Reconstruction was a misguided or cynical attempt to force a social revolution on a suffering people in *Black Reconstruction** (1935), although he overstated the case for black achievements and black radicalism. Nevertheless, historians have generally been won over to the opinion that there were positive aspects to Reconstruction. The best synthesis written from this modern, balanced perspective is Kenneth Stampp's *The Era of Reconstruction, 1865–1877** (1966). Two other surveys are worth consulting: John Hope Franklin's *Reconstruction: After the Civil War** (1961), and Rembert W. Patrick's *The Reconstruction of the Nation** (1967).

An American Crisis* (1963) by W. R. Brock lays great stress on the reality of constitutional issues to the people of the time. John H. and LaWanda Cox, in *Politics, Principle, and Prejudice, 1865–1877* (1963), argue that the radical Republicans were motivated by principles as well as the desire for power and that their chief failure was in not providing land for the freedmen. Eric L. McKitrick, in *Andrew Johnson and Reconstruction** (1960), blames Johnson for its failure but is sympathetic to his policy of moderation in bringing the rebel states back into the Union. Harold M. Hyman, ed., *New Frontiers of the American Reconstruction* (1966) is an ideologically mixed collection of interpretive essays. The great detective story that uncovered hidden levels of the crisis that brought Reconstruction to an end is revealed in C. Vann Woodward's *Reunion and Reaction: The Compromise of 1877 and the End of Reconstruction*,* 2nd ed. (1956).

The response of freedmen to their new condition has been most sensitively gauged thus far by Willie Lee Rose in *Rehearsal for Reconstruction** (1964), though an older work by Vernon Lane Wharton, *The Negro in Mississippi, 1865–1890** (1947), is surprisingly good. Joel R. Williamson, in *After Slavery* (1965), stresses the early hardening of racial lines and segregation in South Carolina in contrast to the observations of C. Vann Woodward in *The Strange Career of Jim Crow** (1955). Williamson has also edited an excellent reader, *The Origins of Segregation** (1968). George B. Tindall's *South Carolina Negroes, 1877–1900* (1952) is solid and straightforward.

A standard text is George R. Bentley's *A History of the Freedmen's Bureau* (1955), which criticizes the Bureau for being too radical. William S. McFeely, in *Yankee Stepfather: General O. O. Howard and the Freedmen* (1968), takes the opposite tack, arguing that General Howard and the Bureau were much too timid. John A. Carpenter, in *Sword and Olive Branch: Oliver Otis Howard* (1964), praises Howard. Martin L. Abbott, *The Freedmen's Bureau in South Carolina, 1865–1872* (1967) is a good, recent state study.

The knitting together of the white portions of the nation is traced and analyzed by Paul H. Buck in *Road to Reunion, 1865–1890** (1937). The southern side of the same story is brilliantly told by C. Vann Woodward in *Origins of the New South, 1877–1913** (1951). Elaborations of Woodward's antiindustrialist bias can be found in the elegant book by Paul M. Gaston, *The New South Creed* (1970). Rayford Logan, in *The Betrayal of the Negro: From Rutherford B. Hayes to Woodrow Wilson** (1954), notes that pawns in the game of sectional reconciliation were black people, and is supported by two overlapping studies: Vincent P. DeSantis' *Republicans Face the Southern Question: The New De-*

parture Years, 1877–1897 (1959), and Stanley P. Hirshson's *Northern Republicans and the Southern Negro, 1877–1893* (1962).

August Meier's *Negro Thought in America, 1880–1915: Racial Ideologies in the Age of Booker T. Washington** (1963) is an exhaustive study. Provocative studies of white attitudes toward blacks include Claude H. Nolen's *The Negro's Image in the South: The Anatomy of White Supremacy* (1967), and Lawrence J. Friedman's *The White Savage: Racial Fantasies in the Postbellum South** (1970).

* Also published in paperback edition.

The New Face
of Society

The Beginnings of
Big Business in
American Industry

Alfred D. Chandler, Jr.

Before the Civil War the United States was
overwhelmingly an agricultural nation of minor
importance in international affairs. Sixty years after
the war it had become the richest and most powerful
nation the world has ever known. Most of the
aggregate growth is attributable to the growth of
population, rather than simply to increased per-capita
productivity. In most ways the growth of the United
States economy is on a par with the performance of
other nations that have undergone economic
modernization. Nevertheless, the performance was
dramatic. During the period from 1840 to 1960
population expanded on the average of 2.2 percent
per year; gross national product increased 3.6 percent
per year; and per capita product grew 1.4 percent per
year. Over these years per capita real income
multiplied sixfold.

It is ironic to note that though this is a nation
conceived in revolution, tempered by a bloody Civil
War, and perpetually excited by uncounted varieties
of social movements and group conflicts, the real
revolutionary force has been the economy and the
leading revolutionary has been the businessman, the
stereotypical defender of the status quo. The energizer

39

of this process of growth was industrialization, which began about 1840 to stimulate structural changes in the primarily agricultural and commercial economy. In 1890, for the first time, industry exceeded agriculture in "value added to product," which is the value of all commodities produced less the value of raw materials used in their production. By 1950, value added by industry was four times the figure for agriculture.

The most striking institutional innovation associated with industrialization is the giant industrial corporation which emerged in the late nineteenth century. It is this phenomenon, the development of big business, that Alfred D. Chandler, Jr., of the Harvard Business School analyzes in the following essay. The literature on business in the Gilded Age, reflecting the prevalent popular fear of bigness in the Gilded Age and later, has been preoccupied with the moral character of such financial freebooters as Jim Fisk, Daniel Drew, and Jay Gould, and with the speculative question of whether or not industrialization could have been accomplished at a lower social cost had businessmen been more responsible or had there been some countervailing force to regulate the process. Was there an alternative to the corporation movement, and if not, does that excuse unethical practices? Given the ecological concerns of today, future historians are bound to ask, as economists have long done, if rapid and unstable growth was really necessary. Why was government not used more to regulate business practices? Recognizing the tremendous power of wealthy men, did they use their wealth wisely? It has also been worthwhile to investigate the social backgrounds of large numbers of successful businessmen in order to destroy the rags-to-riches myth. These are interesting problems, but in a real sense they are peripheral to the central problem of understanding the process by which big business developed.

Chandler's task was to relate the dynamic forces in the economy to the emerging innovations in the world of business. In the late nineteenth century, the dynamic factors that led to larger scale enterprise were the westward shift of population and the building of a railroad network, which created a national and

The Beginnings of Big Business in American Industry. From *Business History Review,* Vol. 33 (Spring 1959), pp. 1–31. Copyright © 1959 by the President and Fellows of Harvard University, and reprinted with their permission.

primarily urban market. The impact of these forces continued after the turn of the century when the exploitation of electricity and the internal combustion engine and the systematic application of organized research and development activities further contributed to the process. All of these forces, in ways that Chandler details, promoted the creation of large, integrated industrial enterprises that were "the major innovation in the American economy between the 1880s and the turn of the century." Consequently, the key economic decisions that affect the lives of millions of people were increasingly made not by some romantic and individualistic robber baron, but by a group of bureaucrats. Cutthroat price competition and other forms of industrial warfare receded as oligopoly came to characterize the marketplace where large corporations operated.

The most interesting and most controversial of Chandler's conclusions is that these new business organizations were innovations made in response to the demands of the new urban market and that they were more a requirement of a firm's internal needs than of external competition, although he does qualify and make exceptions to this point. Another very interesting observation made by Chandler is that firms dealing in staple products tended to become horizontally integrated, while industries trading in urban consumer goods were characterized by vertical integration.

It is a mistake to assume that the big businessmen of the Gilded Age were the masters of the new industrial forces that were disrupting and changing society to such an extent that other elements of society suffered and eventually reacted. Chandler's implied message is that the businessmen were just as much the victims of the disturbing new forces as the farmer, the laborer, and the unaffiliated middle class. Businessmen had to scramble to adapt to the new context into which they were thrust. Those who were able to construct efficient, large-scale enterprises were most successful. The task of the business historian is to analyze the context to determine why this was the best response and how the response itself changed the context in which future businessmen would have to act.

Criteria for Selection and Analysis

The historian, by the very nature of his task, must be concerned with change. What made for change? Why did it come when it did, and in the way it did? These are characteristically historians' questions. For the student of American business history, these basic questions can be put a little more precisely. What in the American past has given businessmen the opportunity or created the need for them to change what they were doing or the way they were doing it? In other words, what stimulated them to develop new products, new markets, new sources of raw materials, new ways of procuring, processing, or marketing the goods they handled? What encouraged them to find new methods of financing, new ways of managing or organizing their businesses? What turned them to altering their relations with their working force, their customers and competitors, and with the larger American public?

The question of what constitutes the dynamic factors in American business history, dynamic in the sense of stimulating change and innovation, can be more clearly defined if the country's land, natural resources, and cultural patterns are taken as given. Land and resources were the raw materials with which the businessmen had to work, and the cultural attitudes and values helped set the legal and ethical rules of the game they had to play. Within this cultural and geographic environment a number of historical developments appear to have stimulated change. These provide a framework around which historical data can be compiled and analyzed.

The following major dynamic forces are visible in the American business economy since 1815: the western expansion of population; the construction and initial operation of the national railroad network; the development of a national and increasingly urban market; the application of two new sources of power: the internal combustion engine and electricity, to industry and transportation; and the systematic application of the natural and physical sciences, particularly chemistry and physics, to industry through the institutionalizing of research and development activities.

The first, the westward expansion, appears to have provided the primary impetus, except possibly in New England, to business innovation in the years from 1815 to about 1850; the building of the railroads appears to have been the major factor from the 1850's to the late 1870's; the growth of the national and urban market from the 1880's until a little after 1900; the coming of electricity and the internal combustion engine from the early 1900's to the 1920's; and, finally, the growth of systematic and institutionalized research and development since the 1920's.

These five factors are essentially aspects of fundamental population changes and technological advances. There were, of course, other factors that encouraged business innovation and change. The coming of the new machines and mechanical devices may have been a more important stimulant to innovation in New England than the growth of her markets and sources of supply in the expanding South and West. Wars usually precipitated change. The business cycle, flow of capital, government policy and legislation all played a significant part in business innovation. But such political and financial developments appear to have intensified or delayed the more basic changes encouraged initially by fundamental population shifts and technological achievements.

The purpose of making such a list is, however, not to argue that one development was more dynamic than the other. Nor are these five factors to be considered as "causes" for change; nor are they "theses" to be argued as representing reality, nor "theories" to provide an over-all explanation of change or possibly of predicting change. They are, rather, a framework on which historical information can be tied and inter-related. They provide a consistent basis upon which meaningful questions can be asked of the data.

This framework and these questions are, it should be emphasized, concerned only with fundamental changes and innovation in the business economy. They do not deal with the day-to-day activities to which businessmen must devote nearly all of their time. They are not concerned with the continuous adaptation to the constant variations of the market, sources of supply, availability of capital, and technological developments. Nor do they consider why some businesses and businessmen responded quickly and creatively to the basic population and technological changes and others did not. But an understanding of the continuous response and adjustment would seem to require first an awareness of the meaning of the more fundamental or "discontinuous" changes.

Since historical compilation and analysis must be selective, it is impossible to undertake any historical study without some criteria either implicit or explicit for selection. Further study and analysis, by indicating the defects of this approach and framework, will suggest more satisfactory ones. In the process, an analysis and interpretation of change in the American business past should come a little nearer to reality.

The purpose of this article then is, by using the framework of basic, dynamic forces, to look a little more closely at the years that witnessed the beginnings of big business in American industry. What types of changes came during these years in the ways of marketing, purchasing, processing, and in the forms of business organization? Why did these changes come when they did in the way they did? Was the growth of the national market a major prerequisite for such innovation and change? If not, what then was? How did these innovations relate to the growth of the railroad network or the coming of electricity and the internal combustion engine?

In addition to secondary works on this period, the data used in seeking answers to these questions have been annual and other corporation reports, government documents, articles in periodicals, histories, and biographies concerning the 50 largest industrial companies in the country in 1909. Nearly all these companies, listed in Table I, had their beginnings in the last years of the nineteenth century.

Major Changes in American Industry at the End of the Nineteenth Century

Between the depression of the 1870's and the beginning of the twentieth century, American industry underwent a significant transformation. In the

1870's, the major industries serviced an agrarian economy. Except for a few companies equipping the rapidly expanding railroad network, the leading industrial firms processed agricultural products and provided farmers with food and clothing. These firms tended to be small, and bought their raw materials and sold their finished goods locally. Where they manufactured for a market more than a few miles away from the factory, they bought and sold through commissioned agents who handled the business of several other similar firms.

By the beginning of the twentieth century, many more companies were making producers' goods, to be used in industry rather than on the farm or by the ultimate consumer. Most of the major industries had become dominated by a few large enterprises. These great industrial corporations no longer purchased and sold through agents, but had their own nation-wide buying and marketing organizations. Many, primarily those in the extractive industries, had come to control their own raw materials. In other words, the business economy had become industrial. Major industries were dominated by a few firms that had become great, vertically integrated, centralized enterprises.

In the terms of the economist and sociologist a significant sector of American industry had become bureaucratic, in the sense that business decisions were made within large hierarchical structures. Externally, oligopoly was prevalent, the decision-makers being as much concerned with the actions of the few other large firms in the industry as with over-all changes in markets, sources of supplies, and technological improvements.

These basic changes came only after the railroads had created a national market. The railroad network, in turn, had grown swiftly primarily because of the near desperate requirements for efficient transportation created by the movement of population westward after 1815.[1] Except for the Atlantic seaboard between Boston and Washington, the construction of the American railroads was stimulated almost wholly by the demand for better transportation to move crops, to bring farmers supplies, and to open up new territories to commercial agriculture.

By greatly expanding the scope of the agrarian economy, the railroads quickened the growth of the older commercial centers, such as New York, Philadelphia, Cincinnati, Cleveland, and St. Louis, and helped create new cities like Chicago, Indianapolis, Atlanta, Kansas City, Dallas, and the Twin Cities. This rapid urban expansion intensified the demand for the products of the older consumer goods industries—particularly those which processed the crops of the farmer and planter into food, stimulants, and clothing.

At the same time, railroad construction developed the first large market in this country for producers' goods. Except for the making of relatively few textile machines, steamboat engines, and ordnance, the iron and nonferrous manufacturers had before 1850 concentrated on providing metals and simple tools for merchants and farmers. Even textile machinery was usually made by the cloth manufacturers themselves. However, by 1860, only a

---

[1] The factors stimulating the growth of the American railroad network and the impact of the earlier construction and operation of this network on the American business economy and business institutions is suggested in Chandler, *Henry Varnum Poor—Business Editor, Analyst, and Reformer* (Cambridge, 1956), especially chaps. 4, 6–9.

decade after beginning America's first major railroad construction boom, railroad companies had already replaced the blacksmiths as the primary market for iron products, and had become far and away the most important market for the heavy engineering industries. By then, too, the locomotive was competing with the Connecticut brass industry as a major consumer of copper. More than this, the railroads, with their huge capital outlay, their fixed operating costs, the large size of their labor and management force, and the technical complexity of their operations, pioneered in the new ways of oligopolistic competition and large-scale, professionalized, bureaucratized management.

The new nation-wide market created by the construction of the railroad network became an increasingly urban one. From 1850 on, if not before, urban areas were growing more rapidly than rural ones. In the four decades from 1840 to 1880 the proportion of urban population rose from 11 per cent to 28 per cent of the total population, or about 4 per cent a decade. In the two decades from 1880 to 1900 it grew from 28 per cent to 40 per cent or an increase of 6 per cent a decade. Was this new urban and national market, then, the primary stimulant for business innovation and change, and for the coming of big business to American industry?

Changes in the Consumers' Goods Industries

The industries first to become dominated by great business enterprises were those making consumer goods, the majority of which were processed from products grown on the farm and sold in the urban markets. Consolidation and centralization in the consumers' goods industries were well under way by 1893. The unit that appeared was one which integrated within a single business organization the major economic processes: production or purchasing of raw materials, manufacturing, distribution, and finance.

Such vertically integrated organizations came in two quite different ways. Where the product tended to be somewhat new in kind and especially fitted for the urban market, its makers created their businesses by first building large marketing and then purchasing organizations. This technique appears to have been true of the manufacturers or distributors of fresh meat, cigarettes, high-grade flour, bananas, harvesters, sewing machines, and typewriters. Where the products were established staple items, horizontal combination tended to precede vertical integration. In the sugar, salt, leather, whiskey, glucose, starch, biscuit, kerosene, fertilizer, and rubber industries a large number of small manufacturers first combined into large business units and then created their marketing and buying organizations. For a number of reasons the makers of the newer types of products found the older outlets less satisfactory and felt more of a need for direct marketing than did the manufacturers of the long-established goods.

INTEGRATION VIA THE CREATION OF MARKETING ORGANIZATION

The story of the changes and the possible reasons behind them can be more clearly understood by examining briefly the experience of a few innovating firms. First, consider the experience of companies that grew large through the creation of a nation-wide marketing and distributing organization. Here the story of Gustavus F. Swift and his brother Edwin is a significant one. Gustavus F. Swift, an Easterner, came relatively late to the Chicago meat-packing business. Possibly because he was from Massachusetts, he appreciated the potential market for fresh western meat in the eastern cities.[2] For after the Civil War, Boston, New York, Philadelphia, and other cities were rapidly outrunning their local meat supply. At the same time, great herds of cattle were gathering on the western plains. Swift saw the possibilities of connecting the new market with the new source of supply by the use of the refrigerated railroad car. In 1878, shortly after his first experimental shipment of refrigerated meat, he formed a partnership with his younger brother, Edwin, to market fresh western meat in the eastern cities.

For the next decade, Swift struggled hard to carry out his plans, the essence of which was the creation, during the 1880's, of the nation-wide distributing and marketing organization built around a network of branch houses. Each "house" had its storage plant and its own marketing organization. The latter included outlets in major towns and cities, often managed by Swift's own salaried representatives. In marketing the product, Swift had to break down, through advertising and other means, the prejudices against eating meat killed more than a thousand miles away and many weeks earlier. At the same time he had to combat boycotts of local butchers and the concerted efforts of the National Butchers' Protective Association to prevent the sale of his meat in the urban markets.

To make effective use of the branch house network, the company soon began to market products other than beef. The "full line" soon came to include lamb, mutton, pork, and, some time later, poultry, eggs, and dairy products. The growing distributing organization soon demanded an increase in supply. So between 1888 and 1892, the Swifts set up meat-packing establishments in Kansas City, Omaha, and St. Louis, and, after the depression of the 1890's, three more in St. Joseph, St. Paul, and Ft. Worth. At the same time, the company systematized the buying of its cattle and other products at the stockyards. In the 1890's, too, Swift began a concerted effort to make more profitable use of by-products.

Before the end of the 1890's, then, Swift had effectively fashioned a great, vertically integrated organization. The major departments—marketing, processing, purchasing, and accounting—were all tightly controlled from the central office in Chicago. A report of the Commissioner of Corporations published in 1905 makes clear the reason for such control:[3]

> Differences in quality of animals and of their products are so great that the closest supervision of the Central Office is necessary to enforce the exercise

[2] Swift's story as outlined in Louis F. Swift in collaboration with Arthur Van Vlissingen, *The Yankee of the Yards—the Biography of Gustavus Franklin Swift* (New York, 1928). The United States Bureau of Corporations, *Report of the Commissioner of Corporations on the Beef Industry, March 3, 1905* (Washington, 1905), is excellent on the internal operations and external activities of the large meat-packing firms. There is additional information in the later three-volume *Report of the Federal Trade Commission on the Meat Packing Industry* (Washington, 1918–1919). R. A. Clemen, *The American Livestock and Meat Industry* (New York, 1923) has some useful background data.

[3] *Report of Commissioner of Corporations on the Beef Industry*, p. 21.

of skill and sound judgement on the part of the agents who buy the stock, and the agents who sell the meat. With this object, the branches of the Selling and Accounting Department of those packing companies which have charge of the purchasing, killing, and dressing and selling of fresh meat, are organized in the most extensive and thorough manner. The Central Office is in constant telegraphic correspondence with the distributing houses, with a view to adjusting the supply of meat and the price as nearly as possible to the demand.

As this statement suggests, the other meat packers followed Swift's example. To compete effectively, Armour, Morris, Cudahy, and Schwarzschild & Sulzberger had to build up similar integrated organizations. Those that did not follow the Swift model were destined to remain small local companies. Thus by the middle of the 1890's, the meat-packing industry, with the rapid growth of these great vertically integrated firms had become oligopolistic (the "Big Five" had the major share of the market) and bureaucratic; each of the five had its many departments and several levels of management.

This story has parallels in other industries processing agricultural products. In tobacco, James B. Duke was the first to appreciate the growing market for the cigarette, a new product which was sold almost wholly in the cities.[4] However, after he had applied machinery to the manufacture of cigarettes, production soon outran supply. Duke then concentrated on expanding the market through extensive advertising and the creation of a national and then world-wide selling organization. In 1884, he left Durham, North Carolina, for New York City, where he set up factories, sales, and administrative offices. New York was closer to his major urban markets, and was the more logical place to manage an international advertising campaign than Durham. While he was building his marketing department, Duke was also creating the network of warehouses and buyers in the tobacco-growing areas of the country.

In 1890, he merged his company with five smaller competitors in the cigarette business to form the American Tobacco Company. By 1895 the activities of these firms had been consolidated into the manufacturing, marketing, purchasing, and finance departments of the single operating structure Duke had earlier fashioned. Duke next undertook development of a full line by handling all types of smoking and chewing tobacco. By the end of the century, his company completely dominated the tobacco business. Only two other firms, R. J. Reynolds & Company and P. Lorillard & Company had been able to build up comparable vertically integrated organizations. When they merged with American Tobacco they continued to retain their separate operating organizations. When the 1911 antitrust decree split these and other units off from the American company, the tobacco industry had become, like the meat-packing business, oligopolistic, and its dominant firms bureaucratic.

What Duke and Swift did for their industries, James S. Bell of the Wash-

---

[4] Some information on James B. Duke and the American Tobacco Company can be found in John W. Jenkins, *James B. Duke, Master Builder* (New York, 1927), chaps. 5–7, 10. More useful was the United States Bureau of Corporations, *Report of the Commissioner of Corporations on the Tobacco Industry* (Washington, 1909).

burn-Crosby Company did during these same years in the making and selling of high-grade flour to the urban bakeries and housewives, and Andrew J. Preston achieved in growing, transporting, and selling another new product for the urban market, the banana.[5] Like Swift and Duke, both these men made their major innovations in marketing, and then went on to create large-scale, departmentalized, vertically integrated structures.

The innovators in new consumer durables followed much the same pattern. Both Cyrus McCormick, pioneer harvester manufacturer, and William Clark, the business brains of the Singer Sewing Machine Company, first sold through commissioned agents. Clark soon discovered that salaried men, working out of branch offices, could more effectively and at less cost display, demonstrate, and service sewing machines than could the agents.[6] Just as important, the branch offices were able to provide the customer with essential credit. McCormick, while retaining the dealer to handle the final sales, came to appreciate the need for a strong selling and distributing organization, with warehouses, servicing facilities, and a large salaried force, to stand behind the dealer.[7] So in the years following the Civil War, both McCormick and Singer Sewing Machine Company concentrated on building up national and then world-wide marketing departments. As they purchased their raw materials from a few industrial companies rather than from a mass of farmers, their purchasing departments were smaller, and required less attention than those in the firms processing farmers' products. But the net result was the creation of a very similar type of organization.

INTEGRATION VIA HORIZONTAL COMBINATION

In those industries making more standard goods, the creation of marketing organizations usually followed large-scale combinations of a number of small manufacturing firms. For these small firms, the coming of the railroad had in many cases enlarged their markets but simultaneously brought them for the first time into competition with many other companies. Most of these firms appear to have expanded production in order to take advantage of the new markets. As a result, their industries became plagued with overproduction and excess capacity; that is, continued production at full capacity threatened to drop prices below the cost of production. So in the 1880's and early 1890's, many small manufacturers in the leather, sugar, salt, distilling and other corn products, linseed and cotton oil, biscuit, petroleum, fertilizer and rubber boot and glove industries, joined in large horizontal combinations.

In most of these industries, combination was followed by consolidation and vertical integration, and the pattern was comparatively consistent. First, the new combinations concentrated their manufacturing activities in locations more advantageously situated to meet the new growing urban

[5] The story of Bell is outlined in James Gray, *Business Without Boundary, the Story of General Mills* (Minneapolis, 1954), and of Preston in Charles M. Wilson, *Empire in Green and Gold* (New York, 1947).

[6] The early Singer Sewing Machine experience is well analyzed in Andrew B. Jack, "The Channels of Distribution for an Innovation: the Sewing Machine Industry in America, 1860–1865," *Explorations in Entrepreneurial History*, Vol. IX (Feb., 1957), pp. 113–141.

[7] William T. Hutchinson, *Cyrus Hall McCormick* (New York, 1935), Vol. II, pp. 704–712.

demands. Next they systematized and standardized their manufacturing processes. Then, except in the case of sugar and corn products (glucose and starch), the combinations began to build large distributing and smaller purchasing departments. In so doing, many dropped their initial efforts to buy out competitors or to drive them out of business by price-cutting. Instead they concentrated on the creation of a more efficient flow from the producers of their raw materials to the ultimate consumer, and of the development and maintenance of markets through brand names and advertising. Since the large majority of these combinations began as regional groupings, most industries came to have more than one great firm. Only oil, sugar, and corn products remained long dominated by a single company. By World War I, partly because of the dissolutions under the Sherman Act, these industries had also become oligopolistic, and their leading firms vertically integrated.

Specific illustrations help to make these generalizations more precise. The best-known is the story of the oil industry, but equally illustrative is the experience of the leading distilling, baking, and rubber companies.

The first permanent combination in the whiskey industry came in 1887 when a large number of Midwestern distillers, operating more than 80 small plants, formed the Distillers' and Cattle Feeders' Trust.[8] Like other trusts, it adopted the more satisfactory legal form of a holding company shortly after New Jersey in 1889 passed the general incorporation law for holding companies. The major efforts of the Distillers Company were, first, to concentrate production in a relatively few plants. By 1895 only 21 were operating. The managers maintained that the large volume per plant permitted by such concentration would mean lower costs, and also that the location of few plants more advantageously in relation to supply and marketing would still reduce expenses further. However, the company kept the price of whiskey up, and since the cost of setting up a distillery was small, it soon had competition from small local plants. The company's answer was to purchase the new competitors and to cut prices. This strategy proved so expensive that the enterprise was unable to survive the depression of the 1890's.

Shortly before going into receivership in 1896, the Distillers Company had begun to think more about marketing. In 1895, it had planned to spend a million dollars to build up a distributing and selling organization in the urban East—the company's largest market. In 1898, through the purchase of the Standard Distilling & Distributing Company and the Spirits Distributing Company, it did acquire a marketing organization based in New York City. In 1903, the marketing and manufacturing units were combined into a single operating organization under the direction of the Distillers Securities Company. At the same time, the company's president announced plans to con-

---

[8] The major sources of information on combination and consolidation in the distilling industry are Jeremiah W. Jenks, "The Development of the Whiskey Trust," *Political Science Quarterly*, Vol. IV (June, 1889), pp. 296–319; J. W. Jenks and W. E. Clark, *The Trust Problem* (rev. ed.; New York, 1917), pp.141–149. The annual reports of the Distilling and Cattle Feeding Company and its various successors provide some useful additional data, as does the Industrial Commission, *Preliminary Report on Trusts and Industrial Combinations* (Washington, 1900), Vol. I, pp. 74–89, 167–259, 813–848, and Victor S. Clark, *History of Manufactures in the United States* (New York, 1929), Vol. II, pp. 505–506. Changes in taxes on liquors also affected the company's policies in the early 1890's.

centrate on the development of brand names and specialties, particularly through advertising and packaging.[9] By the early years of the twentieth century, then, the Distillers Company had become a vertically integrated, departmentalized, centralized operating organization, competing in the modern manner, more through advertising and product differentiation than price.

The experience of the biscuit industry is even more explicit. The National Biscuit Company came into being in 1898 as a merger of three regional combinations: the New York Biscuit Company formed in 1890, the American Biscuit and Manufacturing Company, and the United States Biscuit Company founded a little later.[10] Its initial objective was to control price and production, but as in the case of the Distillers Company, this strategy proved too expensive. The Annual Report for 1901 suggests why National Biscuit shifted its basic policies:[11]

> This Company is four years old and it may be of interest to shortly review its history. . . . When the Company started, it was an aggregation of plants. It is now an organized business. When we look back over the four years, we find that a radical change has been wrought in our methods of business. In the past, the managers of large merchandising corporations have found it necessary, for success, to control or limit competition. So when this company started, it was thought that we must control competition, and that to do this we must either fight competition or buy it. The first meant a ruinous war of prices, and a great loss of profit; the second, a constantly increasing capitalization. Experience soon proved to us that, instead of bringing success, either of those courses, if persevered in, must bring disaster. This led us to reflect whether it was necessary to control competition. . . . we soon satisfied ourselves that within the Company itself we must look for success. We turned our attention and bent our energies to improving the internal management of our business, to getting full benefit from purchasing our raw materials in large quantities, to economizing the expenses of manufacture, to systematizing and rendering more effective our selling department; and above all things and before all things to improve the quality of our goods and the condition in which they should reach the customer.
> It became the settled policy of this Company to buy out no competition. . . .

In concentrating on distribution, the company first changed its policy from selling in bulk to wholesalers to marketing small packages to retailers. It developed the various "Uneeda Biscuit" brands, which immediately became popular. "The next point," the same Annual Report continued, "was to reach the customer. Thinking we had something that the customer wanted, we had to advise the customer of its existence. We did this by extensive advertising." This new packaging and advertising not only quickly

---

[9] *Annual Report of the President of the Distillers Securities Company* for 1903.

[10] The information on National Biscuit comes largely from its annual reports.

[11] *Annual Report of the National Biscuit Company for the Year Ending December, 1901*, January 3, 1902. References to centralizing of manufacturing facilities appear in several early annual reports. As this was written before Theodore Roosevelt had started to make the Sherman Act an effective antitrust instrument and Ida Tarbell and other journalists had begun to make "muck raking" of big business popular and profitable, the Biscuit Company's shift in policy could hardly have been the result of the pressure of public opinion or the threat of government action.

created a profitable business, but also required the building of a sizable marketing organization. Since flour could be quickly and easily purchased in quantity from large milling firms, the purchasing requirements were less complex, and so the company needed a smaller purchasing organization. On the other hand, it spent much energy after 1901 in improving plant layout and manufacturing processes in order to cut production costs and to improve and standardize quality. Throughout the first decade of its history, National Biscuit continued the policy of "centralizing" manufacturing operations, particularly in its great New York and Chicago plants.

In the rubber boot, shoe, and glove industries, the story is much the same. Expansion of manufacturing facilities and increasing competition as early as 1874, led to the formation, by several leading firms, of the Associated Rubber Shoe Companies—an organization for setting price and production schedules through its board of directors.[12] This company continued until 1886. Its successor, the Rubber Boot and Shoe Company, which lasted only a year, attempted, besides controlling prices and production, to handle marketing, which had always been done by commissioned agents. After five years of uncontrolled competition, four of the five firms that had organized the selling company again combined, this time with the assistance of a large rubber importer, Charles A. Flint. The resulting United States Rubber Company came, by 1898, to control 75 per cent of the nation's rubber boot, shoe, and glove output.

At first the new company remained a decentralized holding company. Each constituent company retained its corporate identity with much freedom of action, including the purchasing of raw materials and the selling of finished products, which was done, as before, through jobbers. The central office's concern was primarily with controlling price and production schedules. Very soon, however, the company began, in the words of the 1896 Annual Report, a policy of "perfecting consolidation of purchasing, selling, and manufacturing."[13] This was to be accomplished in four ways. First, as the 1895 Annual Report had pointed out, the managers agreed "so far as practicable, to consolidate the purchasing of all supplies of raw materials for the various manufactures into one single buying agency, believing that the purchase of large quantities of goods can be made at more advantageous figures than the buying of small isolated lots."[14] The second new "general policy" was

> to undertake to reduce the number of brands of goods manufactured, and to consolidate the manufacturing of the remaining brands in those factories which have demonstrated superior facilities for production or advantageous

[12] The background for the creation of the United States Rubber Company can be found in Nancy P. Norton, "Industrial Pioneer: the Goodyear Metallic Rubber Shoe Company" (Ph.D. thesis, Radcliffe College, 1950), Constance McL. Green, *History of Naugatuck, Connecticut* (New Haven, 1948), pp. 126–131, 193–194, and Clark, *History of Manufactures*, Vol. II, pp. 479–481, Vol. III, pp. 235–237. The company's annual reports provide most of the information on its activities.

[13] *The Fifth Annual Report of the United States Rubber Company, March 31, 1897,* pp. 6–7.

[14] This and the following quotations are from the *Fourth Annual Report of the United States Rubber Company, May 25, 1896,* pp. 4–5, 7–8.

labor conditions. This course was for the purpose of utilizing the most efficient instruments of production and closing those that were inefficient and unprofitable.

The third policy was to consolidate sales through the formation of a "Selling Department," which was to handle all goods made by the constituent companies in order to achieve "economy in the distribution expense." Selling was now to be handled by a central office in the New York City headquarters, with branch offices throughout the United States and Europe. Of the three great new departments, actually manufacturing was the slowest to be fully consolidated and centralized. Finally, the treasurer's office at headquarters began to obtain accurate data on profit and loss through the institution of uniform, centralized cost accounting.

Thus United States Rubber, National Biscuit, and the Distillers Securities Company soon came to have organizational structures paralleling those of Swift and American Tobacco. By the first decade of the twentieth century, the leading firms in many consumers' goods industries had become departmentalized and centralized. This was the organizational concomitant to vertical integration. Each major function, manufacturing, sales, purchasing, and finance, became managed by a single and separate department head, usually a vice president, who, assisted by a director or a manager, had full authority and responsibility for the activities of his unit. These departmental chiefs, with the president, coordinated and evaluated the work of the different functional units, and made policy for the company as a whole. In coordinating, appraising, and policy-making, the president and the vice presidents in charge of departments came to rely more and more on the accounting and statistical information, usually provided by the finance department, on costs, output, purchases, and sales.

Changes in the Producers' Goods Industries

Bureaucracy and oligopoly came to the producers' goods industries somewhat later than to those making products for the mass market. Until the depression of the 1890's, most of the combinations and consolidations had been in the consumers' goods industries. After that, the major changes came in those industries selling to other businesses and industrialists. The reason for the time difference seems to be that the city took a little longer to become a major market for producers' goods. Throughout the 1880's, railroad construction and operation continued to take the larger share of the output of steel, copper, power machinery, explosives, and other heavy industries. Then in the 1890's, as railroad construction declined the rapidly growing American cities became the primary market. The insatiable demand for urban lighting, communication, heat, power, transportation, water, sewerage, and other services directly and indirectly took ever growing quantities of electric lighting apparatus, telephones, copper wire, newsprint, streetcars, coal, and iron, steel, copper, and lead piping, structures and fixtures; while the constantly expanding urban construction created new calls on the power machinery and explosives as well as the metals industries. Carnegie's decision in 1887 to shift the Homestead Works, the nation's largest and most modern steel plant, from rails to structures, symbolized the coming change in the market.[15]

Also the new combinations and consolidations in the consumers' goods industries increased the demand for producers' products in the urban areas. Standard Oil, American Tobacco, Swift and other meat packers, McCormick's Harvesting Machinery and other farm implement firms, American Sugar, Singer Sewing Machine, and many other great consumer goods companies concentrated their production in or near major cities, particularly New York and Chicago.

The changes after 1897 differed from the earlier ones not only in types of industries in which they occurred but also in the way they were promoted and financed. Combinations and vertical integration in the consumer goods industries before 1897 had been almost all engineered and financed by the manufacturers themselves, so the stock control remained in the hands of the industrialists. After 1897, however, outside funds and often outside promoters, who were usually Wall Street financiers, played an increasingly significant role in industrial combination and consolidation. The change reflected a new attitude of investor and financier who controlled capital toward the value of industrial securities.[16] Before the depression of the 1890's investment and speculation had been overwhelmingly in railroad stocks and bonds. The institutionalizing of the American security market in Wall Street had come, in fact, as a response to the needs for financing the first great railroad boom in the 1850's.

The railroads, however, had made a poor showing financially in the middle years of the 1890's when one-third of the nation's trackage went through receivership and financial reorganization. The dividend records of some of the new large industrial corporations, on the other hand, proved unexpectedly satisfactory. Moreover, railroad construction was slowing, and the major financial and administrative reorganizations of the 1890's had pretty well stabilized the industry. So there was less demand for investment bankers and brokers to market new issues of railroad securities.

Industrials were obviously the coming field, and by 1898 there was a rush in Wall Street to get in on this new business. The sudden availability of funds stimulated, and undoubtedly overstimulated, industrial combination. Many of the mergers in the years after 1897 came more from the desire of financiers for promotional profits, and because combination had become the thing to do, and less from the special needs and opportunities in the several industries. Moreover, as the financiers and promoters began to provide funds for mergers and expansion, they began to acquire, for the first time, the

<hr>

[15] Clark, *History of Manufactures*, Vol. II, chap. 19.

[16] The story of the shift from rails to industrials as acceptable investments is told in Thomas R. Navin and Marian V. Sears, "The Rise of the Market for Industrial Securities, 1887–1902," *Business History Review*, Vol. XIX (June, 1955), pp. 105–138. Government securities were, of course, important in the years before 1850 and during and after the Civil War, but in the late 1870's and 1880's as in the 1850's, railroads dominated the American security exchanges. As Navin and Sears point out, some coal and mining firms were traded on the New York Exchange, but the only manufacturing securities, outside of those of the Pullman Company, were some textile stocks traded on the local Boston Exchange. The connections between the railroad expansion and the beginnings of modern Wall Street are described in detail in Chandler, *Poor*, chap. 4.

same type of control over industrial corporations that they had enjoyed in railroads since the 1850's.

The changes in the producers' goods industries were essentially like those in the consumer goods firms before the depression. Only after 1897 the changes came more rapidly, partly because of Wall Street pressures; and the differences that did develop between the two types of industries reflected the basic differences in the nature of their businesses. Like the companies making consumer goods, those manufacturing items for producers set up nation-wide and often world-wide marketing and distributing organizations, consolidated production into a relatively few large plants and fashioned purchasing departments. Because they had fewer customers, their sales departments tended to be smaller than those in firms selling to the mass market. On the other hand, they were more concerned with obtaining control over the sources of their supply than were most of the consumer goods companies.

Here a distinction can be made between the manufacturers who made semi-finished products from raw materials taken from the ground, and those who made finished goods from semi-finished products. The former, producing a uniform product for a few large industrial customers, developed only small sales departments and concentrated on obtaining control of raw materials, and often of the means of transporting such materials from mine to market. The latter, selling a larger variety of products and ones that often required servicing and financing, had much larger marketing and distributing organizations. These makers of finished goods, except for a brief period around 1900, rarely attempted to control their raw materials or their semi-finished steel and other metal supplies. They did, however, in the years after 1900, begin to buy or set up plants making parts and components that went into the construction of their finished products.

Except in steel, integration usually followed combination in the producers' goods industries. And for both makers of semi-finished and finished goods, integration became more of a defensive strategy than it was in the consumers' goods industries processing agricultural products. In the latter the manufacturers had an assured supply of raw materials from the output of the nation's millions of farms. In the former, on the other hand, they had to consider the threatening possibility of an outsider obtaining complete control of raw materials or supplies.

INTEGRATION AND COMBINATION IN THE EXTRACTIVE INDUSTRIES

By the early twentieth century nearly all the companies making semi-finished product goods controlled the mining of their own raw materials. The industries in which they operated can, therefore, be considered as extractive. This was also true of two consumers' goods industries: oil and fertilizer. The experience of these two provides a good introduction to the motives for integration and the role it played in the coming of "big business" in steel, copper, paper, explosives and other businesses producing semi-finished goods.

In both the oil and fertilizer industries, control over raw materials came well after combination and consolidation of groups of small manufacturing firms. The Standard Oil Trust, after its formation in 1882, consolidated its manufacturing activities and then created a domestic marketing organization.

Only in the late 1880's, when the new Indiana field began to be developed and the older Pennsylvania ones began to decline, did the Trust consider going into the production of crude oil. Both Allan Nevins in his biography of John D. Rockefeller and the Hidys in their history of Standard Oil agree that the need to be assured of a steady supply of crude oil was the major reason for the move into production.[17] Other reasons, the Hidys indicate, were a fear that the producers might combine and so control supplies, and the desire of the pipeline subsidiaries to keep their facilities operating at full capacity. Although neither Nevins nor the Hidys suggest that the desire to obtain a more efficient flow of oil from the well to the distributor was a motive for this integration, both describe the committees and staff units that were formed at the central office at 26 Broadway to assure more effective coordination between production, refining, and marketing.

What little evidence there is suggests somewhat the same story in the fertilizer industry. Shortly after its organization in the mid-1890's, the Virginia-Carolina Chemical Company, a merger of many small southern fertilizer firms, began, apparently for the same defensive reasons, to purchase phosphate mines. Quickly its major competitor, the American Agricultural Chemical Company, a similar combination of small northeastern companies formed in 1893, responded by making its own purchases of mines. As the latter company explained in a later annual report:

> The growth of the business, as well as the fact that available phosphate properties were being fast taken up, indicated that it was the part of wisdom to make additional provision for the future, and accordingly . . . available phosphate properties were purchased, and the necessary plants were erected and equipped, so the company now has in hand a supply of phosphate rock which will satisfy its growing demand for 60 years and upwards.[18]

However, neither of these companies appeared to have set up organizational devices to guide the flow of materials from mine to plant to market; nor did the managers of a third large integrated fertilizer company, the International Agricultural Corporation, formed in 1909.

Defensive motives were certainly significant in the changes in the steel industry. Here the story can be most briefly described by focusing on the history of the industry's leader, the Carnegie Steel Company.[19] That com-

[17] Ralph W. Hidy and Muriel E. Hidy, *Pioneering in Big Business, 1882–1911* (New York, 1955), pp. 176–188. Allan Nevins, *Study in Power, John D. Rockefeller, Industrialist and Philanthropist* (New York, 1953), Vol. II, pp. 1–3. Nevins adds that another reason for the move into production was "partly to limit the number of active wells and reduce the overproduction of crude oil," Vol. II, p. 2, but he gives no documentation for this statement.

[18] *Annual Report of the American Agricultural Chemical Company, August 14, 1907;* also the same company's *Annual Report* dated August 25, 1902. In addition to the annual reports of the two companies, Clark, *History of Manufactures*, Vol. III, pp. 289–291, provides information. There is a brief summary of the story of the International Agricultural Corporation in Williams Haynes, *American Chemical Industry—A History* (New York, 1945), Vol. III, p. 173.

[19] The information on the Carnegie Steel Company is taken from Burton J. Hendrick, *The Life of Andrew Carnegie*, 2 vols. (New York, 1932), George Harvey, *Henry Clay Frick, the Man* (New York, 1928), James H. Bridge, *The Inside Story of the Carnegie Steel Company* (New York, 1903.)

pany's chairman, Henry C. Frick, had in the early 1890's consolidated and rationalized the several Carnegie manufacturing properties in and about Pittsburgh into an integrated whole. At the same time, he systematized and departmentalized its purchasing, engineering, and marketing activities. The fashioning of a sales department became more necessary since the shift from rails to structures had enlarged the number of the company's customers.

Then in 1896 the Carnegie company made a massive purchase of ore lands when it joined with Henry W. Oliver to buy out the Rockefeller holdings in the Mesabi Range. As Allan Nevins points out, the depression of the 1890's had worked a rapid transformation in the recently discovered Mesabi region.[20] By 1896, the ore fields had become dominated by three great interests: the Oliver Mining Company, the Minnesota Mining Company, and Rockefeller's Consolidated Iron Mines. A fourth, James J. Hill's Great Northern Railroad, was just entering the field. Frick's purchases, therefore, gave the Carnegie company an assured supply of cheap ore, as well as providing it with a fleet of ore ships. Next, Frick and Carnegie bought and rebuilt a railroad from Lake Erie to Pittsburgh to carry the new supplies to the mills.

Yet the steel company's managers did little to coordinate systematically the mining, shipping, and manufacturing units in their industrial empire. These activities did not become departments controlled from one central office but remained completely separate companies under independent managements, whose contact with one another was through negotiated contracts. This was the same sort of relation that existed between the Frick Coke Company and Carnegie Steel from the time Frick had joined Carnegie in 1889. If the Carnegie company's strategy had been to provide a more effective flow of materials as well as to assure itself of not being caught without a supply of ore and the means to transport it, then Frick and Carnegie would have created some sort of central coordinating office.

The steel industry responded quickly to the Carnegie purchases.[21] In 1898, Chicago's Illinois Steel Company, with capital supplied by J. P. Morgan & Company, joined the Lorain Steel Company (with plants on Lake Erie and in Johnstown, Pennsylvania) to purchase the Minnesota Mining Company, a fleet of ore boats, and railroads in the Mesabi and Chicago areas. Again, little attempt was made to coordinate mining and shipping with manufacturing and marketing. In the same year, many iron and steel firms in Ohio and Pennsylvania merged to form the Republic and National Steel

[20] Nevins, *Rockefeller*, Vol. II, p. 252.

[21] The experience of the other steel firms comes primarily from their annual reports and from prospectuses and other reports in the Corporation Records Division of Baker Library. A company publication, *J & L—The Growth of an American Business* (Pittsburgh, 1953) has some additional information on that company. Also, books listed in footnote 26 on the United States Steel Corporation have something on these companies. Two other steel companies listed in Table I made major changes somewhat before and after the period immediately following 1898. One, the Colorado Fuel & Iron Co., established in 1892, quickly became an integrated steel company in the Colorado area. The Bethlehem Steel Corporation was formed in 1904 when Charles F. Schwab, formerly of the Carnegie company and the United States Steel Corporation, reorganized the finances, corporate structure, and administrative organization of the bankrupt United States Shipbuilding Company.

Companies. Shortly thereafter, a similar combination in the Sault Sainte Marie area became the Consolidated Lake Superior Company. These three new mergers began at once to set up their marketing organizations and to obtain control by lease and purchase of raw materials and transportation facilities. In 1900, several small firms making high-grade steel did much the same thing by the formation of the Crucible Steel Company of America. In these same years, the larger, established steel companies, like Lackawanna, Cambria, and Jones & Laughlin obtained control of more supplies of ore, coke, and limestone and simultaneously reorganized their manufacturing and marketing organizations. Like Carnegie and Federal, they at first made little effort to bring their mining and coke operations under the direct control of the central office.

In copper, defensive motives for integration appear to have been somewhat less significant. In the 1890's, mining, smelting and refining were combined on a large scale. During the 'eighties the railroad had opened up many western mining areas, particularly in Montana and Arizona; a little later the new electrical and telephone businesses greatly increased the demand for copper. Mining firms like Anaconda, Calumet & Hecla, and Phelps Dodge moved into smelting and refining, while the Guggenheim's Philadelphia Smelting & Refining Company began to buy mining properties.[22] In the copper industry, the high cost of ore shipment meant that smelting and—after the introduction of the electrolytic process in the early 1890's—even refining could be done more cheaply close to the mines. Of the large copper firms, only Calumet & Hecla and the Guggenheims set up refineries in the East before 1898, and both made use of direct water transportation.

After 1898, several large mergers occurred in the nonferrous metals industries. Nearly all were initially promoted by eastern financiers. Of these, the most important were Amalgamated Copper, engineered by H. H. Rogers of Standard Oil and Marcus Daly of Anaconda, the American Smelting and Refining Company which the Guggenheims came to control, and United Copper promoted by F. Augustus Heinze. United Copper remained little more than a holding company. Amalgamated set up a subsidiary to operate a large refinery at Perth Amboy and another, the United Metals Selling Company, with headquarters in New York City, to market the products of its mining and processing subsidiaries. The holding company's central offices in New York remained small and apparently did comparatively little to coordinate the activities of its several operating companies. The Guggenheims formed a much tighter organization with direct headquarters control of the company's mining, shipping, smelting and marketing departments. On the whole, there appears to have been somewhat closer coordination between mining and processing in the large copper than in the major steel companies.

Lowering of costs through more effective coordination appears to have been a major motive for consolidation and combination in three other businesses whose raw materials came from the ground: explosives, paper, and

---

[22] Information on the mining companies came from their annual reports and from Isaac P. Marcosson's two books, *Magic Metal—the Story of the American Smelting and Refining Company* (New York, 1949), and *Anaconda* (New York, 1957), also Clark, *History of Manufactures*, Vol. II, pp. 368–369.

coal.[23] The mergers that created the Pittsburgh Coal Company in 1899 and greatly enlarged the Consolidation Coal Company in 1903 were followed by a reorganization and consolidation of mining properties and then by the creation of large marketing departments which operated throughout most of the country. The merger of close to 30 paper companies, forming the International Paper Company in 1899, was followed first by consolidation and reorganization of the manufacturing plants, next by the formation of a national marketing organization with headquarters in New York City, and then by the purchase of large tracts of timber in Maine and Canada. These three activities were departmentalized under vice presidents and controlled from the New York office. In all these cases, the central office was responsible for the flow of materials from mine or forest to the customer or retailer.

The explosive industries underwent a comparable sweeping change in 1902 and 1903. Since the 1870's, price and production schedules had been decided by the industry's Gunpowder Trade Association, and almost from its beginning, that Association had been controlled by one firm, the E. I. DuPont de Nemours & Company. However, the member concerns had retained their own corporate identities and managements. In 1902, the DuPonts bought out a large number of these independent companies through exchanges of stock, and then consolidated them into a single centralized organization. In the process, plants were shut down, others enlarged, and new ones built. A nation-wide selling organization was created, and centralized accounting, purchasing, engineering and traffic departments formed. Once the new organization was completed, then the company's executives obtained control of their raw materials through the purchase of nitrate mines and deposits in Chile.

Except possibly in paper, the control of price and production does not appear to have been a major motive for the initial combinations in the extractive industries making producers' goods. In steel before 1901, and in nonferrous metals and coal, there were several combinations, but none acquired as much as 20 per cent of the market. Nor is there any evidence that the creators of the different mergers, while they were forming their organizations, were arranging with one another to set over-all price and production schedules. In explosives, control of competition could not have been a significant reason for the 1902 changes since the DuPont company had enjoyed such control since the 1870's. In coal and explosives, and possibly in copper, the major motive for combination, consolidation, and the integration of supply with the manufacturing and marketing processes seems to have been an expectation of lowered costs through the creation of a national distributing organization, the consolidation of manufacturing activities, and the

---

[23] The story of the leading explosives, paper, salt and coal companies comes from annual reports and also from Charles E. Beachley, *History of the Consolidation Coal Company 1864–1934* (New York, 1934), George H. Love, *An Exciting Century in Coal* (New York, 1955), the company-written, *The International Paper Company, 1898–1948* (n.p., 1948), William S. Dutton, *DuPont—One Hundred and Forty Years* (New York, 1940), and *U.S. v. E. I. DuPont de Nemours & Company et al. in Circuit Court of the United States for the District of Delaware, #280 in Equity (1909), Defendants' Record Testimony*, Vol. I, and for the paper industry, Clark, *History of Manufactures*, Vol. III, pp. 245–252. The American Writing Paper Company, though less successful, had many parallels to International Paper.

effective coordination of the different industrial processes by one central office. In steel and possibly copper, the desire for an assured supply of raw materials appears to have been more significant in encouraging combination and integration.

CHANGES AND INTEGRATION IN THE FINISHED PRODUCERS' GOODS INDUSTRIES

Control of price and production was, on the other hand, much more of an obvious motive for combination and resulting consolidation in the industries manufacturing finished products or machinery from the semi-finished materials produced by the extractive firms. Concern over supply, however, was also a cause for change, for after 1898 the users of steel, copper, coal, and other semi-finished materials felt threatened by the growing number of combinations among their suppliers. In any case, between 1898 and 1900 there was a wave of mergers in these industries, largely Wall Street financed, which led to the formation of American Tin Plate, American Wire & Steel, American Steel Hoop, National Tube, American Bridge, American Sheet Metal, Shelby Steel Tube, American Can, National Enameling & Stamping Company and a number of other combinations among steel-fabricating firms.[24] At the same time, there were many amalgamations in the power machinery and implement businesses, such as American Car & Foundry, American Locomotive, Allis-Chalmers, International Steam Pump, and International Harvester. The largest combination among the copper users, the American Brass Company, came a little later, in 1903, after the Guggenheims, Rogers, and Heinze had completed the major copper mergers.

Nearly all these combinations quickly consolidated their constituent companies into a single operating organization. Manufacturing facilities were unified and systematized, over-all accounting procedures instituted, and national and often world-wide distributing organizations formed. Many set up central traffic and purchasing departments; some even began to assure themselves control over supply by building up their own rolling mills and blast furnaces. As American Wire & Steel and National Tube began to make their own steel, they cancelled contracts with Carnegie and other semi-finished steel producers. This development, in turn, led Carnegie to develop plans for fabricating his own finished products.[25]

The resulting threat of overcapacity and price-cutting led to the formation of the United States Steel Corporation.[26] This giant merger, which included Carnegie, Federal and National Steel, and the first six of the fabricating companies listed above, continued on as a combination. Although the activities of the various subsidiaries were re-formed and redefined, there was no consolidation. United States Steel remained a holding company only,

---

[24] The best brief summary of these mergers and the formation of the United States Steel Corporation is in Eliot Jones, *The Trust Problem in the United States* (New York, 1924), pp. 189–200. The companies' annual reports and prospectuses provide additional material.

[25] Hendrick, *Carnegie*, Vol. II, pp. 116–119.

[26] The beginnings and the operation of the United States Steel Corporation are outlined in Abraham Berglund, *The United States Steel Corporation: A Study of Growth and Combination in the Iron and Steel Industry* (New York, 1907), Arundel Cotter, *The Authentic History of the United States Steel Corporation* (New York, 1916), Ida M. Tarbell, *The Life of Elbert H. Gary, the Story of Steel* (New York, 1925).

and the central office at 72 Broadway did comparatively little to coordinate the operations of its many subsidiary companies.

After 1901, the fabricators and the machinery manufacturers made little attempt to produce their own steel or copper. Nor did the makers of semi-finished products try, for some years to come, to do their own fabricating. Possibly the metal users realized that even with the formation of United States Steel they were fairly certain of alternative sources of supply. Also they may have found that once they had combined they had enough bargaining power to assure themselves of a supply of steel and other materials more cheaply than they could make it themselves.

While such firms no longer sought to control their basic materials, many, particularly the machinery makers like General Electric, Westinghouse, American Car & Foundry, International Harvester and, a little later, General Motors, began to purchase or set up subsidiaries or departments to make parts and components.[27] Here again the motive was essentially defensive. Since much of their manufacturing had now become mainly assembling, they wanted to be sure to have a supply of parts available at all times. The lack of a vital part could temporarily shut down a plant. However, they expected to take only a portion of the output; a major share was sold to outsiders. One outstanding exception to this pattern was Henry Ford. He came to control his raw materials as well as his parts and components, and rarely sold such parts to outside companies. But Ford's insistence on having a completely integrated organization from mine to market, concentrated largely in one huge plant, proved to be one of the most costly mistakes in American business history.

Control of parts and accessory units led to a diversification of the types of products these manufacturing companies made and sold. Such diversification brought, over time, important changes in business organization. Even more significant for stimulating product diversification was the new "full line" strategy adopted by a number of these recently consolidated concerns. Such a policy, initiated largely to help assure the maximum use of the new departments, encouraged technological as well as organizational change.

Pioneers in developing "full lines" in the producers' goods industries were the two great electrical companies: General Electric and Westinghouse. Unlike almost any other of the leading American industrial companies in 1900, these two had begun as research and development rather than manufacturing organizations. Because of their origins, they had the skilled personnel and the necessary equipment to move, in the mid-1890's, from making lighting equipment alone to manufacturing many lines of electric traction and power machinery products.[28] Allis-Chalmers, International Steam Pump, and American Locomotive began, shortly after their formation and subsequent consolidations, to develop new lines using electric and gasoline engines.[29]

[27] This generalization is based on the annual reports of the several companies.

[28] As is well described in Harold C. Passer, *The Electrical Manufacturers* (Cambridge, 1953).

[29] The development of new lines by Allis-Chalmers, International Steam Pump, and American Locomotive is mentioned in their annual reports in the first decade of the twentieth century. International Harvester's similar "full line" policies are described in Cyrus McCormick, *The Century of the Reaper* (New York, 1931), chaps. 6–9, and United States Bureau of Corporations, *The International Harvester Co., March 3, 1913* (Washington, 1913), especially pp. 156–158.

International Harvester, building up a number of farm implement lines, also started to experiment with the use of the gasoline engine for machinery on the farm. In this same first decade of the twentieth century, rubber, explosive, and chemical companies began to turn to industrial chemistry in their search to develop broader lines of products.

Continuing diversification came, however, largely in industries where science, particularly chemistry and physics, could be most easily applied. And it was in these industries, and in those which were directly affected by the coming of two new sources of power, electricity and the internal combustion engine, that the major innovations in American industry came after 1900. The chemical, automotive, power machinery, rubber, and petroleum industries led the way to the development of new processes and products, new ways of internal organization and new techniques of external competition as the new century unfolded. The metals industries and those processing agricultural goods have, on the other hand, changed relatively little since the beginning of the century. In these industries, the same firms make much the same products, use much the same processes, and compete in much the same manner in the 1950's as they did in the 1900's. For them the greatest period of change came in the last decade of the nineteenth century.

Conclusion: The Basic Innovations

The middle of the first decade of the new century might be said to mark the end of an era. By 1903, the great merger movement was almost over, and by then the metals industries and those processing agricultural products had developed patterns of internal organization and external competition which were to remain. In those years, too, leading chemical, electrical, rubber, power machinery and implement companies had initiated their "full line" policy, and had instituted the earliest formal research and development departments created in this country. In this decade also, electricity was becoming for the first time a significant source of industrial power, and the automobile was just beginning to revolutionize American transportation. From 1903 on, the new generators of power and the new technologies appear to have become the dominant stimuli to innovation in American industry, and such innovations were primarily those which created new products and processes. Changes in organizational methods and marketing techniques were largely responses to technological advances.

This seems much less true of the changes during the 20 to 25 years before 1903. In that period, the basic innovations were more in the creation of new forms of organization and new ways of marketing. The great modern corporation, carrying on the major industrial processes, namely, purchasing, and often production of materials and parts, manufacturing, marketing, and finance—all within the same organizational structure—had its beginnings in that period. Such organizations hardly existed, outside of the railroads, before the 1880's. By 1900 they had become the basic business unit in American industry.

Each of these major processes became managed by a corporate department, and all were coordinated and supervised from a central office. Of the departments, marketing was the most significant. The creation of nationwide distributing and selling organizations was the initial step in the growth of many large consumer goods companies. Mergers in both the consumer and producer goods industries were almost always followed by the formation of a centralized sales department.

The consolidation of plants under a single manufacturing department usually accompanied or followed the formation of a national marketing organization. The creation of such a manufacturing department normally meant the concentration of production in fewer and larger plants, and such consolidation probably lowered unit costs and increased output per worker. The creation of such a department in turn led to the setting up of central traffic, purchasing, and often engineering organizations. Large-scale buying, more rational routing of raw materials and finished products, more systematic plant lay-out, and plant location in relation to materials and markets probably lowered costs still further. Certainly the creators of these organizations believed that it did. In the extractive and machinery industries integration went one step further. Here the motives for controlling raw materials or parts and components were defensive as well as designed to cut costs through providing a more efficient flow of materials from mine to market.

These great national industrial organizations required a large market to provide the volume necessary to support the increased overhead costs. Also, to be profitable, they needed careful coordination between the different functional departments. This coordination required a steady flow of accurate data on costs, sales, and on all purchasing, manufacturing, and marketing activities. As a result, the comptroller's office became an increasingly important department. In fact, one of the first moves after a combination by merger or purchase was to institute more effective and detailed accounting procedures. Also, the leading entrepreneurs of the period, men like Rockefeller, Carnegie, Swift, Duke, Preston, Clark, and the DuPonts, had to become, as had the railroad executives of an earlier generation, experts in reading and interpreting business statistics.

Consolidation and departmentalization meant that the leading industrial corporations became operating rather than holding companies, in the sense that the officers and managers of the companies were directly concerned with operating activities. In fact, of the 50 companies with the largest assets in 1909, only United States Steel, Amalgamated Copper, and one or two other copper companies remained purely holding companies. In most others, the central office included the heads of the major functional departments, usually the president, vice presidents, and sometimes a chairman of the board and one or two representatives of financial interests. These men made major policy and administrative decisions and evaluated the performance of the departments and the corporation as a whole. In the extractive industries a few companies, like Standard Oil (N.J.) and some of the metals companies, were partly holding and partly operating companies. At Standard Oil nearly all important decisions were made in the central headquarters, at 26 Broadway, which housed not only the presidents of the subsidiaries but the powerful policy formulating and coordinating committees.[30] But in some of the metals companies, the subsidiaries producing and transporting raw materials retained a large degree of autonomy.

[30] Hidys, *Pioneering in Big Business*, chap. 3 and pp. 323–388.

The coming of the large vertically integrated, centralized, functionally departmentalized industrial organization altered the internal and external situations in which and about which business decisions were made. Information about markets, supplies, and operating performance as well as suggestions for action often had to come up through the several levels of the departmental hierarchies, while decisions and suggestions based on this data had to be transmitted down the same ladder for implementation. Executives on each level became increasingly specialists in one function—in sales, production, purchasing, or finance—and most remained in one department and so handled one function only for the major part of their business careers. Only he who climbed to the very top of the departmental ladder had a chance to see his own company as a single operating unit. Where a company's markets, sources of raw materials, and manufacturing processes remained relatively stable, as was true in the metals industries and in those processing agricultural goods, the nature of the business executive's work became increasingly routine and administrative.

When the internal situation had become bureaucratic, the external one tended to be oligopolistic. Vertical integration by one manufacturer forced others to follow. Thus, in a very short time, many American industries became dominated by a few large firms, with the smaller ones handling local and more specialized aspects of the business. Occasionally industries like oil, tobacco, and sugar, came to be controlled by one company, but in most cases legal action by the federal government in the years after 1900 turned monopolistic industries into oligopolistic ones.

Costs, rather than interfirm competition, began to determine prices. With better information on costs, supplies, and market conditions, the companies were able to determine price quite accurately on the basis of the desired return on investment. The managers of the different major companies had little to gain by cutting prices below an acceptable profit margin. On the other hand, if one firm set its prices excessively high, the other firms could increase their share of the market by selling at a lower price and still maintain a profit. They would, however, rarely cut to the point where this margin was eliminated. As a result, after 1900, price leadership, price umbrellas, and other evidences of oligopolistic competition became common in many American industries. To increase their share of the market and to improve their profit position, the large corporations therefore concerned themselves less with price and concentrated more on obtaining new customers by advertising, brand names, and product differentiations; on cutting costs through further improvement and integration of the manufacturing, marketing, and buying processes; and on developing more diversified lines of products.

The coming of the large vertically integrated corporation changed more than just the practices of American industrialists and their industries. The effect on the merchant, particularly the wholesaler, and on the financier, especially the investment banker, has been suggested here. The relation between the growth of these great industrial units and the rise of labor unions has often been pointed out. Certainly the regulation of the large corporation became one of the major political issues of these years, and the devices created to carry out such a regulation were significant innovations in American constitutional, legal, and political institutions. But an examination of such effects is beyond the scope of this paper.

One question remains to be reviewed. Why did the vertically integrated corporation come when it did, and in the way it did? The creation by nearly all the large firms of nation-wide selling and distributing organizations indicates the importance of the national market. It was necessary that the market be an increasingly urban one. The city took the largest share of the goods manufactured by the processors of agricultural products. The city too, with its demands for construction materials, lighting, heating and many other facilities, provided the major market for the metals and other producers' goods industries after railroad construction slowed. Without the rapidly growing urban market there would have been little need and little opportunity for the coming of big business in American industry. And such a market could hardly have existed before the completion of a nation-wide railroad network.

What other reasons might there have been for the swift growth of the great industrial corporation? What about foreign markets? In some industries, particularly oil, the overseas trade may have been an important factor. However, in most businesses the domestic customers took the lion's share of the output, and in nearly all of them the move abroad appears to have come after the creation of the large corporation, and after such corporations had fashioned their domestic marketing organization.

What about the investor looking for profitable investments, and the promoter seeking new promotions? Financiers and promoters certainly had an impact on the changes after 1897, but again they seem primarily to have taken advantage of what had already proved successful. The industrialists themselves, rather than the financiers, initiated most of the major changes in business organization. Availability of capital and cooperation with the financier figured much less prominently in these industrial combinations and consolidations than had been the case with the earlier construction of the railroads and with the financing of the Civil War.

What about technological changes? Actually, except for electricity, the major innovations in the metals industries seem to have come before or after the years under study here. Most of the technological improvements in the agricultural processing industries appear to have been made to meet the demands of the new urban market. The great technological innovations that accompanied the development of electricity, the internal combustion engine, and industrial chemistry did have their beginning in these years, and were, indeed, to have a fundamental impact on the American business economy. Yet this impact was not to be really felt until after 1900.

What about entrepreneurial talent? Certainly the best-known entrepreneurs of this period were those who helped to create the large industrial corporation. If, as Joseph A. Schumpeter suggests, "The defining characteristic [of the entrepreneur and his function] is simply the doing of new things, and doing things that are already done, in a new way (innovation)," Rockefeller, Carnegie, Frick, Swift, Duke, McCormick, the DuPonts, the Guggenheims, Coffin of General Electric, Preston of United Fruit, and

TABLE 1   The Fifty Largest Industrials

(Numbers indicate relative size according to 1909 assets)

CONSUMERS' GOODS COMPANIES

Agricultural Processing	*Extractive*	*Manufacturing*
3. Am. Tobacco	2. Standard Oil	4. Int'l. Harvester
8. Armour & Co.	26. Va.-Carolina Chem.	10. U.S. Rubber
9. American Sugar	35. American Agri. Chem.	12. Singer Mfg. Co.
13. Swift & Co.		
30. Nat'l. Biscuit		
33. Distillers' Securities		
50. United Fruit		

PRODUCERS' GOODS COMPANIES

Agricultural Processing	*Extractive*	*Manufacturing*
6. Central Leather	1. U.S. Steel	7. Pullman
18. Corn Products Co.	5. Amalgamated	15. Gen. Elec.
21. Am. Woolens	(Anaconda) Copper	16. Am. Car & Foundry
	11. Am. Smelting &	19. Am. Can
	Refining	22. Westinghouse
	14. Pittsburgh Coal	24. DuPont
	17. Colo. Fuel & Iron	29. Am. Locomotive
	20. Lackawanna	36. Allis-Chalmers
	23. Consolidation Coal	44. Int. Steam Pump
	25. Republic Steel	46. Western Electric
	27. Int'l. Paper	
	28. Bethlehem Steel	
	31. Cambria Steel	
	33. Associated Oil	
	34. Calumet & Hecla	
	37. Crucible Steel	
	38. Lake Superior Corp.	
	39. U.S. Smelting & Ref.	
	40. United Copper	
	41. National Lead	
	42. Phelps Dodge	
	43. Lehigh Coal	
	45. Jones & Laughlin	
	48. Am. Writing Paper	
	49. Copper Range	

Clark of Singer Sewing Machine were all major innovators of their time.[31] And their innovations were not in technology, but rather in organization and in marketing. "Doing a new thing," is, to Schumpeter a "creative response" to a new situation, and the situation to which these innovators responded appears to have been the rise of the national urban market.

---

[31] Joseph A. Schumpeter, "The Creative Response in Economic History," *Journal of Economic History*, Vol. VII (May, 1947), p. 151, and also his *Theory of Economic Development*, trans, Redvers Opie (Cambridge, 1934), pp. 74–94.

There must be an emphasis here on the words "seem" and "appear." The framework used is a preliminary one and the data itself, based on readily available printed material rather than on business records are hardly as detailed or accurate as could be desired. More data, more precise and explicit questions, and other types and ranges of questions will modify the generalizations suggested here. For the moment, however, I would like to suggest, if only to encourage the raising of questions and the further compilation and analysis of data, that *the* major innovation in the American economy between the 1880's and the turn of the century was the creation of the great corporations in American industry. This innovation, as I have tried to show, was a response to the growth of a national and increasingly urban market that was created by the building of a national railroad network—the dynamic force in the economy in the quarter century before 1880. After 1900 the newly modified methods of interfirm and intrafirm administration remained relatively unchanged (as did the location of major markets and sources of raw materials) except in those industries directly affected by new sources of power and the systematic application of science to industry. In the twentieth century electricity, the internal combustion engine, and systematic, institutionalized research and development took the place of the national urban market as the dynamic factor in the American industrial economy.[32]

[32] This point has only been considered briefly here, but has been developed at some length in my "Development, Diversification and Decentralization," to be published in a book of essays tentatively titled *The Postwar American Economy* under the sponsorship of the Department of Economics, Massachusetts Institute of Technology.

Urbanization and Criminal Violence in the Nineteenth Century: Massachusetts as a Test Case

Roger Lane

Under the impact of the twin forces of immigration and industrialization, America became an urban nation in the late nineteenth century. During the forty years following 1860, cities grew twice as fast as the nation as a whole. While farm population in these years was increasing by 50 percent, nonfarm population leaped 400 percent. The largest cities were still in the East, but the ones growing most rapidly were in the Midwest: Chicago, Minneapolis, St. Paul, Kansas City. There, as well as in the older and larger cities, industrialization offered an ever-increasing supply of jobs. This was reflected in the fact that in 1890 the census for the first time showed that a majority of the gainfully employed Americans were working in nonagricultural pursuits. Fortunately, at this stage of industrialization, a stage in which the leading sector was composed of heavy industries, the economy was creating a preponderance of unskilled and semiskilled jobs. Otherwise, the untrained immigrants from American farms and from Eastern and Southern

Europe would have suffered far more than they did in the cities. Not only did the number of immigrants entering the country grow from less than 100,000 per year in 1861 to almost 800,000 in 1882, the peak year for the nineteenth-century, but also the sources of the immigration changed during the decade of the 1880s so that WASPs formed a progressively smaller portion of the total annual immigration. Increasingly, the newcomers settled not on the plentiful farmland of the Midwest and West as many previous immigrants had done, but in the wicked cities where they crowded into the already seething turmoil of ethnic ghettos. There they provided the labor for the urban sweat shops; elsewhere they were hired by the herd under a padrone, or leader, to do the dangerous work in the country's mines or in the construction of the railroad network that was rapidly stitching the nation together into one vast, rich, urban market.

We know that changes of this magnitude have disorganizing consequences. In the highly transient urban centers the common set of values and understandings engendered by long-term personal relationships that bind people together into a community are lacking. People tend to be isolated from one another, unable to communicate. Together they form not an integrated society but an audience. In the ethnic ghettos of the late nineteenth century, there were few forces operating to give newcomers a sense of belonging or a sense of purpose, although this role was filled to a certain extent by the ethnic political boss, the padrone who hired gangs of laborers, the church, a few volunteer associations, perhaps the pervasive sense of progress and upward movement in the city, as well as the fact that real wages were rising for those who could stay employed.

According to Roland Berthoff in *An Unsettled People* (1970), the nineteenth century was an era of social disintegration following the stability of the eighteenth century. Fragmented by the disorienting impact of social and geographic mobility, immigration, urbanization, industrialization, and sectional conflict, all social institutions were under strain, and change came at a bewildering pace. Society's centripetal power was being tested as never before, and Berthoff's view is that it was not until the twentieth century that new

Urbanization and Criminal Violence in the Nineteenth Century: Massachusetts as a Test Case. Copyright © 1971 by Peter N. Stearns. Reprinted from the *Journal of Social History*, Vol. IV, No. 4 (Winter 1968), pp. 333–56, by permission of the editor and the author.

forms and new values arose to successfully knit national society back together again. If this is an accurate representation of historical reality, one would expect to find some evidence of disintegration in that most popular index of social disorganization, the crime rate. Americans in the nineteenth century, as well as now, thought of the city as a dangerous place, full of vice and violence, and it was. The question is whether it got more turbulent and unruly as it got more densely populated, more impersonal, and more ethnically diverse.

In a sophisticated interpretation of imaginatively gathered data, Roger Lane of Haverford College maintains that "all evidence points to the long-term drop in criminal activity as normative, and as associated with urbanization." This conclusion derives primarily from his finding that there was a decline in the number of serious crimes detected and a decline in the number of arrests per man in the police force. He goes on to ingeniously point to the rise in the number of punished misdemeanors in Massachusetts as evidence that there was a growing intolerance of public disorder, or perhaps a changing conception of the meaning of public order, in urbanized areas in the nineteenth century. Frontier towns and cities, which were collections of individuals, could tolerate a great deal of disorder, but the highly interdependent nature of living in a modern manufacturing town imposed higher standards of individual conduct. Therefore, the result of industrialization was an increase in the need for more routinized and disciplined lives and a greater public insistence on sobriety. Some uncertainty about the conclusions derives from the interplay in the interpretation between attributing changes in the indices of disorder to real changes in disorderly behavior and changes in public perceptions of disorderly behavior.

Lane's interpretation of the cause for the great increase in the numbers of public safety officials lies at the heart of his theory. The increase was basically due to a changed public perception of the need for more police. But Lane argues that the change in the felt need for police was not the result of a real increase in breaches of public safety but resulted from a changed conception of the meaning of public safety and the location of the responsibility for protecting the society. Formerly, it was everyone for himself. With the increasing realization of the interdependence of life in the changing and growing city came a new conception of the community and what areas of life came under common responsibility. Here Lane has put his finger on the essence of modernization: the collective assumption of previously individual duties and responsibilities.

Roger Lane has produced in this essay an excellent example of the new social history. The essay is tightly constructed around a problem. The problem is conceived and stated in such a way that it can be tested with quantifiable data, and the data are handled with understanding and circumspection. In drawing conclusions and suggesting further hypotheses, the new social historian makes conscious, though not necessarily blatant, use of concepts and ideas harvested from the social sciences. The more humanistically inclined historians are quick to bemoan the lack of a story filled with individuals. Method, the old guard say, is no substitute for insight. They are possibly right, but the reader may judge for himself whether studies such as Lane's essay enhance his historical understanding.

*A*merica is now an urban nation, but Americans are still afraid of cities. There are many dimensions to this fear, but one of them is especially direct, and starkly physical. The current concern with "safety in the streets" echoes a belief, as old as the Republic, that the city is dangerous, the breeding ground of vice and violence. Observers of varying sophistication have pointed out that dark streets hide dark deeds, and that the anonymity and freedom of urban society, its temptations and frenzied pace, all contribute to encourage criminal behavior. From this it is easy to conclude that with metropolitan growth and the multiplication of all these conditions, the rate of violent crime is inexorably multiplied also.

But constant repetition of a myth is no substitute for proof. Under some circumstances it does in fact seem clear that migration to the metropolis has been accompanied by disruption and violence. This does not mean that there is a necessary or inevitable connection between the growth of cities and the growth of crime. In fact the existing historical evidence suggests the very reverse, that over a long term urbanization has had a settling, literally a civilizing, effect on the population involved.

The statistical evidence for such a long-term trend is necessarily fragmentary and local. But for this purpose local studies may well be more reliable than national. Figures for the United States as a whole, compiled by the Federal Bureau of Investigation, have been available only since 1930. Based on the records of police departments with widely varying standards of accuracy, these have provided a generation of criminologists with material for argument.[1] Analyses of crime rates in individual urban areas, on the other hand, are less complicated by discrepancies in definition and in police practice. While few of these reach back to any period before the FBI's Uniform Crime Reports, these few are significant. None points to any clear proportional increase in serious crime within particular cities. And the more recent suggest, on the contrary, a sometimes striking proportional decrease.[2]

Both the decrease and some of the explanation for it may be demonstrated since it is necessary to choose a single area to represent the whole—by an examination of 19th-century Massachusetts. A stable Eastern state, with one growing metropolis and a number of thriving smaller cities, this Commonwealth had a fairly typical experience with industrial urbanization. As a result of the legislature's enormous appetite for statistical information, its official records, including all those relating to criminal behavior, are probably better than any kept elsewhere.[3] And while criminal statistics are notoriously difficult to deal with, and by themselves offer no firm conclusions, the history of the Commonwealth has been abundantly studied, and may be used to help interpret the raw numerical data. Together, the statistics and the social record can illuminate several aspects of the history of criminal violence in America. These include: the changing incidence of disorder itself, the relation of this change to urban growth, the special conditions which may upset this relation, and lastly the problem of public attitudes or concern.

While all criminal statistics are subject to some doubt, the central conclusion about the figures from Massachusetts may be stated with confidence; serious crime in metropolitan Boston has declined sharply between the middle of the 19th century and the middle of the 20th. This often ragged downward trend does not, of course, apply equally to all offenses, but it does to most of the more serious common-law crimes. Three independent studies, by a lawyer, a historian, and a sociologist, confirm this basic direction.[4] While the three cover different periods, and employ somewhat different methods, they do fit together, and all are based essentially on police

[1] See *The Challenge of Crime in a Free Society: A Report by the President's Commission on Law Enforcement and The Administration of Justice* (Washington, 1967), p. 29.

[2] Four studies are especially germane: Harold A. Phelps, "Frequency of Crime and Punishment," *Journal of the American Institute of Criminal Law and Criminology*, vol. XIX, No. 2 (Aug. 1926), pp. 165–180, which covers Rhode Island between 1897 and 1927; Sam Bass Warner, *Crime and Criminal Statistics in Boston* (Boston, 1934), "Crime as a Function of Anomie," *Journal of Criminal Law, Criminology, and Police Science* (June 1966), covering Buffalo from 1854 to 1956; and Theodore Ferdinand, "The Criminal Patterns of Boston Since 1849," *The American Journal of Sociology* (July 1967), pp. 84–99, which runs to 1951. These all differ in purpose and sophistication, and none is directly concerned with the long-term decline, which helps to make their results the more striking.

[3] A survey of many of the official and criminal records of Boston and Massachusetts is contained in Roger Lane, *Policing the City: Boston, 1822–1885* (Cambridge, Mass.: Harvard University Press, 1967), pp. 225–229 and 239–241.

[4] See the works by Ferdinand, Warner, and Lane, in footnotes 2 and 3, above. There is no attempt, in these or in this paper, to measure the extent of statutory or white-collar crime.

arrest statistics, the index most widely used by contemporary criminologists.[5] The most comprehensive, covering the years from 1849 to 1951, shows a drop of nearly two-thirds in those crimes which the FBI classifies as "major."[6]

But only half the story, at best, can be told through the figures from the metropolis alone. Our concern is with the whole society. And it has been argued that the difference in crime rates between urban and nonurban areas may be great enough so that a drop in the incidence of criminality in the cities is more than offset by the fact that a continually greater percentage of the population is living in them.[7] It is necessary, to meet this problem, to look at the statistics for Massachusetts as a whole.

For most of the 19th century, the use of police records is neither possible nor desirable on a statewide basis.[8] But other indices of real criminal activity are available. And four of them may be used to establish the changing incidence of "serious" crime, defined as that which involves real injury to persons or loss of property.[9] These four are lower court cases, jail commitments, grand jury cases, and state prison commitments, all involving the major common-law offenses against persons or property. The first date for which two of these indices were published in trustworthy form is 1834; the first year for which all four were compiled is 1860. The figures for these periods, expressed in 3-year averages, may be compared with those for the end of the century in table 1:[10]

TABLE 1   Average Yearly Incidence of Cases
Per 100,000 Population

	1834–36	1860–62	1899–1901
Lower Court cases		777	707
Jail commitments		333	163
Grand jury cases	89	117	63
Imprisonments	16.8	11.9	5.9

The decline in the officially recorded crime rate is unmistakable here. And it is strongly probable that the real decline is greater than the statistics indicate. The key problem in the interpretation of criminal statistics is posed

[5] Thorstein Sellin and Marvin E. Wolfgang, *The Measurement of Delinquency* (New York, 1964), p. 31.

[6] Ferdinand, "Criminal Patterns of Boston," p. 87. Together with roughly similar results in Powell's study of Buffalo, these figures suggest that the main conclusions of the present paper, which is largely confined to the 19th century, may be projected up to the founding of the Uniform Crime Reports and beyond.

[7] Ferdinand, "Criminal Patterns of Boston," p. 99.

[8] Statewide arrest figures were not compiled until very late in the 19th century, and comparing those for different cities involves many of the same problems as plague students of the Uniform Crime Reports.

[9] In this paper except where specifically noted, no distinction is made between violent crimes—against the person—and other serious offenses. Such terms as "crime" or "disorder" are used to cover both.

[10] For references in this table, see Roger Lane "Crime and Criminal Statistics in Nineteenth Century Massachusetts," *Journal of Social History* (December 1968), footnote 8.

by "the dark figure," representing those illegal activities or incidents which never come to the light of official attention. But since in later years, as will be discussed below, there was both an increasing intolerance of criminal activity and a great growth in the numbers of police and investigative agents, all evidence suggests that this "dark figure" was growing proportionately smaller as the century progressed. Thus table 1 considerably understates the real decline.

For purposes of explanation, it is almost equally important to note the pattern of this decline. The table lists offenses in the order of their severity: lower court cases generally involve the least important crimes, jailings the next, indictments next, and imprisonments the most. And with one exception—the relative rise in indictments between the 1830's and the 1860's, which will be considered later—it is especially notable that the recorded drop in the crime rate is directly proportional to the seriousness of the offense. This is generally true also when the four indices used are examined further and broken into subcategories. Thus for example the combined rate of commitments for homicide, rape, armed robbery, and arson in 1860–62 was 6.8 per 100,000; by 1900 it has dropped to 2.9 per 100,000.[11] Most of the other data point in the same direction—not only a fall over time but a fall most marked in the most serious categories.

Meanwhile, however, while the serious crime rate was falling, the total crime rate—or the officially recorded total—was actually rising. This apparent paradox results from the fact that the downward curve described above may be wholly reversed simply by adding a third official category, "Crimes Against Public Order," to the two above. When these offenses are added in —drunkenness is by far the largest of them—the results for the lower courts may be indicated as follows:[12]

TABLE 2   Yearly Incidence of Cases Per
100,000 Population

	1840	1860	1900
Total lower court cases	595	1,869	3,317

The pattern for these minor crimes is the obverse of that for serious offenses, in that the more trivial the degree of the offense the larger its proportional increase over time. While virtually no indictments or imprisonments resulted from third-class offenses, their addition makes less difference in the case of jailings than of lower court cases:[13]

TABLE 3   Yearly Incidence of Cases Per
100,000 Population

	1841	1860	1900
Total jail commitments	419	548	969

[11] For references, see *ibid.*, footnote 8.

[12] For references, see *ibid.*, footnote 10. 1840 is the first year for which these figures are available.

[13] For references, see *ibid.*, footnote 11. The year 1841 is the first for which these figures are available.

This upward curve in total offenses does not have the same importance as the other, downward curve in the incidence of serious crime. The latter represents the basic statistical conclusion, in that it reflects a real situation, a real decline in the rate of criminal activity. But the former, while it is merely statistical, is nonetheless important. There is a complementary relationship between the two trends, and the nature of this relationship helps account for much that underlies the numbers.

The entire increase in the criminal statistics of Massachusetts, during the period covered, may in fact be attributed wholly to the rise in cases of drunkenness. Indeed this one offense, together with simple assault, its constant companion, may serve as a focus for much more. To understand the reasons for the rise in drunk arrests is to understand much about the social changes occurring in the 19th century, changes which affected all of its criminal patterns.

It is clear, first, that the mounting total of cases fed into the official machinery of justice does not reflect a real increase in the consumption of alcohol. The misuse of drink was throughout the 19th century a problem of enormous dimensions. The continuing debate about the nature of drunkenness, although some of it anticipated the best of current thinking, was on the whole punitive, and tended to blame the use of alcohol for virtually every individual and most social evils.[14] But even the most ardent spirits in the temperance movement did not usually suggest that there was any long-term rise in drunken behavior. They and their opponents generally united in agreeing that the situation, in ragged fashion, was improving with time.[15] Because much of the alcohol was made and sold illegally, especially in the countryside, it is difficult to investigate this statistically. But certainly in the metropolis and probably elsewhere the evidence does suggest a decline. Early in the century even ministerial ordinations, to say nothing of less grave occasions, were frequently bibulous affairs.[16] By the 1830's a substantial portion of the middle class had renounced the use of hard liquor. The prohibition was extended later to all drinks, and its champions carried on a continuous political and educational campaign against it. In the 1830's, and again in the 1850's, law enforcement officers estimated that 1 in every 65 inhabitants of Boston—men, women, and children—were selling alcohol for a living, in the latter period in defiance of a state law which prohibited all private sales.[17] Certainly neither this proportion nor this widespread evasion of the law was matched later in the century; by about 1880 the ratio was down to 1 seller in 150 and rising fast.[18]

On one level, the rising statistics of drunk arrests simply reflect an increase in the numbers of professional police and in the penal apparatus. It

[14] Compare *The Challenge of Crime*, p. 235, and Lane, *Policing the City, passim,* especially pp. 112–113.

[15] For testimony of both reformers and conservatives, see especially Massachusetts House Document No. 415, *Reports on the Subject of a License Law . . . Together With a Stenographic Report of the Testimony* (Boston, 1867), *passim.*

[16] Alice Felt Tyler, *Freedom's Ferment: Phases of American Social History to 1860* (Minneapolis, 1944), ch. 13, especially p. 311.

[17] Lane, *Policing the City*, pp. 41 and 71.

[18] *Ibid.*, p. 211.

was not until 1837 that Boston organized a squad of full-time professionals, and for many years these were the only ones in the Commonwealth. But by 1860 all of the larger cities had organized forces of varying sizes, and these had grown and spread to the smaller towns well before 1900.[19] The effect of this, and of a proportionate increase in the rest of the agents of justice, is easily demonstrated. In the absence of police, ordinary citizens were expected to make complaints on their own, and to call on constables only to execute warrants already sworn. But while private individuals may make the effort to initiate the processes of justice when directly injured, professionals are required to deal, in number, with those whose merely immoral or distasteful behavior hurts no one in particular. It takes real cops, in short, to make drunk arrests.

Again on this level, the relative shortage of official agents of law enforcement accounts for one of the most striking characteristics of table 1 above. The farther back the figures go, as noted, the higher is the relative proportion of serious crimes. The authorities, with limited resources, obviously had to deal with felony first, indictable crime next, and misdemeanor only when resources permitted.

Conversely it is notable that as time advanced and it became easier for injured citizens to complain to a policeman, the tables indicate that proportionately fewer such complaints were being made. In the city of Boston, at least, the result was a progressive decrease in the number of annual arrests made by each patrolman: in 1855, the average was 71 per man, while by 1885 this had dropped to 37.[20]

Drawn as a model, this development may explain the only apparent anomaly in table 1, already referred to. This is the fact that between the 1830's and the 1860's the figures show both a fall in prison commitments and a rise in grand jury indictments. Perhaps—the subject will be investigated further—there is no great paradox at all. District attorneys in the 1830's, faced with a high incidence of truly violent criminal behavior, may have had to concentrate on the more important prisonable offenses, to the neglect of others, even indictable ones. As their resources were increased, and as the real crime rate fell, they would be able by the 1860's to catch up on lesser indictments.

But there remains a more fundamental level of explanation. To account for the rise in lesser offenses or the drop in more serious crimes simply in terms of the expansion of police, courts, and prosecutors is to misplace the emphasis. The expansion is not cause but symptom. The machinery of justice was increased because of a felt need, a growing intolerance of behavior which had earlier been tolerated, coupled with a belief that the state and not the individual citizen was required to do the necessary job.

This process is most evident in Boston itself. Leading citizens and govern-

---

[19] Unfortunately, neither the federal nor the state census permits an accurate statewide count of policemen during the 19th century.

[20] Lane, *Policing the City*, pp. 230–232. The trend has continued. Modern police, despite the introduction of patrol cars and call wagons, make fewer arrests, in general, than did their predecessors, especially when the whole class of minor auto violations is eliminated.

mental officials were always proud of their reputation for maintaining a tidy and well-governed "order" in the city. But the definition of what constituted "order" changed considerably with time.

Josiah Quincy, one of Boston's first mayors, was also the first to boast that in no other city "of equal population, are there fewer instances of those crimes, to which all populous places are subject."[21] He had in fact assumed charge, in 1823, of a newly incorporated city of about 45,000 inhabitants, which officially issued some 697 liquor licenses and ignored the existence of a large number of illegal sellers. Relatively little attention was paid to such common offenses as simple drunkenness and assault. The night watch, largely concerned with the danger of fire or arson, was afraid to enter some of the more notorious neighborhoods. No one patrolled anywhere in the daytime. Quincy's several terms of office were marked by frequent battles between rival gangs of firemen, whose hunger for looting threatened the whole institution of fire insurance. When, after one of the city's numerous "riots, routs, and tumultuous assemblies" had spluttered on for a full week during the long hot summer of 1825, Quincy was forced to take personal charge of a posse of citizens to put it down. This was clearly an unusual action, and the mayor refused later opportunities to risk his limbs and authority in physical combat, preferring to let mob violence burn out by itself. Nevertheless, neither he nor the voters were unduly alarmed by the prevailing level of disorder. Citizens were traditionally supposed to take care of themselves, with the help of family, friends, or servants when available. An organized professional police would certainly be expensive and might be a threat to valued freedoms. And Quincy was proud to point out, at the end of his official career, that he had not added a single constable or watchman to Boston's part-time corps of peace officers.

By the 1880's, when an aldermanic committee echoed Mayor Quincy's earlier claim that Boston was the most orderly of America's larger cities, the situation had changed considerably.[22] In 1837, after three major riots in 4 years, the city had acquired a police force.[23] Since then it had been growing steadily, at a rate faster than the population. By the Civil War, the citizens had abandoned their objection to uniforms, with their paramilitary connotations, and the patrolmen had begun to carry guns.[24] By the 1880's the force had acquired most of its familiar modern characteristics and functions.[25] And the demand for more men continued—despite the fact that the crime rate had been dropping for some time, and with it the workload for each man on the force.

The demand for more men, then, reflected not a worsening situation but higher standards, a change in attitude. Really violent crime brought more severe retribution than formerly; the same offenses which had earned 2-year sentences in the 1830's were now punished by 3 to 4 years or more in the

---

21 Quoted in *ibid.*, p. 25. For the other information in this paragraph see ch. 2 *passim.*
22 *Ibid.*, p. 204.
23 *Ibid.*, pp. 29–35.
24 *Ibid.*, pp. 104–105.
25 *Ibid.*, p. 224.

state penitentiary, and the average was still going up.[26] While the police stations were still being built for "defensibility," there had been—and would be—no large-scale riot for years.[27] It is impossible to imagine a late-century mayor wrestling with mobs as did Quincy in the twenties and Theodore Lyman in the thirties. All of the city had been brought under more or less effective patrol, and the voters were demanding that the streets be cleared not only of arsonists but of drunks, peddlers, and truants. Traffic problems were settled not by teamsters with their fists but by officers with whistles. The responsibility for individual safety had been decisively shifted to these agents of the law; uniformed men with revolvers were stationed not only in potentially dangerous areas but in the quiet confines of the public library.[28] And the end result, reflected in many arrests for minor breaches of conduct, was a degree of "order" which would have astonished and perhaps dismayed an earlier and rougher generation.

The progressive heightening of standards of propriety, and with it the increasing reliance on official law enforcement, were processes which, while most sharply visible in Boston, were common to the whole society. Traditionally, criminologists have interpreted the zigs and zags of recorded criminal statistics in terms of individual events or situations—war, for example, or depression. But the change in social behavior reflected in the two dominant curves of criminality in Massachusetts is so long term and so widespread as to suggest a connection with the most fundamental of contemporary social processes, that of industrial urbanization itself. The nature of that connection has never been studied in detail, but it may at least be outlined.

Massachusetts in 1835 had a population of some 660,940, 81 percent rural, overwhelmingly preindustrial and native born.[29] Its citizens were used to considerable personal freedom. Whether teamsters, farmers, or artisans, they were all accustomed to setting their own schedules, and the nature of their work made them physically independent of each other. None of the more common occupations provided any built-in checks against various kinds of personal excess. Neither fits of violence nor bouts of drunkenness disrupted any vital patterns. Individual problems, sins or even crimes, were not generally cause for wider social concern.

Under these circumstances, while scarcely a frontier, the Commonwealth could afford a fairly high degree of lawlessness. No city in the state boasted a professional police, and the machinery of justice was not equipped to handle many cases. Many of the more common forms of violence or crime were simply not reported to the agents of law, as those affected either shrugged off their injuries or struck back directly.

[26] These figures for the average sentences to the state penitentiary. The range of offenses listed remained about the same through the century. For references, see Lane, "Crime and Criminal Statistics," footnote 14.

[27] *Annual Report of the Commissioners of Police of the City of Boston for . . . 1885* (Boston, 1885), pp. 28–30.

[28] Lane, *Policing the City*, p. 173.

[29] Population figures are from *The Census of Massachusetts . . . 1905* (Boston, 1909), vol. 1, p. xxxi. The urban definition is based on a population of 8,000.

But the impact of the twin movements to the city and to the factory, both just gathering force in 1835, had a progressive effect on personal behavior throughout the 19th century and into the 20th. The factory demanded regularity of behavior, a life governed by obedience to the rhythms of clock and calendar, the demands of foreman and supervisor. In the city or town, the needs of living in closely packed neighborhoods inhibited many actions previously unobjectionable. Both blue- and white-collar employees in larger establishments were mutually dependent on their fellows; as one man's work fit into another's, so one man's business was no longer his own.

The results of the new organization of life and work were apparent by 1900, when some 76 percent of the 2,805,346 inhabitants of Massachusetts were classified as urbanites.[30] Much violent or irregular behavior which had been tolerated in a casual, independent society was no longer acceptable in the more formalized, cooperative atmosphere of the later period. The private, direct response to criminal injury was no longer necessary or approved. All cities and most towns had acquired police forces, constantly expanding to meet greater expectations. Throughout the state, the victims of violence and theft were conditioned to seek official help. The move to the cities had, in short, produced a more tractable, more socialized, more "civilized" generation than its predecessors.[31]

The trend in the direction of higher standards and a lower level of violence may be measured from the early 19th century through much of the 20th. But what is true in the long run is not necessarily evident in the short. While the process of urbanization has helped to raise standards of personal behavior, it may not do so by itself. And there is some indication in the history of 19th-century Massachusetts that under unfavorable conditions migration to the cities may at some times have increased the incidence of violently unsocial behavior. This may well be true, at least, of the long generation between 1835 and 1860.

The existing statistics, alone, are no sure guide to what was actually happening during these crucial early decades. The Boston arrest figures were not kept until 1849. For the state as a whole, much of the remaining evidence remains ambiguous. As explained above, the two main indices, the rate of grand jury indictments and of imprisonments for felony, point stubbornly in opposite directions. But there is good reason to suspect that the period from the mid-1830's to the Civil War illustrates at least a partial, and important, exception to the general developments previously sketched.

From the war on to the end of the century and beyond, the industrial development of Massachusetts, however painful for those involved, was at least proceeding at a pace and along lines already laid out. The era just be-

[30] *Ibid.*

[31] It should be noted that after the 1880's, when Boston already had nearly 2 policemen per 1,000 inhabitants, which is close to the present nationwide average for major cities, it was the smaller places only where the arrest rate continued to climb dramatically. Boston, because of its very small geographical area, was ahead of most American cities in this respect. It was still possible in other places to raise the arrest figures by extending patrol and demanding higher standards in previously neglected areas, such as outlying slums. This process, and the reduction of the "dark figure" which results from better policing in general, may account for many apparent "rises" in crime rates which occur right up to the present.

fore was the one which witnessed the turbulence of transition. No similar timespan in fact encompassed a more rapid increase in the urban population. Between 1835 and 1860, while the total population was growing from 660,940 to 1,231,066, the proportion of city dwellers leaped from 19 to 44 percent of the total.[32] At the same time, too, the major railroad lines were laid in patterns still existing. As steam began to replace waterpower as the major source of industrial energy, the factories, earlier confined to rural sites near waterfalls, began to move into the cities.

Social dislocation, meanwhile, accompanied economic. All through the period, and especially during and after the "hungry forties," heavy Irish immigration exacerbated all of the problems of city living. By 1855, some 68,100 of the 168,031 residents of Boston were natives of Ireland.[33] Uprooted from a rural setting, wholly without skills, the newcomers experienced the kind of culture shock, prejudice, and alienation which would plague other waves of migrants later. Crowded into stinking hovels, some of them underground, their miserable conditions of living strained all of the city's institutions of charity and police. Smallpox, once virtually eliminated, became again a problem, cholera struck hard, and the death rate about the middle of the century climbed to the highest point in the city's recorded history.[34]

In terms of its effect on behavior, all of these rapid and wrenching changes promoted the worst aspects of living in the city without benefit of its compensations. It must be stressed that economic developments were not fully able to keep pace with migration. Between 1837 and 1845, it has been estimated, the amount of large-scale or factory employment did not increase at all.[35] And in the 15 years following, while the total of factory employees grew to something like 25,000 or 30,000, the number of outright paupers in the metropolitan area was increasing at an even faster rate, to reach a peak of nearly 13,000 in 1860.[36] Without the discipline imposed by regular employment, this first large-scale flow of migrants into the city was a kind of mutual disaster. The raw arrivals from the countryside, Yankees as well as Irish, had not yet learned to weave warily through crowds, with their arms held in close. Often radically insecure, in neighborhoods still unstable, they sought release in drink. But to drink with strangers requires different rules, and more restraints, than drinking in more familiar situations. In this era of swinging elbows, bewilderment, and desperate unemployment, it is hard to find evidence that the level of violence was declining.

Indeed it is easy to find the opposite. During this whole period Massachusetts was wracked by political instability, aggravated by one unpopular war and the overhanging threat of another one.[37] The 1850's, in particular,

---

[32] See footnote 29.

[33] Oscar Handlin, *Boston's Immigrants: A Study in Acculturation* (rev. ed., Cambridge, 1959), p. 244.

[34] *Ibid.*, pp. 114–116.

[35] *Ibid.*, p. 74.

[36] *Ibid.*, pp. 74 and 256.

[37] For political conditions in Massachusetts, see William Gleason Bean, "Party Transformation in Massachusetts, 1848–1860, with Special Reference to the Antecedents of Republicanism" (unpublished Ph.D. dissertation, Harvard University archives, 1922), *passim.*

witnessed a resurgence of mob violence as Know-Nothings and Irishmen, opponents and defenders of slavery, all found occasions to take to the streets.[38] These clashes, superimposed on and partly resulting from the already unhealthy social condition of Boston, were deeply disturbing to the inhabitants. If the real incidence of criminal behavior was not actually rising at this time, then surely it was not falling at the rate apparent in the generations following the Civil War.

All evidence points to the long-term drop in criminal activity as normative, and associated with urbanization. But the process was not complete without the accompaniment of rapid industrial development also. It was this which provided the means of absorbing raw migrants, of fitting them into a "system" which socialized and accommodated them into more cooperative habits of life. Without this other process, migration to the city alone, simply by multiplying human contacts, may very well multiply the incidence of criminally violent interaction among inhabitants unsuited to its demands.

Because of its clear connection with ethnic prejudice, and its dangerous political and social implications, the violent state of Boston during the 1850's was the source of considerable public concern. But the relation between concern about violence and violence itself is not always so uncomplicated. Both in the 19th and the 20th centuries, the attitudes of newspapers, scholars, and the public generally have been various and volatile, the product often of special interests or misinformation. This makes such attitudes difficult to measure. But they are nevertheless crucially important to the study of criminal disorder.

In the long run and in the short, popular concern has a direct effect on the shape of criminal statistics. As it was changing public standards which accounted for the rising total of arrests during the 19th century, so police departments still concentrate on those offenses of greatest current interest. Moreover, it is not simply the actual level of criminal activity, but the balance between this and social attitudes, which determines how much violence is a "problem" at any given time.

While public "attitudes" are slippery concepts to compare, it does seem that in the sense above the state of Massachusetts, and the United States in general, had a criminal problem less worrisome in the 19th century than in the 1960's. The citizens of the Commonwealth, still close to their rural antecedents, were indeed afraid of cities, which one legislative committee called "the common sewers of the state."[39] And one major source of this fear was the "poverty, vice, and crime" commonly associated with Boston, in particular.[40] But hostile critics were more interested in the first two than in the last, and reformers endlessly debated the causal relation between them. The charge that the city had lost control of its "dangerous classes" was used in several attempts to limit self-government in Boston, but mob action was the only form of violence which generally figured in these com-

[38] Lane, *Policing the City*, pp. 72–74, 90–91, and 94–95.
[39] *Ibid.*, p. 132.
[40] First used by Josiah Quincy in his "remarks on some of the Provisions of the Massachusetts Affecting Poverty, Vice, and Crime" (Cambridge, 1822), these last four words became a stock phrase among the Commonwealth's reformers.

plaints, and "crime" was used typically as a synonym for "vice."[41] It is significant that the laws concerning drink, especially, were subject to constant revision, but except for a reduction in the number of cases involving the death penalty, the general criminal code was not.[42] Legislative action or inaction mirrored public concern in this case. As the sons and daughters of Massachusetts migrated to the metropolis, the image conjured by the fearful was the rake or tempter, not the robber or rapist.

Nevertheless, however overshadowed by other issues, there were periodic outbursts of concern about violence or other crime. Often these occurred in response to some new development, or threat, for which the public or authorities were unprepared. In fact, the history of these threats, and the responses to them, comprise much of the history of criminal law enforcement.[43]

Thus the multiplication of banks and bank notes, through the 1820's, provided golden opportunities for counterfeiters. The nature of the problem, in this case, required a network of private bankers' agents to cooperate, across state and even national boundaries, with the appropriate public authorities. Anti-Catholic rioting, in the 1830's, was a principal spur to the development of professional police. During the 1870's, the growing sophistication of professional criminals, dramatized by a spectacular series of bank robberies, led to an overhaul of existing detective methods in many American cities. During the same period, bands of healthy native vagrants, fugitives from the new industrial age, were a subject of great concern to the readers of sensational newspapers, who feared the violent potential in these "wild-eyed" strangers. The response in this case was harsher police action, and a tightening of the rules governing charity and soup kitchens.

These concerns were at any rate real, and had often lasting effects, although they had little to do with the overall crime rate. Another and more frequent kind of scare resulted not from some genuinely new problem but from sudden attention focused on an old one. Lincoln Steffens, as a cub reporter in New York, learned how easy it was to manufacture a "crime wave," with techniques still familiar.[44] Thus a particularly brutal murder or a series of muggings could touch off a wave of arrests "on suspicion."[45] Often it was simply an investigation or exposé of some endemic form of crime which generated a sudden excitement, during which the public was assured that Boston was facing a threat of unprecedented proportions.

But it is impossible, from these brief scares, to get any clear sense of direction. While the definition of the tolerable was altering with time, it was altering slowly and imperceptibly. And there is no evidence that, as the century progressed, the gap between the level of order expected and the level actually obtaining was changing in any constant direction. It is true

---

[41] Lane, *Policing the City*, especially pp. 122–125, 128–134, 142–156, and 213–219.

[42] *Ibid., passim*. For the criminal code, summed up in revisions compiled in 1835, 1859, 1881, and 1900, see p. 239.

[43] For references in the following paragraph, see *ibid.*, pp. 55–56, 29–35, 142–156, 157–160, and 193–195.

[44] Lincoln Steffens, *Autobiography* (New York, 1931), pp. 285–291.

[45] In 1865, inspired by a fear of returning veterans much like that following World War II, the police made some 2,532 such arrests. See Lane, *Policing the City*, p. 149.

that the police often felt that they were faced with problems of unprecedented magnitude, and chiefs decades apart warned that the level of juvenile
delinquency, and the general breakdown of authority, threatened the very
basis of society.[46] Other observers too, perhaps beguiled by the image of a
more peaceful golden age in the past, sometimes asserted that crime was
growing faster than the population. But this tendency to fear was balanced
throughout the century by pride in growth and progress. And the many
apocalyptic statements may be countered with an equal number of others,
more optimistic. Thus even in the troubled year of 1859, the State's attorney
general could declare that "at no time in the history of Massachusetts have
life, liberty, and property been more secure than at present."[47]

In short, while it is possible now to discover a long-term drop in the level
of violence, contemporaries were simply not aware of this. The degree of
public concern has never been, nor is it now, an accurate index of the degree
of criminal activity. Indeed the reverse is often true. And it is doubly ironic
that a drop in the actual incidence of disorder has been accompanied by—
and contributed to—a heightened sensitivity to disorder. Such sensitivity, by
leading to a more demanding standard of conduct, has been essential to the
functioning of an interdependent urban society. But unless the process is
recognized and understood, it may have unsettling effects. There are times
when for various reasons the level of violence overbalances current expectations. In such situations the social pressure to maintain and extend high
standards, and to enforce them universally, may result in frustration. The
frustration may translate into fear. And this fear, in turn, may focus on the
very urban process which helped to create those standards, on the growth
of cities itself.

Suggested Reading

The best general economic history of the late nineteenth century is Edward
C. Kirkland's *Industry Comes of Age: Business, Labor and Public Policy, 1860–
1897* (1961),* but one should also consult the relevant chapters of *The Age of
Enterprise: A Social History of Industrial America,** rev. ed. (1961). Samuel
P. Hays has provided a brief but provocative reinterpretation of the period,
*The Response to Industrialism, 1885–1914** (1957). Joseph Dorfman surveys
economic thought in *The Economic Mind in American Civilization, 1865–1918*
(1949). A good analysis of the economy is provided by Rendigs Fels's *American
Business Cycles, 1865–1897* (1959) which should be brought up to date by
Robert Higgs's *The Transformation of the American Economy, 1865–1914*
(1971). Douglas C. North's *Growth and Welfare in the American Past* (1966) is
a stimulating interpretation from a long-term perspective. Milton J. Friedman
and Anna Jacobson Schwartz' *A Monetary History of the United States, 1867–
1960* (1963) is a brilliant application of monetary theory with surprising results.

The classic statement of the antibusinessman bias of the progressive tradition is
Mathew Josephson's *The Robber Barons** (1934). Similar predilections underlie

---

[46] See, e.g., *ibid.*, pp. 68, 137, and 34.
[47] *Ibid.*, p. 117.

Sidney Fine's study *Laissez-Faire and the General Welfare State: A Study of Conflict in American Thought, 1865–1901** (1956), and Sigmund Diamond traces public attitudes toward rich businessmen in *The Reputation of the American Businessman* (1955). The businessman's image is considerably bettered by Allan Nevins, in *Study in Power: John D. Rockefeller, Industrialist and Philanthropist* (2 vols., 1953), and by Ralph W. and Muriel E. Hidy, in *Pioneering in Big Business, 1882–1911: History of the Standard Oil Company* (1955), which is an excellent study. A balanced and insightful treatment of the problems and points of view of businessmen is furnished by Thomas C. Cochran's *Railroad Leaders, 1845–1890** (1953).

Richard Hofstadter's brilliant analysis *Social Darwinism in American Thought** (1944) probably overemphasizes the degree to which businessmen actually based their thinking on Darwin's theories. A more probable reconstruction of the late nineteenth-century businessman's world view is Edward C. Kirkland's *Dream and Thought in the Business Community, 1860–1900* (1956), and *Business in the Gilded Age* (1952). Robert G. McCloskey's *American Conservatism in the Age of Enterprise* (1951) is a comprehensive study. Irvin G. Wyllie in *The Self-Made Man in America: The Myth of Rags to Riches* (1954) studies the propagators of the ruling myth of the era. That the myth had little basis in fact is one of many things one can learn from the essays in William Miller, ed., *Men in Business: Essays on the Historical Role of the Entrepreneur** (1952).

Railroads played a crucial role in the nineteenth century and are described by George R. Taylor and Irene D. Neu in *The American Railroad Network, 1861–1890* (1956). A very revisionist interpretation of the relationship of railroads to government regulation is given by Lee Benson in *Merchants, Farmers, and Railroads* (1955), and Gabriel Kolko in *Railroads and Regulation, 1877–1916* (1965). An even more revisionist interpretation of the relationship, or lack of it, between railroads and economic growth is propounded by Robert Fogel in *Railroads and American Economic Growth* (1964), but Albert Fishlow's *American Railroads and the Transformation of the Antebellum Economy* (1966) should also be consulted.

The history of technology is as yet an underdeveloped field, although H. J. Habakkuk's *American and British Technology in the Nineteenth Century* (1962) is a good start. John W. Oliver surveys technological advances in his *History of American Technology* (1956). A ready reference tool is *A History of Technology*, Vol. V, *The Late Nineteenth Century, c. 1850 to c. 1900* (1958), ed. by Charles Singer *et al.*

For labor history, one must begin with John R. Commons *et al., History of Labour in the United States* (4 vols., 1936). Foster Rhea Dulles' *Labor in America,** 2nd ed. (1961) and Joseph G. Rayback's *A History of American Labor** (1959) are standard works. On the Knights of Labor, see Norman J. Ware's *The Labor Movement in the United States, 1860–1895** (1929). Philip Taft chronicles the rise of the American Federation of Labor in *The AF of L in the Time of Gompers* (1957). Gerald Grob's *Workers and Utopia* (1961) is a sophisticated treatment of ideological conflict within the labor movement which finds the Knights wanting. The radical sectors of the labor movement can be assessed through two good studies: Howard H. Quint's *The Forging of American Socialism* (1953), and David A. Shannon's *The Socialist Party of America** (1955).

For a general overview of the late nineteenth century see John A. Garraty's *The New Commonwealth, 1877–1890* (1968). More specialized essays can be found in H. Wayne Morgan, ed., *The Gilded Age: A Reappraisal* (1963). The political historiography of the period has been diverted into new paths by Richard Jensen's *The Winning of the Midwest* (1971), and Paul Kleppner's *The Cross of Culture: A Social Analysis of Midwestern Politics, 1850–1900* (1970).

Leonard D. White takes up administrative history in *The Republican Era, 1869–1901* (1958). Ray Ginger's *Age of Excess: The United States from 1877 to 1914** (1965) is a comprehensive but idiosyncratic interpretation.

A compendium of the minutia of social history is J. C. Furnas' *The Americans, A Social History, 1587–1914** (2 vols., 1969). Oscar Handlin's account of the psychology of immigrants to urban America in *The Uprooted: The Epic Story of the Great Migrations that Made the American People** (1951) is imaginative but somewhat disembodied. The real facts can be found in Moses Rischin, *The Promised City: New York's Jews, 1870–1914* (1962). M. A. Jones's *American Immigration** (1960) is a general synthesis. Attitudes toward immigrants are the subject of Barbara Solomon's *Ancestors and Immigrants** (1956), and John Higham's *Strangers in the Land** (1955). Attitudes toward poverty are analyzed by Robert Bremner in *From the Depths: The Discovery of Poverty in the United States** (1956). Two good sources on the response to urban immigrant culture and problems are Roy Lubove's *The Progressives and the Slums: Tenement House Reform in New York City, 1890–1917* (1962), and Roy Ginger's *Altgeld America: The Lincoln Ideal Versus Changing Realities* (1958). The better side of the genteel tradition can also be viewed in Arthur Mann's *Yankee Reformers in the Urban Age* (1954), and Nathan Huggins' *Protestants Against Poverty: Boston's Charities, 1870–1900* (1971). E. Digby Baltzell's *Philadelphia Gentlemen: The Making of a National Upper Class* (1958) should not be missed.

Urban history is beginning to be developed at a rapid pace, although there is a relatively low level of generalization in the comprehensive studies. The best introductions are Blake McKelvey's *The Urbanization of America, 1860–1915* (1963), Constance McL. Green's *The Rise of Urban America* (1965), Charles N. Glaab and A. Theodore Brown's *A History of Urban America** (1967), and Christopher Tunnard and H. H. Reed's *American Skyline** (1955). The pioneer in the field is Sam Bass Warner, Jr.'s *Streetcar Suburbs: The Process of Growth in Boston 1870–1900** (1962). The interaction of blacks and the urban environment can be followed in Gilbert Osofsky's *Harlem: The Making of a Ghetto, Negro New York, 1890–1930** (1966), Seth M. Scheiner's *Negro Mecca: A History of the Negro in New York City, 1865–1920* (1965), and Allan H. Spear's *Black Chicago: The Making of a Negro Ghetto, 1890–1920** (1967). The idea of community, threatened by the rapid changes of the Gilded Age, is Jean B. Quandt's subject in *From Small Town to the Great Community: The Social Thought of Progressive Intellectuals* (1970).

Social and intellectual historians have begun to poke around very productively in the byways of culture. A prime example is the work of James Harvey Young, *The Toadstool Millionaires: A Social History of Patent Medicines in America Before Federal Regulation* (1961). Henry F. May, in *Protestant Churches and Industrial America* (1949), and William G. McLaughlin, Jr., in *Modern Revivalism: Charles Grandison Finney to Billy Graham*, study the changing religious scene. Larzer Ziff's *The American 1890s: Life and Times of a Lost Generation** (1966) is an excellent introduction to literature on several levels. A brilliant analysis of educational history is Lawrence A. Cremin's *The Transformation of the School: Progressivism in American Education, 1876–1957* (1961). Higher education is covered by Frederick Rudolph in *The American College and University, A History** (1962), Lawrence R. Veysey in *The Emergence of the American University* (1965), and Richard Hofstadter and Walter Metzger in *The Development of Academic Freedom in the United States* (1955). F. L. Mott's *A History of American Magazines, 1885–1905* (1957) is an excellent study of the popular culture of the period.

* Also published in paperback edition.

Agrarian Radicalism

Populist Dreams and Negro Rights: East Texas as a Case Study

Lawrence C. Goodwyn

Race relations within the Populist Party in the South have been the elusive subject of scholarly interest for a long time. C. Vann Woodward in *Tom Watson, Agrarian Rebel* (1939) left a distinct impression that Georgia Populists attempted a dramatic departure in the direction of equalitarianism. Later, in *The Strange Career of Jim Crow* (1955), he maintained his position in a more carefully qualified form: "It is altogether probable that during the brief Populist upheaval of the 'nineties Negroes and native whites achieved a greater comity of mind and harmony of political purpose than ever before or since in the South."

It is important to understand that no scholar has claimed that the Populists were advocates of social equality between the races. Theirs was a very pragmatic (or perhaps cynical) appeal for political cooperation based on the idea that poor whites and poor blacks had the same economic problems. "This was an equalitarianism of want and poverty," Woodward writes, "the kinship of a common grievance and a common oppressor. As a Texas Populist

87

expressed the new equalitarianism, 'They are in the ditch just like we are.' " Black militants of the current black liberation movement have learned to distrust white radicals who argue that since racism is but a symptom of some more fundamental cause, such as class interests, one should not attack racism directly but rather attack the root cause. A black tenant farmer in the 1890s might have had similar suspicions concerning Populism.

In an article in the *Journal of Negro History* in 1953 Jack Abromowitz surveyed the scanty evidence about blacks and Populism and concluded that in the context of the times the white Populists behaved very well. Had they been able to do what they said they were going to do, they would have softened some of the hard lines of hostility between the races. One must keep in mind, of course, that the 1890s were a period of extraordinary racial tensions, peak years for lynchings, and a time when blacks were being systematically proscribed from the opportunities other citizens enjoyed in the economy, in politics, in public places, and in almost every area of life. The question quickly becomes, were white Populists more or less prejudiced than the average white Southerner? We do know that the Democrats baited the Populists relentlessly with the charge of heresy to the sacred principles of white supremacy and that the Populists, more often than not, denied the charge. Many historians think the Populists were hurt by the Democrats' ability to appeal for white solidarity.

Recently, in 1969, Robert Saunders has argued in the *Journal of Negro History* that in practice the evidence of Populist racial liberalism was very mixed and that there was very little difference between Populists and Democrats in revealed racial attitudes or in political tactics. If this is true, it is difficult to attribute the lack of Populist success to racial attitudes alone. In contrast, Herbert Shapiro, in his essay "The Populists and the Negro: A Reconsideration" (in August Meier and Elliott Rudwick, eds., *The Making of Black America*, II [1969]), argues that racism was the Achilles heel of Populism. Had Populist appeals for black votes not been so crassly expedient, had they addressed themselves to the inherent problems of black men, then black voters would have responded more

Populist Dreams and Negro Rights: East Texas as a Case Study. From *American Historical Review*, LXXVI (December 1971), pp. 1435–56. Copyright © 1972 by Lawrence C. Goodwyn. Reprinted by permission of The Sterling Lord Agency, Inc.

enthusiastically and the Populists would have been more successful. In view of prevalent racial attitudes among white voters, and Democratic party control of the election machinery, a frank appeal to racial equalitarianism was perhaps not realistic for the Populists.

Lawrence C. Goodwyn of Duke University has added the most recent chapter to this continuing scholarly controversy. He has provided a microcosmic study of politics in a county in eastern Texas where Populist success depended on a biracial alliance. His findings tend to confirm that equalitarianism was advocated by Populists, but at the same time they remind us that rural politics in the 1890s were not, as most historians assume, a matter of formal meetings, platforms, rhetoric, and public statements. They depended on family and personal alliances, face-to-face relationships, petty spoils and privileges, and frequently violence. An even more exciting aspect of Goodwyn's local study is its methodological breakthrough. He has successfully used oral sources to recapture some lost history.

*N*early a century later the Populist decade lingers in historical memory as an increasingly dim abstraction. The very word "Populism" no longer carries specific political meaning. It is now invoked to explain George Wallace, as it was used to explain Lyndon Johnson in the sixties, Joe McCarthy in the fifties, and Claude Pepper in the forties. Though afflicting principally the popular mind, this confusion is at least partly traceable to those historians who have insisted on concentrating on Populism as exhortation, so that Ignatius Donnelly's utopian novels or Mary Lease's pronouncements on the respective uses of corn and hell become the explanatory keys to agrarian radicalism. For scholars who mine political movements with a view to extracting cultural nuggets, the focus has been chiefly upon the word, not the deed; in the process of agrarian crusade has become increasingly obscure.[1]

---

[1] Such careful inquiries as C. Vann Woodward, *Origins of the New South* (Baton Rouge, 1951); Woodward, *Tom Watson, Agrarian Rebel* (New York, 1938); and Walter T. K. Nugent, *The Tolerant Populists* (Chicago, 1963), demonstrate how regional and state studies can reconstruct the milieu within which men performed their public political labors. Both historians are careful to set the words of Populists, Democrats, and Republicans against their respective acts. In contrast Richard Hofstadter and Norman Pollack, though in healthy disagreement in their assessment of the quality of Populist agitation, both rest their analysis on elusive cultural and ideological categories that often seem far removed from the inner workings of the agrarian crusade. In *The*

Much of the difficulty centers on the subject of race. There is essential agreement that, on economic issues, Populists were men of the Left, primitive to some, prophetic to others, but leftists to all. But did their banner indicate a highly selective nativist radicalism for whites only, or did they grapple with the inherited legacies of the caste system as part of an effort to create what they considered a more rational social and economic order? The analysis of Populist rhetoric has left us with contradictory answers.

While party platforms can be useful tools in determining professed attitudes, the gap between asserted ideals and performance is sufficiently large to defeat any analysis resting on the implicit assumption that political manifestos have an intrinsic value apart from the milieu in which they existed. In America the distance between assertion and performance is especially evident in matters of race; as a result, on this issue above all, the context of public assertions is central to the task of their political evaluation.[2] An inquiry into the murkiest corner of Populism, interracial politics, should begin not merely with what Populists said but what they did in the course of bidding for power at the local level. What was the stuff of daily life under Populist rule in the rural enclaves where the third party came to exercise all the authority of public office, including police authority? What can we learn not only about Populist insurgency but also about the orthodoxy the third party opposed?

Grimes County, Texas, was one of many counties scattered across the South and West where the People's party achieved a continuing political presence in the latter part of the nineteenth century. Located some sixty miles north of Houston in the heart of what the natives call the Old South part of Texas, Grimes County displayed the cotton-centered economy typical of rural East Texas in 1880. Its largest town, Navasota, contained 1,800 persons in 1890 and its second largest town, Anderson, the county

---

Populist Response to Industrial America (Cambridge, 1962), Pollack strains to find an authentic socialist basis for Populist criticisms of American capitalism. The attempt has the effect of diminishing the provincial generosity and innocence of Populism as well as socialist claims to ideological consistency; it also carries Pollack's inquiry toward the upper reaches of the party hierarchy in a manner frequently unrelated to the substance of third-party survival at the local level. The scholarly assault on Hofstadter's *The Age of Reform* (New York, 1958) has been both telling and recurring—the recurrence a testament to the vitality of this creative and persuasively written book. The criticism that Hofstadter selected a small number of Populist writings as a basis for sweeping generalizations about the nature of the agrarian crusade remains as true as ever.

[2] For example, a central aspect of race relations in the South concerns the question of which classes in Southern society took the lead in the successive processes—black disfranchisement being one of the more essential ones—by which the antebellum caste system, in altered form, was reinstitutionalized after Reconstruction. Analysis of rhetoric that is not intimately related to these processes as they occur cannot be expected to produce evidence that bears on the crucial causal relationships involved. In this connection a recent study by William I. Hair touches directly on one of these processes— the violent suppression of black trade unionism. Hair asserts that the gentry "embraced the kind of Negrophobia elsewhere usually attributed to ignorant poor whites." When Louisiana planters crushed a Knights of Labor strike in the lower delta parishes in 1887 casualties among cane field workers "ran into the hundreds." *Bourbonism and Agrarian Protest: Louisiana Politics, 1877–1900* (Baton Rouge, 1969), 184.

seat, only 574 persons as late as 1900. Farms in Grimes County ranged from plantation size in the rich bottomland country of the Brazos River on the county's western border to small, single-family agricultural units on the poorer land of the northern part of the county.[3] The 1890 census revealed a county population of 21,312, of which 11,664 were black.[4]

Populism in Grimes County is the story of a black-white coalition that had its genesis in Reconstruction and endured for more than a generation. In time this coalition came to be symbolized by its most enduring elected public official, Garrett Scott. The Scotts had roots in Grimes County dating back before the Civil War. Their sons fought for the Confederacy and returned to face a postwar reality by no means unique in the South; possessing moderately large holdings of land but lacking necessary capital to make it productive, the Scotts did not achieve great affluence. During the hard times that continued to afflict undercapitalized Southern agriculture through the 1870's Garrett Scott became a soft-money agrarian radical.[5] His stance was significant in the political climate of Grimes County in the early 1880s. During Reconstruction Negroes in the county had achieved a remarkably stable local Republican organization, headed by a number of resourceful black leaders. When Reconstruction ended and white Democrats regained control of the state governmental machinery in Texas, Grimes County blacks retained local power and sent a succession of black legislators to Austin for the next decade.[6] The local effort to end this Republican rule took the usual postwar Southern form of a political movement of white solidarity under the label of the Democratic party. In supporting the Greenback party Garrett Scott not only was disassociating himself from the politics of white racial solidarity, he was undermining it.

In 1882 a mass meeting of various non-Democratic elements in Grimes County nominated a variegated slate for county offices. Among the candidates were black Republicans, "lily-white" Republicans, and Independent Greenbackers. Garrett Scott was on the ticket as the Independent Greenback candidate for sheriff.[7] Not much is known about the racial climate in Grimes County in 1882, but it must not have been wholly serene, because the "lily-white" nominee for county judge, Lock MacDaniel, withdrew from the ticket rather than publicly associate with black candidates.[8] Garrett Scott did not withdraw, and in November he was elected. Also elected, as district clerk, was a black man who became a lifelong political ally of Scott, Jim Kennard.[9] Thus began an interracial coalition that endured through the years of propagandizing in Texas by the increasingly radical Farmers Alli-

---

[3] The author wishes to acknowledge the assistance of Marcus Mallard of Navasota, chairman of the Grimes County Historical Society. Mr. Mallard provided social, economic, and genealogical information on the county and many of its prominent families.

[4] Bureau of the Census, *Thirteenth Census of the United States, Abstract with Supplement for Texas* (Washington, 1913), 620; *Texas Almanac, 1910* (Dallas, 1910), 133.

[5] Galveston *News*, Sept. 10, 1882; Navasota *Tablet*, Nov. 11, 1900.

[6] Harrell Budd, "The Negro in Politics in Texas, 1877–1898" (master's thesis, University of Texas, 1925), 83; J. Mason Brewer, *Negro Legislators of Texas* (Dallas, 1935), 64, 74–75, 81.

[7] Galveston *News*, Sept. 10, 1882.

[8] *Ibid.*, Sept. 21, 1882.

[9] *Ibid.*, Nov. 11, 1882.

ance and through the ensuing period of the People's party. The success of the coalition varied with the degree of white participation. After the collapse of the Greenback party in the mid-eighties visible white opposition to the Democratic party declined for several years before Grimes County farmers, organized by the Alliance, broke with the Democracy to form the nucleus of the local People's party in 1892. Scott and Kennard were the most visible symbols of the revitalized coalition, but there were others as well. Among them were Morris Carrington, a Negro school principal, and Jack Haynes, both staunch advocates of Populism in the black community, as well as J. W. H. Davis and J. H. Teague, white Populist leaders. These men led the People's party to victory in the county elections of 1896 and again in 1898.[10]

A subtle duality creeps into the narrative of events at this point. To the world outside Grimes County in the 1890s, to both Populists and Democrats, Garrett Scott was simply another Populist officeholder, distinguished for his antimonopoly views and his generally radical approach to monetary policy. To his white supporters within Grimes County he was doubtless respected for the same reasons. But to the Democrats of Grimes County the sheriff symbolized all that was un-Southern and unpatriotic about the third party. Under Populist rule, it was charged, Negro school teachers were paid too much money; furthermore, in Scott's hands the sheriff's office hired Negro deputies. The two Democratic newspapers in Navasota were fond of equating Populist rule with Negro rule and of attributing both evils to Scott. The Navasota *Daily Examiner* asserted that "the Negro has been looking too much to political agitation and legislative enactment. . . . So long as he looks to political agitation for relief, so long will he be simply the means of other men's ambition."[11] To the Navasota *Tablet* Scott was simply "the originator of all the political trouble in Grimes County for years."[12] Both these explanations oversimplify Grimes County politics. The political presence and goals of blacks were definite elements of local Populism, as was, presumably, the personal ambition of Garrett Scott. But the Populists' pro-

---

[10] Carrington and Haynes as well as Kennard had been active in the county Republican organization prior to the emergence of the third party. The information from contemporary sources on the political lives of Negro leaders in Grimes County that was used in this paper was augmented by oral interviews with their descendants. The author wishes to express his gratitude to Maurice Lyons and B. T. Bonner, both former students at the University of Texas, for their assistance in the conduct of oral interviews in the black communities of Navasota, Anderson, Plantersville, and Richards in Grimes County. Largely through the efforts of Mr. Lyons and Mr. Bonner, the author was able to locate the descendants of every known black leader of the People's party in Grimes County. With respect to the third party's white leadership, the political histories of Teague, Davis, and Scott, traced through both oral interviews and contemporary sources, stand as examples of the diverse sources of Southern Populism. Teague, like Scott, spent his entire political life in opposition to the Democratic party—but as a Republican rather than as an agrarian radical. Quietly progressive on the race issue, Teague possessed considerable administrative talents and eventually became chairman of the third party for the first congressional district of Texas. He was elected county judge in 1896 and was reelected in the local third-party sweep of 1898. Davis, a Democrat, became quite radical on economic issues, broke with his party, and became a third-party editor. He displayed an ambivalent stance on the race issue and was not prominent in the events described in this paper.

[11] Navasota *Daily Examiner*, Oct. 13, 1898.

[12] *Tablet*, Nov. 11, 1890.

posed economic remedies had gained a significant following among the county's white farmers, and this was of crucial importance in inducing white Populists to break with Democrats and ally themselves with blacks. Garrett Scott was a living embodiment of white radicalism; he did not cause it.[13] Beyond this the political cohesion of blacks was a local phenomenon that had preceded Scott's entry into Grimes County politics and had remained relatively stable since the end of the war. The ease with which Democratic partisans saw the fine hand of Garrett Scott in Negro voting was more a reflection of their own racial presumptions than an accurate description of the political dynamics at work in the county.

Through the election of 1898 Democrats in Grimes County had labored in vain to cope with the disease of Populism among the county's white farmers. Finally, in the spring of 1899, the Democrats moved in a new direction. The defeated Democratic candidate for county judge, J. G. McDonald, organized a clandestine meeting with other prominent local citizens and defeated Democratic office seekers. At this meeting a new and—for the time being—covert political institution was created: the White Man's Union. A charter was drawn providing machinery through which the Union could nominate candidates for county offices in elections in which only White Man's Union members could vote. No person could be nominated who was not a member; no person could be a member who did not subscribe to these exclusionary bylaws; in effect, to participate in the organization's activities, so adequately expressed in its formal title, one had to support, as a policy matter, black disfranchisement.[14] Throughout the summer and fall of 1899 the White Man's Union quietly organized.

Writing years later McDonald explained that care was taken not to launch the organization publicly "until the public attitude could be sounded."[15] By January 1900 the covert organizing had been deemed sufficiently successful to permit the public unveiling of the White Man's Union through a long story in the *Examiner*. During the spring the *Examiner*'s political reporting began to reflect a significant change of tone. In April, for example, the *Examiner*'s report of a "quiet election" in nearby Bryan noted that friends of the two mayoral candidates "made a display of force and permitted no Negroes to vote. All white citizens went to the polls, quietly deposited their ballots for whom they pleased and went on about their business."[16] The *Examiner* had progressed from vague suggestions for disfranchisement to approval of its forcible imposition without cover of law.

The first public meetings of the White Man's Union, duly announced in the local press,[17] occupied the spring months of 1900 and were soon augmented by some not-quite-so-public night riding. The chronology of these

[13] The characterization of third-party rule as "Negro rule" was common in the Democratic press in counties where Populism was strong. Such accounts must be weighed against other stories, appearing in the same newspapers, that acknowledged the strong appeal of the People's party among white farmers. In this connection, see the *Examiner*, Nov. 4, 1898.

[14] The bylaws of the White Man's Union were published in the *Examiner*, Jan. 6, 1900.

[15] J. G. McDonald to E. L. Blair, July 10, 1928, in E. L. Blair, *Early History of Grimes County* (Austin, 1930), 197.

[16] *Examiner*, Apr. 4, 1900.

[17] *Ibid.*, Apr. 2, 3, June 4, 6, 11, July 17, 18, 19, 20, 30, 1900.

events may be traced through the denials in the local Democratic press of their occurrence. In July the *Examiner* angrily defended the county's honor against charges by the Negro Baptist State Sunday School Conference that the county had become unsafe for Negroes. The Austin *Herald* reported from the state's capital that the Sunday School Board, "after mature thought and philosophical deliberation," had decided to cancel its annual meeting scheduled for Navasota.[18] The *Examiner* cited as "irresponsible slush" the charge that Negroes were being threatened and told to leave the county, but within weeks reports of just such events began cropping up in the *Examiner* itself.[19] One example of terrorism left no one in doubt, for it occurred in broad daylight on the main street of the county seat: in July Jim Kennard was shot and killed within one hundred yards of the court-house. His assailant was alleged to be J. G. McDonald.[20]

Intimidation and murder constituted an even more decisive assault on the People's party than had the ominous bylaws of the White Man's Union. The Populist leadership recognized this clearly enough, and Scott went so far as to attempt to persuade Southern white farmers to shoulder arms in defense of the right of Negroes to vote.[21] Beyond this we know little of the measures attempted by the local Populist constabulary to contain the spreading terrorism. A well-informed member of the Scott family wrote a detailed account of these turbulent months, but the manuscript was subsequently destroyed. In the early autumn of 1900 members of the White Man's Union felt sufficiently strong to initiate visits to white farmers with a known allegiance to the People's party. Under such duress some of these farmers joined the White Man's Union.[22]

In August the Union, aided by a not inconsiderable amount of free publicity in the local press, announced "the Grandest Barbecue of the Year," at

[18] Austin *Herald*, reprinted in *Examiner*, July 17, 1900.

[19] *Examiner*, Sept. 4, 13, Oct. 19, Nov. 5, 1900.

[20] Carrie Meacham, private interview near Plantersville, Texas, Aug. 12, 1970. Mrs. Meacham is the daughter of the slain Populist leader. W. F. McGowan, private interview in Navasota, Apr. 14, 1970. Mr. McGowan, now ninety-four years old, was a personal friend of Jim Kennard. A. P. Wickey, private interview in Anderson, May 14, 1970. Mr. Wickey is the source of the statement attributing Kennard's death to Judge McDonald. Mr. Wickey's stepfather was a prominent member of the White Man's Union; the younger Wickey, now in his eighties, was present in Anderson the day of the slaying. His account is supported by Mrs. Meacham: "Judge McDonald shot my father off his horse on the main street of Anderson."

[21] The Navasota *Tablet* accused Scott of attempting to rally Populists in defense of Negro voting rights, describing his public appeals as "raving speeches." *Tablet*, Nov. 11, 1900.

[22] Edith Hamilton, private interview in Richards, Texas, May 24, 1970. Though specific information about the night-riding activities of the White Man's Union can occasionally be found in the local Democratic press, that source cannot be characterized as zealous in its reporting of extraparliamentary aspects of the campaign of 1900. Accounts of intimidation of Negro Populists have been preserved in the oral tradition of Grimes County Negroes; accounts of intimidation of white Populists have been preserved in the oral tradition of the Scott family. Mrs. Hamilton, now eighty years of age, is the niece of Garrett Scott. Richards, Texas, is located in Grimes County, a few miles from the county seat of Anderson. The lost "Populist history" of Grimes County was written by Mrs. Hamilton's father. It was destroyed after his death by his wife, Cornelia Kelly, because, says Mrs. Hamilton, "my mother felt we had all suffered enough and no purpose would be served by keeping my father's manuscript."

which the "workings of the White Man's Union" would be explained to all. The leadership of the People's party objected to announced plans to include the local state guard unit, the Shaw Rifles, in the program. After some discussion the Texas adjutant general, Thomas Scurry, placed at the discretion of the local commander the question of the attendance of the Shaw Rifles in a body. The commander, Captain Hammond Norwood, a leading Navasota Democrat and a member of the White Man's Union, exercised his option, and the Shaw Rifles appeared en masse at the function. Populist objections were brushed aside.[23]

Shortly after this well-attended barbecue had revealed the growing prestige of the White Man's Union as well as the inability of the People's party to cope with the changing power relationships within the county, a black exodus began. People left by train, by horse and cart, by day and by night. The *Examiner*, with obvious respect for the new political climate its own columns had helped engender, suggested elliptically that the exodus could produce complications. Some citizens, said the *Examiner*, "are beginning to feel a little nervous as the thing progresses, and lean to the idea that the action will bring on detrimental complications in the labor market."[24]

The next day, however, the paper printed a public address that it said had been "ordered published by the executive committee of the White Man's Union in order to combat the many reports that are calculated to injure the Union." After reaffirming the Union's intent to end "Negro rule" in the county, the report concluded with a message "to the Negroes":

> Being the weaker race, it is our desire to protect you from the schemes of those men who are now seeking to place you before them. . . . Therefore, the White Man's Union kindly and earnestly requests you to keep hands off in the coming struggle. Do not let impudent men influence you in that pathway which certainly leads to trouble. . . . In the future, permit us to show you, and convince you by our action, that we are truly your best friends.[25]

Fourteen days later a black Populist leader, Jack Haynes, was riddled with a shotgun blast by unknown assailants. He died instantly in the fields of his cotton farm.[26]

---

[23] *Examiner*, July 30, Aug. 8, 17, 18, 24, 1900. The affair of the Shaw Rifles was described in the *Examiner*, Aug. 21, 1900. The *Examiner* had by this stage become quite committed to the cause of extraparliamentary disfranchisement. On August 24 the paper described the White Man's Union picnic in terms of triumph, asserting that five thousand people had feasted at "1500 feet of tables . . . laden with well-turned and thoroughly seasoned barbecue, pork and mutton." Replying a week later to out-of-town dispatches that Grimes County politics had become complicated by the presence of four political tickets (Democratic, Republican, Populist, and White Man's Union), the paper replied: "Grimes County is in better shape politically than most counties in Texas. There is only one ticket and one piece of a ticket in the field. Anyone who viewed the Anderson picnic parade last week would have left little room for doubt as to which side would win." *Examiner*, Aug. 31, 1900.

[24] *Ibid.*, Sept. 13, 1900.

[25] *Ibid.*, Sept. 14, 1900. The promptness of the reply by the White Man's Union to the *Examiner*'s gentle admonition may be taken as an indication of the confidence and aggressiveness of the organization's leadership.

[26] Jack Haynes, Jr., private interview, Navasota, Texas, Apr. 14, 1970. Mr. Haynes is the son of the slain Populist leader. W. F. McGowan, interview, Apr. 14, 1970. The

The White Man's Union held a rally in Navasota two nights later that featured a reading of original poetry by one of the Union's candidates, L. M. Bragg. The verse concluded:

> Twas nature's laws that drew the lines
> Between the Anglo-Saxon and African races,
> And we, the Anglo-Saxons of Grand Old Grimes,
> Must force the African to keep his place.[27]

Another White Man's Union rally held in Plantersville the same week displayed other Union candidates whose conduct won the *Examiner*'s editorial approval: "They are a solid looking body of men and mean business straight from the shoulder."[28] Apparently this characterization of the Plantersville speakers was not restricted to approving Democrats; Populists, too, responded to events initiated by the men who "meant business." In October the Plantersville school superintendent reported that only five white families remained in his school district and that all the Negroes were gone. The superintendent stated that twelve white families had left that week, and "the end is not in sight."[29]

Amid this wave of mounting terror the People's party attempted to go about its business, announcing its nominating conventions in the local press and moving forward with the business of naming election judges and poll watchers. But there were already signs of a fatal crack in Populist morale. The People's party nominee for county commissioner suddenly withdrew from the race. His withdrawal was announced in the *Examiner*, and no explanation was offered.[30]

Throughout the late summer and autumn of 1900 the demonstrated power of the White Man's Union had protected McDonald from prosecution in the Kennard slaying. Nothing short of a war between the Populist police authority and the White Man's Union could break that extralegal shield. An exasperated and perhaps desperate Garrett Scott angrily challenged a White Man's Union official in October to "go and get your Union force, every damn one of them, put them behind rock fences and trees and I'll fight the whole damn set of cowards."[31] That Scott had to use the first person singular to describe the visible opposition to the Union underscores the extent to which terror had triumphed over the institutions of law in Grimes County. By election eve it was clear that the Populist ticket faced certain defeat. The third party had failed to protect its constituency. White Populists as well as

---

Examiner, Sept. 27, 1900, carried a one-paragraph story on Haynes's murder without, however, attributing to it any political implications. Haynes was not identified as a Populist leader. The murder of another black Populist leader, Morris Carrington, was also reported in the same issue, again without specifying Carrington's role in the People's party. This report had no foundation in fact and was printed either through error or by design to frighten the county's black population. Mr. Carrington died in 1923. The value of received oral traditions in correcting primary—and partisan—sources is briefly discussed at the conclusion of this paper.

[27] *Examiner*, Sept. 29, 1900.
[28] *Ibid.*
[29] *Ibid.*, Oct. 24, 1900.
[30] *Ibid.*, Oct. 30, 1900.
[31] *Tablet*, Nov. 11, 1900.

black were intimidated. Many would not vote; indeed, many were no longer in the county.[32]

Over 4,500 votes had been cast in Grimes in 1898. On November 6, 1900, only 1,800 persons ventured to the polls. The People's party received exactly 366 votes. The Populist vote in Plantersville fell from 256 in 1898 to 5 in 1900. In the racially mixed, lower-income precinct of south Navasota the Populist vote declined from 636 to 23. The sole exception to this pattern came in a geographically isolated, lower-income precinct in the extreme northern part of the county that contained few Negroes and thus, presumably, fewer acts of terrorism. The Populist vote in this precinct actually increased from 108 to 122 and accounted for one-third of the countywide vote of 366. In north Navasota, also almost all white but not geographically isolated from the terror, the Populist vote declined from 120 to 3.[33] An additional element, nonstatistical in nature, stamped the election as unusual. The underlying philosophy of the South's dominant political institution, the Democratic party, has perhaps never been expressed more nakedly than it was in Grimes County in 1900 when "the party of white supremacy," as C. Vann Woodward has called the Southern Democracy, appeared on the official ballot as the White Man's Union.[34]

On the way to its landslide victory the Union had grown more self-confident in its willingness to carry out acts of intimidation and terrorism in defiance of the local Populist police authority. Now that that authority had been deposed and a sheriff friendly to the White Man's Union had been elected, would terrorism become even more public?

On November 7, 1900, the morning after the election, a strange tableau unfolded on the streets of Anderson, the tiny county seat.[35] Horsemen began arriving in town from every section of the county, tied their horses all along the main street, and occupied the second floor of the courthouse. In a nearby house Garrett Scott's sister, Cornelia, and her husband, John Kelly,

[32] The *Examiner*'s pre-election issue foresaw a "quiet election" despite "some unmistakable bitterness in some quarters." The paper reported that "everything points to the success of the White Man's Union ticket." *Examiner*, Nov. 5, 1900.

[33] *Examiner*, Nov. 10, 1898, Nov. 9, 1900. Official Texas election returns are available in the state archives only on a countywide basis.

[34] The twenty-five per cent decline in the Democratic vote showed that not everyone was wholly content with the climate of violence that had developed. The *Examiner* somewhat opaquely expressed this anxiety. After noting that the Negro exodus was not confined to Grimes County, the White Man's Union and its tactics having spread to other counties, the newspaper felt contrained to add: "Yet there is a positive indication that something deep is at the bottom of the removal—some source for the frightful, unchristian and willful fabrications circulated." *Examiner*, Nov. 5, 1900. The *Examiner* can perhaps be pardoned for its failure to comment on its own role as a "source" if not of fabrications then of the advantages of the exclusionary administration of the ballot.

[35] The ensuing account of the events of November 7–11 is derived from a variety of sources. Both Navasota newspapers published versions of the Anderson affair, the *Tablet*, in a lengthy story on November 11 and the *Examiner* on November 8–10. The Galveston *News* carried increasingly detailed accounts on November 8-12. In addition to those persons cited elsewhere herein, a number of Grimes County residents supplied information on a basis not for attribution. In the black community the effect of the terrorism of 1900 has not yet run its course. The adjutant general's account, which is available in the Texas State Archives, Austin, is quite brief. *Report of the Adjutant General, 1899–1900* (Austin, 1900).

watched the buildup of Union supporters on the courthouse square, not fifty yards from the sheriff's official residence on the second floor of the county jail. They decided the situation was too dangerous to permit an adult Populist to venture forth, so the Kellys sent their nine-year-old son with a note to warn Scott not to appear on the street.

At about the same time that this mission was carried out Garrett Scott's younger brother, Emmett Scott, came into town from the family farm, rode past the growing clusters of armed men, and reined up in front of the store belonging to John Bradley, his closest friend in town. Bradley was a Populist but, as befitting a man of trade, a quiet one. His store was adjacent to the courthouse.

Cornelia Kelly's son found the sheriff at Abercrombie's store across the street from the jail and delivered the warning note. As Scott read it an outbreak of gunfire sounded from the direction of Bradley's store. Scott stepped to the street and peered in the direction of the fusillade. Rifle fire from the second floor of the courthouse immediately cut him down. Upon hearing the gunfire Cornelia Kelly ran out of her house and down the long street toward the courthouse. The gunsights of scores of men tracked her progress. Seeing her brother's body in the street she turned and confronted his attackers. "Why don't you shoot me, too," she yelled, "I'm a Scott." She ran to her brother and, with the assistance of her son, dragged him across the street to the county jail. He was, she found, not dead, though he did have an ugly wound in his hip. Inside Bradley's store, however, three men were dead—Emmett Scott, Bradley, and Will McDonald, the son of a Presbyterian minister and a prominent member of the White Man's Union. McDonald had shot Scott shortly after the latter had entered the store; the two men grappled for the gun, and the fatally wounded Scott fired one shot, killing McDonald. Bradley was killed either by a shot fired from outside the store where Union forces had gathered near the courthouse or by a stray bullet during the struggle inside.[36]

The siege of Anderson continued for five days, with the wounded sheriff and his deputies—black and white—in the jail and the White Man's Union forces in the courthouse. Shots crossed the fifty yards between the two buildings intermittently over the next several days. On the evening of the fatal shooting another member of the Scott clan, Mrs. W. T. Neblett, had left Navasota for Austin to plead with the governor, Joseph D. Sayers, for troops. On Friday she returned, accompanied by the adjutant general of the State of Texas, Thomas Scurry—the same official who had earlier acquiesced in the participation of the state guard in the White Man's Union barbecue.

[36] The *Tablet* leaves open the question of how Bradley's death occurred. White oral tradition holds that Scott killed Bradley. This is disputed by the Scott family oral tradition, supplied by Mrs. Hamilton, that Bradley was Scott's "best friend." The Galveston *News* supports Mrs. Hamilton's version: "As a result of some words, McDonald emptied his revolver into Emmett Scott, killing him, hitting him every time. He grabbed Scott's pistol, and the two began scuffling when a shot rang out and Bradley fell." *News*, Nov. 8, 1900. A subsequent bulletin, also printed in that issue, revises the story: "It was first thought Bradley received an accidental shot from Scott's pistol but later reports say he was shot by someone else. It is claimed Bradley had nothing to do with the fight between Scott and McDonald." The *News* described all three victims as men "prominent in the county."

After conferring with the contending forces Scurry pondered various methods to get the wounded Scott out of town and into a hospital; gangrene had set in. For protection, Scurry suggested that he be authorized to select a group of twenty prominent citizens of Navasota to escort the sheriff from the jail to the railroad station. Since most of the "prominent citizens" of Navasota were members of the White Man's Union, it is perhaps understandable that Scott declined this offer. The adjutant general then suggested that the Shaw Rifles be employed as an escort. This idea was respectfully declined for the same reason. Asked what he would consider a trustworthy escort, the wounded sheriff suggested a state guard unit from outside the county.[37]

On Saturday, four days after the shooting, a company of Houston light infantry of the Texas Volunteer State Guard detrained at Navasota and marched the eleven miles to Anderson. On Sunday morning Garrett Scott was placed on a mattress, the mattress put in a wagon, and the procession began. In the wagon train were most of the members of the large Scott clan —Emmett Scott's widow and children, the Kelly family, and the Nebletts, all with their household belongings piled in wagons. A file of infantrymen marched on either side as the procession formed in front of the jail, moved past hundreds of armed men at the courthouse and onto the highway to Navasota, and then boarded a special train bound for Houston.[38]

Thus did Populism leave Grimes County. From that day in 1900 until well after mid-century Negroes were not a factor in Grimes County politics. J. G. McDonald regained his judgeship and served for many years. The White Man's Union continued into the 1950s as the dominant political institution in the county. None of its nominees, selected in advance of the Democratic primary, was ever defeated.[39] The census of 1910 revealed the extent of the Negro exodus. It showed that Grimes County's Negro population had declined by almost thirty per cent from the 1900 total.[40] School census figures for 1901 suggest an even greater exodus.[41]

To this day the White Man's Union, as a memory if no longer as an insti-

---

[37] Report of the Adjutant General, 12. Both the Tablet, November 11, 1900, and Mrs. Hamilton agree in principle on this summation of the conversation between Garrett Scott and the adjutant general.

[38] Galveston News, Nov. 12, 1900; Tablet, Nov. 11, 1900; Report of the Adjutant General says that eight men and six women had taken refuge in the jail (p. 12).

[39] On this point all oral traditions in Grimes County correspond.

[40] Thirteenth Census, 822. The Negro population declined from 14,327 in 1900 to 9,858 in 1910. In 1890 the black population of Grimes had been 11,664.

[41] Scholastic Population and Apportionment of Available School Fund for 1901 (Austin, 1901), 7. While school census figures are available for 1901, I have been unable to locate comparable data for 1900. Nearest available figures prior to 1901 are for 1889. The 1901 school census, though taken a year after the exodus and presumably reflecting the return of some Negroes in addition to in-migration encouraged by the labor shortage, reveals a decline in the number of Negro pupils of fifteen per cent from the 1889 total, despite the fact that census returns show an increase of almost twenty per cent in Negro population between 1890 and 1900. This comparison suggests that the thirty per cent decline in Negro population evident from the census returns for 1900 and 1910 probably substantially minimizes the actual exodus that occurred in the late summer and fall of 1900. An exodus in the range from forty to fifty per cent probably would be a reasonable estimate.

tution, enjoys an uncontested reputation among Grimes County whites as a civic enterprise for governmental reform. In this white oral tradition the general events of 1900 are vividly recounted. Specific events are, however remembered selectively. The exodus of Negroes from the county is not part of this oral tradition, nor is the night riding of the White Man's Union or the assassination of the Negro Populist leaders.

As for Garrett Scott, he endured a long convalescence in a San Antonio hospital, regained his health, married his nurse, and moved to a farm near Houston. He retired from politics and died in his bed. He is remembered in the oral tradition of the black community as the "best sheriff the county ever had." Kennard and Haynes were killed because they "vouched" for Scott among Negroes.[42] In this black oral tradition the Negro exodus plays a central role. It is perhaps an accurate measure of the distance between the races in Grimes County today that two such contradictory versions of famous events could exist side by side without cross-influence.

To these two oral traditions a third must be added—the Scott tradition. The Scotts were, and are, a proud family. One by one, as they died, they were brought home to be buried in the family plot in the Anderson cemetery, little more than a mile from the site of the bloody events of 1900. Tombstones of female members of the clan bear the Scott middle name, defiantly emblazoned in marble. Edith Hamilton of Richards, Grimes County, was ten years old in November 1900 and remembers vividly the day her nine-year-old brother carried her mother's message to Garrett Scott. She remembers the defiance of her mother, the political commitment of her father, the acts of intimidation by the White Man's Union, the Negro exodus, and what she calls the "intelligence of Uncle Garrett." "They said that Uncle Garrett was a nigger-lover," recalls Mrs. Hamilton. "He wasn't a nigger-lover, or a white-lover, he just believed in being fair to all, in justice."[43]

The Scott oral tradition—similar to the black oral tradition and at odds with the white tradition—is virtually the only legacy of the long years of interracial cooperation in Grimes County. Beyond this the substance of political life that came to an end in Grimes County in 1900 cannot be measured precisely from the available evidence. Very little survives to provide insight into the nature of the personal relationship that existed between Garrett Scott and Jim Kennard, between any of the other Populist leaders of both races, or between their respective constituencies. Scott and his third-party colleagues may have been motivated solely by personal ambition, as the White Man's Union charged; on the other hand, the impulses that made them Populists in the first place may have led them toward public coalition with blacks. It is clear that such stridently white supremacist voices as the Navasota *Tablet* were unable to project any reason other than personal ambition to explain the phenomenon of white men willingly associating themselves politically with black men. To what extent this attitude reflected Populist presumptions is another question. White Populists and black Republicans shared an animosity toward the Southern Democracy that

42 W. F. McGowan, interview, Apr. 14, 1970.
43 Edith Hamilton, interview, May 13, 1970.

grew in intensity during the bitter election campaigns of the 1890s. Democratic persistence in raising the cry of "Negro domination" to lure Populist-leaning voters back to the "party of the fathers" was effective enough to keep white Populists on the defensive about the race issue throughout the agrarian revolt in the South. The circumstance of a common political foe nevertheless provided Populists and Republicans with a basis for political coalition that was consummated in a bewildering variety of ways—and sometimes not consummated at all. The stability of local black organizations and their demonstrated capacity to withstand Democratic blandishments or acts of intimidation were only two of the factors governing the complex equation of post-Reconstruction interracial politics. A stable, local black political institution existed in Grimes County, and its enduring qualities obviously simplified the organizational task confronting Garrett Scott. What might be regarded as "normal" Bourbon efforts to split blacks from the Populist coalition—mild intimidation, petty bribery, campaign assertions that the Democrats were the Negroes' "best friends," or a combination of all three—failed to achieve the desired results in Grimes County in the 1890s. The precise reasons are not easily specified. The Navasota *Tablet*, seeing the world through lenses tinted with its own racial presumptions, ascribed the credit for Negro political cohesion solely to the white sheriff. In the face of all Democratic stratagems, the third party's continuing appeal to Negroes was, in the *Tablet*'s view, a thing of "magic." A white supremacist view does not automatically exclude its holder from rendering correct political analyses on occasion, and it is possible that the *Tablet*'s assessment of the cause of Negro political solidarity was correct: however, such an analysis does not explain how the Negro Republican organization was able to send a succession of black legislators to Austin in the 1870s and 1880s, before Garrett Scott became politically active. It seems relevant that when Grimes County Democrats decided upon an overt campaign of terrorism, the men they went after first were the leading black spokesmen of Populism in the county rather than the third party's white leadership. To this extent the actions of Democratic leaders contradicted their public analysis of the causal relationships inherent in the continuing Populist majorities.

Before they indulged in terrorism the Democrats already possessed another method of splitting the Populist coalition: regaining the loyalty of white Populists. Against the historic Democratic campaign cry of white supremacy, the People's party had as its most effective defense the economic appeal of its own platform. The persuasiveness of Populism to white farmers in Grimes County was confirmed by newspaper accounts of the public reaction to the Populist-Democratic debates that occurred during the years of the agrarian uprising. While the reports in the *Examiner* were uniformly partisan and invariably concluded that Democratic spokesmen "won" such debates hands down, the papers conceded that Populist speakers also drew enthusiastic responses from white residents. The absence of reliable racial data by precincts renders a statistical analysis of the Populist vote in Grimes County impossible; however, the fragmentary available evidence suggests that the People's party was generally able to hold a minimum of approximately thirty per cent of the county's white voters in the four elections from 1892 to 1898 while at the same time polling approximately eighty to ninety per cent of the Negro electorate. The inability of the Democratic party to "bloc vote" the county's white citizenry, coupled with the party's failure to win black voters by various means or, alternatively, to diminish the size of the Negro electorate, combined to ensure Democratic defeat at the polls. The fact merits emphasis: both the cohesion of black support for the People's party and the maintenance of substantial white support were essential to the local ascendancy of Populism.

This largely deductive analysis, however, reveals little about the internal environment within the third-party coalition during the bitter struggle for power that characterized the decade of Populist-Democratic rivalry. However scrutinized, the bare bones of voting totals do not flesh out the human relationships through which black and white men came together politically in this rural Southern county. In the absence of such crucial evidence, it seems prudent to measure the meaning of 1900 in the most conservative possible terms. Even by this standard, however, a simple recitation of those elements of Grimes County politics that are beyond dispute isolates significant and lasting ramifications.

An indigenous black political structure persisted in Grimes County for thirty-five years following the Civil War. Out of his own needs as a political insurgent against the dominant Southern Democratic party, Garrett Scott decided in 1882 to identify his Greenback cause with the existing local Republican constituency. Once in office as sheriff he found, among other possible motives, that it was in his own self-interest to preserve the coalition that elected him. It is clear that the style of law enforcement in Grimes County under Scott became a persuasive ingredient in the preservation of black support for the People's party. The presence of black deputy sheriffs and Scott's reputation within the black community seem adequate confirmation of both the existence of this style and its practical effect. The salaries paid Negro school teachers constituted another element of third-party appeal. Comparisons with white salaries are not available, but whatever black teachers received, partisans of the White Man's Union publicly denounced it as "too much." It is evident that Grimes County Negroes supported the People's party for reasons that were grounded in legitimate self-interest—an incontestable basis for political conduct. The point is not so much that the county's Negroes had certain needs, but that they possessed the political means to address at least a part of those needs.

From this perspective the decisive political event of 1900 in Grimes County was not the overwhelming defeat of the local People's party but the political elimination of that part of its constituency that was black. Scott was valuable to Negroes in short-run terms because he helped to translate a minority black vote into a majority coalition that possessed the administrative authority to improve the way black people lived in Grimes County. In the long run, however, it was the presence of this black constituency—not the conduct of a single white sheriff nor even the professed principles of his political party—that provided the Negroes of the county with what protection they had from a resurgent caste system. As long as Negroes retained the right to cast ballots in proportion to their numbers they possessed bargaining power that became particularly meaningful on all occasions when whites divided their votes over economic issues. Disfranchisement destroyed the bargaining power essential to this elementary level of protection. Arrayed against these overriding imperatives for Negroes such questions as the sincerity of Garrett Scott's motives fade in importance. Whatever the sheriff's motives, both the political realities that undergirded the majority coalition and Scott's ability to respond to those realities shaped a course of government conduct under the People's party that was demonstrably of more benefit to Negroes than was the conduct of other administrations before or since. The permanent alteration of those realities through black disfranchisement ensured that no other white administration, whether radical, moderate, or opportunistic, would be able to achieve the patterns in education and law enforcement that had come to exist in the county under Populism. Stated as starkly as possible, after 1900 it was no longer in the interest of white politicians to provide minimal guarantees for people who could not help elect them.

Beyond this crucial significance for the county's black people, disfranchisement also institutionalized a fundamental change in the political environment of whites. More than a third party passed from Grimes County in 1900; in real political terms an idea died. Though a new political idea invariably materializes in democratic societies as an expression of the self-interest of a portion of the electorate, the party that adopts the idea in the course of appealing for the votes of that sector of the electorate inevitably is placed in the position of having to rationalize, defend, explain, and eventually promote the idea. If the concept has substance, this process eventually results in the insinuation of the idea into the culture itself. In this sense it is not necessary to know the precise depth of the commitment to Negro rights of the Grimes County People's party to know that the *idea* of Negro rights had a potential constituency among white people in the county as long as black people were able to project its presence through their votes. Given the endurance of this real and potential constituency, one could reasonably intuit that twentieth-century politics in Grimes County would have contained one, or a dozen, or a thousand Garrett Scotts—each more, or less, "sincere" or "ambitious" than the Populist sheriff. Disfranchisement destroyed the political base of this probability. A political party can survive electoral defeat, even continuing defeat, and remain a conveyor of ideas from one generation to the next. But it cannot survive the destruction of its constituency, for the party itself then dies, taking with it the possibility of transmitting its political concepts to those as yet unborn. It is therefore no longer possible to speak of two white political traditions in Grimes County, for the White Man's Union succeeded in establishing a most effective philosophical suzerainty. Seventy years after disfranchisement Mrs. Hamilton can recall the racial unorthodoxy of Uncle Garrett; she cannot participate in such activity herself. "The Negro people here don't want this school integration any more than the whites do," she now says. "They're not ready for it. They don't feel comfortable in the school with white children. I've talked to my maid. I know."[44]

While Garrett Scott's memory has been preserved, the local presence of the creed of his political party died with the destruction of that party.

[44] *Ibid.,* May 24, 1970.

There has been literally no political place to go for subsequent generations of Scotts and Teagues, or Kennards and Carringtons. This absence of an alternative political institution to the Democratic party, the party of white supremacy, has been a continuing and unique factor in Southern politics.[45] The circumstance is based on the race issue, but in its long-term political and social implications it actually transcends that issue.

The Populist era raises a number of questions about the interaction of the two races in the South, both within the third party and in the larger society. It is widely believed, by no means merely by laymen, that after the failure of Reconstruction meaningful experiments with the social order were finished in the South and that the aspirations of blacks were decisively thwarted. The example of Grimes County suggests, however, the existence of a period of time—a decade perhaps, or a generation—when nascent forms of indigenous interracial activity struggled for life in at least parts of the old Confederacy. Was some opportunity missed and, if so, how? How widespread through the South, and the nation, was this opportunity?

The White Man's Union was organized and led by men who considered themselves the "best people" of the South. If this attitude was typical, major adjustments must be made in our understanding of precisely how, and for what reasons, the antebellum caste system, in altered form, was reinstitutionalized in Southern society a generation after the formal ending of slavery. Was the "red-neck" the source of atrocity, or was he swept along by other stronger currents? And what of the Populist role? To what extent was agrarian racial liberalism in Texas traceable to an overall philosophy within the third-party leadership? Through what intuition of self-interest did the radical organizers of the Farmers Alliance, the parent institution of the People's party, accept the political risks of public coalition with blacks? What were their hopes and fears, and where did they falter? And, finally, what does the substance of their effort tell us about the Democrats in the South and the Republicans in the North who opposed them?

Answers to these questions rest, in part, on detailed knowledge of such events as those in Grimes County, but they require more than compilations of local histories, just as they assuredly require more than cultural assessments based on novels, speeches, and party manifestoes considered apart from their organic milieu. These answers will not provide much of a synthesis—Populism was too diverse, too congregational, and too ideologically thin—but they should tell us more about the larger society that, along with the Populists, failed to erect the foundations for a multiracial society in the nineteenth century. As the inquiry proceeds, it should be remembered that Populism perished before developing a mature philosophy—on race, on money, or on socialism. One must generalize, therefore, not only from contradictory evidence but, more important, from incomplete evidence. An analogy, doubtless unfair, could be made with the plight that would face modern historians of Marxism had that movement been abruptly truncated

[45] V. O. Key, *Southern Politics* (New York, 1949), is an authoritative study of the forms of Democratic orthodoxy in the various states of the old Confederacy, including the dominating orthodoxy of white supremacy; Vincent P. DeSantis, *Republicans Face the Southern Question* (Baltimore, 1959), summarizes the Republican failure to cope with the same imperatives.

at the time, say, of the Brussels Conference in 1903. Who could have predicted on the evidence available to that date the Stalinist reign of terror that evolved from the mature, victorious revolutionary party of 1917? By the same token sweeping generalizations about what Populist radicalism could have become are not only romantic but historically unsound.

It should be sufficient to observe that in the long post-Reconstruction period—a period not yet ended—during which the social order has been organized hierarchically along racial lines, Populism intruded as a brief, flickering light in parts of the South. For a time some white Southerners threw off the romanticism that has historically been a cover for the region's pessimism and ventured a larger, more hopeful view about the possibilities of man in a free society. Under duress and intimidation this public hope failed of persuasion at the ballot box; under terrorism it vanished completely.

The Grimes County story dramatically illustrates this failure, but in the insight it provides into the underlying politics of black disfranchisement and the achievement of a monolithic one-party political environment in the American South it is not unique. Other Populists in East Texas and across the South—white as well as black—died during the terrorism that preceded formal disfranchisement. In Texas the extraparliamentary institutions formed by white Democrats to help create the political climate for disfranchisement bore a variety of local names: the Citizens White Primary of Marion County; the Tax-Payers Union of Brazoria County; the Jaybird Democratic Association of Fort Bend County; and the White Man's Union of Wharton, Washington, Austin, Matagorda, Grimes, and other counties.[46] The available historical material concerning each of these organizations comes largely from the founders themselves, or their descendants, reflecting an incipient or a mature oral tradition—one oral tradition.[47] The secondary literature based

[46] J. A. R. Moseley, "The Citizens White Primary of Marion County," *Southwestern Historical Quarterly*, 49 (1946): 524–31; Pauline Yelderman, "The Jaybird Democratic Association of Fort Bend County" (master's thesis, University of Texas, 1938); Millie L. Kochan, "The Jaybird-Woodpecker Feud: A Study in Social Conflict" (master's thesis, University of Texas, 1929); Ira Brandon, "The Tax Payers Union in Brazoria County," *Texas History Teachers Bulletin*, 14 (1926): 86–92. Roscoe Martin reflects a knowledge of these extraparliamentary institutions, though the closest the author comes to exploring the topic is the following footnote: "One who is willing to undergo the hardships involved may learn many interesting things concerning the White Man's Party from those who have a first hand knowledge of the organization. Practically nothing, however, has been written on the subject." *The People's Party in Texas* (2d ed.: Austin, 1970), 236n. Other than accounts reflecting the perspective of the founders of these institutions, the statement is as true in 1971 as when Martin wrote in 1933.

[47] J. A. R. Moseley is the son of the founder of the Marion County Citizens White Primary. Both the Yelderman and Kochan manuscripts on the Jaybird Democratic Association rest on versions supplied by founders, as does the Brandon article on Brazoria County. The following extract from Brandon may be taken as indicative of the style of this genre: "On the night before the returns were canvassed, a comparatively small band of determined, conservative, honest, white, Christian, representative men of the county assembled . . . and the result of their deliberations was the creation of the present Tax Payers' Union of Brazoria County. . . . According to the rules, only white men can be members of this union and . . . vote in the 'Tax Payers' Primary.' " "Tax Payers Union," 87. Douglas G. Perry makes no inquiry into the structure of the party at the local level, in Grimes or any other Texas county, nor does he investigate the politics of black disfranchisement as it affected the People's party. "Black Populism: The Negro in the People's Party" (master's thesis, Prairie View Agricultural and Mechanical College, 1945).

on these accounts, including scholarly works used in graduate schools as well as primary and secondary textbooks, is correspondingly inadequate.[48]

A surprising amount of uninterpreted material from violently partisan white supremacist sources has found its way into scholarly literature. One example from the Grimes experience pertains directly to the scholarly characterization of Negro political meetings during the Populist era. It is worth attention as an illustration of the impact of white supremacist modes of thought on modern scholarship. The sunup-to-sundown work routine of Southern farm labor obviously precluded daytime political meetings. Accordingly, Kennard, Haynes, and Carrington campaigned among their black constituents by holding political meetings in each of the towns and hamlets of the county at night. Democratic partisans termed these rallies "Owl Meetings" and characterized black Populist leaders as " 'fluence men." Drawing upon their own party's time-honored campaign technique with Negroes, Democrats further asserted that owl meetings were more concerned with sumptuous banquets and whisky than with politics. If partisans of white supremacy had difficulty finding reasons for white acceptance of political coalition with blacks, they were culturally incapable of ascribing reasons for Negro support of the third party to causes other than short-run benefits in terms of money and alcohol. The point is not that Democrats were always insincere in their descriptions (as white supremacists they were quite sincere), but that scholars have subsequently accepted such violently partisan accounts at face value. The darkly sinister picture of " 'fluence men" corrupting innocent blacks with whisky at surreptitious owl meetings served to justify, at least to outsiders, the use of terrorism as the ultimate campaign technique of Democratic interracial politics. This sequential recording of events has found its way into scholarly monographs that otherwise demonstrate no inherent hostility to the Populistic inclinations of Southern farmers, black or white. In *The People's Party in Texas* Roscoe Martin precedes his brief allusion to the White Man's Union with a resumé of owl meetings and " 'fluence men" that reflects in detail the bias of white supremacist sources.[49] Other scholars writing broadly about Gilded Age politics have routinely drawn upon such monographs as Martin's, and by this process " 'fluence men" have materialized as an explanation of Negro

[48] Dewey Grantham, *The Democratic South* (Athens, Ga., 1963), is but one of the more recent manifestations of a long scholarly tradition in the South reflecting an unconscious assumption that reform politics is a function of white Southerners and that the observable victims of "Negrophobia" are Southern white progressives who are forced to employ race-baiting demagoguery in order to prevail at the polls. In this context see also Grantham's *Hoke Smith and the Politics of the New South* (Baton Rouge, 1958), 178: "The publicity given [Smith's] anti-Negro measures during the years 1905–1909 stamped him in the eyes of the nation as a Southern demagogue. It was unfortunate for his reputation as a Progressive leader that his work should have been marred in this respect." The failure of this kind of monoracial Southern scholarship rests less in its detail than in its underlying perspective on the qualifications for being "Southern" and the criteria upon which progressive "reputations" are based. Negroes lived desperately "political" lives during the period covered by Professor Grantham's books, though the substance of this politics, after disfranchisement, rarely took the form of decisions made at a ballot box.

[49] Martin, *People's Party*, 179–83, 236.

political insurgency in the nineties.[50] In the heat of local political combat, however, Democratic leaders often were able to face a wholly different set of facts in the course of persuading their followers, and the citizenry as a whole, to adjust to the necessity of terrorism. As the time approached for actual precinct campaigning in Grimes County in the autumn of 1900, the executive board of the White Man's Union published a notice of the Union's intentions, climaxed by a "fair distinct warning" to the county's Negro leadership. The statement is revealing—not only of the transformation visited upon normal campaign practices when they were viewed through the cultural presumptions of white supremacy but also of the dangers of uncritical acceptance of such perspectives by scholars relying upon monoracial sources. The notice read in part:

> The Union is largely composed of the best citizens of the county. . . . They are the tax payers, representing the worth, the patriotism, the intelligence, and the virtues of the county. . . . We are not fighting any political party or individuals, but only those who band together under any name, who seek to perpetuate negro rule in Grimes County. [Good citizens] are astounded at the manner in which the children's money has been expended. Colored teachers with fat salaries and totally incompetent have been appointed for political "fluence." Our white teachers, male and female, enjoy no such fat salaries as these colored politicians or these sweet colored girls. . . . One of the most corrupting practices in the past has been the system of Owl Meetings which has been in vogue for years. . . . This is the school and hot bed where the negro politician received his inspiration, and riding from one end of the county to the other as an apostle of his race, corrupting his own people who may be in the honest pathway of duty. We give fair warning that any effort to continue these Owl Meetings—by the appointment of special deputies sheriffs to organize and carry them on—will be prevented. No threat of shotguns will deter us from the discharge of this duty.[51]

Even without recourse to other perspectives this view of the existing political situation in Grimes County contains serious internal contradictions. Black Populist leaders were "incompetent" but as "apostles of their race" they had been so effective that their efforts needed to be stopped. Black teachers were paid "fat salaries" solely for political reasons, but among those receiving such gross patronage were "sweet colored girls," who obviously were not conducting owl meetings. The assertion that black teachers were actually paid more than white teachers must be rejected out of hand. In addition to the compelling fact that such an arrangement would have constituted poor political behavior on the part of a third party strenuously endeavoring to hold a substantial portion of the white vote and the further reality that such expenditures were unnecessary since parity for blacks in itself would have represented a notable accomplishment in the eyes of Negro leaders, Democrats had access to the records of all county expenditures and no such charge was ever leveled, much less documented, at any other time during the Populist decade. Whites complained that Negro

[50] See, for example, H. Wayne Morgan, *From Hayes to McKinley* (New York, 1969), 382.
[51] *Examiner*, Sept. 13, 1900. Jack Haynes was murdered two weeks after publication of this statement.

teachers received "too much," not that they received more than white teachers. In any case, it seems necessary only to observe that American political parties have routinely utilized night gatherings without having their opponents characterize them as owl meetings and that persons who benefited from incumbency were not presumed to be acting in sinister ways when they campaigned for their party's re-election. The only thing "special" about Garrett Scott's deputies was that some of them were black. Viewed as some sort of black abstraction Jim Kennard might appear convincing as a shadowy " 'fluence man," but as an intelligent and determined voice of the aspirations of Negro people he merits scholarly attention from perspectives not bounded by the horizons of those who murdered him. To an extent that is perhaps not fully appreciated, decades of monoracial scholarship in the South have left a number of Jim Kennards buried under stereotypes of one kind or another. They sometimes intrude anonymously as " 'fluence men," but they simply do not appear as people in books on Southern politics.

This circumstance suggests that not only the broad topic of interracial life and tension but the entire Southern experience culminated by disfranchisement needs to be tested by a methodology that brings both black and white sources to bear on the admittedly intricate problem of interpreting a free society that was not free. At all events, evidence continues to mount that monoracial scholarship, Northern and Southern, has exhausted whatever merit it possessed as an instrument of investigating the variegated past of the American people. The obvious rejoinder—that written black sources do not exist in meaningful quantity—cannot, of course, be explained away; at the same time, this condition suggests the utility of fresh attempts to devise investigatory techniques that offer the possibility of extracting usable historical material from oral sources. The example of the erroneous report in the Navasota *Examiner* of Morris Carrington's death[52] illustrates, perhaps as well as any single piece of evidence, not only the dangers inherent in relying on such "primary sources" for details of interracial tension in the post-Reconstruction South but also the value of received oral traditions in correcting contemporary accounts. Nevertheless, the problem of evaluating such source material remains; white and black versions of the details of racial conflicts are wildly contradictory. When they are measured against other contemporary evidence, however, the interpretive problem becomes considerably less formidable; indeed, the task of penetrating the substance behind partisan contemporary accounts may be lessened through recourse to available oral sources, as I have attempted to demonstrate.

Since much of the *Realpolitik* of the South, from Reconstruction through the modern civil rights movement, rests on legal institutions that, in turn, rest on extralegal methods of intimidation, the sources of political reality may be found less in public debate than in the various forms of intimidation that matured in the region. However determined a historian may be to penetrate the legal forms to reach this extralegal underside of the political culture of the South he is, in our contemporary climate, blocked off from part of his sources by his skin color. For black scholars there are limits to the availability both of courthouse records in the rural South and of respon-

---

[52] See note 26 above.

sive white oral sources. There are corresponding limits to the information white scholars can gain from interviews in black communities. Here, then, is fertile ground for scholarly cooperation. Methods of achieving this cooperation need to be explored. In its fullest utilization the subject is not black history or Southern history but American history.

The Folklore
of Populism

Richard Hofstadter

The classic accounts of Populism, such as those by
John D. Hicks (*The Populist Revolt* [1931]) and
C. Vann Woodward (*Origins of the New South*
[1951]), describe it as a rational and forward-looking
reform movement in the great American reform
tradition, a movement of simple farmers offering
reasonable solutions to real problems. Then, in the
1950s, at a time when democracy was under attack
because it was associated with the most perverse kind
of anticommunist witch hunting, and when some
historians were discovering that democracy had urban
roots while others found that agrarian societies were
not necessarily democratic, various commentators
began to emphasize the aberrations of Populism to
such an extent that Populism appeared to be a sharp
deviation from the reform tradition. According to
Richard Hofstadter, the most cogent of these critics,
the Populists were plagued with anxiety due to a loss
of social status and were therefore bitterly motivated
by an unreflective belief in the yeoman myth.

The collective charge against Populism comprises a
more lengthy bill of particulars. First, and most
important, the Populists are faulted for thinking that
rural life conferred moral worth. Feeling powerless
and persecuted because of their declining importance
to society and their worsening economic condition as

contrasted with the burgeoning urban sector, farmers naturally took refuge in the myth that gave them a central place. "A generation or two removed from the invigorating influences of the farm wears out both mental and bodily vigor," said Napoleon V. Ashby, the lecturer for the National Farmers Alliance. "Hence, the leaders in the great moral, social, intellectual, and political movements of the race come continually from the descendants of the sturdy yeoman." One must be cautious in criticizing the Populists for some special sin in believing in the yeoman myth. It is a popular conception. As Dwight David Eisenhower wrote in one of his messages to Congress while President, "In America, agriculture is more than an industry; it is a way of life. Throughout our history the family farmer has given strength and vitality to our entire social order. We must keep it healthy and vigorous."

Second, the critics charged Populists with oversimplifying their situation. In the American Manichean tradition, they dichotomized the conflict; there were simply the producers and the nonproducers. Third, rather than coming to terms with changing reality and facing the future, Populists looked backward to a golden age in the early republic. Fourth, Populist thought proceeded from a mistaken belief in natural harmonies. According to them, the sad plight of the farmers was due to the erection of artificial barriers and the intervention of evil men and laws. They were so convinced of this that they fell into their fifth error of tending to interpret history in terms of conspiracy.

Sixth, the critics state that the Populists were fixated on an unrealistic belief in the primacy of money. And last, in all of their actions and outlook, they were guilty of provincialism and narrowness. They were, in fact, nativists. They were nationalistic, jingoistic, imperialistic, and anti-Semitic. Some of the more imaginative and less careful Populist critics even accused them of fascistic tendencies.

For the past fifteen years, the defenders of Populism have been replying to these charges. They have, in the main, been successful. The Populists should be excused, argue the defenders, for believing in the agrarian myth, for every social group tends to believe in the myths that confer worth on itself. Similarly, it can be said that all popular movements dramatize and concretize the enemy. The Populists should not be charged with demagogy simply on those grounds. As for the charge that the Populists believed unrealistically in "natural harmony," they were probably right in thinking that there were artificial reasons for poverty. They were also right in believing that the banking system was stacked against them, and they were correct in thinking that only the government could solve the problem. There is very little evidence that they, as a group, rejected industrialism. If they longed for their old status, they still acted in the present, and hoped for the future. They may have overdone the conspiracy argument, but they were right about the identity of their enemy. They were no more unrealistic in their economic ideas than were Easterners of the time with their insistence on the gold standard; besides, real Populists emphasized credit and not free silver. They may have been guilty of provincialism and narrowness, but that is no great sin, and there is no hard evidence that they were more nativistic or xenophobic than the population at large. Finally, Populism was neither humanitarian nor paternalistic but very pragmatic. As an oppressed group, they could not afford to be other than realistic.

The anti-Semitism of the Populists has been unfairly stressed, argue the defenders of the party. Anti-Semitism was more connected to the silverites than to Populism, and it was associated with the symbolic targets of the silverites: Wall Street, British bankers, and Jewish bankers. That which did exist within the party was verbal and rhetorical; there was no overt anti-Semitic action on the part of the Populists. Anti-Semitism was extremely rare in the South, where Populism was strong, and there were, in fact, Jewish Populists in the South.

In the following selection, the late Richard Hofstadter, former Dewitt Clinton Professor of History at Columbia University, exposes the dual image that farmers had of themselves and argues that Populism was an outgrowth of the soft side of agricultural existence. The discontinuity between agrarian realities and the agrarian myth is the theme of this selection from *The Age of Reform*, which was awarded the Pulitzer Prize for history in 1956. In judging the validity of the charges that Hofstadter brings against Populism, the reader should heed the author's warning: "By 'Populism' I do not mean

only the People's (or Populist) Party of the 1890s; for
I consider the Populist Party to be merely a
heightened expression, at a particular moment of time,
of a kind of popular impulse that is endemic in
American political culture."

The Frontier or the Market?

The American farmer was unusual in the agricultural world in the sense
that he was running a mechanized and commercialized agricultural unit of
a size far greater than the small proprietary holdings common elsewhere,
and yet he was running it as a family enterprise on the assumption that the
family could supply not only the necessary capital and managerial talent
but also most of the labor. This system, however applicable to the subsistence farm or the small yeoman's farm, was hardly adequate to the conditions of commercial agriculture.[1] As a businessman, the farmer was
appropriately hardheaded; he tried to act upon a cold and realistic strategy
of self-interest. As the head of a family, however, the farmer felt that he was
investing not only his capital but his hard work and that of his wife and
children, that when he risked his farm he risked his home—that he was, in
short, a single man running a personal enterprise in a world of impersonal
forces. It was from this aspect of his situation—seen in the hazy glow of the
agrarian myth—that his political leaders in the 1890's developed their rhetoric
and some of their concepts of political action. The farmer's commercial
position pointed to the usual strategies of the business world: combination,
co-operation, pressure politics, lobbying, piecemeal activity directed toward
specific goals. But the bathos of the agrarian rhetoric pointed in a different
direction: broad political goals, ideological mass politics, third parties, the
conquest of the "money power," the united action of all labor, rural and
urban. When times were persistently bad, the farmer tended to reject his
business role and its failures to withdraw into the role of the injured little
yeoman. This made the differences between his situation and that of any
other victim of exploitation seem unimportant to him. As a Southern
journalist wrote of the situation in the cotton country: "The landowner
was so poor and distressed that he forgot that he was a capitalist. . . so
weary of hand and sick of spirit that he imagined himself in precisely the
same plight as the hired man. . . ."[2]

The American farmer thus had a dual character, and one way of understanding our agrarian movements is to observe which aspect of the farmer's
double personality is uppermost at a given time. It is my contention that
both the Populist rhetoric and the modern liberal's indulgent view of the

[1] Malin: "Mobility and History," pp. 182 ff.

[2] Quoted by C. Vann Woodward: *Origins of the New South* (Baton Rouge, 1951),
p. 194. During the late 1880's, when farm discontent was not yet at its peak, such farm
organizations as the Farmers' Alliances developed limited programs based upon economic
self-interest; in the 1890's, when discontent became most acute, it produced a national
third-party movement.

farmers' revolt have been derived from the "soft" side of the farmer's existence—that is, from agrarian "radicalism" and agrarian ideology—while most farm organizations since the decline of the Populists have been based primarily upon the "hard" side, upon agricultural improvement, business methods, and pressure politics. Populism itself had a hard side, especially in the early days of the Farmers' Alliance and the Populist Party, but this became less and less important as the depression of the nineties deepened and other issues were dropped in favor of the silver panacea.

.   .   .

The Two Nations

There is indeed much that is good and usable in our Populist past. While the Populist tradition had defects that have been too much neglected, it does not follow that the virtues claimed for it are all fictitious. Populism was the first modern political movement of practical importance in the United States to insist that the federal government has some responsibility for the common weal; indeed, it was the first such movement to attack seriously the problems created by industrialism. The complaints and demands and prophetic denunciations of the Populists stirred the latent liberalism in many Americans and startled many conservatives into a new flexibility. Most of the "radical" reforms in the Populist program proved in later years to be either harmless or useful. In at least one important area of American life a few Populist leaders in the South attempted something profoundly radical and humane—to build a popular movement that would cut across the old barriers of race—until persistent use of the Negro bogy distracted their following. To discuss the broad ideology of the Populist does them some injustice, for it was in their concrete programs that they added most constructively to our political life, and in their more general picture of the world that they were most credulous and vulnerable. Moreover, any account of the fallibility of Populist thinking that does not acknowledge the stress and suffering out of which that thinking emerged will be seriously remiss. But anyone who enlarges our portrait of the Populist tradition is likely to bring out some unseen blemishes. In the books that have been written about the Populist movement, only passing mention has been made of its significant provincialism; little has been said of its relations with nativism and nationalism; nothing has been said of its tincture of anti-Semitism.

The Populist impulse expressed itself in a set of notions that represent what I have called the "soft" side of agrarianism. These notions, which appeared with regularity in the political literature, must be examined if we are to re-create for ourselves the Populist spirit. To extract them from the full context of the polemical writings in which they appeared is undoubtedly to oversimplify them; even to name them in any language that comes readily to the historian of ideas is perhaps to suggest that they had a formality and coherence that in reality they clearly lacked. But since it is less feasible to have no labels than to have somewhat too facile ones, we may enumerate the dominant themes in Populist ideology as these: the idea of a golden age; the concept of natural harmonies; the dualistic version of social struggles; the conspiracy theory of history; and the doctrine of the primacy of money. The last of these I will touch upon in connection with the free-silver issue. Here I propose to analyze the others, and to show how they were nurtured by the traditions of the agrarian myth.

The utopia of the Populists was in the past, not the future. According to the agrarian myth, the health of the state was proportionate to the degree to which it was dominated by the agricultural class, and this assumption pointed to the superiority of an earlier age. The Populists looked backward with longing to the lost agrarian Eden, to the republican America of the early years of the nineteenth century in which there were few millionaires and, as they saw it, no beggars, when the laborer had excellent prospects and the farmer had abundance, when statesmen still responded to the mood of the people and there was no such thing as the money power.[3] What they meant—though they did not express themselves in such terms—was that they would like to restore the conditions prevailing before the development of industrialism and the commercialization of agriculture. It should not be surprising that they inherited the traditions of Jacksonian democracy, that they revived the old Jacksonian cry: "Equal Rights for All, Special Privileges for None," or that most of the slogans of 1896 echoed the battle cries of 1836.[4] General James B. Weaver, the Populist candidate for the presidency in 1892, was an old Democrat and Free-Soiler, born during the days of Jackson's battle with the United States Bank, who drifted into the Greenback movement after a short spell as a Republican, and from there to Populism. His book, *A Call to Action*, published in 1892, drew up an indictment of the business corporation which reads like a Jacksonian polemic. Even in those hopeful early days of the People's Party, Weaver projected no grandiose plans for the future, but lamented the course of recent history, the growth of economic oppression, and the emergence of great contrasts of wealth and poverty, and called upon his readers to do "All in [their] power to arrest the alarming tendencies of our times."[5]

Nature, as the agrarian tradition had it, was beneficent. The United States was abundantly endowed with rich land and rich resources, and the "natural" consequence of such an endowment should be the prosperity of the people. If the people failed to enjoy prosperity, it must be because of a harsh and arbitrary intrusion of human greed and error. "Hard times, then," said one popular writer,

> as well as the bankruptcies, enforced idleness, starvation, and the crime, misery, and moral degradation growing out of conditions like the present, being unnatural, not in accordance with, or the result of any natural law, must be attributed to that kind of unwise and pernicious legislation which history proves to have produced similar results in all ages of the world. It is

[3] Thomas E. Watson: *The Life and Times of Andrew Jackson* (Thomson, Ga., 1912), p. 325: "All the histories and all the statesmen agree that during the first half-century of our national existence, we had no poor. A pauper class was unthought of: a beggar, or a tramp never seen." Cf. Mrs. S. E. V. Emery: *Seven Financial Conspiracies Which Have Enslaved the American People* (Lansing, ed. 1896), pp. 10–11.

[4] Note for instance the affectionate treatment of Jacksonian ideas in Watson, op. cit., pp. 343–4.

[5] James B. Weaver: *A Call to Action* (Des Moines, 1892), pp. 377–8.

the mission of the age to correct these errors in human legislation, to adopt and establish policies and systems, in accord with, rather than in opposition to divine law.[6]

In assuming a lush natural order whose workings were being deranged by human laws, Populist writers were again drawing on the Jacksonian tradition, whose spokesmen also had pleaded for a proper obedience to "natural" laws as a prerequisite of social justice.[7]

Somewhat akin to the notion of the beneficence of nature was the idea of a natural harmony of interests among the productive classes. To the Populist mind there was no fundamental conflict between the farmer and the worker, between the toiling people and the small businessman. While there might be corrupt individuals in any group, the underlying interests of the productive majority were the same; predatory behavior existed only because it was initiated and underwritten by a small parasitic minority in the highest places of power. As opposed to the idea that society consists of a number of different and frequently clashing interests—the social pluralism expressed, for instance, by Madison in the *Federalist*—the Populists adhered, less formally to be sure, but quite persistently, to a kind of social dualism: although they knew perfectly well that society was composed of a number of classes, for all practical purposes only one simple division need be considered. There were two nations. "It is a struggle," said Sockless Jerry Simpson, "between the robbers and the robbed."[8] "There are but two sides in the conflict that is being waged in this country today," declared a Populist manifesto.

> On the one side are the allied hosts of monopolies, the money power, great trusts and railroad corporations, who seek the enactment of laws to benefit them and impoverish the people. On the other are the farmers, laborers, merchants, and all other people who produce wealth and bear the burdens of taxation. . . . Between these two there is no middle ground.[9]

"On the one side," said Bryan in his famous speech against the repeal of the Sherman Silver Purchase Act, "stand the corporate interests of the United States, the moneyed interests, aggregated wealth and capital, imperious, arrogant, compassionless. . . . On the other side stand an unnumbered throng, those who gave to the Democratic party a name and for whom it has assumed to speak."[10] The people versus the interests, the public versus the

---

[6] B. S. Heath: *Labor and Finance Revolution* (Chicago, 1892), p. 5.

[7] For this strain in Jacksonian thought, see Richard Hofstadter: "William Leggett, Spokesman of Jacksonian Democracy," *Political Science Quarterly*, Vol. XLVIII (December 1943), pp. 581–94, and *The American Political Tradition*, pp. 60–1.

[8] Elizabeth N. Barr: "The Populist Uprising," in William E. Connelley, ed.: *A Standard History of Kansas and Kansans*, Vol. II, p. 1170.

[9] Ray Allen Billington: *Westward Expansion* (New York, 1949), p. 741.

[10] Allan Nevins: *Grover Cleveland* (New York, 1933), p. 540; Heath, op. cit., p. 27: "The world has always contained two classes of people, one that lived by honest labor and the other that lived *off* of honest labor." *Cf.* Governor Lewelling of Kansas: "Two great forces are forming in battle line: the same under different form and guise that have long been in deadly antagonism, represented in master and slave, lord and vassal, king and peasant, despot and serf, landlord and tenant, lender and borrower, organized avarice and the necessities of the divided and helpless poor." James A. Barnes: *John G. Carlisle* (New York, 1931), pp. 254–5.

plutocrats, the toiling multitude versus the money power—in various phrases this central antagonism was expressed. From this simple social classification it seemed to follow that once the techniques of misleading the people were exposed, victory over the money power ought to be easily accomplished, for in sheer numbers the people were overwhelming. "There is no power on earth that can defeat us," said General Weaver during the optimistic days of the campaign of 1892. "It is a fight between labor and capital, and labor is in the vast majority."[11]

The problems that faced the Populists assumed a delusive simplicity: the victory over injustice, the solution for all social ills, was concentrated in the crusade against a single, relatively small but immensely strong interest, the money power. "With the destruction of the money power," said Senator Peffer,

> the death knell of gambling in grain and other commodities will be sounded; for the business of the worst men on earth will have been broken up, and the mainstay of the gamblers removed. It will be an easy matter, after the greater spoilsmen have been shorn of their power, to clip the wings of the little ones. Once get rid of the men who hold the country by the throat, the parasites can be easily removed.[12]

Since the old political parties were the primary means by which the people were kept wandering in the wilderness, the People's Party advocates insisted, only a new and independent political party could do this essential job.[13] As the silver question became more prominent and the idea of a third party faded, the need for a monolithic solution became transmuted into another form: there was only one *issue* upon which the money power could really be beaten and this was the money issue. "When we have restored the money of the Constitution," said Bryan in his Cross of Gold speech, "all other necessary reforms will be possible; but . . . until this is done there is no other reform that can be accomplished."

While the conditions of victory were thus made to appear simple, they did not always appear easy, and it would be misleading to imply that the tone of Populistic thinking was uniformly optimistic. Often, indeed, a deep-lying vein of anxiety showed through. The very sharpness of the struggle, as the Populists experienced it, the alleged absence of compromise solutions and of intermediate groups in the body politic, the brutality and desperation that were imputed to the plutocracy—all these suggested that failure of the people to win the final contest peacefully could result only in a total victory for the plutocrats and total extinction of democratic institutions, possibly after a period of bloodshed and anarchy. "We are nearing a serious crisis," declared Weaver. "If the present strained relations between wealth owners and wealth producers continue much longer they will ripen into frightful disaster. This universal discontent must be quickly interpreted and its causes removed."[14] "We meet," said the Populist platform of 1892,

[11] George H. Knoles: *The Presidential Campaign and Election of 1892* (Stanford, 1942), p. 179.
[12] William A. Peffer: *The Farmer's Side* (New York, 1891), p. 273.
[13] Ibid., pp. 148–50.
[14] Weaver, op. cit., p. 5.

in the midst of a nation brought to the verge of moral, political, and material ruin. Corruption dominates the ballot-box, the Legislatures, the Congress, and touches even the ermine of the bench. The people are demoralized. . . . The newspapers are largely subsidized or muzzled, public opinion silenced, business prostrated, homes covered with mortgages, labor impoverished, and the land concentrating in the hands of the capitalists. The urban workmen are denied the right to organize for self-protection, imported pauperized labor beats down their wages, a hireling standing army, unrecognized by our laws, is established to shoot them down, and they are rapidly degenerating into European conditions. The fruits of the toil of millions are boldly stolen to build up colossal fortunes for a few, unprecedented in the history of mankind; and the possessors of these, in turn, despise the Republic and endanger liberty.

Such conditions foreboded "the destruction of civilization, or the establishment of an absolute despotism."

.   .   .

History as Conspiracy

. . . There was something about the Populist imagination that loved the secret plot and the conspiratorial meeting. There was in fact a widespread Populist idea that all American history since the Civil War could be understood as a sustained conspiracy of the international money power.

The pervasiveness of this way of looking at things may be attributed to the common feeling that farmers and workers were not simply oppressed but oppressed deliberately, consciously, continuously, and with wanton malice by "the interests." It would of course be misleading to imply that the Populists stand alone in thinking of the events of their time as the results of a conspiracy. This kind of thinking frequently occurs when political and social antagonisms are sharp. Certain audiences are especially susceptible to it—particularly, I believe, those who have attained only a low level of education, whose access to information is poor,[15] and who are so completely shut out from access to the centers of power that they feel themselves completely deprived of self-defense and subjected to unlimited manipulation by those who wield power. There are, moreover, certain types of popular movements of dissent that offer special opportunities to agitators with paranoid tendencies, who are able to make a vocational asset out of their psychic disturbances.[16] Such persons have an opportunity to impose their own style of thought upon the movements they lead. It would of course be misleading to imply that there are no such things as conspiracies in history. Anything that partakes of political strategy may need, for a time at least, an element of secrecy, and is thus vulnerable to being dubbed conspiratorial. Corruption itself has the character of conspiracy. In this sense the Crédit Mobilier was a

[15] In this respect it is worth pointing out that in later years, when facilities for realistic exposure became more adequate, popular attacks on "the money power" showed fewer elements of fantasy and more of reality.

[16] See, for instance, the remarks about a mysterious series of international assassinations with which Mary E. Lease opens her book *The Problem of Civilization Solved* (Chicago, 1895).

conspiracy, as was the Teapot Dome affair. If we tend to be too condescending to the Populists at this point, it may be necessary to remind ourselves that they had seen so much bribery and corruption, particularly on the part of the railroads, that they had before them a convincing model of the management of affairs through conspiratorial behavior. Indeed, what makes conspiracy theories so widely acceptable is that they usually contain a germ of truth. But there is a great difference between locating conspiracies *in* history and saying that history *is*, in effect, a conspiracy, between singling out those conspiratorial acts that do on occasion occur and weaving a vast fabric of social explanation out of nothing but skeins of evil plots.

· · ·

. . . Populist thought showed an unusually strong tendency to account for relatively impersonal events in highly personal terms. An overwhelming sense of grievance does not find satisfactory expression in impersonal explanations, except among those with a well-developed tradition of intellectualism. It is the city, after all, that is the home of intellectual complexity. The farmer lived in isolation from the great world in which his fate was actually decided. He was accused of being unusually suspicious,[17] and certainly his situation, trying as it was, made thinking in impersonal terms difficult. Perhaps the rural middle-class leaders of Populism (this was a movement of farmers, but it was not led by farmers) had more to do than the farmer himself with the cast of Populist thinking. At any rate, Populist thought often carries one into a world in which the simple virtues and unmitigated villainies of a rural melodrama have been projected on a national and even an international scale. In Populist thought the farmer is not a speculating businessman, victimized by the risk economy of which he is a part, but rather a wounded yeoman, preyed upon by those who are alien to the life of folkish virtue. A villain was needed, marked with the unmistakable stigmata of the villains of melodrama, and the more remote he was from the familiar scene, the more plausibly his villainies could be exaggerated.

It was not enough to say that a conspiracy of the money power against the common people was going on. It had been going on ever since the Civil War. It was not enough to say that it stemmed from Wall Street. It was international: it stemmed from Lombard Street. In his preamble to the People's Party platform of 1892, a succinct, official expression of Populist views, Ignatius Donnelly asserted: "A vast conspiracy against mankind has been organized on two continents, and it is rapidly taking possession of the world. If not met and overthrown at once it forebodes terrible social convulsions, the destruction of civilization, or the establishment of an absolute despotism." A manifesto of 1895, signed by fifteen outstanding leaders of the People's Party, declared:

> As early as 1865–66 a conspiracy was entered into between the gold gamblers of Europe and America. . . . For nearly thirty years these conspirators have

---

[17] Frederick L. Paxson: "The Agricultural Surplus: a Problem in History," *Agricultural History*, Vol. VI (April 1932), p. 58; cf. the observations of Lord Bryce in *The American Commonwealth* (New York, ed. 1897), Vol. II, pp. 294–5.

kept the people quarreling over less important matters while they have pursued with unrelenting zeal their one central purpose. . . . Every device of treachery, every resource of statecraft, and every artifice known to the secret cabals of the international gold ring are being made use of to deal a blow to the prosperity of the people and the financial and commercial independence of the country."[18]

The financial argument behind the conspiracy theory was simple enough. Those who owned bonds wanted to be paid not in a common currency but in gold, which was at a premium; those who lived by lending money wanted as high a premium as possible to be put on their commodity by increasing its scarcity. The panics, depressions, and bankruptcies caused by their policies only added to their wealth; such catastrophes offered opportunities to engross the wealth of others through business consolidations and foreclosures. Hence the interests actually relished and encouraged hard times. The Greenbackers had long since popularized this argument, insisting that an adequate legal-tender currency would break the monopoly of the "Shylocks." Their demand for $50 of circulating medium per capita, still in the air when the People's Party arose, was rapidly replaced by the less "radical" demand for free coinage of silver. But what both the Greenbackers and free-silverites held in common was the idea that the contraction of currency was a deliberate squeeze, the result of a long-range plot of the "Anglo-American Gold Trust." Wherever one turns in the Populist literature of the nineties one can find this conspiracy theory expressed. It is in the Populist newspapers, the proceedings of the silver conventions, the immense pamphlet literature broadcast by the American Bimetallic League, the Congressional debates over money; it is elaborated in such popular books as Mrs. S. E. V. Emery's *Seven Financial Conspiracies Which Have Enslaved the American People* or Gordon Clark's *Shylock: as Banker, Bondholder, Corruptionist, Conspirator.*

Mrs. Emery's book, first published in 1887, and dedicated to "the enslaved people of a dying republic," achieved great circulation, especially among the Kansas Populists. According to Mrs. Emery, the United States had been an economic Garden of Eden in the period before the Civil War. The fall of man had dated from the war itself, when "the money kings of Wall Street" determined that they could take advantage of the wartime necessities of their fellow men by manipulating the currency. "Controlling it, they could inflate or depress the business of the country at pleasure, they could send the warm life current through the channels of trade, dispensing peace, happiness, and prosperity, or they could check its flow, and completely paralyze the industries of the country."[19] With this great power for good in their hands, the Wall Street men preferred to do evil. Lincoln's war policy of issuing greenbacks presented them with the dire threat of an adequate supply of currency. So the Shylocks gathered in convention and "perfected" a conspiracy to create a demand for their gold.[20] The remainder of the book was a recital of a series of seven measures passed between 1862

[18] Frank L. McVey: *The Populist Movement* (New York, 1896), pp. 201–2.
[19] Emery, op. cit., p. 13.
[20] Ibid., pp. 14–18.

and 1875 which were alleged to be a part of this continuing conspiracy, the total effect of which was to contract the currency of the country further and further until finally it squeezed the industry of the country like a hoop of steel.[21]

Mrs. Emery's rhetoric left no doubt of the sustained purposefulness of this scheme—described as "villainous robbery," and as having been "secured through the most soulless strategy."[22] She was most explicit about the so-called "crime of 1873," the demonetization of silver, giving a fairly full statement of the standard greenback-silverite myth concerning that event. As they had it, an agent of the Bank of England, Ernest Seyd by name, had come to the United States in 1872 with $500,000 with which he had bought enough support in Congress to secure the passage of the demonetization measure. This measure was supposed to have greatly increased the value of American four per cent bonds held by British capitalists by making it necessary to pay them in gold only. To it Mrs. Emery attributed the panic of 1873, its bankruptcies, and its train of human disasters: "Murder, insanity, suicide, divorce, drunkenness and all forms of immorality and crime have increased from that day to this in the most appalling ratio."[23]

.   .   .

The Spirit Militant

The conspiratorial theory and the associated Anglophobic and Judophobic feelings were part of a larger complex of fear and suspicion of the stranger that haunted, and still tragically haunts, the nativist American mind. This feeling, though hardly confined to Populists and Bryanites, was none the less exhibited by them in a particularly virulent form. Everyone remote and alien was distrusted and hated—even Americans, if they happened to be city people. The old agrarian conception of the city as the home of moral corruption reached a new pitch. Chicago was bad; New York, which housed the Wall Street bankers, was farther away and worse; London was still farther away and still worse. This traditional distrust grew stronger as the cities grew larger, and as they were filled with immigrant aliens. As early as 1885 the Kansas preacher Josiah Strong had published *Our Country*, a book widely read in the West, in which the cities were discussed as a great problem of the future, much as though they were some kind of monstrous malignant growths on the body politic.[24] Hamlin Garland recalled that when he first visited Chicago, in the late 1880's, having never seen a town larger than Rockford, Illinois, he naturally assumed that it swarmed with

---

[21] The measures were: the "exception clause" of 1862; the National Bank Act of 1863; the retirement of the greenbacks, beginning in 1866; the "credit-strengthening act" of March 18, 1869; the refunding of the national debt in 1870; the demonetization of silver in 1873; and the destruction of fractional paper currency in 1875.

[22] Ibid., pp. 25, 43.

[23] Ibid., pp. 54–5. For a more elaborate statement of this story see Gordon Clark: *Shylock: as Banker, Bondholder, Corruptionist, Conspirator* (Washington, 1894), pp. 88–99.

[24] Josiah Strong: *Our Country* (New York, 1885), chapter x; for the impact of the city, see Arthur M. Schlesinger: *The Rise of the City* (New York, 1933).

thieves. "If the city is miles across," he wondered, "how am I to get from the railway station to my hotel without being assaulted?" While such extreme fears could be quieted by some contact with the city, others were actually confirmed—especially when the farmers were confronted with city prices.[25] Nativist prejudices were equally aroused by immigration, for which urban manufacturers, with their insatiable demand for labor, were blamed. "We have become the world's melting pot," wrote Thomas E. Watson.

> The scum of creation has been dumped on us. Some of our principal cities are more foreign than American. The most dangerous and corrupting hordes of the Old World have invaded us. The vice and crime which they have planted in our midst are sickening and terrifying. What brought these Goths and Vandals to our shores? The manufacturers are mainly to blame. They wanted cheap labor: and they didn't care a curse how much harm to our future might be the consequence of their heartless policy.[26]

Anglo-Saxons, whether Populist or patrician, found it difficult to accept other peoples on terms of equality or trust. Others were objects to be manipulated—benevolently, it was often said, but none the less firmly. Mary E. Lease, that authentic voice of inland Populism who became famous for advising farmers to "raise less corn and more hell," wrote a book in 1895 under the ingratiating title: *The Problem of Civilization Solved*, in which this ethnic condescension was rather ingenuously displayed. According to Mrs. Lease, Europe and America stood on the brink of one of two immense catastrophes—a universal reign of anarchistic terror or the establishment of a worldwide Russian despotism. The only hope of averting catastrophe was, as she put it, "the most stupendous migration of races the world has ever known, and thereby relieve the congested centers of the world's population of half their inhabitants and provide Free Homes for half of mankind."[27] She proposed a vast reshuffling of peoples in which the tropics in both hemispheres be taken over by white planters with Negroes and Orientals as "tillers of the soil." "Through all the vicissitudes of time, the Caucasian has arisen to the moral and intellectual supremacy of the world, until now this favored race is fitted for the *Stewardship of the Earth and Emancipation from Manual Labor*."[28] This stewardship, far from being an imposition on the lesser breeds without the law, would be an act of mercy; it would take the starved and miserable ryots and coolies of the world and by giving them management and supervision provide them with the means of life, as well as rescue them from paganism. Such a change they would "hail with joy."[29]

.   .   .

. . . Mrs. Lease's peculiar ideas of *Weltpolitik*, her particular views on tropical colonization, were not common currency in Populist thinking. But other assumptions in her book could be found among the Populists with

[25] Hamlin Garland: *A Son of the Middle Border* (New York, ed. 1923), pp. 269, 295.
[26] Watson: *Andrew Jackson*, p. 326; cf. *Cæsar's Column*, p. 131: "The silly ancestors of the Americans called it 'national development' when they imported millions of foreigners to take up the public lands and left nothing for their own children."
[27] Lease, op. cit., p. 17.
[28] Loc. cit.
[29] Ibid., pp. 31–2, 34, 35.

great frequency—the smug assumption of Anglo-Saxon superiority and benevolence, the sense of a need for some new area of expansion, the hatred of England, the fear of Russia,[30] the anxiety over the urban masses as a potential source of anarchy.

The nationalist fervor of Mrs. Lease's book also represents one side of a curiously ambiguous aspect of Populism. On the surface there was a strong note of anti-militarism and anti-imperialism in the Populist movement and Bryan democracy. Populists were opposed to large standing armies and large naval establishments; most of them supported Bryan's resistance to the acquisition of the Philippines. They looked upon the military as a threat to democracy, upon imperialist acquisitions as gains only to financiers and "monarchists," not to the people.[31] But what they chiefly objected to was institutional militarism rather than war itself, imperialism rather than jingoism. Under a patina of pacifist rhetoric they were profoundly nationalistic and bellicose. What the nativist mind most resolutely opposed was not so much war itself as cooperation with European governments for any ends at all.[32] Those who have been puzzled in our own time by the anti-European attitudes of men like Senator Taft and General MacArthur, and by their alternating espousal of dangerously aggressive and near-pacifistic (or antimilitarist) policies, will find in the Populist mentality a suggestive precedent.

The Populists distinguished between wars for humanity and wars of conquest. The first of these they considered legitimate, but naturally they had difficulty in discriminating between the two, and they were quite ready to be ballyhooed into a righteous war, as the Cuban situation was to show. During the early nineteenth century popular sentiment in the United States, especially within the democratic camp, had been strong for the republican

[30] Since this was a commonplace in the nineteenth century, it would be too much to ascribe to Mrs. Lease any special prophetic stature.

[31] See W. H. Harvey: *Coin on Money, Trusts, and Imperialism* (Chicago, 1900), for an expression of popular feelings on these and other issues.

[32] The best illustration was the American bimetallist movement. It was only during the 1870's that the international gold standard can be said to have come into existence, and it did so on the eve of the long price decline of the "Great Depression." The desire of the silver interests in various parts of the world, together with those groups that sought in silver a means of raising the general level of prices, gave rise almost from the beginning to bimetallic movements nearly everywhere in western Europe. Even in England, the commercial center and the creditor nation which did not relish being paid its debts in depreciated currency, there were eminent statesmen who favored bimetallism; and the two greatest economists of the era, Jevons and Marshall, considered it seriously. But everywhere except in the United States the bimetallic movements looked to international action as the method of establishing a bimetallic standard; in the United States alone the silver interests adhered to the possibility of unilateral action. The constant expectation that the United States would act alone to maintain the price of silver was an impediment to action elsewhere. From the 1870's onward conservative American statesmen who sought to initiate action that would lead to an international bimetallic standard had been caught between the difficulty of lining up the other nations and the sharp impatience of domestic silver interests, which insisted with growing asperity as the years went by that reluctance to go it alone was treasonable. See J. B. Condliffe: *The Commerce of Nations* (New York, 1950), chapter xii, "The International Gold Standard"; Jeannette P. Nichols: "Silver Diplomacy," *Political Science Quarterly*, Vol. XXXVIII (December 1933), pp. 565–88. On the relation between silverism and isolationism, see Ray Allen Billington: "The Origins of Middle Western Isolationism," *Political Science Quarterly*, Vol. LX (March 1945), esp. pp. 50–2.

movements in Europe and Latin America. With the coming of the nineties and the great revulsion against the outside world, the emphasis was somewhat changed; where sympathy with oppressed and revolutionary peoples had been the dominant sentiment in the past, the dominant sentiment now seemed rather to be hatred of their governments. That there must always be such an opposition between peoples and governments of the Populist mind did not like to question, and even the most democratic governments of Europe were persistently looked upon as though they were nothing but reactionary monarchies.[33]

.   .   .

It is no coincidence, then, that Populism and jingoism grew concurrently in the United States during the 1890's. The rising mood of intolerant nationalism was a nationwide thing, certainly not confined to the regions of Populist strength; but among no stratum of the population was it stronger than among the Populists. Moreover it was on jingoist issues that the Populist and Bryanite sections of the country, with the aid of the yellow press and many political leaders, achieved that rapport with the masses of the cities which they never succeeded in getting on economic issues. Even conservative politicians sensed that, whatever other grounds of harmony were lacking between themselves and the populace of the hinterland, grounds for unity could be found in war.

.   .   .

. . . The situation of the oppressed Cubans was one with which the Populist elements in the country could readily identify themselves, and they added their voice to the general cry throughout the country for an active policy of intervention. After the defeat of Bryan, popular frustration in the silver areas, blocked on domestic issues, seemed to find expression in the Cuban question. Here at last was a point at which the goldbugs could be vanquished. Neither the big business and banking community nor the Cleveland and McKinley administrations had much sympathy with the crusading fever that pervaded the country at large, and there were bitter mutual recriminations between conservative and Populist papers. Wall Street was accused of a characteristic indifference to the interests of humanity; the Populists in return were charged with favoring war as a cover under which they could smuggle in an inflationary policy. One thing seems clear: "most of the leading Congressional backers of intervention in Cuba represented southern and western states where Populism and silver were strongest."[34] And it appears that one of the reasons why McKinley was advised by many influential Republicans to yield to the popular demand for war was the common fear, still meaningful in 1898, that the Democrats would go into the next presidential election with the irresistible slogan of Free Silver and Free Cuba as its battle cry.[35] Jingoism was confined to no class, section, or party;

[33] See Harvey's *Coin on Money, Trusts, and Imperialism, passim.*
[34] J. E. Wisan: *The Cuban Crisis as Reflected in the New York Press* (New York, 1934), p. 455; for the relation of this crisis to the public temper of the nineties, see Richard Hofstadter: "Manifest Destiny and the Philippines," in Daniel Aaron, ed.: *America in Crisis* (New York, 1952).
[35] Vagts, op. cit., Vol. II, p. 1308 n.

but the Populist areas stood in the vanguard, and their pressure went far to bring about a needless war. When the war was over, the economic and emotional climate in which their movement had grown no longer existed, and their forces were scattered and confused. A majority of them, after favoring war, attempted honorably to spurn the fruits of war by taking up the cause of anti-imperialism. Thomas E. Watson, one of the few Populists who had consistently opposed the war, later insisted that "The Spanish War finished us. The blare of the bugle drowned the voice of the reformer."[36] The cause of reform was, in fact, too resilient to be permanently crushed by a short war; but, for the moment, Free Cuba had displaced Free Silver in public interest, and when reform raised its head again, it had a new face.

As we review these aspects of Populist emotion, an odd parallel obtrudes itself. Where else in American thought during this period do we find this militancy and nationalism, these apocalyptic forebodings and drafts of world-political strategies, this hatred of big businessmen, bankers, and trusts, these fears of immigrants and urban workmen, even this occasional toying with anti-Semitic rhetoric? We find them, curiously enough, most conspicuous among a group of men who are in all obvious respects the antithesis of the Populists. During the late 1880's and the '90's there emerged in the eastern United States a small imperialist elite representing, in general, the same type that had once been Mugwumps, whose spokesmen were such solid and respectable gentlemen as Henry and Brooks Adams, Theodore Roosevelt, Henry Cabot Lodge, John Hay, and Albert J. Beveridge. While the silverites were raging openly and earnestly against the bankers and the Jews, Brooks and Henry Adams were expressing in their sardonic and morosely cynical private correspondence the same feelings, and acknowledging with bemused irony their kinship at this point with the mob. While Populist Congressmen and newspapers called for war with England or Spain, Roosevelt and Lodge did the same, and while Mrs. Lease projected her grandiose schemes of world partition and tropical colonization, men like Roosevelt, Lodge, Beveridge, and Mahan projected more realistic plans for the conquest of markets and the annexation of territory. While Populist readers were pondering over Donnelly's apocalyptic fantasies, Brooks and Henry Adams were also bemoaning the approaching end of their type of civilization, and even the characteristically optimistic T. R. could share at moments in "Brooks Adams' gloomiest anticipations of our gold-ridden, capitalist-bestridden, usurer-mastered future." Not long after Mrs. Lease wrote that "we need a Napoleon in the industrial world who, by agitation and education, will lead the people to a realizing sense of their condition and the remedies,"[37] Roosevelt and Brooks Adams talked about the threat of

---

[36] Woodward: *Tom Watson*, p. 334.

[37] Lease, op. cit., p. 7. Thomas E. Watson wrote in 1902 a lengthy biography: *Napoleon, a Sketch of His Life, Character, Struggles, and Achievements*, in which Napoleon, "the moneyless lad from despised Corsica, who stormed the high places of the world, and by his own colossal strength of character, genius, and industry took them," is calmly described as "the great Democratic despot." Elsewhere Watson wrote: "There is not a railway king of the present day, not a single self-made man who has risen from the ranks to become chief in the vast movement of capital and labor, who will not recognize in Napoleon traits of his own character; the same unflagging purpose, tireless persistence, silent plotting, pitiless rush to victory . . ."—which caused Watson's biographer to ask what a Populist was doing celebrating the virtues of railroad kings and erecting

the eight-hour movement and the danger that the country would be "en-slaved" by the organizers of the trusts, and played with the idea that Roosevelt might eventually lead "some great outburst of the emotional classes which should at least temporarily crush the Economic Man."[38]

Not only were the gentlemen of this imperialist elite better read and better fed than the Populists, but they despised them. This strange convergence of unlike social elements on similar ideas has its explanation, I believe, in this: both the imperialist elite and the Populists had been bypassed and humiliated by the advance of industrialism, and both were rebelling against the domination of the country by industrial and financial capitalists. The gentlemen wanted the power and status they felt due them, which had been taken away from their class and type by the *arriviste* manufacturers and railroaders and the all-too-potent banking houses. The Populists wanted a restoration of agrarian profits and popular government. Both elements found themselves impotent and deprived in an industrial culture and balked by a common enemy. On innumerable matters they disagreed, but both were strongly nationalistic, and amid the despairs and anxieties of the nineties both became ready for war if that would unseat or even embarrass the moneyed powers, or better still if it would topple the established political structure and open new opportunities for the leaders of disinherited farmers or for ambitious gentlemen. But if there seems to be in this situation any suggestion of a forerunner or analogue of modern authoritarian movements, it should by no means be exaggerated. The age was more innocent and more fortunate than ours, and by comparison with the grimmer realities of the twentieth century many of the events of the nineties take on a comic-opera quality. What came in the end was only a small war and a quick victory; when the farmers and the gentlemen finally did coalesce in politics, they produced only the genial reforms of Progressivism; and the man on the white horse turned out to be just a graduate of the Harvard boxing squad, equipped with an immense bag of platitudes, and quite willing to play the democratic game.

Suggested Reading

A good introduction to the controversies over the history of Populism is Sheldon Hackney's *Populism: The Critical Issues** (1971). George B. Tindall's *A Populist Reader** (1966) and Norman Pollack's *The Populist Mind** (1967) provide a fair sampling of Populist rhetoric and thinking.

The best guide to the literature on the part that blacks played in the history of agriculture and agrarian politics is James M. McPherson *et al.*, *Blacks in America:*

---

an image of capitalist acquisitiveness for his people to worship. "Could it be that the Israelites worshipped the same gods as the Philistines? Could it be that the only quarrel between the two camps was over a singular disparity in the favors won?" Woodward, op. cit., pp. 340–2.

[38] Matthew Josephson: *The President Makers* (New York, 1940), p. 98. See the first three chapters of Josephson's volume for a penetrating account of the imperialist elite. Danield Aaron has an illuminating analysis of Brooks Adams in his *Men of Good Hope* (New York, 1951).

Bibliographical Essays (1971). *The Negro Cowboys** (1965) by Philip Durham and Everett L. Jones is a particularly interesting story of a little known aspect of Afro-American history. The role of blacks in politics is a feature of most monographs on politics in the South in this period; Albert D. Kirwan's *Revolt of the Rednecks: Mississippi Politics, 1876–1925** (1951) is a straightforward narrative, and Sheldon Hackney's *Populism to Progressivism in Alabama* (1969) is more analytical. Helen Edmonds, in *The Negro and Fusion Politics in North Carolina, 1894–1901* (1951), exposes the opportunism of the Populist appeal to blacks to join the reform movement. (On the general subject of black Americans refer also to the bibliography following section I.)

Matthew Josephson's *The Politicos, 1865–1896** (1938) emphasizes that the corrupt, self-serving, do-nothing politics of the Gilded Age cried out for reform. David R. Rothman reaches a different evaluation of the politicians in the Senate in *Politics and Power: The United States Senate, 1869–1901* (1966). Harold U. Faulkner's *Politics, Reform and Expansion, 1890–1900** (1959) provides solid coverage of the decade. Eric Goldman's interpretation of the reform spirit, *Rendezvous with Destiny: A History of Modern American Reform** (1952), is highly readable.

On the election of 1892, one should consult George H. Knowles' *The Presidential Campaign and Election of 1892* (1942), and on the critical election of 1896, Stanley Jones's *The Presidential Election of 1896* (1964). Paul Glad's *McKinley, Bryan, and the People** (1964) is a popular narrative of the 1896 campaign employing interpretation of campaign symbolism. Robert Durden, in *The Climax of Populism** (1966), takes a close analytical look at the Populist party in the 1896 election. J. Rogers Hollingsworth's *The Whirligig of Politics: The Democracy of Cleveland and Bryan* (1963) is a history of the Democratic party. Horace Samuel Merrill has produced an unpretentious but solid biography of Cleveland, *Bourbon Leader: Grover Cleveland and the Democratic Party** (1957). William McKinley is the subject of Margaret Leech's *In the Days of McKinley* (1959), and H. Wayne Morgan's *William McKinley and His America* (1963). Paul Glad's *The Trumpet Soundeth: William Jennings Bryan and His Democracy, 1896–1912* (1960) is not as exhaustive as Paolo E. Coletta's *William Jennings Bryan, Political Evangelist, 1860–1908* (1964). Considerable understanding of southern politics can be gained through biography. C. Vann Woodward's *Tom Watson, Agrarian Rebel** (1938) is a beautiful study of the South's foremost Populist leader. Francis Butler Simkins' *Pitchfork Ben Tillman: South Carolinian** (1944) is a portrait of a demogog who never became a Populist.

The charges leveled against Populism by Richard Hofstadter in *The Age of Reform** (1955) have been most categorically denied by Norman Pollack in *The Populist Response to Industrial America** (1962), and most effectively answered by Walter T. K. Nugent in *The Tolerant Populists: Kansas, Populism, and Nativism** (1963). A model of reasoned debate is the essay "The Populist Heritage and the Intellectuals," by C. Vann Woodward, in Woodward, ed., *The Burden of Southern History,** rev. ed. (1968).

The classic account of Populism as the result of the process of settling in the West is John D. Hicks's *The Populist Revolt** (1931). This tendency to underrate the movement in the South is partly corrected by C. Vann Woodward in *Origins of the New South** (1951). Solon J. Buck's *The Granger Movement** (1913) has never been surpassed. Theodore Saloutos' *Farmer Movements in the South, 1865–1933** (1960), Carl C. Taylor's *The Farmers' Movement, 1620–1920* (1953), and Murray R. Benedict's *Farm Policies in the United States, 1790–1950* (1953) provide good background information.

The best general history of the West in the nineteenth century is Ray Allen Billington's *Westward Expansion,* 3rd ed. (1967), but much can also be learned from Thomas D. Clark's *Frontier America: The Story of the Westward Movement* (1959). Frederick Jackson Turner's seminal essay, "The Significance of the Frontier in American History," is contained in his collection *The Frontier in American History** (1920). *The Great Plains** (1931) by Walter Prescott Webb is still one of the most provocative and original applications of the Turner thesis. Ray Allen Billington has brought together more recent scholarly thinking on the subject in *America's Frontier Heritage* (1966). Howard R. Lamar's *The Far Southwest, 1846–1912* (1966) is one of the most significant additions to knowledge about the frontier in recent years. A brilliantly innovative study of the West as symbol and myth by Henry Nash Smith, *Virgin Land** (1950) set the pattern for a genre of analysis.

The pioneer farm on the plains is vividly pictured by Everett Dick in *The Sod-House Frontier, 1854–1890* (1937). Two excellent histories of agriculture during the late nineteenth century are Fred A. Shannon's *The Farmer's Last Frontier: Agriculture, 1860–1897** (1945), and Gilbert C. Fite's *The Farmer's Frontier, 1865–1900* (1966). Allan G. Bogue's *From Prairie to Corn Belt* (1963) and his earlier book *Money at Interest: The Farm Mortgage on the Middle Border* (1955) are fruitful analyses. One might also consult Earl W. Hayter's *The Troubled Farmer, 1850–1900: Rural Adjustment to Industrialism* (1968) and Paul W. Gates's *Fifty Million Acres: Conflicts over Kansas Land Policy, 1854–1890* (1954).

Some of the South's peculiar problems are noted in Robert Brandfon's *Cotton Kingdom of the New South: A History of the Yazoo Mississippi Delta from Reconstruction to the Twentieth Century* (1967), J. Carlyle Sitterson's *Sugar Country: The Cane Sugar Industry in the South, 1753–1950* (1953), and A. M. Tang's *Economic Development in the Southern Piedmont, 1860–1950: Its Impact on Agriculture* (1958). Compounding the agricultural problems were the railroads: see John F. Stover's *The Railroads of the South, 1865–1900* (1955), and Leonard P. Curry's *Rail Routes South: Louisville's Fight for the Southern Market, 1865–1872* (1969). The conjunction of railroads and politics is evident in almost every study of politics in the late nineteenth century, and serves as the focus of James F. Doster's *Railroads in Alabama Politics, 1875–1914* (1957). In addition to Woodward's *Origins of the New South*, Dewey Grantham's *The Democratic South** (1963) and T. Harry Williams' *Romance and Realism in Southern Politics* (1961) also interpret southern politics.

* Also published in paperback edition.

The City on
a Hill Expands

Manifest Destiny and the Philippines

Richard Hofstadter

The expansion of the 1890s—the Spanish-American War and annexation of the Philippines—has long provoked historical controversy. Some historians explain the war and annexation as products of the quest for foreign markets. But most historians deny that the United States entered the war for imperialistic reasons and they view colonialism as an unexpected departure from the nation's earlier policies.

Addressing these problems in 1951, the late Richard Hofstadter of Columbia University, in the influential essay reprinted below, sought to explain the movement to war in terms of a "psychic crisis": "the displacement of feelings of sympathy or social protest generated in domestic affairs" and ultimately discharged in foreign conflict. The searing depression, the burning radicalism, the growing trusts, the closing frontier—all seemed to threaten the nation. For some of the frustrated, especially those left discontented by Bryan's defeat in 1896, the war, according to Hofstadter, promised a way of discharging aggression against the "Wall Street interests," whom he finds opposed the war. The war, he explains, "served as an outlet for aggressive impulses while presenting itself, quite truthfully, as an idealistic and humanitarian crusade." In this analysis, President McKinley, presumably fearing political injury to his party because of his opposition to war, ultimately

131

succumbed to public demands and requested a declaration of war.

Annexation of the Philippines, according to Hofstadter, drew great support from those who had opposed the war: the big business-conservative-Republican-McKinley element. In turn, he contends, the Populist-Democratic-Bryanite element, having supported the war, opposed annexation. The dynamic element in the movement toward colonialism, however, was not the business community, Hofstadter maintains, but a group of upper-class, Anglo-Saxon citizens (such as Henry Cabot Lodge and Theodore Roosevelt) who wanted to extend the nation's influence abroad, expand her markets overseas, and replenish her vitality. According to Hofstadter, President McKinley, presented with the Philippines and supported by public opinion, endorsed annexation. The public belief in "duty" and "destiny," for Hofstadter, confirmed the desires of some that the United States become a colonial nation.

Historians have faulted this important essay, a pioneering effort to use socio-psychological theories in historical analysis, on various grounds. On the theoretical level, some have criticized it for taking from *individual* psychology a model (displaced aggression), which has been challenged by some psychologists, and extending it to *groups* in society. What kinds of possible evidence, critics ask, could confirm or disconfirm the use of this theory? On the factual level, John A. S. Grenville and George B. Young have disputed Hofstadter's statement about Roosevelt's pivotal role in the seizure of the Philippines. They also establish, contrary to Hofstadter, that Spain did not accept the President's terms in April for a settlement: Spain proffered only a conditional armistice, which would have worked to the disadvantage of the insurgents in Cuba, and thereby rejected McKinley's terms (*Politics, Strategy, and American Diplomacy* [1966], pp. 269–70, 262).

On the interpretive level, historians have criticized Hofstadter's analysis (1) for misunderstanding the role of the business community, which Walter LaFeber and William Appleman Williams contend had moved to support war by early 1898, (2) for viewing

---

McKinley as a weak leader and thereby neglecting his desire to go to war in order to secure his goals, and (3) for not understanding that the central goal of policy-makers was economic expansion abroad, which the events in Cuba threatened and the annexation of the Philippines assisted. Even the farmers, contends Williams, did not act out of a "psychic crisis" but supported the war for rational, not irrational, reasons. In addition, critics note that Hofstadter does not explain why President Cleveland reacted so belligerently to the Venezuelan crisis. Was he also caught up in the "psychic crisis" or was he simply pushed by public sentiment?

Hofstadter, when revising this essay in 1965, expanded it but did not modify the interpretation. Addressing some of his critics on that occasion, he disagreed with those who interpreted his essay as "an attempt to offer a psychological alternative to an economic interpretation of American imperialism." He contended that it was "less psychological than institutional; less an alternative than a necessary supplement that is to avoid running aground on certain stubborn facts." Students are encouraged to examine the essay in terms of this later explanation and also to consider whether, as he contends, he shares much common ground with the interpretation advanced by Walter LaFeber in *The New Empire* (1963) and partly summarized in his essay on pages 153–61.

*T*he taking of the Philippine Islands from Spain in 1899 marked a major historical departure for the American people. It was a breach in their traditions and a shock to their established values. To be sure, from their national beginnings they had constantly engaged in expansion, but almost entirely into contiguous territory. Now they were extending themselves to distant extrahemispheric colonies; they were abandoning a strategy of defense hitherto limited to the continent and its appurtenances, in favor of a major strategic commitment in the Far East; and they were now supplementing the spread of a relatively homogeneous population into territories destined from the beginning for self-government with a far different procedure in which control was imposed by force on millions of ethnic aliens. The acquisition of the islands, therefore, was understood by contemporaries on both sides of the debate, as it is readily understood today, to be a turning-point in our history.

To discuss the debate in isolation from other events, however, would be to deprive it of its full significance. American entrance into the Philippine Islands was a by-product of the Spanish-American War. The Philippine crisis is inseparable from the war crisis, and the war crisis itself is inseparable from a larger constellation that might be called "the psychic crisis of the 1890's."

Central in the background of the psychic crisis was the great depression that broke in 1893 and was still very acute when the agitation over the war in Cuba began. Severe depression, by itself, does not always generate an emotional crisis as intense as that of the nineties. In the 1870's the country had been swept by a depression of comparable acuteness and duration which, however, did not give rise to all the phenomena that appeared in the 1890's or to very many of them with comparable intensity and impact. It is often said that the 1890's, unlike the 1870's, form some kind of a "watershed" in American history. The difference between the emotional and intellectual impact of these two depressions can be measured, I believe, not by any difference in severity, but rather by reference to a number of singular events that in the 1890's converged with the depression to heighten its impact upon the public mind.

First in importance was the Populist movement, the free-silver agitation, the heated campaign of 1896. For the first time in our history a depression had created an allegedly "radical" movement strong enough to capture a major party and raise the specter, however unreal, of drastic social convulsion. Second was the maturation and bureaucratization of American business, the completion of its essential industrial plant, and the development of trusts on a scale sufficient to stir the anxiety that the old order of competitive opportunities was approaching an eclipse. Third, and of immense symbolic importance, was the apparent filling up of the continent and disappearance of the frontier line. We now know how much land had not yet been taken up and how great were the remaining possibilities of internal expansion both in business and on the land; but to the mind of the 1890's it seemed that the resource that had engaged the energies of the people for three centuries had been used up; the frightening possibility suggested itself that a serious juncture in the nation's history had come. As Frederick Jackson Turner expressed it in his famous paper of 1893: "Now, four centuries from the discovery of America, at the end of one hundred years of life under the Constitution, the frontier has gone, and with its going has closed the first period of American history."

To middle-class citizens who had been brought up to think in terms of the nineteenth-century order, things looked bad. Farmers in the staple-growing region seemed to have gone mad over silver and Bryan; workers were stirring in bloody struggles like the Homestead and Pullman strikes; the supply of new land seemed at an end; the trust threatened the spirit of business enterprise; civic corruption was at a high point in the large cities; great waves of seemingly unassimilable immigrants arrived yearly and settled in hideous slums. To many historically conscious writers, the nation seemed overripe, like an empire ready for collapse through a stroke from outside or through internal upheaval. Acute as the situation was for all those who lived by the symbols of national power—for the governing and thinking classes—

it was especially poignant for young people, who would have to make their careers in the dark world that seemed to be emerging.

The symptomatology of the crisis might record several tendencies in popular thought and behavior that had not been observable before or had existed only in pale and tenuous form. These symptoms fall into two basic moods. The key to one of them is an intensification of protest and humanitarian reform. Populism, Utopianism, the rise of the Christian Social gospel, the growing intellectual interest in Socialism, the social settlement movement that appealed so strongly to the college generation of the nineties, the quickening of protest in the realistic novel—all of these are expressions of this mood. The other is one of national self-assertion, aggression, expansion. The tone of the first was sympathy, of the second, power. During the 1890's far more patriotic groups were founded than in any other decade of our history; the naval theories of Captain Mahan were gaining in influence; naval construction was booming; there was an immense quickening of the American cult of Napoleon and a vogue of the virile and martial writings of Rudyard Kipling; young Theodore Roosevelt became the exemplar of the vigorous, masterful, out-of-doors man; the revival of European imperialism stirred speculation over what America's place would be in the world of renewed colonial rivalries. But most significant was the rising tide of jingoism, a matter of constant comment among observers of American life during the decade.

Jingoism, of course, was not new in American history. But during the 1870's and '80's the American public had been notably quiescent about foreign relations. There had been expansionist statesmen, but they had been blocked by popular apathy and statecraft had been restrained. Grant had failed dismally in his attempt to acquire Santo Domingo; our policy toward troubled Hawaii had been cautious; in 1877 an offer of two Haitian naval harbors had been spurned. In responding to Haiti, Secretary of State Frelinghuysen had remarked that "the policy of this Government . . . has tended toward avoidance of possessions disconnected from the main continent."[1] Henry Cabot Lodge, in his life of George Washington published in 1889, observed that foreign relations then filled "but a slight place in American politics, and excite generally only a languid interest." Within a few years this comment would have seemed absurd; the history of the 1890's is the history of public agitation over expansionist issues and of quarrels with other nations.

Three primary incidents fired American jingoism between the spring of 1891 and the close of 1895. First came Secretary of State Blaine's tart and

[1] Albert K. Weinberg: *Manifest Destiny* (Baltimore: 1935), p. 252. There is a suggestive similarity to the conditions of the nineties in the circumstances attending the Cuban insurrection of 1868–78. The hostilities were even more bitter and exhausting than those of 1895–8; its latter phases also corresponded with an acute depression in the United States; the case of the *Virginius* offered a pretext for war almost as satisfactory as that of the *Maine*. Some public and press clamor followed. But it did not rise even near to the pitch of overwhelming pressure for war. Two things were supplied in the nineties that were missing in the seventies: a psychic crisis that generated an expansionist mood, and the techniques of yellow journalism. Cf. Samuel Flagg Bemis: *A Diplomatic History of the United States* (New York: 1936), pp. 433–5.

provocative reply to the Italian minister's protest over the lynching of eleven Italians in New Orleans. Then there was friction with Chile over a riot in Valparaiso in which two American sailors were killed and several injured by a Chilean mob. In 1895 occurred the more famous Venezuela boundary dispute with Britain. Discussion of these incidents would take us too far afield, but note that they all had these characteristics in common: in none of them was national security or the national interest vitally involved; in all three American diplomacy was extraordinarily and disproportionately aggressive; in all three the possibility of war was contemplated; and in each case the American public and press response was enthusiastically nationalist.

It is hard to read the history of these events without concluding that politicians were persistently using jingoism to restore their prestige, mend their party fences, and divert the public mind from grave internal discontents. It hardly seems an accident that jingoism and Populism rose together. Documentary evidence for the political exploitation of foreign crises is not overwhelmingly abundant, in part because such a motive is not necessarily conscious and where it is conscious it is not likely to be confessed or recorded. The persistence of jingoism in every administration from Harrison's to Theodore Roosevelt's, however, is too suggestive to be ignored. During the nineties the press of each party was fond of accusing the other of exploiting foreign conflict. We know that Blaine was not above twisting the British lion's tail for political purposes; and there is no reason to believe that he would have exempted Italy from the same treatment. We know too that Harrison, on the eve of the Chile affair, for the acuteness of which he was primarily responsible, was being urged by prominent Republican politicians who had the coming Presidential campaign in mind to pursue a more aggressive foreign policy because it would "have the . . . effect of diverting attention from stagnant political discussions." And although some Democratic papers charged that he was planning to run for re-election during hostilities so that he could use the "don't-swap-horses-in-the-middle-of-the-stream" appeal, many Democrats felt that it was politically necessary for them to back him against Chile so that, as one of their Congressmen remarked, the Republicans could not "run away with all the capital there is to be made in an attempt to assert national self-respect." Grover Cleveland admittedly was a man of exceptional integrity whose stand against pressure for the annexation of Hawaii during 1893–4 does him much credit. But precisely for this act of abnegation his administration fell under the charge made by Republican jingoes like Lodge and by many in his own party that he was indifferent to America's position in the world. And if Cleveland was too high-minded a man to exploit a needless foreign crisis, his Secretary of State, Richard Olney, was not. The Venezuela affair, which came at a very low point in the prestige of Cleveland's administration, offered Olney a rich chance to prove to critics in both parties that the administration was, after all, capable of vigorous diplomacy. That the crisis might have partisan value was not unthinkable to members of Olney's party. He received a suggestive letter from a Texas Congressman encouraging him to "go ahead," on the ground that the Venezuela issue was a "winner" in every section of the country. "When you come to diagnose the country's internal ills," his correspondent continued, "the possibilities of 'blood and iron' loom up immediately. Why, Mr. Secretary, just think of how angry the anarchistic, socialistic, and populistic boil appears on our political surface and who knows how deep its roots extend or ramify? One cannon shot across the bow of a British boat in defense of this principle will knock more *pus* out of it than would suffice to inoculate and corrupt our people for the next two centuries."

This pattern had been well established when the Cuban crisis broke out anew in 1895. It was quite in keeping that Secretary Olney should get a letter during the 1896 campaign from Fitzhugh Lee, the American consul in Havana, advising that the conservative faction of Gold Democrats become identified with the strong policy of mediation or intervention in Cuba. Thus, he argued,

> the 'Sound Democrats' would get, with the Executive, the credit of stopping the wholesale atrocities daily practised here, the acquisition of Cuba by purchase, or by fighting a successful war, if war there be. In the latter case, the enthusiasm, the applications for service, the employment of many of the unemployed, might do much towards directing the minds of the people from imaginary ills, the relief of which is erroneously supposed to be reached by 'Free Silver'.

When President McKinley took office he was well aware that nationalist enthusiasm had reached a pitch that made war very likely. A few months earlier, he had told Senator Lodge that he might be "obliged" to go to war as soon as he entered the Presidency, and had expressed a preference that the Cuban crisis be settled one way or another in the time between his election and inauguration. Although he promised Carl Schurz that there would be "no jingo nonsense under my administration," he proved to have not quite enough strength to resist the current. Members of his own party put a great deal of pressure on him to give the people their war rather than endanger the Republican position. It was held that if war was inevitable, as presumably it was, it would be better for the President to lead than to be pushed; that resistance to war would be ruinous to the party; that going to war would prevent the Democrats from entering the next Presidential campaign with "Free Cuba" and "Free Silver" as their battle cries. After Senator Proctor's speech exposing conditions in Cuba the Chicago *Times-Herald*, a McKinley paper, declared that intervention in Cuba, peaceful or forcible, was

> immediately inevitable. Our own internal political condition will not permit its postponement. . . . Let President McKinley hesitate to rise to the just expectation of the American people, and who can doubt that 'war for Cuban liberty' will be the crown of thorns that Free Silver Democrats and Populists will adopt at the elections this fall. . . . The President would be powerless to stay any legislation, however ruinous to every sober, honest interest of the country.

At the time McKinley sent his war message to Congress he knew quite well, and indeed made a passing reference to the fact, that Spain had already capitulated to the demands the United States had made upon her. This capitulation *could* have been made the basis of a peace message; instead it occupied one sentence tucked away near the end of a war message—a sentence that everyone chose to ignore. Evidently McKinley had concluded that what was wanted in the United States was not so much the freedom of Cuba as a *war* for the freedom of Cuba.

Historians say that the war was brought on by sensational newspapers. The press, spurred by the rivalry between Pulitzer and Hearst, aroused sympathy with the Cubans and hatred of Spain and catered to the bellicosity of the public. No one seems to have asked: *Why was the public so fatally receptive to war propaganda?* I believe the answer must be sought in the causes of the jingoism that had raged for seven years before the war actually broke out. The events of the nineties had brought frustration and anxiety to civically conscious Americans. On one hand, as Mark Sullivan has commented, the American during this period was disposed "to see himself as an underdog in economic situations and controversies in his own country"; but the civic frustrations of the era created also a restless aggressiveness, a desire to be assured that the power and vitality of the nation were not waning. The capacity for sympathy and the need for power existed side by side. That highly typical and symptomatic American William Allen White, recalls in his *Autobiography* how during the nineties he was "bound to my idols—Whitman, the great democrat, and Kipling, the imperialist." In varying stages of solution the democrat and imperialist existed in the hearts of White's countrymen—the democrat disposed to free Cuba, the imperialist to vent his civic spleen on Spain.

I suspect that the readiness of the public to over-react to the Cuban situation can be understood in part through the displacement of feelings of sympathy or social protest generated in domestic affairs; these impulses found a safe and satisfactory discharge in foreign conflict. Spain was portrayed in the press as waging a heartless and inhuman war; the Cubans were portrayed as noble victims of Spanish tyranny, their situation as analogous to that of Americans in 1776. When one examines the sectional and political elements that were most enthusiastic about the war, one finds them not primarily among the wealthy Eastern big-business Republicans who supported McKinley and read the conservative dignified newspapers, but in the Bryan sections of the country, in the *Democratic Party*, and among the patrons of the yellow journals. During the controversy significant charges were hurled back and forth; conservative peace-advocates claimed that many jingoists were hoping for a costly war over Cuba that could be made the occasion of a return to free silver; in return, the inflammatory press often fell into the pattern of Populist rhetoric, declaiming, for example, about "the eminently respectable porcine citizens who—for dollars in the money-grubbing sty, support 'conservative' newspapers and consider the starvation of . . . inoffensive men, women and children, and the murder of 250 American sailors . . . of less importance than a fall of two points in a price of stocks." Although imputations of base economic motives were made by both sides, it is also significant that the current of sympathy and agitation ran strong where a discontented constituency, politically frustrated by Bryan's defeat, was most numerous. An opportunity to discharge aggressions against "Wall Street interests" coolly indifferent to the fate of both Cuban *insurrectos* and staple farmers may have been more important than the more rationalized and abstract linkage between a war and free silver. The primary significance of the war for the psychic economy of the nineties was that it served as an outlet for aggressive impulses while presenting itself, quite truthfully, as an idealistic and humanitarian crusade. The American public was not interested in the material gains of an intervention in Cuba. It never dreamed that the war would lead to the taking of the Philippines. Starting a war for a high-minded and altruistic purpose and then transmuting it into a war for annexation was unthinkable; it would be, as McKinley put it in a phrase that later came back to haunt him, "criminal aggression."

There is one odd paradox in the evolution of sentiment from a war over freeing Cuba to a peace treaty acquiring the Philippines by conquest. The big-business-conservative-Republican-McKinley element, overwhelmingly hostile to this romantic and sentimental war, quickly became interested in the imperialism that grew out of it. The popular Populist-Democratic-Bryanite element, which had been so keen for the war, became the stronghold —although by no means resolute or unbroken—of opposition to the fruits of war. This much, however, must be said of both the populace and the business community: if the matter had been left either to public clamor or to business interests, there would have been no American entrance into the Philippines in 1898.

The dynamic element in the movement for imperialism was a small group of politicians, intellectuals, and publicists, including Senator Henry Cabot Lodge, Theodore Roosevelt, John Hay, Senator Albert J. Beveridge, White-law Reid, editor of the *New York Tribune*, Albert Shaw, editor of the *Review of Reviews*, Walter Hines Page, editor of the *Atlantic Monthly*, and Henry and Brooks Adams.

Most of these men came from what are known as good families. They were well educated, cultivated, patrician in outlook, Anglo-Saxon in background, non-commercial in personal goals and standards, and conservative reformers in politics. Although living in a commercial world, they could not accept business standards for their own careers nor absorb themselves into the business community. Although they lived in a vulgar democracy, they were not democratic by instinct. They could not and did not care to succeed in politics of the corrupt sort that had become so common in America. They had tried their hands at civic reform, had found it futile, and had become bored with it. When they did not, like Henry Adams, turn away from American life in bitterness, they became interested in some large and states-manlike theater of action, broader than American domestic policy. Although there were men of this sort in the Democratic ranks, like Walter Hines Page, they were most influential within the Republican Party, which during the mid-nineties had become committed to a policy of expansion.

In general, this group of imperialists was inspired by the navalist theories of Mahan and by the practical example of what they sometimes referred to as Mother England. They saw that a new phase of imperialism had opened in the Western world at large, and they were fearful that if the United States did not adopt a policy of expansion and preparation for military and naval struggle, it would be left behind in what they referred to as the struggle for life or, at other times, as the march of the nations. They were much concerned that the United States expand its army and particularly its navy; that it dig an isthmian canal; that it acquire the naval bases and colonies in the Caribbean and the Pacific necessary to protect such a canal; that it annex Hawaii and Samoa. At their most aggressive, they also called for the annexation of Canada, and the expulsion of European powers from the Western hemisphere. They were much interested in the Far East as a new theater of political conflict and investment possibilities. They were, indeed, more interested than business itself in the Pacific area, particularly in China, as a potential market. As Professor Pratt has observed: "The need of American business for colonial markets and fields for investment was discovered not by businessmen but by historians and other intellectuals, by journalists and politicians."

The central figure in this group was Theodore Roosevelt, who more than any other single man was responsible for our entry into the Philippines. Throughout the 1890's Roosevelt had been eager for a war, whether it be with Chile, Spain, or England. A war with Spain, he felt, would get us "a proper navy and a good system of coast defenses," would free Cuba from Spain, and would help to free America from European domination, would give "our people . . . something to think of that isn't material gain," and would try "both the army and navy in actual practice." Roosevelt feared that the United States would grow heedless of its defense, take insufficient care to develop its power, and become "an easy prey for any people which still retained those most valuable of all qualities, the soldierly virtues." "All the great masterful races have been fighting races," he argued. There were higher virtues than those of peace and material comfort. "No triumph of peace is quite so great as the supreme triumphs of war." Such was the philosophy of the man who secured Commodore Dewey's appointment to the Far Eastern Squadron and alerted him before the actual outbreak of hostilities to be prepared to engage the Spanish fleet at Manila.

Our first step into the Philippines presented itself to us as a "defensive" measure. Dewey's attack on the Spanish fleet in Manila Bay was made on the assumption that the Spanish fleet, if unmolested, might cross the Pacific and bombard the West Coast cities of the United States. I do not know whether American officialdom was aware that this fleet was so decrepit that it could hardly have gasped its way across the ocean. Next, Dewey's fleet seemed in danger unless its security were underwritten by the dispatch of American troops to Manila. To be sure, having accomplished his mission, Dewey could have removed this "danger" simply by leaving Manila Bay. However, in war one is always tempted to hold whatever gains have been made, and at Dewey's request American troops were dispatched very promptly after the victory and arrived at Manila in July 1898. Thus our second step into the Philippines was again a "defensive" measure. The third step was the so-called "capture" of Manila, which was actually carried out in co-operation with the Spaniards, who were allowed to make a token resistance, and in exclusion of the Filipino patriots under Aguinaldo. The fourth step was an agreement, incorporated in the protocol suspending hostilities between the United States and Spain, that the United States would occupy the city, bay, and harbor of Manila pending a final settlement in the peace treaty. The fifth step came much later, on December 21, 1898, when McKinley instructed the War Department to extend the military government already in force at Manila to the entire archipelago. This began a fierce revolt by the

Filipino patriots, who felt that they had been led to expect a much different policy from the American government. Two days before the vote was taken in the Senate on the ratification of the peace treaty, the patriots and the American forces fought their first battle and American soldiers were killed, a fact that seems to have had an important influence on public discussion. Once again, administrative action had given a sharp bias to the whole process of political decision. Tyler Dennett goes so far as to say that by authorizing a campaign of conquest while the Senate was still discussing the situation, McKinley "created a situation . . . which had the effect of coercing the Senate." This is a doubtful conclusion, but there is some reason to believe that the hand of expansionists was strengthened by the feeling that opposition to the administration's policy would be unpatriotic.

This much can certainly be said: by the time our policy could be affected by public discussion a great deal had already been accomplished by the annexationists. The tone of the argument was already weighted towards staying in simply because we were there. As McKinley put it: "It is not a question of keeping the islands of the East, but of leaving them." It is not an easy thing to persuade a people or a government during the pitch of war enthusiasm to abandon a potential gain already in hand. Moreover, a great social interest hitherto indifferent to the Philippines, the business community, quickly swung around to an expansionist position. The Protestant clergy, seeing a potential enlargement of missionary enterprise, also threw in its weight. For the first time the group of imperialists and navalists had powerful allies. Business began to talk about the Philippines as a possible gateway to the markets of eastern Asia, the potentialities of which were thought to be very large. The little imperialist group was much heartened and, with the help of Navy officers, put increasing pressure upon a rather hesitant administration to follow through.

There seemed four possible ways of disposing of the Philippine problem. The first, returning the islands to Spain, found favor nowhere. The second, selling or otherwise alienating the Philippines to some other power, seemed to invite a possible general European war; and it would hardly be more justified morally than remaining in possession ourselves. Moreover, we were being encouraged by England to remain in the Philippines, for American possession of those islands was much more palatable to England than possession by any other power. The third possibility, leaving the Philippines to themselves and giving them the independence Aguinaldo's men had been fighting for, was equivalent in most American minds to leaving them to anarchy. It also seemed to be another way of encouraging a scramble among other powers interested in the Far East. The final possibility was some form of American possession, in the form of protectorate or otherwise. In the beginning there was much sentiment for merely retaining a naval base and coaling station on the island of Luzon, or perhaps the island of Luzon itself. Second thought suggested, however, that such a base would be endangered if the rest of the islands were left open to possible occupation by other nations. The dynamics of the situation suggested an all-or-none policy, and the administration drifted rapidly towards annexation of the entire archipelago.

The American public had not previously been either informed about or interested in the Philippines. In the entire eighty-year period from 1818 through May 1898, only thirty-five articles about the islands had appeared in American magazines. At the moment of Dewey's victory the press, although given over to encouraging the public jubilation, did not show an immediate interest in taking the islands. However, sentiment grew with considerable rapidity. As early as July 1898, the *Literary Digest* noted that the leading Republican papers were pro-expansion. A sample of 65 newspapers taken by the magazine *Public Opinion* in August showed that 43 per cent were for permanent retention of the Philippines, 24.6 per cent were opposed, and 32.4 per cent were wavering. In this case, "wavering" usually meant formerly opposed to expansion but apparently changing views. By December 1898, when the crucial debate in the Senate was beginning, the *New York Herald* polled 498 newspapers on the subject of expansion and found that 305, or 61.3 per cent, were favorable. New England and the Middle States showed clear margins in favor of expansion, the West an overwhelming margin; the South alone, by a thin margin, was opposed. The state of press opinion does not *measure* public feeling, but probably does indicate the direction in which public opinion was moving.

To President McKinley, a benign and far from aggressive man, public sentiment was of great importance. He was not a man to lead the American people in a direction in which their sympathies were not already clearly bent. There was a current joke: "Why is McKinley's mind like a bed? Because it has to be made up for him every time he wants to use it." However unjust to the President, this does characterize his response to public opinion. He was not by temperament an expansionist, but if his immediate advisers and the public at large were preponderantly for annexation, he was willing to go along, and was thoroughly capable of finding good reasons for doing so. During the fall of 1898 he left Washington for a tour of the West, and made a great many brief speeches sounding out public opinion on annexation of the Philippines, on which he seems to have tentatively been determined in his own mind. He found a warm reception for himself and an enthusiastic response to the idea of expansion. Evidently his intent was confirmed by this exposure to public opinion and also by advices concerning the state of the public mind from correspondents and advisers, and when he returned to Washington those who were opposed to expansion found him unmovable. The Peace Commission negotiating the treaty in Paris was instructed to ask for all the Philippine Islands, and this provision was included in the peace treaty signed on December 10, 1898.

The debate over the retention of the Philippines then went through two phases. During the first, which lasted from December 1898 to the second week in February 1899, the question was argued both in the Senate and in the forums of public opinion. This phase neared its end when, on February 6, the Senate narrowly voted to ratify the peace treaty; it was definitively closed on February 14, when a resolution sponsored by Senator Bacon of Georgia, calling for early Philippine independence, was rejected by the preciously narrow margin of one vote—the casting vote of the Vice President, which resolved a 29–29 tie. The second phase of the debate extended throughout 1899 and 1900, when American policy toward the Philippines was a matter of general public discussion and a partisan issue in the Presidential campaign of 1900.

Who was for and who against annexation? In a large measure it was a party issue. The *New York Herald* poll showed that of 241 Republican papers 84.2 per cent were *for* expansion, and of 174 Democratic papers 71.3 per cent were *against* expansion. In some degree it was also a young man's movement. Geographically it extended throughout all sections of the country, and seems to have been favored everywhere but in the South, although even there it was strong. We do not have a clear index of public opinion for the period, but the practical politicians, whose business it was to gauge public sentiment in the best way they knew, concluded that the preponderant feeling was overwhelmingly for annexation.

The debate over the acquisition of the Philippines was perhaps no more than a ceremonial assertion of the values of both sides. The real decisions were made in the office of Theodore Roosevelt, in the Senate cloakroom, in the sanctums of those naval officers from whom the McKinley administration got its primary information about the Philippines during its period of doubt over annexation, and, by McKinley's own testimony, in the privacy of his chambers late at night. The public was, by and large, faced with a *fait accompli* that, although theoretically reversible, had the initial impetus of its very existence to carry it along. The intensity of the public discussion, at any rate, showed that the American conscience had really been shocked. No type of argument was neglected on either side. Those who wanted to take the Philippines pointed to the potential markets of the East, the White Man's Burden, the struggle for existence, "racial" destiny, American traditions of expansion, the dangers of a general war if the Philippines were left open to a European scramble, the almost parental duty of assuming responsibility for the allegedly child-like Filipinos, the incapacity of the Filipinos for self-government, and so on. The anti-imperialists based their essential appeal on political principle. They pointed out that the United States had come into existence pledged to the idea that man should not be governed without his consent. They suggested that the violation of these political traditions (under which the nation had prospered) was not only a gross injustice to others, of which we should feel deeply ashamed, but also a way of tempting Providence and risking degeneration and disintegration as a sort of punishment for the atrophy of one's own principles. They pointed also to the expense of overseas dominions, standing armies and navalism, and the danger of being embroiled in imperialist wars.

Many leading anti-imperialists were men of great distinction; their ranks included by far the greater part of the eminent figures of the literary and intellectual world. Most of them were, however, in the unfortunate position of opposing the fruits of a war that they had either favored or failed to oppose. Unlike the expansionists, they did not have complete control of a major party (there were more expansionists among the Democrats than there were anti-expansionists among the Republicans). They were hopelessly heterogeneous: Gold Democrats, Bryan Democrats, New-England conscience Republicans, and a scattering of reformers and intellectuals.

They organized late—the Anti-Imperialist League grew up in the months after November 1898—and their political leadership, however ardent in sentiment, pursued a hesitant and uncertain course. Their most eminent political leaders were chiefly old men, and the strongest appeal of the anti-imperialist movement seems to have been to the old, high-principled elements in the country, while the imagination of the young was fired far more by the rhetoric of expansionism. It seems clear that the main chance of this minority was to use its position in the Senate to deny the necessary two-thirds approval to the peace treaty acquiring the islands from Spain. Here the opponents of annexation might have delayed it long enough to give themselves a chance to reach the public. But William Jennings Bryan, for reasons that are not altogether clear, persuaded enough members of his party to vote for the treaty to lose the case. Bryan hoped to continue the fight, of course, and grant independence later, but over his conduct and his explanations there hangs a heavy sense of inevitable defeat, stemming from his recognition that the voice of the majority demanded the bold and aggressive policy.

In the arguments for annexation two essential moral and psychological themes appeared over and over again. These themes were expressed in the words Duty and Destiny. According to the first, to reject annexation of the Philippines would be to fail of fulfilling a solemn obligation. According to the second, annexation of the Philippines in particular, and expansion generally, were inevitable and irresistible.

The people had entered the war for what they felt to be purely altruistic and humanitarian reasons—the relief and liberation of the Cubans. The idea that territorial gains should arise out of this purehearted war of liberation, and the fact that before long the Americans stood in the same relation to the Filipinos as the Spaniards had stood to the Cubans, was most uncomfortable. These things raised moral questions that the anti-imperialists did not neglect to express and exploit. The imperialists were accused of breaking our national word, of violating the pledge made by McKinley himself that by our moral code forcible annexation would be "criminal aggression." They were also accused of violating the solemn injunctions of the Founding Fathers, particularly the principles of the Declaration of Independence. The rhetoric of Duty was a reassuring answer to this attempt to stir feelings of guilt.

The feeling that one may be guilty of wrongdoing can be heightened when the questionable act is followed by adversity. Conversely, it may be minimized by the successful execution of a venture. Misfortune is construed as providential punishment; but success, as in the Calvinist scheme, is taken as an outward sign of an inward state of grace. One of the most conspicuous things about the war was the remarkable successes achieved by American arms, of which the most astonishing was Dewey's destruction, without losing a single American life, of the entire Spanish Eastern fleet in Manila Bay. Victories of this sort could readily be interpreted as Providential signs, tokens of Divine approval. It was widely reported in the United States that this was Dewey's own interpretation. "If I were a religious man, and I hope I am," he said, "I should say that the hand of God was in it." This was precisely the sort of reassurance that was needed. "The magnificent fleets of Spain," declared a writer in a Baptist periodical, concerning Spain's senile and decrepit navy, "have gone down as marvelously, I had almost said, as miraculously, as the walls of Jericho went down." The victory, said an editor of the *Christian and Missionary Alliance*, "read almost like the stories of the ancient battles of the Lord in the times of Joshua, David, and Jehoshophat."

Furthermore, what might have seemed a sin became transformed into a positive obligation, a duty. The feeling was: *Providence has been so indulgent to us, by giving us so richly of success, that we would be sinful if we did not accept the responsibility it has asked us to assume.* The Protestant clergy, those tender guardians of the national conscience, did not hesitate to make lavish use of such arguments. "To give to the world the life more abundant both for here and hereafter," reasoned a writer in the *Baptist Missionary Review*, "is the duty of the American people by virtue of the call of God. This is very plain. The hand of God in history has ever been plain." "If God has brought us to the parting of the ways," insisted a writer in the *Churchman*, "we cannot hold back without rejecting divine leadership." The rhetoric of secular leaders was hardly less inspired. "We will not renounce our part in the mission of our race, trustees under God, of the civilization of the world," said Senator Albert J. Beveridge.

> God has not been preparing the English-speaking and Teutonic peoples for a thousand years for nothing but vain and idle self-contemplation and self-admiration. No! He has made us the master organizers of the world to establish system where chaos reigns. He has made us adepts in government that we may administer government among savages and senile peoples.

The theme of Destiny was a corollary of the theme of Duty. Repeatedly it was declared that expansion was the result of a "cosmic tendency," that "destiny always arrives," that it was in the "inexorable logic of events," and so on. The doctrine that expansion was inevitable had of course long been familiar to Americans: We all know how often Manifest Destiny was invoked throughout the nineteenth century. Albert Weinberg has pointed out, however, that this expression took on a new meaning in the nineties. Previously destiny had meant primarily that American expansion, *when we willed it*, could not be resisted *by others* who might wish to stand in our way. During the nineties it came to mean that expansion "could not be resisted by Americans themselves, caught, willing or unwilling," in the coils of fate. A certain reluctance on our part was implied. This was not quite so much what we *wanted* to do; it was what we *had* to do. Our aggression was implicitly defined as compulsive—the product not of our own wills but of objective necessity (or the will of God).

"Duty," said President McKinley, "determines destiny." While Duty meant that we had a moral obligation, Destiny meant that we would certainly fulfill it, that the capacity to fulfill it was inherent in us. Our history had been a continuous history of expansion; it had always succeeded before, therefore it was certain to succeed in the future. Expansion was a national and "racial" inheritance, a deep and irresistible inner necessity. Here was a plausible traditionalist answer to the accusation of a grave breach of tradition.

It is not surprising that the public should have found some truth in this concept of inevitable destiny, for the acts that first involved their country with the fate of the Philippines were willed and carried out by others and were made objects for public discussion and decision only *after* the most important commitments had been made. The public will was not freely exercised upon the question, and for the citizens at large, who were in the presence of forces they could not understand or control, the rhetoric of

Destiny may have been a way of softening and ennobling the *fait accompli* with which they were presented. But what of the men whose wills were really effective in the matter? If we examine their case, we find that the manufacturers of inevitability believed deeply in their own product. Indeed, while the extent to which the idea of Destiny was generally accepted is unknown, its wide prevalence among influential politicians, editors, and publicists is beyond argument. When Senator Lodge wrote to Theodore Roosevelt in 1898 that "the whole policy of annexation is growing rapidly under the irresistible pressure of events," when President McKinley remarked in private to his secretary, concerning the taking of Hawaii, "It is manifest destiny," when he declared in his private instructions to the peace commissioners that "the march of events rules and overrules human action"—what was involved was not an attempt to sell an idea to the public but a mode of communication in which the insiders felt thoroughly at home; perhaps a magical mode of thought by which they quieted their own uncertainties. It is easy to say, from the perspective of the twentieth century, that where contemporaries heard the voice of God we think we can discern the carnal larynx of Theodore Roosevelt. But if the insiders themselves imagined that they heard the voice of God, we must be careful of imputing hypocrisy. It is significant that the idea of Destiny was effective even among people who had very grave doubts about the desirability of remaining in the Philippines. Secretary of the Navy John D. Long, who was affectionately regarded by Theodore Roosevelt as an old fuddy-duddy on this score, confided to a friend in 1898 that we would really have preferred the United States to remain what it had been during the first half of the nineteenth century—"provincial," as he expressed it, and "dominated by the New England idea. But," he added, "I cannot shut my eyes to the march of events —a march which seems to be beyond human control."

It would be false to give the impression that only high moral and metaphysical concepts were employed in the imperialistic argument. Talk about entry into the markets of Asia was heard often after Dewey's victory; but even those who talked about material gains showed a conspicuous and symptomatic inability to distinguish between interests, rights, and duties. Charles Denby, former minister to China and a member of McKinley's commission to study the Philippines, contributed to the *Forum* two interesting articles full of this confusion. The central business of diplomacy, confessed Denby, was to advance commerce. Our right to hold the Philippines was the right of conquerors. So far, Mr. Denby was all *Realpolitik*. But he continued that he favored keeping the islands because he could not conceive any alternative to doing so except seizing territory in China, and he did not want to oppress further, "the helpless Government and people of China"! Thus a rather odd scruple crept in; but Mr. Denby quickly explained that this was simply because China's strength and prosperity were in America's interest. "We are after markets," he went on, sliding back into *Realpolitik*, and "along with these markets"—sliding back into morality—"will go our beneficent institutions; and humanity will bless us." In a second article Mr. Denby shuttled back to "the cold, hard practical question. . . . Will the possession of these islands benefit us as a nation? If it will not, set them free tomorrow, and let their people, if they please, cut each other's throats." And yet, Mr.

Denby made it clear, we did come as benefactors, bringing to our cut-throat friends "the choicest gifts—liberty and hope and happiness."

There was, besides the oscillatory rhetoric of Mr. Denby, a let's-be-candid school, whose views were expressed by the Washington *Post:*

> All this talk about benevolent assimilation; all this hypocritical pretense of anxiety for the moral, social, and intellectual exaltation of the natives . . . deceives nobody, avails nothing. . . . We all know, down in our hearts, that these islands . . . are important to us only in the ratio of their practical possibilities, and by no other. . . . Why not be honest?

There were others who found the primary benefit of our new imperial status in the social cohesion and military spirit that would result, hoping that the energies of the country would be deflected from internal to external conflict. "Marse" Henry Watterson, the well-known editor of the Louisville *Courier-Journal*, told a New York reporter:

> From a nation of shopkeepers we become a nation of warriors. We escape the menace and peril of socialism and agrarianism, as England has escaped them, by a policy of colonization and conquest. From a provincial huddle of petty sovereignties held together by a rope of sand we rise to the dignity and prowess of an imperial republic incomparably greater than Rome. It is true that we exchange domestic dangers for foreign dangers; but in every direction we multiply the opportunities of the people. We risk Caesarism, certainly; but even Caesarism is preferable to anarchism. We risk wars; but a man has but one time to die, and either in peace or war, he is not likely to die until his time comes. . . . In short, *anything is better than the pace we are going before these present forces were started into life.* Already the young manhood of the country is as a goodly brand snatched from the burning, and given a perspective replete with noble deeds and elevating ideas.

Since Julius W. Pratt published his *Expansionists of 1898* fifteen years ago it has been obvious that any interpretation of America's entry upon the paths of imperialism in the nineties in terms of rational economic motives would not fit the facts, and that a historian who approached the event with preconceptions no more supple than those, say, of Lenin's *Imperialism* would be helpless. This is not to say that markets and investments have no bearing; they do, but there are innumerable features of the situation that they do not explain at all. In so far as the economic factor was important, it can be better studied in terms of the relation between the depression and the public mood.

The alternative explanation has been the equally simple idea that the war was a newspapers' war. This notion, once again, has some point, but it certainly does not explain the war itself, much less its expansionist result. The New Deal period showed that the press is not powerful enough to impose upon the public mind a totally uncongenial view of public events. It must operate roughly within the framework of public predispositions. Moreover, not all the papers of the nineties were yellow journals. We must inquire into the structure of journalistic power and also into the personnel of its ownership and editorship to find out what differentiated the sensational editors and publishers from those of the conservative press, and what it was about their readership that led the former to the (correct) conclusion that they could expand their circulations by resorting to jingo sensationalism.

There is still another qualification that must be placed upon the role of the press: the press itself, whatever it can do with opinion, does not have the power to precipitate opinion into action. That is something that takes place within the *political* process, and we cannot tell that part of the story without examining the state of party rivalries, the derivation and goals of the political elites, and indeed the entire political context. We must then supplement our story about the role of the newspapers with at least two other factors: the state of the public temper upon which the newspapers worked, and the manner in which party rivalries deflected domestic clashes into foreign aggression.

When we examine the public temper, we will find that the depression, together with such other events as the approaching completion of continental settlement, the growth of trusts, and the intensification of internal social conflict, had brought to large numbers of people intense frustrations in their economic lives and their careers. To others they had brought anxiety that a period of stagnation in national wealth and power had set in. The restlessness of the frustrated classes had been heightened by the defeat of Bryan in 1896. The anxieties about the national position had been increased among statesmen and publicists by the revival of world imperialism, in particular by the feeling that the nation was threatened by the aims of Germany, Russia, and Japan. The expansionist statesmen themselves were largely drawn from a restless upper-middle-class elite that had been fighting an unrewarding battle for conservative reform in domestic politics and that looked with some eagerness toward a more spacious field of action.

It is a psychological commonplace that we tend to respond to frustration with acts of aggression, and to allay anxieties by threatening acts against others. It seems suggestive that the underdog elements in American society showed a considerably higher responsiveness to the idea of war with Spain than the groups that were more satisfied with their economic or political positions. Our entry into the Philippines then aroused the interest of conservative groups that had been indifferent to the quixotism of freeing Cuba but were alert to the idea of capturing new markets. Imperialism appealed to members of both the business and political elites as an enlargement of the sphere of American power and profits. Many of the underdog elements also responded to this new note of national self-assertion; others, however, looked upon our conduct in the Philippines as a betrayal of national principles. Anti-expansionists attempted to stir a sense of guilt and foreboding in the nation at large. But the circumstances of the period 1898–1900—the return of prosperity and the quick spectacular victories in war—made it difficult for them to impress this feeling upon the majority. The rhetoric of Duty and Destiny carried the day. The anti-expansionists had neither the numbers nor the morale of their opponents. The most conspicuous result of their lack of drive and confidence can be seen in the lamentable strategy of Bryan over the ratification of the treaty.

Clearly this attempt to see the war and expansion in the light of social history has led us onto the high and dangerous ground of social psychology. On this terrain we historians are at a great disadvantage; we are inexpert psychologists, and in any event we cannot get the kind of data for this period which would satisfactorily substantiate any psychological hypotheses. However, we have little other choice than to move into this terrain wherever simple rationalistic explanations of national behavior leave us dissatisfied. What I have attempted here is merely a preliminary sketch of a possible explanatory model that would enlarge our conception of our task. It needs further inquiry—which might make it seem more plausible at some points, more questionable at others.

A further warning is necessary: this study has been narrowly focused on a single incident. No effort has been made—and an effort should be made—to compare this crisis with other expansionist crises in our own history, which I suspect will show important differences. No effort has been made to compare American imperialism with that of other countries. No claim has been made either that the various features of our behavior are unique to our own country or that they are the same as those which will be found elsewhere. Many parallels can be found in the history of other nations to the role of the press and the parties in whipping up foreign crises. Parallels without number could be found to the role of the administration in largely committing the nation to a foreign policy before it could be made a matter of public discussion. The rhetoric and ideology of expansion also were not singular to us; duty, destiny, racism, and the other shibboleths can be found elsewhere. Only a careful comparative inquiry will tell us how our behavior in this situation compares with other instances of our own behavior, or with the behavior of other peoples in roughly comparable situations.

I cannot refrain from adding to these notes on the methods of historical understanding another note on the tragicomical procedure of history itself. It may be of some value to us to be reminded how some of the more grandiose expectations of the nineties were realized. Cuba, to be sure, which could have been freed in peace, was freed in the war—in so far as the little country of Batistas and Machados can be considered free. The sensational newspapers that had boomed the war lost money on expensive extras, costly war-news coverage, and declining advertising. I do not know whether those silverites who wanted the war really expected that it would remonetize silver, but if they did they were rewarded with McKinley's renewed triumph and the Gold Standard Act of 1900. As for business, the gigantic markets of the East never materialized, and the precise value of the Philippines in getting at them is arguable. The islands themselves proved to be a mildly profitable colony that came to absorb a little over one per cent of all United States investments abroad. Yet within a generation the United States had committed itself to restoring independence to the Philippines. When this promise was enacted in 1934 many descendants of Auguinaldo's rebels were unenthusiastic about their new economic and strategic position. Finally, the exact estimation that is to be put on our strategic commitment in the Far East, which began with the Philippines, is still a matter of debate. We should, however, make note of the earlier opinion of one of our most brilliant and farsighted statesmen, who declared in 1907 that the Philippines were the Achilles' heel of our strategic position and should be given "nearly complete independence" at the "earliest possible moment." The author of these remarks was Theodore Roosevelt.

That "Splendid Little War" in Historical Perspective

Walter LaFeber

During the Great Depression, when many scholars were sympathetic to economic interpretations of the American past, Julius Pratt, in *The Expansionists of 1898* (1936), dramatically reversed the tide of interpretation of the Spanish-American War when he contended that the business community did not want war in the early months of 1898. Almost twenty-five years later, however, his conclusion, by then the reigning orthodoxy, was boldly challenged by William Appleman Williams in *The Tragedy of American Diplomacy* (1959, 1962) and by Walter LaFeber in *The New Empire* (1963). They found that important businessmen had become advocates of war by at least late March 1898.

In the following essay based partly on his book, LaFeber, of Cornell University, concludes that the war was conceived to preserve and extend the "American system": the war was designed to eliminate the insurrection in Cuba which disrupted American conditions and to allow policy-makers to promote American expansion in China, thereby providing the overseas markets then considered essential to the economy. The American economy, recently deep in depression, was suffering from what many diagnosed as overproduction. The rivalry of the great powers for spheres in China, according to LaFeber, made

necessary an American business-government alliance
in order to secure the needed markets there. (In his
book, LaFeber also notes that American businessmen
with investments or trade interests in Cuba wanted
war, as did some business interests that expected to
prosper in the war.) In this analysis, President
McKinley and some other policy-makers and
businessmen wished to obtain Manila and other ports
in the Pacific as bases—stepping stones—to China.
LaFeber views the annexation of the Philippines not as
part of a "large policy" of colonialism but as a tactic
to guarantee the security of the desired port—a tactic
that Thomas McCormick, in *The China Market*
(1967), terms "insular imperialism." For LaFeber,
then, the purposes of the war and of annexation are
the same: economic expansion abroad. Put bluntly,
annexation was not a "Great Aberration," to cite a still
popular alternative theory first advanced by Samuel
Flagg Bemis (*Diplomatic History of the United States*,
5th ed. [1936, 1965]). Nor was the war a product of a
"psychic crisis," as Richard Hofstadter contended.

The general quest for markets, LaFeber maintains,
was shared by farmers, businessmen, and even members
of the labor movement. Farmers, not industrialists or
financiers, first recognized the need for overseas
markets, and this agrarian analysis was later accepted
by businessmen. The Populists, in LaFeber's
interpretation, shared the capitalist consensus and were
expansionist.

A critical point in LaFeber's analysis is the
contention that the Cuban revolution had to be settled
before the possibilities of the China markets could be
exploited. Why? Certainly the desire for a future
isthmian canal, which might be delayed by the
radicals' victory in Cuba, does not adequately explain
the concern. In his book LaFeber also notes the fears
of some American businessmen that the triumph of
Cuban radicals might unsettle the American economy.
But surely this is not an adequate explanation. Perhaps
the question can be addressed more satisfactorily by
examining a statement endorsed by McKinley in 1897:
"The chronic condition of trouble in Cuba causes
disturbance in the social condition of our peoples. . . .
A continuous irritation within our own borders,
injuriously affects the normal functions of business,
and tends to delay the condition of prosperity to

That "Splendid Little War" in Historical Perspective. From *The Texas Quarterly*
(Winter 1968), pp. 89–98. Reprinted by permission of *The Texas Quarterly*.

which this country is entitled" (Secretary of State
John Sherman to Stewart Woodford, Minister to
Spain, July 16, 1897). The historian who takes this
document seriously must conclude either that the
McKinley-Sherman analysis was flawed or,
alternatively, that they accurately diagnosed mass
sentiment. LaFeber and Williams, among others, treat
this as an astute assessment of sentiment. But can one
explain this sentiment as rational, as an example of
ideology, as do LaFeber and Williams? Or is it in
fact an irrational impulse? Why had Cuba become an
American obsession? Perhaps there was *some* form
of a "psychic crisis," as Richard Hofstadter
maintains in his study of 1898, "Manifest Destiny and
the Philippines," reprinted on pp. 131–49.

LaFeber's analysis has also been criticized on other
grounds. Marilyn Blatt Young, for example, contends
that businessmen were often reluctant to exploit
opportunities in China, and she suggests, contrary to
LaFeber, that there may have been a disjunction
between the views of policy-makers and businessmen,
or at least a gap between the words and actions of
businessmen ("American Expansion, 1870–1900," in
Barton J. Bernstein, ed., *Towards a New Past*
[1968]). How, then, should one interpret the
statements about the need for overseas markets? Paul
Varg, among others, has questioned the importance of
the China market ("The Myth of the China Market,
1890–1914," *American Historical Review*, LXXIII
[1967]), though defenders of the LaFeber-
McCormick-Williams position reply that the market
was growing and seemed then to represent rich
prospects for the future. The best test of the China
market's importance, according to this rejoinder, is
not simply the magnitude of trade with China in 1897
or 1898, or even in 1900 or thereafter, but the faith of
Americans in 1898 in the "myth" that millions of
Chinese would purchase American goods. There is
also a related question: How important were foreign
markets to the survival of the American political
economy in the 1890s?

LaFeber's important study, by concentrating on the
ideology of the American political economy and the
quest for markets, helped restore economic
interpretations to an important place in the analysis of
American history. His particular emphasis on the
relations of business and government and his
explanation of imperialism as a carefully conceived

policy have helped promote a reassessment of the
1890s in particular and of American foreign policy in
general.

*T*he "splendid little war" of 1898, as Secretary of State
John Hay termed it at the time, is rapidly losing its splendor for those concerned with American foreign policy in the 1960s. Over the past decade few
issues in the country's diplomatic history have aroused academics more than
the causes of the Spanish-American War, and in the last several years the
argument has become not merely academic, but a starting point in the debate over how the United States evolved into a great power, and more particularly how Americans got involved in the maelstrom of Asian nationalism.
The line from the conquest of the Philippines in 1898 to the attempted paci-
fication of Vietnam in 1968 is not straight, but it is quite traceable, and if
Frederick Jackson Turner was correct when he observed in the 1890s that
"The aim of history, then, is to know the elements of the present by understanding what came into the present from the past," the causes of the war in
1898 demand analysis from our present viewpoint.

Historians have offered four general interpretations to explain these causes.
First, the war has been traced to a general impulse for war on the part of
American public opinion. This interpretation has been illustrated in a famous
cartoon showing President William McKinley, in the bonnet and dress of a
little old lady, trying to sweep back huge waves marked "Congress" and
"public opinion," with a very small broom. The "yellow journalism" generated by the Hearst-Pulitzer rivalry supposedly both created and reflected
this sentiment for war. A sophisticated and useful version of this interpretation has been advanced by Richard Hofstadter. Granting the importance of
the Hearst-Pulitzer struggle, he has asked why these newspaper titans were
able to exploit public opinion. Hofstadter has concluded that psychological
dilemmas arising out of the depression of the 1890s made Americans react
somewhat irrationally because they were uncertain, frightened, and consequently open to exploitation by men who would show them how to cure
their frustrations through overseas adventures. In other words, the giddy
minds of the 1890s could be quieted by foreign quarrels.

A second interpretation argues that the United States went to war for
humanitarian reasons, that is, to free the Cubans from the horrors of Spanish
policies and to give the Cubans democratic institutions. That this initial impulse resulted within ten months in an American protectorate over Cuba
and Puerto Rico, annexation of the Philippines, and American participation
in quarrels on the mainland of Asia itself, is explained as accidental, or, more
familiarly, as done in a moment of "aberration" on the part of American
policy-makers.

A third interpretation emphasizes the role of several Washington officials who advocated a "Large Policy" of conquering a vast colonial empire in the Caribbean and Western Pacific. By shrewd maneuvering, these few imperialists pushed the vacillating McKinley and a confused nation into war. Senator Henry Cabot Lodge, of Massachusetts, Captain Alfred Thayer Mahan, of the U.S. Navy, and Theodore Roosevelt, Assistant Secretary of the Navy in 1897–1898, are usually named as the leaders of the "Large Policy" contingent.

A fourth interpretation believes the economic drive carried the nation into war. This drive emanated from the rapid industrialization which characterized American society after the 1840s. The immediate link between this industrialization and the war of 1898 was the economic depression which afflicted the nation in the quarter-century after 1873. Particularly important were the 1893–1897 years when Americans endured the worst of the plunge. Government and business leaders, who were both intelligent and rational, believed an oversupply of goods created the depression. They finally accepted war as a means of opening overseas markets in order to alleviate domestic distress caused by the overproduction. For thirty years the economic interpretation dominated historians' views of the war, but in 1936 Professor Julius Pratt conclusively demonstrated that business journals did not want war in the early months of 1898. He argued instead the "Large Policy" explanation, and from that time to the present, Professor Pratt's interpretation has been pre-eminent in explaining the causes of the conflict.

As I shall argue in a moment, the absence of economic factors in causing the war has been considerably exaggerated. At this point, however, a common theme which unites the first three interpretations should be emphasized. Each of the three deals with a superficial aspect of American life; each is peculiar to 1898, and none is rooted in the structure, the bed-rock, of the nation's history. This theme is important, for it means that if the results of the war were distasteful and disadvantageous (and on this historians do largely agree because of the divisive problems which soon arose in the Philippines and Cuba), those misfortunes were endemic to episodes unique to 1898. The peculiarities of public sentiment or the Hearst-Pulitzer rivalry, for example, have not reoccurred; the wide-spread humanitarian desire to help Cubans has been confined to 1898; and the banding together of Lodge, Mahan, and Roosevelt to fight for "Large Policies" of the late 1890s was never repeated by the three men. Conspiracy theories, moreover, seldom explain history satisfactorily.

The fourth interpretation has different implications. It argues that if the economic was the primary drive toward war, criticism of that war must begin not with irrational factors or flights of humanitarianism or a few stereotyped figures, but with the basic structure of the American system.

United States foreign policy, after all, is concerned primarily with the nation's domestic system and only secondarily with the systems of other nations. American diplomatic history might be defined as the study of how United States relations with other nations are used to insure the survival and increasing prosperity of the American system. Foreign policymakers are no more motivated by altruism than is the rest of the human race, but are instead involved in making a system function at home. Secretary of State, as the Founding Fathers realized, is an apt title for the man in charge of American foreign policy.

Turning this definition around, it also means that domestic affairs are the main determinant of foreign policy. When viewed within this matrix, the diplomatic events of the 1890s are no longer aberrations or the results of conspiracies and drift; American policymakers indeed grabbed greatness with both hands. As for accident or chance, they certainly exist in history, but become more meaningful when one begins with J. B. Bury's definition of "chance": "The valuable collision of two or more independent chains of causes." The most fruitful approach to the war of 1898 might be from the inside out (from the domestic to the foreign), and by remembering that chance is "the valuable collision of two or more independent chains of causes."

Three of these "chains" can be identified: the economic crisis of the 1890s which caused extensive and dangerous maladjustments in American society; the opportunities which suddenly opened in Asia after 1895 and in the Caribbean and the Pacific in 1898, opportunities which officials began to view as poultices, if not cure-alls, for the illnesses at home; and a growing partnership between business and government which reached its nineteenth-century culmination in the person of William McKinley. In April 1898, these "chains" had a "valuable collision" and war resulted.

The formation of the first chain is the great success story of American history. Between 1850 and 1910 the average manufacturing plant in the country multiplied its capital thirty-nine times, its number of wage-earners nearly seven times, and the value of its output by more than nineteen times. By the mid-1890s American iron and steel producers joked about their successful underselling of the vaunted British steel industry not only in world markets, but also in the vicinity of Birmingham, England, itself. The United States traded more in international markets than any nation except Great Britain.

But the most accelerated period of this development, 1873–1898, was actually twenty-five years of boom hidden in twenty-five years of bust. That quarter-century endured the longest and worst depression in the nation's history. After brief and unsatisfactory recoveries in the mid-1880s and early 1890s, the economy reached bottom in 1893. Unparalleled social and economic disasters struck. One out of every six laborers was unemployed, with most of the remainder existing on substandard wages; not only weak firms but many companies with the best credit ratings were forced to close their doors; the unemployed slept in the streets; riots erupted in Brooklyn, California, and points in between, as in the calamitous Pullman Strike in Chicago; Coxey's Army of broken farmers and unemployed laborers made their famous march on Washington; and the Secretary of State, Walter Quentin Gresham, remarked privately in 1894 that he saw "symptoms of revolution" appearing. Federal troops were dispatched to Chicago and other urban areas, including a cordon which guarded the Federal Treasury building in New York City.

Faced with the prospect of revolution and confronted with an economy that had almost ground to a stop, American businessmen and political officials faced alternative policies: they could attempt to re-examine and reorient the economic system, making radical modifications in the means of distribution and particularly the distribution of wealth; or they could look for new physical frontiers, following the historic tendency to increase production and then ferreting out new markets so the surplus, which the nation supposedly was unable to consume, could be sold elsewhere and Americans then put back to work on the production lines.

To the business and political communities, these were not actually alternatives at all. Neither of those communities has been known historically for political and social radicalism. Each sought security, not new political experiments. Some business firms tried to find such security by squashing competitors. Extremely few, however, searched for such policies as a federal income tax. Although such a tax narrowly passed through Congress in 1894, the Supreme Court declared it unconstitutional within a year and the issue would not be resurrected for another seventeen years. As a result, business and political leaders accepted the solution which was traditional, least threatening to their own power, and (apparently) required the least risk: new markets. Secretary of the Treasury John G. Carlisle summarized this conclusion in his public report of 1894: "The prosperity of our people, therefore, depends largely upon their ability to sell their surplus products in foreign markets at remunerative prices."

This consensus included farmers and the labor movement among others, for these interests were no more ingenious in discovering new solutions than were businessmen. A few farmers and laborers murmured ominously about some kind of political and/or economic revolution, but Richard Hofstadter seems correct in suggesting that in a sense Populism was reactionary rather than radical. The agrarians in the Populist movement tended to look back to a Jeffersonian utopia. Historians argue this point, but beyond dispute is the drive by farmers, including Populists, for foreign markets. The agrarians acted out of a long and successful tradition, for they had sought overseas customers since the first tobacco surplus in Virginia three hundred and fifty years before. Farmers initially framed the expansionist arguments and over three centuries created the context for the growing consensus on the desirability of foreign markets, a consensus which businessmen and others would utilize in the 1890's.

The farmers' role in developing this theme in American history became highly ironic in the late nineteenth century, for businessmen not only adopted the argument that overseas markets were necessary, but added a proviso that agrarian interests would have to be suppressed in the process. Industrialists observed that export charts demonstrated the American economy to be depending more upon industrial than agrarian exports. To allow industrial goods to be fully competitive in the world market, however, labor costs would have to be minimal, and cheap bread meant sacrificing the farmers. Fully comprehending this argument, agrarians reacted bitterly. They nevertheless continued searching for their own overseas markets, agreeing with the industrialist that the traditional method of discovering new outlets provided the key to prosperity, individualism, and status.

The political conflict which shattered the 1890s revolved less around the question of whether conservatives could carry out a class solution than the question of which class would succeed in carrying out a conservative solution. This generalization remains valid even when the American labor movement is examined for its response to the alternatives posed. This movement, primarily comprised of the newly-formed American Federation of Labor, employed less than 3 per cent of the total number of employed workers in nonfarm occupations. In its own small sphere of influence, its membership largely consisted of skilled workers living in the East. The AFL was not important in the West or South, where the major discontent seethed. Although Samuel Gompers was known by some of the more faint-hearted as a "socialist," the AFL's founder never dramatized any radical solutions for the restructuring of the economy. He was concerned with obtaining more money, better hours, and improved working conditions for the Federation's members. Gompers refused, moreover, to use direct political action to obtain these benefits, content to negotiate within the corporate structure which the businessman had created. The AFL simply wanted more, and when overseas markets seemed to be a primary source of benefits, Gompers did not complain. As Louis Hartz has noted, "wage consciousness," not "class consciousness," triumphed.

The first "chain of causes" was marked by a consensus on the need to find markets overseas. Fortunately for the advocates of this policy, another "chain," quite complementary to the first, began to form beyond American borders. By the mid-1890's, American merchants, missionaries, and ship captains had been profiting from Asian markets for more than a century. Between 1895 and 1900, however, the United States for the first time became a mover-and-pusher in Asian affairs.

In 1895 Japan defeated China in a brief struggle that now appears to be one of the most momentous episodes in the nineteenth century. The Japanese emerged as the major Asian power, the Chinese suddenly seemed to be incapable of defending their honor or existence, Chinese nationalism began its peculiar path to the 1960s, and European powers which had long lusted after Asian markets now seized a golden opportunity. Russia, Germany, France, and ultimately Great Britain initiated policies designed to carve China and Manchuria into spheres of influence. Within a period of months, the Asian mainland suddenly became the scene of international power politics at its worst and most explosive.

The American reaction to these events has been summarized recently by Professor Thomas McCormick: "The conclusion of the Sino-Japanese War left Pandora's box wide open, but many Americans mistook it for the Horn of Plenty." Since the first American ship sailed to sell goods in China in 1784, Americans had chased that most mysterious phantom, the China Market. Now, just at the moment when key interest groups agreed that overseas markets could be the salvation of the 1890s crisis, China was almost miraculously opening its doors to the glutted American factories and farms. United States trade with China jumped significantly after 1895, particularly in the critical area of manufactures; by 1899 manufactured products accounted for more than 90 per cent of the nation's exports to the Chinese, a quadrupling of the amount sent in 1895. In their moment of need, Americans had apparently discovered a Horn of Plenty.

But, of course, it was Pandora's box. The ills which escaped from the box were threefold. Least important for the 1890s, a nascent Chinese nationalism appeared. During the next quarter-century, the United States attempted to minimize the effects of this nationalism either by cooperating with Japan or European powers to isolate and weaken the Chinese, or by siding with the most conservative groups within the nationalist movement. Americans also faced the competition of European and Japanese products, but they were nevertheless confident in the power of their newly-tooled industrial power-house. Given a "fair field and no favor," as the Secretary of State phrased the wish in 1900, Americans would undersell and defeat any competitors. But could fair fields and no favors be guaranteed? Within their recently-created spheres of influence European powers began to grant themselves trade preferences, thus effectively shutting out American competition. In 1897, the American business community and the newly-installed administration of William McKinley began to counter these threats.

The partnership between businessmen and politicians, in this case the Mc-Kinley administration, deserves emphasis, for if the businessman hoped to exploit Asian markets he required the aid of the politician. Americans could compete against British or Russian manufacturers in Asia, but they could not compete against, say, a Russian manufacturer who could turn to his govern-ment and through pressure exerted by that government on Chinese officials receive a prize railroad contract or banking concession. United States busi-nessmen could only compete against such business-government coalitions if Washington officials helped. Only then would the field be fair and the favors equalized. To talk of utilizing American "rugged individualism" and a free enterprise philosophy in the race for the China market in the 1890s was silly. There consequently emerged in American policy-making a classic example of the business community and the government grasping hands and, march-ing shoulder to shoulder, leading the United States to its destiny of being a major power on a far-Eastern frontier. As one high Republican official remarked in the mid-1890s: "diplomacy is the management of international business."

William McKinley fully understood the need for such a partnership. He had grown to political maturity during the 1870s when, as one Congressman remarked, "The House of Representatives was like an auction room where more valuable considerations were disposed of under the speaker's hammer than in any other place on earth." Serving as governor of Ohio during the 1890s depression, McKinley learned firsthand about the dangers posed by the economic crisis (including riots in his state which he terminated with overwhelming displays of military force). The new Chief Executive be-lieved there was nothing necessarily manifest about Manifest Destiny in American history, and his administration was the first in modern American history which so systematically and completely committed itself to helping businessmen, farmers, laborers, and missionaries in solving their problems in an industrializing, supposedly frontierless America. Mr. Dooley caught this aggressive side of the McKinley administration when he described the intro-duction of a presidential speech: "Th' proceedin's was opened with a prayer that Providence might r-remain undher th' protection iv th' administration."

Often characterized as a creation of his campaign manager Mark Hanna, or as having, in the famous but severely unjust words of Theodore Roose-velt, the backbone of a chocolate eclair, McKinley was, as Henry Adams and others fully understood, a master of men. McKinley was never pushed into a policy he did not want to accept. Elihu Root, probably the best mind and most acute observer who served in the McKinley cabinets, commented that on most important matters the President had his ideas fixed, but would convene the Cabinet, direct the members toward his own conclusions, and thereby allow the Cabinet to think it had formulated the policy. In responding to the problems and opportunities in China, however, McKinley's power to exploit that situation was limited by events in the Caribbean.

In 1895 revolution had broken out in Cuba. By 1897 Americans were becoming increasingly belligerent on this issue for several reasons: more than $50,000,000 of United States investments on the island were endangered; Spaniards were treating some Cubans inhumanely; the best traditions of the Monroe Doctrine had long dictated that a European in the Caribbean was a sty in the eye of any red-blooded American; and, finally, a number of Americans, not only Lodge, Roosevelt, and Mahan, understood the strategic and political relationship of Cuba to a proposed isthmian canal. Such a canal would provide a short-cut to the west coast of Latin America as well as to the promised markets of Asia. Within six months after assuming office, McKinley demanded that the island be pacified or the United States would take a "course of action which the time and the transcendent emergency may demand." Some Spanish reforms followed, but in January 1898, new revolts wracked Havana and a month later the "Maine" dramatically sank to the bottom of Havana harbor.

McKinley confronted the prospect of immediate war. Only two restraints appeared. First, a war might lead to the annexation of Cuba, and the multitude of problems (including racial) which had destroyed Spanish authority would be dumped on the United States. Neither the President nor his close advisers wanted to leap into the quicksands of noncontiguous, colonial empire. The business community comprised a second restraining influence. By mid-1897 increased exports, which removed part of the agricultural and industrial glut, began to extricate the country from its quarter-century of turmoil. Finally seeing light at the end of a long and treacherous tunnel, businessmen did not want the requirements of a war economy to jeopardize the growing prosperity.

These two restraints explain why the United States did not go to war in 1897, and the removal of these restraints indicates why war occurred in April 1898. The first problem disappeared because McKinley and his advisers entertained no ideas of warring for colonial empire in the Caribbean. After the war Cuba would be freed from Spain and then ostensibly returned to the Cubans to govern. The United States would retain a veto power over the more important policy decisions made on the island. McKinley discovered a classic solution in which the United States enjoyed the power over, but supposedly little of the responsibility for, the Cubans.

The second restraint disappeared in late March 1898, exactly at the time of McKinley's decision to send the final ultimatum to Madrid. The timing is crucial. Professor Pratt observed in 1936 that the business periodicals began to change their antiwar views in mid-March 1898, but he did not elaborate upon this point. The change is significant and confirms the advice McKinley received from a trusted political adviser in New York City who cabled on

March 25 that the larger corporations would welcome war. The business journal and their readers were beginning to realize that the bloody struggle in Cuba and the resulting inability of the United States to operate at full-speed in Asian affairs more greatly endangered economic recovery than would a war.

McKinley's policies in late March manifested these changes. This does not mean that the business community manipulated the President, or that he was repaying those businessmen who had played vital roles in his election in 1896. Nor does it mean that McKinley thought the business community was forcing his hand or circumscribing his policies in late March. The opinions and policies of the President and the business community had been hammered out in the furnace of a terrible depression and the ominous changes in Asia. McKinley and pivotal businessmen emerged from these unforgettable experiences sharing a common conclusion: the nation's economy increasingly depended upon overseas markets, including the whole of China; that to develop these markets not only a business-government partnership but also tranquillity was required; and, finally, however paradoxical it might seem, tranquillity could be insured only through war against Spain. Not for the first or last time, Americans believed that to have peace they would have to wage war. Some, including McKinley, moved on to a final point. War, if properly conducted, could result in a few select strategic bases in the Pacific (such as Hawaii, Guam, and Manila) which would provide the United States with potent starting-blocks in the race for Asian markets. McKinley sharply distinguished between controlling such bases and trying to rule formally over an extensive territorial empire. In the development of the "chains of causes" the dominant theme was the economic, although not economic in the narrow sense. As discussed in the 1890's, business recovery carried most critical political and social implications.

Some historians argue that McKinley entered the war in confusion and annexed the Philippines in a moment of aberration. They delight in quoting the President's announcement to a group of Methodist missionaries that he decided to annex the Philippines one night when after praying he heard a mysterious voice. Most interesting, however, is not that the President heard a reassuring voice, but how the voice phrased its advice. The voice evidently outlined the points to be considered; in any case, McKinley numbered them in order, demonstrating, perhaps, that either he, the voice, or both had given some thought to putting the policy factors in neat and logical order. The second point is of particular importance: "that we could not turn them [the Philippines] over to France or Germany—our commercial rivals in the Orient—that would be bad business and discreditable. . . ." Apparently everyone who had been through the 1890s knew the dangers of "bad business." Even voices.

Interpretations which depend upon mass opinion, humanitarianism, and "Large Policy" advocates do not satisfactorily explain the causes of the war. Neither, however, does Mr. Dooley's famous one-sentence definition of American imperialism in 1898: "Hands acrost th' sea an' into somewan's pocket." The problem of American expansion is more complicated and historically rooted than the flippancy indicates. George Eliot once observed, "The happiest nations, like the happiest women, have no history." The

United States, however, endured in the nineteenth century a history of growing industrialism, supposedly closing physical frontiers, rapid urbanization, unequal distribution of wealth, and an overdependence upon export trade. These historical currents clashed in the 1890s. The result was chaos and fear, then war and empire.

In 1898 McKinley and the business community wanted peace, but they also sought benefits which only a war could provide. Viewed from the perspective of the 1960's, the Spanish-American conflict can no longer be viewed as only a "splendid little war." It was a war to preserve the American system.

Suggested Reading

Ernest R. May's *Imperial Democracy* (1961) relies partly on the "psychic crisis" theory, as does Marilyn Blatt Young's "American Expansion, 1870–1900," in Barton J. Bernstein, ed., *Toward a New Past** (1968). May's *American Imperialism: A Speculative Essay** (1968) theorizes that American imperialism resulted from the fact that American "opinion leaders" gained the conception of colonialism from Europe and then converted their fellow citizens. H. Wayne Morgan's *America's Road to Empire: The War with Spain and Overseas Expansion** (1965) is a useful volume.

Walter LaFeber's initial analysis of the expansion of the 1890s appears in *The New Empire: An Interpretation of American Expansion** (1963), and should be supplemented by similar interpretations by Thomas J. McCormick in *China Market: America's Quest for Informal Empire, 1893–1901** (1967), and by William Appleman Williams in *The Tragedy of American Diplomacy*,* 2nd rev. ed. (1972), *The Contours of American History** (1961), *The Great Evasion** (1964), and *The Roots of the Modern American Empire** (1970).

The interpretations of this so-called Wisconsin School have been attacked by Irwin Unger in "The 'New Left' and American History: Some Recent Trends in United States Historiography," *American Historical Review*, LXXII (1967), and more thoughtfully by Robert Tucker in *The Radical Left and American Foreign Policy** (1971). Paul Holbo's "Economics, Expansion and Emotion: An Emerging Foreign Policy," in H. Wayne Morgan, ed., *The Gilded Age*,* rev. ed. (1970), is sharply critical of LaFeber's analysis.

A Marxist interpretation of expansion is Philip Foner's "Why the United States Went to War With Spain in 1898," *Science and Society*, XXXII (1968). The relationship between businessmen and expansion in the 1890s is treated differently in Julius Pratt's *The Expansionists of 1898** (1936), and in Charles S. Campbell, Jr.'s *Special Business Interests and the Open Door Policy* (1951). Paul Varg's "The Myth of the China Market, 1890–1914," *American Historical Review*, LXXIII (1967), stresses the erroneous hopes for, and the failures of, that market.

Analyses of the ideas behind expansion are available in Frederick Merk's *Manifest Destiny and Mission in American History** (1963), Albert Weinberg's *Manifest Destiny** (1935), Richard Van Alstyne's *The Rising American Empire** (1960), and Charles Vevier's "American Continentalism: An Idea of Expansion, 1845–1910," *American Historical Review*, LXV (1960).

Foreign policy before McKinley is the subject of David Pletcher in *The Awkward Years: American Foreign Relations Under Garfield and Arthur* (1962), and

Milton Plesur in *America's Outward Thrust: Approaches to Foreign Affairs, 1865–1890* (1971).

Important studies of antiimperialism include Fred H. Harrington's "The Anti-Imperialist Movement in the United States," *Mississippi Valley Historical Review* (1935), and "The Literary Aspects of American Anti-Imperialism," *New England Quarterly*, X (1937), Robert Beisner's *Twelve Against Empire: The Anti-Imperialists, 1898–1900* (1968); E. Berkeley Tompkins' *Anti-Imperialism in the United States: The Great Debate, 1890–1920* (1970), and John Rollins' "The Anti-Imperialists and Twentieth Century American Foreign Policy," and Thomas McCormick's "A Commentary on the Anti-Imperialists and Twentieth-Century Foreign Policy," both in *Studies on the Left*, III (1962).

* Also published in paperback edition.

The Poverty
of Progress

The Politics of Reform
in Municipal Government
in the Progressive Era

Samuel P. Hays

Despite the fact that the Progressive movement was so
variegated and multifaceted that some historians have
denied that it existed, it was vividly real to those who
lived through it. Some historians have found the
coherence of Progressivism in the desires of reformers
to curb immoral or irresponsible aggregations of
private economic power, to solve the problem of
political corruption, and to extend some protections
to those weak members of society unable to protect
themselves against the harsh forces of the new
industrial order. Most importantly, the reformers
sought to achieve all these goals by the reinvigoration
of government at all levels. The historians who hold
this view of Progressivism appear to be explaining the
developments of the period by extending the
categories used by the participants themselves. To
accept at face value the rhetoric of the antagonists
results in an interpretation that is highly compatible
with the liberal-conservative cycle theory. According
to this theory, whose best known exponent is Arthur
M. Schlesinger, Jr., the principal pattern of American
political history is determined by the struggle on the
part of the business community to dominate the state,
and the recurrent attempts of the rest of society, led

by liberals, to check the political power of business. During periods of conservative ascendancy, social problems pile up unsolved until the demand for reform brings a liberal government to power. There follows a flood of change until the liberal impulse is spent, whereupon the conservatives return to enforce a new period of inaction, but one in which the reforms generated in the preceding liberal period are still in effect.

Progressivism was explained as an example of the liberal phase of this cycle until the 1950s. It is interesting to note that such an explanation is consistent with one of the themes that historians seem to agree was central to the Progressive movement. Reformers of the time saw themselves as champions of the public interest against the unwarranted power of special interests, and historians concur that one of the central problems of the time was the relationship of public to private power. One of the earliest and most active arenas in which Progressives allegedly pursued the public interest was the municipality, and some of the most celebrated political innovations connected with Progressivism were new forms of municipal government such as the city manager plan and the city commission plan. Rule by experts or by the disinterested were the alternatives acceptable to the reform movement which was oriented toward the urban middle class.

According to Samuel P. Hays of the University of Pittsburgh, however, the central thrust of reform at the local level was not democratization and decentralization, as one might infer from such structural reforms as the initiative, referendum, and recall, but concentration of decision-making authority in the hands of a smaller number of officials who could confidently be expected to represent the new elites. Hays dismisses the old interpretation of Progressivism as the liberal phase in a liberal-conservative cycle and calls into question the status-squeeze theory that attributes the Progressive impulse to the anxieties felt by members of the middle class who are afraid of both the lower and upper classes. The problem, writes Hays, is that status anxiety is a better description of what the middle-class reformers said than of how they acted. In addition, it does not conform very well to the available evidence, which indicates that municipal

The Politics of Reform in Municipal Government in the Progressive Era. From *Pacific Northwest Quarterly,* LV (October 1964), pp. 157–69. Reprinted by permission of the author and the publisher.

reform was initiated by the organized business community and professionals, that its purpose was to foster
economic growth through greater efficiency on the
model of business, and that the business elite that
initiated the reforms expected that the reforms would
result in an increase of political power for them.

Hays's view of Progressivism at the local level is
echoed on the national level by Gabriel Kolko in his
*The Triumph of Conservatism: A Reinterpretation of
American History, 1900–1916* (1963). Kolko argues
that "there were any number of options involving
government and economics abstractly available to
national political leaders during the period 1900–1916,
and in virtually every case they chose those solutions
to problems advocated by the representatives of
concerned business and financial interests."

The student of Progressivism is faced with a serious
problem. Were the Progressives crusading altruists,
conservative businessmen disguised as reformers,
insecure members of the middle class anxious about
their social status in view of the rising power of
organized labor on the one hand and the accretion of
power and prestige on the part of the new economic
men of big business on the other hand, or were they
something else altogether? It is certainly worth
wondering whether a scholar can be as sure as Hays
seems to be that the social position of the proponent
of a certain action is a sufficient clue to his motivation.

*I*n order to achieve a more complete understanding of
social change in the Progressive Era, historians must now undertake a deeper
analysis of the practices of economic, political, and social groups. Political
ideology alone is no longer satisfactory evidence to describe social patterns
because generalizations based upon it, which tend to divide political groups
into the moral and the immoral, the rational and the irrational, the efficient
and the inefficient, do not square with political practice. Behind this contemporary rhetoric concerning the nature of reform lay patterns of political
behavior which were at variance with it. Since an extensive gap separated
ideology and practice, we can no longer take the former as an accurate description of the latter, but must reconstruct social behavior from other types
of evidence.

Reform in urban government provides one of the most striking examples
of this problem of analysis. The demand for change in municipal affairs,
whether in terms of over-all reform, such as the commission and city-manager
plans, or of more piecemeal modifications, such as the development of city-

wide school boards, deeply involved reform ideology. Reformers loudly proclaimed a new structure of municipal government as more moral, more rational, and more efficient and, because it was so, self-evidently more desirable. But precisely because of this emphasis, there seemed to be no need to analyze the political forces behind change. Because the goals of reform were good, its causes were obvious, rather than being the product of particular people and particular ideas in particular situations, they were deeply imbedded in the universal impulses and truths of "progress." Consequently, historians have rarely tried to determine precisely who the municipal reformers were or what they did, but instead have relied on reform ideology as an accurate description of reform practice.

The reform ideology which became the basis of historical analysis is well known. It appears in classic form in Lincoln Steffens' *Shame of the Cities*. The urban political struggle of the Progressive Era, so the argument goes, involved a conflict between public impulses for "good government" against a corrupt alliance of "machine politicians" and "special interests."

During the rapid urbanization of the late 19th century, the latter had been free to aggrandize themselves, especially through franchise grants, at the expense of the public. Their power lay primarily in their ability to manipulate the political process, by bribery and corruption, for their own ends. Against such arrangements there gradually arose a public interest, a demand by the public for honest government, for officials who would act for the public rather than for themselves. To accomplish their goals, reformers sought basic modifications in the political system, both in the structure of government and in the manner of selecting public officials. These changes, successful in city after city, enabled the "public interest" to triumph.[1]

Recently, George Mowry, Alfred Chandler, Jr., and Richard Hofstadter have modified this analysis by emphasizing the fact that the impulse for reform did not come from the working class.[2] This might have been suspected from the rather strained efforts of National Municipal League writers in the "Era of Reform" to go out of their way to demonstrate working-class support for commission and city-manager governments.[3] We now know that they clutched at straws, and often erroneously, in order to prove to themselves as well as to the public that municipal reform was a mass movement.

The Mowry-Chandler-Hofstadter writings have further modified older views by asserting that reform in general and municipal reform in particular sprang from a distinctively middle-class movement. This has now become the prevailing view. Its popularity is surprising not only because it is based upon faulty logic and extremely limited evidence, but also because it, too, emphasizes the analysis of ideology rather than practice and fails to contrib-

[1] See, for example, Clifford W. Patton, *Battle for Municipal Reform* (Washington, D.C., 1940), and Frank Mann Stewart, *A Half-Century of Municipal Reform* (Berkeley, 1950).

[2] George E. Mowry, *The California Progressives* (Berkeley and Los Angeles, 1951), 86–104; Richard Hofstadter, *The Age of Reform* (New York, 1955), 131–269; Alfred D. Chandler, Jr., "The Origins of Progressive Leadership," in Elting Morrison *et al.*, eds., *Letters of Theodore Roosevelt* (Cambridge, 1951-54), VIII, Appendix III, 1462–64.

[3] Harry A. Toulmin, *The City Manager* (New York, 1915), 156–68; Clinton R. Woodruff, *City Government by Commission* (New York, 1911), 243–53.

ute much to the understanding of who distinctively were involved in reform and why.

Ostensibly, the "middle-class" theory of reform is based upon a new type of behavioral evidence, the collective biography, in studies by Mowry of California Progressive party leaders, by Chandler of a nationwide group of that party's leading figures, and by Hofstadter of four professions—ministers, lawyers, teachers, editors. These studies demonstrate the middle-class nature of reform, but they fail to determine if reformers were distinctively middle class, specifically if they differed from their opponents. One study of 300 political leaders in the state of Iowa, for example, discovered that Progressive party, Old Guard, and Cummins Republicans were all substantially alike, the Progressives differing only in that they were slightly younger than the others and had less political experience.[4] If its opponents were also middle-class, then one cannot describe Progressive reform as a phenomenon, the special nature of which can be explained in terms of middle-class characteristics. One cannot explain the distinctive behavior of people in terms of characteristics which are not distinctive to them.

Hofstadter's evidence concerning professional men fails in yet another way to determine the peculiar characteristics of reformers. For he describes ministers, lawyers, teachers, and editors without determining who within these professions became reformers and who did not. Two analytical distinctions might be made. Ministers involved in municipal reform, it appears, came not from all segments of religion, but peculiarly from upper-class churches. They enjoyed the highest prestige and salaries in the religious community and had no reason to feel a loss of "status," as Hofstadter argues. Their role in reform arose from the class character of their religious organizations rather than from the mere fact of their occupation as ministers.[5] Professional men involved in reform (many of whom—engineers, architects, and doctors—Hofstadter did not examine at all) seem to have come especially from the more advanced segments of their professions, from those who sought to apply their specialized knowledge to a wider range of public affairs.[6] Their role in reform is related not to their attempt to defend earlier patterns of culture, but to the working out of the inner dynamics of professionalization in modern society.

The weakness of the "middle-class" theory of reform stems from the fact that it rests primarily upon ideological evidence, not on a thorough-going description of political practice. Although the studies of Mowry, Chandler, and Hofstadter ostensibly derive from behavioral evidence, they actually derive largely from the extensive expressions of middle-ground ideological position, of the reformers' own descriptions of their contemporary society,

---

[4] Eli Daniel Potts, "A Comparative Study of the Leadership of Republican Factions in Iowa, 1904–1914," M.A. thesis (State University of Iowa, 1956). Another satisfactory comparative analysis is contained in William T. Kerr, Jr., "The Progressives of Washington, 1910-12," *Pacific Northwest Quarterly*, Vol. 55 (1964), 16–27.

[5] Based upon a study of eleven ministers involved in municipal reform in Pittsburgh, who represented exclusively the upper-class Presbyterian and Episcopal churches.

[6] Based upon a study of professional men involved in municipal reform in Pittsburgh, comprising eighty-three doctors, twelve architects, twenty-five educators, and thirteen engineers.

and of their expressed fears of both the lower and the upper classes, of the fright of being ground between the millstones of labor and capital.[7]

Such evidence, though it accurately portrays what people thought, does not accurately describe what they did. The great majority of Americans look upon themselves as "middle class" and subscribe to a middle-ground ideology, even though in practice they belong to a great variety of distinct social classes. Such ideologies are not rationalizations or deliberate attempts to deceive. They are natural phenomena of human behavior. But the historian should be especially sensitive to their role so that he will not take evidence of political ideology as an accurate representation of political practice.

In the following account I will summarize evidence in both secondary and primary works concerning the political practices in which municipal reformers were involved. Such an analysis logically can be broken down into three parts, each one corresponding to a step in the traditional argument. First, what was the source of reform? Did it lie in the general public rather than in particular groups? Was it middle class, working class, or perhaps of other composition? Second, what was the reform target of attack? Were reformers primarily interested in ousting the corrupt individual, the political or business leader who made private arrangements at the expense of the public, or were they interested in something else? Third, what political innovations did reformers bring about? Did they seek to expand popular participation in the governmental process?

There is now sufficient evidence to determine the validity of these specific elements of the more general argument. Some of it has been available for several decades; some has appeared more recently; some is presented here for the first time. All of it adds up to the conclusion that reform in municipal government involved a political development far different from what we have assumed in the past.

Available evidence indicates that the source of support for reform in municipal government did not come from the lower or middle classes, but from the upper class. The leading business groups in each city and professional men closely allied with them initiated and dominated municipal movements. Leonard White, in his study of the city manager published in 1927, wrote:

> The opposition to bad government usually comes to a head in the local chamber of commerce. Business men finally acquire the conviction that the growth of their city is being seriously impaired by the failures of city officials to perform their duties efficiently. Looking about for a remedy, they are captivated by the resemblance of the city-manager plan to their corporate form of business organization.[8]

In the 1930's White directed a number of studies of the origin of city-manager government. The resulting reports invariably begin with such statements as, "the Chamber of Commerce spearheaded the movement," or

---

[7] See especially Mowry, *The California Progessives.*
[8] Leonard White, *The City Manager* (Chicago, 1927), ix–x.

commission government in this city was a "businessmen's government."[9] Of thirty-two cases of city-manager government in Oklahoma examined by Jewell C. Phillips, twenty-nine were initiated either by chambers of commerce or by community committees dominated by businessmen.[10] More recently James Weinstein has presented almost irrefutable evidence that the business community, represented largely by chambers of commerce, was the overwhelming force behind both commission and city-manager movements.[11]

Dominant elements of the business community played a prominent role in another crucial aspect of municipal reform: the Municipal Research Bureau movement.[12] Especially in the larger cities, where they had less success in shaping the structure of government, reformers established centers to conduct research in municipal affairs as a springboard for influence.

The first such organization, the Bureau of Municipal Research of New York City, was founded in 1906; it was financed largely through the efforts of Andrew Carnegie and John D. Rockefeller. An investment banker provided the crucial support in Philadelphia, where a Bureau was founded in 1908. A group of wealthy Chicagoans in 1910 established the Bureau of Public Efficiency, a research agency. John H. Patterson of the National Cash Register Company, the leading figure in Dayton municipal reform, financed the Dayton Bureau, founded in 1912. And George Eastman was the driving force behind both the Bureau of Municipal Research and city-manager government in Rochester. In smaller cities data about city government was collected by interested individuals in a more informal way or by chambers of commerce, but in larger cities the task required special support, and prominent businessmen supplied it.

The character of municipal reform is demonstrated more precisely by a brief examination of the movements in Des Moines and Pittsburgh. The Des Moines Commercial Club inaugurated and carefully controlled the drive for the commission form of government.[13] In January, 1906, the Club held a so-called "mass meeting" of business and professional men to secure an enabling act from the state legislature. P. C. Kenyon, president of the Club, selected a Committee of 300, composed principally of business and professional men, to draw up a specific proposal. After the legislature approved their plan, the same committee managed the campaign which persuaded the

[9] Harold A. Stone et al., *City Manager Government in Nine Cities* (Chicago, 1940); Frederick C. Mosher et al., *City Manager Government in Seven Cities* (Chicago, 1940); Harold A. Stone et al., *City Manager Government in the United States* (Chicago, 1940). Cities covered by these studies include: Austin, Texas; Charlotte, North Carolina; Dallas, Texas; Dayton, Ohio; Fredericksburg, Virginia; Jackson, Michigan; Janesville, Wisconsin; Kingsport, Tennessee; Lynchburg, Virginia; Rochester, New York; San Diego, California.

[10] Jewell Cass Phillips, *Operation of the Council-Manager Plan of Government in Oklahoma Cities* (Philadelphia, 1935), 31–39.

[11] James Weinstein, "Organized Business and the City Commission and Manager Movements," *Journal of Southern History*, XXVIII (1962), 166–82.

[12] Norman N. Gill, *Municipal Research Bureaus* (Washington, D.C., 1944).

[13] This account of the movement for commission government in Des Moines is derived from items in the Des Moines *Register* during the years from 1905 through 1908.

electorate to accept the commission form of government by a narrow margin in June, 1907.

In this election the lower-income wards of the city opposed the change, the upper-income wards supported it strongly, and the middle-income wards were more evenly divided. In order to control the new government, the Committee of 300, now expanded to 530, sought to determine the nomination and election of the five new commissioners, and to this end they selected an avowedly businessman's slate. Their plans backfired when the voters swept into office a slate of anticommission candidates who now controlled the new commission government.

Proponents of the commission form of government in Des Moines spoke frequently in the name of the "people." But their more explicit statements emphasized their intent that the new plan be a "business system" of government, run by businessmen. The slate of candidates for commissioner endorsed by advocates of the plan was known as the "businessman's ticket." J. W. Hill, president of the committees of 300 and 530, bluntly declared: "The professional politician must be ousted and in his place capable business men chosen to conduct the affairs of the city." I. M. Earle, general counsel of the Bankers Life Association and a prominent figure in the movement, put the point more precisely: "When the plan was adopted it was the intention to get businessmen to run it."

Although reformers used the ideology of popular government, they in no sense meant that all segments of society should be involved equally in municipal decision-making. They meant that their concept of the city's welfare would be best achieved if the business community controlled city government. As one businessman told a labor audience, the businessman's slate represented labor "better than you do yourself."

The composition of the municipal reform movement in Pittsburgh demonstrates its upper-class and professional as well as its business sources.[14] Here the two principal reform organizations were the Civic Club and the Voters' League. The 745 members of these two organizations came primarily from the upper class. Sixty-five per cent appeared in upper-class directories which contained the names of only 2 per cent of the city's families. Furthermore, many who were not listed in these directories lived in upper-class areas. These reformers, it should be stressed. comprised not an old but a new upper class. Few came from earlier industrial and mercantile families. Most of them had risen to social position from wealth created after 1870 in the iron, steel, electrical equipment, and other industries, and they lived in the newer rather than the older fashionable areas.

Almost half (48 per cent) of the reformers were professional men: doctors, lawyers, ministers, directors of libraries and museums, engineers, architects, private and public school teachers, and college professors. Some of these belonged to the upper class as well, especially the lawyers, ministers,

---

[14] Biographical data constitutes the main source of evidence for this study of Pittsburgh reform leaders. It was found in city directories, social registers, directories of corporate directors, biographical compilations, reports of boards of education, settlement houses, welfare organizations, and similar types of material. Especially valuable was the clipping file maintained at the Carnegie Library of Pittsburgh.

and private school teachers. But for the most part their interest in reform stemmed from the inherent dynamics of their professions rather than from their class connections. They came from the more advanced segments of their organizations, from those in the forefront of the acquisition and application of knowledge. They were not the older professional men, seeking to preserve the past against change; they were in the vanguard of professional life, actively seeking to apply expertise more widely to public affairs.

Pittsburgh reformers included a large segment of businessmen; 52 per cent were bankers and corporation officials or their wives. Among them were the presidents of fourteen large banks and officials of Westinghouse, Pittsburgh Plate Glass, U.S. Steel and its component parts (such as Carnegie Steel, American Bridge, and National Tube), Jones and Laughlin, lesser steel companies (such as Crucible, Pittsburgh, Superior, Lockhart, and H. K. Porter), the H. J. Heinz Company, and the Pittsburgh Coal Company, as well as officials of the Pennsylvania Railroad and the Pittsburgh and Lake Erie. These men were not small businessmen; they directed the most powerful banking and industrial organizations of the city. They represented not the old business community, but industries which had developed and grown primarily within the past fifty years and which had come to dominate the city's economic life.

These business, professional, and upper-class groups who dominated municipal reform movements were all involved in the rationalization and systematization of modern life; they wished a reform of government which would be more consistent with the objectives inherent in those developments. The most important single feature of their perspective was the rapid expansion of the geographical scope of affairs which they wished to influence and manipulate, a scope which was no longer limited and narrow, no longer within the confines of pedestrian communities, but was now broad and city-wide, covering the whole range of activities of the metropolitan area.

The migration of the upper class from central to outlying areas created a geographical distance between its residential communities and its economic institutions. To protect the latter required involvement both in local ward affairs and in the larger city government as well. Moreover, upper-class cultural institutions, such as museums, libraries, and symphony orchestras, required an active interest in the larger municipal context from which these institutions drew much of their clientele.

Professional groups, broadening the scope of affairs which they sought to study, measure, or manipulate, also sought to influence the public health, the educational system, or the physical arrangements of the entire city. Their concerns were limitless, not bounded by geography, but as expansive as the professional imagination. Finally, the new industrial community greatly broadened its perspective in governmental affairs because of its recognition of the way in which factors throughout the city affected business growth. The increasing size and scope of industry, the greater stake in more varied and geographically dispersed facets of city life, the effect of floods on many business concerns, the need to promote traffic flows to and from work for both blue-collar and managerial employees—all contributed to this larger interest. The geographically larger private perspectives of upper-class, professional, and business groups gave rise to a geographically larger public perspective.

These reformers were dissatisfied with existing systems of municipal government. They did not oppose corruption per se—although there was plenty of that. They objected to the structure of government which enabled local and particularistic interests to dominate. Prior to the reforms of the Progressive Era, city government consisted primarily of confederations of local wards, each of which was represented on the city's legislative body. Each ward frequently had its own elementary schools and ward-elected school boards which administered them.

These particularistic interests were the focus of a decentralized political life. City councilmen were local leaders. They spoke for their local areas, the economic interests of their inhabitants, their residential concerns, their educational, recreational, and religious interests—i.e., for those aspects of community life which mattered most to those they represented. They rolled logs in the city council to provide streets, sewers, and other public works for their local areas. They defended the community's cultural practices, its distinctive languages or national customs, its liberal attitude toward liquor, and its saloons and dance halls which served as centers of community life. One observer described this process of representation in Seattle:

> The residents of the hill-tops and the suburbs may not fully appreciate the faithfulness of certain downtown ward councilmen to the interests of their constituents. . . . The people of a state would rise in arms against a senator or representative in Congress who deliberately misrepresented their wishes and imperilled their interests, though he might plead a higher regard for national good. Yet people in other parts of the city seem to forget that under the old system the ward elected councilmen with the idea of procuring service of special benefit to that ward.[15]

In short, pre-reform officials spoke for their constituencies, inevitably their own wards which had elected them, rather than for other sections or groups of the city.

The ward system of government especially gave representation in city affairs to lower- and middle-class groups. Most elected ward officials were from these groups, and they, in turn, constituted the major opposition to reforms in municipal government. In Pittsburgh, for example, immediately prior to the changes in both the city council and the school board in 1911 in which city-wide representation replaced ward representation, only 24 per cent of the 387 members of those bodies represented the same managerial, professional, and banker occupations which dominated the membership of the Civic Club and the Voters' League. The great majority (67 per cent) were small businessmen—grocers, saloonkeepers, livery-stable proprietors, owners of small hotels, druggists—white-collar workers such as clerks and bookkeepers, and skilled and unskilled workmen.[16]

This decentralized system of urban growth and the institutions which arose from it reformers now opposed. Social, professional, and economic

[15] *Town Crier* (Seattle), Feb. 18, 1911, p.13.
[16] Information derived from same sources as cited in footnote 14.

life had developed not only in the local wards in a small community context, but also on a larger scale had become highly integrated and organized, giving rise to a superstructure of social organization which lay far above that of ward life and which was sharply divorced from it in both personal contacts and perspective.

By the late 19th century, those involved in these larger institutions found that the decentralized system of political life limited their larger objectives. The movement for reform in municipal government, therefore, constituted an attempt by upper-class, advanced professional, and large business groups to take formal political power from the previously dominant lower- and middle-class elements so that they might advance their own conceptions of desirable public policy. These two groups came from entirely different urban worlds, and the political system fashioned by one was no longer acceptable to the other.

Lower- and middle-class groups not only dominated the pre-reform governments, but vigorously opposed reform. It is significant that none of the occupational groups among them, for example, small businessmen or white-collar workers, skilled or unskilled artisans, had important representation in reform organizations thus far examined. The case studies of city-manager government undertaken in the 1930's under the direction of Leonard White detailed in city after city the particular opposition of labor. In their analysis of Jackson, Michigan, the authors of these studies wrote: "The *Square Deal*, oldest Labor paper in the state, has been consistently against manager government, perhaps largely because labor has felt that with a decentralized government elected on a ward basis it was more likely to have some voice and to receive its share of privileges."[17]

In Janesville, Wisconsin, the small shopkeepers and workingmen on the west and south sides, heavily Catholic and often Irish, opposed the commission plan in 1911 and in 1912 and the city-manager plan when adopted in 1923.[18] "In Dallas there is hardly a trace of class consciousness in the Marxian sense," one investigator declared, "yet in city elections the division has been to a great extent along class lines."[19] The commission and city-manager elections were no exceptions. To these authors it seemed a logical reaction, rather than an embarrassing fact that had to be swept away, that workingmen should have opposed municipal reform.[20]

In Des Moines working-class representatives, who in previous years might have been council members, were conspicuously absent from the "businessman's slate." Workingmen acceptable to reformers could not be found. A workingman's slate of candidates, therefore, appeared to challenge the reform slate. Organized labor, and especially the mineworkers, took the lead; one of their number, Wesley Ash, a deputy sheriff and union member, made "an astonishing run" in the primary, coming in second among a field of

---

[17] Stone *et al.*, *Nine Cities*, 212.

[18] *Ibid.*, 3–13.

[19] *Ibid.*, 329.

[20] Stone *et al.*, *City Manager Government*, 26, 237–41, for analysis of opposition to city-manager government.

more than twenty candidates.[21] In fact, the strength of anticommission candidates in the primary so alarmed reformers that they frantically sought to appease labor.

The day before the final election they modified their platform to pledge both an eight-hour day and an "American standard of wages." They attempted to persuade the voters that their slate consisted of men who represented labor because they had "begun at the bottom of the ladder and made a good climb toward success by their own unaided efforts."[22] But their tactics failed. In the election on March 30, 1908, voters swept into office the entire "opposition" slate. The business and professional community had succeeded in changing the form of government, but not in securing its control. A cartoon in the leading reform newspaper illustrated their disappointment; John Q. Public sat dejectedly and muttered, "Aw, What's the Use?"

The most visible opposition to reform and the most readily available target of reform attack was the so-called "machine," for through the "machine" many different ward communities as well as lower- and middle-income groups joined effectively to influence the central city government. Their private occupational and social life did not naturally involve these groups in larger city-wide activities in the same way as the upper class was involved; hence they lacked access to privately organized economic and social power on which they could construct political power. The "machine" filled this organizational gap.

Yet it should never be forgotten that the social and economic institutions in the wards themselves provided the "machine's" sustaining support and gave it larger significance. When reformers attacked the "machine" as the most visible institutional element of the ward system, they attacked the entire ward form of political organization and the political power of lower- and middle-income groups which lay behind it.

Reformers often gave the impression that they opposed merely the corrupt politician and his "machine." But in a more fundamental way they looked upon the deficiencies of pre-reform political leaders in terms not of their personal shortcomings, but of the limitations inherent in their occupational, institutional, and class positions. In 1911 the Voters' League of Pittsburgh wrote in its pamphlet analyzing the qualifications of candidates that "a man's occupation ought to give a strong indication of his qualifications for membership on a school board."[23] Certain occupations inherently disqualified a man from serving:

> Employment as ordinary laborer and in the lowest class of mill work would naturally lead to the conclusion that such men did not have sufficient education or business training to act as school directors. . . . Objection might also be made to small shopkeepers, clerks, workmen at many trades, who by lack of educational advantages and business training, could not, no matter how honest, be expected to administer properly the affairs of an educational system, requiring special knowledge, and where millions are spent each year.

[21] Des Moines *Register and Leader*, March 17, 1908.
[22] *Ibid.*, March 30, March 28, 1908.
[23] Voters' Civil League of Allegheny County, "Bulletin of the Voters' Civic League of Allegheny County Concerning the Public School System of Pittsburgh," Feb. 14, 1911, pp. 2–3.

These, of course, were precisely the groups which did dominate Pittsburgh government prior to reform. The League deplored the fact that school boards contained only a small number of "men prominent throughout the city in business life . . . in professional occupations . . . holding positions as managers, secretaries, auditors, superintendents and foremen" and exhorted these classes to participate more actively as candidates for office.

Reformers, therefore, wished not simply to replace bad men with good; they proposed to change the occupational and class origins of decision-makers. Toward this end they sought innovations in the formal machinery of government which would concentrate political power by sharply centralizing the process of decision-making rather than distribute it through more popular participation in public affairs. According to the liberal view of the Progressive Era, the major political innovations of reform involved the equalization of political power through the primary, the direct election of public officials, and the initiative, referendum, and recall. These measures played a large role in the political ideology of the time and were frequently incorporated into new municipal charters. But they provided at best only an occasional and often incidental process of decision-making. Far more important in continuous, sustained, day-to-day processes of government were those innovations which centralized decision-making in the hands of fewer and fewer people.

The systematization of municipal government took place on both the executive and the legislative levels. The strong-mayor and city-manager types became the most widely used examples of the former. In the first decade of the 20th century, the commission plan had considerable appeal, but its distribution of administrative responsibility among five people gave rise to a demand for a form with more centralized executive power; consequently, the city-manager or the commission-manager variant often replaced it.[24]

A far more pervasive and significant change, however, lay in the centralization of the system of representation, the shift from ward to city-wide election of councils and school boards. Governing bodies so selected, reformers argued, would give less attention to local and particularistic matters and more to affairs of city-wide scope. This shift, an invariable feature of both commission and city-manager plans, was often adopted by itself. In Pittsburgh, for example, the new charter of 1911 provided as the major innovation that a council of twenty-seven, each member elected from a separate ward, be replaced by a council of nine, each elected by the city as a whole.

Cities displayed wide variations in this innovation. Some regrouped wards into larger units but kept the principle of areas of representation smaller than the entire city. Some combined a majority of councilmen elected by wards with additional ones elected at large. All such innovations, however, constituted steps toward the centralization of the system of representation.

[24] In the decade 1911 to 1920, 43 per cent of the municipal charters adopted in eleven home-rule states involved the commission form and 35 per cent the city-manager form; in the following decade the figures stood at 6 per cent and 71 per cent respectively. The adoption of city-manager charters reached a peak in the years 1918 through 1923 and declined sharply after 1933. See Leonard D. White, "The Future of Public Administration," *Public Management*, XV (1933), 12.

Liberal historians have not appreciated the extent to which municipal reform in the Progressive Era involved a debate over the system of representation. The ward form of representation was universally condemned on the grounds that it gave too much influence to the separate units and not enough attention to the larger problems of the city. Harry A. Toulmin, whose book, *The City Manager*, was published by the National Municipal League, stated the case:

> The spirit of sectionalism had dominated the political life of every city. Ward pitted against ward, alderman against alderman, and legislation only effected by "log-rolling" extravagant measures into operation, mulcting the city, but gratifying the greed of constituents, has too long stung the conscience of decent citizenship. This constant treaty-making of factionalism has been no less than a curse. The city manager plan proposes the commendable thing of abolishing wards. The plan is not unique in this for it has been common to many forms of commission government. . . .[25]

Such a system should be supplanted, the argument usually went, with citywide representation in which elected officials could consider the city "as a unit." "The new officers are elected," wrote Toulmin, "each to represent all the people. Their duties are so defined that they must administer the corporate business in its entirety, not as a hodge-podge of associated localities."

Behind the debate over the method of representation, however, lay a debate over who should be represented, over whose views of public policy should prevail. Many reform leaders often explicitly, if not implicitly, expressed fear that lower- and middle-income groups had too much influence in decision-making. One Galveston leader, for example, complained about the movement for initiative, referendum, and recall:

> We have in our city a very large number of negroes employed on the docks; we also have a very large number of unskilled white laborers; this city also has more barrooms, according to its population, than any other city in Texas. Under these circumstances it would be extremely difficult to maintain a satisfactory city government where all ordinances must be submitted back to the voters of the city for their ratification and approval.[26]

At the National Municipal League convention of 1907, Rear Admiral F. E. Chadwick (USN Ret.), a leader in the Newport, Rhode Island, movement for municipal reform, spoke to this question even more directly:

> Our present system has excluded in large degree the representation of those who have the city's well-being most at heart. It has brought, in municipalities . . . a government established by the least educated, the least interested class of citizens.
>
> It stands to reason that a man paying $5,000 taxes in a town is more interested in the well-being and development of his town than the man who pays no taxes. . . . It equally stands to reason that the man of the $5,000

[25] Toulmin, *The City Manager*, 42.

[26] Woodruff, *City Government*, 315. The Galveston commission plan did not contain provisions for the initiative, referendum, or recall, and Galveston commercial groups which had fathered the commission plan opposed movements to include them. In 1911 Governor Colquitt of Texas vetoed a charter bill for Texarkana because it contained such provisions; he maintained that they were "undemocratic" and unnecessary to the success of commission government. *Ibid.*, 314–15.

tax should be assured a representation in the committee which lays the tax
and spends the money which he contributes. . . . Shall we be truly democratic and give the property owner a fair show or shall we develop a tyranny of ignorance which shall crush him.[27]

Municipal reformers thus debated frequently the question of who should be
represented as well as the question of what method of representation should
be employed.

That these two questions were intimately connected was revealed in other
reform proposals for representation, proposals which were rarely taken seriously. One suggestion was that a class system of representation be substi-
tuted for ward representation. For example, in 1908 one of the prominent
candidates for commissioner in Des Moines proposed that the city council
be composed of representatives of five classes: educational and ministerial
organizations, manufacturers and jobbers, public utility corporations, retail
merchants including liquor men, and the Des Moines Trades and Labor Assembly. Such a system would have greatly reduced the influence in the
council of both middle- and lower-class groups. The proposal revealed the
basic problem confronting business and professional leaders: how to reduce
the influence in government of the majority of voters among middle- and
lower-income groups.[28]

A growing imbalance between population and representation sharpened
the desire of reformers to change from ward to city-wide elections. Despite
shifts in population within most cities, neither ward district lines nor the
apportionment of city council and school board seats changed frequently.
Consequently, older areas of the city, with wards that were small in geographical size and held declining populations (usually lower and middle class
in composition), continued to be overrepresented, and newer upper-class
areas, where population was growing, became increasingly underrepresented.
This intensified the reformers' conviction that the structure of government
must be changed to give them the voice they needed to make their views
on public policy prevail.[29]

It is not insignificant that in some cities (by no means a majority) municipal reform came about outside of the urban electoral process. The original
commission government in Galveston was appointed rather than elected.
"The failure of previous attempts to secure an efficient city government
through the local electorate made the business men of Galveston willing to
put the conduct of the city's affairs in the hands of a commission dominated
by state-appointed officials."[30] Only in 1903 did the courts force Galveston
to elect the members of the commission, an innovation which one writer
described as "an abandonment of the commission idea," and which led to
the decline of the influence of the business community in the commission
government.[31]

In 1911 Pittsburgh voters were not permitted to approve either the new

[27] *Ibid.,* 207–208.
[28] Des Moines *Register and Leader,* Jan. 15, 1908.
[29] Voters' Civic League of Allegheny County, "Report on the Voters' League in the
Redistricting of the Wards of the City of Pittsburgh," (Pittsburgh, n.d.).
[30] Horace E. Deming, "The Government of American Cities," in Woodruff, *City
Government,* 167.
[31] *Ibid.,* 168.

city charter or the new school board plan, both of which provided for city-wide representation; they were a result of the state legislature enactment. The governor appointed the first members of the new city council, but thereafter they were elected. The judges of the court of common pleas, however, and not the voters, selected members of the new school board.

The composition of the new city council and new school board in Pittsburgh, both of which were inaugurated in 1911, revealed the degree to which the shift from ward to city-wide representation produced a change in group representation.[32] Members of the upper class, the advanced professional men, and the large business groups dominated both. Of the fifteen members of the Pittsburgh Board of Education appointed in 1911 and the nine members of the new city council, none were small businessmen or white-collar workers. Each body contained only one person who could remotely be classified as a blue-collar worker; each of these men filled a position specifically but unofficially designed as reserved for a "representative of labor," and each was an official of the Amalgamated Association of Iron, Steel, and Tin Workers. Six of the nine members of the new city council were prominent businessmen, and all six were listed in upper-class directories. Two others were doctors closely associated with the upper class in both professional and social life. The fifteen members of the Board of Education included ten businessmen with city-wide interests, one doctor associated with the upper class, and three women previously active in upper-class public welfare.

Lower- and middle-class elements felt that the new city governments did not represent them.[33] The studies carried out under the direction of Leonard White contain numerous expressions of the way in which the change in the structure of government produced not only a change in the geographical scope of representation, but also in the groups represented. "It is not the policies of the manager or the council they oppose," one researcher declared, "as much as the lack of representation for their economic level and social groups."[34] And another wrote:

> There had been nothing unapproachable about the old ward aldermen. Every voter had a neighbor on the common council who was interested in serving him. The new councilmen, however, made an unfavorable impression on the less well-to-do voters. . . . Election at large made a change that, however desirable in other ways, left the voters in the poorer wards with a feeling that they had been deprived of their share of political importance.[35]

The success of the drive for centralization of administration and representation varied with the size of the city. In the smaller cities, business, professional, and elite groups could easily exercise a dominant influence. Their

[32] Information derived from same sources as cited in footnote 14.

[33] W. R. Hopkins, city manager of Cleveland, indicated the degree to which the new type of government was more responsive to the business community: "It is undoubtedly easier for a city manager to insist upon acting in accordance with the business interests of the city than it is for a mayor to do the same thing." Quoted in White, *The City Manager*, 13.

[34] Stone *et al.*, *Nine Cities*, 20.

[35] *Ibid.*, 225.

close ties readily enabled them to shape informal political power which they could transform into formal political power. After the mid-1890's the widespread organization of chambers of commerce provided a base for political action to reform municipal government, resulting in a host of small-city commission and city-manager innovations. In the larger, more heterogeneous cities, whose sub-communities were more dispersed, such community-wide action was extremely difficult. Few commission or city-manager proposals materialized here. Mayors became stronger, and steps were taken toward centralization of representation, but the ward system or some modified version usually persisted. Reformers in large cities often had to rest content with their Municipal Research Bureaus through which they could exert political influence from outside the municipal government.

A central element in the analysis of municipal reform in the Progressive Era is governmental corruption. Should it be understood in moral or political terms? Was it a product of evil men or of particular socio-political circumstances? Reform historians have adopted the former view. Selfish and evil men arose to take advantage of a political arrangement whereby unsystematic government offered many opportunities for personal gain at public expense. The system thrived until the "better elements," "men of intelligence and civic responsibility," or "right-thinking people" ousted the culprits and fashioned a political force which produced decisions in the "public interest." In this scheme of things, corruption in public affairs grew out of individual personal failings and a deficient governmental structure which could not hold those predispositions in check, rather than from the peculiar nature of social forces. The contestants involved were morally defined: evil men who must be driven from power, and good men who must be activated politically to secure control of municipal affairs.

Public corruption, however, involves political even more than moral considerations. It arises more out of the particular distribution of political power than of personal morality. For corruption is a device to exercise control and influence outside the legal channels of decision-making when those channels are not readily responsive. Most generally, corruption stems from an inconsistency between control of the instruments of formal governmental power and the exercise of informal influence in the community. If powerful groups are denied access to formal power in legitimate ways, they seek access through procedures which the community considers illegitimate. Corrupt government, therefore, does not reflect the genius of evil men, but rather the lack of acceptable means for those who exercise power in the private community to wield the same influence in governmental affairs. It can be understood in the Progressive Era not simply by the preponderance of evil men over good, but by the peculiar nature of the distribution of political power.

The political corruption of the "Era of Reform" arose from the inaccessability of municipal government to those who were rising in power and influence. Municipal government in the United States developed in the 19th century within a context of universal manhood suffrage which decentralized political control. Because all men, whatever their economic, social, or cultural conditions, could vote, leaders who reflected a wide variety of community interests and who represented the views of people of every circumstance arose to guide and direct municipal affairs. Since the majority of urban voters were workingmen or immigrants, the views of those groups carried great and often decisive weight in governmental affairs. Thus, as Herbert Gutman has shown, during strikes in the 1870's city officials were usually friendly to workingmen and refused to use police power to protect strikebreakers.[36]

Ward representation on city councils was an integral part of grass-roots influence, for it enabled diverse urban communities, invariably identified with particular geographical areas of the city, to express their views more clearly through councilmen peculiarly receptive to their concerns. There was a direct, reciprocal flow of power between wards and the center of city affairs in which voters felt a relatively close connection with public matters and city leaders gave special attention to their needs.

Within this political system the community's business leaders grew in influence and power as industrialism advanced, only to find that their economic position did not readily admit them to the formal machinery of government. Thus, during strikes, they had to rely on either their own private police, Pinkertons, or the state militia to enforce their use of strikebreakers. They frequently found that city officials did not accept their views of what was best for the city and what direction municipal policies should take. They had developed a common outlook, closely related to their economic activities, that the city's economic expansion should become the prime concern of municipal government, and yet they found that this view had to compete with even more influential views of public policy. They found that political tendencies which arose from universal manhood suffrage and ward representation were not always friendly to their political conceptions and goals and had produced a political system over which they had little control, despite the fact that their economic ventures were the core of the city's prosperity and the hope for future urban growth.

Under such circumstances, businessmen sought other methods of influencing municipal affairs. They did not restrict themselves to the channels of popular election and representation, but frequently applied direct influence —if not verbal persuasion, then bribery and corruption. Thereby arose the graft which Lincoln Steffens recounted in his *Shame of the Cities*. Utilities were only the largest of those business groups and individuals who requested special favors, and the franchises they sought were only the most sensational of the prizes which included such items as favorable tax assessments and rates, the vacating of streets wanted for factory expansion, or permission to operate amid antiliquor and other laws regulating personal behavior. The relationships between business and formal government became a maze of accommodations, a set of political arrangements which grew up because effective power had few legitimate means of accomplishing its ends.

Steffens and subsequent liberal historians, however, misread the significance of these arrangements, emphasizing their personal rather than their more fundamental institutional elements. To them corruption involved per-

[36] Herbert Gutman, "An Iron Workers' Strike in the Ohio Valley, 1873–74," *Ohio Historical Quarterly*, LXVIII (1959), 353–70; "Trouble on the Railroads, 1873–1874: Prelude to the 1877 Crisis," *Labor History*, II (Spring, 1961), 215–36.

sonal arrangements between powerful business leaders and powerful "machine" politicians. Just as they did not fully appreciate the significance of the search for political influence by the rising business community as a whole, so they did not see fully the role of the "ward politician." They stressed the argument that the political leader manipulated voters to his own personal ends, that he used constituents rather than reflected their views.

A different approach is now taking root, namely, that the urban political organization was an integral part of community life, expressing its needs and its goals. As Oscar Handlin has said, for example, the "machine" not only fulfilled specific wants, but provided one of the few avenues to success and public recognition available to the immigrant.[37] The political leader's arrangements with businessmen, therefore, were not simply personal agreements between conniving individuals; they were far-reaching accommodations between powerful sets of institutions in industrial America.

These accommodations, however, proved to be burdensome and unsatisfactory to the business community and to the upper third of socioeconomic groups in general. They were expensive; they were wasteful, they were uncertain. Toward the end of the 19th century, therefore, business and professional men sought more direct control over municipal government in order to exercise political influence more effectively. They realized their goals in the early 20th century in the new commission and city-manager forms of government and in the shift from ward to city-wide representation.

These innovations did not always accomplish the objectives that the business community desired because other forces could and often did adjust to the change in governmental structure and reëstablish their influence. But businessmen hoped that reform would enable them to increase their political power, and most frequently it did. In most cases the innovations which were introduced between 1901, when Galveston adopted a commission form of government, and the Great Depression, and especially the city-manager form which reached a height of popularity in the mid-1920's, served as vehicles whereby business and professional leaders moved directly into the inner circles of government, brought into one political system their own power and the formal machinery of government, and dominated municipal affairs for two decades.

Municipal reform in the early 20th century involves a paradox: the ideology of an extension of political control and the practice of its concentration. While reformers maintained that their movement rested on a wave of popular demands, called their gatherings of business and professional leaders "mass meetings," described their reforms as "part of a world-wide trend toward popular government," and proclaimed an ideology of a popular upheaval against a selfish few, they were in practice shaping the structure of municipal government so that political power would no longer be broadly distributed, but would in fact be more centralized in the hands of a relatively small segment of the population. The paradox became even sharper when new city charters included provisions for the initiative, referendum,

[37] Oscar Handlin, *The Uprooted* (Boston, 1951), 209–17.

and recall. How does the historian cope with this paradox? Does it represent deliberate deception or simply political strategy? Or does it reflect a phenomenon which should be understood rather than explained away?

The expansion of popular involvement in decision-making was frequently a political tactic, not a political system to be established permanently, but a device to secure immediate political victory. The prohibitionist advocacy of the referendum, one of the most extensive sources of support for such a measure, came from the belief that the referendum would provide the opportunity to outlaw liquor more rapidly. The Anti-Saloon League, therefore, urged local option. But the League was not consistent. Towns which were wet, when faced with a county-wide local-option decision to outlaw liquor, demanded town or township local option to reinstate it. The League objected to this as not the proper application of the referendum idea.

Again, "Progressive" reformers often espoused the direct primary when fighting for nominations for their candidates within the party, but once in control they often became cool to it because it might result in their own defeat. By the same token, many municipal reformers attached the initiative, referendum, and recall to municipal charters often as a device to appease voters who opposed the centralization of representation and executive authority. But, by requiring a high percentage of voters to sign petitions—often 25 to 30 per cent—these innovations could be and were rendered relatively harmless.

More fundamentally, however, the distinction between ideology and practice in municipal reform arose from the different roles which each played. The ideology of democratization of decision-making was negative rather than positive; it served as an instrument of attack against the existing political system rather than as a guide to alternative action. Those who wished to destroy the "machine" and to eliminate party competition in local government widely utilized the theory that these political instruments thwarted public impulses, and thereby shaped the tone of their attack.

But there is little evidence that the ideology represented a faith in a purely democratic system of decision-making or that reformers actually wished, in practice, to substitute direct democracy as a continuing system of sustained decision-making in place of the old. It was used to destroy the political in-situations of the lower and middle classes and the political power which those institutions give rise to, rather than to provide a clear-cut guide for alternative action.[38]

The guide to alternative action lay in the model of the business enterprise. In describing new conditions which they wished to create, reformers drew on the analogy of the "efficient business enterprise," criticizing current practices with the argument that "no business could conduct its affairs that way and remain in business," and calling upon business practices as the guides to

[38] Clinton Rodgers Woodruff of the National Municipal League even argued that the initiative, referendum, and recall were rarely used. "Their value lies in their existence rather than in their use." Woodruff, *City Government*, 314. It seems apparent that the most widely used of these devices, the referendum, was popularized by legislative bodies when they could not agree or did not want to take responsibility for a decision and sought to pass that responsibility to the general public, rather than because of a faith in the wisdom of popular will.

improvement. As one student remarked: "The folklore of the business elite came by gradual transition to be the symbols of governmental reformers. Efficiency, system, orderliness, budgets, economy, saving, were all injected into the efforts of reformers who sought to remodel municipal government in terms of the great impersonality of corporate enterprise."[39] Clinton Rodgers Woodruff of the National Municipal League explained that the commission form was "a simple, direct, businesslike way of administering the business affairs of the city . . . an application to city administration of that type of business organization which has been so common and so successful in the field of commerce and industry."[40] The centralization of decision-making which developed in the business corporation was now applied in municipal reform.

The model of the efficient business enterprise, then, rather than the New England town meeting, provided the positive inspiration for the municipal reformer. In giving concrete shape to this model in the strong-mayor, commission, and city-manager plans, reformers engaged in the elaboration of the processes of rationalization and systematization inherent in modern science and technology. For in many areas of society, industrialization brought a gradual shift upward in the location of decision-making and the geographical extension of the scope of the area affected by decisions.

Experts in business, in government, and in the professions measured, studied, analyzed, and manipulated ever wider realms of human life, and devices which they used to control such affairs constituted the most fundamental and far-reaching innovations in decision-making in modern America, whether in formal government or in the informal exercise of power in private life. Reformers in the Progressive Era played a major role in shaping this new system. While they expressed an ideology of restoring a previous order, they in fact helped to bring forth a system drastically new.[41]

The drama of reform lay in the competition for supremacy between two systems of decision-making. One system, based upon ward representation and growing out of the practices and ideas of representative government, involved wide latitude for the expression of grass-roots impulses and their involvement in the political process. The other grew out of the rationalization of life which came with science and technology, in which decisions arose from expert analysis and flowed from fewer and smaller centers outward to the rest of society. Those who espoused the former looked with fear upon the loss of influence which the latter involved, and those who espoused the latter looked only with disdain upon the wastefulness and inefficiency of the former.

The Progressive Era witnessed rapid strides toward a more centralized system and a relative decline for a more decentralized system. This develop-

---

[39] J. B. Shannon, "County Consolidation," *Annals of the American Academy of Political and Social Science*, Vol. 207 (January, 1940), 168.

[40] Woodruff, *City Government*, 29–30.

[41] Several recent studies emphasize various aspects of this movement. See, for example, Loren Baritz, *Servants of Power* (Middletown, 1960); Raymond E. Callahan, *Education and the Cult of Efficiency* (Chicago, 1962); Samuel P. Hays, *Conservation and the Gospel of Efficiency* (Cambridge, 1959); Dwight Waldo, *The Administrative State* (New York, 1948), 3–61.

ment constituted an accommodation of forces outside the business community to the political trends within business and professional life rather than vice versa. It involved a tendency for the decision-making processes inherent in science and technology to prevail over those inherent in representative government.

Reformers in the Progressive Era and liberal historians since then misread the nature of the movement to change municipal government because they concentrated upon dramatic and sensational episodes and ignored the analysis of more fundamental political structure, of the persistent relationships of influence and power which grew out of the community's social, ideological, economic, and cultural activities. The reconstruction of these patterns of human relationships and of the changes in them is the historian's most crucial task, for they constitute the central context of historical development. History consists not of erratic and spasmodic fluctuations, of a series of random thoughts and actions, but of patterns of activity and change in which people hold thoughts and actions in common and in which there are close connections between sequences of events. These contexts give rise to a structure of human relationships which pervade all areas of life; for the political historian the most important of these is the structure of the distribution of power and influence.

The structure of political relationships, however, cannot be adequately understood if we concentrate on evidence concerning ideology rather than practice. For it is becoming increasingly clear that ideological evidence is no safe guide to the understanding of practice, that what people thought and said about their society is not necessarily an accurate representation of what they did. The current task of the historian of the Progressive Era is to quit taking the reformers' own description of political practice at its face value and to utilize a wide variety of new types of evidence to reconstruct political practice in its own terms. This is not to argue that ideology is either important or unimportant. It is merely to state that ideological evidence is not appropriate to the discovery of the nature of political practice.

Only by maintaining this clear distinction can the historian successfully investigate the structure of political life in the Progressive Era. And only then can he begin to cope with the most fundamental problem of all: the relationship between political ideology and political practice. For each of these facets of political life must be understood in its own terms, through its own historical record. Each involves a distinct set of historical phenomena. The relationship between them for the Progressive Era is not now clear; it has not been investigated. But it cannot be explored until the conceptual distinction is made clear and evidence tapped which is pertinent to each. Because the nature of political practice has so long been distorted by the use of ideological evidence, the most pressing task is for its investigation through new types of evidence appropriate to it. The reconstruction of the movement for municipal reform can constitute a major step forward toward that goal.

Social Tensions and the Origins of Progressivism

David P. Thelen

The history of Progressivism as seen by David P. Thelen of the University of Missouri provides an example of one of the constants of human nature—the reluctance of society to embark on new departures simply on the basis of intellectual arguments without some dramatic demonstration of the necessity of the innovation. Progressivism, that congeries of political and social reform activity concentrated between the depression of the 1890s and the end of the First World War, was the response to the social problems incidental to the industrialization, urbanization, and immigration that had been under way for the preceding sixty years or so. Public affairs and public attitudes had continued to function in the old grooves with the old definitions and understandings while these new problems grew and multiplied and remained unsolved. Then, a crisis intruded on the collective mind in such an insistent way that the need for change became obvious and all of the previously ignored problems bubbled to the surface clamoring for attention. If this is a fair model of how change occurs in society, progress arrives by fits and starts rather than through the smooth and constant application of human intelligence to man's problems.

In the essay that follows, Thelen defends the application of this "disaster first" model to the Progressive movement. Individuals and groups of reformers extending far back into the Gilded Age had identified the major problems facing society and had proposed solutions. The reformers remained fragmented and ineffective, however, and political life and governmental action up to the Progressive period centered around outdated issues. Reformers were considered to be cranks and were dismissed by the press as unwanted "calamity howlers." The business of America was getting rich, and woe to those who saw through the emperor's new clothes.

Thelen argues that the depression of the 1890s was the catalytic event that brought together the various proponents of reform and created an audience responsive to their messages. The vision of social chaos revealed by the depression and the welling up of radical movements on the tide of popular discontent was enough to convince the middle classes that change was required in order to conserve the social system (and the place of the middle class in it). Previously disparate groups came together in the interests of reform, and it is this urge to cooperate that historians must understand.

One should not think that Thelen's thesis entails an unduly pessimistic view of human nature. Rational perception and intelligent planning are eventually applied to problems. What is disheartening is that it takes some extraordinary crisis to get enough people motivated so that change can occur. There was a time when historians regarded Progressivism as an even more rational movement and viewed the reformers as altruists who through some special perception or experience were convinced that reform was needed. They were "men of good hope" who believed that "the people" would share their vision of the future if only they were informed. Muckraking was used to create the constituency for reform through intellectual processes. This view, of course, takes the Progressives pretty much at their own evaluation as men and women not motivated by partisan or special interests. They were working for "the public interest," a concept that has gotten lost as the twentieth century has grown more cynical.

For the last twenty years this lollipop view of

Social Tensions and the Origins of Progressivism From *Journal of American History*, LVI (September 1969), pp. 323–41. Reprinted by permission of the Organization of American Historians.

Progressivism has been out of favor and has been replaced by theories that locate the reform impulse in class and status conflicts. According to these interpretations, one must not believe what the reformers said about why they were doing what they were doing, or at least their description of their own motivations is not to be taken as sufficient explanation for their behavior. One must instead look to the tensions and insecurities of the actor's social position for clues to his motivations.

The burden of the following essay is a critique of this socio-psychological approach to Progressivism on two points. First, Thelen argues that the sort of selective borrowing of dubious psychological principles would not meet the standards of many professional psychologists and does not in fact provide complete explanations for such problems as why the reform movement occurred when it did and why only certain members of a presumably anxiety-ridden social group were attracted to the movement. The reader should wonder whether the fact that a socio-psychological theory does not enjoy universal acceptance should make it unusable by historians. One should have reservations as well about Thelen's attempt to discredit the explanatory potential of social stratification, a subject that is much more controversial than a reader might assume from Thelen's treatment. Second, Thelen empirically isolates a group of (typical?) Progressives and compares their social profiles with those of their moderate and conservative colleagues. Unfortunately for the social tensions approach, no significant differences in social position appear among the three groups. This should also call into question the interpretation put forward by Samuel P. Hays in the preceding selection.

One question the reader should seriously ponder is whether Thelen's interpretation differs significantly from the old liberal framework which was essentially an elaboration of the ideologies of the combatants themselves. This old, and now discarded, theory assumed a political structure that was manned by people motivated by moralistic and rationalistic perceptions. In its reductionist form, it pictured social conflict as a battle between the people and their leaders on the one hand, and special interest groups on the other. Resolution of the conflict is achieved through the activation of enough rational and moral forces of cohesion to overcome the temporary advantage that the special interest groups had enjoyed because of the lack of information on the part of the people. The new view offered by Thelen is not a perfect replica of the old liberal view, but it is close enough so that one should wonder whether it fits one's understanding of human nature and the political process.

*R*ecent historians have explained the origins of the Progressive movement in several ways. They have represented progressivism, in turn, as a continuation of the western and southern farmers' revolt,[1] as a desperate attempt by the urban gentry to regain status from the new robber barons,[2] as a thrust from the depths of slum life,[3] and as a campaign by businessmen to prevent workers from securing political power.[4] Behind such seemingly conflicting theories, however, rests a single assumption about the origins of progressivism: the class and status conflicts of the late-nineteenth century formed the driving forces that made men become reformers. Whether viewed by the historian as a farmer, worker, urban elitist, or businessman, the progressive was motivated primarily by his social position; and each scholar has painted a compelling picture of the insecurities and tensions felt by the group that he placed in the vanguard of progressivism. Pressures and threats from other social groups drove men to espouse reform. In these class and status conflicts can be found the roots of progressivism.

How adequately does this focus on social tensions and insecurities explain the origins of progressivism? Since some of these scholars have invoked concepts from social science to support their rejection of earlier approaches, the validity and application of some of the sociological and psychological assumptions which make up the conceptual framework for the idea that social tensions impelled the progressive require analysis. Is the focus on social classes relevant to the rise of political movements like progressivism? Is it useful to rely upon a narrow, untestable and unproved conception of motivation when other approaches are available? How much of a concrete situation does an abstract model explain?

[1] John D. Hicks, *The Populist Revolt: A History of the Farmers' Alliance and the People's Party* (Minneapolis, 1931), 404–23; George E. Mowry, *Theodore Roosevelt and the Progressive Movement* (Madison, 1947), 3–35.

[2] Influential statements of this view include George E. Mowry, *The California Progressives* (Berkeley, 1951), 86–104; George E. Mowry, *The Era of Theodore Roosevelt: 1900–1912* (New York, 1958), 85–105; Richard Hofstadter, *The Age of Reform: From Bryan to F.D.R.* (New York, 1955), 131–72.

[3] J. Joseph Huthmacher, "Urban Liberalism in the Age of Reform," *Mississippi Valley Historical Review*, XLIX (Sept. 1962), 231–41.

[4] Samuel P. Hays, "The Politics of Reform in Municipal Government in the Progressive Era," *Pacific Northwest Quarterly*, 55 (Oct. 1964), 157–69; James Weinstein, "Organized Business and the City Commission and Manager Movements," *Journal of Southern History*, XXVIII (May 1962), 166–82.

First, theories borrowed from one discipline are not designed to encompass the data of another. In questioning the application of models from physiology and physics to psychology, the noted personality theorist George A. Kelly explained: "We are skeptical about the value of copying ready-made theories which were designed for other foci of convenience"; and he urged his fellow psychologists to resist the temptation of "poking about in the neighbors' back yards for methodological windfalls."[5] Just as physiology and physics encompass only part of the psychologist's realm, so psychology, sociology, and political science are concerned with only part of the historian's realm.

Those historians who have borrowed the idea that social stratification explains the rise of political movements like progressivism illustrate the dangers inherent in borrowing theories from other fields. Most sociologists and political scientists now doubt the relevance of social stratification to the emergence of political movements. Reinhard Bendix, for example, maintained that "the study of social stratification, whether or not it is adumbrated by psychological analysis, is not the proper approach to an understanding of the role of cumulative political experience."[6] In their pleas for more pluralistic approaches to political power, such political scientists as Nelson W. Polsby and Robert A. Dahl have found that social stratification is largely irrelevant to the exercise of political power.[7] So severe were these criticisms of the assumption that social class determined political power that one sociologist, reviewing the literature of the field in 1964, concluded that "the problem has simply been dropped."[8]

But an even greater problem with placing emphasis on social tensions is that it is ahistorical. Even sociologists like Seymour M. Lipset and Bendix have complained about the "increasingly ahistorical" drift of the focus of this field.[9] After analyzing the major models of social change, another sociologist concluded that the fundamental error of these models was their failure to incorporate the dimension of time.[10] Few scholars would deny that social tensions exist at all times and in all societies.[11] For at least twenty

[5] George A. Kelly, *A Theory of Personality: The Psychology of Personal Constructs* (New York, 1963), 22–23.

[6] Reinhard Bendix, "Social Stratification and Political Power," Reinhard Bendix and Seymour Martin Lipset, eds., *Class, Status and Power: A Reader in Social Stratification* (Glencoe, 1953), 609. In the same article which Richard Hofstadter cited, Seymour Lipset and Reinhard Bendix averred that "the exercise of power cannot be fully explained by the facts of social stratification as this subject is conceived by American sociologists." Seymour M. Lipset and Reinhard Bendix, "Social Status and Social Structure: A Reexamination of Data and Interpretations: II," *British Journal of Sociology*, Two (Sept. 1951), 254.

[7] Nelson W. Polsby, *Community Power and Political Theory* (New Haven, 1963), 98; Robert A. Dahl, *Who Governs* (New Haven, 1962).

[8] M. Herbert Danzger, "Community Power Structure: Problems and Continuities," *American Sociological Review*, 29 (Oct. 1964), 711.

[9] Lipset and Bendix, "Social Status and Social Structure," 246, 247. See also C. Wright Mills' review of W. Lloyd Warner and Paul S. Lunt, *The Social Life of a Modern Community*, in *American Sociological Review*, VII (April 1942), 267–68.

[10] Max Heirich, "The Use of Time in the Study of Social Change," *American Sociological Review*, 29 (June 1964), 386–97.

[11] See, for example, Wilbert E. Moore, "Predicting Discontinuities in Social Change," *American Sociological Review*, 29 (June 1964), 337.

years before 1900, various business groups had tried to take political power away from workers and bosses. But to focus on the social class motivation of businessmen is to obscure the basic historical problem of why progressivism emerged *when* it did. Conflicts between businessmen and workers were hardly unique to the years around 1900. The emphasis on social tensions obscures chronology. When sociologists are disturbed about this problem, historians should be wary indeed.

The assumption that progressivism derived from social tensions is at least as vulnerable to attack by psychologists. If the kinds of questions historians generally ask about the origins of political and social movements are reduced to the psychological level, then the theories of class and status motivation would seem to be premised on very debatable assumptions about individual motivation. Most historians would want to know the conditions that existed before a change occurred, why the change happened, and what were the results of that change.

The first problem—the conditions before a change occurred—reduces in psychological terms to the way an individual perceives himself, his self-image. Psychologists have approached this question in many ways, but a theory of change which assumes that social tensions were the basic cause implicitly accepts only one of these approaches. It assumes that an individual defines himself primarily in terms of his particular social role, that his behavior is motivated mainly by his class and status role perceptions. Only about one out of every three psychologists, however, would accept this premise to any real extent.[12] Even some sociologists and anthropologists, who have traditionally seen individual behavior as primarily determined by culture, have retreated from that position and now see a more symmetrical interaction in which personality also influences culture.[13] An overwhelming majority of psychologists have rejected a role theory as an adequate explanation for the way an individual who enlists in a reform movement forms his self-image.

The second problem—why the change happened—reduces in psychological terms to the mechanism by which an individual feels impelled to join a political movement like progressivism. Here again those scholars who emphasize social tensions have implicitly chosen only one of several alternatives offered by psychologists. They assume that the threat from some other social group frustrated the would-be progressive who, in turn, reacted aggressively against that threat. Very few psychologists, however, would claim that social tensions are the main source of frustration. Furthermore, individuals are generally capable of reacting to new roles without experiencing any major frustrations. The different ways in which Theodore Roosevelt and Calvin Coolidge, for example, remade the role of the presidency to fit their own personalities suggest how flexible roles can be without

[12] Calvin S. Hall and Gardner Lindzey, *Theories of Personality* (New York, 1957), 26, 548. Gordon W. Allport, for example, attacked role theory in "What units shall we employ?" Gardner Lindzey, ed., *Assessment of Human Motives* (New York, 1958), 244–46.

[13] See, for example, Melford E. Spiro, "Social Systems, Personality, and Functional Analysis," Bert Kaplan, ed., *Studying Personality Cross-Culturally* (New York, 1961), 93–128.

deeply frustrating an individual. Furthermore, different members of the same social class will perceive social challenges in different ways; many will experience no frustration at all.[14]

Even if historians concede that socal stresses can frustrate an individual, does it follow that he will react aggressively toward the source of that frustration? The frustration-produces-aggression model is one of the most debated propositions in psychology.[15] Extreme critics have called it "nonsensical."[16] Others have shown that frustration more often produces anxiety, submission, dependence, or avoidance than aggression.[17] Even presumably simpleminded creatures like rats and pigeons do not necessarily react aggressively when they are frustrated.[18] If some psychologists have shown that aggression is only one possible result of frustration, others have shown that frustration is only one possible source of aggression. Indeed, prior to 1939 most psychologists accepted Sigmund Freud's *Beyond the Pleasure Principle*, which contended that aggression derived from the Death Wish.[19] Others have found the source of aggression in neither frustration nor the Death Wish.[20] The assumption that social tensions will frustrate an individual and drive him to react aggressively has been riddled by the artillery of a great many psychologists.[21] For historians to continue to assume that men react primarily to social threats is to ignore an impressive body of psychological literature.

The third problem—what were the results of that change—reduces in psychological terms to the way an individual outwardly expresses the internal

[14] A. H. Maslow, "Deprivation, Threat, and Frustration," Chalmers L. Stacey and Manfred F. DeMartino, eds., *Understanding Human Motivation* (Cleveland, 1958), 259–61, argues that the threat from other groups must be extraordinarily deep before an individual will be frustrated. Saul Rosenzweig, "An Outline of Frustration Theory," J. McV. Hunt, ed., *Personality and the Behavior Disorders* (2 vols., New York, 1944), I, 383, claims that men can completely ignore a frustrating situation.

[15] The original statement of the frustration-produces-aggression model is John Dollard, Neal E. Miller, and others, *Frustration and Aggression* (New Haven, 1939).

[16] Karl Menninger, *Love Against Hate* (New York, 1942), 295.

[17] Kenneth R. Wurtz, "Some Theory and Data Concerning the Attenuation of Aggression," *Journal of Abnormal and Social Psychology*, 60 (Jan. 1960), 134–36; John W. M. Whiting, "The Frustration Complex in Kwoma Society," *Man*, XLIV (Nov.–Dec. 1944), 140–44; Irving L. Janis, *Air War and Emotional Stress: Psychological Studies of Bombing and Civilian Defense* (New York, 1951), 4–66, 98–125; J. P. Scott and Emil Fredericson, "The Causes of Fighting in Mice and Rats," *Physiological Zoology*, XXIV (Oct. 1951), 280–81, 284, 307–08.

[18] John P. Seward, "Aggressive Behavior in the Rat. III: The Role of Frustration," *Journal of Comparative Psychology*, 38 (Aug. 1945), 233; N. H. Azrin, R. R. Hutchinson, and D. F. Hake, "Extinction-Induced Aggression," *Journal of the Experimental Analysis of Behavior*, 9 (May 1966), 191–204.

[19] O. H. Mowrer and Clyde Kluckhohn, "Dynamic Theory of Personality," Hunt, *Personality and the Behavior Disorders*, I, 112–13.

[20] See, for example, Scott and Fredericson, "Causes of Fighting in Mice and Rats," 273–309; Seward, "Aggressive Behavior in the Rat," 235. Leonard Berkowitz, *Aggression: A Social Psychological Analysis* (New York, 1962), 29–36, reviews many experiments which showed that aggression has other sources than frustration.

[21] Studies which accept the basic outlines of the frustration-aggression thesis while insisting on modifying it significantly are Berkowitz, *Aggression*; Nicholas Pastore, "The Role of Arbitrariness in the Frustration-Aggression Hypothesis," *Journal of Abnormal and Social Psychology*, 47 (July 1952), 728–31.

change. If an individual felt angry following threats from another social group, how would he express that anger? The idea that he will sublimate his aggressive propensities into cries for political reform is one which is endorsed by many Freudians who follow *Civilization and Its Discontents*.[22] But even some psychoanalysts claim that Freud never adequately explained sublimation. Other personality theorists have asserted that "everyone recognizes . . . that at present we have no theory which really explains the dynamics" of sublimation.[23] Many psychologists have seen sublimation as only one possible way of expressing aggressive proclivities. Political reform is only one of hundreds of directions an individual can channel hostile impulses. But most personality theorists are so unimpressed by the concept of sublimation that they simply ignore it in their own theories.[24]

By assuming that social tensions produced progressivism, historians have approached the basic questions about social and political movements from a very narrow psychological viewpoint. Even more important, the psychological underpinnings of this assumption are either disproved, disputed, ignored, or "untestable" by modern psychologists.

Moreover, the whole psychological framework which includes these theories has recently come under attack. Both behaviorists and psychoanalysts had previously assumed that individuals were motivated by "a state of tenseness that leads us to seek equilibrium, rest, adjustment, satisfaction, or homeostasis. From this point of view, personality is nothing more than our habitual modes of reducing tension."[25] Men became reformers to relieve tensions, perhaps impelled by class and status anxieties. Now, however, many psychologists contend that personality theorists too long overemphasized the irrational components in motivation.[26] As early as 1953 Gordon Allport reported that the trend in motivational theory was away from the tension reduction approach and toward an emphasis on the rational and healthy side of individuals.[27] By stressing the rationality of free choice, these psychologists have argued that a commitment to reform, for example, may in fact be the ultimate expression of a mature personality and reflect a man who is capable of getting outside of his self-preoccupation. Indeed, Erich Fromm has said that the revolutionary leader might well be the only "sane person in an insane world."[28] The decision to embrace progressivism may

[22] Menninger, *Love Against Hate*, 126–33.

[23] Kurt Lewin, *A Dynamic Theory of Personality: Selected Papers* (New York, 1935), 181.

[24] Of all the approaches analyzed by Hall and Lindzey, *Theories of Personality*, only those of Sigmund Freud, Carl Jung, Harry Stack Sullivan, Kurt Lewin, and Raymond B. Cattell incorporate sublimation.

[25] Gordon W. Allport, *Becoming: Basic Considerations for a Psychology of Personality* (New Haven, 1955), 48–49.

[26] Roy Schafer, "Regression in the service of the ego: The relevance of a psychoanalytic concept for personality assessment," Lindzey, *Assessment of Human Motives*, 119–48; Irving L. Janis, "The psychoanalytic interview as an observational method," *ibid.*, 149–81.

[27] Gordon W. Allport, "The Trend in Motivational Theory," *American Journal of Orthopsychiatry*, XXIII (Jan. 1953), 107–19. See also Ernest R. Hilgard and Gordon H. Bower, *Theories of Learning* (3rd ed., New York, 1966), 430–33.

[28] Erich Fromm, *The Dogma of Christ and Other Essays on Religion, Psychology and Culture* (New York, 1955), 165.

simply represent a conscious choice between alternative programs, not an attempt to reduce tensions which grew out of a man's efforts to maintain his social position.[29]

There is another problem in borrowing models: the more inclusive the model, the farther it is removed from the reality it is attempting to explain. The data must be squeezed and distorted to make them conform to the model. Many social scientists themselves have revolted against the top-heavy and abstract models which have prevailed in their fields. One student of social stratification, for example, concluded from a review of 333 studies that his field suffered from "the disease of overconceptualization."[30] Similarly, many psychologists have rejected the abstract personality constructs used to explain motivation because they are too far removed from the reality of individual people. Arguing for a focus on the "life-style" of each person, Allport has attacked theories which emphasize "the abstract motivation of an impersonal and therefore non-existent mind-in-general," preferring "the concrete, viable motives of each and every mind-in-particular."[31] In a like vein, Kelly has argued that most psychological constructs ignore an individual's "private domain, within which his behavior aligns itself within its own lawful system." These abstract constructs can only account for the individual as "an inert object wafted about in a public domain by external forces, or as a solitary datum sitting on its own continuum."[32] Allport even charged that psychologists who build universal models to explain human motivation are seeking a "scientific will of the wisp"; the " 'irreducible unlearned motives' of men" they are seeking cannot be found because they do not exist.[33]

This is not a critique of any particular psychological theory or approach to behavior. Rather it is a plea to be aware of the dangers in building a conceptual approach to such a problem as progressivism upon so many rickety psychological foundations. Historians should recognize that psychologists are not that different; they are at least as divided in their interpretations as we are. For historians to accept the assumptions that underlie the idea that social tensions produced progressivism would be similar to a psychologist borrowing Frederick Jackson Turner's frontier hypothesis for his research. Many of us would complain that there are other explanations for the development of American history; and a great many psychologists, in effect, are shuddering at the weak psychological underpinnings of the assumption that their social backgrounds made men become reformers.

The real test for the soundness of any approach is not theoretical, of

[29] Martin B. Duberman has used the writings of some of these psychologists to argue that the abolitionists were not hopeless neurotics. Martin Duberman, "The Abolitionists and Psychology," *Journal of Negro History*, XLVII (July 1962), 183–91; Martin Duberman, "The Northern Response to Slavery," Martin Duberman, ed., *The Anti-Slavery Vanguard: New Essays on the Abolitionists* (Princeton, 1965), 406–13.

[30] Harold W. Pfautz, "The Current Literature on Social Stratification: Critique and Bibliography," *American Journal of Sociology*, LVIII (Jan. 1953), 392.

[31] Gordon W. Allport, "The Functional Autonomy of Motives," Stacey and De-Martino, *Understanding Human Motivation*, 81. See also Allport, *Becoming*, 19–101; Allport, "What units shall we employ?" 239–60.

[32] Kelly, *Theory of Personality*, 39–40. See also George A. Kelly, "Man's construction of his alternatives," Lindzey, *Assessment of Human Motives*, 33–64.

[33] Gordon W. Allport, "Motivation in Personality: Reply to Peter A. Bertocci," Stacey and DeMartino, *Understanding Human Motivation*, 111.

course, but empirical. In this case the inadequacy of the sociological and psychological ideas which inform the assumption that social tensions produced progressivism becomes obvious after an explanation of the types of men who became progressives and conservatives. If social tensions were relevant to the rise of progressivism, then clearly the class and status experiences of progressives should have differed in some fundamental way from those of the conservatives.

How different, in fact, were the social origins of progressives and conservatives? Following George E. Mowry's publication in 1951 of *The California Progressives*, several scholars examined the external social class attributes of progressive leaders and concluded that the reformers were drawn from the young urban gentry.[34] But because they neglected to sample a comparable group of conservatives, these studies failed to prove their contention that class and status experiences impelled the progressives. Subsequent profiles of both progressive and conservative leaders in the election of 1912 and the legislative sessions of 1911 in Washington and 1905 in Missouri showed that both groups came from nearly the same social background.[35] Objective measures of their social origins failed to predict the programs and ideologies of political leaders.

Scholars may not accept this finding because they question whether the 1912 campaign reflected political ideologies so much as the personalities of leaders and the desire for office. The studies of legislatures in Washington and Missouri might be questioned because in a single session such extraneous pressures as the personality of a powerful governor or the use of bribes might have interfered with a legislator's expression of his natural preferences. Furthermore, neither Washington nor Missouri was ever noted as a banner progressive state. Perhaps the issues in these states were not as hotly contested—and hence did not reveal as sharp social tensions—as in the more radical states.

The following profile of Wisconsin legislators was designed to avoid some of the possible objections to the other studies. Since contemporaries and historians alike have agreed on the pivotal position of Wisconsin, it is an ideal state to test whether social tensions were important in the development of progressivism. This sample begins with the 1897 session because it was

---

[34] Mowry, *California Progressives*, 86–104; Mowry, *Era of Theodore Roosevelt*, 85–105; Alfred D. Chandler, Jr., "The Origins of Progressive Leadership," Elting E. Morison, ed., *The Letters of Theodore Roosevelt* (8 vols., Cambridge, 1954), VIII, 1462–65; Hoyt Landon Warner, *Progessivism in Ohio, 1897–1917* (Columbus, 1964), 22–23, 46. Gerhard E. Lenski, "American Social Classes: Statistical Strata or Social 'Groups?'" *American Journal of Sociology*, LVIII (Sept. 1952), 139–44, finds these external traits to be valid measures of social class affiliation.

[35] Richard B. Sherman, "The Status Revolution and Massachusetts Progressive Leadership," *Political Science Quarterly*, LXXVIII (March 1963), 59–65; William T. Kerr, Jr., "The Progessives of Washington, 1910–1912," *Pacific Northwest Quarterly*, 55 (Jan. 1964), 16–27; E. Daniel Potts, "The Progressive Profile in Iowa," *Mid-America*, XLVII (Oct. 1965), 257–68; Norman M. Wilensky, *Conservatives in the Progressive Era: The Taft Republicans of 1912* (Gainesville, 1965), 32–39; David Rosenblatt, "1905 Missouri Legislature Statistical Profile" (seminar paper, University of Missouri, 1967). Jack Tager, "Progressives, Conservatives, and the Theory of the Status Revolution," *Mid-America*, XLVIII (July 1966), 162–75, found that social origins failed to distinguish progressives from conservatives in Toledo.

then, for the first time, that the Progressive Republicans identified in their speeches, platforms, and votes the issues which divided them from the stalwarts, and concludes with the 1903 session, when many of their programs were enacted. The index for "progressivism" was based on votes growing out of the campaigns for a more equitable distribution of the tax burden, for regulation of quasi-public corporations, and for purification of the electoral and legislative processes. These were the issues which gave the thrust and tone to Wisconsin progressivism and served as the dividing lines between the old guard and the insurgents.[36]

During these four sessions there were 286 roll calls on these issues. A "progressive" legislator was defined as one who voted for more than 75 percent of the progressive measures; a "moderate" favored between 50 and 75 percent of the progressive measures; and a "conservative" opposed more than half of the progressive measures. Of the 360 Republican legislators included in this profile, 40 percent were progressives, 38 percent were moderates, and 22 percent were conservatives.[37]

If social conflicts were important to the emergence of progressivism, the variable which would be most likely to reveal that fact would be the occupations of legislators. Convincing generalizations from the following chart would need to be based upon large statistical differences, since the relatively small sample is divided so many ways. Occupation clearly made little difference in a legislator's vote on progressive measures.

TABLE 1

	Farmer	Merchant	Professional	Manufacturer	Financier	Worker
	Percent	Percent	Percent	Percent	Percent	Percent
Progressives	20	27	26	13	9	5
Moderates	22	24	29	6	13	6
Conservatives	12	27	32	16	10	3

The extent of a man's education helps to locate his social position. In Wisconsin neither progressives (22 percent), moderates (24 percent), nor conservatives (27 percent) were dominated by college graduates. At a time and place where college degrees were rare, perhaps a better measure of educational aspirations would be the proportion of men who sought any kind of formal schooling—high school, business college, night school—beyond the level of the common school. Here again, however, the differences in

36 David P. Thelen, "The Social and Political Origins of Wisconsin Progressivism, 1885–1900" (doctoral dissertation, University of Wisconsin, 1967), 220–38, 249–52, 261–70, 272–316, 330–402, 445–57.

37 The handful of Democrats, who seldom comprised over one tenth of the legislators, were excluded because they contributed no programs to the development of Wisconsin progressivism and because they used their meagre numbers primarily to embarrass the conflicting Republican factions. Because absences could be interpreted in many ways, those legislators who were absent for more than 20 percent of the roll calls on these issues were also excluded from the sample.

achievement between progressives (58 percent), moderates (60 percent), and conservatives (66 percent) are insignificant.

The place of a man's birth also indicates his social background. But the nativity of Wisconsin's legislators failed to differentiate progressives from conservatives (see Table 2).

TABLE 2

	Midwest	East and New England	Canada	Europe
	Percent	Percent	Percent	Percent
Progressives	47	29	6	18
Moderates	61	24	2	13
Conservatives	49	30	5	16

If the Wisconsin sample corresponds roughly to those of other states in the occupations, education, and nativity of political leaders, it differs from them in two other respects. Students of the 1912 election found the progressives to be considerably younger than the conservatives in both age and political experience, a fact which led them to see progressivism as a revolt of the young, would-be politicians. In Wisconsin, however, progressives and conservatives both had an average age of forty-eight, and the moderates averaged forty-six. The median ages of progressives (49), moderates (45), and conservatives (47) likewise fail to suggest the existence of any generational conflict between progressives and conservatives.

Nor were Wisconsin's progressives the most politically immature of the rival factions. While service in the legislature is only one measure of political experience, it does reveal the effectiveness of politicians in winning renomination from their local organizations. Although Wisconsin's conservatives had the longest tenure in the legislature, they contrasted not so much with the progressives as with the moderates. Table 3 indicates the number of previous sessions attended by legislators.

The social origins of Wisconsin legislators between 1897 and 1903 clearly suggest that no particular manner of man became a progressive. Such variables as occupation, education, nativity, age, and previous legislative experience fail to differentiate the average progressive from the average conservative. The theories that progressivism was motivated by status or class tensions felt by the urban gentry, the businessmen, the workers, the farmers, or the incipient politicians are challenged in Wisconsin by the fact that

TABLE 3

	None	One	Two or More
	Percent	Percent	Percent
Progressive	52	28	20
Moderates	62	27	11
Conservatives	35	37	28

members of these groups were as likely to become conservatives as progressives. And the Wisconsin profile parallels other studies. To the extent that social class allegiance can be measured by such attributes as occupation, nativity, education, and age, social tensions were apparently irrelevant to the formation of progressivism since the "typical" progressive and conservative came from the same social background.

Collective statistical profiles can, however, obscure more than they reveal. The five more prominent early Wisconsin progressive leaders, the men who forged the issues which Robert M. La Follette subsequently adopted, were most noteworthy for their different social origins. The man contemporaries hailed as the "father of Wisconsin progressivism" was Albert R. Hall, a small dairy farmer in the western part of the state. Nephew of national Grange head Oliver Kelley, Hall was basically an agrarian radical who developed the reputation of a fearless enemy of the railroads and other large corporations.[38] No less important was John A. Butler, the lengthened shadow of the powerful Milwaukee Municipal League. A sharper contrast to Hall could scarcely be found than this independently wealthy and highly educated Brahmin who seemed to spend more time in his villa than he did in his Milwaukee law office.[39] Milwaukee also contributed Julius E. Roehr, organized labor's leading champion in the legislature. Born in New York City—the son of German immigrants—this hardworking lawyer and dissident Republican politician would have been extremely uncomfortable with the smells of either Hall's farm or Butler's villa.[40] James H. Stout, the most respected of the early progressives in the legislature, was born and raised in Iowa and educated at the University of Chicago. A fabulously wealthy lumber baron, Stout used his company town of Menomonie to pioneer in vocational education and in welfare benefits for his workers.[41] The orator of these early legislative progressives was James J. McGillivray, a self-made Canadian-born architect and manufacturer who lived in Black River Falls and authored the state's antitrust acts.[42] It would seem almost pointless to hunt for a common social "type" in these early progressives. A Brahmin man of leisure and self-made manufacturer, an agrarian radical who knew

[38] George W. Chowen to Albert R. Hall, March 30, 1871; Hall's mother to Hall, June 7, 1873; Eugene Elliott to Hall, July 20, 1896; Sara M. Dodge to Caroline A. Hall, Oct. 29, 1909, Albert R. Hall Papers (State Historical Society of Wisconsin, Madison); Madison *Wisconsin State Journal*, April 16, 1895; Milwaukee *Sentinel*, Dec. 16, 1894; *Weekly Madisonian*, March 30, 1895; La Crosse *Leader-Press*, June 6, 1905; Albert O. Barton, *La Follette's Winning of Wisconsin, 1894-1904* (Des Moines, 1922), 93–101; Nils P. Haugen, *Pioneer and Political Reminiscences* (Madison, 1930[?]), 97, 126.

[39] *National Cyclopedia of American Biography* (49 vols. to date, New York, 1898–), XXI, 55–56; John A. Butler to Jerome H. Raymond, Nov. 10, 1895, J. H. Raymond File, Extension Division Correspondence, University of Wisconsin Archival Series 18/1/1–4 (Memorial Library, University of Wisconsin).

[40] *The Blue Book of the State of Wisconsin . . . 1909*, pp. 730–31; Milwaukee *Sentinel*, Aug. 25, 1896, Feb. 27, April 4, 1899; Madison *Wisconsin State Journal*, April 23, 24, 1897.

[41] Madison *Wisconsin State Journal*, March 5, May 10, 1895, Jan. 22, May 8, 1897; Kathryn Saucerman, "A Study of the Wisconsin Library Movement, 1850–1900" (master's thesis, University of Wisconsin, 1944), 84–85; Ann M. Keppel and James I. Clark, "James H. Stout and the Menomonie Schools," *Wisconsin Magazine of History*, 42 (Spring 1959), 200–10; *Blue Book . . . 1901*, p. 737.

[42] *Blue Book . . . 1901*, p. 738; Madison *Wisconsin State Journal*, Feb. 8, 1895.

no workers and a lawyer who never lived outside a large city and was the workers' champion, young men and old men, Yankees and immigrants, these were the leaders who made common cause in Wisconsin and developed the progressive program.

The widely scattered backgrounds of the most prominent early leaders and the remarkable collective similarity between the average progressive and conservative confirm the weaknesses in the sociological and psychological framework for the assumption that progressivism was rooted in social tensions. The widespread emphasis on social tensions is unsound sociologically because it draws upon only a narrow spectrum of personality theory, and those models upon which it does draw are either unproved or unprovable. The statistical profiles from Wisconsin and elsewhere reveal empirically that the origins of progressivism cannot be found by studying the social backgrounds and tensions of progressive leaders. Remembering Kelly's injunction to avoid "poking about in the neighbors' back yards for methodological windfalls," historians must develop alternative approaches which encompass not only the realm of sociology and psychology but also that of history.

Such an alternative approach should at least restore chronology, a major casualty in the repeated emphasis on men's class and status feelings, to a more prominent position. At this point it is possible to offer a tentative explanation for the origins of progressivism when that movement is placed in the context of the chronological evolution of both industrialism and reform.

When the Progressive era is put against the backdrop of the growth of industrialism in America, the remarkable fact about that period is its relative freedom from social tensions. If conflicts between city and farm, worker and boss, younger and older generations, native-born and immigrant are more or less natural results of industrialization, then the years between the late 1890s and the early 1910s stand as a period of social peace when contrasted with either the Gilded Age or the 1920's, when those conflicts were raw and ragged. Not competition but cooperation between different social groups —ministers, businessmen, workers, farmers, social workers, doctors, and politicians—was what distinguished progressivism from such earlier reform movements as Mugwumpery, Populism, the labor movement, and civil service reform. To the extent that men and groups were motivated by tensions deriving from their class and status perceptions, they would have been unable to cooperate with men from different backgrounds. In focusing on the broadly based progressive thrust, the real question is not what drove groups apart, but what drove them together? To answer this question, progressivism must be located in the development of reform in the late-nineteenth century.

The roots of progressivism reach far back into the Gilded Age. Dozens of groups and individuals in the 1880s envisioned some change that would improve society. Reformers came forward to demand civil service reform, the eight hour day, scientific agriculture, woman suffrage, enforcement of vice laws, factory inspection, nonpartisan local elections, trust-busting, wildlife conservation, tax reform, abolition of child labor, businesslike local government, regulation of railway rates, less patronizing local charity, and hundreds of other causes which would subsequently be identified with progressivism. Younger social scientists, particularly economists, were not only beginning to lambast the formalism and conservatism in their fields and to advocate the ideas which would undergird progressivism but they were also seeking to force governments to accept their ideas. Richard T. Ely's work on the Maryland Tax Commission in the mid-1880s, for example, pioneered in the application of the new economics to government and generated many of the programs which future reformers and politicians would soon adopt.

But this fertility of reform in the Gilded Age did not conceal the basic fact that individuals and groups remained fragmented. There was no common program which could rally all groups, and the general prosperity tended to reassure people that industrialism might cure its own ills. As late as 1892 one editor, reflecting this optimistic frame of mind, could state that "the rich are growing richer, some of them, and the poor are growing richer, all of them."[43] Men and groups seeking major changes, whether elitists or Populists, were generally stereotyped as cranks who were blind to the vast blessings and bright future of industrialism. Circumscribed by such problems and attitudes reformers were understandably fragmented in the Gilded Age.

The catastrophic depression of 1893–1897 radically altered this pattern of reform. It vividly dramatized the failures of industrialism. The widening chasm between the rich and the poor, which a few observers had earlier called a natural result of industrialism, could no longer be ignored. As several tattered bands of men known as Coxey's Army tramped from town to town in 1894, they drew attention to the plight of the millions of unemployed and vividly portrayed the striking contrasts between the way of life of the poor and the "conspicuous consumption" of the rich. Furthermore, as Thorstein Veblen observed, they showed that large numbers of Americans no longer cherished the old gospel of self-help, the very basis for mobility in a democratic society.[44] As desperation mounted, businessmen and politicians tried the traditional ways of reversing the business cycle, but by 1895 they realized that the time-honored formulas of the tariff and the currency simply could not dispel the dark pall that hung over the land.[45] Worse still, President Grover Cleveland seemed utterly incapable of comprehending, let alone relieving, the national crisis.

The collapse of prosperity and the failure of national partisan politicians to alleviate the crisis by the traditional methods generated an atmosphere of restless and profound questioning which few could escape. "On every corner stands a man whose fortune in these dull times has made him an ugly

[43] Milwaukee *Sentinel*, Oct. 22, 1892.

[44] Thorstein Veblen, "The Army of the Commonweal," *Journal of Political Economy*, II (June 1894), 456–61. See also Douglas W. Steeples, "The Panic of 1893: Contemporary Reflections and Reactions," *Mid-America*, XLVII (July 1965), 155–75; and Samuel Rezneck, "Unemployment, Unrest, and Relief in the United States During the Depression of 1893–1897," *Journal of Political Economy*, LXI (Aug. 1953), 324–45, for other aspects of the depression.

[45] Walter LaFeber, *The New Empire: An Interpretation of American Expansion: 1860–1898* (Ithaca, 1963), 150–96, suggests that many businessmen recognized the failure of traditional methods when they began the aggressive search for world markets in 1895.

critic of everything and everybody," wrote one editor.[46] A state university president warned his graduates in 1894 that

> you will see everywhere in the country symptoms of social and political discontent. You will observe that these disquietudes do not result from the questions that arise in the ordinary course of political discussion . . . but that they spring out of questions that are connected with the very foundations of society and have to do with some of the most elemental principles of human liberty and modern civilization.[47]

Was the American dream of economic democracy and mobility impossible in an industrial society? Would the poor overthrow an unresponsive political and economic system? Such questions urgently demanded answers, and it was no longer either wise or safe to summarily dismiss as a crank anyone who had an answer. "The time is at hand," cried one editor, "when some of the great problems which the Nineteenth century civilization has encountered are crying for a solution. . . . Never before in the history of the world were people so willing to accept true teaching on any of these subjects and give to them a just and practical trial."[48] A man's social origins were now less important than his proposals, and many men began to cooperate with people from different backgrounds to devise and implement solutions.

This depression-inspired search for answers sprouted hundreds of discussion groups at which men met, regardless of background, to propose remedies. These groups gave men the habit of ignoring previously firm class lines in the face of the national crisis. When Victor Berger urged the Milwaukee Liberal Club to adopt socialism as the answer, for example, his audience included wealthy bankers, merchants, and lawyers.[49] In the same city, at the Church and Labor Social Union, banker John Johnston urged a "new society" where "class privileges will be abolished because all will belong to the human family," and the discussion was joined by Populists and Socialists as well as clergymen and conservative editors.[50] In this context, too, all types of people sought the wisdom of the men who had made a career of studying the social and economic breakdown. No one was surprised when unions, Granges, women's clubs, and other groups wanted University of Wisconsin economists like Ely to address them.[51] Maybe they had an answer. The social unrest accompanying the depression weakened class and status allegiances.

The direct political effects of the depression also broke down the previous rigidity and fragmentation of reform. The depression created a clear sense of priorities among the many causes which Gilded Age reformers had advocated. It generated broadly based new issues which all classes could unite

[46] Superior *Evening Telegram*, March 21, 1896.
[47] Milwaukee *Sentinel*, June 18, 1894.
[48] Superior *Evening Telegram*, July 12, 1893.
[49] Milwaukee *Sentinel*, March 4, 1895.
[50] *Ibid.*, March 2, 1894.
[51] W. A. Hilton to Richard T. Ely, Sept. 6, 1893; John O'Connell to Ely, Aug. 6, 1894; Jerome H. Raymond to Ely, Nov. 14, 1895, Richard T. Ely Papers (State Historical Society of Wisconsin, Madison); W. A. McEwan to Raymond, Nov. 13, 1895, Raymond File, Extension Division Correspondence; *Proceedings of the 24th Annual Session of the Wisconsin State Grange Patrons of Husbandry* (1895), 18–19.

behind. One such program was the urgent necessity for tax reform. When the depression struck, individuals and corporations were forced to devise ways of economizing as property values, sales, and revenues declined precipitously. Caught between higher taxes to cover the rising costs of local government and their own diminishing revenues, many wealthy individuals and corporations began to hide their personal assets from the assessors, to lobby tax relief through local governments, and even to refuse to pay any taxes. The progressive program was forged and received widespread popular support as a response to these economies. Citizens who lacked the economic or political resources to dodge their taxes mounted such a crusade against these tax dodgers that former President Benjamin Harrison warned the wealthiest leaders that unless they stopped concealing their true wealth from the tax assessors they could expect a revolution led by enraged taxpayers.[52] The programs for tax reform—including inheritance, income, and ad valorem corporation taxes—varied from place to place, but the important fact was that most citizens had developed specific programs for tax reform and had now agreed that certain individuals and corporations had evaded a primary responsibility of citizenship.

A second major area which proved capable of uniting men of different backgrounds was "corporate arrogance." Facing declining revenues, many corporations adopted economies which ranged from raising fares and rates to lobbying all manner of relief measures through city and state governments. Even more important, perhaps, they could not afford necessary improvements which elementary considerations of safety and health had led local governments to demand that they adopt. Corporate arrogance was no longer a doctrinaire cry of reformers. Now it was an unprotected railway crossing where children were killed as they came home from school or the refusal of an impoverished water company to make improvements needed to provide the healthful water which could stop the epidemics of typhoid fever.[53] Such incidents made the corporation look like a killer. These specific threats united all classes: anyone's child might be careless at a railroad crossing, and typhoid fever was no respecter of social origins.

From such new, direct, and immediate threats progressivism developed its thrust. The more corporations used their political influence to resist making the small improvements, the more communities developed increasingly radical economic programs like municipal ownership or consumer-owned utilities and fought to overthrow the machines that gave immunity to the corporations. Political reforms like the initiative, direct primary, and home rule became increasingly important in the early stages of progressivism because, as William Allen White said, men had first to get the gun before they could hit anything with it.[54] But it was the failure of the political system to respond to the new and immediate threats of the depression that convinced people that more desperate programs were needed.

[52] Superior *Evening Telegram*, Feb. 22, 1898.

[53] Henry F. Bedford, *Socialism and the Workers in Massachusetts, 1886–1912* (Amherst, 1966), 63–136, implies that such issues became the basis for early Socialist victories in Haverhill and Brockton.

[54] William Allen White, "The Insurgence of Insurgency," *American Magazine*, LXXI (Dec. 1910), 170–73.

Perhaps there are, after all, times and places where issues cut across class lines. These are the times and places where men identify less with their occupational roles as producers and more with their roles as consumers—of death-dealing water, unsafe railway crossings, polluted air, high streetcar rates, corrupt politicians—which serve to unite them across social barriers. There are also universal emotions—anger and fear—which possess all men regardless of their backgrounds.[55] The importance of the depression of the 1890s was that it aroused those universal emotions, posed dramatic and desperate enough threats to lead men of all types to agree that tax dodging and corporate arrogance had to be ended and thereby served to unite many previously fragmented reformers and to enlist the support of the majority that had earlier been either silent or enthusiastic only about partisan issues like the tariff or symbols like Abraham Lincoln. The conversion of the National Municipal League showed how issues were becoming more important than backgrounds. Originally composed of elitists who favored such Mugwumpish concerns as civil service reform, the League by 1898 had become so desperate with the domination over political machines by utility companies that it devoted its energies to municipal ownership and to political devices which promised "more trust in the people, more democracy" than its earlier elitism had permitted.[56] The attitude of moral indignation, such an obvious feature of the early stages of progressivism, was not rooted in social tensions but in the universal emotion of anger.

Whether this emphasis on the results of the depression—unrest, new threats and new issues, and cooperation among social groups—has widespread relevance or validity remains to be seen, but it does help to explain the roots of progressivism in Wisconsin. The most important factor in producing the intensity of Wisconsin progressivism was the cooperation between previously discrete and fragmented social groups both in forging popular issues and getting reforms adopted. And the most important factor in defining the popular issues was the arrogance of certain corporations. In Milwaukee the traction and electricity monopoly between 1894 and 1896 alone, for reasons ranging from extreme overcapitalization to confidence in its political powers, raised both its lighting and streetcar fares, refused to arbitrate with its striking employees, enjoined the city from enforcing ordinances lowering its fares, and used its political power—the company's chief manager was the state's leading Republican boss—to cut its tax bill in half, kill an ordinance which would have prevented it from polluting the air, and thwart generally popular attempts at regulation. Each time the monopoly refused to obey an order, lobbied special favors from the city or state, or prostituted the Republican party to the company, the progressive coalition grew. By the end of the depression, the coalition drew together both ends of the economic spectrum—the Merchants and Manufacturers Association and the Chamber of Commerce as well as several labor unions and the Federated Trades Council. Politically it included the country Republican Club, the Democratic Jefferson Club, and the Socialists and Populists. The Mug-

[55] Robert H. Wiebe, *The Search for Order, 1877–1920* (New York, 1967), 111–32, argues that growing cooperation resulted not from the depression but from modernization in general and professionalization and bureaucratization in particular.
[56] Edward W. Bemis to Ely, Dec. 29, 1898, Ely Papers.

wumpish and upper-class Municipal League was joined by German social clubs like the Turnvereine. So defiant was the company—so desperate were the people—that the traction managers became the state's most hated men by 1899; and humorist-politician George Peck observed that Wisconsin's parents "frighten children when they are bad, by telling them that if they don't look out," the traction magnates "will get them."[57] Four hundred miles away, in Superior, the story was remarkably similar. Angered by the repeated refusals of that city's water company to provide the city with healthful enough water to prevent the typhoid fever epidemics that killed dozens of people each year, and blaming the company's political power within both parties for the failure of regulation, labor unions and Populists cooperated with business and professional men and with dissident politicians to try to secure pure water and to overthrow the politicians owned by the company. In Superior, political debate had indeed narrowed, as an editor observed, to a fight of "the people against corporate insolence."[58] The water company, like the traction monopoly at Milwaukee, stood isolated and alone, the enemy of men from all backgrounds. In Wisconsin, at least, the community's groups continued to perform their special functions; and, by the end of the depression, they were all agreed that corporate arrogance had to be abolished. Their desperation made them willing to speak, lobby, and work together.

If, as the Wisconsin experience suggests, cooperation was the underpinning of progressivism, historians should focus on reformers not as victims of social tensions, but as reformers. At any given time and place, hundreds of men and groups are seeking supporters for their plans to change society and government. The basic problem for the reformer is to win mass support for his program. In Wisconsin a reformer's effectiveness depended on how well he manipulated acts of corporate and individual arrogance that infuriated everyone in order to demonstrate the plausibility of his program. Desperate events had made tax dodging, corporate defiance and control of politics the main political issues and had allowed this program to swallow the older reformers at the same time that they created a much broader constituency for reform. The question then becomes: Why did some succeed while others failed? North Dakota never developed a full-blown progressive movement because that state's progressives never demonstrated the plausibility of their programs.[59] Wisconsin's early progressives did succeed in drawing together such diverse groups as unions, businessmen, Populists, and dissident politicians because they adapted their program and rhetoric to the menacing events which angered everyone. Reformers operate in their

[57] John A. Butler, "Street Railway Problem in Milwaukee," *Municipal Affairs*, IV (March 1900), 212–18; Charles E. Monroe, "The Time to Deal with Corporations Asking Public Franchises," *Municipality*, I (Aug. 1900), 5–14; Milwaukee *Sentinel*, Nov. 24, 26, 27, Dec. 2, 8, 1897, Dec. 19, 1899, Jan. 4, 6, 1900; Thelen, "Origins of Wisconsin Progressivism," 330–402.

[58] Superior *Evening Telegram*, Aug. 14, Sept 4, 11, Oct. 23, 1895, March 12, 16, 18, 20, 27, 28, April 18, 21, 1896, Feb. 2, March 30, 31, April 1, 1898; Superior *Leader*, Aug. 15, 1895, March 15, 1896, March 27, 1898; Superior *Sunday Forum*, Feb. 6, 20, 27, 1898; Thelen, "Origins of Wisconsin Progressivism," 225–40.

[59] Charles N. Glaab, "The Failure of North Dakota Progressivism," *Mid-America*, XXXIX (Oct. 1957), 195–209.

hometowns and not in some contrived social background which could as easily apply to New York or Keokuk, and it is in their hometowns that they should be studied. Historians should determine why they succeeded or failed to rally the support of their communities to their programs, for the most significant criterion for any reformer is, in the end, his effectiveness.

When the progressive characteristically spoke of reform as a fight of "the people" or the "public interest" against the "selfish interests," he was speaking quite literally of his political coalition because the important fact about progressivism, at least in Wisconsin, was the degree of cooperation between previously discrete social groups now united under the banner of the "public interest." When the progressive politician denounced the arrogance of quasi-public corporations and tax-dodgers, he knew that experiences and events had made his attacks popular with voters from all backgrounds. Both conceptually and empirically it would seem safer and more productive to view reformers first as reformers and only secondarily as men who were trying to relieve class and status anxieties. The basic riddle in progressivism is not what drove groups apart, but what made them seek common cause.

Suggested Reading

An excellent introduction to the issues in the historiography of Progressivism is David M. Kennedy, ed., *Progressivism: The Critical Issues** (1971), which also has a good bibliography. The older view of the movement, against which Hays is reacting, is contained in Harold U. Faulkner's *The Quest for Social Justice* (1931), and *The Decline of Laissez-Faire, 1897–1917** (1951). Daniel Aaron, in *Men of Good Hope** (1951), and Sidney Fine, in *Laissez-Faire and the General-Welfare State** (1956), approach the subject from much the same point of view.

A number of the general syntheses of the Progressive era deviate from the old view. Richard Hofstadter's *The Era of Reform** (1955) and George Mowry's *The Era of Theodore Roosevelt, 1900–1912** (1958) stress the status-seeking motivations of a reform movement led by an old elite. Arthur Link, in *Woodrow Wilson and the Progressive Era, 1910–1917** (1954), finds considerable continuity between Progressivism and the old agrarian reform tradition. Samuel P. Hays, in *The Response to Industrialism** (1957), emphasizes the forward-looking, rational, self-interested nature of Progressivism as a movement led by upwardly mobile, middle-class elements of the city. This break with the older notion of Progressivism as the effort of the unorganized people to regulate the business community is made more complete by Robert Wiebe in *Businessmen and Reform: A Study of the Progressive Movement** (1962). Wiebe's *The Search for Order, 1877–1920** (1967) describes Progressivism as a search for a new principle of order by elite groups who were in the process of shifting their frames of reference from the local geographic community to national professional and business networks. Gabriel Kolko, in *The Triumph of Conservatism: A Reinterpretation of American History, 1900–1916** (1963), argues that Progressivism actually achieved the goals of corporate capitalism, and James Weinstein plays variations on that theme in *The Corporate Ideal in the Liberal State, 1900–1918** (1968).

Inquiry into the social thought of Progressivism may enjoyably start with Eric Goldman's *Rendezvous with Destiny** (1952). One of Goldman's themes, that a prerequisite of Progressivism was the breaking up of social Darwinism, was analyzed earlier by Morton White in *Social Thought in America: The Revolt Against Formalism** (1949). Charles B. Forcey's *The Crossroads of Liberalism* (1961) and David W. Noble's *The Paradox of Progressive Thought* (1958) deal with other aspects of Progressive thought. David M. Chalmers' *The Social and Political Ideas of the Muckrakers** (1964), and Aileen S. Kraditor's *The Ideas of the Woman Suffrage Movement, 1890–1920* (1965) are specialized studies. One of the few studies of the conservative mind of the Progressive era is Richard Leopold's *Elihu Root and the Conservative Tradition* (1954). A watershed of literary history is explored by Henry F. May in *The End of American Innocence* (1959).* Perhaps the most imaginative recent study of the intellectual history of the period is Christopher Lasch's *The New Radicalism in America: The Intellectual as a Social Type** (1965).

There are numerous sources of special insight into Progressivism. David Thelen's ideas are elaborated in *The New Citizenship: Origins of Progressivism in Wisconsin, 1885–1900* (1972). State and regional studies are frequently the source of fresh conceptions, demonstrated by *The California Progressives** (1952) by George Mowry, which was the first full statement of the theory against which Thelen argues. Russell Nye's *Midwestern Progressive Politics* (1951) is a more conventional treatment. C. Vann Woodward's *Origins of the New South** (1951) is the best survey of the movement in the South and emphasizes the tragically limited horizons of Progressivism. R. E. Noble's *New Jersey Progressivism Before Wilson* (1947) and H. L. Warner's *Progressivism in Ohio, 1897–1917* (1964) are useful. Richard M. Abrams' *Conservatism in a Progressive Era: Massachusetts Politics, 1900–1912* (1964) and Arthur Mann's *Yankee Reformers in the Urban Age** (1954) have overlapping interests but different points of view.

Biography is another mine of information. John M. Blum's *The Republican Roosevelt** (1954) is an excellent and stimulating essay. More admiring but less perceptive is Carlton Putnam's *Theodore Roosevelt: The Formative Years* (1958). Henry Pringle's *Theodore Roosevelt** (1931), though old, is still useful. W. H. Harbough's study of Roosevelt *Power and Responsibility** (1961) is learned and balanced. The other commanding presidential figure of the era, Woodrow Wilson, is the subject of an ongoing, multivolume biography by Arthur Link, who is also the editor-in-chief of the Woodrow Wilson Papers. Five volumes have appeared thus far, which bring Wilson up to the brink of American entry into the First World War: *Wilson: The Road to the White House** (1947), *Wilson: The New Freedom** (1956) *Wilson: Struggle for Neutrality, 1914–1915* (1960), *Wilson: Confusions and Crises, 1915–1916* (1964), and *Wilson: Campaigns for Progressivism and Peace, 1916–1917* (1965). A briefer biography is John A. Garraty's *Woodrow Wilson* (1956); and John M. Blum's *Woodrow Wilson and the Politics of Morality** (1956) is hostile and acerbic, but very interesting.

Progressivism can also be approached through the issues of the day. Allen F. Davis, in *Spearheads for Reform: The Social Settlements and the Progressive Movement, 1890–1914** (1967) suggests that one result of such an approach might be to revive the old belief that social justice was one of the aims of Progressivism; he is supported in this opinion by Robert Bremner's study of the discovery of poverty, *From the Depths* (1956) and Henry F. May's *Protestant Churches and Industrial America** (1949). Roy Lubove's interest in the housing question led to *The Progressives and the Slums: Tenement House Reform in New York City, 1890–1917*

(1963) and *The Urban Community: Housing and Planning in the Progressive Era** (1967). A more popular and more general social history is *The Good Years** (1960) by Walter Lord.

Conflicting interpretations of prohibition are provided by James H. Timberlake's *Prohibition and the Progressive Movement, 1900–1920* (1963) and Joseph R. Gusfield's *Symbolic Crusade: Status Politics and the American Temperance Movement* (1963). An elegant interpretation of the conservation movement is contained in Samuel P. Hays's *The Gospel of Efficiency: The Progressive Conservation Movement, 1890–1920* (1959); E. R. Richardson, in *The Politics of Conservation, Crusades and Controversies, 1897–1913* (1962), treats the subject from a different perspective. A leading actor on this stage is studied by M. N. McGeary in *Gifford Pinchot: Forester Politician* (1960). A more quiet crusader is presented by O. E. Anderson in *The Health of a Nation: Harvey W. Wiley and the Fight for Pure Food* (1958). The role of unions is examined by R. J. Cornell and Marc Karson in *American Labor Unions and Politics, 1900–1918* (1958).

* Also published in paperback edition.

The First
World War and
the Peace

Wilson the Diplomatist: The Problems of Neutrality and the Decisions for War

Arthur S. Link

Partly because wars are among the most cataclysmic
events in the lives of modern nation-states, historians
are usually interested both in explaining their causes
and in asserting whether (and on what terms) they
could or should have been avoided. Accordingly,
America's intervention in the First World War, which
cost the United States 107,000 dead and led to an
uneasy peace, has provoked a continuing dialog among
historians on the causes and desirability of that
conflict.

In the 1920s and 1930s, a group of historians known
as the revisionists—Harry Elmer Barnes, Charles C.
Tansill, and C. Hartley Grattan, most notably
—contended, among other points, that intervention in
the First World War had been contrary to America's
interests and that the United States had been lured
into war to aid financiers and munition-makers. The
revisionists also raised other questions that have
influenced later historical analysis: Were Wilson's
policies unneutral? Did his pro-British sympathies
lead him to favor the British and thereby lead the
nation to war? Why did he not ban the munitions

211

trade and passenger travel to Europe and thereby either avoid America's confrontation with Germany's submarine warfare or perhaps make that warfare unnecessary? Did Wilson exploit the issue of unrestricted submarine warfare in order to lead America to a war that he wanted to enter for other reasons?

A later generation of scholars called realists, decrying the innocence, moralism and legalism of American foreign policy, raised new questions and challenges. George Kennan, Walter Lippmann, and Robert Osgood, among others, concluded that American intervention after Sarajevo was in the national interest, and some like Kennan and Osgood charged that Wilson had failed to understand that America's security rested on a strong England and the balance of power in Europe. They lamented that he did not intervene earlier in the war and they regretted that he had offered an idealistic or utopian reason ("to make the world safe for democracy") rather than a realistic one: protecting England and the balance of power.

Many of the issues raised by the revisionists and the realists are among the problems that Arthur Link of Princeton University, author of the definitive biography of Wilson, considers in the following selection from *Wilson: The Diplomatist* (1957). He portrays Wilson as a man struggling to remain neutral despite the pressures at home and abroad that narrowed his options and made his course progressively more difficult. Yet, according to Link, Wilson maintained neutrality and kept the nation out of war until Germany's renewal of unrestricted submarine warfare compelled the President reluctantly to go to war. There is, in Link's analysis, a sense of tragedy and a great sympathy for the beleaguered President whose struggles proved ultimately unsuccessful: Wilson was coerced by events beyond his effective control.

Wilson's critics have maintained that he had more options than he exploited and that he chose wrongly, or at least unwisely, in guiding the nation. For example, had Wilson (1) accepted a proposed Congressional ban in 1914 on munitions exports, or (2) not relaxed the government's restrictions in 1915

Wilson the Diplomatist: The Problems of Neutrality and the Decisions for War. From *Wilson the Diplomatist* by Arthur S. Link (Baltimore: Johns Hopkins University Press, 1957), pp. 31–33, 35–50, 73–90. Copyright © 1957 by Arthur S. Link. Reprinted by permission of the author.

on loans to the belligerents, or (3) secured a prohibition on travel overseas for Americans in late 1916 (when Congress would probably have agreed), he might well have avoided the conditions that led to war. In none of these cases could he *know* that war would result from his decisions, but there was certainly mounting evidence that war would become more likely, especially in 1916 when overseas travel was still not prohibited and war was looming in the near future. In rejecting a proposed ban on munitions exports in 1914 the administration was wrong in concluding that an embargo would legally violate neutrality. In relaxing restrictions on loans to belligerents in 1915, Link notes that the reversal was partly for economic reasons but believes also that Wilson thought that the ban would have been unneutral—a judgment about Wilson that Link later admitted was speculative. Some other historians have concluded that Wilson relaxed the ban for only one reason: he recognized that the American economy required the trade that the loans would finance (Paul Birdsall, "Neutrality and Economic Pressures, 1914–1917," *Science and Society*, III [1939]). To restrict overseas travel by Americans, Wilson would have had to surrender his conception of freedom of the seas, give up his struggle to preserve the rights of neutrals, and yield in his self-defined quest to defend American honor. These were values on which he would not yield. Perhaps, then, he was not a prisoner of history, as some historians suggest, but a prisoner of his own values. But would he have chosen differently if he had foreseen the casualties at Meuse-Argonne or Chateau-Thierry? Perhaps Wilson felt that the nation could uphold the values he cherished precisely because in 1917 the future cost did not seem so great.

Germany's renewal of unrestricted warfare, according to Link, compelled Wilson to go to war in 1917. He saw no other way to protect American rights as a neutral. Beneath these *immediate* circumstances, Link suspects, there were deeper considerations subtly influencing Wilson. "It was Wilson's apparent fear," Link wrote in 1957, "that the threat of a German victory imperiled the balance of power and all his hopes for the future reconstruction of the world community." After additional research, however, Link altered his judgment in 1963. He no longer believed that the President knew, or was influenced by the fear, that the Central Powers in 1917 were about to win. Nor was Wilson concerned about national security in his decision to go to war. Link stressed "Wilson's conviction that the war was in its final stages, American belligerency would have the effect of shortening, not prolonging the war, and belligerency had the one advantage of guaranteeing him an important role in peacemaking."

Perhaps, then, Wilson had more freedom to maneuver than Link finds. And perhaps his decision to go to war, like his earlier decision not to ban passenger travel, was part of his ideological commitment to advance the values of a liberal capitalist order—as William Appleman Williams, in *The Tragedy of American Diplomacy* (1959, 1972), and N. Gordon Levin, in *Woodrow Wilson and World Politics* (1968), have contended.

*F*or Woodrow Wilson and the American people, who had a positive disinclination to play the game of power politics, events on the international stage intruded in an ironic if fateful way from 1914 to 1917. By the spring of 1915 the United States was the only great power not directly involved in the war then raging from western Europe to the Far East. Desiring only to deal fairly with both sides and to avoid military involvement, the President soon found that neutrality, as well as war, has its perplexities and perils.

The way in which Wilson met the challenges to America's peace and security raised by the death grapple between the opposing alliances has never been fully explained, notwithstanding scores of books and articles. Too often, historians, in company with public men, have looked for culprits instead of facts. Too often they have misunderstood the facts even when they found them. Too often they have written as if Wilson and his advisers made policy in a vacuum independent of the interplay of conflicting pressures. If we can see the President's policies of neutrality in the light of his convictions and objectives, the pressures and events (both domestic and foreign) that bore constantly upon him, and the alternatives between which he was often forced to choose—if we can do this, then perhaps we will see that his task in foreign policy at this juncture was not as simple as it has sometimes been described.

Among the most pervasive pressures controlling Wilson's decisions throughout the period 1914–1917 were the attitudes and opinions of the American people concerning the war and America's proper relation to it. Few presidents in American history have been more keenly aware of risks that the leader runs when he ceases to speak for the preponderant majority.

"The ear of the leader must ring with the voice of the people. He cannot be of the school of the prophets; he must be of the number of those who studiously serve the slow-paced daily need." Thus Wilson had written in 1890;[1] thus he believed and practiced while formulating his policies toward the belligerents in the First World War.

The dominant American sentiment throughout the period of nonintervention can be summarily characterized by the single adjective "neutral." This is not to say that Americans had no opinions on the merits of the war and the claims of the opposing alliances, or that there were no differences among the popular reactions. It is simply to state the fairly obvious fact that the preponderant majority, whose opinions played a decisive role in shaping Wilson's policies, did not believe that their interests and security were vitally involved in the outcome of the war and desired to avoid participation if that were possible without sacrificing rights that should not be yielded. The prevalence and astounding vitality of neutralism, in spite of the severest provocations and all the efforts of propagandists on both sides, formed at once the unifying principle of American politics and the compelling reality with which Wilson had to deal from 1914 to 1917.

On the other hand, it would be a large error to imply that Wilson was a prisoner of the public opinion of the majority, and that his will to adopt sterner policies toward one group of belligerents or the other was paralyzed by the stronger counterforce of neutralism. Actually, the evidence points overwhelmingly to the conclusion that Wilson personally shared the opinions of the majority, in brief, that he was substantially neutral in attitude, and that his policies were controlled as much by his own convictions as by the obvious wishes of the people.

. . .

. . . it would be a difficult task to prove that Wilson's pro-British sympathies were ever controlling or indeed even very strong. At no time did he act like a man willing to take measures merely to help his supposed friends. On the contrary, all his policies were aimed either at averting American participation on Britain's side or at ending the war on terms that would have denied the spoils of victory to Britain and her allies. If this is too big an assertion to be taken on faith, then perhaps the reasons for making it will become apparent as we see the way in which Wilson executed policies toward the two leading antagonists.

All authorities, whether friendly or hostile to Wilson, would agree that the acid tests of his neutrality were the policies that he worked out and applied vis-à-vis the British from 1914 to 1917. He has been most condemned by the group of historians highly censorious of his policies, generally known as revisionists, on this score—for becoming the captive of pro-Allied influences within his administration, for condoning such sweeping British control of neutral commerce that the Germans were forced to resort to drastic countermeasures, for permitting American prosperity to become dependent upon loans and exports to the Allies, in short, for permitting a situation to develop that made it inevitable that the United States would go to war if the success of Allied arms was ever seriously threatened.

[1] T. H. Vail Motter (ed.), *Leaders of Men* (Princeton, N.J., 1952), p. 43.

Like most fallacious arguments, this one contains a certain element of plausibility. Wilson did condone a far-reaching British maritime system. American neutrality did work greatly to the benefit of the Allies. The error arises in saying that these things occurred because Wilson and his advisers necessarily wanted them to occur.

Perhaps the best way to gain a clear understanding of why Anglo-American relations developed as they did from 1914 to 1917 is to see how the policies that decisively shaped those relations emerged in several stages in response to certain pressures, events, and forces. The first stage, lasting from August, 1914, to about August, 1915, was in many ways the most critical, because the basic American response to the war and to the British maritime system was formulated then. That response was governed in the first instance by two domestic realities: the overwhelming, virtually unanimous, American desire to be neutral, and the pressures in the United States for a large measure of free trade with Britain's enemies.

In view of the prevailing American sentiment at the outbreak of the war, a policy of strict official neutrality was the only possible course for the United States government. This fact prompted the President's official proclamations of neutrality, supplemented by his appeal to the American people for impartiality in thought; the subsequent working out by the State Department of the elaborate technical rules to preserve American neutrality; and the establishment of a Joint State and Navy Neutrality Board to advise the various departments upon the correct interpretation of international law.

One cannot read the records revealing how these policies were formulated without being convinced that their authors were high-minded in their determination to be fair to both sides. Indeed, Wilson and the man who chiefly influenced him in the formulation of the rules of neutrality, Secretary of State Bryan, were so intent upon being fair to the Germans that they adopted policies during the first months of the war that were highly disadvantageous to the British, if not unneutral. One was to prevent the sale of submarine parts, and hence parts for any naval craft, by a private American firm to the British government, on the ground that such a sale would be "contrary to . . . strict neutrality." Wilson persisted in supporting Bryan in this matter, in spite of advice from Counselor Lansing and the Joint Neutrality Board to the effect that their position was contrary to international law.

Infinitely more damaging to the Allies was the administration's second effort to lean over backward in being "strictly" neutral—the ban of loans by American bankers to the belligerent governments that the President permitted Bryan to impose in August, 1914. From a technical viewpoint, the ban was not unneutral, but it was highly prejudicial to the Allies because its effect was potentially to deny them their otherwise legal right to purchase supplies in the American market. These two incidents are not to be understood as revealing any anti-British bias on the part of Wilson and Bryan, although British officials at the time were convinced that they did. I mention them only to show what an important role the administration's desire to be impartial played in the formation of policies vis-à-vis the British during the early period of American neutrality.

The other pressure shaping American policies at this time was the force of combined demands at home for the virtually free transit of American ships and goods to the European neutrals and the belligerent Central Powers. So powerful were these demands, especially from cotton growers and exporters and their spokesmen in Congress, that Wilson personally sponsored two measures highly disadvantageous to the British and unneutral in fact as well as in spirit. One was a change in the ship registry law, put into effect by an act approved August 18, 1914, which made it easy for German or other foreign shipping firms to take out American registry for their vessels. The other was a plan to establish a federal corporation to purchase German ships in American ports and to use them to carry supplies to the belligerents, particularly to Germany. Wilson applied heavy pressure to obtain congressional approval of this, the so-called ship-purchase bill, during the short term from December, 1914, to March, 1915; he failed only because of a stout senatorial filibuster.

In negotiations with the British government during the early months of the war, Wilson fought hard in response to domestic pressures to keep the channels of international commerce open to American ships and goods. He did not go as far in defense of neutral rights as some of his predecessors, but he did suggest a code so sweeping that an enforcement of it would have meant almost total destruction of the British system of maritime controls. Specifically, the President first proposed on August 6, 1914, that the belligerents adopt the rules of naval warfare laid down in the Declaration of London of 1909, a convention never ratified by Great Britain or the United States, which permitted the free transit of all goods except those obviously contraband. When the British rejected this suggestion, the President came back on October 16, proposing a compromise that would have still seriously impaired the effectiveness of British sea power. When this effort also failed, Wilson then announced that his government would assert and defend all its rights under international law and treaties.

I have described these policies and proposals because they so clearly reveal Wilson's neutral intentions and what he would have done in matters of trade had he been able to make the rules himself. But he obviously could not follow his personal preferences alone or respond only to domestic pressures. In seeking to assert and defend American neutral rights he ran head-on into a reality as important as the reality of the pressures at home. It was the British determination to use sea power to prevent American ships and goods from going to the sustenance of the German economy and military forces.

British assumption of a nearly absolute control of the seas washing western Europe began with relatively mild measures in August, 1914, and culminated in the suppression of virtually all commerce to the Central Powers in March, 1915. For the British, this was not a question of adhering to the laws of blockade or of violating them, or of doing things merely to be nice to American friends. It was a question of achieving their supreme objective, to deprive their enemies of vital raw materials and goods, without risking the alienation of the United States. The controlling fact for the British was the necessity of preserving American friendship, in order to assure the uninterrupted rhythm of the North Atlantic trade. . . .

The crucial question all along, therefore, was whether the United States, the only neutral power strong enough successfully to challenge the British measures, would acquiesce or resist to the point of threatening or using force. The American response during the formative period of neutrality was, in brief, to accept the British system and to limit action against it to a vigorous assertion of American legal rights for future adjudication. All this is too well known to require any further exposition. What is not so well understood are the reasons why Wilson and his advisers acquiesced in a solution that denied the objectives that they and a large segment of the American public demanded. These reasons may be briefly summarized, as follows:

First, the British maritime system, in spite of American allegations to the contrary, enjoyed the advantage of being legitimate and usually legal, or nearly so, by traditional criteria. It was legitimate rather than fraudulent, and legal rather than capricious or terroristic, in its major aspects because the British did in fact hold undisputed sea supremacy and were therefore able to execute their controls in an orderly fashion. In asserting their own rights, the Americans could not well deny the advantages that accrued to the British by virtue of their sea power. The British, for example, had an undoubted right to establish a blockade of the Central Powers, and the American attempt to persuade the London government to use techniques effective only in the days of the sailing ship did not have much cogency in the twentieth century.

Second, much of the success of the British in establishing their control depended upon the way in which they went about it. Had they instituted their total blockade at the outset of the war, the American reaction would undoubtedly have been violent. Instead, the British applied their controls gradually, with a careful eye upon American opinion, using the opportunities provided by recurrent crises in German-American relations to institute their severest measures.

Third, the British were careful never to offend so many American interests at one time that retaliation would have been inevitable, or any single interest powerful enough by itself to compel retaliation. . . .

Fourth, there was great significance in the language and symbolism that the British Foreign Office used in defending the measures of the Admiralty and Ministry of Blockade. By justifying their maritime system in terms of international law and the right of retaliation, and (at least before the summer of 1916) by making an honest effort to meet American objections half way when possible, the British made it almost inevitable that the Washington authorities would have to reply in the same language, thus giving a purely *legal* character to the issues involved and for the most part avoiding raising the issues of sovereignty and inherent national rights. The significance of this achievement can be seen in the conviction of Wilson and the majority of Americans that the Anglo-American disputes did involve only property rights, which should be vindicated only by an appeal to much-controverted international law. Moreover, by appealing to the American government and people in the name of friendship and by always professing their devotion to the cause of humanity, the British succeeded in evoking strong feelings of sympathy and understanding on the other side of the water.

Finally, the British were able partially to justify their own blockade measures as legitimate adaptations to a changing technology by pointing to precedents established by the Washington government itself during the American Civil War. To be sure, the British drew some incorrect analogies (as Lansing pointed out) between American and British practice; even so, their main contention—that the American government had also stretched the rules of blockade to allow for technological changes—was essentially correct.

Wilson's refusal to challenge the British maritime system, in short, to break the British blockade, was almost inevitable in view of the facts we have just reviewed, *if the President's objective was simply to maintain as best he could the neutral position of the United States.* An absolute neutrality was in any event impossible because of the total character of the war and America's importance in the world economy. It often happened that any action by the United States inevitably conferred a benefit on one side and thereby injured the other, at least indirectly. In these circumstances, neutrality often consisted of doing the things that would give the least unwarranted or undeserved advantages.

By this standard, it would have been more unneutral than neutral for Wilson to have broken the British maritime system by enforcing highly doubtful technical rights under international law. Judged by practical standards rather than by the often conflicting criteria of neutrality, Wilson's acceptance of the British system seems realistic and wise—indeed, the only choice that he could have made in the circumstances. This is true because the results of destroying the British blockade would have been the wrecking of American friendship with the two great European democracies and the probable victory of the Central Powers, without a single compensating gain for the interests and security of the United States. Only the sure achievement of some great political objective like a secure peace settlement, certainly not the winning of a commercial advantage or the defense of doubtful neutral rights, would have justified Wilson in undertaking a determined challenge to British sea power.

The second stage in Anglo-American relations, lasting from the summer of 1915 to the late spring of 1916, saw the development of the natural economic consequence of the American adjustment to tightening British control of the seas. That consequence was the burgeoning of an enormous war trade between the United States and the Allies. The United States became the storehouse and armory of the Allies neither because there was any conspiracy on the part of certain pro-Allied leaders in Washington to make American prosperity dependent upon an Allied victory, nor because American businessmen and bankers were willing to incur the risks of war in order to increase their profits. The United States became the storehouse of the Allies for the simple reason that Great Britain and not Germany controlled the seas.

The war trade itself was entirely neutral. Indeed, any action by the United States government to impede it, unless undertaken for overriding political motives, would have been grossly prejudicial and unneutral. If it had been permitted to develop in a normal way, this commerce would have raised no important problems in the relations of the United States with the Allies. A problem of the first magnitude did arise, however, because the

President, in the summer of 1914, had permitted Secretary Bryan to enforce his own private moral views by imposing a ban on loans by American bankers to the belligerents.

. . .

Bryan's ban could not survive the development of the war trade on a large scale because, in the first place, it (like the Embargo of 1808) was potentially nearly as disastrous to the United States as to the Allies. American material well-being was in large measure dependent upon foreign trade, and particularly upon trade with the Allied world. Such trade was possible during wartime only if American businessmen were willing to do for the Allies what they always did for solvent customers in temporary straits, namely, sell them goods on credit.

The most important reason that Bryan's embargo could not survive, however, was that it was an essentially unneutral policy that impeded the growth of the chief economic consequence of American neutrality, the legitimate war trade. The credit embargo and the war trade could not both survive. The former gave way because Wilson finally realized that it would be as unneutral to interfere with the extension of credit as it would be to stop the flow of goods. Bryan's ban was in a sense, therefore, a casualty chiefly of American neutrality.

. . .

The second stage in Anglo-American relations also witnessed the apparent convergence of the diplomatic policies of the two countries on the high level. During the summer and autumn of 1915 Colonel Edward M. House, Wilson's confidant and principal adviser on foreign policy, conceived a plan by which the American and British leaders would join hands to press for an end to the war through Wilson's meditation. The British Foreign Secretary, Sir Edward Grey, replied that his government would co-operate only if the Washington administration were willing to go beyond simple mediation and would agree to join a postwar international organization established for the purpose of effecting disarmament, maintaining freedom of the seas, and preserving peace. Wilson hopefully consented, and House went to Berlin, Paris, and London in January, 1916, to lay the diplomatic basis of mediation.

In London, House worked out in documentary form with Grey and the other members of the British Cabinet the specific terms of Anglo-American co-operation. Initialed by House and Grey on February 22, 1916, and known as the House-Grey Memorandum or Agreement, this document declared that President Wilson was ready, upon hearing from England and France that the time was ripe, to propose that a conference be called to end the war. Should the Allies accept and Germany refuse the invitation, the United States would "probably" enter the war against Germany. Should the conference meet and Germany refuse to accept a reasonable settlement, then the United States would also "probably" enter the war on the Allied side.

To the so-called revisionists the conclusion of the House-Grey Agreement is irrefutable proof that Wilson had abandoned neutrality and meant to take the country into war at the first opportunity. . . .

.   .   .

The revisionists are correct in asserting that the conclusion of the House-Grey Agreement marked the beginning of a new and epochal phase in Wilson's policies toward the belligerents. Otherwise they have missed the entire meaning of the affair, for the House-Grey Agreement was in Wilson's purpose *not an instrument of intervention, but a means of averting American involvement*. The truth of this important generalization will perhaps become evident when we recall the realities of the American diplomatic situation during late 1915 and early 1916, and when we understand Wilson's motives and intentions in devising a solution.

The overshadowing reality confronting the makers of American foreign policy at this time was the grave possibility of war with Germany over the submarine issue. It caused Wilson and Lansing, for example, to abandon ambitious plans for further intervention in Mexico. It speeded the American acquiescence in the British maritime system. Most important, it prompted the President and his advisers to search for ways to avert the rupture that might draw the United States into the maelstrom.

One way out of the predicament was to come to a full understanding with the German government over the issues involved in the submarine controversy. This is what Lansing attempted to do and almost succeeded in accomplishing during his negotiations over the *Lusitania* affair. Another way out and a surer means of averting the peril of American involvement in the future was to bring the war itself to an end through Wilson's mediation. It seemed at the time that the best hope of peace lay in Anglo-American co-operation for a peace of compromise, specifically in the kind of co-operation detailed in the House-Grey Agreement.

Thus Wilson approved this plan of mediation, but with a full realization that certain obligations and risks were involved. There was the necessity of giving positive assurances to the Allies, for they would have been at a fatal disadvantage in a peace conference without American support, in view of the strategic advantages that the Germans then enjoyed on the Continent of Europe. There was, moreover, the risk of war if the Germans refused to approve an armistice or proved to be unreasonable at a peace conference after agreeing to end the fighting. However, Wilson gave the necessary assurances in the belief that the risk of war involved was insignificant as compared to the greater danger of hostilities with Germany if he could not somehow bring the war to an end. This, then, was his dominant motive in sending House to Europe in January, 1916, and in approving the House-Grey Agreement at the cost of Lansing's proposed compromise for submarine warfare.

In the final analysis, our judgment of Wilson's mediation plans must depend upon the kind of settlement that he had in mind and for which he was willing to run the risk of war in order to achieve peace. It is clear that Wilson envisaged a "reasonable" settlement based upon recognition that the war was a stalemate and upon a return for the most part of the *status quo ante bellum*. It meant, Wilson also hoped, the kind of settlement in which all the belligerents would forego annexations and indemnities, put aside past differences, and join hands with the United States to create a new international order. In his final discussions with the British Cabinet, Colonel House made it clear that this, and this only, was the kind of settlement that Wilson was prepared to use the House-Grey Agreement to achieve. In other words, as House told the British leaders, the President would "throw the weight of the United States on the side of those wanting a just settlement—a settlement which would make another such war impossible."[2]

.   .   .

In the circumstances prevailing during the late autumn and early winter of 1916–1917, the Germans had three possible choices of policy. These were, first, to join hands with Wilson in a drive for peace generally on the President's terms; second, to make a limited bid for victory by intensifying the submarine war at the risk of alienating the United States; and, third, to make a supreme bid for victory by instituting a total blockade of all commerce to the British Isles. The situation from the German point of view was such that this choice would not depend upon anything that Wilson did or said, unless, of course, the President could be used as a German pawn or was willing openly to support Germany's war objectives. The German decision would depend entirely upon a realistic evaluation of the possibilities of the military situation, that is, upon whether the Imperial army and navy were capable of imposing terms upon the enemies of the Reich.

Discussions of these possibilities had begun in Germany in earnest in mid-August, 1916, as a consequence of the urgent demand of the Admiralty for permission to resume unrestricted submarine attacks in the near future. The civilian and military leaders rejected the demand at a conference at Pless Castle on August 31, 1916, on the ground that the navy did not have enough submarines to enforce a blockade and that it would obviously be foolhardy to risk American retaliation at this time. Actually, it was the new commanders of the army, Generals Paul von Hindenburg and Erich von Ludendorff, who made this decision. The military situation, they said, was too menacing to justify assuming the risk of war with America. There was heavy Allied pressure on the western front; above all, there was the grave danger of an Allied invasion of the Balkans, which might cause the collapse of Austria-Hungary.

Events of the late summer and early autumn combined inexorably to create a new situation in which a different decision would be made. First, the great British offensive on the Somme, aimed at tearing a huge hole in the German lines and a thrust into Belgium, failed; as a result, the German position in the West was again secure. Second, after dawdling in the matter for nearly two years, the Admiralty had finally launched a large program of submarine construction and the training of crews; by the end of the year it would be possible to talk in terms of dealing England a death-

---

[2] The Diary of Edward M. House, February 14, 1916, MS in the Yale University Library.

blow underseas. Finally, the army's counteroffensive against the Russians and its smashing victory over Rumania removed all cause for concern about the security of Austria-Hungary and the Balkans.

.   .   .

Almost formless at the outset of the war, German war objectives had grown in a direct ratio to the progress of the Imperial armies in the field. By the late autumn of 1916 the military situation was so favorable and the potentialities of an effective submarine blockade were so great that the German leaders inevitably abandoned thought of a compromise peace and began to plan for a settlement that would remove all threats to future German security. As drawn up by [Theobald von] Bethmann-Hollweg, amended by Hindenburg, and approved by the German and Austrian governments, the German peace terms were breathtaking in scope. They included, in the East, the establishment of a Polish kingdom under German control and German annexation of Lithuania and Courland on the Baltic; in the West, destruction of British naval supremacy, an indemnity from England and France, the annexation of strategic parts of France and Belgium, and the reconstruction of Belgium as a German vassal; and, overseas, the annexation of all or part of the Belgian Congo. To be sure, these were the maximum German objectives at the time; a realization of even part of them, however, would have secured German domination of Europe for years to come.

This was the kind of settlement that the German leaders were determined to obtain through peace negotiations. They knew that they could never obtain such terms, or even a large part of them, through Wilson's mediation. They knew that Wilson would demand, among other things, the restitution of a free and independent Belgium and perhaps the return of Alsace-Lorraine to France. Acceptance of Wilson's mediation and a compromise peace, even one based entirely upon the *status quo ante bellum,* would, in German eyes, be tantamount to defeat, for it would mean the frustration of everything for which so much German blood had been shed. As a consequence, no German leader, civilian or military, ever seriously considered accepting Wilson's *mediation.* During all the high-level discussions about peace plans, no German leader ever seriously mentioned such a possibility. On the contrary, all German diplomatic efforts were concentrated upon the goal of preventing Wilson's mediation, or "meddling," as the Germans called it.

This statement needs some clarification. The Germans were eager, almost desperately eager, to win the President's support for their peace plans. They wanted Wilson's help in forcing the Allies to the peace table at a time when all the odds favored the winning of a German peace. They were willing to give pledges of postwar disarmament and membership in a League of Nations, if this were necessary to win the President's support. But they did not want, indeed, they would not permit, Wilson's mediation or even his presence at the peace conference.

Wilson did not know these facts during the first stages of the peace discussions, but the truth finally came out in January, 1917, when the President begged the Foreign Office in Berlin to come out frankly and fully in acceptance of his mediation. Then the German leaders had to say that they would welcome Wilson's co-operation only after the peace treaty had been signed, not at the conference of belligerents itself. Shrewdly perceiving the German intentions, Wilson refused to be a pawn in Berlin's game.

Wilson's refusal meant that the German leaders would now proceed to consider means of achieving through force what they had failed to win by their inept diplomacy. The High Command had already made the decision by late December; it was confirmed by a conference of all leaders at Pless Castle on January 9, 1917. That decision was, in brief, to begin unrestricted submarine warfare against all shipping, belligerent and neutral, in the approaches to the British Isles and the eastern Mediterranean after January 31.

It was easily the most fateful decision made by any government during the course of the war, and the German records fully reveal the reasons for its adoption. It now seemed beyond all doubt that the navy had sufficient power to establish an effective submarine blockade of the British Isles, for it could send between twenty-five and thirty submarines into western waters by February 1, 1917, and a growing number after that date. Moreover, other circumstances, particularly a short wheat crop in the New World, augured well for the success of the blockade. Indeed, on a basis of elaborate calculations the Admiralty spokesmen guaranteed absolutely to reduce the British to actual starvation within five months after the submarine blockade began. If this were possible, then Germany had it within her power to win a total victory and a settlement that would establish the Reich in an unassailable position. To the military leaders, who had despaired of winning the war in the trenches, it was an opportunity that could not be refused.*

Fear of American belligerency no longer had any effect on German policy in such an atmosphere of confident expectation. The German leaders all assumed that a wholesale attack on American maritime commerce would drive the United States into the war. These same leaders also concluded that American belligerency would not make any difference. On the contrary, American participation would have certain positive advantages, for it would mean the diversion of huge quantities of food and matériel to an American army in training during the very period when the U-boats would be winning the war on the seas. But in any event, American participation was in the circumstances necessary to the success of the German plans, because the submarine blockade could succeed only if it were total, that is, only if American as well as British ships were prevented from carrying life-giving supplies to the beleaguered British Isles. Of course, no German leader wanted recklessly to provoke an American declaration of war; all Germans, however, were prepared to incur American belligerency if they could win the war by so doing.

---

* *Editors' note.* "Additional work in German sources," Link later wrote, "has persuaded me that the decision was born not only of hope but of desperate despair occasioned by the Allied rebuff of the German peace offer and the conviction that Germany would inevitably lose the war if she could not obtain some decision by 1917" (*Wilson the Diplomatist*, 2nd ed. [1963], p. xiv).

It was the only decision that seemed possible to the Imperial military commanders. No nation involved in a desperate war for survival will fail to use a weapon, whether it be the submarine or the atomic bomb, when that weapon promises to bring quick and overwhelming victory. But the submarine campaign brought catastrophic defeat to Germany and misfortunes unnumbered to the world because it destroyed all possibility of a peace of reconciliation. . . .

There remains only one further question, whether the Germans decided to go the whole length and to attack American shipping because they believed that the United States would enter the war in any case if they violated the *Sussex* pledge. In other words, did the Germans conclude that there was little point in confining unrestricted attacks to armed merchantmen or to *belligerent* shipping, armed and unarmed, because any deviations from the rules of cruiser warfare would provoke American intervention? This is an academic question, but an important one, because the answer to it sheds additional light upon Wilson's intentions and the German choice of alternatives.

There is much evidence that by the end of 1916 Wilson was prepared to effect a sharp diplomatic withdrawal if both belligerent groups refused to heed his peace appeal. He knew that if the war proceeded the belligerents would use every means at their command to end it, and that this would mean a severe intensification of the struggle on the seas, to the further detriment of neutral rights. It seems almost certain that he would have accepted unrestricted submarine attacks against *armed* merchantmen. On January 10, 1917, the German government informed the State Department that its submarines would hereafter attack armed merchant ships without warning, because these ships had all been offensively armed and instructed to attack submarines. . . .

We can go further and say that it seems also possible that Wilson would not have broken diplomatic relations over unrestricted submarine attacks against all *belligerent* merchantmen, exclusive, perhaps, of passenger liners. Much would have depended upon American public opinion, which then seemed overwhelmingly opposed to war for the vindication of the right of Americans to travel on belligerent vessels. Much would have depended upon the President himself, but his determination to avoid participation had never been stronger than at this time. "There will be no war," he told Colonel House on January 4, 1917. "This country does not intend to become involved in this war. We are the only one of the great white nations that is free from war to-day, and it would be a crime against civilization for us to go in."

The Germans never seriously considered adopting these limited alternatives, not because they believed that any infraction of the *Sussex* pledge would automatically provoke American intervention, but because they thought that they could win only by enforcing a total blockade. But if it is true that Wilson would not have gone to war if the Germans had confined their attacks to belligerent merchantmen, then we are confronted with one of the supreme ironies of history. By doing the thing that seemed the best guarantee of victory, the Germans assured their own defeat. By failing to adopt the limited policies, they threw away their one chance of success, which might well have come after the collapse of Russia and a devastating attack on Allied commerce.

President Wilson's response to the German blockade proclamation lends additional evidence to my theory that the United States might not have broken diplomatic relations if the Germans had exempted American shipping from the wrath of their underseas campaign. The German Ambassador delivered copies of the German blockade announcement to Lansing and House on January 31, 1917. Wilson did not act like a man who had a predetermined course of action in mind. Even in the face of a German declaration of war against American commerce, he hesitated to take any step that might lead to war. He was willing, he told Lansing, to go to almost any lengths "rather than to have this nation actually involved in the conflict."

There was, however, only one decision that Wilson could now make. No great power could continue to maintain diplomatic intercourse with a government that promised to destroy its shipping and slaughter its citizens in violation of national and treaty rights and solemn pledges. Small neutral states like Holland and Norway had no choice but to suffer under protest, but a great nation like the United States had responsibilities commensurate with its power and influence. Continuing to maintain relations with Berlin after the issuance of the blockade proclamation of January 31 would have meant nothing less than Wilson's condoning of the German assault upon American rights and lives. The remarkable thing is not that Wilson severed diplomatic relations as he did on February 3, but that he hesitated at all.

To engage in a debate at this point over the reasons for Wilson's severance of diplomatic relations with Germany would obscure a development that was vastly more important than the handing of passports to the German Ambassador. It was Wilson's announcement, made in an address to Congress on February 3, 1917, that the United States would accept the new submarine blockade and would not go to war, in spite of the break in relations, provided that the Germans did not carry out their threat to destroy American ships and lives. This is the clear meaning of the following paragraph in Wilson's address:

> Notwithstanding this unexpected action of the German Government, . . . I refuse to believe that it is the intention of the German authorities to do in fact what they have warned us they will feel at liberty to do. I cannot bring myself to believe that they will indeed pay no regard to the ancient friendship between their people and our own or to the solemn obligations which have been exchanged between them and destroy *American ships and take the lives of American citizens* in the wilful prosecution of the ruthless naval programme they have announced their intention to adopt. Only actual overt acts on their part can make me believe it even now.

Wilson then announced what he would do in the event that his confidence in the "sobriety and prudent foresight" of the German leaders proved unfounded: "I shall take the liberty of coming again before the Congress, to ask that authority be given me to use any means that may be necessary for the protection of our seamen and our people in the prosecution of their peaceful and legitimate errands on the high seas."[3]

In short, Wilson was saying that he would follow a policy of watchful waiting and govern his future policies in response to what the Germans did. If they spared American ships and lives, presumably upon American ships of all categories and upon belligerent unarmed passenger vessels, then he would do nothing. If they attacked American ships, then he would defend them by an armed neutrality. This, obviously, was not the language of war, such as Lansing had urged the President to use. It was the language of a man determined to avoid such full-fledged commitment as a war declaration would imply, willing in the worst event only to protect "our seamen and our people in the prosecution of their peaceful and legitimate errands on the high seas."

Throughout the first weeks of February, 1917, the President waited patiently to see what the future would bring. At any moment the German government could have removed the possibility of war with the United States by declaring that it would respect American shipping and take all possible care to protect American lives on belligerent ships. But when the Swiss Minister in Washington offered to serve as an intermediary in any discussions between Berlin and Washington, the German Foreign Office replied that not even the re-establishment of diplomatic relations with the United States would prompt the Imperial government to reconsider "its resolution to completely stop by submarines all importations from abroad by its enemies."

In spite of the obvious German determination to enforce a total blockade, Wilson refused to permit the defense departments to make any important preparations for war. He would not do anything to cause the Germans to think that he was contemplating hostilities. As the days passed, however, the pressures for an end to watchful waiting and for the adoption of at least an armed neutrality mounted almost irresistibly. Members of the Cabinet, shipowners, a large majority of the newspapers, and a growing body of public opinion combined in the demand that the President either convoy merchantmen or arm them with naval guns and crews. Still protesting that the people wanted him to avert any risk of war, Wilson gave in to their wishes on about February 25. Going to Congress the following day to request authority to arm merchantmen and to "employ any other instrumentalities or methods that may be necessary and adequate to protect our ships and our people in their legitimate and peaceful pursuits on the seas," he carefully explained that he was not contemplating war or any steps that might lead to war. "I merely request," he said,

> that you will accord me by your own vote and definite bestowal the means and the authority to safeguard in practice the right of a great people who are at peace and who are desirous of exercising none but the rights of peace to follow the pursuits of peace in quietness and good will—rights recognized time out of mind by all the civilized nations of the world. No course

[3] Ray S. Baker and William E. Dodd (eds.), *The Public Papers of Woodrow Wilson, The New Democracy* (2 vols.; New York, 1926), II, 425. Italics added.

of my choosing or of theirs will lead to war. War can come only by the wil-ful acts and aggressions of others.[4]

Although a small group of senators prevented approval of a bill au-thorizing Wilson to arm merchantmen, the President took such action any-way on March 9, 1917. At the same time, he called Congress into special session for April 16, 1917, presumably in order to ask the legislative branch to sanction a more elaborate program of armed neutrality, which he set to work with his advisers in the Navy Department to devise.

By the middle of March, therefore, it seemed that Wilson had made his decision in favor of a limited defensive war on the seas. "We stand firm in armed neutrality," he declared, for example, in his second inaugural ad-dress on March 5, "since it seems that in no other way we can demonstrate what it is we insist upon and cannot forego." Yet on April 2 (he had mean-while convened Congress for this earlier date), scarcely more than a month after he had uttered these words, he stood before Congress and asked for a declaration of full-fledged war. What events occurred, what forces were at work, what pressures were applied during this brief interval to cause Wil-son to make the decision that he had been trying so desperately to avoid? We should perhaps put the question in a less positive way, as follows: What caused the President to abandon armed neutrality and to *accept* the decision for war?

There was first the fact that from the end of February to the end of March the Germans gave full evidence of their determination to press a relentless, total attack against all ships passing through the war zones that enveloped western Europe. The sinking of the British liner *Laconia* with-out warning on February 25 and with loss of American life, the ruthless de-struction of three American merchantmen (*City of Memphis, Illinois,* and *Vigilancia*)* on March 18, and the relentless attacks against the vessels of other neutral nations, to say nothing of the slashing attacks against Allied merchant shipping, removed all doubt in Wilson's mind about the deadly seriousness of the German intention to conduct total warfare against all commerce and human life within the broad war zones.

The more the character of the submarine blockade became apparent, the stronger the conviction grew in the President's mind that armed neu-trality was neither a sufficient response physically, nor a proper or legally possible one. He explained this conviction in his war message:

> It is a war against all nations. . . . The challenge is to all mankind. When I addressed the Congress on the 26th of February last, I thought that it would suffice to assert our neutral rights with arms, our right to use the seas against unlawful interference, our right to keep our people safe against unlawful violence. But armed neutrality, it now appears, is impracticable. Because submarines are in effect outlaws when used as the German subma-rines have been used against merchant shipping, it is impossible to defend ships against their attacks as the law of nations has assumed that merchant-men would defend themselves. . . . It is common prudence in such circum-

[4] *Ibid.,* pp. 428–32.
* *Editors' note.* "Only the *Illinois* and the *Vigilancia*," Link later noted, "were sunk without warning; the *City of Memphis* was destroyed after warning and evacuation of crew" (*Wilson the Diplomatist,* 2nd ed. [1963], p. xv).

stances, grim necessity indeed, to endeavour to destroy them before they show their own intention. They must be dealt with upon sight, if dealt with at all. The German Government denies the right of neutrals to use arms at all within the areas of the sea which it has proscribed, even in the defense of rights which no modern publicist has ever before questioned their right to defend. The intimation is conveyed that the armed guards which we have placed on our merchant ships will be treated as beyond the pale of law and subject to be dealt with as pirates would be. Armed neutrality is ineffectual enough at best; in such circumstances and in the face of such pretensions it is worse than ineffectual; it is likely only to produce what it was meant to prevent; it is practically certain to draw us into the war without either the rights or the effectiveness of belligerents.[5]

This passage, in my opinion, reveals the *immediate* reason why Wilson made his decision for war. It was simply that the German assault upon American lives and property was so overwhelming and so flagrant that the only possible way to cope with it was to claim the status of a belligerent in order to strike at the sources of German power. "I would be inclined to adopt . . . [armed neutrality]," the President wrote only two days before he delivered his war message, "indeed, as you know, I had already adopted it, but this is the difficulty: . . . To make even the measures of defense legitimate we must obtain the status of belligerents."[6]

Certainly Wilson had convinced himself that this was true, but I have a strong suspicion that he would have stood doggedly by his first decision to limit American action to a defense of rights on the seas if this decision had not been overridden by convictions, events, pressures, and ambitions that were themselves decisive in Wilson's final shift from armed neutrality to war, in forcing him to the conclusion that the *immediate* circumstances left the United States with no choice but full-scale participation.

One of the most important of these factors was the subtlest and the one for which the least direct evidence can be adduced. It was Wilson's apparent fear that the threat of a German victory imperiled the balance of power and all his hopes for the future reconstruction of the world community. We must be careful here not to misinterpret his thoughts and motives. There is little evidence that he accepted the decision for war because he thought that a German victory would seriously endanger American security, because he wanted to preserve Anglo-American control of the North Atlantic sea lanes, or because he desired to maintain the traditional balance of European power because it served American interests. Nor is there any convincing evidence that Wilson's attitude toward the objectives of the rival alliances had changed by the time that he made his final decision.*

[5] *Papers Relating to the Foreign Relations of the United States, 1917, Supplement 1, The World War* (Washington, 1931), pp. 196–97.

[6] Wilson to Matthew Hale, March 31, 1917, Wilson Papers, Library of Congress.

* *Editors' note.* In 1963, Link modified these judgments. He doubted that the President knew, or was influenced by the fear, that the Central Powers were about to win the war. Nor is there any evidence "that Wilson was importantly motivated by considerations of national security in his own decision for war." Link "would have given greater emphasis . . . to Wilson's conviction that the war was in its final stages, American belligerency would have the effect of shortening, not prolonging the war, and belligerency had the advantage of guaranteeing him an important role in peacemaking" (*Wilson the Diplomatist*, 2nd ed. [1963], p. xv).

On the other hand, there was now a great and decisive difference in the relative position of the belligerents: The Allies seemed about to lose the war and the Central Powers about to win it. This, almost certainly, was a governing factor in Wilson's willingness to think in terms of war. Germany, he told Colonel House, was a madman who must be curbed. A German victory meant a peace of domination and conquest; it meant the end of all Wilson's dreams of helping to build a secure future.

As the President pondered America's duty at this juncture in history, the answer must have seemed obvious to him—to accept belligerency, because now only through belligerency could the United States fulfill its mission to insure a just and lasting peace of reconciliation. This could be accomplished only by preventing a German victory and only by the assertion of such power and influence among the Allies as would come to the United States by virtue of its sacrifice of blood and treasure.

If the immediate events made a war resolution necessary, then the goal of a righteous peace was the objective that justified full-scale participation in Wilson's mind and raised that effort to a high and noble plane. It was, therefore, not war in anger that he advocated, not war sheerly in defense of national rights, but, as he put it in his war message,

> [war] for democracy, for the right of those who submit to authority to have a voice in their own governments, for the rights and liberties of small nations, for a universal dominion of right by such a concert of free peoples as shall bring peace and safety to all nations and make the world itself at last free.

The combined weight of official and public opinion was another pressure meanwhile driving Wilson toward acceptance of the decision for war. It was a fact of no little consequence that by the end of March every important member of the administration, including those members of the Cabinet who had heretofore opposed any bellicose measures, urged the President to admit that a state of war with Germany in fact existed. Public opinion had remained stubbornly pacific until near the end of February, 1917. Then the publication of the Zimmermann telegram, in which the German government proposed to Mexico a war alliance against the United States, the sinking of the *Laconia*, and above all, the destruction of American ships in the war zones after mid-March generated a demand for war that grew with mounting crescendo in all sections and among all classes, until it seemed beyond doubt to be a national and a majority demand. It was further stimulated by news of the downfall of the czarist regime and the establishment of a provisional republican government in Russia—news that convinced many wavering Americans that the Allies were indeed fighting for democracy and also changed overnight the large and influential American Jewish community from a position of strong hostility toward the Allies to one of friendship.

This was all a development of profound importance for a leader as keenly sensitive to public opinion as was Woodrow Wilson. He could have joined forces with the large antiwar minority to resist the demand for war; indeed, he probably would have done so had he been convinced that it was the wise and right thing to do. The point is not, therefore, that public opinion *forced* Wilson to accept the decision for war, but that it facilitated doing what Wilson for other reasons now thought was necessary and right to do.

All this is said without any intention of implying that Wilson ever *wanted* war. The agony of his soul was great as he moved through the dark valley of his doubts. He had no illusions about the merits of the conflict into which he and his people were being drawn. He saw the risks of intervention, both to his own nation and to the world, with remarkable clarity. But he could devise no alternative; and he set aside his doubts in the hope that acting now as a belligerent, with all the power and idealism of the American people sustaining him, he could achieve objectives to justify the misery of mankind.

Wilsonian Liberalism, the League of Nations, and the German Problem

N. Gordon Levin, Jr.

N. Gordon Levin of Amherst College, in his volume
*Woodrow Wilson and World Politics: America's
Response to War and Revolution* (1968), analyzes
Wilson's thought and action as an integrated effort to
establish a liberal-capitalist international order. Wilson,
in Levin's conception, opposed the imperialism of
Germany and the revolutionary theories of Bolshevik
Russia, and sought to spread the blessings of the
American way of life to the rest of the world. His
aim was to end colonialism and militarism, stop
revolution, establish self-determination, advance
capitalism, create and expand free trade, and eliminate
power politics.

Levin's subtle analysis seeks to transcend the dispute
as to whether Wilson was a realist or idealist by
establishing that these aspects of thought can be
integrated within the ideology of promoting a liberal-
capitalist world order. For Wilson, the national
interest and liberal ideology dictated the same policies:
internationalism and antiimperialism. In the Wilsonian
world order, America would flourish amid peace and
international law, and the nation would achive a
preeminent moral and economic position. Put simply,
what served America served humanity, and vice versa.

Levin emphasizes that Wilson's ideology contained contradictions and ambiguities. In dealing with the problem of Germany at the Paris Peace Conference, for example, the President was torn between the wish to integrate a democratic Germany into the new world order and the desire to punish Germany for its sins. Among the reasons for this contradiction, according to Levin, is that Wilson feared the strength of the German right in the postwar years, but he was unwilling to risk having the right destroyed by the left, for that could mean Bolshevism and the loss of Germany's participation in the (liberal) world order. Nor could Wilson be sure that German liberalism would be able or willing to control the right. Given the conflict between Wilson's desires for integration and punishment of Germany, and his fears of the resurgent right, he ended by treating Germany as a suspect nation, assumed that she was guilty and should pay substantial reparations, and thereby, as Levin notes, contributed to the "self-fulfilling prophecy about the character of the postwar German State" (p. 158).

Levin also emphasizes that Wilson, in his effort to involve America in world politics as a moderate reformer, risked having her succumb to power politics or become simply another nation struggling to advance her own interests. The League of Nations, as Levin explains in the following section from *Woodrow Wilson and World Politics*, allowed Wilson to resolve this problem.

Levin's study, which he acknowledges was influenced by the work of Louis Hartz, William Appleman Williams, and Arno Mayer, has received a surprisingly favorable reception in view of its left framework. Undoubtedly one reason for this is its calm tone and its respect for Wilson. Another reason may be that Levin only occasionally mentions economic expansion as a part of the Wilsonian ideology and therefore avoids provoking the ire of historians who are prepared to accept Levin's interpretation of the Wilsonian world order in the abstract terms that he employs. By not stressing the American quest for markets or economic penetration of colonial areas, Levin makes his study more

Wilsonian Liberalism, the League of Nations, and the German Problem. From *Woodrow Wilson and World Politics: America's Response to War and Revolution* by N. Gordon Levin, Jr. (New York: Oxford University Press, 1968), pp. 171–82. Copyright © 1968 by Oxford University Press, Inc. Reprinted by permission of Oxford University Press.

acceptable to many historians than, say, the related
analysis of Wilsonianism advanced by William
Appleman Williams. Perhaps Levin's analysis reflects
a certain ambivalence on his part about the hierarchy
of values within the Wilsonian ideology and about
whether American economic expansion meant
noncolonial imperialism—an ambivalence that many of
his readers apparently resolved in accord with their
own preconceptions and desires.

. . . *I*n its efforts to check Allied extremism and to
provide for the reintegration of a liberalized Germany into a new non-rev-
olutionary world order, the Wilson Administration was partly inhibited by
the fact that the President, and many of his advisers, retained a punitive and
a suspicious orientation toward the postwar German polity. Yet, even when
they did disagree on German questions with the British and French, Wilsonians were also inhibited from more direct conflict with the Allies by the
fear that an overt U.S.-Entente break might somehow give encouragement
to manifest and latent revolutionary-socialist tendencies in postwar Europe.
It followed, therefore, that to whatever extent the President and his advisers
did choose to oppose Allied, and especially French, extremism at Paris, the
Americans were not prepared to rely on the tactic of radical mass mobilization against imperialism. Instead, Wilsonians sought to moderate Allied policies behind the scenes by the implicit and explicit use of America's one
viable weapon: namely the threat of the possible withdrawal of the economic, political, and military power of the United States from the immense
task of· guaranteeing the final European settlement. It must be noted, however, that, paradoxically, the employment of such tactics meant that every
concession on the German question which the Administration won in negotiation with the Entente only served to bind American power more securely
to the task of guaranteeing the peace settlement. The willingness of Wilson
and House, despite the reintegrationist objections of Lansing, White, and
Bliss, to join Great Britain and France in a special anti-German security
treaty in return for French concessions to moderation in Rhineland negotiations was the classic case in point. In sum, then, part of the American
conception of the League of Nations involved anti-German security considerations.

For their own part, unlike Wilson and his advisers, the postwar leaders
of France saw the League only as a *de facto* military alliance to protect
France from Germany.[1] The French would accept moderation of their demands in the Rhineland only after the United States and Great Britain

---

[1] David H. Miller, *Drafting of the Covenant*, I, pp. 243–60; R. S. Baker, *Woodrow Wilson and World Settlement*, III, pp. 236–7; *Foreign Relations: Paris Peace Conference, 1919*, I, p. 335; *FR, PPC, 1919*, III, p. 301; George Noble, *Policies and Opinions*, pp. 103–4, 136–47.

agreed to sign a special security treaty guaranteeing France against unprovoked German aggression.[2] Thus, so deeply interrelated at Paris were the Wilsonian reintegrationist and punitive orientations toward Germany that, whatever the inherent tension between them, both these approaches often coexisted in the Wilsonian response to such issues as the reparations tangle and the question of the League and French security.

In any event, there is no doubt that on one level Wilsonians were definitely prepared to conceive of the League partly as an instrument for enforcing the final peace terms on Germany, notwithstanding whatever inherent contradiction such a view might involve for the Administration's equally strong desire to reintegrate a democratized Germany into a nonrevolutionary liberal-capitalist world order. In this sense, the Wilsonian orientation toward the League tended to merge well with the world views of such leading British statesmen as Lloyd George, who envisioned the absorption of American power permanently into the maintenance of a peace settlement in Europe which would fuse punitive and reintegrationist features in an uneasy balance.[3] It is also interesting to observe that, during 1919, many security-conscious elements of the French Center and Right moved from opposition to later support of the President, as it became clear that he meant to pledge American power to the protection of France and to the maintenance of the severe peace settlement through the League of Nations and the related security treaty.[4]

Yet if, during 1919, the French and British leaders moved to support Wilson and the League, it is true that, conversely, Europe's democratic-socialists and Left-liberals tended to move from initial support of the President to an increased rejection of Wilsonian policies. Desperate in their search of a way to end imperialism without socialist revolution, many democratic-socialists hoped that Wilson would create a League which, rather than being made up exclusively of the representatives of various foreign offices, would instead reflect the diversity of class and party interests in each member country, and would, thereby, provide a world forum capable both of being strongly influenced by socialist values and of transcending the nation-state system of world politics.[5] However, having underestimated Wilson's loyalty to liberal-nationalist legitimacy, his distaste for any form of socialist politics, and his desire to control Germany by reliance on Allied armed power rather than through more radical means, the democratic-socialists were necessarily disillusioned by the actual League of Nations, which emerged as a union of governments implicitly pledged, in part, to enforce an anti-German peace.[6] Radicals could see clearly that, far from

[2] Harold Nelson, *Land and Power*, pp. 198–248; Lewis Yates, *U.S. and French Security*, pp. 45–63.

[3] Nelson, *Land and Power*, pp. 51–2, 95–7, 138–9, 212–13, 216–20, 248, 366–8, 375, 379–80; Seth Tillman, *Anglo-American Relations*, pp. 394–9; Henry Winkler, *League Movement*, pp. 241–2.

[4] Noble, *Policies and Opinions*, pp. 124–5, 363, 367, 375–6, 388, n. 112, 406–9; Allan Nevins, *Henry White, Thirty Years of American Diplomacy*, p. 477.

[5] Carl Brand, *British Labor*, pp. 246–8; Winkler, *League Movement*, pp. 172–4, 187–9, 192–3; Austin Van der Slice, *Labor, Diplomacy, and Peace*, p. 322.

[6] Noble, *Policies and Opinions*, p. 411; Brand, *British Labor*, pp. 250–54; Stephen Bonsal, *Unfinished Business*, p. 166.

ending such contradictions in world politics as the German question by any sort of revolutionary transformation, the League created by the statesmen at Paris was itself partially based on those very contradictions.

Within the Wilsonian delegation itself, at Paris, a critical approach toward the postwar Allied-American political agreements also developed among such ardent reintegrationists as Lansing, Bliss, White, and Hoover. Convinced of the necessity strongly to oppose the Allies in the interests of a moderate settlement which would strengthen Germany as a bastion of liberal political and economic stability, these committed reintegrationists were often fearful that, in secret negotiations, House and Wilson would allow American power to be absorbed fully by the Allies into the maintenance of a severely anti-German peace capable of producing war or social revolution.[7] Lansing, for one, even went so far as to be deeply critical of the League of Nations, which he saw as basically an alliance of the victorious powers formed primarily to enforce harsh peace terms on Germany.[8] Lansing had envisioned instead a League with no real powers of enforcement which, by immediately including a liberalized Germany and by bringing all nations to pledge allegiance to the principles of liberal-internationalism on an equalitarian basis, could not have implicitly become a postwar extension of the Entente alliance.[9] In part, then, Lansing, Hoover, and Bliss became somewhat "isolationist" in their reactions to events at Paris, in that they sought to keep America free from entangling economic and political ties to the Allies. Yet, their "isolationism" was always ambivalent at best, since these ardent reintegrationists also hoped, in their own way, to make possible, under the guidance of a liberal-exceptionalist America uncontaminated by power politics, the creation of a more inclusive international system of political and economic liberalism, safe from either traditional imperialism or Bolshevism.

It is true that at Paris neither Wilson nor House was indifferent either to general reintegrationist criticism of Allied policy or to the desire of the most committed American reintegrationists to defend America's political and economic freedom against possible Allied absorption. At the same time, and to a greater extent than Lansing, Bliss or White, both Wilson and

[7] Lansing MSS Diary, Apr. 7, 1919; Lansing, "Confidential Memoranda and Notes, Feb. 3, Mar. 7, 16, 20, Apr. 2, 12, 15, 19, May 5, 1919," Lansing MSS; Hoover to Wilson, Apr. 11, 1919, Lansing to Wilson, Apr. 12, 1919, White to Wilson, Apr. 12, 1919, Wilson MSS, File 8A; Bliss to N. D. Baker, Jan. 11, 1919, N. D. Baker MSS; Bliss to Gen. E. Crowder, Mar. 3, 1919, Bliss to Mrs. Bliss, June 19, 1919, Bliss to Gen. B. H. Wells, Mar. 26, 1919, Bliss MSS; Lansing to Polk, Mar. 14, 1919, Polk MSS; FR, PPC, 1919, I, pp. 294–7; FR, PPC, 1919, II, pp. 547–9; FR, PPC, 1919, XI, p. 130; Frederick Palmer, Bliss, Peacemaker, The Life and Letters of General Tasker Howard Bliss, pp. 376, 387, 420–21; Lansing, Peace Negotiations, pp. 178–86; David Trask, General Bliss, pp. 39, 43–7.

[8] Lansing, "Confidential Memoranda and Notes, May 6, 1919," Lansing MSS; FR, PPC, 1919, II, pp. 568–9; Robert Lansing, The Big Four and Others of the Peace Conference (Boston, 1921), pp. 34–5, 50–55, 130–31; Lansing, Peace Negotiations, pp. 45, 77–80, 85, 146–8, 272–5; Roland N. Stromberg, Collective Security and American Foreign Policy From the League of Nations to NATO (New York, 1963), pp. 30–31.

[9] Lansing, "Confidential Memoranda and Notes, Sept. 30, Oct. 27, Nov. 12, 22, 1918," Lansing MSS; Lansing to House, Apr. 8, 1918, Lansing MSS; Lansing to Wilson, with enclosures, Dec. 23, 1918, Jan. 31, 1919, Wilson MSS, File 8A; Lansing, Peace Negotiations, pp. 36–41, 43, 50–59, 67–9, 124–35, 164–7; R. S. Baker, WW&WS, III, p. 494.

House were also prepared to view the League as a device making possible the involvement of American power in the tasks of controlling Germany and of enforcing the peace settlement. Indeed, Wilson's defense of the League Covenant in America during the summer and early fall of 1919 was partly based on the argument that the League was needed to maintain American-Allied unity in the face of a Germany which had suffered severe but just punishment.[10] This apparent contradiction could be wholly resolved in the realm of ideology, if not so completely in the area of practice, since both House and the President also saw the League of Nations as having strong counterbalancing reintegrationist potentialities.

Along with their more static vision of the League as a defender of the Versailles settlement, both the President and Colonel House also saw the League as a potentially flexible instrument through which the imperfect decisions made at Paris could be readjusted in the future.[11] Unwilling completely to share the view of such reintegrationist critics as Lansing, Wilson and House preferred to view the League more broadly and hopefully as a living liberal institution capable of constant adaptation and growth. "A living thing is born," said Wilson of the League at one point, "and we must see to it that the clothes we put on it do not hamper it—a vehicle of power, but a vehicle in which power may be varied at the discretion of those who exercise it and in accordance with the changing circumstances of the times."[12] Similarly, the President hoped that America's postwar participation in the work of the Reparations Commission would make possible a rational readjustment of the problematic reparations settlement which Wilsonians had been forced to accept at Paris. For Wilson, then, the League was the means of extending to the world scene an American vision of pragmatic and progressive change within the confines of a liberal order.

In this general context it is of interest to note that even such ardent reintegrationists and critics of the Paris settlement as Hoover, Lansing, Bliss, and White were in no sense immune to the notion that the League might prove to be useful in an imperfect world, by assuring some degree of continued international cooperation in the interests of world stability.[13] Lansing's memoirs make clear that, for him, his eventual support of the cause of treaty ratification represented no change of heart from his critical stance at Paris, but rather a sense that American ratification of the Treaty and the League Covenant was necessary to the prevention of social chaos:

> My own position was paradoxical. I was opposed to the Treaty, but signed it and favored its ratification. The explanation is this: Convinced after conversations with the President in July and August, 1919, that he would not consent to any effective reservations, the politic course seemed to be to

[10] Roy S. Baker and William E. Dodd, eds., *Public Papers of Woodrow Wilson*, VI, pp. 181, 212–13, 230–31, 245–7, 294–5, 302, 322–3, 345–6, 356–7, 402, 413–15.

[11] Bonsal, *Unfinished Business*, p. 206; *Intimate Papers of Colonel House*, IV, pp. 281, 410, 487–9; *PPWW*, V, pp. 354, 395, 544–5; Wilson to Hoover, Apr. 15, 1919, Wilson MSS, File 8A; R. S. Baker, *WW&WS*, III, pp. 478–9; "Conversation with Colonel House, May 19, 1919," Bullitt MSS; *FR, PPC, 1919*, II, pp. 620–23.

[12] *PPWW*, V, p. 426.

[13] Hoover, *Ordeal*, pp. 248–9; *FR, PPC, 1919*, II, pp. 612–14; Nevins, *White*, pp. 474–6; Trask, *General Bliss*, pp. 68–70.

endeavor to secure ratification without reservations. It appeared to be the only possible way of obtaining that for which all the world longed and which in the months succeeding the signature appeared absolutely essential to prevent the widespread disaster resulting from political and economic chaos which seemed to threaten many nations if not civilization itself. Even if the Treaty was bad in certain provisions, so long as the President remained inflexible and insistent, its ratification without change seemed a duty to humanity.[14]

It is quite probable that, considering his general world view, Lansing had Bolshevism in mind when he referred to a "widespread disaster resulting from political and economic chaos which seemed to threaten many nations if not civilization itself." Ironically, Colonel House, a man whose constant efforts to compromise with the Allies had drawn Lansing's wrath at Paris, had been himself moved to compromise in the interests of a speedy peace partly because of a fear that Bolshevism was growing in the atmosphere of postwar uncertainty.[15] In any event, it could be said that, in the aftermath of the Paris Peace Conference, the differences between Wilson and such reintegrationist critics within the Administration as Hoover and Lansing tended to be submerged in a unified Wilsonian effort to attain both Treaty ratification and the maintenance of world liberal-capitalist stability in the face of intransigent criticism of the Versailles Peace from the Left and the Right in the United States.

In the realm of ideology, Wilson's reintegrationist conception of the League was more powerful than his somewhat contradictory vision of the League as a means for controlling Germany and enforcing the peace settlement. After all, the President did feel that Germany would be admitted to the League after having proved her liberal sincerity, and that Germany's eventual admittance could help to ease certain problems latent in the terms of the Treaty.[16] On September 13, 1919, Wilson clearly affirmed his idea of the future reintegration, after a period of probation, of a truly liberalized Germany:

> I read you these figures in order to emphasize and set in a higher light, if I may, the substitute which is offered to us, the substitute for war, the substitute for turmoil, the substitute for sorrow and despair. That substitute is offered in the Covenant of the League of Nations. America alone cannot underwrite civilization. All the great free peoples of the world must underwrite it, and only the free peoples of the world can join the League of Nations. The membership is open only to self-governing nations. Germany is for the present excluded, because she must prove that she has changed the processes of her constitution and the purposes of her policy; but when she has proved these things she can become one of the partners in guaranteeing that civilization shall not suffer again the intolerable thing she attempted.[17]

[14] Lansing, *Peace Negotiations*, p. 276.

[15] House MSS Diary, Mar. 24, 1919; *Intimate Papers*, IV, pp. 389–91, 397–403; Alexander and Juliette George, *Woodrow Wilson and Colonel House, A Personality Study* (New York, 1956), p. 247.

[16] R. S. Baker, *WW&WS*, III, p. 500.

[17] *PPWW*, VI, p. 167.

Thus, Wilson's conception of the League as an inter-Allied instrument to control a justly punished Germany was ultimately transcended by the President's related but broader vision of the League of Nations as an inclusive concert of liberal powers into which a reformed Germany could eventually be reintegrated.

As early as spring 1918 the President had urged that the League ought not to be "an alliance or a group formed to maintain any sort of balance of power, but must be an association which any nation is at liberty to join which is willing to cooperate in its objects and qualify in respect of its guarantees."[18] Similarly, at Paris, Wilson affirmed that "there must now be, not a balance of power, not one powerful group of nations set off against another, but a single overwhelming, powerful group of nations who shall be the trustee of the peace of the world."[19] Of course, it is clear that, for a time, the powerful trustees would be the victorious Allied powers, but it is significant, as Colonel House made plain, that one of the reasons for America's rejection of the French plan for an official League army was the Wilsonian concern lest the French succeed in turning the League completely into an anti-German instrument.[20] In sum, then, the basic Wilsonian reintegrationist conception of the League, as an inclusive community of liberal states mutually pledged to defend international law and one another's territorial integrity, had the potential of ideologically transcending the actual anti-German context from within which the League emerged at Paris.[21]

At one point, while in England late in 1918, the President spoke of the League in terms which contained many of the ambiguities already discussed:

> I wish that it were possible for us to do something like some of my very stern ancestors did, for among my ancestors are those very determined persons who were known as the Covenanters. I wish we could, not only for Great Britain and the United States, but for France and Italy and the world, enter into a great league and covenant, declaring ourselves, first of all, friends of mankind and uniting ourselves together for the maintenance and the triumph of right.[22]

On the one hand, both the direct mention of the Allied powers as forming the moral core of the League, and the reference to stern covenanted unity in "the maintenance and the triumph of right," could imply the creation of a League simply to defend a righteously punitive settlement against Germany. On the other hand, however, such phrases as "and the world" and "friends of mankind" obviously suggest the more inclusive and reintegrationist possibilities of Wilsonian liberal-internationalism.

There can be no doubt that the President saw the League of Nations, in part, as a postwar inter-Allied police force growing naturally out of the progressive nucleus of the Allied-American liberal alliance which had de-

18 Wilson to J. S. Strachey, Apr. 5, 1919, R. S. Baker MSS, DLC
19 *PPWW*, V, p. 343; see also Chapter IV, p. 126, and note 2, p. 285.
20 House MSS Diary, Mar. 16, 1919.
21 In this connection, see Thompson, *Peace Conference*, pp. 410–11.
22 *PPWW*, V, pp. 355–6.

feated the special reactionary challenge to world liberalism posed by German autocratic imperialism.[23] Yet, beyond the necessary defeat of atavistic German imperialism, there also existed the larger Wilsonian hope to so reorganize world politics as to prevent any other nation from repeating Germany's imperialistic actions in the future. In his defense of the Versailles settlement, the President was concerned not only with reforming and controlling Imperial Germany; he also sought to liberalize the entire imperialistic system of European politics within which an autocratic Germany had simply played the most militant and aggressive single role.[24] The President often combined an argument to the effect that the League was the necessary culmination to the triumph of world liberalism over German imperialism with a broader argument that the League was also the means by which world liberalism would finally reform the Old World's traditional balance-of-power system.

The point is that, speaking theoretically, Germany's eventual reintegration was latent in the Wilsonian critique of the traditional imperialistic system. Had Wilson joined the French in merely seeking to punish and to control German imperialism alone, the League of Nations would have been only a postwar extension of the Entente alliance. To be sure, the League was, in part, just such a peacetime extension of the anti-German wartime alliance, yet the Wilsonian critique of European imperialism also contained an implicit condemnation both of any continued Allied reliance on the old diplomacy of the balance of power and of any Allied failure to live up to liberal values in the future. For the President, then, the League Covenant projected the vision of a liberal world order, transcending the historical and traditional restraints of power politics, into which a liberalized Germany could eventually be reintegrated as a full partner.

Wilson conceived the essence of the League as an orderly social contract among the nations. The international social contract represented by the Covenant of the League was to rescue the world from an insecure "Hobbesian" state of nature in which nations could find temporary security only through armaments and the balance of power. The President saw the League Covenant as establishing a new co-operative international society, governed by liberal norms, whose nation-state members would be pledged to substitute public discussion and peaceful arbitration under world law for the reactionary diplomatic practices of secret diplomacy or armed conflict.[25] Indeed, Wilson always put far more emphasis on the universal moral force of world liberal opinion, focused in an association of self-governing states, than he did on the armed power of the League members.[26]

In Wilson's new "Lockeanized" international environment, in which formerly hostile nations had been theoretically transformed into equal law-

[23] *PPWW*, V, pp. 603–4; *PPWW*, VI, pp. 113, 121, 164–6, 205–6, 273, 281, 301, 323–4, 327–30, 340, 366–8.

[24] *PPWW*, V, pp. 548, 593–4, 597, 609, 619, 622–3; *PPWW*, VI, pp. 5–6, 45–8, 51–2, 116–18, 203, 218, 277–8, 295, 310, 346, 388–9.

[25] *PPWW*, V, pp. 608–13, 626–9, 642–3; *PPWW*, VI, pp. 28–9, 34–7, 53–5, 71–2, 80–82, 95–6, 134–6, 146–7, 168–9, 177–8, 182–4, 190, 255–9, 274–6, 290–91, 299, 306, 325–6, 360–61, 364, 391–2, 402–3.

[26] David Hunter Miller, *The Drafting of the Covenant*, I, pp. 164–6; *PPWW*, V, pp. 330–38, 347–8, 363–4, 397, 410, 425–6.

abiding liberal world citizens, all countries, weak and strong alike, were to eschew power politics and were also to covenant together, under Article X of the League of Nations Covenant, to defend each other's legal rights and territorial integrity.[27] On one occasion, the President pithily expressed his orderly liberal desire to transform a world political system in which, historically, might had made right, by remarking that he hoped "to make a society instead of a set of barbarians out of the governments of the world."[28] The League Covenant, then, ultimately represented for Wilson the fulfillment of America's historic mission to lead the Old World away from the traditional war-producing diplomacy of the balance of power to an harmonious American-inspired liberal world order of international responsibility under law. In the eyes of the President the League Covenant was the embodiment of American and world liberalism's final triumph over the imperialistic and atavistic restraints of the pre-liberal historical past.[29]

There can be little doubt that, without his faith that the League offered a new liberal beginning in world politics, in which the concept of a universal concert of powers replaced the old notion of a balance of power, the President would not have been willing to involve the United States so permanently in European affairs.[30] Given Wilson's missionary conception of the universality of America's liberal-nationalism, the League legitimized for him the involvement of American power in world politics by permitting him the assumption that, far from being absorbed as another competing element into the traditional global political reality, American strength was enabled, by the League, to enter world politics at the very moment that world politics was transcended by liberal-internationalism. For Wilson America's involvement in world affairs was inseparably joined with America's effort to lead a liberal anti-imperialist transformation of global reality through the League of Nations. In a theoretical sense, then, the League may be seen as Wilson's answer to reintegrationist critics, such as Hoover and Lansing, who feared lest Allied absorption of America's political and economic power might end hopes for the establishment of an American-inspired world of liberal-capitalist harmony.

For Wilson, the ultimate mission of a liberal exceptionalist America was to lead the rest of the world, without socialist revolution, to a universal liberal triumph over all elements of pre-bourgeois reaction and atavistic imperialism. The war years had seen a strengthening of the President's faith that, under his leadership, the United States was fulfilling this historic destiny by uniting America, the Allies, and common peoples of all countries in a liberal people's war on behalf of freedom and the creation of a new anti-imperialist world order.[31] In the postwar period as well, Wilson was more than ever

[27] FR, PPC, 1919, V, pp. 128–9; PPWW, V, pp. 593, 610–11, 621, 623–6, 631–3; PPWW, VI, pp. 11, 25, 90–91, 98, 111–12, 122, 129, 150–52, 186, 203–4, 217, 267, 281, 350–53, 380.

[28] PPWW, VI, p. 55.

[29] See PPWW, VI, pp. 326–33, for a clear statement of Wilson's vision of the Paris Peace Conference as the culmination of the Enlightenment's long struggle against European traditional reaction.

[30] PPWW, V, pp. 353, 397, 452–3; House MSS Diary, Mar. 24, 1919.

[31] PPWW, V, pp. 3-4, 49–53, 56–7, 85, 95, 111, 133–5, 138, 162, 174, 180–81, 184, 224–5, 231–7, 246–8, 254, 258–9, 264.

certain that it was the duty of the American state to continue to act self-
lessly as the leader of world liberalism in the effort to create a new international system free of power politics and Europe's traditional balance of
power.[32] In this connection, it is not surprising that the President saw the
American-inspired League of Nations as a logical extension, to the entire
world, of America's effort, under the Monroe Doctrine, to keep European
reaction out of the Western Hemisphere.[33] In essence, therefore, Wilson
saw a powerful postwar America as the leader of the liberal opinion of the
world, as the selfless and trusted arbiter of international problems, and as
the disinterested defender of a new world order against both traditional imperialism and revolutionary socialism.[34] For the President, America's political, economic, and military self-interest was inseparably joined to America's
missionary idealism, in the Wilsonian struggle for international liberal stability.

In the final analysis the League of Nations proved to be the central element in the Wilsonian vision of an Americanized post-war world order in
which the contradictions of international politics would be resolved in a new
liberal harmony. While it is true that the League provided a means to enforce a severe peace on Germany, it is also true that, for Wilson, the League
held out the promise of the eventual reintegration of a reformed Germany
into an American-inspired liberal-capitalist world order safe from war and/
or socialist revolution. Moreover, by maintaining the basic legitimacy of the
nation-state system, the League was a logical expression of Wilson's effort,
based on his ideology of American liberal-exceptionalism, to combine the
leadership of world liberal anti-imperialism with his somewhat contradictory
position as the leader of the militarily powerful American nation-state.
Finally, by permitting Wilson to link ideologically American nationalism
with liberal-internationalism, the League was the culmination of the President's vision of an orderly American-inspired reform of the traditional
world political-economy. Such Wilsonian international reform, by using the
League to establish a universal liberal-capitalist stability without class conflict, would ultimately defeat both atavistic imperialism and revolutionary
socialism, the two mutually reinforcing barriers to the final realization of
America's true national interest and pre-eminence in a liberal world order.

Suggested Reading

The best guides to the literature on American intervention in the First World
War are Daniel M. Smith's "National Interest and American Intervention, 1917:
An Historiographical Appraisal," *Journal of American History*, LIII (1965),

[32] *PPWW*, V, pp. 325, 333, 337, 353, 380, 397-9, 433-40, 447-55, 483, 502-3, 538-9.

[33] *Intimate Papers*, IV, pp. 281, 427; Miller, *Drafting*, I, pp. 444-50; Alfred Zimmern,
The League of Nations and the Rule of Law, 1918-1935 (London, 1936), pp. 215-22.

[34] Wilson to Senator Key Pittman, Nov. 7, 1918, Wilson MSS, File 2; Bonsal, *Un-
finished Business*, p. 48; Thompson, *Peace Conference*, p. 409; Harold Whiteman (ed.),
Letters from the Paris Peace Conference by Seymour, p. 24; *Intimate Papers*, IV, p. 280;
PPWW, V, pp. 447-8; Joseph Tumulty, *Woodrow Wilson as I Know Him*, pp. 368-9.

Richard Leopold's "The Problem of American Intervention in 1917: An Historical Retrospect," *World Politics*, II (1950), Richard L. Watson's "Woodrow Wilson and His Interpreters, 1947–1957," *Mississippi Valley Historical Review*, XLIV (1957), and Ernest May's *American Intervention, 1917 and 1941* (1960).

An important volume is Ernest May's *The World War and American Isolation, 1914–1917.** The foreign policy of the period is also examined by Daniel Smith in *The Great Departure: The United States and World War I** (1965). A still useful defense of Wilson is Charles Seymour's, "American Neutrality: The Experience of 1914–17," *Foreign Affairs*, XIII (1935).

Among the revisionist studies are Charles C. Tansill's *America Goes to War* (1938), C. Hartley Grattan's *Why We Fought* (1929), Walter Millis' *Road to War: America, 1914–1917* (1935), and Edwin Borchard and W. P. Lage's *Neutrality for the United States*, 2nd ed. (1940).

Among the realist studies are Walter Lippmann's *U.S. Foreign Policy: Shield of the Republic** (1943), Edward Beuhrig's *Woodrow Wilson and the Balance of Power* (1955), Robert Osgood's *Ideals and Self-Interest in America's Foreign Relations** (1953), and George Kennan's *American Diplomacy, 1900–1950** (1951).

Herbert Bass's collection *America's Entry into World War I** (1964) is useful.

Wilson's conception of collective security is examined by Edward Buehrig in "Woodrow Wilson and Collective Security," in Buehrig, ed., *Wilson's Foreign Policy in Perspective* (1957), and by Denna Frank Fleming in "Woodrow Wilson and Collective Security Today," *Journal of Politics*, XVIII (1956). An interpretation similar to Levin's is presented by Arno Mayer in two important volumes: *Political Origins of the New Diplomacy, 1917–1918** (1959) and *Politics and Diplomacy of Peacemaking: Containment and Counterrevolution at Versailles, 1918–1919** (1967). The influence of the Russian Revolution on Wilson's programs also receives consideration in George Kennan's *Russia Leaves the War** (1967) and *The Decision to Intervene** (1958), as well as in Christopher Lasch's "American Intervention in Siberia: A Reinterpretation," *Political Science Quarterly*, LXXVII (1962).

Different interpretations of Wilson's struggle for the League are available in Denna Frank Fleming's *The United States and the League of Nations* (1932), and Thomas A. Bailey's *Woodrow Wilson and the Lost Peace** (1945). Herbert Hoover's *The Ordeal of Woodrow Wilson** (1957) is a sympathetic study of the President's struggles.

Preparations for Versailles are examined by Lawrence Gelfand in *The Inquiry: American Preparations for Peace, 1917–1919* (1963).

* Also published in paperback edition.

The Twenties

What Happened to the Progressive Movement in the 1920's?

Arthur S. Link

Writing nearly three decades after the Great Depression, Arthur Link of Princeton University, author of the multivolume biography of Wilson, sought to reexamine the 1920s and the place of reform in that decade. He rejected the older notion that the decade was characterized by "an extraordinary reaction against idealism and reform," and found instead the continuation, though in weakened form, of Progressivism in the 1920s. Put simply, the movement declined but did not die; Progressivism survived in fragmented form.

In the years before 1918, he concluded that Progressivism, though never an actual organization with political machinery, had a definable constituency and shared common ideals and goals. The Progressive coalition of 1916—southern and western farmers, organized labor, and social justice elements that elected Wilson—crumbled between 1917 and 1920. In the 1920s, unity became impossible because the various components could not agree on programs and goals. The southern and western farmers, for example, split with their urban allies on such issues as prohibition, immigration restriction, and the Ku Klux Klan. There

247

was also a "paralysis of the progressive mind" and an inability to find adequate leadership. Torn by internal dissension, Progressivism in this period also confronted conditions unsuitable for reform—prosperity, materialism, and general contentment.

Still, Link finds important elements of the movement were active in the 1920s: farmers, organized labor, and urban lower classes. There were the efforts of the Farm Bloc, for example, on behalf of McNary-Haugen, public ownership and regulation of utilities, and regional development. Even prohibition, tariff protection, and promotion of trade associations were related to Progressive theory, and in the last two cases to the practices of Wilson. In the cities, too, Progressivism was still alive, as zoning, planning, and establishment of the city manager system demonstrated.

Link's reassessment, which has never been adequately challenged, does offer an important new perspective on the 1920s. Unfortunately much of his essay rests on a loose and overly broad conception of Progressivism "as the popular effort . . . to insure the survival of democracy . . . by the enlargement of government power to control and offset the power of private economic groups over the nation's institutions and life." The utility of even this definition is further weakened by his acknowledgment that most progressive efforts were the "work of special interest groups or classes" seeking benefits even when "convincing themselves that they sought the welfare of society rather than their own interests primarily." Having defined Progressivism as special-interest politics, Link's analysis is left in the uneasy position of simply admitting that Progressivism was not the politics of laissez faire. Such a loose conception raises serious problems and underlines the difficulty that historians face in trying to come to terms with the many, and sometimes contradictory, reform movements that have been called progressive. Perhaps Link's greatest achievement in this essay is his evidence that the 1920s did not represent the triumph of laissez-faire government. That recognition constitutes an early, not the final, step in providing a synthesis

What Happened to the Progressive Movement in the 1920's? From *American Historical Review*, LXIV (July 1959), pp. 833–51. Copyright © 1959 by Arthur S. Link. Reprinted by permission of the author.

This paper was read in a slightly different form before a joint meeting of the American Historical Association and the Mississippi Valley Historical Association in New York City on December 28, 1957.

of the decade in which Warren G. Harding and Calvin Coolidge occupied the presidency and in which promises of "normalcy" and a "New Era" offered competing visions to citizens.

*I*f the day has not yet arrived when we can make a definite synthesis of political developments between the Armistice and the Great Depression, it is surely high time for historians to begin to clear away the accumulated heap of mistaken and half-mistaken hypotheses about this important transitional period. Writing often without fear or much research (to paraphrase Carl Becker's remark), we recent American historians have gone on indefatigably to perpetuate hypotheses that either reflected the disillusionment and despair of contemporaries, or once served their purpose in exposing the alleged hiatus in the great continuum of twentieth-century reform.

Stated briefly, the following are what might be called the governing hypotheses of the period under discussion: The 1920's were a period made almost unique by an extraordinary reaction against idealism and reform. They were a time when the political representatives of big business and Wall Street executed a relentless and successful campaign in state and nation to subvert the regulatory structure that had been built at the cost of so much toil and sweat since the 1870's, and to restore a Hanna-like reign of special privilege to benefit business, industry, and finance. The surging tides of nationalism and mass hatreds generated by World War I continued to engulf the land and were manifested, among other things, in fear of communism, suppression of civil liberties, revival of nativism and anti-Semitism most crudely exemplified by the Ku Klux Klan, and in the triumph of racism and prejudice in immigration legislation. The 1920's were an era when great traditions and ideals were repudiated or forgotten, when the American people, propelled by a crass materialism in their scramble for wealth, uttered a curse on twenty-five years of reform endeavor. As a result, progressives were stunned and everywhere in retreat along the entire political front, their forces disorganized and leaderless, their movement shattered, their dreams of a new America turned into agonizing nightmares.

To be sure, the total picture that emerges from these generalizations is overdrawn. Yet it seems fair to say that leading historians have advanced each of these generalizations, that the total picture is the one that most of us younger historians saw during the years of our training, and that these hypotheses to a greater or lesser degree still control the way in which we write and teach about the 1920's, as a reading of textbooks and general works will quickly show.

This paper has not been written, however, to quarrel with anyone or to make an indictment. Its purposes are, first, to attempt to determine the degree to which the governing hypotheses, as stated, are adequate or inadequate to explain the political phenomena of the period, and, second, to discover whether any new and sounder hypotheses might be suggested. Such an effort, of course, must be tentative and above all imperfect in view of the absence of sufficient foundations for a synthesis.

Happily, however, we do not have to proceed entirely in the dark. Historians young and old, but mostly young, have already discovered that the period of the 1920's is the exciting new frontier of American historical research and that its opportunities are almost limitless in view of the mass of manuscript materials that are becoming available. Thus we have (the following examples are mentioned only at random) excellent recent studies of agrarian discontent and farm movements by Theodore Saloutos, John D. Hicks, Gilbert C. Fite, Robert L. Morlan, and James H. Shideler; of nativism and problems of immigration and assimilation by John Higham, Oscar Handlin, Robert A. Devine, and Edmund D. Cronon; of intellectual currents, the social gospel, and religious controversies by Henry F. May, Paul A. Carter, Robert M. Miller, and Norman F. Furniss; of left-wing politics and labor developments by Theodore Draper, David A. Shannon, David Bell, Paul M. Angle, and Matthew Josephson; of the campaign of 1928 by Edmund A. Moore; and of political and judicial leaders by Alpheus T. Mason, Frank Friedel, Arthur M. Schlesinger, Jr., Merlo J. Pusey, and Joel F. Paschal.[1] Moreover, we can look forward to the early publication of studies that will be equally illuminating for the period, like the biographies of George W. Norris, Thomas J. Walsh, and Albert B. Fall now being prepared by Richard Lowitt, Leonard Bates, and David Stratton, respec-

---

[1] Theodore Saloutos and John D. Hicks, *Agrarian Discontent in the Middle West, 1900–1939* (Madison, Wis., 1951); Gilbert C. Fite, *Peter Norbeck: Prairie Statesman* (Columbia, Mo., 1948), and *George N. Peek and the Fight for Farm Parity* (Norman, Okla., 1954); Robert L. Morlan, *Political Prairie Fire: The Nonpartisan League, 1915–1922* (Minneapolis, Minn., 1955); James H. Shideler, *Farm Crisis, 1919–1923* (Berkeley, Calif., 1957); John Higham, *Strangers in the Land: Patterns of American Nativism, 1860–1925* (New Brunswick, N.J., 1955); Oscar Handlin, *The American People in the Twentieth Century* (Cambridge, Mass., 1954); Robert A. Devine, *American Immigration Policy, 1924–1952* (New Haven, Conn. 1957); Edmund D. Cronon, *Black Moses: The Story of Marcus Garvey and the Universal Negro Improvement Association* (Madison, Wis., 1955); Henry F. May, "Shifting Perspectives on the 1920's," *Mississippi Valley Historical Review*, XLIII (Dec., 1956), 405–27; Paul A. Carter, *The Decline and Revival of the Social Gospel* (Ithaca, N.Y., 1956); Robert M. Miller, "An Inquiry into the Social Attitudes of American Protestantism, 1919–1939," doctoral dissertation, Northwestern University, 1955; Norman F. Furniss, *The Fundamentalist Controversy, 1918–1931* (New Haven, Conn., 1954); Theodore Draper, *The Roots of American Communism* (New York, 1957); David A. Shannon, *The Socialist Party of America: A History* (New York, 1955); Daniel Bell, "The Background and Development of Marxian Socialism in the United States," *Socialism and American Life*, ed. Donald D. Egbert and Stow Persons (2 vols., Princeton N.J., 1952), I, 215–405; Paul M. Angle, *Bloody Williamson* (New York, 1952); Matthew Josephson, *Sidney Hillman: Statesman of American Labor* (New York, 1952); Edmund A. Moore, *A Catholic Runs for President: The Campaign of 1928* (New York, 1956); Alpheus Thomas Mason, *Brandeis: A Free Man's Life* (New York, 1946), and *Harlan Fiske Stone: Pillar of the Law* (New York, 1956); Frank Freidel, *Franklin D. Roosevelt: The Ordeal* (Boston, 1954); Arthur M. Schlesinger, Jr., *The Age of Roosevelt: The Crisis of the Old Order* (Boston, 1957); Merlo J. Pusey, *Charles Evans Hughes* (2 vols., New York, 1951); Joel Francis Paschal, *Mr. Justice Sutherland: A Man against the State* (Princeton, N.J., 1951).

tively, and the recently completed study of the campaign and election of 1920 by Wesley M. Bagby.[2]

Obviously, we are not only at a point in the progress of our research into the political history of the 1920's when we can begin to generalize, but we have reached the time when we should attempt to find some consensus, however tentative it must now be, concerning the larger political dimensions and meanings of the period.

In answering the question of what happened to the progressive movement in the 1920's, we should begin by looking briefly at some fundamental facts about the movement before 1918, facts that in large measure predetermined its fate in the 1920's, given the political climate and circumstances that prevailed.

The first of these was the elementary fact that the progressive movement never really existed as a recognizable organization with common goals and a political machinery geared to achieve them. Generally speaking (and for the purposes of this paper), progressivism might be defined as the popular effort, which began convulsively in the 1890's and waxed and waned afterward to our own time, to insure the survival of democracy in the United States by the enlargement of governmental power to control and offset the power of private economic groups over the nation's institutions and life. Actually, of course, from the 1890's on there were many "progressive" movements on many levels seeking sometimes contradictory objectives. Not all, but most of these campaigns were the work of special interest groups or classes seeking greater political status and economic security. This was true from the beginning of the progressive movement in the 1890's; by 1913 it was that movement's most important characteristic.

The second fundamental fact—that the progressive movements were often largely middle class in constituency and orientation—is of course well known, but an important corollary has often been ignored. It was that several of the most important reform movements were inspired, staffed, and led by businessmen with very specific or special-interest objectives in view. Because they hated waste, mismanagement, and high taxes, they, together with their friends in the legal profession, often furnished the leadership of good government campaigns. Because they feared industrial monopoly, abuse of power by railroads, and the growth of financial oligarchy, they were the backbone of the movements that culminated in the adoption of the Hepburn and later acts for railroad regulation, the Federal Reserve Act, and the Federal Trade Commission Act. Among the many consequences of their participation in the progressive movement, two should be mentioned because of their significance for developments in the 1920's: First, the strong identification of businessmen with good government and economic reforms for which the general public also had a lively concern helped preserve the good reputation of the middle-class business community (as opposed to its

[2] Wesley M. Bagby, "Woodrow Wilson and the Great Debacle of 1920," MS in the possession of Professor Bagby; see also his "The 'Smoke-Filled Room' and the Nomination of Warren G. Harding," *Mississippi Valley Historical Review*, XLI (Mar. 1955), 657–74, and "Woodrow Wilson, a Third Term, and the Solemn Referendum," *American Historical Review*, LX (Apr., 1955), 567–75.

alleged natural enemies, monopolists, malefactors of great wealth, and railroad barons) and helped to direct the energies of the progressive movement toward the strengthening instead of the shackling of the business community. Second, their activities and influence served to intensify the tensions within the broad reform movement, because they often opposed the demands of farm groups, labor unions, and advocates of social justice.

The third remark to be made about the progressive movement before 1918 is that despite its actual diversity and inner tensions it did seem to have unity; that is, it seemed to share common ideals and objectives. This was true in part because much of the motivation even of the special-interest groups was altruistic (at least they succeeded in convincing themselves that they sought the welfare of society rather than their own interests primarily); in part because political leadership generally succeeded in subordinating inner tensions. It was true, above all, because there were in fact important idealistic elements in the progressive ranks—social gospel leaders, social justice elements, and intellectuals and philosophers—who worked hard at the task of defining and elevating common principles and goals.

Fourth and finally, the substantial progressive achievements before 1918 had been gained, at least on the federal level, only because of the temporary dislocations of the national political structure caused by successive popular uprisings, not because progressives had found or created a viable organization for perpetuating their control. Or, to put the matter another way, before 1918 the various progressive elements had failed to destroy the existing party structure by organizing a national party of their own that could survive. They, or at least many of them, tried in 1912; and it seemed for a time in 1916 that Woodrow Wilson had succeeded in drawing the important progressive groups permanently into the Democratic party. But Wilson's accomplishment did not survive even to the end of the war, and by 1920 traditional partisan loyalties were reasserting themselves with extraordinary vigor.

With this introduction, we can now ask what happened to the progressive movement or movements in the 1920's. Surely no one would contend that after 1916 the political scene did not change significantly, both on the state and national levels. There was the seemingly obvious fact that the Wilsonian coalition had been wrecked by the election of 1920, and that the progressive elements were divided and afterward unable to agree upon a program or to control the national government. There was the even more "obvious" fact that conservative Republican presidents and their cabinets controlled the executive branch throughout the period. There was Congress, as Eric F. Goldman had said, allegedly whooping through procorporation legislation, and the Supreme Court interpreting the New Freedom laws in a way that harassed unions and encouraged trusts.[3] There were, to outraged idealists and intellectuals, the more disgusting spectacles of Red hunts, mass arrests and deportations, the survival deep into the 1920's of arrogant nationalism, crusades against the teaching of evolution, the attempted suppression of the

---

[3] Eric F. Goldman, *Rendezvous with Destiny* (New York, 1953), 284. The "allegedly" in this sentence is mine, not Professor Goldman's.

right to drink, and myriad other manifestations of what would now be called a repressive reaction.[4]

Like the hypotheses suggested at the beginning, this picture is overdrawn in some particulars. But it is accurate in part, for progressivism was certainly on the downgrade if not in decay after 1918. This is an obvious fact that needs explanation and understanding rather than elaborate proof. We can go a long way toward answering our question if we can explain, at least partially, the extraordinary complex developments that converge to produce the "obvious" result.

For this explanation we must begin by looking at the several progressive elements and their relation to each other and to the two major parties after 1916. Since national progressivism was never an organized or independent movement (except imperfectly and then only temporarily in 1912), it could succeed only when its constituent elements formed a coalition strong enough to control one of the major parties. This had happened in 1916, when southern and western farmers, organized labor, the social justice elements, and a large part of the independent radicals who had heretofore voted the Socialist ticket coalesced to continue the control of Wilson and the Democratic party.

The important fact about the progressive coalition of 1916, however, was not its strength but its weakness. It was not a new party but a temporary alliance, welded in the heat of the most extraordinary domestic and external events. To be sure, it functioned for the most part successfully during the war, in providing the necessary support for a program of heavy taxation, relatively stringent controls over business and industry, and extensive new benefits to labor. Surviving in a crippled way even in the months following the Armistice, it put across a program that constituted a sizable triumph for the progressive movement—continued heavy taxation, the Transportation Act of 1920, the culmination of the long fight for railroad regulation, a new child labor act, amendments for prohibition and woman suffrage, immigration restriction, and water power and conservation legislation.

Even so, the progressive coalition of 1916 was inherently unstable. Indeed, it was so wracked by inner tensions that it could not survive, and destruction came inexorably, it seemed systematically, from 1917 to 1920. Why was this true?

First, the independent radicals and antiwar agrarians were alienated by the war declaration and the government's suppression of dissent and civil liberties during the war and the Red scare. Organized labor was disaffected by the administration's coercion of the coal miners in 1919, its lukewarm if not hostile attitude during the great strikes of 1919 and 1920, and its failure to support the Plumb Plan for nationalization of the railroads. Isolationists and idealists were outraged by what they thought was the President's betrayal of American traditions or the liberal peace program at Paris. These tensions were strong enough to disrupt the coalition, but a final one would have been fatal even if the others had never existed. This was the alienation

[4] H. C. Peterson and Gilbert C. Fite, *Opponents of War, 1917–1918* (Norman, Okla., 1957); Robert K. Murray, *Red Scare: A Study in National Hysteria, 1919–1920* (Minneapolis, Minn., 1955).

of farmers in the Plains and western states produced by the administration's refusal to impose price controls on cotton while it maintained ceilings on the prices of other agricultural commodities,[5] and especially by the administration's failure to do anything decisive to stem the downward plunge of farm prices that began in the summer of 1920.[6] Under the impact of all these stresses, the Wilsonian coalition gradually disintegrated from 1917 to 1920 and disappeared entirely during the campaign of 1920.

The progressive coalition was thus destroyed, but the components of a potential movement remained. As we will see, these elements were neither inactive nor entirely unsuccessful in the 1920's. But they obviously failed to find common principles and a program, much less to unite effectively for political action on a national scale. I suggest that this was true, in part at least, for the following reasons:

First, the progressive elements could never create or gain control of a political organization capable of carrying them into national office. The Republican party was patently an impossible instrument because control of the GOP was too much in the hands of the eastern and midwestern industrial, oil, and financial interests, as it had been since about 1910. There was always the hope of a third party. Several progressive groups—insurgent midwestern Republicans, the railroad brotherhoods, a segment of the AF of L, and the moderate Socialists under Robert M. La Follette—tried to realize this goal in 1924, only to discover that third party movements in the United States are doomed to failure except in periods of enormous national turmoil, and that the 1920's were not such a time. Thus the Democratic party remained the only vehicle that conceivably could have been used by a new progressive coalition. But that party was simply not capable of such service in the 1920's. It was so torn by conflicts between its eastern, big city wing and its southern and western rural majority that it literally ceased to be a national party. It remained strong in its sectional and metropolitan components, but it was so divided that it barely succeeded in nominating a presidential candidate at all in 1924 and nominated one in 1928 only at the cost of temporary disruption.[7]

Progressivism declined in the 1920's, in the second place, because, as has been suggested, the tensions that had wrecked the coalition of 1916 not only persisted but actually grew in number and intensity. The two most numerous progressive elements, the southern and western farmers, strongly supported the Eighteenth Amendment, were heavily tinged with nativism and therefore supported immigration restriction, were either members of, friendly to, or politically afraid of the Ku Klux Klan, and demanded as the principal plank in their platform legislation to guarantee them a larger share of the

[5] On this point, see Seward W. Livermore, "The Sectional Issue in the 1918 Congressional Elections," *Mississippi Valley Historical Review*, XXXV (June, 1948), 29–60.

[6] Arthur S. Link, "The Federal Reserve Policy and the Agricultural Depression of 1920–1921," *Agricultural History*, XX (July, 1946), 166–75; and Herbert F. Margulies, "The Election of 1920 in Wisconsin: The Return to 'Normalcy' Reappraised," *Wisconsin Magazine of History*, XXXVIII (Autumn, 1954), 15–22.

[7] For a highly partisan account of these events see Karl Schriftgiesser, *This Was Normalcy* (Boston, 1948). More balanced are the already cited Freidel, *Franklin D. Roosevelt: The Ordeal*, and Schlesinger, *The Age of Roosevelt: The Crisis of the Old Order*.

national income. On all these points and issues the lower and lower middle classes in the large cities stood in direct and often violent opposition to their potential allies in the rural areas. Moreover, the liaison between the farm groups and organized labor, which had been productive of much significant legislation during the Wilson period, virtually ceased to exist in the 1920's. There were many reasons for this development, and I mention only one—the fact that the preeminent spokesmen of farmers in the 1920's, the new Farm Bureau Federation, represented the larger commercial farmers who (in contrast to the members of the leading farm organization in Wilson's day, the National Farmers' Union) were often employers themselves and felt no identification with the rank and file of labor.

It was little wonder, therefore (and this is a third reason for the weakness of progressivism in the 1920's), that the tension-ridden progressive groups were never able to agree upon a program that, like the Democratic platform of 1916, could provide the basis for a revived coalition. So long as progressive groups fought one another more fiercely than they fought their natural opponents, such agreement was impossible; and so long as common goals were impossible to achieve, a national progressive movement could not take effective form. Nothing illustrates this better than the failure of the Democratic conventions of 1924 and 1928 to adopt platforms that could rally and unite the discontented elements. One result, among others, was that southern farmers voted as Democrats and western farmers as Republicans. And, as Professor Frank Freidel once commented to the author, much of the failure of progressivism in the 1920's can be explained by this elementary fact.

A deeper reason for the failure of progressives to unite ideologically in the 1920's was what might be called a substantial paralysis of the progressive mind. This was partly the result of the repudiation of progressive ideals by many intellectuals and the defection from the progressive movement of the urban middle classes and professional groups, as will be demonstrated. It was the result, even more importantly, of the fact that progressivism as an organized body of political thought found itself at a crossroads in the 1920's, like progressivism today, and did not know which way to turn. The major objectives of the progressive movement of the prewar years had in fact been largely achieved by 1920. In what direction should progressivism now move? Should it remain in the channels already deeply cut by its own traditions, and, while giving sincere allegiance to the ideal of democratic capitalism, work for more comprehensive programs of business regulation and assistance to disadvantaged classes like farmers and submerged industrial workers? Should it abandon these traditions and, like most similar European movements, take the road toward a moderate socialism with a predominantly labor orientation? Should it attempt merely to revive the goals of more democracy through changes in the political machinery? Or should it become mainly an agrarian movement with purely agrarian goals?

These were real dilemmas, not academic ones, and one can see numerous examples of how they confused and almost paralyzed progressives in the 1920's. The platform of La Follette's Progressive party of 1924 offers one revealing illustration. It embodied much that was old and meaningless by this time (the direct election of the president and a national referendum before the adoption of a war resolution, for example) and little that had any real significance for the future.[8] And yet it was the best that a vigorous and idealistic movement could offer. A second example was the plight of the agrarians and insurgents in Congress who fought so hard all through the 1920's against Andrew Mellon's proposals to abolish the inheritance tax and to make drastic reductions in the taxes on large incomes. In view of the rapid reduction of the federal debt, the progressives were hard pressed to justify the continuation of nearly confiscatory tax levels, simply because few of them realized the wide social and economic uses to which the income tax could be put. Lacking any programs for the redistribution of the national income (except to farmers), they were plagued and overwhelmed by the surpluses in the federal Treasury until, for want of any good arguments, they finally gave Secretary Andrew Mellon the legislation he had been demanding.[9] A third and final example of this virtual paralysis of the progressive mind was perhaps the most revealing of all. It was the attempt that Woodrow Wilson, Louis D. Brandeis, and other Democratic leaders made from 1921 to 1924 to draft a new charter for progressivism. Except for its inevitable proposals for an idealistic world leadership, the document that emerged from this interchange included little or nothing that would have sounded new to a western progressive in 1912.

A fourth reason for the disintegration and decline of the progressive movement in the 1920's was the lack of any effective leadership. Given the political temper and circumstances of the 1920's, it is possible that such leadership could not have operated successfully in any event. Perhaps the various progressive elements were so mutually hostile and so self-centered in interests and objectives that even a Theodore Roosevelt or a Woodrow Wilson, had they been at the zenith of their powers in the 1920's, could not have drawn them together in a common front. We will never know what a strong national leader might have done because by a trick of fate no such leader emerged before Franklin D. Roosevelt.

Four factors, then, contributed to the failure of the progressive components to unite successfully after 1918 and, as things turned out, before 1932: the lack of a suitable political vehicle, the severity of the tensions that kept progressives apart, the failure of progressives to agree upon a common program, and the absence of a national leadership, without which a united movement could never be created and sustained. These were all weaknesses that stemmed to a large degree from the instability and failures of the progressive movement itself.

There were, besides, a number of what might be called external causes for the movement's decline. In considering them one must begin with what was seemingly the most important—the alleged fact that the 1920's were a very unpropitious time for any new progressive revolt because of the ever-increasing level of economic prosperity, the materialism, and the general contentment of the decade 1919 to 1929. Part of this generalization is valid

[8] For a different picture see Belle C. La Follette and Fola La Follette, *Robert M. La Follette* (2 vols., New York, 1953); and Russel B. Nye, *Midwestern Progressive Politics, 1870–1950* (East Lansing, Mich., 1951). Both works contribute to an understanding of progressive politics in the 1920's.

[9] Here indebtedness is acknowledged to Sidney Ratner, *American Taxation: Its History as a Social Force in Democracy* (New York, 1942).

when applied to specific elements in the population. For example, the rapid rise in the real wages of industrial workers, coupled with generally full employment and the spread of so-called welfare practices among management, certainly did much to weaken and avert the further spread of organized labor, and thus to debilitate one of the important progressive components. But to say that it was prosperity per se that created a climate unfriendly to progressive ideals would be inaccurate. There was little prosperity and much depression during the 1920's for the single largest economic group, the farmers, as well as for numerous other groups. Progressivism, moreover, can flourish as much during periods of prosperity as during periods of discontent, as the history of the development of the progressive movement from 1901 to 1917 and of its triumph from 1945 to 1956 prove.

Vastly more important among the external factors in the decline of progressivism was the widespread, almost wholesale, defection from its ranks of the middle classes—the middling businessmen, bankers, and manufacturers, and the professional people closely associated with them in ideals and habits —in American cities large and small. For an understanding of this phenomenon no simple explanations like "prosperity" or the "temper of the times" will suffice, although they give some insight. The important fact was that these groups found a new economic and social status as a consequence of the flowering of American enterprise under the impact of the technological, financial, and other revolutions of the 1920's. If, as Professor Richard Hofstadter had claimed,[10] the urban middle classes were progressive (that is, they demanded governmental relief from various anxieties) in the early 1900's because they resented their loss of social prestige to the *nouveaux riches* and feared being ground under by monopolists in industry, banking, and labor—if this is true, then the urban middle classes were not progressive in the 1920's for inverse reasons. Their temper was dynamic, expansive, and supremely confident. They knew that they were building a new America, a business civilization based not upon monopoly and restriction but upon a whole new set of business values—mass production and consumption, short hours and high wages, full employment, welfare capitalism. And what was more important, virtually the entire country (at least the journalists, writers in popular magazines, and many preachers and professors) acknowledged that the nation's destiny was in good hands. It was little wonder, therefore, that the whole complex of groups constituting the urban middle classes, whether in New York, Zenith, or Middletown, had little interest in rebellion or even in mild reform proposals that seemed to imperil their leadership and control.

Other important factors, of course, contributed to the contentment of the urban middle classes. The professionalization of business and the full-blown emergence of a large managerial class had a profound impact upon social and political ideals. The acceleration of mass advertising played its role, as did the beginning disintegration of the great cities with the spread of middle- and upper-middle-class suburbs, a factor that diffused the remaining reform energies among the urban leaders.

A second external factor in the decline of the progressive movement after

[10] Richard Hofstadter, *The Age of Reform: From Bryan to F.D.R.* (New York, 1955), 131 ff.

1918 was the desertion from its ranks of a good part of the intellectual leadership of the country. Indeed, more than simple desertion was involved here; it was often a matter of a cynical repudiation of the ideals from which progressivism derived its strength. I do not mean to imply too much by this generalization. I know that what has been called intellectual progressivism not only survived in the 1920's but actually flourished in many fields.[11] I know that the intellectual foundations of our present quasi-welfare state were either being laid or reinforced during the decade. Even so, one cannot evade the conclusion that the intellectual-political climate of the 1920's was vastly different from the one that had prevailed in the preceding two decades.

During the years of the great progressive revolt, intellectuals—novelists, journalists, political thinkers, social scientists, historians, and the like—had made a deeply personal commitment to the cause of democracy, first in domestic and then in foreign affairs. Their leadership in and impact on many phases of the progressive movement had been profound. By contrast, in the 1920's a large body of this intellectual phalanx turned against the very ideals they had once deified. One could cite, for example, the reaction of the idealists against the Versailles settlement; the disenchantment of the intellectuals with the extension of government authority when it could be used to justify the Eighteenth Amendment or the suppression of free speech; or the inevitable loss of faith in the "people" when en masse they hounded so-called radicals, joined Bryan's crusade against evolution, or regaled themselves as Knights of the Ku Klux Klan. Whatever the case, many alienated intellectuals simply withdrew or repudiated any identification with the groups they had once helped to lead. The result was not fatal to progressivism, but it was serious. The spark plugs had been removed from the engine of reform.

The progressive movement, then, unquestionably declined, but was it defunct in the 1920's? Much, of course, depends upon the definition of terms. If we accept the usual definition for "defunct" as "dead" or "ceasing to have any life or strength," we must recognize that the progressive movement was certainly not defunct in the 1920's; that on the contrary at least important parts of it were very much alive; and that it is just as important to know how and why progressivism survived as it is to know how and why it declined.

To state the matter briefly, progressivism survived in the 1920's because several important elements of the movement remained either in full vigor or in only slightly diminished strength. These were the farmers, after 1918 better organized and more powerful than during the high tide of the progressive revolt; and politically conscious elements among organized labor, particularly the railroad brotherhoods, who wielded a power all out of proportion to their numbers; the Democratic organizations in the large cities, usually vitally concerned with the welfare of the so-called lower classes; a remnant of independent radicals, social workers, and social gospel writers and preachers; and finally, an emerging new vocal element, the champions of public power and regional developments.

---

[11] *Ibid.*, 5, 131, 135 ff. For a recent excellent survey, previously cited, see Henry F. May, "Shifting Perspectives on the 1920's." Schlesinger's previously cited *Age of Roosevelt* sheds much new light on the economic thought of the 1920's.

Although they never united effectively enough to capture a major party and the national government before 1932, these progressive elements controlled Congress from 1921 to about 1927 and continued to exercise a near control during the period of their greatest weakness in the legislative branch, from 1927 to about 1930.

Indeed, the single most powerful and consistently successful group in Congress during the entire decade from 1919 to 1929 were the spokesmen of the farmers. Spurred by an unrest in the country areas more intense than at any time since the 1890's,[12] in 1920 and 1921 southern Democrats and midwestern and western insurgents, nominally Republican, joined forces in an alliance called the Farm Bloc. By maintaining a common front from 1921 to 1924 they succeeded in enacting the most advanced agricultural legislation to that date, legislation that completed the program begun under Wilsonian auspices. It included measures for high tariffs on agricultural products, thoroughgoing federal regulation of stockyards, packing houses, and grain exchanges, the exemption of agricultural cooperatives from the application of the antitrust laws, stimulation of the export of agricultural commodities, and the establishment of an entirely new federal system of intermediate rural credit.

When prosperity failed to return to the countryside, rural leaders in Congress espoused a new and bolder plan for relief—the proposal made by George N. Peek and Hugh S. Johnson in 1922 to use the federal power to obtain "fair exchange" or "parity" prices for farm products. Embodied in the McNary-Haugen bill in 1924, this measure was approved by Congress in 1927 and 1928, only to encounter vetoes by President Calvin Coolidge.

In spite of its momentary failure, the McNary-Haugen bill had a momentous significance for the American progressive movement. Its wholesale espousal by the great mass of farm leaders and spokesmen meant that the politically most powerful class in the country had come full scale to the conviction that the taxing power should be used directly and specifically for the purpose of underwriting (some persons called it subsidizing) agriculture. It was a milestone in the development of a comprehensive political doctrine that it was government's duty to protect the economic security of all classes and particularly depressed ones. McNary-Haugenism can be seen in its proper perspective if it is remembered that it would have been considered almost absurd in the Wilson period, that it was regarded as radical by nonfarm elements in the 1920's; and that it, or at any rate its fundamental objective, was incorporated almost as a matter of course into basic federal policy in the 1930's.

A second significant manifestation of the survival of progressivism in the 1920's came during the long controversy over public ownership or regulation of the burgeoning electric power industry. In this, as in most of the conflicts that eventually culminated on Capitol Hill, the agrarian element constituted the core of progressive strength. At the same time a sizable and well-organized independent movement developed that emanated from urban centers and was vigorous on the municipal and state levels. Throughout

---

12 It derived from the fact that farm prices plummeted in 1920 and 1921, and remained so low that farmers, generally speaking, operated at a net capital loss throughout the balance of the decade.

the decade this relatively new progressive group fought with mounting success to expose the propaganda of the private utilities, to strengthen state and federal regulatory agencies, and to win municipal ownership for distributive facilities. Like the advocates of railroad regulation in an earlier period, these proponents of regulation or ownership of a great new natural monopoly failed almost as much as they had succeeded in the 1920's. But their activities and exposures (the Federal Trade Commission's devastating investigation of the electric power industry in the late 1920's and early 1930's was the prime example) laid secure foundations for movements that in the 1930's would reach various culminations.

Even more significant for the future of American progressivism was the emergence in the 1920's of a new objective, that of committing the federal government to plans for large hydroelectric projects in the Tennessee Valley, the Columbia River watershed, the Southwest, and the St. Lawrence Valley for the purpose, some progressives said, of establishing "yardsticks" for rates, or for the further purpose, as other progressives declared, of beginning a movement for the eventual nationalization of the entire electric power industry. The development of this movement in its emerging stages affords a good case study in the natural history of American progressivism. It began when the Harding and Coolidge administrations attempted to dispose of the government's hydroelectric and nitrate facilities at Muscle Shoals, Alabama, to private interests. In the first stage of the controversy, the progressive objective was merely federal operation of these facilities for the production of cheap fertilizer—a reflection of its exclusive special-interest orientation. Then, as new groups joined the fight to save Muscle Shoals, the objective of public production of cheap electric power came to the fore. Finally, by the end of the 1920's, the objective of a multipurpose regional development in the Tennessee Valley and in other areas as well had taken firm shape.

In addition, by 1928 the agrarians in Congress led by Senator George W. Norris had found enough allies in the two houses and enough support in the country at large to adopt a bill for limited federal development of the Tennessee Valley. Thwarted by President Coolidge's pocket veto, the progressives tried again in 1931, only to meet a second rebuff at the hands of President Herbert Hoover.

All this might be regarded as another milestone in the maturing of American progressivism. It signified a deviation from the older traditions of mere regulation, as President Hoover had said in his veto of the second Muscle Shoals bill, and the triumph of new concepts of direct federal leadership in large-scale development of resources. If progressives had not won their goal by the end of the 1920's, they had at least succeeded in writing what would become perhaps the most important plank in their program for the future.

The maturing of an advanced farm program and the formulation of plans for public power and regional developments may be termed the two most significant progressive achievements on the national level in the 1920's. Others merit only brief consideration. One was the final winning of the old progressive goal of immigration restriction through limited and selective admission. The fact that this movement was motivated in part by racism, nativism, and anti-Semitism (with which, incidentally, a great many if not a majority of progressives were imbued in the 1920's) should not blind us to the fact that it was also progressive. It sought to substitute a so-called scientific and a planned policy for a policy of laissez-faire. Its purpose was admittedly to disturb the free operation of the international labor market. Organized labor and social workers had long supported it against the opposition of large employers. And there was prohibition, the most ambitious and revealing progressive experiment of the twentieth century. Even the contemned anti-evolution crusade of Bryan and the fundamentalists and the surging drives for conformity of thought and action in other fields should be mentioned. All these movements stemmed from the conviction that organized public power could and should be used purposefully to achieve fundamental social and so-called moral change. The fact that they were potentially or actively repressive does not mean that they were not progressive. On the contrary, they superbly illustrated the repressive tendencies that inhered in progressivism precisely because it was grounded so much upon majoritarian principles.

Three other developments on the national level that have often been cited as evidences of the failure of progressivism in the 1920's appear in a somewhat different light at second glance. The first was the reversal of the tariff-for-revenue-only tendencies of the Underwood Act with the enactment of the Emergency Tariff Act of 1921 and the Fordney-McCumber Act of 1922. Actually, the adoption of these measures signified, on the whole, not a repudiation but a revival of progressive principles in the realm of federal fiscal policy. A revenue tariff had never been an authentic progressive objective. Indeed, at least by 1913, many progressives, except for some southern agrarians, had concluded that it was retrogressive and had agreed that the tariff laws should be used deliberately to achieve certain national objectives—for example, the crippling of noncompetitive big business by the free admission of articles manufactured by so-called trusts, or benefits to farmers by the free entry of farm implements. Wilson himself had been at least partially converted to these principles by 1916, as his insistence upon the creation of the Federal Tariff Commission and his promise of protection to the domestic chemical industry revealed. As for the tariff legislation of the early 1920's, its only important changes were increased protection for aluminum, chemical products, and agricultural commodities. It left the Underwood rates on the great mass of raw materials and manufactured goods largely undisturbed. It may have been economically shortsighted and a bad example for the rest of the world, but for the most part it was progressive in principle and was the handiwork of the progressive coalition in Congress.

Another development that has often been misunderstood in its relation to the progressive movement was the policies of consistent support that the Harding and Coolidge administrations adopted for business enterprise, particularly the policy of the Federal Trade Commission in encouraging the formation of trade associations and the diminution of certain traditional competitive practices. The significance of all this can easily be overrated. Such policies as these two administrations executed had substantial justification in progressive theory and in precedents clearly established by the Wilson administration.

A third challenge to usual interpretations concerns implications to be drawn from the election of Harding and Coolidge in 1920 and 1924. These elections seem to indicate the triumph of reaction among the mass of American voters. Yet one could argue that both Harding and Coolidge were political accidents, the beneficiaries of grave defects in the American political and constitutional systems. The rank and file of Republican voters demonstrated during the preconvention campaign that they wanted vigorous leadership and a moderately progressive candidate in 1920. They got Harding instead, not because they wanted him, but because unusual circumstances permitted a small clique to thwart the will of the majority.[13] They took Coolidge as their candidate in 1924 simply because Harding died in the middle of his term and there seemed to be no alternative to nominating the man who had succeeded him in the White House. Further, an analysis of the election returns in 1920 and 1924 will show that the really decisive factor in the victories of Harding and Coolidge was the fragmentation of the progressive movement and the fact that an opposition strong enough to rally and unite the progressive majority simply did not exist.

There remains, finally, a vast area of progressive activity about which we yet know very little. One could mention the continuation of old reform movements and the development of new ones in the cities and states during the years following the Armistice: For example, the steady spread of the city manager form of government, the beginning of zoning and planning movements, and the efforts of the great cities to keep abreast of the transportation revolution then in full swing. Throughout the country the educational and welfare activities of the cities and states steadily increased. Factory legislation matured, while social insurance had its experimental beginnings. Whether such reform impulses were generally weak or strong, one cannot say; but what we do know about developments in cities like Cincinnati and states like New York, Wisconsin, and Louisiana[14] justifies a challenge to the assumption that municipal and state reform energies were dead after 1918 and, incidentally, a plea to young scholars to plow this unworked field of recent American history.

Let us, then, suggest a tentative synthesis as an explanation of what happened to the progressive movement after 1918:

First, the national progressive movement, which had found its most effective embodiment in the coalition of forces that reelected Woodrow Wilson in 1916, was shattered by certain policies that the administration pursued from 1917 to 1920, and by some developments over which the administration had no or only slight control. The collapse that occurred in 1920 was not inevitable and cannot be explained by merely saying that "the war killed the progressive movement."

Second, large and aggressive components of a potential new progressive coalition remained after 1920. These elements never succeeded in uniting effectively before the end of the decade, not because they did not

[13] Much that is new on the Republican preconvention campaign and convention of 1920 may be found in William T. Hutchinson, *Lowden of Illinois: The Life of Frank O. Lowden* (2 vols., Chicago, 1957).

[14] See e.g., Allan P. Sindler, *Huey Long's Louisiana: State Politics, 1920–1952* (Baltimore, Md., 1956).

exist, but because they were divided by conflicts among themselves. National leadership, which in any event did not emerge in the 1920's, perhaps could not have succeeded in subduing these tensions and in creating a new common front.

Third, as a result of the foregoing, progressivism as an organized national force suffered a serious decline in the 1920's. This decline was heightened by the defection of large elements among the urban middle classes and the intellectuals, a desertion induced by technological, economic, and demographic changes, and by the outcropping of certain repressive tendencies in progressivism after 1917.

Fourth, in spite of reversals and failures, important components of the national progressive movement survived in considerable vigor and succeeded to a varying degree, not merely in keeping the movement alive, but even in broadening its horizons. This was true particularly of the farm groups and of the coalition concerned with public regulation or ownership of electric power resources. These two groups laid the groundwork in the 1920's for significant new programs in the 1930's and beyond.

Fifth, various progressive coalitions controlled Congress for the greater part of the 1920's and were always a serious threat to the conservative administrations that controlled the executive branch. Because this was true, most of the legislation adopted by Congress during this period, including many measures that historians have inaccurately called reactionary, was progressive in character.

Sixth, the progressive movement in the cities and states was far from dead in the 1920's, although we do not have sufficient evidence to justify any generalizations about the degree of its vigor.

If this tentative and imperfect synthesis has any value, perhaps it is high time that we discard the sweeping generalizations, false hypotheses, and clichés that we have so often used in explaining and characterizing political developments from 1918 to 1929. Perhaps we should try to see these developments for what they were—the normal and ordinary political behavior of groups and classes caught up in a swirl of social and economic change. When we do this we will no longer ask whether the progressive movement was defunct in the 1920's. We will ask only what happened to it and why.

Sources and Nature
of Intolerance in
the 1920's

Paul Murphy

The 1920s, whether viewed as the continuation or
disintegration of Progressivism, are also usually
examined in terms of the sour impulses of the decade:
intolerance, nativism, xenophobia, and sometimes even
religious fundamentalism. Beneath the surface
frivolity, the speakeasies, jazz and flappers, were often
bitter antagonisms that created what many historians
consider to be an ugly part of the American past: the
Red Scare, the Scopes trial, the Sacco-Vanzetti case,
the Ku Klux Klan, prohibition, and immigration
restriction.

Most historians have viewed these developments as
rational or irrational attempts to preserve older values
and to remove or defeat threats to that embattled
social order. Historians disagree, however, on whether
the developments of the 1920s are simply heightened
expressions of attitudes located deep in the American
past or whether the events of the 1920s should be
traced back only to about the turn of the century
when American attitudes changed. Put simply, do the
Red Scare and the Alien-Sedition acts flow from
similar sources? Do the Know-Nothings of the 1840s
and the immigration restriction movements express
similar attitudes and social tensions? Had a new

concept of Americanism arisen in the years around the turn of the century, or were native-born citizens acting on an older conception?

In his analysis of the "Sources and Nature of Intolerance in the 1920s," Paul Murphy of the University of Minnesota is often ambivalent on these matters. He concludes, for example, that much of the intolerance, though not "traditional," "was merely an outbreak of familiar subsurface prejudices with antecedents in earlier expressed antipathies," and he also traces intolerance explicitly back to at least the Progressive period.

The immediate postwar source for peacetime sedition and criminal syndicalist laws, according to Murphy, was the business community. He implies that the broader public would not have feared Bolshevism so much, nor have supported these restrictions, if the business community had not encouraged fears and pushed for the legislation. The Red Scare, he notes, also allowed self-serving individuals or special interest groups to exploit fears for personal advantage.

Basic to much of the division of the decade, according to the author, is what Ferdinand Tönnies termed the Gemeinschaft-Gesellschaft structure: the shift from the rural-oriented, ethnically and religiously homogeneous society of traditional status arrangements and low mobility (Gemeinschaft) to the urban-industrial, ethnically and religiously heterogeneous society, where social and economic relations are defined by contract and high mobility prevails (Gesellschaft). These competing modes, often explained more simply as the conflict between urban and rural values, have been located at the core of much of the antagonism of the decade. Prohibition, Murphy notes, can be explained within the framework of "superimposed Gemeinschaft values."

While the Gemeinschaft-Gesellschaft theory has much to recommend it, and many historians rely on it to explain the deep antagonisms of the 1920s, there are also some problems with this analysis. Some of the events and attitudes of the 1920s do not comfortably fit the theory. For example, some rural areas violated prohibition laws and found them antithetical to their practices and values. Also, historians using the theory

Sources and Nature of Intolerance in the 1920's. From *Journal of American History*, LI (June 1964), pp. 60–76. Copyright © 1964 by the Organization of American Historians. Reprinted by permission of the Organization of American Historians.

assume that many urban middle-class Americans clung to Gemeinschaft values despite the evidence suggesting that they were also willing to embrace portions of Gesellschaft values. How, for example, can the theory adequately explain why these Americans wanted prohibition and also accepted industrialization and the new forms of the organizational society? Is the answer that these Americans were ambivalent an adequate response or is it a description and not an explanation? And, finally, the Gemeinschaft-Gesellschaft distinction assumes the stability of the small town and farming areas, yet studies suggest that even small towns, whose total population and social structure might remain stable, were subject to considerable flux because of substantial in- and out-migration. Indeed, there is some evidence to challenge the familiar image of stable rural America. Curiously, even though Murphy himself is troubled about relying on social theory for historical analysis, he, nevertheless, uncritically uses this theory in his explanation of intolerance in the 1920s.

Moving beyond the Gemeinschaft-Gesellschaft framework, Murphy ultimately concludes with an eclectic interpretation: "many interwoven factors produced a concatenation of syndromes which made the country a peculiarly fertile seedbed for both intolerance and its shrewd manipulation." Among the tensions he cites were those created by economic growth, the inequitable distribution of income, urbanization and its attendant dislocations, the disillusionment with democracy, and the contradictory responses to the war experience.

*I*n approaching that seamy side of the national character which periodically displays broad-scale intolerance, prejudice, nativism, and xenophobia, many American historians have sought in recent years to draw upon the findings of scholars in related disciplines in their attempts at meaningful analysis. Especially suggestive in this area has been recent work in sociology, social psychology, cultural anthropology, and American studies.[1] Differences exist, however, as to how such findings can actually aid

[1] Particularly suggestive in this regard are the works of Gordon Allport, Bruno Bettelheim, Kenneth B. Clark, Allison Davis, E. Franklin Frazier, Marie Jahoda, Morris Janowitz, Clyde Kluckhohn, Kurt Lewin, Herbert Muller, Gunnar Myrdal, Arnold Rose, Gerhart Saenger, Edward A. Shils, James Vander Zanden, Robin Williams, and J. Milton Yinger.

the historian and the degree of reliance he can confidently place upon them. Given the fact that the average historian must work in a past context in which precise empirical research is impossible, particularly as it applies to a broad spectrum of public attitudes, and given the fact that modern social science studies draw the great body of their evidence from current materials, a question of relevance is raised. How safe is it for the historian to project such modern findings backwards in an attempt better to understand and grasp the tensions and pressures of a prior era? Are modern social science techniques reliable in the analysis of imprecise historical materials?

Some members of the historical guild feel that such borrowing of either materials or techniques is too dangerous to be acceptable. Others at times have relied too heavily upon such interdisciplinary aids in order to validate general presumptions otherwise difficult of documentation. Still others have used such materials cautiously and carefully, so cautiously and so carefully that they have come to differ among themselves concerning their applicability. In the study of past intolerance, for example, there have been those who drew heavily upon a sociologically oriented emphasis on status rivalries and who have emphasized ongoing tensions ever present in the slow process of ethnic integration in our dynamic society.[2] Yet such persons have subsequently been challenged to explain the plausibility of the cyclical nature of waves of intolerance and its frequently differing character as unique situations have produced unique expressions geared to immediate needs. Others who have made careful use of stereotyping or who have placed reliance upon ideological factors have been questioned. So too have those who have focused upon the concrete facts of the immediate situation, especially upon the influence of men of passion with ability to create or nurture moods of alarm by exploiting irrational myths. This has forced such persons to de-emphasize the constant factor of human irrationality in normal times even though it is always basic in assessing causation in all historical events.[3]

In many ways the study of intolerance in the 1920s raises in exaggerated form both a question of the applicability of related materials and of proper permissible use of such materials. That decade, despite its surface prosperity and supposed gaiety and exuberance, was characterized by waves of public intolerance seldom felt in the American experience. Much of this intolerance was merely an outbreak of familiar subsurface prejudices with antecedents in earlier expressed antipathies toward radicals, Catholics, Jews, Negroes, Orientals, and other minority groups. Yet such intolerance was not traditional. Fostered frequently, although seldom led directly by an appre-

[2] For example, John Higham, "Another Look at Nativism," *Catholic Historical Review*, XLIV (July 1958), 150, in denigrating an ideological approach, argues: "Except on the subject of race (and in related forms anti-Semitism), the kind of accusations which nativists leveled against foreign elements remained relatively constant. . . . For the history of nativism, therefore, emotional intensity provided the significant measure of change."

[3] David B. Davis confronts this dilemma with healthy open-mindedness in "Some Themes of Counter-Subversion: An Analysis of Anti-Masonic, Anti-Catholic, and Anti-Mormon Literature," *Mississippi Valley Historical Review*, XLVII (Sept. 1960), 205–24.

hensive business community or aggravated by men seeking gratuities as brokers for that community or as brokers for men of property, it quickly gained its sanctions from that national consensus so clumsily branded "normalcy" and involved many Americans previously immune to its toxicity. As such it was an integral part of the 1920s, participated in consciously or unconsciously by the great majority of Americans. That it took on a changing character as the decade advanced is apt testimony to its virulence. That it either disappeared or took on different forms with the depression seems to reveal that it was specially suited to the peculiar culture and society of the jazz age.

The historian would be delighted if by merely adding the materials and utilizing the techniques of the social scientists he could say precise and scientific things both about the roots, nature, and manifestations of intolerance at this time. Yet, despite the siren's call of being able through empirical social research to reach quantitative answers, he is tempted to concentrate on the imprecise approaches of history, relying upon interdisciplinary tools as analytical devices only when they seem to have an obvious relation to known and documentable reality.

Clearly the sources of the intolerance of the 1920s can be traced to at least the late Progressive period, with obvious roots in the immediately preceding years. Clearly such intolerance had a relation to growing Progressive apprehensions over alarming developments which did not seem to be responding to normal controls. The IWW, the first effectively organized movement of militant workingmen to challenge the whole American economic system, sent chills through the hearts and outrage through the souls of upper and middle class Americans. Here in the early years of the century was a group with the effrontery to make demands no decent citizen could honor and employ techniques no moral American could tolerate. But worse than this, these people and their Socialist "cousins" rejected the premises upon which the American system rested, namely that rights and privileges were open in a free society to anyone who was willing to work up patiently within the system. Or if the individual was incapable of utilizing this technique he would eventually be taken care of in a spirit of paternalism by the affluent class, as long as he stood with his hat in his hand and patiently waited. The alarming fact was that the IWWs and Socialists were no longer willing to wait. They were unwilling to accept the fact that only after one had gained a stake in society was he warranted in becoming a critic or a reformer. As one Progressive editor wrote during the Lawrence textile strike of 1912 (at the point which Paul Brissenden called "the high tide of the I.W.W. activity"):

> On all sides people are asking, Is this a new thing in the industrial world? . . . Are we to see another serious, perhaps successful, attempt to organize labor by whole industrial groups instead of by trades? Are we to expect that instead of playing the game respectably, or else frankly breaking out into lawless riot which we know well enough how to deal with, the laborers are to listen to a subtle anarchistic philosophy which challenges the fundamental ideas of law and order, inculcating such strange doctrines as those of "direct

action," "sabotage," "syndicalism," "the general strike," and "violence"? . . .
We think that our whole current morality as to the sacredness of property
and even of life is involved in it.[4]

Also involved in it was the IWW practice of utilizing the rhetoric of
American democracy as a device for obtaining their ends. The "free-speech
fight" which assumed national proportions after 1910 was distressingly
successful at times and was painfully difficult to counteract. For while many
Americans could argue that utilizing free speech to gain personal economic
ends was an abuse of American ideals, the alternative of arbitrary suppression hardly preserved them.

For those in this dilemma World War I afforded a satisfying rationalization for suppression. Woodrow Wilson's prediction, "once lead this people
into war and they'll forget there ever was such a thing as tolerance,"[5] was
clairvoyant, as the government quickly set out to turn the President's words
into official policy that succeeded frighteningly well. Every element of
American public opinion was mobilized behind "my country, right or
wrong," dissent was virtually forbidden, democracy at home was drastically
curtailed so that it could be made safe abroad, while impressionable children
were either "educated" in Hun atrocities, or their time was employed in
liberty loan, Red Cross, war saving stamp, or YMCA campaigns. It was not
difficult then to channel an aroused nation's wrath against earlier boatrockers
—a development made easier by the fact that many IWWs and Socialists
stood out boldly against the war from the start. The Espionage Act of 1917,
while ostensibly a measure to strike at illegal interference with the war
effort, was so worded that it could be, and was, used to stamp out radical
criticism of the war. Its subsequent 1918 amendment, the Sedition Act,
was a less subtle device. Passed by the pressure of western senators, and
modeled after a Montana IWW statute, its purpose was to undercut both
the performance and advocacy of undesirable activity. There was a clear
implication that people who utilized speech as a means of gaining im-
proper ends had to be restricted.[6] And with the subsequent federal prosecution of 184 members of the IWW in 1918 and 1919,[7] to say nothing of a
crackdown on Socialists, German-Americans, conscientious objectors, and
Non-Partisan Leaguers, the intent of the federal legislative and administrative program became crystal clear.

With peace and the end of conservative labor's wartime honeymoon,
there was renewed fear on the part of the reinvigorated business com-

[4] "After the Battle," Survey, XXVIII (April 6, 1912), 1–2. Such attitudes are explored
in provocative detail in Reinhard Bendix, Work and Authority in Industry: Ideologies
of Management in the Course of Industrialization (New York, 1956), 254–340.

[5] Ray Stannard Baker, Woodrow Wilson, Life and Letters (8 vols., New York, 1927–
1939), VI, 506–07. On the persecution of anti-war groups generally, see H. C. Peterson
and Gilbert C. Fite, Opponents of War: 1917–18 (Madison, 1957), and O. A. Hilton,
"The Minnesota Commission of Public Safety in World War I, 1917–1919," Bulletin of
the Oklahoma Agricultural and Mechanical College, LXVIII (May 15, 1951).

[6] Zechariah Chafee, Jr., Free Speech in the United States (Cambridge, 1941), 39–41.

[7] Philip Taft, "The Federal Trials of the IWW," Labor History, III (Winter 1962),
57–91.

munity that an unholy union of dissident malcontents and elements of more orthodox labor, now feeling callously betrayed, was not only possible but probable. The strikes of the immediate postwar period could only be rationalized by business in these terms. And to create further alarm, not only was Bolshevism a reality in Russia, but American workers and even some influential leaders were studying its economic and political implications with interest if not with admiration. Catholics, when under fire in the past, had consistently denied their allegiance to the Vatican, but some of these Bolshevik admirers even proclaimed proudly and openly their allegiance to a new order functioning from the Kremlin.[8]

Fear led to irrationality and business found it impossible to analyze the meaning and implications of these developments or to understand what Gutzon Borglum called in 1919 the "real labor problem," which was labor's dependent condition. In response to a speech by Nicholas Murray Butler, rebuking labor for its lack of "reasonableness."[9] Borglum wrote:

> Labor's recent political activity is due to a deep consciousness of the neces-sity of self-reliance to secure any and all improvement in its condition. And further, the political color that has recently appeared in its methods, is forced because of the utter faithlessness and failure of partisan government to give it relief.[10]

But to conservative leaders, protection was more important than under-standing. With the wartime legislation now generally inapplicable, they sought to get onto the statute books peacetime sedition and criminal syn-dicalism laws to take its place. To accomplish this, business was frequently able to transfer its own fears of Bolshevism both to a broader public and to state legislators who served that public. The result was that such propa-gandizing, plus added apprehensions triggered by frequently specious bomb scares, produced wide demand for restriction. Thus, although much of the new legislation was enacted in a sincere desire to control agitators and dangerous seditionists, other more responsive legislators took care to be sure that resultant laws were carefully worded and did not appear to be class legislation. By 1920 thirty-five states had enacted some form of restrictive, precautionary legislation enabling the rapid crackdown on speech that might by its expression produce unlawful actions geared toward stimulating im-proper political or economic change. Such legislation was couched in terms which in Connecticut permitted punishment of "disloyal, scurrilous, or abusive language about the form of government of the United States," and in Colorado, "advocacy by word or in print of forcible resistance to con-

---

[8] Roger N. Baldwin, "The Myth of Law and Order," in Samuel D. Schmalhausen, ed., *Behold America!* (New York, 1931), 660–61. The appeal of the Soviet experiment in its early years stands out in various liberal organs. See, for example, *The Advance* (New York), 1919–1923. See also Matthew Josephson, *Sidney Hillman: Statesman of American Labor* (Garden City, 1952), 274 ff., and Christopher Lasch, *The American Liberals and the Russian Revolution* (New York, 1962).

[9] Nicholas Murray Butler, *The Real Labor Problem* (n.p., [1919]), an address de-livered before the Institute of Arts and Sciences, Columbia University, October 13, 1919, and published as a pamphlet.

[10] Gutzon Borglum, *The Real Labor Problem* (n.p., [1919]), a confidential pamphlet, privately printed.

stituted government either as a general principle, or in particular instances as a means of affecting governmental, industrial, social or economic conditions."[11]

That there was no legal need or justification for such legislation (the criminal codes of the states adequately covered conspiracy and libel)[12] further underlined the fact that its purpose was devious. It constituted intimidating legislation by which business subtly sought to institutionalize forms of prior curtailment and thereby free itself from the necessity of having personally to restrict those it considered a threat to the existing order. Henceforth such restriction and subtle regimentation could be left to the discretion of administrative officials who could develop standards to fit immediate and local needs,[13] and who, as the decade progressed, were to add the injunction as a further precautionary weapon.

Although this legislation was quickly implemented in 1919 in a number of states, it did not quiet all malcontents. Prompted by a multiplication of strikes and labor discontent, the more hysterical began to fear that local sanctions were not enough and proceeded to advocate a form of federal "direct action." Powerful federal activity such as the Palmer raids, the army-conducted deportation of 249 "dangerous Reds" aboard the "Soviet Ark" *Buford,* the contemporaneous effort of representatives and senators to rush through a federal peacetime sedition act, while a product of and response to excessive public hysteria should also be understood as the partial culmination of an increasingly more pressing apprehensiveness which had obsessed conservatives for well over a decade. And the fact that many Americans were at the time able to rationalize and condone the most disgraceful, wholesale departure from fundamental guarantees of basic liberty and due process of law in American history further underscores the extent of their fears.[14]

Yet the Red scare of the 1920s introduced a new permanent dimension of intolerance. This was the aspiring, self-seeking individual or special interest group which sought to exploit the hysteria and intolerance of the moment for personal advantage. Such individuals and groups were not new in American history.[15] But the breadth of their operations was more sweeping

[11] See Fund for the Republic, *Digest of the Public Record of Communism in the United States* (New York, 1955), 266 ff. For a detailed history of this legislation and a careful state-by-state record of its framing see Eldridge F. Dowell, "A History of the Enactment of Criminal Syndicalism Legislation in the United States" (2 vols., doctoral dissertation, Johns Hopkins University, 1936).

[12] "Criminal Syndicalism," *Columbia University Law Review,* XX (Feb. 1920), 232. The point was made regularly by liberals in the 1920s. See, for example, Brandeis' famous concurring opinion in the Whitney case (1927), 274 U.S., 357, 372 ff.

[13] American Civil Liberties Union, *The Police and Radicals: What 88 Police Chiefs Think and Do About Radical Meetings* (New York, 1921). See also *Investigation of Communist Propaganda. Hearings before a Special Committee to Investigate Communist Activities in the United States.* House Exec. Docs., 71 Cong., 2 Sess., Pt. IV, Vol. I, 3; Vol. II, 574 ff. (1930).

[14] National Popular Government League, *To the American People: Report upon Illegal Practices of the United States Department of Justice* (Washington, 1920). On the impact of the report see Robert K. Murray, *Red Scare: A Study in National Hysteria* (Minneapolis, 1955), 255.

[15] One is immediately reminded of the careful attempt of the Adams Federalists to exploit the half-war with France in 1798, Know-Nothingism in various periods of

in the 1920s, and the ambitiousness of their calculations was greater, as was the number of Americans they sought to affect. For aggressive politicians like A. Mitchell Palmer, Leonard Wood, or Albert S. Burleson, the ability to project themselves into the role of master defender of the endangered order could mean nomination to high office, hopefully the presidency. To an Anthony Caminetti, the first person of Italian extraction to be elected to Congress and by then Commissioner of Immigration, this was an opportunity to demonstrate that he, as well as others of his national origin, were fully 100 percent American. To an aggressive bureaucrat like William J. Flynn, head of the Bureau of Investigation, or J. Edgar Hoover, head of the Bureau's newly created General Intelligence (antiradical) Division, here was a chance to enhance the power of the Bureau, and his own power and domain simultaneously.[16] To Flynn's successor, William J. Burns, the ability to guide public fears and even create fears where only apprehensions had existed was also an opportunity to stimulate a brisk private business for the Burns International Detective Agency until an increasingly more hostile public forced a curtailment and a housecleaning in the Department of Justice.[17]

At the group level motivations were equally divergent. The American Legion epitomized the service-oriented organizations, obligated to deliver a variety of specific benefits to its wide membership. To do this entailed sufficient flattering and assisting of those in power to convince them that the organization deserved favors. But to write the Legion off as "apple-polishing, flag-wavers of patriotism" is to miss the fact that most legionnaires received great satisfaction from ousting "Reds" and Americanizing everyone completely. Such patrioteering afforded an opportunity for members to demonstrate and articulate their faith and allegiance to basic ideals and institutions and thereby to gain acceptance and status with those who felt a similar need.[18] Thus in this and similar organizations there was a natural tie between aiding the "establishment" and crusading to save America. The professional patriots, on the other hand, had simpler and even less commendable motives. Primarily propaganda organizations, and the mouthpieces of single leaders or small cabals, their purpose was to ingratiate themselves with large private or corporate donors and thereby insure their continuation. This meant showing results, not only in broad distribution of literature but in providing speakers to help in mobilizing large elements of the general public against all manner of enemies of "the American way." Thus Harry A. Jung of the powerful National Clay Products Industries As-

---

American History, bloody-shirt waving in the post-Civil War years, among other things. See James M. Smith, *Freedom's Fetters: The Alien and Sedition Laws and American Civil Liberties* (Ithaca, 1956).

[16] Max Lowenthal, *The Federal Bureau of Investigation* (New York, 1950), 71–72, 90, 298 ff.

[17] Don Whitehead, *The F.B.I. Story* (New York, 1956), 55–59; Alpheus T. Mason, *Harlan Fiske Stone: Pillar of the Law* (New York, 1956), 149–50; Methodist Federation for Social Service, *The Social Service Bulletin* (Feb. 1920), 1–4; *ibid.* (Sept. 1924), 1–4; Dowell, *Criminal Syndicalism Legislation*, 1026, 1129.

[18] Rodney G. Minott, *Peerless Patriots: Organized Veterans and the Spirit of Americanism* (Washington, 1963), 112 ff.

sociation and later the American Vigilant Intelligence Federation could write to a potential subscriber:

> We cooperate with over 30 distinctly civic and patriotic organizations. . . . It would take me too long to relate how I "put over" this part of our activities, namely, "trailing the Reds." Should you ever be in Chicago, drop in and see me and I will explain. That it has been a paying proposition for our organization goes without saying. . . .[19]

And again, Fred R. Marvin, head of the Keymen of America, could for six dollars per annum supply potential private radical hunters with his *Daily Data Sheets* which conveyed the doings of the Bolsheviks and parlor pinks to nervous and apprehensive individuals.[20] It was Marvin's aim to inspire the leadership of such a group as the DAR to draw up and enforce a national "black-list" of undesirable speakers that included such public disturbers of the peace as Jane Addams, Sherwood Eddy, James Harvey Robinson, and William Allen White.[21] In all, over thirty such ultra-patriotic organizations came and went in the 1920s, all to a greater or lesser degree dependent upon the success with which they could mobilize and direct public intolerance and intemperance.[22]

In this context the Ku Klux Klan played a unique role. Although it was geared to financial gain, especially as the decade progressed and its leadership fell more and more into the hands of those who sought to utilize it solely for personal profit, it was content to draw its money and support largely from private citizens in small towns and rural communities, a fact which set it apart from most other intolerance purveyors in the 1920s. This also meant, however, that it operated upon poorly underpinned grounds, a fact graphically illustrated by its rapid collapse well before the onset of the economic crisis of the depression years.

The success which all these individuals and groups achieved would still not have been possible if great segments of the American public had not been highly susceptible to the various types of appeal which they made. The source of this susceptibility was neither simple, nor always rational. It stemmed from the turbulence of the decade as value patterns underwent modification from the impact both of external pressures and internal conflict. When the German sociologist Ferdinand Tönnies delineated in his 1926 volume[23] between what he called Gemeinschaft-Gesellschaft social

---

[19] Jung to Henry E. Niles, March 23, 1926, American Civil Liberties Union Collection, Microfilm Reel 333 (New York Public Library). The ACLU files are filled with material concerning the various professional patriot groups.

[20] There is a complete run of the *Daily Data Sheets* in the ACLU Collection, Microfilm Reel 332.

[21] On the blacklist see Martha Strayer, *The D.A.R., An Informal History* (Washington, 1958), 133 ff., and Walter Johnson, ed., *Selected Letters of William Allen White, 1899–1943* (New York, 1947), 278–83.

[22] Norman Hapgood, ed., *Professional Patriots* (New York, 1927), concentrates on twenty-five or so of the major ones, although Fred R. Marvin, *Our Government and Its Enemies* (New York, 1932), by adding a variety of local auxiliaries, lists fifty-four organizations as making up the American Coalition of Patriotic Societies at the height of the movement.

[23] Ferdinand Tönnies, *Gemeinschaft und Gesellschaft*, translated and edited by Charles P. Loomis (East Lansing, 1957). The danger for the historian in utilizing such a concept

structure, he inadvertently suggested the root of one of the sources of the chronic distress of the American middle class mind. Tönnies' Gemeinschaft structure well described that segment of American society which was basically rural or rural oriented, homogeneous in its ethnic and religious structure and values, a society which functioned through traditional status arrangements and which was characterized by low mobility. The members of such a society had always in America fought off what they considered the deleterious effect of foreign values endemic in a Gesellschaft structure with its urban orientation, secular focus, heterogeneous ethnic makeup, its preference for ordering social and economic relations through contract, and its tradition of high mobility which too often seemed to operate on questionable standards. In fact, the decade had opened on the crest of a successful counterattack of superimposed Gemeinschaft values in the "noble experiment," prohibition. But such a victory was a nervous one as open defiance and hostility grew and as erosion seemed to be occurring elsewhere with the nation succumbing to the excitement and immediacy of a new, generally urban dispersed popular culture. Formerly insulated value orientations now were subjected to the lure of new behavioral patterns suggested by the radio, the movies, romance magazines, and national service clubs. Moreover, the automobile, and in time the airplane, were affording the physical mobility which inevitably speeded up actual social contact with those whose values may earlier have only been slightly known.[24] This does not suggest that either form of social organization was bound to prevail. What it does suggest is that with the pressures to standardize, elements of formerly isolated groups were being subjected to a new challenge to modify the intensity with which they held to their own unique ways as the only acceptable ones.

Those who were thus disturbed accepted dominant American values. However, they found that their interpretation of these values or the techniques that they found acceptable in attaining them frequently had to undergo more modification than they found comfortable. Yet "normalcy," incorporating as it did a multitude of simple virtues along with carefully contrived selfish ends, proved an acceptable home for most rural Victorians and Babbitts alike. Their concern, and often it was held with equal intensity by each, was not the system, but the deviator, who for one reason or another was unwilling to accept the system with its fairly rigid formulae as to how to succeed and who might succeed. Here two types of troublemakers invariably stood out. The one was made up of those who sought unjustifiably to reach the pinnacle of full attainment of the success symbols which the system held out. The other consisted of those whose hierarchy of values and, of necessity, methods for attaining them were totally at odds with the standards of the day. In the former group one inevitably found the targets

is well delineated by Robin M. Williams, Jr., *American Society* (2nd rev. ed., New York, 1960), 482–83. Highly provocative in this context is the assessment of value orientation within a culture in Florence R. Kluckhohn and Fred L. Strodtbeck, *Variations in Value Orientation* (Evanston, 1961), 24 ff., 340–44.

[24] A perceptive contemporary understanding of this development was given by Judge Learned Hand in 1930; see Irving Dilliard, *The Spirit of Liberty: Papers and Addresses of Learned Hand* (New York, 1960), 66–83.

of Klan antipathy, for example: the ambitious immigrant, non-Anglo-Saxon, non-Protestant, whose frequent tendency to "overachieve" led to actions to "keep him in his place." But the quiet "consensus" of the 1920s backed up the Klan's overt censuring with a type of silent coercion which was often far more effective, especially if a Jew wanted admission to the local country club, or a Catholic wanted the presidency of the nation. Although Americans may never be fully ready for "the functionally strategic convergence of the standards by which conduct is evaluated," to use Robin Williams' phrase,[25] they were not ready in the 1920s even to consider such a possibility as a desirable national objective. The deviators, although small in number, were even more of a threat. Radicals, militant labor leaders, other loud and unreasonable critics of the system, and the honest and misguided average citizens whom they seemed to be perverting, had to be clamped into place even more quickly and thoroughly and by virtually any means possible. In this many welcomed the aid of any and all self-proclaimed champions of 100 percent Americanism.[26]

This position constituted an interesting modification of an earlier confidence in progress through broad public participation and discussion, a process long boasted as inherent in American institutions. In 1931 Roger Baldwin attributed this to the manifestly declining postwar faith in democracy.[27] Others attributed it to the general insecurity of all Americans and especially the chronic dissatisfaction with what many had been led to believe would be the glorious life of a postwar world.[28] Regardless of the cause, the effect was to undercut one of the potentially important sources which might have brought significant relief. Having convinced themselves that deviators from the status quo were potential Bolsheviks, many Americans found it a simple step to renounce the mildest type of reformer or reform program, a view in which they had the most thorough encouragement from the self-seeking patriots of the decade. An organization like the American Civil Liberties Union, the Federal Council of Churches, various social justice elements within specific religious groups,[29] explicit social reform organizations like the American Birth Control League, the Consumer's League, the National Child Labor Committee, although in reality seeking to strengthen the system by eliminating its many defects, found

[25] Williams, *American Society*, 557. In this regard see John P. Roche, *The Quest for the Dream* (New York, 1963), 261 ff.

[26] Such champions sometimes used aggressive campaigns of "Americanization" geared especially toward education. See "Program for Promoting American Ideals," *American Bar Association Journal*, VIII (Sept. 1922), 587. See also Bessie L. Pierce, *Public Opinion and the Teaching of History in the United States* (New York, 1926), and the same author's *Citizens' Organizations and the Civic Training of Youth* (New York, 1933).

[27] Baldwin, "Myth of Law and Order," 658-59.

[28] Walter Lippmann, whose own writings had reflected intense disillusionment with the "phantom public," attempted to analyze the general disillusionment of the decade in his volume, *A Preface to Morals* (New York, 1929). Revealing in this regard is the broad study of Joseph E. Clark, "The American Critique of the Democratic Idea, 1919–1929" (doctoral dissertation, Stanford University, 1958).

[29] The Methodist Federation for Social Service, Unitarian Fellowship for Social Justice, Church League for Industrial Democracy (Episcopal), National Catholic Welfare Council, and Central Conference of American Rabbis are leading examples.

basic communication difficult with a public conditioned to look askance at any but practitioners of normalcy.[30]

Despite the general similarity through the decade of the sources of broad scale intolerance, its public manifestations took a variety of changing forms. The early fears of Bolshevism could not be exploited indefinitely especially when the sins committed in the name of its suppression were revealed and its purveyors were shown to be using it as a device for unscrupulous personal gain. Public indignation toward the excesses of the Palmer raids, for example, came quickly following the issuance by the National Popular Government League of the devastating report on the *Illegal Practices of the United States Department of Justice* in late May 1920.[31] Such indignation was sufficient to drive those who might have sought to extend similar techniques to adopt far more subtle and clandestine modes of approach, and also to turn hysteria-making over to the private professional patriot organizations. Thus, William J. Burns, for example, after carefully instituting the Bridgeman raids of August 1922 turned to Ralph Easley of the National Civic Federation, Richard M. Whitney of the American Defense Society, and Joseph T. Cashman of the National Security League to arouse the public to a fever pitch over their implications.[32]

Yet even Burns's string ran out in 1923–1924 as the misrule of the Department of Justice could no longer be ignored[33] and as antiradicalism (labor by this time having been quite thoroughly tamed) was becoming a tiresome broken record. This is not to say, as Sidney Howard wrote bitterly at the time, that certain business interests might not find it useful to tar their critics by turning to the "services of radicalism in almost any one of their patriotic clashes with social liberalism or rambunctious unions, or, even, child labor reformers."[34] But for the moment different targets were needed.

For those distressed with the growing disruption of their Gemeinschaft society, the Ku Klux Klan offered avenues for assaulting those most surely responsible. And while all Americans might not have agreed with C. Lewis Fowler, editor of the *American Standard,* that a heinous conspiracy to destroy America was afoot between Roman Catholicism and anti-Christian Jewry,[35] the irrational myths and stereotyping surrounding these groups

[30] Clarke A. Chambers, "Creative Effort in an Age of Normalcy, 1913–1933," *The Social Welfare Forum* (1961), 252–71.

[31] See National Popular Government League, *To the American People.*

[32] Burns's dealings with Easley are revealed in some detail in the files of the National Civic Federation. See Easley to Howard E. Coffin, Oct. 9 and 19, 1922, National Civic Federation Collection (New York Public Library). See also Richard M. Whitney, *The Reds in America* (New York, 1923), and Joseph T. Cashman, *America Asleep: The Menace of Radicalism* (New York, 1923).

[33] American Civil Liberties Union, *The Nation-Wide Spy System Centering in the Department of Justice* (New York, 1924); Mason, *Harlan Fiske Stone;* Whitehead, *F.B.I. Story.*

[34] Sidney Howard, "Our Professional Patriots: V, The New Crusade," *New Republic,* XL (Sept. 24, 1924), 93.

[35] A typical *American Standard* story caption read: "Ochs (Jew) wants Smith (R.C.): Owner of 'New York Times' Would Give Wet Papist Life Tenure of New York Governorship," Sept. 1, 1925. On the modern Klan and southern racism generally see: James W. Vander Zanden, "The Southern White Resistance Movement to Integration" (doctoral dissertation, University of North Carolina, 1958).

were sufficient to convince many they needed surveillance, if not repression. The Klan also impressed many with its pious objectives of uplifting the nation's morality through attacking its immoral desecrators. Atypical of the conservative, service-and-fellowship oriented organizations, or the professional patriot groups, stemming primarily from outside the urban business community, the Klan, nonetheless, for three or four years in the mid-1920s successfully attacked and insidiously exploited the shattering of old moral standards. Thereby the Klan could resort to direct action against progenitors of public immorality, as it did in the case of Judge Ben "Companionate Marriage" Lindsey in Denver.[36] Indirectly, it could also inspire others to heed the clarion call to expose the evil forces which had to be behind the callous disregard of traditional ways, a call answered by Calvin Coolidge, for example, in his public exposé of "Reds" in our women's colleges,[37] or by Texas representative Thomas L. Blanton's public assault on the ACLU which he branded the "UnAmerican Criminal License Union."[38]

For those patriots seeking essentially to play a broker's role for powerful interests, intriguing new opportunities were opening up in antipacifism and the baiting of antimilitarists. The official demise of Burns left the tradition of his office to the War Department. By that time the department was growing more apprehensive over the potential threat to its authority from antiwar sentiments that were increasingly prevalent as disillusion with the war experience intensified. As early as 1923, General Amos Fries, head of the Chemical Warfare Service, had publicly committed the government to support Preparedness Day, and by inference the continuation of an expanded military establishment. Fries had also encouraged Mrs. Lucia R. Maxwell, librarian of the Service, to prepare and circulate the famed "Spider Web Chart," which purported to study women's peace organizations in the United States and show, by ramification and association, that they were all Bolshevik inspired or at least deep pink.[39] Although the War Department eventually ordered retraction, and directed Fries to inform persons to whom the chart had been circulated that its information was erroneous, the retraction fell on few careful ears. The chart was still being used by the Legion and the DAR in the early 1930s as an authentic exposé of the enemies of America. Such sentiments were also purveyed by such a professional militarist as General John J. Pershing, who in a series of lectures for the American Defense Society warned that "our situation is seriously complicated by the teachings of numerous pacifist organizations. . . ."[40]

The concern with pacifism does not imply, however, that earlier hostility toward radicals, social reformers, and other public disrupters had ended.

[36] Ben B. Lindsey and Rube Borough, *The Dangerous Life* (New York, 1931), 388 ff.

[37] Calvin Coolidge, "Enemies of the Republic: Are the 'Reds' Stalking Our College Women?" *The Delineator*, XCVIII (June 1921), 4 ff.

[38] *Cong. Record*, LXVII, Pt. 2, 1217 ff. (Dec. 19, 1925). The story of the assault was widely reprinted. Harry A. Jung wrote to 600 trade secretaries urging support for Blanton in his fight against the ACLU. ACLU Collection, Microfilm Reel 333.

[39] Howard, "Our Professional Patriots," 94. Howard quotes Fries as referring to "the insidious pacifist, who is more to be feared than the man with the torch, gun or sword."

[40] ACLU Collection, Microfilm Reel 331, contains pamphlet reprints of a number of Pershing's public addresses.

On the contrary, the development of pacifism as a term of opprobrium was merely adding another liability to the large series of undesirable personality traits that these enemies of America were supposed to possess, one which could be stressed more strongly when public apprehensions of radicalism were relatively deflated. Certainly as explosive public episodes developed—the Passaic Textile Strike,[41] the furor over New York City's Stuyvesant High School, and by implication the use of any public building as a public forum even for liberals,[42] the Colorado Mine War of late 1927,[43] and above all the execution of Sacco and Vanzetti,[44]—the "Reds" and their dupes were held largely to blame, both for the episodes and for any number of people taking a remotely liberal view on the questions they raised. However, the dangers of such people could be brought home to a far more diversified audience if one talked of the "whole Pacifist-Radical-Communist movement in America [which] is foreign in its conception, if not actually under foreign influence, direction and control,"[45] or referred to such a leader as Roger Baldwin as a "slacker, radical, draft evader, and Leavenworth ex-convict."[46]

And the most effective agents of intolerance came more and more to have this focus. By 1925, the heyday of the Klan was over. The enactment of the National Origins Act in 1924, internal strife (endemic in the order from its beginnings), and burgeoning prosperity, all undercut prior strength. In its annual report for 1927, the American Civil Liberties Union announced that the principal purveyors of intolerance in the country were the War Department, the American Legion, and professional patriot societies. It declared that the American Legion had by then "replaced the Klan as the most active agency of intolerance and repression in the country."[47] The report was editorially criticized by Joseph Pulitzer's liberal New York World for such a value judgment, stating: "With scores of different organizations seeking to curtail liberty in scores of different ways, it is a wise

[41] The material on Passaic is voluminous. See especially Albert Weisbord, Passaic (Chicago, 1926); Mary Heaton Vorse, The Passaic Textile Strike (New York, 1927); Joseph Freeman, An American Testament (New York, 1936), 392 ff.; American Labor Year Book, 1927 (New York, 1927), 105 ff., 156.

[42] The Annual Report of the American Civil Liberties Union for 1927, Free Speech, 1926 (New York, 1927), referred to the ACLU's struggle with the New York City School Board in the Stuyvesant case as "the most important 'free speech fight' of the year." This struggle revealed the existence of a "blacklist" against individuals whose opinions did not conform to those of board members.

[43] American Civil Liberties Union, The War on Colorado Miners (New York, 1928); Donald J. McClurg, "The Colorado Coal Strike of 1927: Tactical Leadership of the IWW," Labor History, IV (Winter 1963), 68–92; Dowell, "Criminal Syndicalism Legislation," 806 ff.; The Advance (New York), Dec. 2, 16, 27, 1929.

[44] See especially G. Louis Joughin and Edmund M. Morgan, The Legacy of Sacco and Vanzetti (New York, 1948), and Francis Russell, Tragedy in Dedham (New York, 1962).

[45] Fred R. Marvin, quoted in Marcus Duffield, King Legion (New York, 1931), 177–78.

[46] This was the standard indictment of Baldwin by his enemies throughout the decade. The quote here is by Col. Leroy F. Smith of the Better America Federation of Los Angeles in an "expose" entitled: The American Civil Liberties Union: Its Mental Processes, Its Chums, Its Program and Purpose (Los Angeles, 1930), 1. On the early activities of the Federation see Edwin Layton, "The Better America Federation: A Case Study of Superpatriotism," Pacific Historical Review, XXX (May 1961), 137–47.

[47] Free Speech, 1926, p. 2.

man who can say that one is more active than any of the others."[48] To which Forrest Bailey, Director of the ACLU, responded by merely pointing out that this was the consensus of all the state units reporting to national headquarters for the year.[49]

It is not the purpose of this paper to attempt to explain the effect of the depression upon what had become fairly standard patterns of intolerance and intolerance-making. Nonetheless, certain clear developments can be recognized. On one hand, the professional patriots quickly found their traditional sources of income drying up. The National Civic Federation, for example, previously one of the bellwethers of such groups, was reduced to such belt-tightening by 1930 and the years following that its activities had to be cut to virtual ineffectiveness.[50] Other comparable groups collapsed completely. Faced with similar problems the American Legion and the DAR found it expedient to do some of their cutting back in the area of antiradical activity. Pacifist-baiting no longer seemed a highly meaningful or relevant response to public problems.

On the other hand, vast evidence suggests that many businesses stepped up their antiradical activity. Deserting the intolerance purveyors who had formerly performed the function of subtly undermining and discrediting their critics, they now preferred to spend their money for direct action in the form of company guards, labor spies, strike breakers, and arms. Thus the American Civil Liberties Union could report a vast increase in the number of cases it received in the early depression years and generally the greatest suppression of individual liberties in the country since the days of the Red scare. Similarly, the number of instances of police brutality and flagrant abuse of local governmental power were well known.[51]

If one is to talk in terms of meaningful and internally consistent cycles of public intolerance, an era ends in 1929–1930. By this time, to defend the status quo as unassailable was to make oneself ludicrous, since a casual glance revealed the magnitude of its defects. Significantly, when Representative Hamilton Fish auspiciously launched a series of congressional investigations in 1930 in an attempt to throw the blame for the depression on domestic "Reds,"[52] the results of his crusade were to produce either large-scale public apathy or large-scale public antipathy.

The imperfect public record of the 1920s then would seem to reveal that many interwoven factors produced a concatenation of syndromes which

[48] Editorial, "The American Civil Liberties Union," New York *World*, May 17, 1927, p. 12.

[49] Letters column, *ibid.*, May 18, 1927, p. 12.

[50] Prior to 1929 the organization's subversive activities program was lavishly supported. In that year the only contribution so earmarked was $1,000 from John Hays Hammond. In 1930 the only contribution was $5,000 from Samuel Insull. By 1931 the amount had been reduced to $138, and in 1932, 1933, and 1934 there were no entries of money received for that purpose. National Civic Federation Receipt Book, National Civic Federation Collection.

[51] See the popular summarization of the findings of the Wickersham Commission, Ernest J. Hopkins, *Our Lawless Police: A Study of the Unlawful Enforcement of the Law* (New York, 1931).

[52] See footnote 13. *The Hearings* of the so-called Fish committee were published in nineteen volumes. The hearings were responsible for a large "Deport the Reds," rally in Carnegie Hall on Jan. 10, 1931. A good cross section of national newspaper opinion on the rally (which was primarily hostile) is in the ACLU Collection, Microfilm Reel 464.

made the country a peculiarly futile seedbed both for intolerance and its shrewd manipulation. These undoubtedly included the tensions of economic dynamism, grossly unequal distribution of wealth, enhanced urbanization with the dislocation it produced both in the urban area and in its rural recruitment grounds, virulent disillusionment with democracy, and the confusing and contradictory assumptions concerning the increasingly unpopular war experience.

A moot question still exists as to whether more precise results could not have been reached by placing heavier reliance on social science. Undoubtedly if public opinion poll information were available or if scientific attempts had been made at the time to quantify a variety of public attitudes, the record would be more approachable. Certainly steeping ourselves in a more sophisticated analysis of present and future events enhances the understanding of social and human processes in general and affords a more precise appreciation of human behavior in a past context. Certainly the types of questions which the empirical social researcher is currently asking can be asked of that decade and the historian is derelict if he fails to ask them. Yet the basic problem is still how to gain essential information now lacking and difficult or impossible to obtain. The social science researcher is not much help here. In fact, he operates on the assumption that unless sufficient information is available to permit arrival at quantitative answers, little of value can be produced and one's energies are wasted in the effort.

The historian, proceeding on the assumption that almost all important questions are important precisely because of their subtle implications and overtones, their complexities, ambiguities, and ambivalences—because in other words, they are not susceptible to quantitative answers—then must plod on his dogged and imperfect way. He must approach incomplete materials not only semi-analytically, but impressionistically and eclectically, even at times attempting to devise his own ways to evaluate a great divergency of data which the social scientist scarcely feels worth considering due to its impreciseness and unsuitability to quantitative analysis. But the historian likes to feel that only if serious attempt is made to assess all the data, regardless of its nature or its incompleteness, can anything resembling past reality possibly be attained. And as a humanist viewing essentially human phenomena, even if in so imprecise a fashion, the historian also likes to feel that he may, as Arthur M. Schlesinger, Jr., has suggested, "yield truths about both individual and social experience which quantitative social research by itself could never reach."[53]

Suggested Reading

Herbert Margulies in "Recent Opinion on the Decline of the Progressive Movement," *Mid-America*, XL (1963), summarizes historical thought on the problem. Paul Glad in "Progressives and the Business Culture of the 1920's," *Journal of American History*, LIII (1966), and George Tindall in "Business Progressivism: Southern Politics in the Twenties," *South Atlantic Quarterly*, LXII (1963), challenge some of Link's conclusions. Clark Chamber in *Seedtime*

[53] Arthur M. Schlesinger, Jr., "The Humanist Looks at Empirical Social Research," *American Sociological Review*, XXVII (Dec. 1962), 771.

of Reform: Social Service and Social Action, 1918–1933 (1963) analyzes the continuation of the reform impulse. Two important studies considering the place of Progressivism in the 1920s are Otis L. Graham, Jr.'s *An Encore for Reform** (1967) and *The Great Campaigns: Reform and War in America, 1900–1928** (1971). The problems of the Democratic Party are examined by David Burner in *The Politics of Provincialism* (1968).

Business-government relations in the decade are examined by Louis Galambos in *Competition and Cooperation: The Emergence of a National Trade Association* (1966), a study of the Cotton Textile Institute; by G. Cullom Davis, in "The Transformation of the Federal Trade Commission, 1914–1929," *Mississippi Valley Historical Review*, LIV (1962); and by James Weinstein in "Organized Business and the City Commission and Manager Movements," *Journal of Southern History*, XXVIII (1962). Labor and labor relations are treated by Marguerite Green in *The National Civic Federation and the American Labor Movement, 1900–1925** (1956), David Brody in "The Rise and Decline of Welfare Capitalism," in John Braeman et al., eds., *Change and Continuity in Twentieth-Century America: The 1920's* (1968), Ronald Radosh in "The Corporate Ideology of Labor Leaders from Gompers to Hillman," *Studies on the Left*, VI (1966), and Robert H. Zieger in *Republicans and Labor, 1919–1929* (1969).

There is a substantial literature on the so-called sour aspects of the decade. Paul Murphy examines these issues in "Normalcy, Tolerance, and the American Character," *Virginia Quarterly Review*, XL (1964). The Red Scare is the subject of Robert K. Murray's *The Red Scare* (1955); William Preston, Jr.'s *Aliens and Dissenters: Federal Suppression of Radicals, 1903–1933** (1963), Stanley Coben's "A Study in Nativism: The American Red Scare of 1919–1920," *Political Science Quarterly*, LXXIX (1964), and John Blum's "Nativism, Anti-Radicalism, and the Foreign Scare, 1917–1920," *Midwest Journal*, III (1950–51).

Nativism is analyzed by John Higham in *Strangers in the Land** (1955), and Oscar Handlin in *The American People in the Twentieth Century** (1954).

The Klan is the subject of Kenneth Jackson's *The Ku Klux Klan in City, 1915–1930** (1968), David Chalmers' *Hooded Americanism** (1965), Arnold Rice's *The Ku Klux Klan in American Politics* (1962), Charles C. Alexander's *The Ku Klux Klan in the Southwest* (1965), and Robert Moats Miller's "The Ku Klux Klan," in John Braeman et al., eds., *Change and Continuity in Twentieth-Century America: The 1920's* (1968).

Important studies of fundamentalism and the conflicts it raised include Paul Carter's "The Fundamentalist Defense of the Faith," in John Braeman et al., eds., *Change and Continuity in Twentieth-Century America: The 1920's* (1968), Robert M. Miller's *American Protestantism and Social Issues, 1919–1939* (1958), Ray Ginger's *Six Days or Forever? Tennessee vs. John Thomas Scopes** (1958), Norman Furniss' *The Fundamentalist Controversy, 1918–1931* (1954), and Lawrence Levine's *Defender of the Faith: William Jennings Bryan** (1965).

For an examination of prohibition, see James Timberlake's *Prohibition and the Progressive Movement** (1963), Andrew Sinclair's *Prohibition: The Era of Excess** (1962), Joseph Gusfield's *Symbolic Crusade: Status Politics and the American Temperance Movement** (1963) and "Prohibition: The Impact of Political Utopianism," in John Braeman et al., eds., *Change and Continuity in Twentieth-Century America: The 1920's*, and John Burnham's "New Perspectives on the Prohibition 'Experiment' of the 1920's," *Journal of Social History*, II (1968).

Burl Noggle's "The Twenties: A New Historiographical Frontier," *Journal of American History*, LII (1966), and Don S. Kirschner's "Conflicts and Politics in the 1920's: Historiography and Prospects," *Mid-America*, XLVIII (1966), are fine introductions to the literature on the decade.

* Also published in paperback edition.

The New Deal

The Roosevelt Reconstruction: Retrospect

William Leuchtenburg

Few administrations and Presidents have provoked
more passion, more hatred and affection, than the
New Deal and Franklin D. Roosevelt. His efforts to
centralize power in the federal government, his
contributions to the activist state, and his expansion of
the office of President seemed threatening to a
generation of conservatives who feared the destruction
of the values they cherished. Many liberal historians,
in contrast, have celebrated the New Deal as the
triumph of the middle way: American reform that
avoided the extremism of ideology while extending
benefits to many citizens and making business more
socially responsible. In short, the New Deal was a
monumental step along the route to the healthy
reform of democratic capitalism. To some enthusiastic
liberals, looking back on these years, the New Deal
was even, in Carl Degler's phrase, a "Third American
Revolution" (*Out of Our Past* [1959, 1970]).

In *Franklin D. Roosevelt and the New Deal* (1963),
from which the following selection is drawn, William
E. Leuchtenburg of Columbia University presented
a more moderate but still friendly judgment: the
New Deal was a "half-way revolution." The New
Deal, among its achievements, advanced justice by

285

recognizing largely unrepresented groups—staple farmers, industrial workers, ethnic groups—but still left many Americans, including sharecroppers, slum dwellers, and most blacks, outside the system.

Leuchtenburg's conception of a "half-way revolution" raises some serious problems. While none of the critics of this liberal analysis denies that the New Deal changed America, some stress the continuities with the past and the limitations of reform. Walter Lippmann, writing in the third year of the New Deal, anticipated some of these criticisms when he assessed Herbert Hoover not as the last of the old, but the first of the new, Presidents. Under Hoover, according to Lippmann, "the national government undertook to make the whole economic order operate prosperously." Hoover, not Roosevelt, "first abandoned the principles of *laissez faire* in relation to the business cycle, established the conviction that prosperity and depression can be properly controlled by political action, and drove out of the public consciousness the old idea that depression must be overcome by private adjustment" ("The Permanent New Deal," *Yale Review* [1935], p. 651).

Moving beyond Lippmann's position, critics of Leuchtenburg's analysis also ask whether the New Deal made significant changes in the structure of the American political economy—in power relations, business-government relations, and income distribution. Without such changes, they maintain, it was neither a "revolution" nor a "half-way revolution." Leuchtenburg argues that the New Deal transformed the distribution of power, substantially weakened big business, and gave labor an important place in the New Deal coalition and in the national system of power, but admits that the New Deal did not appreciably change the distribution of income. Some New Left critics contend, however, that the New Deal did not transform the structure: the New Deal maintained big business' dominance, enabled organized labor simply to become a junior partner in the political economy, and did not alter the distribution of income.

The Roosevelt Reconstruction: Retrospect. From *Franklin D. Roosevelt and the New Deal 1932–1940* by William E. Leuchtenburg (New York: Harper & Row, 1963), pp. 326–48 with deletion of two paragraphs on pp. 334–35 "Even . . . Washington." Copyright © 1963 by William E. Leuchtenburg. Reprinted by permission of Harper & Row, Publishers, Inc.

In examining the New Deal, historians of a liberal or radical persuasion usually also consider another set of issues: Why did the administration not achieve more in social welfare, in extending benefits and representation to other groups, and perhaps in promoting racial equality? Were the limitations primarily in the New Deal ideology? Or was the main impediment actual or feared opposition by the enemies of the New Deal? Put simply, perhaps too simply, did the New Deal run out of ideas, as Richard Hofstadter suggested in *The American Political Tradition* (1948), or did it run into great conservative opposition, as many liberal historians have maintained?

Most historical studies of the New Deal, as that of Leuchtenburg makes clear, involve not only an analysis of what happened and why, but also estimates of what might have been accomplished and appraisals of what was achieved. An appraisal depends in part on the historian's own values; it clearly moves beyond the orbit of objective history to value-laden questions that most historians wish to address and that many readers want answered. It is not the particular political persuasion of the historians—whether conservative, liberal, or radical—but a shared sense of purpose that leads to offering evaluations in recent American history.

*I*n eight years, Roosevelt and the New Dealers had almost revolutionized the agenda of American politics. "Mr. Roosevelt may have given the wrong answers to many of his problems," concluded the editors of *The Economist*. "But he is at least the first President of modern America who has asked the right questions." In 1932, men of acumen were absorbed to an astonishing degree with such questions as prohibition, war debts, and law enforcement. By 1936, they were debating social security, the Wagner Act, valley authorities, and public housing. The thirties witnessed a rebirth of issues politics, and parties split more sharply on ideological lines than they had in many years past. "I incline to think that for years up to the present juncture thinking Democrats and thinking Republicans had been divided by an imaginary line," reflected a Massachusetts congressman in 1934. "Now for the first time since the period before the Civil War we find vital principles at stake." Much of this change resulted simply from the depression trauma, but much too came from the force of Roosevelt's personality and his use of his office as both pulpit and lectern. "Of course you have fallen into some errors—that is human," former Supreme Court Justice John

Clarke wrote the President, "but you have put a new face upon the social and political life of our country."[1]

Franklin Roosevelt re-created the modern Presidency. He took an office which had lost much of its prestige and power in the previous twelve years and gave it an importance which went well beyond what even Theodore Roosevelt and Woodrow Wilson had done. Clinton Rossiter has observed: "Only Washington, who made the office, and Jackson, who remade it, did more than [Roosevelt] to raise it to its present condition of strength, dignity, and independence."[2] Under Roosevelt, the White House became the focus of all government—the fountainhead of ideas, the initiator of action, the representative of the national interest.

Roosevelt greatly expanded the President's legislative functions. In the nineteenth century, Congress had been jealous of its prerogatives as the law-making body, and resented any encroachment on its domain by the Chief Executive. Woodrow Wilson and Theodore Roosevelt had broken new ground in sending actual drafts of bills to Congress and in using devices like the caucus to win enactment of measures they favored. Franklin Roosevelt made such constant use of these tools that he came to assume a legislative role not unlike that of a prime minister. He sent special messages to Congress, accompanied them with drafts of legislation prepared by his assistants, wrote letters to committee chairmen or members of Congress to urge passage of the proposals, and authorized men like Corcoran to lobby as presidential spokesmen on the Hill. By the end of Roosevelt's tenure in the White House, Congress looked automatically to the Executive for guidance; it expected the administration to have a "program" to present for consideration.[3]

Roosevelt's most important formal contribution was his creation of the Executive Office of the President on September 8, 1939. Executive Order 8248, a "nearly unnoticed but none the less epoch-making event in the history of American institutions," set up an Executive Office staffed with six administrative assistants with a "passion for anonymity."[4] In 1939, the President not only placed obvious agencies like the White House Office in the Executive Office but made the crucial decision to shift the Bureau of the Budget from the Treasury and put it under his wing. In later years, such pivotal agencies as the Council of Economic Advisers, the National Security Council, and the Central Intelligence Agency would be moved into the Executive Office of the President. Roosevelt's decision, Rossiter has concluded,

---

[1] The Editors of the Economist, *The New Deal* (New York, 1937), p. 149; Representative Robert Luce to Herbert Claiborne Pell, November 14, 1934, Pell MSS., Box 7; Elliott Roosevelt (ed.), *F.D.R.: His Personal Letters, 1928–1945* (2 vols., New York, 1950), I, 723.

[2] Clinton Rossiter, *The American Presidency* (Signet edition, New York, 1956), p. 114.

[3] *Ibid.*, pp. 81–84; Edward S. Corwin, *The President: Office and Powers 1787–1957* (New York, 1957), pp. 274–275. Yet despite the growth of the Presidency, this was a period in which Congress had great influence. Much of the specific New Deal legislation was the consequence of the work of a Robert Wagner or a Robert La Follette, Jr. The expansion of the Presidency resulted in a reinvigoration of the whole political system.

[4] Luther Gulick, cited in Rossiter, *American Presidency*, p. 96.

converts the Presidency into an instrument of twentieth-century government; it gives the incumbent a sporting chance to stand the strain and fulfill his constitutional mandate as a one-man branch of our three-part government; it deflates even the most forceful arguments, which are still raised occasionally, for a plural executive; it assures us that the Presidency will survive the advent of the positive state. Executive Order 8248 may yet be judged to have saved the Presidency from paralysis and the Constitution from radical amendment.[5]

Roosevelt's friends have been too quick to concede that he was a poor administrator. To be sure, he found it difficult to discharge incompetent aides, he procrastinated about decisions, and he ignored all the canons of sound administration by giving men overlapping assignments and creating a myriad of agencies which had no clear relation to the regular departments of government.[6] But if the test of good administration is not an impeccable organizational chart but creativity, then Roosevelt must be set down not merely as a good administrator but as a resourceful innovator. The new agencies he set up gave a spirit of excitement to Washington that the routinized old-line departments could never have achieved. The President's refusal to proceed through channels, however vexing at times to his subordinates, resulted in a competition not only among men but among ideas, and encouraged men to feel that their own beliefs might win the day. "You would be surprised, Colonel, the remarkable ideas that have been turned loose just because men have felt that they can get a hearing," one senator confided.[7] The President's "procrastination" was his own way both of arriving at a sense of national consensus and of reaching a decision by observing a trial by combat among rival theories. Periods of indecision—as in the spring of 1935 or the beginning of 1938—were inevitably followed by a fresh outburst of new proposals.[8]

Most of all, Roosevelt was a successful administrator because he attracted to Washington thousands of devoted and highly skilled men. Men who had been fighting for years for lost causes were given a chance: John Collier, whom the President courageously named Indian Commissioner; Arthur Powell Davis, who had been ousted as chief engineer of the Department of the Interior at the demand of power interests; old conservationists like Harry Slattery, who had fought the naval oil interests in the Harding era. When Harold Ickes took office as Secretary of the Interior, he looked up Louis Glavis—he did not even know whether the "martyr" of the Ballinger-Pinchot affair was still alive—and appointed him to his staff.[9]

[5] Rossiter, *American Presidency*, p. 100. Cf. Emile Giraud, *La Crise de la démocratie et le renforcement du pouvoir exécutif* (Paris, 1938).

[6] "At times Roosevelt acted as if a new agency were almost a new solution. His addiction to new organizations became a kind of nervous tic which disturbed even avid New Dealers." Arthur Schlesinger, Jr., *The Coming of the New Deal* (Boston, 1959), p. 535. Schlesinger has an excellent discussion of Roosevelt's administrative talent.

[7] Elbert Thomas to Colonel E. LeRoy Bourne, January 6, 1934, Elbert Thomas MSS., Box 23.

[8] Richard Neustadt, *Presidential Power* (New York, 1960), pp. 156–158.

[9] In Roosevelt's first year in office, he signed an order restoring Glavis to the civil service status he had lost when President Taft fired him. Ironically, Ickes found Glavis as

The New Dealers displayed striking ingenuity in meeting problems of governing. They coaxed salmon to climb ladders at Bonneville; they sponsored a Young Choreographers Laboratory in the WPA's Dance Theatre; they gave the pioneer documentary film maker Pare Lorentz the opportunity to create his classic films *The Plow That Broke the Plains* and *The River*. At the Composers Forum-Laboratory of the Federal Music Project, William Schuman received his first serious hearing. In Arizona, Father Bernard Haile of St. Michael's Mission taught written Navajo to the Indians.[10] Roosevelt, in the face of derision from professional foresters and prairie states' governors, persisted in a bold scheme to plant a mammoth "shelterbelt" of parallel rows of trees from the Dakotas to the Panhandle. In all, more than two hundred million trees were planted—cottonwood and willow, hackberry and cedar, Russian olive and Osage orange; within six years, the President's visionary windbreak had won over his former critics.[11] The spirit behind such innovations generated a new excitement about the potentialities of government. "Once again," Roosevelt told a group of young Democrats in April, 1936, "the very air of America is exhilarating."[12]

Roosevelt dominated the front pages of the newspapers as no other President before or since has done. "Frank Roosevelt and the NRA have taken the place of love nests," commented Joe Patterson, publisher of the tabloid New York *Daily News*. At his very first press conference, Roosevelt abolished the written question and told reporters they could interrogate him without warning. Skeptics predicted the free and easy exchange would soon be abandoned, but twice a week, year in and year out, he threw open the White House doors to as many as two hundred reporters, most of them representing hostile publishers, who would crowd right up to the President's desk to fire their questions. The President joshed them, traded wisecracks with them, called them by their first names; he charmed them by his good-humored ease and impressed them with his knowledge of detail.[13] To a degree, Roosevelt's press conference introduced, as some observers claimed, a new institution like Britain's parliamentary questioning; more to the point, it was a device the President manipulated, disarmingly and adroitly, to win support for his program.[14] It served too as a classroom to instruct the country in the new economics and the new politics.

---

intolerable a subordinate as Taft had, and concluded that he had "been very unjust to Ballinger all of these years." *The Secret Diary of Harold Ickes* (3 vols., New York, 1954), III, 111.

[10] John Collier to Louis Brandeis, April 5, 1937, Brandeis MSS., SC 19.

[11] H. H. Chapman, "Digest of Opinions Received on the Shelterbelt Project," *Journal of Forestry*, XXXII (1934), 952–957; Bristow Adams, "Some Fence!" *Cornell Countryman*, XXXII (1934), 4; *Science News Letter*, CXXXIV (1938), 409; "Prairie Tree Banks," *American Forester*, CXLVII (1941), 177.

[12] Samuel Rosenman (ed.), *The Public Papers and Addresses of Franklin D. Roosevelt* (13 vols., New York, 1938–50), V, 165.

[13] Elmer Cornwell, Jr., "Presidential News: The Expanding Public Image," *Journalism Quarterly*, XXXVI (1959), 275–283; "The Chicago Tribune," *Fortune*, IX (May, 1934), 108; *Editor and Publisher*, March 4, 1933; Thomas Stokes, *Chip Off My Shoulder* (Princeton, 1940), p. 367.

[14] Erwin Canham, "Democracy's Fifth Wheel," *Literary Digest*, CXIX (January 5, 1935), 6; Douglass Cater, *The Fourth Branch of Government* (Boston, 1959), pp. 13–14, 142–155; James Pollard, *The Presidents and the Press* (New York, 1947), pp. 773–845.

Roosevelt was the first president to master the technique of reaching people directly over the radio. In his fireside chats, he talked like a father discussing public affairs with his family in the living room. As he spoke, he seemed unconscious of the fact that he was addressing millions. "His head would nod and his hands would move in simple, natural, comfortable gestures," Frances Perkins recalled. "His face would smile and light up as though he were actually sitting on the front porch or in the parlor with them." Eleanor Roosevelt later observed that after the President's death people would stop her on the street to say "they missed the way the President used to talk to them. They'd say 'He used to talk to me about my government.' There was a real dialogue between Franklin and the people," she reflected. "That dialogue seems to have disappeared from the government since he died."[15]

For the first time for many Americans, the federal government became an institution that was directly experienced. More than state and local governments, it came to be *the* government, an agency directly concerned with their welfare. It was the source of their relief payments; it taxed them directly for old age pensions; it even gave their children hot lunches in school. As the role of the state changed from that of neutral arbiter to a "powerful promoter of society's welfare," people felt an interest in affairs in Washington they had never had before.[16]

Franklin Roosevelt personified the state as protector. It became commonplace to say that people felt toward the President the kind of trust they would normally express for a warm and understanding father who comforted them in their grief or safeguarded them from harm. An insurance man reported: "My mother looks upon the President as someone so immediately concerned with her problems and difficulties that she would not be greatly surprised were he to come to her house some evening and stay to dinner." From his first hours in office, Roosevelt gave people the feeling that they could confide in him directly. As late as the Presidency of Herbert Hoover, one man, Ira Smith, had sufficed to take care of all the mail the White House received. Under Roosevelt, Smith had to acquire a staff of fifty people to handle the thousands of letters written to the President each week. Roosevelt gave people a sense of membership in the national community. Justice Douglas has written: "He was in a very special sense the people's President, because he made them feel that with him in the White House they shared the Presidency. The sense of sharing the Presidency gave even the most humble citizen a lively sense of belonging."[17]

When Roosevelt took office, the country, to a very large degree, responded to the will of a single element: the white, Anglo-Saxon, Protestant propertyholding class. Under the New Deal, new groups took their place in the sun. It was not merely that they received benefits they had not had before but

[15] Frances Perkins, *The Roosevelt I Knew* (New York, 1946), p. 72; Bernard Asbell, *When F.D.R. Died* (New York, 1961), p. 161.

[16] Felix Frankfurter, "The Young Men Go to Washington," *Fortune*, XIII (1936), 61; E. W. Bakke, *Citizens Without Work* (New Haven, 1940), pp. 52–53.

[17] Richard Neuberger, "They Love Roosevelt," *Forum and Century*, CI (1939), 15; Corwin, *The President*, p. 471; William O. Douglas, *Being an American* (New York, 1948), p. 88.

that they were "recognized" as having a place in the commonwealth. At the beginning of the Roosevelt era, charity organizations ignored labor when seeking "community" representation; at the end of the period, no fund-raising committee was complete without a union representative. While Theodore Roosevelt had founded a lily-white Progressive party in the South and Woodrow Wilson had introduced segregation into the federal government, Franklin Roosevelt had quietly brought the Negro into the New Deal coalition. When the distinguished Negro contralto Marian Anderson was denied a concert hall in Washington, Secretary Ickes arranged for her to perform from the steps of Lincoln Memorial. Equal representation for religious groups became so well accepted that, as one priest wryly complained, one never saw a picture of a priest in a newspaper unless he was flanked on either side by a minister and a rabbi.

The devotion Roosevelt aroused owed much to the fact that the New Deal assumed the responsibility for guaranteeing every American a minimum standard of subsistence. Its relief programs represented an advance over the barbaric predepression practices that constituted a difference not in degree but in kind. One analyst wrote: "During the ten years between 1929 and 1939 more progress was made in public welfare and relief than in the three hundred years after this country was first settled." The Roosevelt administration gave such assistance not as a matter of charity but of right. This system of social rights was written into the Social Security Act. Other New Deal legislation abolished child labor in interstate commerce and, by putting a floor under wages and a ceiling on hours, all but wiped out the sweatshop.[18]

Roosevelt and his aides fashioned a government which consciously sought to make the industrial system more humane and to protect workers and their families from exploitation. In his acceptance speech in June, 1936, the President stated:

> Governments can err, Presidents do make mistakes, but the immortal Dante tells us that divine justice weighs the sins of the cold-blooded and the sins of the warm-hearted in different scales.
>
> Better the occasional faults of a Government that lives in a spirit of charity than the constant omission of a Government frozen in the ice of its own indifference.

Nearly everyone in the Roosevelt government was caught up to some degree by a sense of participation in something larger than themselves. A few days after he took office, one of the more conservative New Deal administrators wrote in his diary: "This should be a Gov't of humanity."[19]

The federal government expanded enormously in the Roosevelt years. The crisis of the depression dissipated the distrust of the state inherited from the eighteenth century and reinforced in diverse ways by the Jeffersonians and the Spencerians. Roosevelt himself believed that liberty in America was im-

[18] Josephine Chapin Brown, *Public Relief 1929–1939* (New York, 1940), p. ix; Thomas Paul Jenkin, *Reactions of Major Groups to Positive Government in the United States, 1930–1940* (University of California Publications in Political Science [Berkeley and Los Angeles, 1945]), p. 284.

[19] *Public Papers*, V, 235; J. F. T. O'Connor MS. Diary, June 25, 1933.

periled more by the agglomerations of private business than by the state. The New Dealers were convinced that the depression was the result not simply of an economic breakdown but of a political collapse; hence, they sought new political instrumentalities. The reformers of the 1930's accepted almost unquestioningly the use of coercion by the state to achieve reforms.[20] Even Republicans who protested that Roosevelt's policies were snuffing out liberty voted overwhelmingly in favor of coercive measures.[21]

This elephantine growth of the federal government owed much to the fact that local and state governments had been tried in the crisis and found wanting. When one magazine wired state governors to ask their views, only one of the thirty-seven who replied announced that he was willing to have the states resume responsibility for relief.[22] Every time there was a rumored cutback of federal spending for relief, Washington was besieged by delegations of mayors protesting that city governments did not have the resources to meet the needs of the unemployed.

Even more dramatic was the impotence of local governments in dealing with crime, a subject that captured the national imagination in a decade of kidnapings and bank holdups. In September, 1933, the notorious bank robber John Dillinger was arrested in Ohio. Three weeks later, his confederates released him from jail and killed the Lima, Ohio, sheriff. In January, 1934, after bank holdups at Racine, Wisconsin, and East Chicago, Indiana, Dillinger was apprehended in Tucson, Arizona, and returned to the "escape-proof" jail of Crown Point, Indiana, reputedly the strongest county prison in the country. A month later he broke out and drove off in the sheriff's car. While five thousand law officers pursued him, he stopped for a haircut in a barber shop, bought cars, and had a home-cooked Sunday dinner with his family in his home town. When he needed more arms, he raided the police station at Warsaw, Indiana.

Dillinger's exploits touched off a national outcry for federal action. State and local authorities could not cope with gangs which crossed and recrossed jurisdictional lines, which were equipped with Thompson submachine guns and high-powered cars, and which had a regional network of informers and fences in the Mississippi Valley. Detection and punishment of crime had always been a local function; now there seemed no choice but to call in the federal operatives. In July, 1934, federal agents shot down Dillinger outside a Chicago theater. In October, FBI men killed Pretty Boy Floyd near East Liverpool, Ohio; in November, they shot Baby Face Nelson, Public Enemy No. 1, near Niles Center, Illinois. By the end of 1934, the nation had a new kind of hero: the G-man Melvin Purvis and the chief of the Division of Investigation of the Department of Justice, J. Edgar Hoover. By the end of that year, too, Congress had stipulated that a long list of crimes would

[20] Paul Carter has noted the change in the social gospel. The editors of *The Baptist*, he has written, "recognized that the transfer of social privilege involves the use of social coercion, a fact which the Right and Center of the old Social Gospel had not always faced up to." Carter, "The Decline and Revival of the Social Gospel" (unpublished Ph.D. dissertation, Columbia University, 1954).

[21] On the compulsory Potato Act, only six Republicans (and just nine Democrats) voted in opposition.

[22] *Today*, III (January 12, 1935), 4.

henceforth be regarded as federal offenses, including holding up a bank insured by the Federal Deposit Insurance Corporation. The family of a kidnaped victim could call in the federal police simply by phoning National 7117 in Washington.[23]

Under the New Deal, the federal government greatly extended its power over the economy. By the end of the Roosevelt years, few questioned the right of the government to pay the farmer millions in subsidies not to grow crops, to enter plants to conduct union elections, to regulate business enterprises from utility companies to air lines, or even to compete directly with business by generating and distributing hydroelectric power. All of these powers had been ratified by the Supreme Court, which had even held that a man growing grain solely for his own use was affecting interstate commerce and hence subject to federal penalties.[24] The President, too, was well on his way to becoming "the chief economic engineer," although this was not finally established until the Full Employment Act of 1946. In 1931, Hoover had hooted that some people thought "that by some legerdemain we can legislate ourselves out of a world-wide depression." In the Roosevelt era, the conviction that government both should and could act to forestall future breakdowns gained general acceptance. The New Deal left a large legacy of antidepression controls—securities regulation, banking reforms, unemployment compensation—even if it could not guarantee that a subsequent administration would use them.[25]

In the 1930's, the financial center of the nation shifted from Wall Street to Washington. In May, 1934, a writer reported: "Financial news no longer originates in Wall Street." That same month, *Fortune* commented on a revolution in the credit system which was "one of the major historical events of the generation." "Mr. Roosevelt," it noted, "seized the Federal Reserve without firing a shot." The federal government had not only broken down the old separation of bank and state in the Reserve system but had gone into the credit business itself in a wholesale fashion under the aegis of the RFC, the Farm Credit Administration, and the housing agencies. Legislation in 1933 and 1934 had established federal regulation of Wall Street for the first time. No longer could the New York Stock Exchange operate as a private club free of national supervision. In 1935, Congress leveled the mammoth holding-company pyramids and centralized yet more authority over the banking system in the federal government. After a tour of the United States in 1935, Sir Josiah Stamp wrote: "Just as in 1929 the whole country was 'Wall Street-conscious' now it is 'Washington-conscious.' "[26]

Despite this encroachment of government on traditional business prerogatives, the New Deal could advance impressive claims to being regarded as a

[23] "The Marines Are Coming," *Fortune*, X (August, 1934), 56 ff.; *Literary Digest*, CXVII (May 5, 1934), 9; CXVIII (July 28, 1934), 6; CXVIII (December 8, 1934), 7; *Time*, XXIII (March 12, 1934), 14; *Public Papers*, III, 242 ff.

[24] Wickard *v.* Filburn, 317 U.S. 111 (1942).

[25] Sidney Hyman, *The American President* (New York, 1954), pp. 263–264; Carl Degler, *Out of Our Past* (New York, 1959), pp. 391–393. In a few pages, Degler has written the best analysis of the permanent significance of the New Deal.

[26] Ferdinand Lunberg, "Wall Street Dances to Washington's Tune," *Literary Digest*, CXVII (May 12, 1934), 46; "Federal Reserve," *Fortune*, IX (May, 1934), 65–66, 125; Sir Josiah Stamp, "Six Weeks in America," *The Times* (London), July 4, 1935.

"savior of capitalism." Roosevelt's sense of the land, of family, and of the community marked him as a man with deeply ingrained conservative traits. In the New Deal years, the government sought deliberately, in Roosevelt's words, "to energize private enterprise." The RFC financed business, housing agencies underwrote home financing, and public works spending aimed to revive the construction industry. Moreover, some of the New Deal reforms were Janus-faced. The NYA, in aiding jobless youth, also served as a safety valve to keep young people out of the labor market. A New Deal congressman, in pushing for public power projects, argued that the country should take advantage of the sea of "cheap labor" on the relief rolls. Even the Wagner Act and the movement for industrial unionism were motivated in part by the desire to contain "unbalanced and radical" labor groups. Yet such considerations should not obscure the more important point: that the New Deal, however conservative it was in some respects and however much it owed to the past, marked a radically new departure. As Carl Degler writes: "The conclusion seems inescapable that, traditional as the words may have been in which the New Deal expressed itself, in actuality it was a revolutionary response to a revolutionary situation."[27]

Not all of the changes that were wrought were the result of Roosevelt's own actions or of those of his government. Much of the force for change came from progressives in Congress, or from nongovernmental groups like the C.I.O., or simply from the impersonal agency of the depression itself. Yet, however much significance one assigns the "objective situation," it is difficult to gainsay the importance of Roosevelt. If, in Miami in February, 1933, an assassin's bullet had been true to its mark and John Garner rather than Roosevelt had entered the White House the next month, or if the Roosevelt lines had cracked at the Democratic convention in 1932 and Newton Baker had been the compromise choice, the history of America in the thirties would have been markedly different.

At a time when democracy was under attack elsewhere in the world, the achievements of the New Deal were especially significant. At the end of 1933, in an open letter to President Roosevelt, John Maynard Keynes had written:

> You have made yourself the trustee for those in every country who seek to mend the evils of our condition by reasoned experiment within the framework of the existing social system. If you fail, rational change will be gravely prejudiced throughout the world, leaving orthodoxy and revolution to fight it out.

In the next few years, teams of foreigners toured the TVA, Russians and Arabs came to study the shelterbelt, French writers taxed Léon Blum with importing "Rooseveltism" to France, and analysts characterized Paul Van Zeeland's program in Belgium as a "New Deal." Under Roosevelt, observed

[27] *Public Papers,* IX, 11; Walter Pierce to Bureau of Publicity, Democratic National Committee, January 4, 1940, Pierce MSS., File 7.1; Robert Wagner to Harold McCollom, April 24, 1935, Wagner MSS; Sidney Lens, *Left, Right and Center* (Hinsdale, Ill., 1949), pp. 286 ff.; Degler, *Out of Our Past,* p. 416. Not only did the New Deal borrow many ideas and institutions from the Progressive era, but the New Dealers and the progressives shared more postulates and values than is commonly supposed. Nonetheless, the spirit of the 1930's seems to me to be quite different from that of the Progressive era.

a Montevideo newspaper, the United States had become "as it was in the eighteenth century, the victorious emblem around which may rally the multitudes thirsting for social justice and human fraternity."[28]

In their approach to reform, the New Dealers reflected the tough-minded, hard-boiled attitude that permeated much of America in the thirties. In 1931, the gangster film *Public Enemy* had given the country a new kind of hero in James Cagney: the aggressive, unsentimental tough guy who deliberately assaulted the romantic tradition. It was a type whose role in society could easily be manipulated; gangster hero Cagney of the early thirties was transformed into G-man hero Cagney of the later thirties. Even more representative was Humphrey Bogart, creator of the "private eye" hero, the man of action who masks his feelings in a calculated emotional neutrality.[29] Bogart, who began as the cold desperado Duke Mantee of *Petrified Forest* and the frightening Black Legionnaire, soon turned up on the right side of anti-Fascist causes, although he never surrendered the pose of noninvolvement. This fear of open emotional commitment and this admiration of toughness ran through the vogue of the "Dead End Kids," films like *Nothing Sacred*, the popularity of the St. Louis Cardinals' spike-flying Gas House Gang, and the "hard-boiled" fiction of writers like James Cain and Dashiell Hammett.

Unlike the earlier Progressive, the New Dealer shied away from being thought of as sentimental.[30] Instead of justifying relief as a humanitarian measure, the New Dealers often insisted it was necessary to stimulate purchasing power or to stabilize the economy or to "conserve manpower." The justification for a better distribution of income was neither "social justice" nor a "healthier national life," wrote Adolf Berle. "It remained for the hard-boiled student to work out the simple equation that unless the national income was pretty widely diffused there were not enough customers to keep the plants going."[31] The reformers of the thirties abandoned—or claimed they had abandoned—the old Emersonian hope of reforming man and sought only to change institutions.[32] This meant that they did not seek to "uplift" the people they were helping but only to improve their economic position. "In other words," Tugwell stated bluntly, "the New Deal is attempting to do nothing to *people*, and does not seek at all to alter their way of life, their wants and desires."[33]

[28] *The New York Times*, December 31, 1933; Ludovic Naudeau, "Le Rooseveltisme ou la troisième solution," *L'Illustration*, XCCV (November 28, 1936), 375; Otto Veit, "Franklin Roosevelt's Experiment," *Die Neue Rundschau*, XLV (1934), 718–734; Nicholas Halasz, *Roosevelt Through Foreign Eyes* (Princeton, 1961); Donald Dozer, *Are We Good Neighbors?* (Gainesville, 1959), p. 30.

[29] Lewis Jacobs, *The Rise of the American Film* (New York, 1939), pp. 509–512; Lincoln Kirstein, "James Cagney and the American Hero," *Hound and Horn*, V (1932), 465–467; Alistair Cooke, *A Generation on Trial* (New York, 1950), p. 11.

[30] A New Deal social worker, obviously moved by something she had seen, would preface her report apologetically: "At the risk of seeming slobbery . . ." Martha Gellhorn to Harry Hopkins, April 25, 1935, Hopkins MSS.

[31] A. A. Berle, Jr., "The Social Economics of the New Deal," *The New York Times Magazine*, October 29, 1933, pp. 4–5.

[32] Edgar Kemler, *The Deflation of American Ideals* (Washington, 1941), p. 69.

[33] Tugwell, *The Battle for Democracy* (New York, 1935), p. 319. "The excuse for us being in this thing," Aubrey Williams explained to NYA leaders, "is that we are trying

Reform in the 1930's meant *economic* reform; it departed from the Methodist-parsonage morality of many of the earlier Progressives, in part because much of the New Deal support, and many of its leaders, derived from urban immigrant groups hostile to the old Sabbatarianism. While the progressive grieved over the fate of the prostitute, the New Dealer would have placed Mrs. Warren's profession under a code of authority. If the archetypical progressive was Jane Addams singing "Onward, Christian Soldiers," the representative New Dealer was Harry Hopkins betting on the horses at Laurel Race Track. When directing FERA in late 1933, Hopkins announced: "I would like to provide orchestras for beer gardens to encourage people to sit around drinking their beer and enjoying themselves. It would be a great unemployment relief measure." "I feel no call to remedy evils," Raymond Moley declared. "I have not the slightest urge to be a reformer. Social workers make me very weary. They have no sense of humor."[34]

Despite Moley's disclaimer, many of the early New Dealers like himself and Adolf Berle did, in fact, hope to achieve reform through regeneration: the regeneration of the businessman. By the end of 1935, the New Dealers were pursuing a quite different course. Instead of attempting to evangelize the Right, they mobilized massive political power against the power of the corporation. They relied not on converting industrial sinners but on using sufficient coercion. New Dealers like Thurman Arnold sought to ignore "moral" considerations altogether; Arnold wished not to punish wrongdoers but to achieve price flexibility. His "faith" lay in the expectation that "fanatical alignments between opposing political principles may disappear and a competent, practical, opportunistic governing class may rise to power."[35] With such expectations, the New Dealers frequently had little patience with legal restraints that impeded action. "I want to assure you," Hopkins told the NYA Advisory Committee, "that we are not afraid of exploring anything within the law, and we have a lawyer who will declare anything you want to do legal."[36]

In the thirties, nineteenth-century individualism gave ground to a new emphasis on social security and collective action.[37] In the twenties, America hailed Lindbergh as the Lone Eagle; in the thirties, when word arrived that Amelia Earhart was lost at sea, the *New Republic* asked the government to prohibit citizens from engaging in such "useless" exploits. The NRA sought to drive newsboys off the streets and took a Blue Eagle away from a com-

---

to reform the structure of things rather than try to reform the people." National Advisory Committee, NYA, Minutes, August 15, 1937, Charles Taussig MSS., Box 6. In a speech to TVA employees, David Lilienthal derided "uplift." George Fort Milton to Lilienthal, July 10, 1936, Milton MSS., Box 20.

[34] *Time*, XXIII (January 1, 1934), 10; XXI (May 8, 1933), 10. Cf. Richard Hofstadter, *The Age of Reform* (New York, 1955), pp. 300–322.

[35] Arnold, *Symbols of Government*, pp. 270–271. Cf. Sidney Hook, *Reason, Social Myths and Democracy* (New York, 1940), pp. 41–61.

[36] National Advisory Committee, NYA, *Minutes*, August 15, 1935, Charles Taussig MSS., Box 6.

[37] In Ernest Hemingway's *To Have and Have Not*, Harry Morgan says: "No matter how a man alone ain't got no bloody . . . chance." Hemingway, *To Have and Have Not* (New York, 1937), p. 225.

pany in Huck Finn's old town of Hannibal, Missouri, because a fifteen-year-old was found driving a truck for his father's business. Josef Hofmann urged that fewer musicians become soloists, Hollywood stars like Joan Crawford joined the Screen Actors Guild, and Leopold Stokowski canceled a performance in Pittsburgh because theater proprietors were violating a union contract.[38] In New York in 1933, after a series of meetings in Heywood Broun's penthouse apartment, newspapermen organized the American Newspaper Guild in rebellion against the dispiriting romanticism of Richard Harding Davis.[39] "We no longer care to develop the individual as a unique contributor to a democratic form," wrote the mordant Edgar Kemler. "In this movement each individual sub-man is important, not for his uniqueness, but for his ability to lose himself in the mass, through his fidelity to the trade union, or cooperative organization, or political party."[40]

The liberals of the thirties admired intellectual activity which had a direct relation to concrete reality. Stuart Chase wrote of one government report: "This book is live stuff—wheelbarrow, cement mixer, steam dredge, generator, combine, power-line stuff; library dust does not gather here."[41] If the poet did not wish to risk the suspicion that his loyalties were not to the historic necessities of his generation, wrote Archibald MacLeish, he must "soak himself not in books" but in the physical reality of "by what organization of men and railroads and trucks and belts and book-entries the materials of a single automobile are assembled."[42] The New Dealers were fascinated by "the total man days per year for timber stand improvement," and Tugwell rejoiced in the "practical success" of the Resettlement Administration demonstrated by "these healthy collection figures." Under the Special Skills Division of the RA, Greenbelt was presented with inspirational paintings like *Constructing Sewers, Concrete Mixer,* and *Shovel at Work.* On one occasion, in attempting to mediate a literary controversy, the critic Edmund Wilson wrote: "It should be possible to convince Marxist critics of the importance of a work like 'Ulysses' by telling them that it is a great piece of engineering—as it is."[43] In this activist world of the New Dealers, the aesthete and the man who pursued a life of contemplation, especially the man whose interests centered in the past, were viewed with scorn. In Robert Sherwood's *The Petrified Forest,* Alan Squier, the ineffectual aesthete, meets his death in the desert and is buried in the petrified forest where the living turn to stone. He is an archaic type for whom the world has no place.

The new activism explicitly recognized its debt to Dewey's dictum of

[38] *New Republic,* XCI (1937), 262; *Time,* XXIII (February 19, 1934), 14; Herbert Harris, *American Labor* (New Haven, 1938), p. 175.

[39] Cf. *Editor and Publisher,* LXVI (December 23, 1933), 7, 28.

[40] Kemler, *Deflation of Ideals,* pp. 109–110. Kemler, it hardly need be said, grossly overstated his argument.

[41] Stuart Chase, "Old Man River," *New Republic,* LXXXII (1935), 175. "I speak in dispraise of dusty learning, and in disparagement of the historical technique," declared Tugwell. "Are our plans wrong? Who knows? Can we tell from reading history? Hardly." Tugwell, *Battle for Democracy,* pp. 70–71.

[42] MacLeish, *A Time to Speak* (Boston, 1941), p. 45. Cf. MacLeish, "The Social Cant," *New Republic,* LXXIII (1932), 156–158.

[43] *The New York Times,* October 29, 1936; Paul Conkin, *Tomorrow a New World* (Ithaca, 1959), p. 196; Edmund Wilson, "The Literary Class War: I," *New Republic,* LXX (1932), 323.

"learning by doing" and, like other of Dewey's ideas, was subject to exaggeration and perversion. The New Deal, which gave unprecedented authority to intellectuals in government, was, in certain important respects, anti-intellectual. Without the activist faith, perhaps not nearly so much would have been achieved. It was Lilienthal's conviction that "there is almost nothing, however fantastic, that (given competent organization) a team of engineers, scientists, and administrators cannot do today" that helped make possible the successes of TVA.[44] Yet the liberal activists grasped only a part of the truth; they retreated from conceptions like "tragedy," "sin," "God," often had small patience with the force of tradition, and showed little understanding of what moved men to seek meanings outside of political experience. As sensitive a critic as the poet Horace Gregory could write, in a review of the works of D. H. Lawrence: "The world is moving away from Lawrence's need for personal salvation; his 'dark religion' is not a substitute for economic planning."[45] This was not the mood of all men in the thirties—not of a William Faulkner, an Ellen Glasgow—and many of the New Dealers recognized that life was more complex than some of their statements would suggest. Yet the liberals, in their desire to free themselves from the tyranny of precedent and in their ardor for social achievement, sometimes walked the precipice of superficiality and philistinism.

The concentration of the New Dealers on public concerns made a deep mark on the sensibility of the 1930's. Private experience seemed self-indulgent compared to the demands of public life. "Indeed the public world with us has *become* the private world, and the private world has become the public," wrote Archibald MacLeish. "We live, that is to say, in a revolutionary time in which the public life has washed in over the dikes of private existence as sea water breaks over into the fresh pools in the spring tides till everything is salt."[46] In the thirties, the Edna St. Vincent Millay whose candle had burned at both ends wrote the polemical *Conversation at Midnight* and the bitter "Epitaph for the Race of Man" in *Wine from These Grapes*.

The emphasis on the public world implied a specific rejection of the values of the 1920's. Roosevelt dismissed the twenties as "a decade of debauch," Tugwell scored those years as "a decade of empty progress, devoid of contribution to a genuinely better future," Morris Cooke deplored the "gilded-chariot days" of 1929, and Alben Barkley saw the twenties as a "carnival" marred by "the putrid pestilence of financial debauchery."[47] The depression was experienced as the punishment of a wrathful God visited on a nation

[44] David Lilienthal, *TVA: Democracy on the March* (New York, 1944), p. 3.

[45] Waldo Frank, "Our Guilt in Fascism," *New Republic*, CII (1940), 603–608; Murray Kempton, *Part of Our Time* (New York, 1955); p. 2; Cushing Strout, "The Twentieth-Century Enlightenment," *American Political Science Review*, XLIX (1955), 321–339; Morton White, *Social Thought in America* (New York, 1949), p. 241; *New Republic*, LXXIII (1932), 133.

[46] MacLeish mocked "the nineteenth-century poet, the private speaker, the whisperer to the heart, the unworldly romantic, the quaint Bohemian, the understander of women, the young man with the girl's eyes." MacLeish, *A Time to Speak*, pp. 62, 88.

[47] *Public Papers*, V, 179; Tugwell, *Battle for Democracy*, p. 54; Morris Cooke to Louis Howe, July 3, 1933, Cooke MSS., Box 51; *Literary Digest*, CXXII (July 4, 1936), 27.

that had strayed from the paths of righteousness.[48] The fire that followed the Park Avenue party in Thomas Wolfe's *You Can't Go Home Again,* like the suicide of Eveline at the end of John Dos Passos' *The Big Money,* symbolized the holocaust that brought to an end a decade of hedonism.[49] In an era of reconstruction, the attitudes of the twenties seemed alien, frivolous, or—the most cutting word the thirties could visit upon a man or institution —"escapist." When Morrie Ryskind and George Kaufman, authors of the popular *Of Thee I Sing,* lampooned the government again in *Let 'em Eat Cake* in the fall of 1933, the country was not amused. The New York *Post* applauded the decision of George Jean Nathan and his associates to discontinue the *American Spectator:* "Nihilism, dadaism, smartsetism—they are all gone, and this, too, is progress."[50] One of H. L. Mencken's biographers has noted: "Many were at pains to write him at his new home, telling him he was a sophomore, and those writing in magazines attacked him with a fury that was suspect because of its very violence."[51]

Commentators on the New Deal have frequently characterized it by that much-abused term "pragmatic." If one means by this that the New Dealers carefully tested the consequences of ideas, the term is clearly a misnomer. If one means that Roosevelt was exceptionally anti-ideological in his approach to politics, one may question whether he was, in fact, any more "pragmatic" in this sense than Van Buren or Polk or even "reform" Presidents like Jackson and Theodore Roosevelt. The "pragmatism" of the New Deal seemed remarkable only in a decade tortured by ideology, only in contrast to the rigidity of Hoover and of the Left.

The New Deal was pragmatic mainly in its skepticism about utopias and final solutions, its openness to experimentation, and its suspicion of the dogmas of the Establishment. Since the advice of economists had so often been wrong, the New Dealers distrusted the claims of orthodox theory—"All this is perfectly terrible because it is all pure theory, when you come down to it," the President said on one occasion—and they felt free to try new approaches.[52] Roosevelt refused to be awed by the warnings of economists and

[48] "We were all miserable sinners," announced the Harvard economist Oliver Sprague. *The New York Times,* December 10, 1933. Cf. "Special Week of Penitence and Prayer, October 2–8," *Federal Council Bulletin,* XV (September, 1932), 14–15; Milton Garber, Radio Address, 1932, Garber MSS.

[49] Melvin Landsberg, "A Study of the Political Development of John Dos Passos from 1912 to 1936" (unpublished Ph.D. dissertation, Columbia University, 1959).

[50] Hiram Motherwell, "Political Satire Scores on the Stage," *Today,* II (July 28, 1934), 24; *The New York Times,* November 12, 1933; New York *Post, Press Time* (New York, 1936), pp. 317 ff.

[51] William Manchester, *Disturber of the Peace* (New York, 1951), p. 258. "Empty stomachs became more important than hurt sensibilities," commented one critic. "The vexations and hurt feelings of a Carol Kennecott or the spiritual frustration of an Amory Blaine in *This Side of Paradise,* or the frantic dash for personal freedom of a Janet Marsh seemed trifling themes when the dominant feature of the national scene was twelve million unemployed." Halford Luccock, *American Mirror* (New York, 1940), p. 36. Cf. Margaret Mitchell to Mrs. Julian Harris, April 28, 1936, Mitchell MSS.

[52] *Public Papers,* II, 269. "In the months and years following the stock market crash," Professor Galbraith has concluded, "the burden of reputable economic advice was invariably on the side of measures that would make things worse." John Kenneth Galbraith, *The Great Crash* (Boston, 1955), pp. 187–188. For a typical example, see N. S. B. Gras to Edward Costigan, July 22, 1932, Costigan MSS., V.F. 1.

financial experts that government interference with the "laws" of the economy was blasphemous. "We must lay hold of the fact that economic laws are not made by nature," the President stated. "They are made by human beings."[53] The New Dealers denied that depressions were inevitable events that had to be borne stoically, most of the stoicism to be displayed by the most impoverished, and they were willing to explore novel ways to make the social order more stable and more humane. "I am for experimenting . . . in various parts of the country, trying out schemes which are supported by reasonable people and see if they work," Hopkins told a conference of social workers. "If they do not work, the world will not come to an end."[54]

Hardheaded, "anti-utopian," the New Dealers nonetheless had their Heavenly City: the greenbelt town, clean, green, and white, with children playing in light, airy, spacious schools; the government project at Longview, Washington, with small houses, each of different design, colored roofs, and gardens of flowers and vegetables; the Mormon villages of Utah that M. L. Wilson kept in his mind's eye—immaculate farmsteads on broad, rectangular streets; most of all, the Tennessee Valley, with its model town of Norris, the tall transmission towers, the white dams, the glistening wire strands, the valley where "a vision of villages and clean small factories has been growing into the minds of thoughtful men."[55] Scandinavia was their model abroad, not only because it summoned up images of the countryside of Denmark, the beauties of Stockholm, not only for its experience with labor relations and social insurance and currency reform, but because it represented the "middle way" of happy accommodation of public and private institutions the New Deal sought to achieve. "Why," inquired Brandeis, "should anyone want to go to Russia when one can go to Denmark?"[56]

Yet the New Deal added up to more than all of this—more than an experimental approach, more than the sum of its legislative achievements, more than an antiseptic utopia. It is true that there was a certain erosion of values in the thirties, as well as a narrowing of horizons, but the New Dealers inwardly recognized that what they were doing had a deeply moral significance however much they eschewed ethical pretensions. Heirs of the Enlightenment, they felt themselves part of a broadly humanistic movement to make man's life on earth more tolerable, a movement that might someday even achieve a co-operative commonwealth. Social insurance, Frances

[53] *Public Papers*, I, 657. The Boston *Transcript* commented: "Two more glaring misstatements of the truth could hardly have been packed into so little space." J. Joseph Huthmacher, *Massachusetts People and Politics, 1919-1933* (Cambridge, 1959), p. 244. Cf. Eccles, *Beckoning Frontiers*, p. 73.

[54] *Public Papers*, II, 302; V, 497; Josephine Chapin Brown, *Public Relief*, p. 152. Cf. Clarke Chambers, "FDR, Pragmatist-Idealist," *Pacific Northwest Quarterly*, LII (1961), 50-55; F. S. C. Northrop, *The Meeting of East and West* (New York, 1947), p. 152; Jacob Cohen, "Schlesinger and the New Deal," *Dissent*, VIII (1961), 466-468.

[55] Tugwell, *Battle for Democracy*, p. 22. This is a vision caught, in different ways, in the paintings of Paul Sample, Charles Sheeler, Grant Wood, and Joe Jones.

[56] Marquis Childs, *Sweden: The Middle Way* (New Haven, 1936); David Lilienthal to George Fort Milton, July 9, 1936; Milton to F.D.R., July 8, 1936, Milton MSS., Box 20; Irving Fisher to F.D.R., September 28, 1934, Fisher MSS.; John Commons to Edward Costigan, July 25, 1932, Costigan MSS., V.F. 1; Arthur Schlesinger, Jr., *The Politics of Upheaval* (Boston, 1960), p. 221.

Perkins declared, was "a fundamental part of another great forward step in that liberation of humanity which began with the Renaissance."[57]

Franklin Roosevelt did not always have this sense as keenly as some of the men around him, but his greatness as a President lies in the remarkable degree to which he shared the vision. "The new deal business to me is very much bigger than anyone yet has expressed it," observed Senator Elbert Thomas. Roosevelt "seems to really have caught the spirit of what one of the Hebrew prophets called the desire of the nations. If he were in India to-day they would probably decide that he had become Mahatma—that is, one in tune with the infinite."[58] Both foes and friends made much of Roosevelt's skill as a political manipulator, and there is no doubt that up to a point he delighted in schemes and stratagems. As Donald Richberg later observed: "There would be times when he seemed to be a Chevalier Bayard, *sans peur et sans reproche*, and times in which he would seem to be the apotheosis of a prince who had absorbed and practiced all the teachings of Machiavelli." Yet essentially he was a moralist who wanted to achieve certain human reforms and instruct the nation in the principles of government. On one occasion, he remarked: "I want to be a *preaching President*—like my cousin."[59] His courtiers gleefully recounted his adroitness in trading and dealing for votes, his effectiveness on the stump, his wicked skill in cutting corners to win a point. But Roosevelt's importance lay not in his talents as a campaigner or a manipulator. It lay rather in his ability to arouse the country and, more specifically, the men who served under him, by his breezy encouragement of experimentation, by his hopefulness, and—a word that would have embarrassed some of his lieutenants—by his idealism.

The New Deal left many problems unsolved and even created some perplexing new ones. It never demonstrated that it could achieve prosperity in peacetime. As late as 1941, the unemployed still numbered six million, and not until the war year of 1943 did the army of the jobless finally disappear. It enhanced the power of interest groups who claimed to speak for millions, but sometimes represented only a small minority.[60] It did not evolve a way to protect people who had no such spokesmen, nor an acceptable method for disciplining the interest groups. In 1946, President Truman would resort to a threat to draft railway workers into the Army to avert a strike. The New Deal achieved a more just society by recognizing groups which had been largely unrepresented—staple farmers, industrial workers, particular ethnic groups, and the new intellectual-administrative class. Yet this was still a halfway revolution; it swelled the ranks of the bourgeoisie but left many Americans—sharecroppers, slum dwellers, most Negroes—outside of the new equilibrium.

Some of these omissions were to be promptly remedied. Subsequent Congresses extended social security, authorized slum clearance projects, and raised minimum-wage standards to keep step with the rising price level.

[57] Frances Perkins, "Basic Idea Behind Social Security Program," *The New York Times*, January 27, 1935.

[58] Thomas to Colonel E. LeRoy Bourne, January 6, 1934, Elbert Thomas MSS.

[59] Donald Richberg, *My Hero* (New York, 1954), p. 279; Schlesinger, *Coming of the New Deal* (Boston, 1959), p. 558.

[60] Henry Kariel, *The Decline of American Pluralism* (Stanford, 1961).

Other shortcomings are understandable. The havoc that had been done before Roosevelt took office was so great that even the unprecedented measures of the New Deal did not suffice to repair the damage. Moreover, much was still to be learned, and it was in the Roosevelt years that the country was schooled in how to avert another major depression. Although it was war which freed the government from the taboos of a balanced budget and revealed the potentialities of spending, it is conceivable that New Deal measures would have led the country into a new cycle of prosperity even if there had been no war. Marked gains had been made before the war spending had any appreciable effect. When recovery did come, it was much more soundly based because of the adoption of the New Deal program.

Roosevelt and the New Dealers understood, perhaps better than their critics, that they had come only part of the way. Henry Wallace remarked: "We are children of the transition—we have left Egypt but we have not yet arrived at the Promised Land." Only five years separated Roosevelt's inauguration in 1933 and the adoption of the last of the New Deal measures, the Fair Labor Standards Act, in 1938. The New Dealers perceived that they had done more in those years than had been done in any comparable period in American history, but they also saw that there was much still to be done, much, too, that continued to baffle them. "I believe in the things that have been done," Mrs. Roosevelt told the American Youth Congress in February, 1939. "They helped but they did not solve the fundamental problems. . . . I never believed the Federal government could solve the whole problem. It bought us time to think." She closed not with a solution but with a challenge: "Is it going to be worth while?"[61]

"This generation of Americans is living in a tremendous moment of history," President Roosevelt stated in his final national address of the 1940 campaign.

> The surge of events abroad has made some few doubters among us ask: Is this the end of a story that has been told? Is the book of democracy now to be closed and placed away upon the dusty shelves of time?
>
> My answer is this: All we have known of the glories of democracy—its freedom, its efficiency as a mode of living, its ability to meet the aspirations of the common man—all these are merely an introduction to the greater story of a more glorious future.
>
> We Americans of today—all of us—we are characters in the living book of democracy.
>
> But we are also its author. It falls upon us now to say whether the chapters that are to come will tell a story of retreat or a story of continued advance.[62]

[61] Henry Wallace, *The Christian Bases of World Order* (New York, 1943), p. 17; Dorothy Dunbar Bromley, "The Future of Eleanor Roosevelt," *Harper's*, CLXXX (1939), 136.
[62] *Public Papers*, IX, 545.

The New Deal:
The Conservative
Achievements of
Liberal Reform

Barton J. Bernstein

As the liberal consensus started to break down in the middle 1960s, American intellectuals once more became critical of their nation's recent past and began to reexamine sharply the assumptions of liberal reform. The New Deal, no longer a volatile issue in American politics after the Eisenhower years, was subjected to new questions and new appraisals by intellectuals on the left. The three most prominent analyses were by Howard Zinn, Paul Conkin, and Barton J. Bernstein, whose essay on the New Deal follows.

Bernstein, a radical historian at Stanford University and editor of *Towards a New Past* (1968), an early statement by so-called New Left historians, stresses the limitations of New Deal reform and the restrictive ideology of the Roosevelt Administration; Bernstein believes that there was more latitude for bolder reform than Roosevelt and his associates were willing to exploit. The New Deal, he concludes, did not significantly improve the inequitable distribution of income, substantially improve race relations, or even greatly change the structure of power. Even the organization of labor, often presented as a great redistribution of power, is interpreted by Bernstein as a more limited achievement. It integrated many workingmen into the system of large-scale corporate capitalism by making organized labor a junior partner in the American political economy.

The analysis of the New Deal by Bernstein and others on the left has drawn only a few published criticisms. The sharpest, as well as the earliest, by Jerold Auerbach ("New Deal, Old Deal, or Raw Deal: Some Thoughts on New Left Historiography," *Journal of Southern History*, XXXV [February 1969]) attacks Bernstein and the others on two main grounds. First, if the New Deal did so little for the poor, the black, and the unemployed, why did these groups of the population overwhelmingly support Roosevelt? Auerbach rejects Bernstein's contention that "the marginal men . . . were seduced by rhetoric, by the style and movement, by the symbolism of efforts seldom reaching beyond words," and concludes that the masses of Americans received important benefits and that they had an accurate understanding of their real self-interest. Auerbach, by this contention, seems to believe that black leaders who were critical of the New Deal were also in serious error and did not understand the interests of the masses. Second, Auerbach criticizes Bernstein and the others for being ahistorical, for using the standards of the 1960s to appraise the New Deal, and for establishing criteria that no administration in American history could have met. The American public, Auerbach stresses, did not want a radical program, and no presidential administration, including the New Deal, has been willing to end capitalism and abandon private property. Auerbach contends that judged by these standards, which he believes are at the heart of radical interpretations that the New Deal was conservative, all past administrations would be considered conservative. Some historians on the left, in rebuttal, might respond that Auerbach misunderstood part of the left argument: the New Deal did not exploit the

The New Deal: The Conservative Achievements of Liberal Reform. From *Towards a New Past: Dissenting Essays in American History* by Barton J. Bernstein, ed. (New York: Pantheon Books, 1968), pp. 263–88. Reprinted by permission of the author and publisher.

The author wishes to express his gratitude to David M. Potter, Allen J. Matusow, and Otis L. Graham for their generous criticism. This acknowledgment was accidentally omitted from the original and has been restored at the author's request.

possibilities that it had (especially in the early 1930s); substantial reforms short of socialism were possible; and the New Deal saved not simply capitalism but large-scale corporate capitalism. The reader is encouraged to read Bernstein's essay, as well as the works of other analysts on the left, and to assess Auerbach's position.

*W*riting from a liberal democratic consensus, many American historians in the past two decades have praised the Roosevelt administration for its nonideological flexibility and for its far-ranging reforms. To many historians, particularly those who reached intellectual maturity during the depression,[1] the government's accomplishments, as well as the drama and passion, marked the decade as a watershed, as a dividing line in the American past.

Enamored of Franklin D. Roosevelt and recalling the bitter opposition to welfare measures and restraints upon business, many liberal historians have emphasized the New Deal's discontinuity with the immediate past. For them there was a "Roosevelt Revolution," or at the very least a dramatic achievement of a beneficent liberalism which had developed in fits and spurts during the preceding three decades.[2] Rejecting earlier interpretations which

[1] The outstanding examples are Arthur Schlesinger, Jr., Frank Freidel, Carl Degler, and William Leuchtenburg. Schlesinger, in *The Crisis of the Old Order* (Boston, 1957), emphasized the presence of reform in the twenties but criticized the federal government for its retreat from liberalism and condemned Hoover for his responses to the depression. The next two volumes of his *The Age of Roosevelt, The Coming of the New Deal* (Boston, 1958) and *The Politics of Upheaval* (Boston, 1960), praise the New Deal, but also contain information for a more critical appraisal. His research is quite wide and has often guided my own investigations. For his theory that the New Deal was likely even without the depression, see "Sources of the New Deal: Reflections on the Temper of a Time," *Columbia University Forum*, II (Fall 1959), 4–11. Freidel affirmed that the New Deal was a watershed (*American Historical Review*, October 1965, p. 329), but in *The New Deal in Historical Perspective* (Washington, 1959), he has suggested the conservatism of the New Deal as a reform movement. Degler, in *Out of Our Past* (New York, 1959), pp. 379–416, extolled the New Deal as a "Third American Revolution." But also see his "The Ordeal of Herbert Hoover," *Yale Review*, LII (Summer 1963), 565–83. Leuchtenburg, *Franklin D. Roosevelt and the New Deal, 1932–1940* (New York, 1963), offers considerable criticism of the New Deal, but finds far more to praise in this "half-way revolution." He cites Degler approvingly but moderates Degler's judgment (pp. 336–47). The book represents years of research and has often guided my own investigations.

[2] Eric Goldman, *Rendezvous with Destiny* (New York, 1952); Henry Steele Commager, "Twelve Years of Roosevelt," *American Mercury*, LX (April 1945), 391–401; Arthur Link, *American Epoch* (New York, 1955), pp. 377–440. In his essay on "Franklin D. Roosevelt: the Patrician as Opportunist" in *The American Political Tradition* (New York, 1948), pp. 315–52, Richard Hofstadter was critical of the New Deal's lack of ideology but treated it as a part of the larger reform tradition. In *The Age of Reform* (New York, 1955), however, while chiding the New Deal for opportunism, he emphasized the discontinuity of the New Deal with the reform tradition of Populism and Progressivism.

viewed the New Deal as socialism[3] or state capitalism,[4] they have also disregarded theories of syndicalism[5] or of corporate liberalism.[6] The New Deal has generally commanded their approval for such laws or institutions as minimum wages, public housing, farm assistance, the Tennessee Valley Authority, the Wagner Act, more progressive taxation, and social security. For most liberal historians the New Deal meant the replenishment of democracy, the rescuing of the federal government from the clutches of big business, the significant redistribution of political power. Breaking with laissez faire, the new administration, according to these interpretations, marked the end of the passive or impartial state and the beginning of positive government, of the interventionist state acting to offset concentrations of private power, and affirming the rights and responding to the needs of the unprivileged.

From the perspective of the late 1960s these themes no longer seem adequate to characterize the New Deal. The liberal reforms of the New Deal did not transform the American system; they conserved and protected American corporate capitalism, occasionally by absorbing parts of threatening programs. There was no significant redistribution of power in American society, only limited recognition of other organized groups, seldom of unorganized peoples. Neither the bolder programs advanced by New Dealers nor the final legislation greatly extended the beneficence of government beyond the middle classes or drew upon the wealth of the few for the needs of the many. Designed to maintain the American system, liberal activity was directed toward essentially conservative goals. Experimentalism was most frequently limited to means; seldom did it extend to ends. Never questioning private enterprise, it operated within safe channels, far short of Marxism or even of native American radicalisms that offered structural critiques and structural solutions.

All of this is not to deny the changes wrought by the New Deal—the extension of welfare programs, the growth of federal power, the strengthening of the executive, even the narrowing of property rights. But it is to assert that the elements of continuity are stronger, that the magnitude of change has been exaggerated. The New Deal failed to solve the problem of depression, it failed to raise the impoverished, it failed to redistribute income, it failed to extend equality and generally countenanced racial discrimination and segregation. It failed generally to make business more responsible to the social welfare or to threaten business's pre-eminent political power. In this sense, the New Deal, despite the shifts in tone and spirit from the earlier decade, was profoundly conservative and continuous with the 1920s.

I

Rather than understanding the 1920s as a "return to normalcy," the period is more properly interpreted by focusing on the continuation of progressive

[3] Edgar E. Robinson, *The Roosevelt Leadership, 1933–1945* (Philadelphia, 1955), the work of a conservative constitutionalist, does accuse the administration of having objectives approaching the leveling aims of communism (p. 376).

[4] Louis Hacker, *American Problems of Today* (New York, 1938).

[5] William Appleman Williams, *The Contours of American History* (Chicago, 1966), pp. 372–488; and his review, "Schlesinger: Right Crisis—Wrong Order," *Nation*, CLXXXIV (March 23, 1957), 257–60. Williams' volume has influenced my own thought.

[6] Ronald Radosh, "The Corporate Ideology of American Labor Leaders from Gompers to Hillman," *Studies on the Left*, VI (November–December 1966), 66–88.

impulses, demands often frustrated by the rivalry of interested groups, sometimes blocked by the resistance of Harding and Coolidge, and occasionally by Hoover.[7] Through these years while agriculture and labor struggled to secure advantages from the federal government, big business flourished. Praised for creating American prosperity, business leaders easily convinced the nation that they were socially responsible, that they were fulfilling the needs of the public.[8] Benefiting from earlier legislation that had promoted economic rationalization and stability, they were opponents of federal benefits to other groups but seldom proponents of laissez faire.[9]

In no way did the election of Herbert Hoover in 1928 seem to challenge the New Era. An heir of Wilson, Hoover promised an even closer relationship with big business and moved beyond Harding and Coolidge by affirming federal responsibility for prosperity. As Secretary of Commerce, Hoover had opposed unbridled competition and had transformed his department into a vigorous friend of business. Sponsoring trade associations, he promoted industrial self-regulation and the increased rationalization of business. He had also expanded foreign trade, endorsed the regulation of new forms of communications, encouraged relief in disasters, and recommended public works to offset economic declines.[10]

By training and experience, few men in American political life seemed better prepared than Hoover to cope with the depression. Responding promptly to the crisis, he acted to stabilize the economy and secured the agreement of businessmen to maintain production and wage rates. Unwilling to let the economy "go through the wringer," the President requested easier money, self-liquidating public works, lower personal and corporate income taxes, and stronger commodity stabilization corporations.[11] In reviewing these unprecedented actions, Walter Lippmann wrote, "The national government undertook to make the whole economic order operate prosperously."[12]

But these efforts proved inadequate. The tax cut benefitted the wealthy and failed to raise effective demand. The public works were insufficient. The commodity stabilization corporations soon ran out of funds, and agricultural prices kept plummeting. Businessmen cut back production, dismissed employees, and finally cut wages. As unemployment grew, Hoover struggled to inspire confidence, but his words seemed hollow and his understanding of the depression limited. Blaming the collapse on European failures, he could not admit that American capitalism had failed. When prodded by Congress to increase public works, to provide direct relief, and to fur-

[7] Arthur Link, "What Happened to the Progressive Movement?" *American Historical Review*, LXIV (July 1959), 833–51.

[8] James Prothro, *The Dollar Decade* (Baton Rouge, La., 1954).

[9] Louis Galambos, *Competition and Cooperation* (Baltimore, 1966), pp. 55–139; Link, "What Happened to the Progressive Movement?"

[10] Joseph Brandes, *Herbert Hoover and Economic Diplomacy* (Pittsburgh, 1962); Hofstadter, *American Political Tradition*, pp. 283–99.

[11] William S. Myers, ed., *The State Papers and Other Writings of Herbert Hoover* (New York, 1934), I, 84–88 (easier money), 137, 411, 431–33; II, 202 (public works); I, 142–43, 178–79 (lower taxes). The Commodity Stabilization Corporation was created before the crash.

[12] Lippmann, "The Permanent New Deal," *Yale Review*, XXIV (June 1935), 651.

ther unbalance the budget, he doggedly resisted. Additional deficits would destroy business confidence, he feared, and relief would erode the principles of individual and local responsibility.[13] Clinging to faith in voluntarism, Hoover also briefly rebuffed the efforts by financiers to secure the Reconstruction Finance Corporation (RFC). Finally endorsing the RFC,[14] he also supported expanded lending by Federal Land Banks, recommended home-loan banks, and even approved small federal loans (usually inadequate) to states needing funds for relief. In this burst of activity, the President had moved to the very limits of his ideology.

Restricted by his progressive background and insensitive to politics and public opinion, he stopped far short of the state corporatism urged by some businessmen and politicians. With capitalism crumbling he had acted vigorously to save it, but he would not yield to the representatives of business or disadvantaged groups who wished to alter the government.[15] He was reluctant to use the federal power to achieve through compulsion what could not be realized through voluntary means. Proclaiming a false independence, he did not understand that his government already represented business interests; hence, he rejected policies that would openly place the power of the state in the hands of business or that would permit the formation of a syndicalist state in which power might be exercised (in the words of William Appleman Williams) "by a relatively few leaders of each functional bloc formed and operating as an oligarchy."[16]

Even though constitutional scruples restricted his efforts, Hoover did more than any previous American president to combat depression. He "abandoned the principles of laissez faire in relation to the business cycle, established the conviction that prosperity and depression can be publicly controlled by political action, and drove out of the public consciousness the old idea that depressions must be overcome by private adjustment," wrote Walter Lippmann.[17] Rather than the last of the old presidents, Herbert Hoover was the first of the new.

II

A charismatic leader and a brilliant politician, his successor expanded federal activities on the basis of Hoover's efforts. Using the federal government to stabilize the economy and advance the interests of the groups, Franklin D. Roosevelt directed the campaign to save large-scale corporate capitalism. Though recognizing new political interests and extending benefits to them, his New Deal never effectively challenged big business or the organization of the economy. In providing assistance to the needy and by rescuing them from starvation, Roosevelt's humane efforts also protected the established

---

[13] Myers, ed., *State Papers*, II, 195–201, 214–15, 224–26, 228–33 (on the budget); II, 405, 496–99, 503–5 (on relief).

[14] Gerald Nash, "Herbert Hoover and the Origins of the Reconstruction Finance Corporation," *Mississippi Valley Historical Review*, XLVI (December 1959), 455–68.

[15] W. S. Myers and W. H. Newton, eds., *The Hoover Administration: A Documentary History* (New York, 1936), p. 119; "Proceedings of a Conference of Progressives," March 11–12, 1931, Hillman Papers, Amalgamated Clothing Workers (New York).

[16] *Contours of American History*, p. 428.

[17] Lippmann, "The Permanent New Deal," p. 651.

system: he sapped organized radicalism of its waning strength and of its potential constituency among the unorganized and discontented. Sensitive to public opinion and fearful of radicalism, Roosevelt acted from a mixture of motives that rendered his liberalism cautious and limited, his experimentalism narrow. Despite the flurry of activity, his government was more vigorous and flexible about means than goals, and the goals were more conservative than historians usually acknowledge.[18]

Roosevelt's response to the banking crisis emphasizes the conservatism of his administration and its self-conscious avoidance of more radical means that might have transformed American capitalism. Entering the White House when banks were failing and Americans had lost faith in the financial system, the President could have nationalized it—"without a word of protest," judged Senator Bronson Cutting.[19] "If ever there was a moment when things hung in the balance," later wrote Raymond Moley, a member of the original "brain trust," "it was on March 5, 1933—when unorthodoxy would have drained the last remaining strength of the capitalistic system."[20] To save the system, Roosevelt relied upon collaboration between bankers and Hoover's Treasury officials to prepare legislation extending federal assistance to banking. So great was the demand for action that House members, voting even without copies, passed it unanimously, and the Senate, despite objections by a few Progressives, approved it the same evening. "The President," remarked a cynical congressman, "drove the money-changers out of the Capitol on March 4th—and they were all back on the 9th."[21]

Undoubtedly the most dramatic example of Roosevelt's early conservative approach to recovery was the National Recovery Administration (NRA). It was based on the War Industries Board (WIB) which had provided the model for the campaign of Bernard Baruch, General Hugh Johnson, and other former WIB officials during the twenties to limit competition through industrial self-regulation under federal sanction. As trade associations flourished during the decade, the FTC encouraged "codes of fair competition" and some industries even tried to set prices and restrict production. Operating without the force of law, these agreements broke down. When the depression struck, industrial pleas for regulations increased.[22] After the Great Crash, important business leaders including Henry I. Harriman of the Chamber of Commerce and Gerard Swope of General Electric called for suspension of antitrust laws and federal organization of business collabora-

---

[18] For an excellent statement of this thesis, see Howard Zinn's introduction to his *New Deal Thought* (New York, 1966), pp. xv–xxxvi. So far historians have not adequately explored the thesis that F.D.R. frequently acted as a restraining force on his own government, and that bolder reforms were often thwarted by him and his intimates.

[19] Bronson Cutting, "Is Private Banking Doomed?" *Liberty*, XI (March 31, 1934), 10; cf. Raymond Moley, *The First New Deal* (New York, 1966), pp. 177–80.

[20] Moley, *After Seven Years* (New York, 1939), p. 155; Arthur Ballantine, "When All the Banks Closed," *Harvard Business Review*, XXVI (March 1948), 129–43.

[21] William Lemke, later quoted in Lorena Hickok to Harry Hopkins, November 23, 1933, Hopkins Papers, Franklin D. Roosevelt Library (hereafter called FDRL).

[22] Baruch to Samuel Gompers, April 19, 1924, Baruch Papers, Princeton University; Schlesinger, *Coming of the New Deal*, pp. 88–89; Gerald Nash, "Experiments in Industrial Mobilization: WIB and NRA," *Mid-America*, XLV (July 1963), 156–75.

tion.[23] Joining them were labor leaders, particularly those in "sick" industries—John L. Lewis of the United Mine Workers and Sidney Hillman of Amalgamated Clothing Workers.[24]

Designed largely for industrial recovery, the NRA legislation provided for minimum wages and maximum hours. It also made concessions to pro-labor congressmen and labor leaders who demanded some specific benefits for unions—recognition of the worker's right to organization and to collective bargaining. In practice, though, the much-heralded Section 7a was a disappointment to most friends of labor.[25] (For the shrewd Lewis, however, it became a mandate to organize: "The President wants you to join a union.") To many frustrated workers and their disgusted leaders, NRA became "National Run Around." The clause, unionists found (in the words of Brookings economists), "had the practical effect of placing NRA on the side of anti-union employers in their struggle against trade unions. . . . [It] thus threw its weight against labor in the balance of bargaining power."[26] And while some far-sighted industrialists feared racialism and hoped to forestall it by incorporating unions into the economic system, most preferred to leave their workers unorganized or in company unions. To many businessmen, large and independent unions as such seemed a radical threat to the system of business control.[27]

Not only did the NRA provide fewer advantages than unionists had anticipated, but it also failed as a recovery measure. It probably even retarded recovery by supporting restrictionism and price increases, concluded a Brookings study.[28] Placing effective power for code-writing in big business, NRA injured small businesses and contributed to the concentration of American industry. It was not the government-business partnership as envisaged by Adolf A. Berle, Jr., nor government managed as Rexford Tugwell had hoped, but rather, business managed, as Raymond Moley had desired.[29] Calling NRA "industrial self-government," its director, General Hugh Johnson, had explained that "NRA is exactly what industry organized in trade associations makes it." Despite the annoyance of some big business-

[23] Gerard Swope, *The Swope Plan* (New York, 1931); Julius H. Barnes, "Government and Business," *Harvard Business Review*, X (July 1932), 411–19; Harriman, "The Stabilization of Business and Employment," *American Economic Review*, XXII (March 1932), 63–75; House Committee on Education and Labor, 73rd Cong., 1st Sess., *Thirty-Hour Week Bill, Hearings*, pp. 198–99.

[24] *Ibid.*, pp. 884–97; Hillman, "Labor Leads Toward Planning," *Survey Graphic*, LXVI (March 1932), 586–88.

[25] Irving Bernstein, *The New Deal Collective Bargaining Policy* (Berkeley, Cal., 1950), pp. 57–63.

[26] Quotes from Hofstadter, *American Political Tradition*, p. 336. "It is not the function of NRA to organize . . . labor," asserted General Hugh Johnson. "Automobile Code Provides for Thirty-Five Hour Week," *Iron Age*, CXXXII (August 3, 1933), 380.

[27] Richard C. Wilcock, "Industrial Management's Policy Toward Unionism," in Milton Derber and Edwin Young, eds., *Labor and the New Deal* (Madison, Wis., 1957), pp. 278–95.

[28] Leverett Lyon, *et al.*, *The National Recovery Administration* (Washington, 1935).

[29] The characterization of Berle, Tugwell, and Moley is from Schlesinger, *Coming of the New Deal*, pp. 181–84, and Johnson's address at the NAM is from NRA press release 2126, December 7, 1933, NRA Records, RG 9, National Archives.

men with Section 7a, the NRA reaffirmed and consolidated their power at a time when the public was critical of industrialists and financiers.

III

Viewing the economy as a "concert of organized interests,"[30] the New Deal also provided benefits for farmers–the Agricultural Adjustment Act. Reflecting the political power of larger commercial farmers and accepting restrictionist economics, the measure assumed that the agricultural problem was overproduction, not underconsumption. Financed by a processing tax designed to raise prices to parity, payments encouraged restricted production and cutbacks in farm labor. With benefits accruing chiefly to the larger owners, they frequently removed from production the lands of sharecroppers and tenant farmers, and "tractored" them and hired hands off the land. In assisting agriculture, the AAA, like the NRA, sacrificed the interests of the marginal and the unrecognized to the welfare of those with greater political and economic power.[31]

In large measure, the early New Deal of the NRA and AAA was a "broker state." Though the government served as a mediator of interests and sometimes imposed its will in divisive situations, it was generally the servant of powerful groups. "Like the mercantilists, the New Dealers protected vested interests with the authority of the state," acknowledges William Leuchtenburg. But it was some improvement over the 1920s when business was the only interest capable of imposing its will on the government.[32] While extending to other groups the benefits of the state, the New Deal, however, continued to recognize the pre-eminence of business interests.

The politics of the broker state also heralded the way of the future–of continued corporate dominance in a political structure where other groups agreed generally on corporate capitalism and squabbled only about the size of the shares. Delighted by this increased participation and the absorption of dissident groups, many liberals did not understand the dangers in the emerging organization of politics. They had too much faith in representative institutions and in associations to foresee the perils–of leaders not representing their constituents, of bureaucracy diffusing responsibility, of officials serving their own interests. Failing to perceive the dangers in the emerging structure, most liberals agreed with Senator Robert Wagner of New York: "In order that the strong may not take advantage of the weak, every group must be equally strong."[33] His advice then seemed appropriate for organiz-

[30] "Concert of interests" was used by F.D.R. in a speech of April 18, 1932, in Samuel Rosenman, ed., *The Public Papers and Addresses of Franklin D. Roosevelt* (13 vols.; New York, 1938–52), I, 627–39. (Hereafter referred to as *FDR Papers*.)

[31] M. S. Venkataramani, "Norman Thomas, Arkansas Sharecroppers, and the Roosevelt Agricultural Policies," *Mississippi Valley Historical Review*, XLVII (September 1960), 225–46; John Hutson, Columbia Oral History Memoir, pp. 114 ff.; Mordecai Ezekiel, Columbia Oral History Memoir, pp. 74 ff.

[32] Quoted from Leuchtenburg, *F.D.R.*, p. 87, and this discussion draws upon pp. 87–90; John Chamberlain, *The American Stakes* (Philadelphia, 1940): James MacGregor Burns, *Roosevelt: The Lion and the Fox* (New York, 1956), pp. 183–202.

[33] Quoted from House Committee on Education and Labor, 74th Cong., 1st Sess., *National Labor Relations Board Hearings*, p. 35.

ing labor, but it neglected the problems of unrepresentative leadership and of the many millions to be left beyond organization.[34]

In dealing with the organized interests, the President acted frequently as a broker, but his government did not simply express the vectors of external forces.[35] The New Deal state was too complex, too loose, and some of Roosevelt's subordinates were following their own inclinations and pushing the government in directions of their own design.[36] The President would also depart from his role as a broker and act to secure programs he desired. As a skilled politician, he could split coalitions, divert the interests of groups, or place the prestige of his office on the side of desired legislation.

In seeking to protect the stock market, for example, Roosevelt endorsed the Securities and Exchange measure (of 1934), despite the opposition of many in the New York financial community. His advisers split the opposition. Rallying to support the administration were the out-of-town exchanges, representatives of the large commission houses, including James Forrestal of Dillon, Read, and Robert Lovett of Brown Brothers, Harriman, and such commission brokers as E. A. Pierce and Paul Shields. Opposed to the Wall Street "old guard" and their companies, this group included those who wished to avoid more radical legislation, as well as others who had wanted earlier to place trading practices under federal legislation which they could influence.[37]

Though the law restored confidence in the securities market and protected capitalism, it alarmed some businessmen and contributed to the false belief that the New Deal was threatening business. But it was not the disaffection of a portion of the business community, nor the creation of the Liberty League, that menaced the broker state.[38] Rather it was the threat of the Left—expressed, for example, in such overwrought statements as Minnesota Governor Floyd Olson's: "I am not a liberal . . . I am a radical. . . . I am not satisfied with hanging a laurel wreath on burglars and thieves . . . and calling them code authorities or something else."[39] While Olson, along with some others who succumbed to the rhetoric of militancy, would back

[34] For a warning, see Paul Douglas, "Rooseveltian Liberalism," *Nation*, CXXXVI (June 21, 1933), 702–3.

[35] Leuchtenburg, *F.D.R.*, p. 88, uses the image of "a parallelogram of pressures."

[36] For example see the Columbia Oral Histories of Louis Bean, Hutson, and Ezekiel.

[37] *New York Times*, January 30, 1934; House Interstate and Foreign Commerce Committee, 73rd Cong., 2nd Sess., House Report No. 1383, *Securities Exchange Bill of 1934*, p. 3; "SEC," *Fortune*, XXI (June 1940), 91–92, 120 ff.; Ralph De Bedts, *The New Deal's SEC* (New York, 1964), pp. 56–85.

[38] Frederick Rudolph, "The American Liberty League, 1934–1940," *American Historical Review*, LVI (October 1950), 19–33; George Wolfskill, *The Revolt of the Conservatives* (Boston, 1962). Emphasizing the Liberty League and focusing upon the rhetoric of business disaffection, historians have often exaggerated the opposition of the business communities. See the correspondence of James Forrestal, PPF 6367, FDRL, and at Princeton; of Russell Leffingwell, PPF 886, FDRL; of Donald Nelson, PPF 8615, FDRL, and at the Huntington Library; and of Thomas Watson, PPF 2489, FDRL. On the steel industry, see *Iron Age*, CXXXV (June 13, 1935), 44. For very early evidence of estrangement, however, see Edgar Mowrer to Frank Knox, November 8, 1933, Knox Papers, Library of Congress.

[39] Quoted from Donald McCoy, *Angry Voices: Left of Center Politics in the New Deal Era* (Lawrence, Kan., 1958), pp. 55, from *Farmer-Labor Leader*, March 30, 1934.

down and soften their meaning, their words dramatized real grievances: the failure of the early New Deal to end misery, to re-create prosperity. The New Deal excluded too many. Its programs were inadequate. While Roosevelt reluctantly endorsed relief and went beyond Hoover in support of public works, he too preferred self-liquidating projects, desired a balanced budget, and resisted spending the huge sums required to lift the nation out of depression.

IV

For millions suffering in a nation wracked by poverty, the promises of the Left seemed attractive. Capitalizing on the misery, Huey Long offered Americans a "Share Our Wealth" program—a welfare state with prosperity, not subsistence, for the disadvantaged, those neglected by most politicians. "Every Man a King": pensions for the elderly, college for the deserving, home and cars for families—that was the promise of American life. Also proposing minimum wages, increased public works, shorter work weeks, and a generous farm program, he demanded a "soak-the-rich" tax program. Despite the economic defects of his plan, Long was no hayseed, and his forays into the East revealed support far beyond the bayous and hamlets of his native South.[40] In California discontent was so great that Upton Sinclair, food faddist and former socialist, captured the Democratic nomination for governor on a platform of "production-for-use"—factories and farms for the unemployed. "In a cooperative society," promised Sinclair, "every man, woman, and child would have the equivalent of $5,000 a year income from labor of the able-bodied young men for three or four hours per day."[41] More challenging to Roosevelt was Francis Townsend's plan—monthly payments of $200 to those past sixty who retired and promised to spend the stipend within thirty days.[42] Another enemy of the New Deal was Father Coughlin, the popular radio priest, who had broken with Roosevelt and formed a National Union for Social Justice to lead the way to a corporate society beyond capitalism.

To a troubled nation offered "redemption" by the Left, there was also painful evidence that the social fabric was tearing—law was breaking down. When the truckers in Minneapolis struck, the police provoked an incident and shot sixty-seven people, some in the back. Covering the tragedy, Eric Sevareid, then a young reporter, wrote, "I understood deep in my bones and blood what fascism was."[43] In San Francisco union leaders embittered by police brutality led a general strike and aroused national fears of class warfare. Elsewhere, in textile mills from Rhode Island to Georgia, in cities like

[40] Long, *My First Days in the White House* (Harrisburg, Pa., 1935).

[41] Quoted from Sinclair, *The Way Out* (New York 1933), p. 57. See Sinclair to Roosevelt, October 5 and 18, 1934, OF 1165, FDRL.

[42] Nicholas Roosevelt, *The Townsend Plan* (Garden City, N.Y., 1935). Not understanding that the expenditures would increase consumption and probably spur production, critics emphasized that the top 9 percent would have received 50 percent of the income, but they neglected that the top income-tenth had received (before taxes) nearly 40 percent of the national income in 1929. National Industrial Conference Board, *Studies in Enterprise and Social Progress* (New York, 1939), p. 125.

[43] Sevareid, *Not So Wild a Dream* (New York, 1946), p. 58.

Des Moines and Toledo, New York and Philadelphia, there were brutality and violence, sometimes bayonets and tear gas.[44]

Challenged by the Left, and with the new Congress more liberal and more willing to spend, Roosevelt turned to disarm the discontent. "Boys—this is our hour," confided Harry Hopkins. "We've got to get everything we want —a works program, social security, wages and hours, everything—now or never. Get your minds to work on developing a complete ticket to provide security for all the folks of this country up and down and across the board."[45] Hopkins and the associates he addressed were not radicals: they did not seek to transform the system, only to make it more humane. They, too, wished to preserve large-scale corporate capitalism but unlike Roosevelt or Moley, they were prepared for more vigorous action. Their commitment to reform was greater, their tolerance for injustice far less. Joining them in pushing the New Deal left were the leaders of industrial unions, who, while also not wishing to transform the system, sought for workingmen higher wages, better conditions, stronger and larger unions, and for themselves a place closer to the fulcrum of power.

The problems of organized labor, however, neither aroused Roosevelt's humanitarianism nor suggested possibilities of reshaping the political coalition. When asked during the NRA about employee representation, he had replied that workers could select anyone they wished—the Ahkoond of Swat, a union, even the Royal Geographical Society.[46] As a paternalist, viewing himself (in the words of James MacGregor Burns) as a "partisan and benefactor" of workers, he would not understand the objections to company unions or to multiple unionism under NRA. Nor did he foresee the political dividends that support of independent unions could yield to his party.[47] Though presiding over the reshaping of politics (which would extend the channels of power to some of the discontented and redirect their efforts to competition within a limited framework), he was not its architect, and he was unable clearly to see or understand the unfolding design.

When Senator Wagner submitted his labor relations bill, he received no assistance from the President and even struggled to prevent Roosevelt from joining the opposition. The President "never lifted a finger," recalls Miss Perkins. ("I, myself, had very little sympathy with the bill," she wrote.[48]) But after the measure easily passed the Senate and seemed likely to win the House's endorsement, Roosevelt reversed himself. Three days before the Supreme Court invalidated the NRA, including the legal support for unionization, Roosevelt came out for the bill. Placing it on his "must" list, he may have hoped to influence the final provisions and turn an administration defeat into victory.[49]

[44] Sidney Lens, *Left, Right and Center* (Hinsdale, Ill., 1949), pp. 280–89.

[45] Quoted in Robert Sherwood, *Roosevelt and Hopkins*, rev. ed. (New York, 1950), p. 65.

[46] Roosevelt's press conference of June 15, 1934, *FDR Papers*, III, 301; cf., Roosevelt to John L. Lewis, February 25, 1939, Philip Murray Papers, Catholic University.

[47] Burns, *The Lion and the Fox*, pp. 217–19; quotation from p. 218.

[48] Perkins, Columbia Oral History Memoir, VII, 138, 147, quoted by Leuchtenburg, *F.D.R.*, p. 151.

[49] Irving Bernstein, *The New Deal Collective Bargaining Policy*, pp. 100–8; Burns, *The Lion and the Fox*, p. 219.

Responding to the threat from the Left, Roosevelt also moved during the Second Hundred Days to secure laws regulating banking, raising taxes, dissolving utility-holding companies, and creating social security. Building on the efforts of states during the Progressive Era, the Social Security Act marked the movement toward the welfare state, but the core of the measure, the old-age provision, was more important as a landmark than for its substance. While establishing a federal-state system of unemployment compensation, the government, by making workers contribute to their old-age insurance, denied its financial responsibility for the elderly. The act excluded more than a fifth of the labor force leaving, among others, more than five million farm laborers and domestics without coverage.[50]

Though Roosevelt criticized the tax laws for not preventing "an unjust concentration of wealth and economic power,"[51] his own tax measure would not have significantly redistributed wealth. Yet his message provoked an "amen" from Huey Long and protests from businessmen.[52] Retreating from his promises, Roosevelt failed to support the bill, and it succumbed to conservative forces. They removed the inheritance tax and greatly reduced the proposed corporate and individual levies. The final law did not "soak the rich."[53] But it did engender deep resentment among the wealthy for increasing taxes on gifts and estates, imposing an excess-profits tax (which Roosevelt had not requested), and raising surtaxes. When combined with such regressive levies as social security and local taxes, however, the Wealth Tax of 1935 did not drain wealth from higher-income groups, and the top one percent even increased their shares during the New Deal years.[54]

V

Those historians who have characterized the events of 1935 as the beginning of a second New Deal have imposed a pattern on those years which most participants did not then discern.[55] In moving to social security, guarantees of collective bargaining, utility regulation, and progressive taxation, the government did advance the nation toward greater liberalism, but the shift was exaggerated and most of the measures accomplished far less than either friends or foes suggested. Certainly, despite a mild bill authorizing destruction of utilities-holding companies, there was no effort to atomize business, no real threat to concentration.

Nor were so many powerful businessmen disaffected by the New Deal. Though the smaller businessmen who filled the ranks of the Chamber

[50] Margaret Grant, *Old Age Security* (Washington, 1939), p. 217. Under social security, payments at sixty-five ranged from $100 a month to $85 a month, depending on earlier earnings.

[51] Roosevelt's message to Congress on June 19, 1935, *FDR Papers*, IV, 271.

[52] *New York Times*, June 20 and 21, 1935; *Business Week*, June 22, 1935, p. 5.

[53] John Morton Blum, *From the Morgenthau Diaries: Years of Crisis, 1928–1938* (Boston, 1959), pp. 302–4.

[54] Simon Kuznets, *Shares of Upper Income Groups in Income and Savings*, National Bureau of Economic Research, Occasional Paper 35 (New York, 1950), pp. 32–40.

[55] Otis L. Graham, Jr., "Historians and the New Deals: 1944–1960," *Social Studies*, LIV (April 1963), 133–40.

of Commerce resented the federal bureaucracy and the benefits to labor and thus criticized NRA,[56] representatives of big business found the agency useful and opposed a return to unrestricted competition. In 1935, members of the Business Advisory Council—including Henry Harriman, outgoing president of the Chamber, Thomas Watson of International Business Machines, Walter Gifford of American Telephone and Telegraph, Gerard Swope of General Electric, Winthrop Aldrich of the Chase National Bank, and W. Averell Harriman of Union Pacific—vigorously endorsed a two-year renewal of NRA.[57]

When the Supreme Court in 1935 declared the "hot" oil clause and the NRA unconstitutional, the administration moved to measures known as the "little NRA." Re-establishing regulations in bituminous coal and oil, the New Deal also checked wholesale price discrimination and legalized "fair trade" practices. Though Roosevelt never acted to revive the NRA, he periodically contemplated its restoration. In the so-called second New Deal, as in the "first," government remained largely the benefactor of big business, and some more advanced businessmen realized this.[58]

Roosevelt could attack the "economic royalists" and endorse the TNEC investigation of economic concentration, but he was unprepared to resist the basic demands of big business. While there was ambiguity in his treatment of oligopoly, it was more the confusion of means than of ends, for his tactics were never likely to impair concentration. Even the antitrust program under Thurman Arnold, concludes Frank Freidel, was "intended less to bust the trusts than to forestall too drastic legislation." Operating through consent decrees and designed to reduce prices to the consumer, the program frequently "allowed industries to function much as they had in NRA days." In effect, then, throughout its variations, the New Deal had sought to cooperate with business.[59]

Though vigorous in rhetoric and experimental in tone, the New Deal was narrow in its goals and wary of bold economic reform. Roosevelt's sense of what was politically desirable was frequently more restricted than others' views of what was possible and necessary. Roosevelt's limits were those of ideology; they were not inherent in experimentalism. For while

[56] *New York Times*, November 19, 1933; May 1, September 30, November 17, December 23, 1934; May 1, 3, 5, 28, 1935; "Chamber to Vote on NIRA," *Nation's Business*, XXII (December 1934), 51; "Business Wants a New NRA," *ibid.*, XXIII (Feburary 1935), 60; "Listening in as Business Speaks," *ibid.*, XXIII (June 1935), 18, 20; William Wilson, "How the Chamber of Commerce Viewed the NRA," *Mid-America*, XLIII (January, 1962), 95–108.

[57] *New York Times*, May 3, 4, 12, 1935. On the steel industry see L. W. Moffet, "This Week in Washington," *Iron Age*, CXXXV (March 21, 1935), 41; *ibid.* (April 18, 1935), 49; "NRA Future Not Settled by Senate Committee's Action for Extension," *ibid.* (May 9, 1935), 58.

[58] Ellis W. Hawley, *The New Deal and the Problem of Monopoly* (Princeton, 1966), pp. 205–86.

[59] Freidel, *The New Deal*, pp. 18–19. On Arnold's efforts, see Wendell Berge Diary, 1938–1939, Berge Papers, Library of Congress; and Gene Gressley, "Thurman Arnold, Antitrust, and the New Deal," *Business History Review*, XXXVIII (Summer, 1964), 214–31. For characteristic Roosevelt rhetoric emphasizing the effort of his government to subdue "the forces of selfishness and of lust for power," see his campaign address of October 31, 1936, his press conference of January 4, 1938, and his message of April 29, 1938, in *FDR Papers*, V, 568–69, and VII, 11, 305–32.

the President explored the narrow center, and some New Dealers considered bolder possibilities, John Dewey, the philosopher of experimentalism, moved far beyond the New Deal and sought to reshape the system. Liberalism, he warned, "must now become radical. . . . For the gulf between what the actual situation makes possible and the actual state itself is so great that it cannot be bridged by piecemeal policies undertaken *ad hoc*."[60] The boundaries of New Deal experimentalism, as Howard Zinn has emphasized, could extend far beyond Roosevelt's cautious ventures. Operating within very safe channels, Roosevelt not only avoided Marxism and the socialization of property, but he also stopped far short of other possibilities—communal direction of production or the organized distribution of surplus. The President and many of his associates were doctrinaires of the center, and their maneuvers in social reform were limited to cautious excursions.[61]

VI

Usually opportunistic and frequently shifting, the New Deal was restricted by its ideology. It ran out of fuel not because of the conservative opposition,[62] but because it ran out of ideas.[63] Acknowledging the end in 1939, Roosevelt proclaimed, "We have now passed the period of internal conflict in the launching of our program of social reform. Our full energies may now be released to invigorate the processes of recovery in order to preserve our reforms. . . ."[64]

The sad truth was that the heralded reforms were severely limited, that inequality continued, that efforts at recovery had failed. Millions had come to accept the depression as a way of life. A decade after the Great Crash, when millions were still unemployed, Fiorello LaGuardia recommended that "we accept the inevitable, that we are now in a new normal."[65] "It was reasonable to expect a probable minimum of 4,000,000 to 5,000,000 unemployed," Harry Hopkins had concluded.[66] Even that level was never reached, for business would not spend and Roosevelt refused to countenance the necessary expenditures. "It was in economics that our troubles lay," Tugwell wrote. "For their solution his [Roosevelt's] progressivism, his new deal was pathetically insufficient. . . ."[67]

Clinging to faith in fiscal orthodoxy even when engaged in deficit

[60] Dewey, *Liberalism and Social Action* (New York, 1935), p. 62.

[61] Howard Zinn, in *New Deal Thought*, pp. xxvi–xxxi, discusses this subject and has influenced my thought. Also consider those whom Zinn cites: Edmund Wilson, "The Myth of Marxist Dialectic," *Partisan Review*, VI (Fall, 1938), 66–81; William Ernest Hocking, "The Future of Liberalism," *The Journal of Philosophy*, XXXII (April 25, 1935), 230–47; Stuart Chase, "Eating Without Working: A Moral Disquisition," *Nation*, CXXXVII (July 22, 1933), 93–94.

[62] See James T. Patterson, "A Conservative Coalition Forms in Congress, 1933–1939," *Journal of American History*, LII (March 1966), 757–72.

[63] Hofstadter, *American Political Tradition*, p. 342; cf., Freidel, *The New Deal*, p. 20.

[64] Roosevelt's annual message to the Congress on January 4, 1939, *FDR Papers*, VIII, 7.

[65] Fiorello LaGuardia to James Byrnes, April 5, 1939, Box 2584, LaGuardia Papers, Municipal Archives, New York City.

[66] Hopkins, "The Future of Relief," *New Republic*, XC (February 10, 1937), 8.

[67] Tugwell, *The Stricken Land* (Garden City, N.Y., 1947), p. 681.

spending, Roosevelt had been unwilling to greatly unbalance the budget. Having pledged in his first campaign to cut expenditures and to restore the balanced budget, the President had at first adopted recovery programs that would not drain government finances. Despite a burst of activity under the Civil Works Administration during the first winter, public works expenditures were frequently slow and cautious. Shifting from direct relief, which Roosevelt (like Hoover) considered "a narcotic, a subtle destroyer of the human spirit," the government moved to work relief.[68] ("It saves his skill. It gives him a chance to do something socially useful," said Hopkins.[69]) By 1937 the government had poured enough money into the economy to spur production to within 10 percent of 1929 levels, but unemployment still hovered over seven million. Yet so eager was the President to balance the budget that he cut expenditures for public works and relief, and plunged the economy into a greater depression. While renewing expenditures, Roosevelt remained cautious in his fiscal policy, and the nation still had almost nine million unemployed in 1939. After nearly six years of struggling with the depression, the Roosevelt administration could not lead the nation to recovery, but it had relieved suffering.[70] In most of America, starvation was no longer possible. Perhaps that was the most humane achievement of the New Deal.

Its efforts on behalf of humane *reform* were generally faltering and shallow, of more value to the middle classes, of less value to organized workers, of even less to the marginal men. In conception and in practice, seemingly humane efforts revealed the shortcomings of American liberalism. For example, public housing, praised as evidence of the federal government's concern for the poor, was limited in scope (to 180,000 units) and unfortunate in results.[71] It usually meant the consolidation of ghettos, the robbing of men of their dignity, the treatment of men as wards with few rights. And slum clearance came to mean "Negro clearance" and removal of the other poor. Of much of this liberal reformers were unaware, and some of the problems can be traced to the structure of bureaucracy and to the selection of government personnel and social workers who disliked the poor.[72] But the liberal conceptions, it can be argued, were also flawed for there was no willingness to consult the poor, nor to encourage their participation. Liberalism was elitist. Seeking to build America in their own image, liberals wanted to create an environment which they thought would restructure character and personality more appropriate to white, middle-class America.

[68] Roosevelt's speech of January 4, 1935, *FDR Papers*, IV, 19.

[69] Hopkins, "Federal Emergency Relief," *Vital Speeches*, I (December 31, 1934), 211.

[70] Broadus Mitchell, *Depression Decade: From New Era Through New Deal* (New York, 1947), pp. 37–54.

[71] Housing and Home Finance Agency, *First Annual Report* (Washington, 1947), pp. 24–25. Timothy McDonnell, *The Wagner Housing Act* (Chicago, 1957), pp. 53, 186–88, concludes that the Wagner bill would have passed earlier if Roosevelt had supported it.

[72] Jane Jacobs, *The Life and Death of Great American Cities* (New York, 1963). Racial policy was locally determined. U.S. Housing Authority, *Bulletin No. 18 on Policy and Procedure* (1938), pp. 7–8; Robert C. Weaver, "The Negro in a Program of Public Housing," *Opportunity*, XVI (July 1938), 1–6. Three fifths of all families, reported Weaver, were earning incomes "below the figure necessary to afford respectable living quarters without undue skimping on other necessities." (p. 4).

While slum dwellers' received little besides relief from the New Deal, and their needs were frequently misunderstood, Negroes as a group received even less assistance—less than they needed and sometimes even less than their proportion in the population would have justified. Under the NRA they were frequently dismissed and their wages were sometimes below the legal minimum. The Civilian Conservation Corps left them "forgotten" men—excluded, discriminated against, segregated. In general, what the Negroes gained—relief, WPA jobs, equal pay on some federal projects —was granted them as poor people, not as Negroes.[73] To many black men the distinction was unimportant, for no government had ever given them so much. "My friends, go home and turn Lincoln's picture to the wall," a Negro publisher told his race. "That debt has been payed in full."[74]

Bestowing recognition on some Negro leaders, the New Deal appointed them to agencies as advisers—the "black cabinet." Probably more dramatic was the advocacy of Negro rights by Eleanor Roosevelt. Some whites like Harold Ickes and Aubrey Williams even struggled cautiously to break down segregation. But segregation did not yield, and Washington itself remained a segregated city. The white South was never challenged, the Fourteenth Amendment never used to assist Negroes. Never would Roosevelt expend political capital in an assault upon the America caste system.[75] Despite the efforts of the NAACP to dramatize the Negroes' plight as second-class citizens, subject to brutality and often without legal protection, Roosevelt would not endorse the anti-lynching bill. ("No government pretending to be civilized can go on condoning such atrocities," H. L. Mencken testified. "Either it must make every possible effort to put them down or it must suffer the scorn and contempt of Christendom.")[76] Unwilling to risk schism with Southerners ruling committees, Roosevelt capitulated to the forces of racism.[77]

Even less bold than in economic reform, the New Deal left intact the race relations of America. Yet its belated and cautious recognition of the black man was great enough to woo Negro leaders and even to court the

[73] Allen Kifer, "The Negro Under the New Deal, 1933–1941," (unpublished Ph.D. dissertation, University of Wisconsin, 1961), *passim*. The National Youth Agency was an exception, concludes Kifer, p. 139. For Negro protests about New Deal discrimination, John P. Davis, "What Price National Recovery?," *Crisis*, XL (December 1933), 272; Charles Houston and Davis, "TVA: Lily-White Construction," *Crisis*, XLI (October 1934), 291.

[74] Robert Vann of the *Pittsburgh Courier*, quoted in Joseph Alsop and William Kintner, "The Guffey," *Saturday Evening Post*, CCX (March 26, 1938), 6. Vann had offered this advice in 1932.

[75] See Eleanor Roosevelt to Walter White, May 2, 29, 1934, April 21, 1938, White Papers, Yale University; Frank Freidel, *F.D.R. and the South* (Baton Rouge, La., 1965), pp. 71–102.

[76] Quoted from Senate Judiciary Committee, 74th Cong., 1st Sess., *Punishment for the Crime of Lynching, Hearings*, p. 23. Cf. Harold Ickes, "The Negro as a Citizen," June 29, 1936, Oswald Garrison Villard Papers, Harvard University.

[77] Roy Wilkins, Columbia Oral History Memoir, p. 98; Lester Granger, Columbia Oral History Memoir, p. 105, complains that Wagner had refused to include in his labor bill a prohibition against unions excluding workers because of race. When Wagner counseled a delay, Negroes felt, according to Granger, that the New Deal "was concerned with covering up, putting a fine cover over what there was, not bothering with the inequities."

masses. One of the bitter ironies of these years is that a New Dealer could tell the NAACP in 1936: "Under our new conception of democracy, the Negro will be given the chance to which he is entitled. . . ." But it was true, Ickes emphasized, that "The greatest advance [since Reconstruction] toward assuring the Negro that degree of justice to which he is entitled and that equality of opportunity under the law which is implicit in his American citizenship, has been made since Franklin D. Roosevelt was sworn in as President. . . ."[78]

It was not in the cities and not among the Negroes but in rural America that the Roosevelt administration made its (philosophically) boldest efforts: creation of the Tennessee Valley Authority and the later attempt to construct seven little valley authorities. Though conservation was not a new federal policy and government-owned utilities were sanctioned by municipal experience, federal activity in this area constituted a challenge to corporate enterprise and an expression of concern about the poor. A valuable example of regional planning and a contribution to regional prosperity, TVA still fell far short of expectations. The agency soon retreated from social planning. ("From 1936 on," wrote Tugwell, "the TVA should have been called the Tennessee Valley Power Production and Flood Control Corporation.") Fearful of antagonizing the powerful interests, its agricultural program neglected the tenants and the sharecroppers.[79]

To urban workingmen the New Deal offered some, but limited, material benefits. Though the government had instituted contributory social security and unemployment insurance, its much-heralded Fair Labor Standards Act, while prohibiting child labor, was a greater disappointment. It exempted millions from its wages-and-hours provisions. So unsatisfactory was the measure that one congressman cynically suggested, "Within 90 days after appointment of the administrator, she should report to Congress whether anyone is subject to this bill."[80] Requiring a minimum of twenty-five cents an hour ($11 a week for 44 hours), it raised the wages of only about a half-million at a time when nearly twelve million workers in interstate commerce were earning less than forty cents an hour.[81]

More important than these limited measures was the administration's support, albeit belated, of the organization of labor and the right of collective bargaining. Slightly increasing organized workers' share of the national income,[82] the new industrial unions extended job security to millions who were previously subject to the whim of management. Unionization freed them from the perils of a free market.

By assisting labor, as well as agriculture, the New Deal started the institutionalization of larger interest groups into a new political economy. Joining business as tentative junior partners, they shared the consensus on the value of large-scale corporate capitalism, and were permitted to partic-

[78] Ickes, "The Negro as a Citizen." Ickes had said, "since the Civil War."
[79] Schlesinger, *Politics of Upheaval*, pp. 362–80; quotations from Tugwell, p. 371.
[80] Martin Dies, quoted by Burns, *Congress on Trial* (New York, 1949), p. 77.
[81] The law raised standards to thirty cents and forty-two hours in 1939 and forty cents and forty hours in 1945. U.S. Department of Labor, BLS, *Labor Information Bulletin* (April 1939), pp. 1–3.
[82] Arthur M. Ross, *Trade Union Wage Policy* (Berkeley, Cal., 1948), pp. 113–28.

ipate in the competition for the division of shares. While failing to redistribute income, the New Deal modified the political structure at the price of excluding many from the process of decision-making. To many what was offered in fact was symbolic representation, formal representation. It was not the industrial workers necessarily who were recognized, but their unions and leaders; it was not even the farmers, but their organizations and leaders. While this was not a conscious design, it was the predictable result of conscious policies. It could not have been easily avoided, for it was part of the price paid by a large society unwilling to consider radical new designs for the distribution of power and wealth.

VII

In the deepest sense, this new form of representation was rooted in the liberal's failure to endorse a meaningful egalitarianism which would provide actual equality of opportunity. It was also the limited concern with equality and justice that accounted for the shallow efforts of the New Deal and left so many Americans behind. The New Deal was neither a "third American Revolution," as Carl Degler suggests, nor even a "half-way revolution," as William Leuchtenburg concludes. Not only was the extension of representation to new groups less than full-fledged partnership, but the New Deal neglected many Americans—sharecroppers, tenant farmers, migratory workers and farm laborers, slum dwellers, unskilled workers, and the unemployed Negroes. They were left outside the new order.[83] As Roosevelt asserted in 1937 (in a classic understatement), one third of the nation was "ill-nourished, ill-clad, ill-housed."[84]

Yet, by the power of rhetoric and through the appeals of political organization, the Roosevelt government managed to win or retain the allegiance of these peoples. Perhaps this is one of the crueler ironies of liberal politics, that the marginal men trapped in hopelessness were seduced by rhetoric, by the style and movement, by the symbolism of efforts seldom reaching beyond words. In acting to protect the institution of private property and in advancing the interests of corporate capitalism, the New Deal assisted the middle and upper sectors of society. It protected them, sometimes, even at the cost of injuring the lower sectors. Seldom did it bestow much of substance upon the lower classes. Never did the New Deal seek to organize these groups into independent political forces. Seldom did it risk antagonizing established interests. For some this would constitute a puzzling defect of liberalism; for some, the failure to achieve true liberalism. To others it would emphasize the inherent shortcomings of American liberal democracy. As the nation prepared for war, liberalism, by accepting private property and federal assistance to corporate capitalism, was not

[83] Leuchtenburg, *F.D.R.*, pp. 346–47. The Bankhead-Jones Farm Tenancy Act of 1937 provided some funds for loans to selected tenants who wished to purchase farms. In 1935, there were 2,865,155 tenants (about 42 percent of all farmers), and by 1941, 20,748 had received loans. *Farm Tenancy: Report of the President's Committee* (Washington, February 1937), Table I, p. 89; *Report of the Administrator of the Farm Security Administration*, 1941 (Washington, 1941), p. 17.

[84] Roosevelt's Inaugural Address of January 20, 1937, *FDR Papers*, VI, 5.

prepared effectively to reduce inequities, to redistribute political power, or to extend equality from promise to reality.

Suggested Reading

Fine surveys of scholarship on the New Deal include Richard Kirkendall's "The Great Depression: Another Watershed in History?" in John Braeman et al., eds., *Change and Continuity in Twentieth-Century America** (1964), and "The New Deal as Watershed: The Recent Literature," *Journal of American History*, LIV (1968), and Albert B. Rollins' "Was There Really a Man Named Roosevelt," in George Billias and Gerald Grob, eds., *American History: Retrospect and Prospect** (1971).

Important liberal interpretations of the New Deal include Frank Freidel's *The New Deal in Historical Perspective** (1965), the second and third volumes of Arthur Schlesinger, Jr.'s *The Age of Roosevelt—The Coming of the New Deal** (1958) and *The Politics of Upheaval** (1960), James M. Burns's *Roosevelt: The Lion and the Fox** (1956), Rexford Tugwell's *The Democratic Roosevelt* (1957), Richard Hofstadter's *The Age of Reform** (1955) and *The American Political Tradition** (1948), though the latter anticipates portions of later radical analyses, Eric Goldman's *Rendezvous with Destiny** (1952), Clark Chambers' "FDR: Pragmatist-Idealist," *Pacific Northwest Quarterly*, LII (1961), and Arthur Schlesinger, Jr.'s "Sources of the New Deal: Reflections on the Temper of a Time," *Columbia University Forum*, II (1959). The authoritative multivolume biography of Roosevelt is Frank Freidel's *Franklin D. Roosevelt* (3 vols., 1952–   ), which takes him to the election of 1932.

Howard Zinn's analysis in Zinn, ed., *New Deal Social Thought** (1966), Paul Conkin's in *The New Deal** (1967), Brad Wiley's in "The Myth of New Deal Reform," a pamphlet reprinted in Tom Christoffel *et al.*, eds., *Up Against the American Myth** (1970), and Ronald Radosh's "The Myth of the New Deal," in Radosh and Murray Rothbard, eds., *A New History of Leviathan** (1972) have all been classified as radical or New Left interpretations. Conkin's book does not comfortably fit this classification, for often his concern is that the New Deal lacked a coherent ideology, though he notes and laments its shortcomings and suggests that much greater accomplishments were probably unlikely in America. An important intellectual influence on radical analyses of the New Deal is William Appleman Williams' *The Contours of American History** (1961).

Developments in labor can be examined in Irving Bernstein's *The Turbulent Years: A History of the American Worker, 1933–1941* (1970) and *New Deal Collective Bargaining* (1950), Walter Galenson's *The CIO Challenge to the AFL* (1960); David Brody's "The Emergence of Mass Production Unionism," in John Braeman *et al.*, eds., *Change and Continuity in Twentieth-Century America** (1964), and Sidney Fine's *The Automobile Under the Blue Eagle* (1963).

The relationship of the Administration to blacks is the subject of John B. Kirby's "The Roosevelt Administration and Blacks: An Ambivalent Legacy," in Barton J. Bernstein and Allen J. Matusow, eds., *Twentieth-Century America: Recent Interpretations,** 2nd ed. (1972), Leslie Fishel's "The Negro in the New Deal Era," *Wisconsin Magazine of History*, XLVIII (1964–65), and Raymond Wolters' *Negroes and the Great Depression* (1970). Bernard Sternsher, ed., *The Negro in Depression and War** (1969) is a useful collection of essays.

Business-government relations are examined by Ralph DeBedts in *The New*

Deal's SEC: The Formative Years (1964), Michael Parrish in *Securities Regulation and the New Deal* (1970), Charles Jackson in *Food and Drug Legislation in the New Deal* (1970), and Ellis W. Hawley in *The New Deal and the Problem of Monopoly** (1966).

An important study of politics is James Patterson's *Congressional Conservatives and the New Deal** (1967). Daniel Aaron's *Writers on the Left** (1961) is a valuable examination of literary artists and radicalism. Broadus Mitchell's *Depression Decade** (1947) is still the best survey of the economy between 1929 and 1941.

A fine collection of interpretations of the New Deal is Otis L. Graham, ed., *The New Deal** (1971).

* Also published in paperback edition.

The Coming of
the Second
World War

The Axis Alliance
and Japanese-American
Relations, 1941:
An Appraisal of
American Policy

Paul Schroeder

For more than a decade before Pearl Harbor the
United States and Japan coexisted uneasily in the
Pacific. Under Herbert Hoover the United States
condemned Japanese aggression in Manchuria, which
had technically been under China's sovereignty, and
withheld recognition of Manchukuo, the puppet
state created by Japan to replace the Chinese
province. Nonrecognition, since it was unaccompanied
by sanctions, impaired Japanese-American relations
without assisting China. The Roosevelt
Administration, while continuing the policy of
nonrecognition, refrained from moralistic denunciations. Japanese-American relations improved until
1937 when war erupted in China and the United
States resumed its condemnation of Japan. As the
war continued, the administration in 1939 began
granting loans to China and also terminated the
treaty with Japan, thereby preparing the way for a
future trade embargo.

327

When Japan occupied the northern half of
Indo-China in June 1940, and then joined an alliance
with Germany and Italy in September, the Roosevelt
government placed an embargo on shipments of scrap
metal and iron to Japan. Because Roosevelt feared
that a total embargo might provoke a Japanese
invasion of the Dutch East Indies in order to secure
oil, the President decided not to cut off exports of oil
at that time. But, when Japan moved into south
Indo-China in July 1941, and prepared to expand into
the rest of Southeast Asia, Roosevelt finally terminated
Japan's supply of American oil. Japan, then, had
basically two choices: she could negotiate a settlement
with the United States or expand and conquer her
own source of oil. Fearing war with the western
powers, Prime Minister Fumimaro Konoye asked in
August for a meeting with the President in order to
work out a settlement. But the President refused,
apparently on the advice of Secretary of State Cordell
Hull who insisted on specific concessions about China
in advance. Konoye refused to make these
concessions. Roosevelt's rebuff weakened the Prime
Minister's position and his cabinet was forced to resign
in October, giving way to the extremist General
Hideki Tojo.

Tojo's government, acting at the behest of the
Emperor, agreed to make a last attempt at peace. It
would offer a general settlement (Plan A), and if that
was refused, a temporary truce (Plan B) would be
presented. If agreement was not reached by
November 25, Japan would renew expansion.
Washington, having broken the Japanese secret code,
knew in advance the contents of Plan B when Hull
rejected the first plan on the grounds that it would
mean a sell-out of China. In Plan B, which was then
presented, Japan promised, in effect, to halt expansion
in Southeast Asia and the south Pacific, to withdraw
from south Indo-China, and to leave north Indo-China
after the conclusion of a general peace. As part of
Plan B, the United States was to resume exports of oil
to Japan and to agree to a vaguely worded statement
(Point 5) on China: "The Government of the United
States undertakes to refrain from such measures and

The Axis Alliance and Japanese-American Relations, 1941: An Appraisal of American
Policy. From The Axis Alliance and Japanese-American Relations, 1941 by Paul W.
Schroeder (Ithaca, N.Y.: Cornell University Press 1958), pp. 200–16. Copyright © 1958
by the American Historical Association. Used by permission of Cornell University
Press.

actions as will be prejudicial to the endeavors for restoration of general peace between China and Japan."

Though Point 5 has been variously interpreted, Hull contended that it required the immediate American abandonment of China and on November 26 he rejected Plan B. Hull and Roosevelt knew that war was likely to follow, for the United States had decoded a message on November 22 from Tokyo to the Japanese ambassador in Washington: If the agreement is not signed by November 29, "things are automatically going to happen." On December 7 Hull and Roosevelt learned the particulars: Pearl Harbor.

In late November, Hull had briefly considered a counter-offer: a temporary (three-month) agreement or *modus vivendi*, and the outline of a permanent agreement. The temporary agreement, which would have required Japan to withdraw from south Indo-China and reduce her forces in the north, would have compelled the United States to resume oil exports for civilian consumption. Hull, who understood the value of this three-month peace in aiding the United States to prepare for war, discarded the proposal when China charged that she was being abandoned and Winston Churchill warned that the agreement would impair China's morale and therefore leave Japan even more powerful in the Far East. On November 26, Hull instead presented ten demands (considered by many an "ultimatum") that, among other points, required Japan's withdrawal from Indo-China and China. Hull knew, on the basis of the intercepted message of November 22, that these demands would be unacceptable.

Since Pearl Harbor some historians have challenged the wisdom of the American government's policy. In moving beyond an analysis of events and decisions to an *appraisal* of policy, these historians have self-consciously broadened their mandate. Among the more penetrating of those critics is Paul Schroeder of the University of Illinois at Urbana, author of *The Axis Alliance and Japanese-American Relations, 1941* (1958). In the following section drawn from that book, he criticizes the general assumptions of policy as well as its execution. About Plan B, for example, he writes, "It is far from certain that Point 5 actually was a demand for immediate cessation of aid [to China] or that the Japanese would have insisted upon this as a *sine qua non* for agreement."

Schroeder does not analyze why Hull and other American leaders subscribed to principles that made compromise, and maybe even avoidance of war, impossible. Why for example did Hull and most American policy-makers seek to maintain the Open Door policy in China? Is it, as William Appleman Williams contends, that they believed that America's welfare depended on expanding trade and that the Open Door policy was considered essential to peace and prosperity? According to this interpretation, as areas of the world were conquered or moved toward autarky, world trade and American trade would decline, and American democracy, which depended on the prosperity created by trade, would be in danger. If this analysis is correct, then Hull was acting to preserve not simply moralistic or legalistic values but what many considered the national interest: maintenance of the Open Door as a necessary condition for the liberal-capitalist system deemed essential to American democracy and prosperity.

*I*n judging American policy toward Japan in 1941, it might be well to separate what is still controversial from what is not. There is no longer any real doubt that the war came about over China. Even an administration stalwart like Henry L. Stimson and a sympathetic critic like Herbert Feis concur in this.[1] Nor is it necessary to speculate any longer as to what could have induced Japan to launch such an incredible attack upon the United States and Great Britain as occurred at Pearl Harbor and in the South Pacific. One need not, as Winston Churchill did in wartime, characterize it as "an irrational act" incompatible "with prudence or even with sanity."[2] The Japanese were realistic about the position throughout; they did not suddenly go insane. The attack was an act of desperation, not madness. Japan fought only when she had her back to the wall as a result of America's diplomatic and economic offensive.

The main point still at issue is whether the United States was wise in maintaining a "hard" program of diplomatic and economic pressure on Japan from July 1941 on. Along with this issue go two subsidiary questions:

[1] "If at any time the United States had been willing to concede Japan a free hand in China, there would have been no war in the Pacific" (Henry Stimson and McGeorge Bundy, *On Active Service* [New York: Harper & Row, 1948], 256). "Our full induction into this last World War followed our refusal to let China fend for itself. We had rejected all proposals which would have allowed Japan to remain in China and Manchuria. . . . Japan had struck—rather than accept frustration" (Herbert Feis, *The China Tangle* [Princeton: Princeton University Press, 1953], 3).

[2] Speech to U.S. Congress, Washington, Dec. 26, 1941, *War Speeches of Churchill*, II, 150.

the first, whether it was wise to make the liberation of China the central aim of American policy and the immediate evacuation of Japanese troops a requirement for agreement; the second, whether it was wise to decline Premier Konoye's invitation to a meeeting of leaders in the Pacific. On all these points, the policy which the United States carried out still has distinguished defenders. The paramount issue between Japan and the United States, they contend, always was the China problem. In her China policy, Japan showed that she was determined to secure domination over a large area of East Asia by force. Apart from the legitimate American commercial interests which would be ruined or excluded by this Japanese action, the United States, for reasons of her own security and of world peace, had sufficient stake in Far Eastern questions to oppose such aggression. Finally, after ten years of Japanese expansion, it was only sensible and prudent for the United States to demand that it come to an end and that Japan retreat. In order to meet the Japanese threat, the United States had a perfect right to use the economic power she possessed in order to compel the Japanese to evacuate their conquered territory. If Japan chose to make this a cause for war, the United States could not be held responsible.

A similar defense is offered on the decision to turn down Konoye's Leaders' Conference. Historians may concede, as do Langer and Gleason, that Konoye was probably sincere in wanting peace and that he "envisaged making additional concessions to Washington, including concessions on the crucial issue of the withdrawal of Japanese troops from China." But, they point out, Konoye could never have carried the Army with him on any such concession.[3] If the United States was right in requiring Japan to abandon the Co-Prosperity Sphere, then her leaders were equally right in declining to meet with a Japanese Premier who, however conciliatory he might have been personally, was bound by his own promises and the exigencies of Japanese politics to maintain this national aim. In addition, there was the serious possibility that much could be lost from such a meeting—the confidence of China, the cohesiveness of the coalition with Great Britain and Russia. In short, there was not enough prospect of gain to merit taking the chance.

This is a point of view which must be taken seriously. Any judgment on the wisdom or folly of the American policy, in fact, must be made with caution—there are no grounds for dogmatic certainty. The opinion here to be developed, nonetheless, is that the American policy from the end of July to December was a grave mistake. It should not be necessary to add that this does not make it treason. There is a "back door to war" theory, espoused in various forms by Charles A. Beard, George Morgenstern, Charles C. Tansill, and, most recently, Rear Admiral Robert A. Theobald, which holds that the President chose the Far East as a rear entrance to the war in Europe and to that end deliberately goaded the Japanese into an attack.[4] This theory is

3 William L. Langer and S. Everett Gleason, *The Undeclared War, 1940–1941* (New York: Harper & Row, 1953), 706–707.

4 Charles A. Beard, *President Roosevelt and the Coming of the War, 1941* (New Haven: Yale University Press, 1948); George E. Morgenstern, *Pearl Harbor: The Story of the Secret War* (New York: Devin-Adair, 1947); Charles C. Tansill, *Back Door to War* (Chicago: Regnery, 1952); Rear Admiral A. Theobald, *The Final Secret of Pearl Harbor* (New York: Devin-Adair, 1954).

quite different and quite incredible. It is as impossible to accept as the idea that Japan attacked the United States in a spirit of overconfidence or that Hitler pushed the Japanese into war. Roosevelt's fault, if any, was not that of deliberately provoking the Japanese to attack, but of allowing Hull and others to talk him out of impulses and ideas which, he had pursued them, might have averted the conflict. Moreover, the mistake (assuming that it was a mistake) of a too hard and rigid policy with Japan was, as has been pointed out, a mistake shared by the whole nation, with causes that were deeply organic. Behind it was not sinister design or warlike intent, but a sincere and uncompromising adherence to moral principles and liberal doctrines.

This is going ahead too fast, however; one needs first of all to define the mistake with which American policy is charged. Briefly, it was this. In the attempt to gain everything at once, the United States lost her opportunity to secure immediately her essential requirements in the Far East and to continue to work toward her long-range goals. She succeeded instead only in making inevitable an unnecessary and avoidable war—an outcome which constitutes the ultimate failure of diplomacy. Until July 1941, as already demonstrated, the United States consistently sought to attain two limited objectives in the Far East, those of splitting the Axis and of stopping Japan's advance southward. Both aims were in accordance with America's broad strategic interests; both were reasonable, attainable goals. Through a combination of favorable circumstance and forceful American action, the United States reached the position where the achievement of these two goals was within sight. At this very moment, on the verge of a major diplomatic victory, the United States abandoned her original goals and concentrated on a third, the liberation of China. This last aim was not in accord with American strategic interests, was not a limited objective, and, most important, was completely incapable of being achieved by peaceful means and doubtful of attainment even by war. Through her single-minded pursuit of this unattainable goal, the United States forfeited the diplomatic victory which she had already virtually won. The unrelenting application of extreme economic pressure on Japan, instead of compelling the evacuation of China, rendered war inevitable, drove Japan back into the arms of Germany for better or for worse, and precipitated the wholesale plunge by Japan into the South Seas. As it ultimately turned out, the United States succeeded in liberating China only at great cost and then it was too late to do the cause of the Nationalist Chinese much real good.

This is not, of course, a new viewpoint. It is in the main simply that of Ambassador Grew, who has held and defended it since 1941. The arguments he advances seem cogent and sensible in the light of present knowledge. Briefly summarized, they are the following: First is his insistence on the necessity of distinguishing between long-range and immediate goals in foreign policy and on the folly of demanding the immediate realization of both.[5] Second is his contention that governments are brought to abandon aggressive policies not by sudden conversion through moral lectures, but by

---

[5] Joseph Grew, *Turbulent Era*, edited by Walter Johnson (Boston: Houghton Mifflin, 1952), II, 1255.

the gradual recognition that the policy of aggression will not succeed. According to Grew, enough awareness of failure existed in the government of Japan in late 1941 to enable it to make a beginning in the process of reversal of policy—but not nearly enough to force Japan to a wholesale surrender of her conquests and aims.[6] Third was his conviction that what was needed on both sides was time—time in which the United States could grow stronger and in which the tide of war in Europe could be turned definitely against Germany, time in which the sense of failure could grow in Japan and in which moderates could gain better control of the situation. A victory in Europe, Grew observed, would either automatically solve the problem of Japan or make that problem, if necessary, much easier to solve by force.[7] Fourth was his belief that Japan would fight if backed to the wall (a view vindicated by events)[8] and that a war at this time with Japan could not possibly serve the interests of the United States. Even if one considered war as the only final answer to Japanese militarism, still, Grew would answer, the United States stood to gain nothing by seeking a decision in 1941. The time factor was entirely in America's favor. Japan could not hope to gain as much from a limited relaxation of the embargo as the United States could from time gained for mobilization; Roosevelt and the military strategists were in fact anxious to gain time by a *modus vivendi*.[9]

There is one real weakness in Grew's argument upon which his critics have always seized. This is his contention that Konoye, faced after July 26 with the two clear alternatives of war or a genuine peace move, which would of necessity include a settlement with China, had chosen the latter course and could have carried through a policy of peace had he been given the time. "We believed," he writes, "that Prince Konoye was in a position to carry the country with him in a program of peace" and to make commitments to the United States which would "eventually, if not immediately" meet the conditions of Hull's Four Points.[10] The answer of critics is that, even if one credits Konoye's sincerity and takes his assurances at face value, there is still no reason to believe that he could have carried even his own cabinet, much less the whole nation, with him on any program approximating that of Hull. In particular, as events show, he could not have persuaded the Army to evacuate China.[11]

The objection is well taken; Grew was undoubtedly over-optimistic about Konoye's capacity to carry through a peaceful policy. This one objec-

---

[6] *Ibid.*, 1290.

[7] *Ibid.*, 1268–1269, 1286.

[8] The opposite belief, that Japan would give way, not only was inconsonant with the best available political and military intelligence, but was also a bad estimate of Japanese national psychology and of expansionist psychology in general. F. C. Jones rightly criticizes it as "the folly of supposing that the rulers of a powerful nation, having committed themselves to an expansionist policy, will abandon or reverse that policy when confronted by the threat of war. So long as they see, or think they see, any possibility of success, they will elect to fight rather than face the humiliation and probable internal revolt which submission to the demands of their opponents would entail" (F. C. Jones, *Japan's New Order in East Asia* [Toronto: Oxford University Press, 1954], 461).

[9] Grew, *Turbulent Era*, II, 1276–1277.

[10] *Ibid.*, 1263–1264.

[11] Herbert Feis, *Road to Pearl Harbor* (Princeton: Princeton University Press, 1950), 275–277; Jones, *Japan's New Order*, 457–458.

334   PAUL SCHROEDER

tion, however, does not ruin Grew's case. He countered it later with the argument that a settlement with Japan which allowed Japanese garrisons to remain in China on a temporary basis would not have been a bad idea. Although far from an ideal solution, it would have been better, for China as well, than the policy the United States actually followed. It would have brought China what was all-important—a cessation of fighting—without involving the United States, as many contended, in either a sacrifice of principle or a betrayal of China. The United States, Grew points out, had never committed herself to guaranteeing China's integrity. Further, it would not have been necessary to agree to anything other than temporary garrisons in North China which, in more favorable times, the United States could work to have removed. The great mistake was to allow American policy to be guided by a sentimental attitude toward China which in the long run could do neither the United States nor China any good. As Grew puts it:

> Japan's advance to the south, including her occupation of portions of China, constituted for us a real danger, and it was definitely in our national interest that it be stopped, by peaceful means if possible, by force of arms if necessary. American aid to China should have been regarded, as we believe it was regarded by our Government, as an indirect means to this end, and not from a sentimental viewpoint. The President's letter of January 21, 1941, shows that he then sensed the important issues in the Far East, and that he did not include China, purely for China's sake, among them. . . . The failure of the Washington Administration to seize the opportunity presented in August and September, 1941, to halt the southward advance by peaceful means, together with the paramount importance attached to the China question during the conversations in Washington, gives rise to the belief that not our Government but millions of quite understandably sympathetic but almost totally uninformed American citizens had assumed control of our Far Eastern policy.[12]

There remains the obvious objection that Grew's solution, however plausible it may now seem, was politically impracticable in 1941. No American government could then have treated China as expendable, just as no Japanese government could have written off the China Affair as a dead loss. This is in good measure true and goes a long way to explain, if not to justify, the hard American policy. Yet it is not entirely certain that no solution could have been found which would both have averted war and have been accepted by the American people, had a determined effort been made to find one. As F. C. Jones points out, the United States and Japan were not faced in July 1941 with an absolute dilemma of peace or war, of complete settlement or open conflict. Hull believed that they were, of course; but his all-or-nothing attitude constituted one of his major shortcomings as a diplomat. Between the two extremes existed the possibility of a *modus vivendi*, an agreement settling some issues and leaving others in abeyance. Had Roosevelt and Konoye met, Jones argues, they might have been able to agree on a relaxation of the embargo in exchange for satisfactory assurances on the Tripartite Pact and southward expansion, with the China issue laid aside. The United States would not have had to cease aid, nor Japan to remove her troops. The final settlement of the Far Eastern question, Jones concludes,

[12] Grew, *Turbulent Era*, II, 1367–1368.

would then have depended upon the issue of the struggle in Europe. If Germany prevailed, then the United States would be in no position to oppose Japanese ambitions in Asia; if Germany were defeated, Japan would be in no position to persist in those ambitions in the face of the United States, the USSR, and the British Commonwealth.[13]

Such an agreement, limited and temporary in nature, would have involved no sacrifice of principle for either nation, yet would have removed the immediate danger of war. As a temporary expedient and as an alternative to otherwise inevitable and useless conflict, it could have been sold by determined effort to the public on both sides. Nor would it have been impossible, in the writer's opinion, to have accompanied or followed such an agreement with a simple truce or standstill in the China conflict through American mediation.

This appraisal, to be sure, is one based on realism. Grew's criticism of Hull's policy and the alternative he offers to it are both characterized by fundamental attention to what is practical and expedient at a given time and to limited objectives within the scope of the national interest. In general, the writer agrees with this point of view, believing that, as William A. Orton points out, it is foolish and disastrous to treat nations as morally responsible persons, "because their nature falls far short of personality," and that, as George F. Kennan contends, the right role for moral considerations in foreign affairs is not to determine policy, but rather to soften and ameliorate actions necessarily based on the realities of world politics.[14]

From this realistic standpoint, the policy of the State Department would seem to be open to other criticisms besides those of Grew. The criticisms, which may be briefly mentioned here, are those of inconsistency, blindness to reality, and futility. A notable example of the first would be the inconsistency of a strong no-compromise stand against Japan with the policy of broad accommodation to America's allies, especially Russia, both before and after the American entrance into the war.[15] The inconsistency may perhaps best be seen by comparing the American stand in 1941 on such questions as free trade, the Open Door in China, the territorial and administrative integrity of China, the maintenance of the prewar *status quo* in the Far East, and the sanctity of international agreements with the position taken on the same questions at the Yalta Conference in 1945.[16]

[13] Jones, *Japan's New Order*, 459.

[14] William A. Orton, *The Liberal Tradition* (New Haven: Yale University Press, 1944), 239; George F. Kennan, *American Diplomacy, 1900–1950* (Chicago: University of Chicago Press, 1951), 95–103.

[15] One notes with interest, for example, a pre-Pearl Harbor statement by Senator Lister Hill of Alabama, a strong proponent of a radical anti-Japanese policy, as to America's attitude toward the Soviet Union: "It is not the business of this government to ask or to receive any assurance from Stalin about what he will do with regard to Finland after the war. . . . It is the business of this government to look for and defend the vital interests of the United States" (*New York Times*, Nov. 5, 1941). If in the above quotation one reads "Tojo" for "Stalin" and "China" for "Finland," the result is a statement of the extreme isolationist position on the Far East which Hill and other supporters of the administration found so detestable.

[16] The writer has no desire to enter here into controversy over the merits of the Yalta decisions, but only to draw a certain parallel. The standard defense for the Yalta policy on the Far East has been the contention that the United States conceded to Soviet Russia only what the U.S.S.R. could and would have seized without American

The blindness to reality may be seen in the apparent inability of American policy makers to take seriously into account the gravity of Japan's economic plight or the real exigencies of her military and strategic position, particularly as these factors would affect the United States over the long run.[17] Equally unrealistic and more fateful was the lack of appreciation on the part of many influential people and of wide sections of the public of the almost certain consequences to be expected from the pressure exerted on Japan—namely, American involvement in a war her military strategists considered highly undesirable. The attitude has been well termed by Robert Osgood, "this blind indifference toward the military and political consequences of a morally-inspired position."[18]

The charge of futility, finally, could be laid to the practice of insisting on a literal subscription to principles which, however noble, had no chance of general acceptance or practical application. The best example is the per-

---

leave, that the only alternative to agreement would have been war with Russia, and that securing Russian entrance into the Far Eastern war was considered militarily necessary (George F. Lensen, "Yalta and the Far East," in John L. Snell, Forrest C. Pogue, Charles F. Delzell, and George F. Lensen, *The Meaning of Yalta: Big Three Diplomacy and the New Balance of Power* [Baton Rouge: Louisiana State University Press, 1956], 163–164). The argument may be quite sound, but surely it would serve equally well—indeed, much better, *mutatis mutandis*—to justify a policy of conciliation toward Japan in 1941. Applied to Japan, the argument would then read as follows: The United States would have conceded to Japan only the temporary possession of a part of what Japan had already seized without American leave; the only alternative to agreement would have been war with Japan; and preventing Japanese entrance into the European war was considered militarily necessary. The great difference between the two situations would seem to be that the concessions envisioned by Japan in 1941 were temporary and reversible; those gained by Russia in 1945 were not. The very necessity of pursuing the Yalta policy in 1945 casts doubt on the wisdom of the hard-and-fast stand of 1941. Felix Morley has put the parallel neatly: "To assert that the sudden and complete reversal of the long-established Far Eastern policy was justified was also to say, by implication, that the policy reversed was fundamentally faulty, that to fight a war with Japan in behalf of Chinese nationalism had been a dreadful mistake" (*The Foreign Policy of the United States* [New York: Alfred A. Knopf, 1951], 87–88). One may, as Morley does, reject both the above premise and the conclusion, or one may accept both; but it is difficult to see how one may affirm the premise and deny the conclusion. For those who believe that a vital moral difference existed between the two cases, the problem would seem to be how to show that it is morally unjustifiable to violate principle in order to keep a potential enemy out of a war, yet morally justifiable to sacrifice principle in order to get a potential ally into it. The dilemma appears insoluble.

[17] In his very interesting book, *America's Strategy in World Politics* (New York: Harcourt, Brace, 1942), Nicholas Spykman displays some of the insights which seem to have been lacking in the American policy of the time. He points out, for example, that Japan's economic and geographic position was essentially the same as that of Great Britain; that her position vis-à-vis the United States was also roughly equivalent to England's; that therefore it made little sense for America to aid Great Britain in maintaining a European balance of power, while at the same time trying to force Japan to give up all her buffer states in Asia; that the Japanese war potential could not compare to that of a revivified and unified China; and that one day (a striking prediction in 1942!) the United States would have to undertake to protect Japan from Soviet Russia and China (pp. 135–137, 469–470). Spykman saw then what is today so painfully evident—that without a Japanese foothold on the Asiatic mainland no real balance of power is possible in Asia.

[18] Robert E. Osgood, *Ideals and Self-Interest in America's Foreign Relations* (Chicago: University of Chicago Press, 1953), 361.

sistent demand that the Japanese pledge themselves to carrying out nine-teenth-century principles of free trade and equal access to raw materials in a twentieth-century world where economic nationalism and autarchy, trade barriers and restrictions were everywhere the order of the day, and not the least in the United States under the New Deal. Not one of America's major allies would have subscribed whole heartedly to Hull's free-trade formula; what good it could have done to pin the Japanese down to it is hard to determine.[19]

But these are all criticisms based on a realistic point of view, and to judge the American policy solely from this point of view is to judge it unfairly and by a standard inappropriate to it. The policy of the United States was avowedly not one of realism, but of principle. If then it is to be understood on its own grounds and judged by its own standards, the main question will be whether the policy was morally right—that is, in accord with principles of peace and international justice. Here, according to its defenders, the American policy stands vindicated. For any other policy, any settlement with Japan at the expense of China, would have meant a betrayal not only of China, but also of vital principles and of America's moral task in the world.

This, as we know, was the position of Hull and his co-workers. It has been stated more recently by Basil Rauch, who writes:

> No one but an absolute pacifist would argue that the danger of war is a greater evil than violation of principle. . . . The isolationist believes that appeasement of Japan without China's consent violated no principle worth a risk of war. The internationalist must believe that the principle did justify a risk of war.[20]

This is not an argument to be discussed lightly. The contention that the United States had a duty to fulfill in 1941, and that this duty consisted in holding to justice and morality in a world given to international lawlessness and barbarism and in standing on principle against an unprincipled and ruth-less aggressor, commands respect. It is not answered by dismissing it as unrealistic or by proscribing all moral considerations in foreign policy. An answer may be found, however, in a closer definition of America's moral duty in 1941. According to Hull, and apparently also Rauch, the task was primarily one of upholding principle. This is not the only possible definition. It may well be contended that the moral duty was rather one of doing the most practical good possible in a chaotic world situation and, further, that this was the main task President Roosevelt and the administration had in mind at least till the end of July 1941.

If the moral task of the United States in the Far East was to uphold a principle of absolute moral value, the principle of nonappeasement of ag-gressors, then the American policy was entirely successful in fulfilling it.

---

[19] A memorandum by the Chief of the State Department Division of Commercial Policy and Agreements (Hawkins) to Ballantine, Washington, Nov. 10, 1941, offers interesting comments on the extent and nature of the trade discriminations then being practiced against Japan by nations throughout the world, including the United States (*Foreign Relations, 1941*, IV, 576–577).

[20] Basil Rauch, *Roosevelt, From Munich to Pearl Harbor* (Creative Age, 1950), 472.

The American diplomats proved that the United States was capable of holding to its position in disregard and even in defiance of national interests narrowly conceived. If, however, the task was one of doing concrete good and giving practical help where needed, especially to China, then the American policy falls fatally short. For it can easily be seen not only that the policy followed did not in practice help China, but also that it could not have been expected to. Although it was a pro-China and even a China-first policy in principle, it was not in practical fact designed to give China the kind of help needed.

What China required above all by late 1941 was clearly an end to the fighting, a chance to recoup her strength. Her chaotic financial condition, a disastrous inflation, civil strife with the Communists, severe hunger and privation, and falling morale all enfeebled and endangered her further resistance. Chiang Kai-shek, who knew this, could hope only for an end to the war through the massive intervention of American forces and the consequent liberation of China. It was in this hope that he pleaded so strongly for a hard American policy toward Japan. Chiang's hopes, however, were wholly unrealistic. For though the United States was willing to risk war for China's sake, and finally did incur it over the China issue, the Washington government never intended in case of war to throw America's full weight against Japan in order to liberate China. The American strategy always was to concentrate on Europe first, fighting a defensive naval war in the Far East and aiding China, as before, in order to keep the Japanese bogged down. The possibility was faced and accepted that the Chinese might have to go on fighting for some years before eventual liberation through the defeat of Japan. The vehement Chinese protests over this policy were unavailing, and the bitter disillusionment suffered by the Chinese only helped to bring on in 1942 the virtual collapse of the Chinese war effort during the latter years of the war.[21]

As a realistic appraisal of America's military capabilities and of her world-wide strategic interests, the Europe-first policy has a great deal to recommend it. But the combination of this realistic strategy with a moralistic diplomacy led to the noteworthy paradox of a war incurred for the sake of China which could not then be fought for the sake of China and whose practical value for China at the time was, to say the least, dubious. The plain fact is that the United States in 1941 was not capable of forcing Japan out of China by means short of war and was neither willing nor, under existing circumstances, able to throw the Japanese out by war. The American government could conceivably have told the Chinese this and tried to work out the best possible program of help for China under these limitations. Instead, it yielded to Chinese importunities and followed a policy almost sure to eventuate in war, knowing that if the Japanese did attack, China and her deliverance would have to take a back seat. It is difficult to conceive of such a policy as a program of practical aid to China.

The main, though not the only, reason why this policy was followed is

[21] Werner Levi, *Modern China's Foreign Policy* (Minneapolis: University of Minnesota Press, 1953), 229–237. On the danger of internal collapse in China as early as 1940, see U.S. Department of State, *Foreign Relations of the United States: 1940*, vol. IV, *The Far East* (Washington: Government Printing Office, 1955), 672–677.

clearly the overwhelming importance of principle in American diplomacy, particularly the principle of nonappeasement of aggressors. Once most leaders in the administration and wide sections of the public became convinced that it was America's prime moral duty to stand hard and fast against aggressors, whatever the consequences, and once this conviction became decisive in the formulation of policy, the end result was almost inevitable: a policy designed to uphold principle and to punish the aggressor, but not to save the victim.[22]

It is this conviction as to America's moral duty, however sincere and understandable, which the writer believes constitutes a fundamental misreading of America's moral task. The policy it gave rise to was bad not simply because it was moralistic but because it was obsessed with the wrong kind of morality—with that abstract "Let justice be done though the heavens fall" kind which so often, when relentlessly pursued, does more harm than good. It would be interesting to investigate the role which this conception of America's moral task played in the formulation of the American war aims in the Far East, with their twin goals of unconditional surrender and the destruction of Japan as a major power, especially after the desire to vindicate American principles and to punish the aggressor was intensified a hundredfold by the attack on Pearl Harbor.[23] To pursue the later implications of this kind of morality in foreign policy, with its attendant legalistic and vindictive overtones, would, however, be a task for [a] volume.

In contrast, the different kind of policy which Grew advocated and toward which Roosevelt so long inclined need not really be considered immoral or unprincipled, however much it undoubtedly would have been denounced as such. A limited *modus vivendi* agreement would not have required the United States in any way to sanction Japanese aggression or to abandon her stand on Chinese integrity and independence. It would have

---

[22] It is Secretary of War Henry L. Stimson who gives evidence on how strong was the role of avenging justice in the prevailing picture of America's moral duty. He displays a striking anxiety to acquit the administration of the charge of being "soft" on Japan and to prove that the administration was always fully aware of the Japanese crimes and morally aroused by them. The nation's leaders, he insists in one place, were "as well aware as their critics of the wickedness of the Japanese." Avenging justice, too, plays an important role in the defense he makes of the postwar Nuremberg and Tokyo war crimes trials. These trials, he claims, fulfilled a vital moral task. The main trouble with the Kellogg Pact and the policy of nonrecognition and moral sanctions, according to Stimson, was that they named the international lawbreakers but failed to capture and punish them. The United States, along with other nations in the prewar world, had neglected "a duty to catch the criminal. . . . Our offense was thus that of the man who passed by on the other side." Now, this is a curious revision of the parable of the Good Samaritan, to which the Secretary here alludes. According to the Stimson version, the Good Samaritan should not have stopped to bind up the victim's wounds, put him on his beast of burden, and arranged for his care. Had he been cognizant of his real moral duty, he would rather have mounted his steed and rode off in hot pursuit of the robbers, to bring them to justice. This is only an illustration, but an apt one, of the prevailing concept of America's moral duty, with its emphasis on meting out justice rather than doing good (Stimson and Bundy, *On Active Service*, 384, 262).

[23] Admiral William D. Leahy (*I Was There* [New York: McGraw-Hall, 1950], 81) expresses his view of America's war aims in dubious Latin but with admirable forthrightness: "*Delenda est Japanico.*" He was, of course, not the only American leader to want to emulate Cato.

constituted only a recognition that the American government was not then in a position to enforce its principles, reserving for America full freedom of action at some later, more favorable time. Nor would it have meant the abandonment and betrayal of China. Rather it would have involved the frank recognition that the kind of help the Chinese wanted was impossible for the United States to give at that time. It would in no way have precluded giving China the best kind of help then possible—in the author's opinion, the offer of American mediation for a truce in the war and the grant of fuller economic aid to try to help the Chinese recover—and promising China greater assistance once the crucial European situation was settled. Only that kind of morality which sees every sort of dealing with an aggressor, every instance of accommodation or conciliation, as appeasement and therefore criminal would find the policy immoral.[24]

What the practical results of such a policy, if attempted, would have been is of course a matter for conjecture. It would be rash to claim that it would have saved China, either from her wartime collapse or from the final victory of communism. It may well be that already in 1941 the situation in China was out of control. Nor can one assert with confidence that, had this policy enabled her to keep out of war with Japan, the United States would have been able to bring greater forces to bear in Europe much earlier, thus shortening the war and saving more of Europe from communism. Since the major part of the American armed forces were always concentrated in Europe and since in any case a certain proportion would have had to stand guard in the Pacific, it is possible that the avoidance of war with Japan, however desirable in itself, would not have made a decisive difference in the duration of the European conflict. The writer does, however, permit himself the modest conclusions that the kind of policy advocated by Grew presented real possibilities of success entirely closed to the policy actually followed and that it was by no means so immoral and unprincipled that it could not have been pursued by the United States with decency and honor.

---

[24] See the introductory remarks on the possibilities of appeasement, under certain circumstances, as a useful diplomatic tool, along with an excellent case study in the wrong use of it, in J. W. Wheeler-Bennett, *Munich: Prologue to Tragedy* (London: Macmillan, 1948), 3–8.

War Came at
Pearl Harbor:
Suspicions Considered

Herbert Feis

Herbert Feis, a former economic adviser in the State
Department and special consultant to the Secretary of
War, has written a series of widely respected books on
the diplomatic history of the Second World War. His
The Road to Pearl Harbor (1950) is a detailed, largely
sympathetic, account of American relations with
Japan before the outbreak of war. Critics have
attacked the volume on the grounds that it stresses
Japanese imperialism without acknowledging the
imperialistic impulses behind America's involvement
in the Far East.

In the following article Feis presents the case for
the Roosevelt Administration's policies toward Japan.
Much of his early analysis defends the Administration
from charges that received a brief hearing in the
1950s: (1) that Roosevelt placed the fleet at Pearl
Harbor in order to lure a Japanese attack, (2) that
he left the fleet there when he knew that it would be
attacked, or (3) that his policy toward Japan was
devised to provoke the Japanese to attack and thereby
to provide "a back door" into the war with Germany.
These contentions, argued in various ways by such
revisionists as Charles A. Beard, Charles C. Tansill,
Harry Elmer Barnes, and Admiral Robert Theobald,

have generally disappeared from the dialog of historians in the past decade.

Other issues still linger. Did the United States miss opportunities, especially in the summer and autumn of 1941, for a satisfactory understanding that would have averted war? Critics of the Roosevelt-Hull policy often point to the Administration's failure to meet with Prime Minister Konoye in the autumn and its responsibility for the breakdown of negotiations in late November. Feis (contrary to Schroeder) concludes that there was probably no chance of a settlement even if Roosevelt had met with Konoye. A subsidiary, but important theme in Feis's analysis is the possibly dangerous consequences of a Roosevelt-Konoye agreement that did not adequately protect China— such as a "deal" by the Chinese government with Japan, or maybe even the Soviet Union's withdrawal from the war with Hitler. The fears of Munich and the dangers of appeasement resonate throughout much of Feis's analysis.

In analyzing the negotiations of November 1941, Feis concludes (again contrary to Schroeder) that had the United States accepted the second Japanese offer (Plan B), it "would have required the American Government to end its support of China." As for an American counter-offer of a truce, Hull believed it would have been "unheeded" in Japan, and, in Feis's words, "it might shake the coalition to which by then the opponents of the Axis had pledged their lives and national destinies." Feis finds that "the situation had grown too entangled by then for minor measures, its momentum too great." This seems curiously elliptical and quite ambiguous. Does Feis mean that the United States was already committed in a significant moral way to the anti-Axis alliance and, therefore, that U.S. leaders were unable, ideologically or psychologically, to accept a temporary settlement? Or does he mean that American leaders *concluded* that America's future security depended on this alliance and, therefore, that they could find no advantage in risking its destruction for the short-run gain of Japan's promise not "to press on farther for the time being"? In an earlier unpublished draft of his essay, he noted that "once a nation has leaned far over the edge, it is almost impossible to

War Came at Pearl Harbor: Suspicions Considered. Originally published in *The Yale Review*, XLV (March 1956), pp. 378–90. Copyright © 1956 by Yale University Press. Reprinted by permission of *The Yale Review*.

pull back, to change the pitch of gravitation toward war" (Feis Papers, Library of Congress).

Underlying much of Feis's analysis is his assumption that the Administration's policy toward Japan, and even involvement in the war, was in America's interest. In other words, he finds, and is pleased, that the Administration's policy was not a "back door" to war (as the revisionists charged) but a willingness to defend by force American interests in Asia and to join the Allies in Europe before the Axis powers extended their conquests there and left the United States with few powerful friends. Not only do some critics sharply challenge the Administration's policies and Feis's defense, but they also assail Roosevelt for (as Feis admits) not explaining his strategy to the people and even camouflaging the risks. For some historians, a "credibility gap" existed as the United States moved toward the confrontation in the Pacific.

*T*en years after victory, we look ruefully at the way the world has gone. It is right and natural to search out any errors of judgment or faults of character that have led us to our present pass. But such self-scrutiny can go awry if governed by a wish to revile rather than a wish to understand. Unless we are alert, that could happen as a result of the suspicions that have come to cluster around the way in which the United States became engaged in the Second World War—torch-lit by the Pearl Harbor disaster.

The more recently available sources have added but little to our knowledge of the events that led to our entry into the war. The books of memoirs written by Japanese witnesses have told us something more, especially about the struggle within the Japanese Government. But in my reading, while they may improve our knowledge of details, they do not change the fundamental view of this experience or its main features. In American and British records still kept secret there may be information or explanations that would do so. But even this I doubt. With no new great revealing facts to display, and no great new insights to impart, the most useful service would seem to be to act as caretaker of what is known, and in particular to deal with certain warped comments and inferences that seasonally must feel the straightening edge of evidence.

Of all the accusations made, the one most shocking to me is that Roosevelt and his chief advisers deliberately left the Pacific Fleet and base at Pearl Harbor exposed as a lure to bring about a direct Japanese attack upon us. This has been diffused in the face of the fact that the Japanese High

Military Command conference before the Imperial Throne on September 6, 1941, resolved that "If by the early part of October there is no reasonable hope of having our demands agreed to in the diplomatic negotiations mentioned above, we will immediately make up our minds to get ready for war against America (and England and Holland)." This is September 6. The plan for the attack on Pearl Harbor was not approved and adopted until October; and Secret Operation Order #1, the execution of the plan, was not issued until November 5. The presence of the Pacific Fleet at Pearl Harbor was not a lure but an obstacle.

The literature of accusation ignores or rejects the real reasons why the Pacific Fleet was kept in Hawaii. It must do so, since one of the main reasons was the hope that its presence there would deter the Japanese from making so threatening a move south or north that American armed forces might have to join in the war. It scorns the fact that the American military plans—to be executed in the event that we became engaged in war—assigned vital tasks to this Pacific Fleet. A mind must indeed be distracted if it can believe that the American Government could, at one and the same time, use the Pacific Fleet as a target and count on having it as part of its main defending force.

A variant of this accusation, which at least does not require such a willingness to believe the worst, might also be noted—that despite ample knowledge that Pearl Harbor was about to be attacked, the American Government purposefully left it exposed and allowed the event to happen.

Those who do not find such an idea at odds with their view of the sense of duty and regard for human life of President Roosevelt and his chief advisers can find striking points about the occurrence that may be construed to correspond with this conception. How they glare out of the record in hindsight: Ambassador Grew's warnings; Secretary Hull's acute gleam put into words at least three times in Cabinet Councils in November that the Japanese attack might come "at any moment, anywhere"; the intercepted Japanese messages telling of the Japanese effort to secure minute information as to the location of the ships of our Pacific Fleet in the Harbor; carelessness in checking up on the protective measures taken by the local commanders; failure to use the chance to give an effective last-minute warning to Hawaii. How else, it is asked, can these be explained except in terms of secret and conscious purpose?

However, just as hindsight makes the failure of perception plain, so it also makes it understandable—but only by bringing back to mind the total circumstances. That can be done here only in the barest way. Up to then Japanese strategy had been wary, one small creeping step after another, from Manchuria to North China into China and down into Indo-China. American military circles came to take it for granted that it would go on that way. Then there was the fact that Japan's basic objectives lay to the south and southeast; there and there only it could get what it needed—raw materials, oil, and island bases to withstand the attack from the West. Expectation already set in that direction was kept there by impressive and accurate intelligence reports of movements under way. Against this flow of preconception, the signs pointing to Pearl Harbor were not heeded.

Such features of contemporary thinking within the American Government explain, though they do not excuse, the failure to discern that Pearl Harbor was going to be attacked. To think the contrary is to believe that the President and the heads of the American Army, Navy, and Air Force were given to deep deception, and in order to have us enter the war were ready to sacrifice not only the Pacific Fleet but the whole war plan for the Pacific. This, I think, is the difference between history and police court history.

I have taken note of these accusations that have been built about the disaster at Pearl Harbor because they appeal to the sense of the sinister which is so lively in our times. But I am glad to turn to ideas and interpretations of broader historical import.

The first of these is that Roosevelt and the Joint Chiefs of Staff were obligated by secret agreements with Churchill and their British colleagues to enter the war at some time or other, in one way or other. Therefore, it is further supposed, the American authors of this agreement had to cause either Germany or Japan, or both, to attack us.

This view derives encouragement from the fact that the American Government *did* enter into a secret agreement about strategy with the British. The accord, known as ABC-1 Staff Agreement, adopted at Washington in March, 1941, set down the respective missions of the British and American elements in the event that the United States should be at war with Germany or Japan, or both; and subsequently the American basic joint war plan, Rainbow-5, was adjusted to fit this combined plan of operations. An attempt was made at a similar conference in Singapore soon after to work out a more detailed United States—British—Dutch operating plan for the Pacific. This attempt failed; but the discussion that took place there left a lasting mark on American official thinking, for the conferees defined the limits on land and sea beyond which Japanese forces could not be permitted to go without great risk to the defenders.

The ABC-1 agreement did not place the Roosevelt Administration under *political* obligation to enter the war against either Germany or Japan, not even if Japan attacked British or Dutch areas in the Far East. Nor did Roosevelt give a promise to this effect to Churchill when they met at Newfoundland in August, 1941. Up to the very eve of the Japanese assault the President refused to tell the British or Dutch what we would do. In short, the Government kept itself officially free from any obligation to enter the war, certainly free of any obligation to thrust itself into the war.

But I do think this accord conveyed responsibilities of a moral sort. After ABC-1 was adopted, production of weapons in the United States and the British Commonwealth took it into account; and the allocation of weapons, troops, ships, and planes as between threatened areas was based on the expectation that the United States would carry out the assignments set down in the plan.

Thus, it may be fairly thought, Roosevelt and his administration were obligated to try to gain the consent of Congress and the American people to play the part designated in the joint plans if Japanese assaults crossed the land and sea boundaries of resistance that were defined at these joint staff conferences. In the last November weeks when the end of the diplomatic talks with Japan came into sight, and General Marshall and Admiral Stark were asked what measures should be taken in face of the threatened Japanese advances, they advised the President to declare the limits defined at Singapore, and to warn the Japanese that we would fight if these were crossed. There is much reason to think this would have been done even had the Japanese not struck at Pearl Harbor and the Philippines, and this boundary would have been the line between peace and war. But this reaffirmation was made not as a measure required to carry out a secret accord, but because it was believed to be the best course.

A variant explanation of the way we dealt with Japan runs somewhat as follows: that Roosevelt was determined to get into the war against Germany; that he had to find a release from his public promises that the United States would not enter "foreign wars" unless attacked; that his efforts to do so by unneutral aid to Britain and the Soviet Union had failed because Hitler had refused to accept the challenge; and so he sought another door into war, a back door, by inviting or compelling the Japanese attack.

This interpretation, with its kick at the end, twists the record around its own preconception. The actions taken did not flow from a settled wish to get us into war. They trailed along the rim of necessity of the true purpose —which was to sustain resistance against the Axis. How many times the American Government refused to do what the British, French, Chinese, Russians, Dutch asked it to do, because it might involve us in actual combat!

This slant of reasoning about American action passes by the course of Japanese conduct which aroused our fears and stimulated our opposition: the way in which, despite all our pleas and warnings, Japan pressed on. By not recognizing that these Japanese actions called for American counteraction, it excuses them. Thus our resistance is made to appear as nothing else but a deceitful plot to plunge us into war. Furthermore, it dismisses as insincere the patient attempt to calm Japan by diplomatic talks, by offers to join in safeguarding its security.

There were influential individuals in the Roosevelt Administration who wanted to get into the war and indifferent as to how we got into it. Of these, Secretary of the Interior Ickes was, I believe, the most candid, at any rate in his diary entries. Secretary of the Treasury Morgenthau and his staff also had a positive wish that we should engage in war—but against Germany, not against Japan, for what might have brought a diversion of forces to the Pacific. Secretary of War Stimson thought that it would not be possible for Great Britain to sustain the fight unless we entered it; but toward the very end, particularly as it was becoming plain that the Soviet Union was going to survive the Nazi assault, he began to wish for delay. However, time and time again the memoirs and diaries record the impatience of these officials, and those who thought like them, with Hull's caution and Roosevelt's watchful indirection.

The most genuine point made by those who dissent, one that merits thorough analysis, is that the American Government, in conjunction with the British and Dutch, refused to continue to supply Japan with machines and materials vital to it—especially oil. It is contended that they thereby compelled Japan to resort to war, or at least fixed a time period in which Japan was faced with the need of deciding to yield to our terms or go to war.

In reflecting upon this action, the reasons for it must not be confused with the Japanese response to it. Japan showed no signs of curbing its aggressive course. It paid no heed to repeated and friendly warnings that unless it did, the threatened countries would have to take counter-measures. As when on February 14, 1941, while the Lend-Lease Act was being argued in Congress, Dooman, Counsellor of the American Embassy in Japan and known to be a firm and straightforward friend of that country, carried back from Washington the message for the Vice-Minister for Foreign Affairs: that the American people were determined to support Britain even at the risk of war; that if Japan or any other country menaced that effort "it would have to expect to come in conflict with the United States"; and that the United States had abstained from an oil embargo in order not to impel Japan to create a situation that could only lead to the most serious outcome. Japan's answer over the following months had been to force its way further into Indo-China and threaten the Dutch East Indies.

This sustained proof that Japan was going on with its effort to dominate Asia, and the alliance pledging it to stand by Germany if that country got into war with the United States, made a continuation of trade with Japan an act of meekness on our part. Japan was concentrating its foreign purchases on products needed for war, while reducing civilian use by every means, and was thus accumulating great reserve stocks. These were enabling it to maintain its invasion of China without much strain, while continuing to expand its war-making power. Had *effective* restraints—note that I do not say *total* restraints—not been imposed, the American Government would have been in the strange position of having declared an unlimited national emergency, of calling upon the American people to strengthen their army, navy, and air force in great urgency, while at the same time nourishing the opponent that might have to be met in battle. This was a grave, if not intolerable, responsibility.

It is hard to tell how squarely the American and British Governments faced the possible consequence of their restrictive measures. My impression is that they knew the danger of war with Japan was being increased; that Japan might try to get by force the means denied it. The Japanese Government served plain warnings that this game of thrust and counterthrust might so end. These were soberly regarded, but did not weaken the will that Japan was not to have its way by threat.

Mingled with the anxiety lest these restrictive measures would make war more likely, there was a real hope that they might be a deterrent to war. Conceivably they would bring home to the Japanese people that if it came to war, they might soon run out of the means for combat, while the rapid growth of American military strength would make it clear that they could not in the end win. And, as evidence of these probabilities became plain, the conciliatory elements in the Japanese Government would prevail over the more militant ones.

This almost happened. But the reckless ones, those who would rather court fatality than accept frustration, managed to retain control of Japanese decision. The pressure applied by us did not prevent war, and may have brought the time of decision for war closer. The valid question, however, is not whether the American Government resorted to these restrictions *in order* to drive Japan to attack; it is whether the American Government failed to grasp a real chance, after the restraints had begun to leave their mark in Japanese official circles, to arrive at a satisfactory understanding that would have averted war. Twice, in the opinion of some qualified students of the subject, such a chance emerged, or at least appeared on the horizon of diplomacy. Were they real opportunities or merely mirages or decoys?

The first of these was the occasion when in the autumn of 1941, the Japanese Prime Minister, Prince Konoye, sought a personal meeting with the President. It is averred that the President's failure to respond lost a chance to avert the war without yielding any American principle or purpose. Some think the reason was that American diplomacy was inflexible, dull in its insight, and too soaked in mistrust. Others, more accusatory, explain the decision by a lack of desire for an agreement that would have thwarted the design for war.

Since there is no conclusive evidence of what Konoye intended to propose or could have achieved, comment on this subject must enter into "the boggy ground of what-might-have-been." Some observers, including Ambassador Grew, believe that Konoye could have made a real, and an irreversible, start toward meeting American terms. It will always be possible to think that this is so. But to the Americans in authority, the chance seemed small. Konoye was a man who in every past crisis had allowed himself to flounder between criss-crossed promises; hence there was good reason to fear an attempt at deception. Such glimpses as we have of what he might have proposed do not support the view that he could have offered a suspension or end of the fight against China. His freedom to negotiate would have been subject to the conditions stated by those who had controlled Japan's course up to then—their price for allowing him to go to meet the President.

Even so, to repeat, it is possible that skilled and more daring American diplomacy might have handled the meeting so as to get a satisfactory accord; or, failing that—and this is the more likely chance—to bring about so deep a division within the Japanese circle of decision as to have prevented warlike action. These alluring historical queries will continue to roam in the land of might-have-been.

But the risks were great. The echoes of Munich and its aftermath were still loud. The American Government might have found itself forced to make a miserable choice: either to accept an accord which would have left Japan free to complete its conquest of China and menace the rest of Asia, or to face a deep division among the American people. Any understanding with Japan that was not clear and decisive would have had unpredictable consequences. The Chinese Government might have felt justified in making a deal following our own. The Soviet Union, at this time just managing with the greatest effort and agony to prevent German victory, might also have chosen to compromise with Hitler rather than to fight it out. Speculations such as these must leave the subject unsettled. But in any case I think it clear that the American decision was one of judgment, not of secret intent. Konoye was not told that the President would not meet with him; he was told that he would not do so until more progress had been made toward defining what the Japanese Government was prepared to propose.

The same basic question had to be faced in the final crisis of negotiation in November, 1941; whether to relax restraints on Japan and leave it in a position to keep on trying to control much of Asia in return for a promise not to press on farther for the time being.

The opinion that the Japanese truce offer made at this last juncture accepted the main purposes and principles for which the American Government had been standing may be summarily dismissed. It was ambiguously worded, it was silent about the alliance with Germany, and it would have required the American Government to end its support of China—for the last of its numbered five points read: "The Government of the United States undertakes to refrain from such measures and actions as will be prejudicial to the endeavors for the restoration of general peace between Japan and China." This scant and unclear proposal was at once deemed "entirely unacceptable." Furthermore, there seemed little use and much possible damage in making a counter truce-offer of the same variety. The intercepted Japanese messages stated flatly that this was Japan's last and best offer. They told of the swift dismissal of a much more nearly acceptable one that Nomura and Kurusu asked their superiors in Tokyo to consider. A deadline had been set. Thus it was all but sure that the reduced counter-offer which had been patched together in Washington would be unheeded. But it might shake the coalition to which by then the opponents of the Axis had pledged their lives and national destinies.

This seems to have been the thought uppermost in Hull's mind in recommending to the President that the counter truce-offer be withheld. As set down in his historic memo of November 26, he had been led to this conclusion by the opposition of the Chinese, the half-hearted support or actual opposition of the British, Dutch, and Australian governments, and the further excited opposition to be expected because of lack of appreciation of the importance and value of a truce. This I believe to have been the true determining reason for a decision reluctantly taken. Even if by then Japan was genuinely ready for reform, the repentance had come too late. The situation had grown too entangled by then for minor measures, its momentum too great. Germany-Italy-Japan had forced the creation of a defensive coalition more vast than the empire of the Pacific for which Japan plotted. This was not now to be quieted or endangered by a temporary halt along the fringe of the Japanese advance.

Even though these reasons for dropping the idea of a truce may seem sufficient, they leave the question why the American Government could not have given a softer and less declaratory answer. Why had it to give one so "bleakly uncompromising"? It could have said simply that the Japanese offer did not convey the assurances that would warrant us and the alliance for which we spoke to resume the shipment of war materials to Japan and end our aid to China. Why was it deemed advisable or essential at this juncture to state fully and forcibly our maximum terms for a settlement in the Pacific? Was it foreseen that, scanned with mistrust as it would almost surely be, this would be construed as a demand for the swift abandonment of Japan's whole program? Was it done, as the accusation runs, with the deliberate intent of banning any last chance for an accord? Of propelling the Japanese attack?

That this was not the reason I am as sure as anyone can be on a matter of this sort; but I can offer only conjecture as to what the inspiring purposes were. Perhaps to vindicate past actions and decisions. Perhaps a wish to use the dramatic chance to put in the record a statement of the aims for which the risk of war was being accepted, and of the basis on which the Americans would found the peace when the time came. Such an idea was in accord with the usual mode of thought of the men in charge of the Executive Branch of the Government and of most of the American people. It gave vent to the propensity exemplified in Hull to find a base in general principles meant to be at once political standards and moral ideals. After long caution, it appealed as a defiant contradiction of the Axis program. All this, however, is surmise rather than evidenced history.

But I think it is well within the realm of evidenced history that the memo of November 26 was not in any usual sense of the word an ultimatum. It did not threaten the Japanese with war or any other form of forceful punishment if our terms were not accepted. It simply left them in the state of distress in which they were, with the prospect that they might later have to submit to our requirements. The Japanese Government could have, as Konoye and Nomura pleaded with it to do, allowed the situation to drag along, with or without resuming talks with the American Government. Its power to make war would have been depleted, but neither quickly nor crucially. The armed forces and even the position in China could have been maintained.

Notably, the final Japanese answer which ended negotiations on December 7, 1941, does not accuse the American Government of confronting it with an ultimatum, but only of thwarting the larger Japanese aims. Part 14—the clinching part of this note—reads:

> Obviously it is the intention of the American Government to conspire with Great Britain and other countries to obstruct Japan's efforts toward the establishment of peace through the creation of a New Order in East Asia, and especially to preserve Anglo-American rights and interests by keeping Japan and China at war. This intention has been revealed clearly during the course of the present negotiations. Thus, the earnest hope of the Japanese Government to adjust Japanese-American relations and to preserve and promote the peace of the Pacific through coöperation with the American Government has finally been lost.

This is a more nearly accurate description of the purposes of the American Government under Roosevelt than those attributed to it by hostile and suspicious American critics. Our Government did obstruct Japanese efforts, believing them to be unjust, cruel, and a threat to our national security, especially after Japan became a partner with Hitler's Germany and Mussolini's Italy and bent its efforts toward bringing the world under their combined control.

This determination stood on the proposition that it was better to take the risks of having to share in the suffering of the war than of finding ourselves moved or compelled to fight a more desperate battle against the Axis later on. The American Government, I believe, knew how serious a risk of war was being taken. But in its addresses to the American people it chose to put in the forefront the perils we would face if the Axis won, and to leave in the background, even to camouflage, the risks of finding ourselves plunged into wars which during the election campaign it had promised would not occur. Whether any large number of Americans were fooled by this, or whether most of them, in reality, were content to have the prospect presented that way rather than in a more blunt and candid way, I do not know.

This essay in interpretation has compelled me to recall and stress the aggressive Japanese assault—though I should have been glad to let that slip into the past. The passage of time does not alter facts, but it can bring a fuller and calmer understanding of them. It frees the mind for fairer appreciation of the causes and circumstances which impelled Japan along its tragic course and which impelled us to resist it. For both countries there are many common lessons. One of them is that continued friendliness requires mutual effort to relieve the other, to the extent it can, of deep cause for anxiety— the Japanese people of their anxiety over the means of living decently, the American people of anxiety about their security and power to defend the free world. Another is that they must both feel, speak, and act so honestly and steadily that their view of each other will be cleared of mistrust, and brightened by trust.

Suggested Reading

The best bibliographic survey of the literature is still Wayne Cole's "American Entry into World War II: A Historiographical Appraisal," *Mississippi Valley Historical Review*, XLIII (1957). Surveys of the period include Robert Divine's *The Reluctant Belligerent** (1965), John Wiltz' *From Isolation to War, 1931–1941** (1968), and Keith Eubank's *The Origins of World War II** (1969), which deals only with the European side and not American policy. Important analyses of Administration policy include Robert Divine's *The Illusion of Neutrality** (1962) and James M. Burns's *Roosevelt: The Soldier of Freedom** (1970). Useful collections of essays on the period include Robert Divine, ed., *Causes and Consequences of World War II** (1969) and Arnold Offner, ed., *America and the Origins of World War II** (1971).

Recent studies of relations between Germany and the United States include James Compton's *The Swastika and the Eagle* (1967) and Alton Frye's *Nazi Germany and the American Hemisphere* (1967), both of which conclude that Hitler threatened American security. A. J. P. Taylor's *The Origins of the Second World War** (1962) and Bruce Russett's *No Clear and Present Danger: A Skeptical View of U.S. Entry into World War II** (1972) challenge these conclusions. Arnold Offner in *American Appeasement, 1933–1938* (1969) is critical of American policy-makers for not recognizing the "threat of Nazi Germany." The best study of isolationism is Manfred Jonas' *Isolationism in America, 1935–1941** (1966).

Francis Jones in *Japan's New Order in Asia, Its Rise and Fall, 1937–1945* (1954) is critical of the Administration's policies in Asia. James Crowley's *Japan's Quest for Autonomy* (1966) and Dorothy Borg's *The United States and the Far Eastern Crisis, 1933–1938* (1964) should also be consulted.

The most notable of the revisionists is Charles A. Beard, whose *President*

Roosevelt and the Coming of the War, 1941* (1948), an indictment of the President's policies, stresses the danger of presidential power in foreign relations and the Chief Executive's capacity to circumvent constitutional restraints. Beard's work was savagely criticized by Samuel Eliot Morison in "Did Roosevelt Start the War?—History Through a Beard," *Atlantic Monthly*, CLXXXII (1949). Among the other critics of revisionism are William L. Langer and Everett S. Gleason in *The Challenge to Isolation, 1937–1940* (1952) and *The Undeclared War, 1940–1941* (1953), important volumes written on the basis of privileged access to classified materials; Dexter Perkins in "Was Roosevelt Wrong?" *Virginia Quarterly Review*, XXX (1954); and Robert Ferrell in "Pearl Harbor and the Revisionists," *Historian*, XVII (1955). The best study of Pearl Harbor is Roberta Wohlstetter's *Pearl Harbor: Warning and Decision** (1962), which concludes that weaknesses in the gathering and assessment of intelligence data largely account for the surprise at Pearl Harbor.

William Appleman Williams' *The Tragedy of American Diplomacy,** 2nd rev. ed. (1972) emphasizes the role of American ideology, and the concern for expanding markets, in the responses of policy-makers to Japan and Germany. Similar analyses are developed by Lloyd Gardner in *Economic Aspects of New Deal Diplomacy** (1964) and Robert F. Smith in "American Foreign Relations, 1920–1942," in Barton J. Bernstein, ed., *Towards a New Past** (1968). The framework of Williams and the others is criticized by Robert Tucker in *The Radical Left and American Foreign Policy** (1971).

* Also published in paperback edition.

The Origins of
the Cold War

How Did the
Cold War Begin?

Gar Alperovitz

Using a review of Martin F. Herz's *Beginnings of the
Cold War* (1966) as a springboard for his own views
on the subject, Gar Alperovitz of the Cambridge
Institute explains in the following essay why he
believes that the United States was largely responsible
for the Cold War. First, he argues that President
Truman regrettably reversed Roosevelt's policy of
accepting spheres of influence in Eastern Europe. By
attempting instead to impose Western notions of
democracy on the entire area, Truman forced the
Russians to give up hope for a *modus vivendi*. Second,
Alperovitz believes that American policy-makers must
bear much of the blame for the division of Germany.
America's refusal to grant the U.S.S.R. a loan for
postwar reconstruction left the Russians economically
dependent on reparations from their zone in
Germany. Although the American government
apparently hoped that its atomic monopoly would
make its views impossible to resist, the American
position on reparations was so contrary to Russian
interests that early attempts to negotiate the German
question broke down, and the division of Germany
began to harden.

Alperovitz's analysis conflicts at a number of points
with the views of other historians. First of all, many
nonrevisionists disagree with his interpretation of

355

Stalin and contend instead that the dictator's apparent moderation merely concealed evil intentions, or that he was not moderate and that he even needed the Cold War in order to maintain control in the Soviet Union. Second, many historians deny that the atom bomb had an important role in shaping foreign policy, especially in influencing the handling of German reparations and the larger issue of American policy toward Germany.

A third issue is the complex problem of Roosevelt's tactics and goals and whether Truman continued or reversed Roosevelt's policy. Some historians, including such revisionists as William Appleman Williams and Gabriel Kolko, disagree with Alperovitz and contend that Roosevelt never accepted spheres of influence in Eastern Europe and never yielded in his aim of opening Eastern Europe to American and Western European economic penetration. Many revisionists and nonrevisionists, though differing greatly on the nature of Roosevelt's policy, conclude that Truman continued, rather than reversed, that policy. According to most nonrevisionists, Truman followed Roosevelt's policy of accommodation with the Soviet Union until Soviet intransigence compelled a reversal in late 1945 or afterward. According to revisionists, Truman was following Roosevelt's policy *but* it was *not* one of accommodation: it meant instead using American strength to impose an American design on the world. For evidence that Roosevelt was not sincerely pursuing a long-range policy of cooperation with Russia, these revisionists often point to his decision to avoid responding at Yalta to the Soviet request for a loan and his systematic effort to conceal even the fact of the atom bomb project from the Soviets. Put simply, they contend that Truman's use of "atomic diplomacy" and economic coercion was made possible by Roosevelt.

Until recently, most historians who viewed Roosevelt as following a policy of accommodation have relied heavily for evidence on his last message (of April 11, 1945) to Winston Churchill: "I would minimize the general Soviet problem as much as possible, because these problems, in one form or another, seem to arise every day, and most of them straighten out." Recently, however, an important, and previously

classified, Roosevelt-to-Churchill message, of April 5,
has become available, thereby compelling a reappraisal,
though not necessarily a reversal, of interpretations. In
replying to Churchill's proposal that the Anglo-
American combination should act "tougher" and that
their armies should push "as far east as possible" and
even try to take Berlin while the Soviets were bogged
down with the bulk of Germany's troops, Roosevelt
responded on April 5 that he was "in general agreement" and declared that "our armies will in a very
few days be in a position that will permit us to become
'tougher' than has heretofore appeared advantageous"
(Roosevelt-Churchill Correspondence, F.D.R.
Library).

Alperovitz, eschewing an analysis of ideology or of
the earlier sources of Soviet-American antagonism,
chose to focus on the events of 1945–46 and to stress
America's policies as the major cause of the Cold War.
By implication, then, this essay does not *seem* to view
the Cold War as inevitable, and certainly not as the
inevitable result of American capitalism, but primarily
as the consequence of a series of missed opportunities
or errors. (In *Cold War Essays* [1970], Chapter IV,
however, Alperovitz made clear his belief that the
causes of the Cold War were actually more
fundamental, and had to do with the American
"ideology" that the nation's democracy and economy
required unrestricted markets and opposition to
Communism and revolutions of the left.) This
seemingly moderate form of the revisionist argument
has compelled many to reexamine their conceptions of
the Cold War, to reassess more conventional
interpretations that stress Soviet responsibility, and
also to reappraise radical analyses that often assert or
imply that the Cold War was the inevitable product
of American capitalism.

Writing as "Mr. X," George Kennan suggested twenty
years ago that the mechanism of Soviet diplomacy "moves inexorably along
the prescribed path, like a persistent toy automobile wound up and headed
in a given direction, stopping only when it meets with some unanswerable
force."[1] A generation of Americans quickly embraced Kennan's view as an
explanation of the tension, danger, and waste of the Cold War. But was his

[1] *Foreign Affairs*, July, 1947.

theory of inexorable Soviet expansion—and its matching recommendation of "containment"—correct? A cautious but important book, *Beginnings of the Cold War*, suggests we might well have been more critical of so mechanistic an idea of the way Great Powers act and how the Cold War began.

Martin F. Herz is currently a United States diplomat serving in Teheran. His book is mainly concerned with the few months between the 1945 Yalta and Potsdam Conferences. It is well-documented and contains no polemic; indeed, as he says, "the author expresses few views of his own . . ." The book begins by recapitulating the main issues in dispute when Truman became President: Poland, German reparations, lend-lease aid. It moves from the Polish issue to a broader discussion of spheres of influence, and from reparations and lend-lease to a general analysis of aid to Russia and its relation to other diplomatic considerations. The two issues are integrated in a brief concluding discussion of how the "die was cast" in 1945, and the Cold War began.

Any examination of the very earliest postwar period forces us to think about developments *before* 1947 when it was decided to contain the Soviet Union by "unanswerable force." Herz's study is important because it makes two serious judgments about this period: first, that in 1945 Soviet policy was by no means inexorably prescribed and expansionist; second, that mistakes made by American officials just after the war may well have prevented the kind of compromise and accommodation which is just beginning to emerge in Europe today.

These suggestions recall Walter Lippmann's *The Cold War*, published in 1947, which also argued—with greater candor and less detail—that the Russians might have been willing to accept a negotiated settlement in 1945 and 1946, but that US policy ignored opportunities to meet them halfway. Lippmann's now little-remembered book offered a powerful critique of Kennan's theory of Soviet expansion and American containment. If Herz's view is correct, accepted interpretations of American Russian relations are called into question. And if Lippmann was right in saying that American policy helped to prevent an accommodation in 1945 and 1946, the Cold War itself must be regarded, at least in part, as the result of fundamental errors of American diplomacy. These are startling conclusions, but anyone willing to bring an open mind to Herz's book or to Lippmann's will find that they have exposed many weaknesses in the usual explanations of early events in the Cold War.

No one, of course, can be certain of "what might have been." But Herz refutes at least one accepted myth. Contrary to current historical reconstructions, there is abundant evidence that American leaders in 1945 were not much worried about the expansion of communism into *Western* Europe. That worry came later. In the days just after the war, most Communists in Italy, France, and elsewhere were cooperating with bourgeois governments. At Potsdam, in 1945, Truman regarded the Russians' desires for concessions beyond their area of occupation as largely bluff. The major issues in dispute were all in Eastern Europe, deep within the zone of Soviet military occupation. The real expansion of Soviet power, we are reminded, took place in Poland, Hungary, Bulgaria, Rumania, Czechoslovakia, and the eastern regions of Germany and Austria.

The US in 1945 wanted Russia to give up the control and influence the Red Army had gained in the battle against Hitler. American demands may have been motivated by an idealistic desire to foster democracy, but Herz's main point is that in countries like Rumania and Bulgaria they were about as realistic as would be Soviet demands for changes in, say, Mexico. Any such parallel has obvious limits, the most significant of which is not that democracy and communism cannot so easily be compared, but that Eastern Europe is of far greater importance to Soviet security than is Mexico to American security: from the time of Napoleon—and twice in the lifetime of millions of present day Russians—bloody invasions have swept through the area to their "Middle West."

In the early Spring of 1945, negotiations concerning one border state—Poland—brought the main issue into the open. At Yalta and immediately thereafter, the US had mainly mediated between Stalin and Churchill on Poland; Roosevelt had warned Churchill that to make extreme demands would doom the negotiations. A month later, in the faltering last days of Roosevelt's life, the US itself adopted a new tough line, demanding that pro-Western and openly anti-Russian Polish politicians be given more influence in negotiations to set up a new government for Poland. As was predicted, the Russians balked at the idea of such an expansion of anti-Soviet influence in a country so important to their security, and the negotiations ground to a halt.[2] Moreover, at this precise moment, Russian suspicions about the West deepened with Allen Dulles's concurrent but unrelated secret negotiations with Nazi generals in Switzerland.[3] The result was a violent quarrel which shook the entire structure of American-Soviet relations. But this was only the beginning. The demands on the Polish question reflected the ideas of the men who were to surround the new President; led by Joseph Grew and James F. Byrnes, they soon convinced Truman to attempt to make stronger demands elsewhere in Eastern Europe.

For most of the year Roosevelt had been highly ambivalent toward such matters. By late 1944, however (in spite of wavering on the politically sensitive Polish issue in his dying days), Roosevelt concluded it would be a fundamental error to put too much pressure on Russia over other regions vital to her security. In September and October 1944, and in early January 1945, he gave form to his conclusion by entering into armistice agreements with Britain and Russia, which gave the Soviet military almost complete control of internal politics in each Eastern European ex-Nazi satellite. It was understood, for instance, that the Soviets would have authority to issue

[2] The details of this history are often greatly misunderstood. Herz also vacillates in describing Roosevelt's Polish policy. See Appendix I of my *Atomic Diplomacy: Hiroshima and Potsdam* for a discussion of this question. Documentation for other facts and quotations not specifically given in this review can also be found here.

[3] See *The New York Review*, October 8, 1965. The only important new information in Cornelius Ryan's popularized history, *The Last Battle* (Simon and Schuster, 1966, 571 pp., $7.50) suggests that Stalin was so aroused by Dulles's negotiations (and the West's blatant denial they were taking place) that he suspiciously concluded other Western statements at this time were also lies. According to Ryan, when Eisenhower informed Stalin he did not intend to capture Berlin, Stalin thought this was another Western attempt to deceive him. On this basis he, in turn, lied to Eisenhower, misleading him about the timing of the Red Army's own thrust to take the city.

orders to the Rumanian government, and that, specifically, the Allied Control Commission would be "under the general direction of the Allied (Soviet) High Command acting on behalf of the Allied Powers." The Rumanian accords, and the similar but slightly less severe Bulgarian and Hungarian armistice agreements, served to formalize the famous Churchill-Stalin spheres-of-influence arrangement which, without FDR's agreement, had previously given the Russians "90 per cent" influence in Rumania, "80 per cent" influence in Bulgaria, and "75 per cent" influence in Hungary, in exchange for "90 per cent" British influence in Greece and a "50-50" split of influence in Yugoslavia. The armistice accords were also modeled after a previous understanding which had contained Soviet endorsement of dominant American-British influence in Italy. The Eastern European armistice agreements have been available to the public for years, but have been successfully buried, or avoided by most scholars. Herz has exhumed them, and he shows that they contain American endorsement of dominant Soviet influence in the ex-Nazi satellites.

At Yalta, in early February, 1945, Roosevelt pasted over these specific texts the vague and idealistic rhetoric of the famous Declaration on Liberated Europe. The President apparently wished to use the Declaration mainly to appease certain politically important ethnic groups in America; he devoted only a few minutes to the matter at the Yalta Conference, and the familiar rhetoric promising democracy was almost devoid of practical meaning. For example, who was to decide in given instances between the American and Soviet definitions of common but vague terms like "democratic"? Much more important, as Herz shows, in the broad language of the Declaration the Allies agreed merely to "consult" about matters within the liberated countries, not to "act," and they authorized consultations only when all parties agreed they were necessary. Thus the United States itself confirmed the Russians' right to refuse to talk about the ex-Nazi satellites. The State Department knew this and, in fact, had tried to insert operative clauses into the Declaration. But Roosevelt, having just signed the armistice agreements, rejected this unrealistic proposal. Moreover, when the Soviets after Yalta crudely tossed out a Rumanian government they did not like, the President, though unhappy that he had not been consulted, reaffirmed his basic position by refusing to intervene.

Ironically, Herz's book lends credence to the old Republican charge that Roosevelt accepted a compromise at Yalta which bolstered Stalin's position in Eastern Europe. The charge, while correct in essentials, was silly in assuming that much else, short of war, could have been done while the Red Army occupied the area. The Republican politicians also ignored the fact that at Yalta Roosevelt could not expect a continued American military presence in Europe for very long after the war. This not only deprived him of leverage, it made an accommodation with Russia much more desirable for another reason: Red Army help became essential as a guarantee that Germany would not rise from defeat to start yet a third World War. Stalin also needed American help, as he too made clear, to hold down the Germans. Hence, underlying the American-Soviet plans for peace at Yalta was not "faith" but a common interest—the German threat—which had cemented the World War II alliance. From this 1945 perspective the crucial portion of the Yalta agreement was not the Declaration on Liberated Europe, nor even the provisions on Poland, but rather the understanding that the United States and Russia (with Britain and France as minor partners) would work together to control Germany. This meant, among other things, joint action to reduce Germany's physical power by extracting reparations from German industry.

Although Herz tends to play down the German issue, he does take up important economic matters that relate to it. He understands that Moscow was in a cruel dilemma which, had the US been shrewd enough, might have been resolved to the benefit of both American diplomacy and the economic health of Europe. The Russians were greatly in need of aid for their huge postwar reconstruction program. Importing industrial equipment from Eastern Europe was a possible solution, though a doubtful one, for taking this equipment would inevitably cause political problems. Reparations from Germany were another, but the key industrial sectors were in American hands. Finally, the United States itself was a potential source. Herz argues (as did Ambassadors Harriman and Winant at the time) that a US reconstruction loan for Russia would have been wise; it would have given US diplomacy strong leverage in a variety of negotiations. (Without other sources of aid for reconstruction the Russians were almost inevitably reduced to extracting industrial goods from either Germany or Eastern Europe.) American officials seriously considered such a loan, but, as Herz shows, they did not actively pursue it with the Russians—though one or two crude attempts were made to use a loan as a bludgeon in negotiations. With a future US troop commitment unlikely, and a large loan ruled out, the United States had no real bargaining power. Hence its attempts at intervention in Eastern Europe amounted to little more than bluster.

The State Department wanted to have it both ways: it wanted to hold the Russians to the vague promises of the Yalta Declaration; it also wanted to avoid the specific texts of the armistice agreements. But the Republicans, and even Secretary Byrnes in his later writings, understood the weakness of this position. The Republicans, for their part, also wanted to have it both ways. They wanted to argue both that Roosevelt gave the Russians all the authority they needed for their actions *and* that the Russians broke their agreements.

The Republican attack on Yalta came late in the Cold War, and was combined with a new demand that the US "roll back" Soviet influence. Few now realize how unoriginal the demand was, for a "roll back" effort—without its latter-day label—was, in fact, at the center of Harry Truman's first postwar policy. The President, we now know, made this effort in a spurt of confidence derived from the new atomic bomb. But the policy failed in its continuing attempt to reduce Soviet control by expanding Western influence in Poland. It also failed in its bold follow-up effort to force the Russians to change the Bulgarian and Rumanian governments. Nevertheless, these opening moves of the postwar period helped to set the tone of the new Administration's attitude toward Russia. Truman, although publicly proclaiming his adherence to Roosevelt's policy of cooperation, seems to have understood that his approach differed fundamentally from his predecessor's. (In private, as Secretary of State Stettinius has written, he complained that the intervention in Poland rested on rather shaky diplomatic ground.) Indeed, by September 1945, the basic change in US policy was so clearly defined that, as Secretary of State Byrnes later wrote, the Russian complaint that Roosevelt's policy had been abandoned was "understandable."[4]

What was the result? Like Herz, John Foster Dulles (who assisted Byrnes at the time) also believed that the Cold War began in 1945. Dulles emphasized in his book *War or Peace* (1950) that a new tough line of US policy was adopted at this time over dimly remembered issues deep within the Soviet-controlled Balkans. Herz prints almost the full text of the crucial 1945 Hopkins-Stalin talks, which reveal the equally important point that, in Russia, the change in American policy produced what Stalin termed "a certain alarm." A few thoughtful US officials recognized the significance of these developments. Secretary of War Henry L. Stimson, for example, tried to block the campaign to engage American prestige in Eastern Europe. In White House discussions he argued, first, that the demand for more Western influence in Poland was a mistake: "The Russians perhaps were being more realistic than we were in regard to their own security. . . ." He then tried to cut short efforts to intervene elsewhere, reminding Truman, as Stimson's diary shows, that "we have made up our minds on the broad policy that it was not wise to get into the Balkan mess even if the thing seemed to be disruptive of policies which the State Department thought were wise." Stimson pointed out that "we have taken that policy right from the beginning, Mr. Roosevelt having done it himself or having been a party to it himself."

When Stimson failed in his conservative effort to limit American objectives, the stage was set for one of the great tragedies of the Cold War. As Stimson understood, the Russians, though extremely touchy about the buffer area, were not impossible to deal with. Had their security requirements been met, there is evidence that their domination of Eastern Europe might have been much different from what it turned out to be. Churchill, too, thought the Russians were approachable. Obviously, conditions in Eastern Europe would not meet Western ideals; but Churchill judged, in late 1944 and early 1945, that Moscow was convinced it would be much easier to secure its objectives through moderate policies. In Greece at this time, as Churchill was to stress in *Triumph and Tragedy*, Stalin was "strictly and faithfully" holding to his agreement *not* to aid the Greek Communists. Even in much of the border area the Russians seemed willing to accept substantial capitalism and some form of democracy—with the crucial proviso that the Eastern European governments had to be "friendly" to Russia in defense and foreign policies. Finland serves as a rough model of a successful border state. Here, too, the armistice made the Soviets supreme, giving rights parallel to the Bulgarian and Rumanian accords plus the right to maintain Soviet military installations. However, the US made no independent effort to intervene; Finland maintained a foreign policy "friendly" to Russia; and the Russians were —as they still seem to be—prepared to accept a moderate government.

Although it is often forgotten, a modified application of the Finnish formula seemed to be shaping up elsewhere in 1945 and much of 1946. In Hungary, Soviet-sponsored free elections routed the Communist Party in 1945. In Bulgaria, a country with rather weak democratic traditions, the 1945 elec-

[4] *Speaking Frankly*, Harper, 1947.

tions were complicated by competition for Great Power support among the various internal factions. Certainly the results were not perfect, but most Western observers (except the State Department) felt they should have been accepted. In Austria, the Communists were swamped in Soviet-run free elections in their zone in 1945, and, after a hesitant start, a free democratic government emerged for the entire country. In Czechoslovakia, from which the Red Army withdrew in December of 1945, democracy was so clearly acceptable to Soviet policy that the US had little to protest at the time.[5]

Almost all of this was to change, of course. The freedoms in Hungary were to end in 1947. The initial pattern in Czechoslovakia was to be reversed in 1948. But writers who focus only on the brutal period of totalitarian control after 1947 and 1948 often ignore what happened earlier. The few who try to account for the known facts of the 1945–46 interlude usually do so in passing, either to suggest that the democratic governments "must have been" mere smokescreens, formed while Moscow waited for the US to leave the Continent; or that the Russians "must have been" secretly planning to take full control, but were methodically using the early period to prepare the groundwork for what came later. (Communists, too, like to ignore the 1945–46 period, for it suggests the possibility that Soviet Russia was more interested in an old-fashioned *modus vivendi* with the capitalists than in spreading World Communism. This was the essence of Tito's bitter complaint that Stalin tried to turn back the Yugoslav revolution.)

The Russians have displayed so much duplicity, brutality, and intransigence that it is easy to imagine the 1945–46 interlude as a mere smokescreen. But they also have a long history of protecting "socialism in one country" in a rather conservative, nationalistic way: the moderation of the 1945–46 interlude can be viewed as a logical extension of this tradition. That at least two quite different interpretations of their 1945–46 policy are conceivable is now rarely admitted, and the relative merits of each have not been seriously examined. Herz's study calls for a careful reappraisal of early postwar Soviet objectives.[6] If the Russians were secretly harboring plans for an ultimate take over, they certainly were preparing a lot of trouble for themselves by sponsoring free politics, by pulling out the Red Army (it is not particularly shrewd to have to *re*-introduce foreign troops), by ripping up the Red Army's main rail connections across Poland—as they did in the fall of 1945. As well informed an observer as Averell Harriman believed, as he once testified to Congress, that Soviet policy in 1945 was ambivalent, that it could

[5] W. H. McNeill's *America, Britain and Russia* provides a good general survey of this period. Note that early in 1946 the Red Army also withdrew from control of two other border areas: Northern Iran and Manchuria.

[6] Today most writers simply take the mechanistic theory of Soviet expansion for granted. An example of what this can lead to is John Toland's *The Last 100 Days* (Random House, 1965), an account of the closing months of World War II which assumes that the Russians were inevitably evil and expansionistic, and that therefore the "good" Germans had to be used to help contain them. Toland dwells on details of the Western Front. He devotes much less attention to the Eastern Front, taking much of his material from German sources. Accordingly, the book popularizes a one-sided caricature of Russians as pillaging sadists and irrepressible rapists. (As for the Germans, it is only the rare Nazi camp guard who is a brutal exception to the rule of "the other guards, who generally treated the prisoners well"!)

have become either more moderate within a framework of security and understanding with the West, or that it could have become hard-line and totalitarian, within the framework of insecurity and conflict. Harriman, though puzzled by the ultimate Russian decision in favor of the iron-fisted policy, clearly saw that Soviet expansion was neither inexorable nor inevitable.

At least one reason for Russia's shift to a tough line may be traced to mistakes made by US officials. As Stimson argued—and as history later showed —the demand for more influence in Soviet-controlled areas was almost certainly doomed from the start. This basic miscalculation stemmed, finally, from an attempt to overextend *American* diplomatic sway. Lippmann was, I believe, correct in seeing that the other error was the failure of US policy makers to turn their energies to an early solution of the crucial German problem. Bolstered by the atomic bomb, which eliminated the threat that had been Roosevelt's central concern, American leaders dallied over Germany. Moreover, by refusing to hold to Roosevelt's agreement that a specific target for German reparations would be set (July, 1945), by permitting France to hamstring the German Control Commission (Fall, 1945), by halting German reparations shipments (Spring, 1946)—US policy suggested the very prospect Russia feared most: the abandonment of economic and political controls and the possibility that a new and powerful Germany would rise from the ashes of Nazism to become the bastion of Western capitalistic aggression in Europe. The United States had no such aggressive intent. Nonetheless, the US chose not to negotiate seriously on Germany until a full year-and-a-half after the war's end. Especially after Secretary Byrnes's tough speech in Stuttgart in the Fall of 1946, American policy was shortsighted enough to suggest a threat to Russia at the very time it was attempting to weaken Soviet control in the vital area which lay—protectively or threateningly—between German power and the Russian heartland. The Russians, who had no nuclear weapons, were far less casual about the question of security; their grip seemed to tighten in the buffer area month by month, as their worst fears about Germany seemed to come true.

The Russians were not easy to deal with, either in Germany or elsewhere. Nevertheless, if the hypothesis suggested by Lippmann's book is correct— and Herz's study indirectly supports it—there are reasons to believe that US policy itself may have to share responsibility for the imposition of totalitarian control in Eastern Europe, and possibly also for the subsequent expanding Communist agitation in Western Europe. The *addition* of increased insecurity to known Soviet paranoid tendencies may explain the rigidity which Soviet leaders displayed in their satellite policy after 1946. The first pattern seemed crudely similar to the Finnish or Austrian models. Would it have been reversed had the US seriously tried from the first to resolve the European security problem—as Lippmann urged? That Soviet actions may have been in part reactions to their judgments of American intentions may also help to explain why sustained Communist opposition developed in the West only *after* the clear breakdown of German control arrangements. It was not in 1945, but late in 1946 and in 1947 that the Italian and French Communists began to reverse their initial policy of cooperation with bourgeois governments. Was the changed focus of Communist politics part of the inexorable plan? Or was it primarily a rather shortsighted response to American policy itself?

Once the Communists became active in Western Europe, of course, the United States was faced with quite another set of issues. Disputes with Russia moved out of the border regions. The threat some officials had anticipated while reading Marx and listening to Communist propaganda began to become a political reality. In 1947, those who proposed a mechanical theory of Soviet expansion had to deal with expanding Communist political activity in the West. And it was in July of that year, precisely two years after Truman faced Stalin in his first Potsdam showdown over Eastern Europe, that Kennan's containment recommendation was publicly offered.

We do not yet have answers to all the questions about postwar American-Russian relations, but we know enough to consider afresh whether either of the Great Powers ever really did move inexorably, like a wound-up toy automobile, as "Mr. X" argued. Herz's sturdy little book suggests they did not, and is at least the beginning of a more subtle explanation of the complex sequence of interacting events which produced the Cold War.

Origins of
the Cold War

Arthur Schlesinger, Jr.

Until the late 1960s most Americans agreed that the
Cold War was the inevitable result of Soviet
malevolence and expansionist impulses. Within the
United States the historical dialog was usually
restricted to such issues as whether Roosevelt had been
naive in trusting the Soviets and whether the Truman
Administration was also slow in recognizing the Soviet
menace. Occasional dissents, most notably from William Appleman Williams and D. F. Fleming, usually
were ignored or quickly rejected. But, beginning in
the late 1960s, as younger scholars began to exploit
recently opened American archives on the Cold War
and as citizens began to question their nation's
involvement in Vietnam, revisionist challenges to the
orthodox views began making inroads among students
and historians.

Among those who have been troubled by this wave
of revisionism is Arthur Schlesinger, Jr., Pulitzer
Prize–winning historian of the ages of Jackson and
Franklin Roosevelt, founding member of the Americans
for Democratic Action, and memoirist-scholar of the
Kennedy Administration. In the following essay
written in 1967, Schlesinger, now of the City
University of New York, formulated his rebuttal to
the revisionists, thereby hoping to turn back the tide.

In approximately the first three quarters of his essay,
Schlesinger, curiously, seems to agree with much of
the moderate revisionist case. He notes the contradic-

tions between America's efforts to establish spheres of interest near home and universalism elsewhere. He also acknowledges that the United States made mistakes that contributed to the Cold War, and he finds Soviet policies cautious and designed to create a security zone. "In other words," writes Schlesinger of Stalin, "his initial objectives were very probably not world conquest but Russian security." Perhaps, Schlesinger suggests, the Soviet leader even believed that the Yalta Declaration on Liberated Europe, with its heady rhetoric about democratic elections, was simply a piety and did not cancel the earlier Stalin-Churchill agreement dividing Eastern Europe into spheres of influence.

Abruptly retreating from this line of analysis in about the last quarter of his essay, Schlesinger contends that the Cold War cannot be explained in terms of mutual mistakes nor as simply a clash between nation states: Russia was no ordinary state but a Marxist-Leninist "totalitarian state . . . still in a somewhat messianic mood, . . . and ruled by a dictator who . . . had his paranoid moments." In short, the Cold War was inevitable and nothing the United States might have done could have avoided the conflict. Marxism-Leninism, according to Schlesinger, interpreted the United States as implacably hostile, and this ideology also "compelled a steady expansion of communist power." Only Stalin, according to Schlesinger, could have modified the ideology or diverted policy, but his paranoia was too great for any accommodation with the West. "These factors—the intransigence of Leninist ideology, the sinister dynamics of a totalitarian society and the madness of Stalin"—also meant that the West was correct in refusing to believe that Russia only sought security and would settle for control of Eastern Europe. Schlesinger, in effect, has offered a slightly new argument to defend the old orthodoxy.

His analysis has been criticized on a number of grounds. In dealing with the argument about Stalin's paranoia, revisionists maintain that (1) no American decision-maker ever based policy on the assumption that Stalin was paranoid; and (2) the Soviet leader, in view of earlier Western hostility to the Bolshevik state, had ample reason to suspect American policy.

Origins of the Cold War. From *Foreign Affairs*, XLVI (October 1967), pp. 22–52. Copyright © by the Council on Foreign Relations, Inc., New York. Reprinted by permission of the author.

Was not American "universalism," they ask, implicitly anticommunist? Also, contrary to Schlesinger, the revisionists conclude that most American leaders did not fear Soviet military expansion into Western Europe in the near future. Many revisionists contend that Stalin's policies were conservative in 1943–45, that Western communist parties (perhaps under his direction) were still pursuing electoral politics, and that the failure to reach a *modus vivendi* cannot be explained by Marxism-Leninism, by Stalin's paranoia, or by the Soviet leadership's fear of peace, but by American action. In this interpretation, the abrupt cut-off of lend-lease in May, the refusal of a large loan (the request was not lost, contrary to Schlesinger), and the dispute over German reparations made a critical difference. To many revisionists, America's nuclear monopoly and the practice of "atomic diplomacy" also contributed to the Cold War. The Marshall Plan, according to this interpretation, was not simply the generous proposal that Schlesinger implies, but, rather, a program conceived in part to be unacceptable to the Soviets and even to pry Eastern Europe out of the Soviet sphere and put it back into the Western orbit. The Truman-Doctrine and the Marshall Plan, as Truman acknowledged, were "two halves of the same walnut": containment.

*T*he Cold War in its original form was a presumably mortal antagonism, arising in the wake of the Second World War, between two rigidly hostile blocs, one led by the Soviet Union, the other by the United States. For nearly two somber and dangerous decades this antagonism dominated the fears of mankind; it may even, on occasion, have come close to blowing up the planet. In recent years, however, the once implacable struggle has lost its familiar clarity of outline. With the passing of old issues and the emergence of new conflicts and contestants, there is a natural tendency, especially on the part of the generation which grew up during the Cold War, to take a fresh look at the causes of the great contention between Russia and America.

Some exercises in reappraisal have merely elaborated the orthodoxies promulgated in Washington or Moscow during the boom years of the Cold War. But others, especially in the United States (there are no signs, alas, of this in the Soviet Union), represent what American historians call "revisionism"—that is, a readiness to challenge official explanations. No one should be surprised by this phenomenon. Every war in American history has been followed in due course by skeptical reassessments of supposedly sacred assumptions. So the War of 1812, fought at the time for the freedom of the seas, was in later years ascribed to the expansionist ambitions of Congressional war hawks; so the Mexican War became a slaveholders' conspiracy. So the Civil War has been pronounced a "needless war," and Lincoln has even been accused of manœuvring the rebel attack on Fort Sumter. So too the Spanish-American War and the First and Second World Wars have, each in its turn, undergone revisionist critiques. It is not to be supposed that the Cold War would remain exempt.

In the case of the Cold War, special factors reinforce the predictable historiographical rhythm. The outburst of polycentrism in the communist empire has made people wonder whether communism was ever so monolithic as official theories of the Cold War supposed. A generation with no vivid memories of Stalinism may see the Russia of the forties in the image of the relatively mild, seedy and irresolute Russia of the sixties. And for this same generation the American course of widening the war in Viet Nam—which even non-revisionists can easily regard as folly—has unquestionably stirred doubts about the wisdom of American foreign policy in the sixties which younger historians may have begun to read back into the forties.

It is useful to remember that, on the whole, past exercises in revisionism have failed to stick. Few historians today believe that the war hawks caused the War of 1812 or the slaveholders the Mexican War, or that the Civil War was needless, or that the House of Morgan brought America into the First World War or that Franklin Roosevelt schemed to produce the attack on Pearl Harbor. But this does not mean that one should deplore the rise of Cold War revisionism.[1] For revisionism is an essential part of the process by which history, through the posing of new problems and the investigation of new possibilities, enlarges its perspectives and enriches its insights.

More than this, in the present context, revisionism expresses a deep, legitimate and tragic apprehension. As the Cold War has begun to lose its purity of definition, as the moral absolutes of the fifties become the moralistic clichés of the sixties, some have begun to ask whether the appalling risks which humanity ran during the Cold War were, after all, necessary and inevitable; whether more restrained and rational policies might not have guided the energies of man from the perils of conflict into the potentialities of collaboration. The fact that such questions are in their nature unanswerable does not mean that it is not right and useful to raise them. Nor does it mean that our sons and daughters are not entitled to an accounting from the generation of Russians and Americans who produced the Cold War.

The orthodox American view, as originally set forth by the American government and as reaffirmed until recently by most American scholars, has been that the Cold War was the brave and essential response of free men to communist aggression. Some have gone back well before the Second World War to lay open the sources of Russian expansionism. Geopoliticians traced the Cold War to imperial Russian strategic ambitions which in the nine-

---

[1] As this writer somewhat intemperately did in a letter to *The New York Review of Books*, October 20, 1966.

teenth century led to the Crimean War, to Russian penetration of the Balkans and the Middle East and to Russian pressure on Britain's "lifeline" to India. Ideologists traced it to the Communist Manifesto of 1848 ("the violent overthrow of the bourgeoisie lays the foundation for the sway of the proletariat"). Thoughtful observers (a phrase meant to exclude those who speak in Dullese about the unlimited evil of godless, atheistic, militant communism) concluded that classical Russian imperialism and Pan-Slavism, compounded after 1917 by Leninist messianism, confronted the West at the end of the Second World War with an inexorable drive for domination.[2]

The revisionist thesis is very different.[3] In its extreme form, it is that, after the death of Franklin Roosevelt and the end of the Second World War, the United States deliberately abandoned the wartime policy of collaboration

---

[2] Every student of the Cold War must acknowledge his debt to W. H. McNeill's remarkable account, *America, Britain and Russia: Their Cooperation and Conflict, 1941–1946* (New York, 1953) and to the brilliant and indispensable series by Herbert Feis: *Churchill, Roosevelt, Stalin: The War They Waged and the Peace They Sought* (Princeton, 1957); *Between War and Peace: The Potsdam Conference* (Princeton, 1960); and *The Atomic Bomb and the End of World War II* (Princeton, 1966). Useful recent analyses include André Fontaine, *Histoire de la Guerre Froide* (2 v., Paris, 1965, 1967); N. A. Graebner, *Cold War Diplomacy, 1945–1960* (Princeton, 1962); L. J. Halle, *The Cold War as History* (London, 1967); M. F. Herz, *Beginnings of the Cold War* (Bloomington, 1966) and W. L. Neumann, *After Victory: Churchill, Roosevelt, Stalin and the Making of the Peace* (New York, 1967).

[3] The fullest statement of this case is to be found in D. F. Fleming's voluminous *The Cold War and Its Origins* (New York, 1961). For a shorter version of this argument, see David Horowitz, *The Free World Colossus* (New York, 1965); the most subtle and ingenious statements come in W. A. Williams' *The Tragedy of American Diplomacy* (rev. ed., New York, 1962) and in Gar Alperowitz's *Atomic Diplomacy: Hiroshima and Potsdam* (New York, 1965) and in subsequent articles and reviews by Mr. Alperowitz in *The New York Review of Books*. The fact that in some aspects the revisionist thesis parallels the official Soviet argument must not, of course, prevent consideration of the case on its merits, nor raise questions about the motives of the writers, all of whom, so far as·I know, are independent-minded scholars.

I might further add that all these books, in spite of their ostentatious display of scholarly apparatus, must be used with caution. Professor Fleming, for example, relies heavily on newspaper articles and even columnists. While Mr. Alperowitz bases his case on official documents or authoritative reminiscences, he sometimes twists his material in a most unscholarly way. For example, in describing Ambassador Harriman's talk with President Truman on April 20, 1945, Mr. Alperowitz writes, "He argued that a reconsideration of Roosevelt's policy was necessary" (p. 22, repeated on p. 24). The citation is to p. 70–72 in President Truman's *Years of Decision*. What President Truman reported Harriman as saying was the exact opposite: "Before leaving, Harriman took me aside and said, 'Frankly, one of the reasons that made me rush back to Washington was the fear that you did not understand, as I had seen Roosevelt understand, that Stalin is breaking his agreements.'" Similarly, in an appendix (p. 271) Mr. Alperowitz writes that the Hopkins and Davies missions of May 1945 "were opposed by the 'firm' advisers." Actually the Hopkins mission was proposed by Harriman and Charles E. Bohlen, who Mr. Alperowitz elsewhere suggests were the firmest of the firm—and was proposed by them precisely to impress on Stalin the continuity of American policy from Roosevelt to Truman. While the idea that Truman reversed Roosevelt's policy is tempting dramatically, it is a myth. See, for example, the testimony of Anna Rosenberg Hoffman, who lunched with Roosevelt on March 24, 1945, the last day he spent in Washington. After luncheon, Roosevelt was handed a cable. "He read it and became quite angry. He banged his fists on the arms of his wheelchair and said, 'Averell is right; we can't do busines with Stalin. He has broken every one of the promises he made at Yalta.' He was very upset and continued in the same vein on the subject."

and, exhilarated by the possession of the atomic bomb, undertook a course of aggression of its own designed to expel all Russian influence from Eastern Europe and to establish democratic-capitalist states on the very border of the Soviet Union. As the revisionists see it, this radically new American policy —or rather this resumption by Truman of the pre-Roosevelt policy of insensate anti-communism—left Moscow no alternative but to take measures in defense of its own borders. The result was the Cold War.

These two views, of course, could not be more starkly contrasting. It is therefore not unreasonable to look again at the half-dozen critical years between June 22, 1941, when Hitler attacked Russia, and July 2, 1947, when the Russians walked out of the Marshall Plan meeting in Paris. Several things should be borne in mind as this reëxamination is made. For one thing, we have thought a great deal more in recent years, in part because of writers like Roberta Wohlstetter and T. C. Schelling, about the problems of communication in diplomacy—the signals which one nation, by word or by deed, gives, inadvertently or intentionally, to another. Any honest reappraisal of the origins of the Cold War requires the imaginative leap—which should in any case be as instinctive for the historian as it is prudent for the statesman —into the adversary's viewpoint. We must strive to see how, given Soviet perspectives, the Russians might conceivably have misread our signals, as we must reconsider how intelligently we read theirs.

For another, the historian must not overindulge the man of power in the illusion cherished by those in office that high position carries with it the easy ability to shape history. Violating the statesman's creed, Lincoln once blurted out the truth in his letter of 1864 to A. G. Hodges: "I claim not to have controlled events, but confess plainly that events have controlled me." He was not asserting Tolstoyan fatalism but rather suggesting how greatly events limit the capacity of the statesman to bend history to his will. The physical course of the Second World War—the military operations undertaken, the position of the respective armies at the war's end, the momentum generated by victory and the vacuums created by defeat—all these determined the future as much as the character of individual leaders and the substance of national ideology and purpose.

Nor can the historian forget the conditions under which decisions are made, especially in a time like the Second World War. These were tired, overworked, aging men: in 1945, Churchill was 71 years old, Stalin had governed his country for 17 exacting years, Roosevelt his for 12 years nearly as exacting. During the war, moreover, the importunities of military operations had shoved postwar questions to the margins of their minds. All—even Stalin, behind his screen of ideology—had became addicts of improvisation, relying on authority and virtuosity to conceal the fact that they were constantly surprised by developments. Like Eliza, they leaped from one cake of ice to the next in the effort to reach the other side of the river. None showed great tactical consistency, or cared much about it; all employed a certain ambiguity to preserve their power to decide big issues; and it is hard to know how to interpret anything any one of them said on any specific occasion. This was partly because, like all princes, they designed their expressions to have particular effects on particular audiences; partly because the entirely genuine intellectual difficulty of the questions they faced made a degree of vacillation and mind-changing eminently reasonable. If historians cannot solve their problems in retrospect, who are they to blame Roosevelt, Stalin and Churchill for not having solved them at the time?

Peacemaking after the Second World War was not so much a tapestry as it was a hopelessly raveled and knotted mess of yarn. Yet, for purposes of clarity, it is essential to follow certain threads. One theme indispensable to an understanding of the Cold War is the contrast between two clashing views of world order: the "universalist" view, by which all nations shared a common interest in all the affairs of the world, and the "sphere-of-influence" view, by which each great power would be assured by the other great powers of an acknowledged predominance in its own area of special interest. The universalist view assumed that national security would be guaranteed by an international organization. The sphere-of-interest view assumed that national security would be guaranteed by the balance of power. While in practice these views have by no means been incompatible (indeed, our shaky peace has been based on a combination of the two), in the abstract they involved sharp contradictions.

The tradition of American thought in these matters was universalist—*i.e.* Wilsonian. Roosevelt had been a member of Wilson's subcabinet; in 1920, as candidate for Vice President, he had campaigned for the League of Nations. It is true that, within Roosevelt's infinitely complex mind, Wilsonianism warred with the perception of vital strategic interests he had imbibed from Mahan. Moreover, his temperamental inclination to settle things with fellow princes around the conference table led him to regard the Big Three—or Four—as trustees for the rest of the world. On occasion, as this narrative will show, he was beguiled into flirtation with the sphere-of-influence heresy. But in principle he believed in joint action and remained a Wilsonian. His hope for Yalta, as he told the Congress on his return, was that it would "spell the end of the system of unilateral action, the exclusive alliances, the spheres of influence, the balances of power, and all the other expedients that have been tried for centuries—and have always failed."

Whenever Roosevelt backslid, he had at his side that Wilsonian fundamentalist, Secretary of State Cordell Hull, to recall him to the pure faith. After his visit to Moscow in 1943, Hull characteristically said that, with the Declaration of Four Nations on General Security (in which America, Russia, Britain and China pledged "united action . . . for the organization and maintenance of peace and security"), "there will no longer be need for spheres of influence, for alliances, for balance of power, or any other of the special arrangements through which, in the unhappy past, the nations strove to safeguard their security or to promote their interests."

Remembering the corruption of the Wilsonian vision by the secret treaties of the First World War, Hull was determined to prevent any sphere-of-influence nonsense after the Second World War. He therefore fought all proposals to settle border questions while the war was still on and, excluded as he largely was from wartime diplomacy, poured his not inconsiderable moral energy and frustration into the promulgation of virtuous and spacious general principles.

In adopting the universalist view, Roosevelt and Hull were not indulging personal hobbies. Sumner Welles, Adolf Berle, Averell Harriman, Charles Bohlen—all, if with a variety of nuances, opposed the sphere-of-influence approach. And here the State Department was expressing what seems clearly to have been the predominant mood of the American people, so long mistrustful of European power politics. The Republicans shared the true faith. John Foster Dulles argued that the great threat to peace after the war would lie in the revival of sphere-of-influence thinking. The United States, he said, must not permit Britain and Russia to revert to these bad old ways; it must therefore insist on American participation in all policy decisions for all territories in the world. Dulles wrote pessimistically in January 1945, "The three great powers which at Moscow agreed upon the 'closest coöperation' about European questions have shifted to a practice of separate, regional responsibility."

It is true that critics, and even friends, of the United States sometimes noted a discrepancy between the American passion for universalism when it applied to territory far from American shores and the preëminence the United States accorded its own interests nearer home. Churchill, seeking Washington's blessing for a sphere-of-influence initiative in Eastern Europe, could not forbear reminding the Americans, "We follow the lead of the United States in South America"; nor did any universalist of record propose the abolition of the Monroe Doctrine. But a convenient myopia prevented such inconsistencies from qualifying the ardency of the universalist faith.

There seem only to have been three officials in the United States Government who dissented. One was the Secretary of War, Henry L. Stimson, a classical balance-of-power man, who in 1944 opposed the creation of a vacuum in Central Europe by the pastoralization of Germany and in 1945 urged "the settlement of all territorial acquisitions in the shape of defense posts which each of these four powers may deem to be necessary for their own safety" in advance of any effort to establish a peacetime United Nations. Stimson considered the claim of Russia to a preferred position in Eastern Europe as not unreasonable: as he told President Truman, "he thought the Russians perhaps were being more realistic than we were in regard to their own security." Such a position for Russia seemed to him comparable to the preferred American position in Latin America; he even spoke of "our respective orbits." Stimson was therefore skeptical of what he regarded as the prevailing tendency "to hang on to exaggerated views of the Monroe Doctrine and at the same time butt into every question that comes up in Central Europe." Acceptance of spheres of influence seemed to him the way to avoid "a head-on collision."

A second official opponent of universalism was George Kennan, an eloquent advocate from the American Embassy in Moscow of "a prompt and clear recognition of the division of Europe into spheres of influence and of a policy based on the fact of such division." Kennan argued that nothing we could do would possibly alter the course of events in Eastern Europe; that we were deceiving ourselves by supposing that these countries had any future but Russian domination; that we should therefore relinquish Eastern Europe to the Soviet Union and avoid anything which would make things easier for the Russians by giving them economic assistance or by sharing moral responsibility for their actions.

A third voice within the government against universalism was (at least after the war) Henry A. Wallace. As Secretary of Commerce, he stated the sphere-of-influence case with trenchancy in the famous Madison Square Garden speech of September 1946 which led to his dismissal by President Truman:

> On our part, we should recognize that we have no more business in the *political* affairs of Eastern Europe than Russia has in the *political* affairs in Latin America, Western Europe, and the United States. . . . Whether we like it or not, the Russians will try to socialize their sphere of influence just as we try to democratize our sphere of influence. . . . The Russians have no more business stirring up native Communists to political activity in Western Europe, Latin America, and the United States than we have in interfering with the politics of Eastern Europe and Russia.

Stimson, Kennan and Wallace seem to have been alone in the government, however, in taking these views. They were very much minority voices. Meanwhile universalism, rooted in the American legal and moral tradition, overwhelmingly backed by contemporary opinion, received successive enshrinements in the Atlantic Charter of 1941, in the Declaration of the United Nations in 1942 and in the Moscow Declaration of 1943.

The Kremlin, on the other hand, thought *only* of spheres of interest; above all, the Russians were determined to protect their frontiers, and especially their border to the west, crossed so often and so bloodily in the dark course of their history. These western frontiers lacked natural means of defense—no great oceans, rugged mountains, steaming swamps or impenetrable jungles. The history of Russia had been the history of invasion, the last of which was by now horribly killing up to twenty million of its people. The protocol of Russia therefore meant the enlargement of the area of Russian influence. Kennan himself wrote (in May 1944), "Behind Russia's stubborn expansion lies only the age-old sense of insecurity of a sedentary people reared on an exposed plain in the neighborhood of fierce nomadic peoples," and he called this "urge" a "permanent feature of Russian psychology."

In earlier times the "urge" had produced the tsarist search for buffer states and maritime outlets. In 1939 the Soviet-Nazi pact and its secret protocol had enabled Russia to begin to satisfy in the Baltic states, Karelian Finland and Poland, part of what it conceived as its security requirements in Eastern Europe. But the "urge" persisted, causing the friction between Russia and Germany in 1940 as each jostled for position in the area which separated them. Later it led to Molotov's new demands on Hitler in November 1940—a free hand in Finland, Soviet predominance in Rumania and Bulgaria, bases in the Dardanelles—the demands which convinced Hitler that he had no choice but to attack Russia. Now Stalin hoped to gain from the West what Hitler, a closer neighbor, had not dared yield him.

It is true that, so long as Russian survival appeared to require a second front to relieve the Nazi pressure, Moscow's demand for Eastern Europe was a little muffled. Thus the Soviet government adhered to the Atlantic Charter (though with a significant if obscure reservation about adapting its principles to "the circumstances, needs, and historic peculiarities of particular countries"). Thus it also adhered to the Moscow Declaration of 1943, and Molotov then, with his easy mendacity, even denied that Russia had any desire to divide Europe into spheres of influence. But this was guff, which the Russians were perfectly willing to ladle out if it would keep the Americans, and especially Secretary Hull (who made a strong personal impression at the Moscow conference) happy. "A declaration," as Stalin once observed to Eden, "I regard as algebra, but an agreement as practical arithmetic. I do not wish to decry algebra, but I prefer practical arithmetic."

The more consistent Russian purpose was revealed when Stalin offered the British a straight sphere-of-influence deal at the end of 1941. Britain, he suggested, should recognize the Russian absorption of the Baltic states, part of Finland, eastern Poland and Bessarabia; in return, Russia would support any special British need for bases or security arrangements in Western Europe. There was nothing specifically communist about these ambitions. If Stalin achieved them, he would be fulfilling an age-old dream of the tsars. The British reaction was mixed. "Soviet policy is amoral," as Anthony Eden noted at the time; "United States policy is exaggeratedly moral, at least where non-American interests are concerned." If Roosevelt was a universalist with occasional leanings toward spheres of influence and Stalin was a sphere-of-influence man with occasional gestures toward universalism, Churchill seemed evenly poised between the familiar realism of the balance of power, which he had so long recorded as an historian and manipulated as a statesman, and the hope that there must be some better way of doing things. His 1943 proposal of a world organization divided into regional councils represented an effort to blend universalist and sphere-of-interest conceptions. His initial rejection of Stalin's proposal in December 1941 as "directly contrary to the first, second and third articles of the Atlantic Charter" thus did not spring entirely from a desire to propitiate the United States. On the other hand, he had himself already reinterpreted the Atlantic Charter as applying only to Europe (and thus not to the British Empire), and he was, above all, an empiricist who never believed in sacrificing reality on the altar of doctrine.

So in April 1942 he wrote Roosevelt that "the increasing gravity of the war" had led him to feel that the Charter "ought not to be construed so as to deny Russia the frontiers she occupied when Germany attacked her." Hull, however, remained fiercely hostile to the inclusion of territorial provisions in the Anglo-Russian treaty; the American position, Eden noted, "chilled me with Wilsonian memories." Though Stalin complained that it looked "as if the Atlantic Charter was directed against the U.S.S.R.," it was the Russian season of military adversity in the spring of 1942, and he dropped his demands.

He did not, however, change his intentions. A year later Ambassador Standley could cable Washington from Moscow: "In 1918 Western Europe attempted to set up a *cordon sanitaire* to protect it from the influence of bolshevism. Might not now the Kremlin envisage the formation of a belt of pro-Soviet states to protect it from the influences of the West?" It well might; and that purpose became increasingly clear as the war approached its end. Indeed, it derived sustenance from Western policy in the first area of liberation.

The unconditional surrender of Italy in July 1943 created the first major test of the Western devotion to universalism. America and Britain, having won the Italian war, handled the capitulation, keeping Moscow informed at a distance. Stalin complained:

> The United States and Great Britain made agreements but the Soviet Union received information about the results . . . just as a passive third observer. I have to tell you that it is impossible to tolerate the situation any longer. I propose that the [tripartite military-political commission] be established and that Sicily be assigned . . . as its place of residence.

Roosevelt, who had no intention of sharing the control of Italy with the Russians, suavely replied with the suggestion that Stalin send an officer "to General Eisenhower's headquarters in connection with the commission." Unimpressed, Stalin continued to press for a tripartite body; but his Western allies were adamant in keeping the Soviet Union off the Control Commission for Italy, and the Russians in the end had to be satisfied with a seat, along with minor Allied states, on a meaningless Inter-Allied Advisory Council. Their acquiescence in this was doubtless not unconnected with a desire to establish precedents for Eastern Europe.

Teheran in December 1943 marked the high point of three-power collaboration. Still, when Churchill asked about Russian territorial interests, Stalin replied a little ominously, "There is no need to speak at the present time about any Soviet desires, but when the time comes we will speak." In the next weeks, there were increasing indications of a Soviet determination to deal unilaterally with Eastern Europe—so much so that in early February 1944 Hull cabled Harriman in Moscow:

> Matters are rapidly approaching the point where the Soviet Government will have to choose between the development and extension of the foundation of international cooperation as the guiding principle of the postwar world as against the continuance of a unilateral and arbitrary method of dealing with its special problems even though these problems are admittedly of more direct interest to the Soviet Union than to other great powers.

As against this approach, however, Churchill, more tolerant of sphere-of-influence deviations, soon proposed that, with the impending liberation of the Balkans, Russia should run things in Rumania and Britain in Greece. Hull strongly opposed this suggestion but made the mistake of leaving Washington for a few days; and Roosevelt, momentarily free from his Wilsonian conscience, yielded to Churchill's plea for a three-months' trial. Hull resumed the fight on his return, and Churchill postponed the matter.

The Red Army continued its advance into Eastern Europe. In August the Polish Home Army, urged on by Polish-language broadcasts from Moscow, rose up against the Nazis in Warsaw. For 63 terrible days, the Poles fought valiantly on, while the Red Army halted on the banks of the Vistula a few miles away, and in Moscow Stalin for more than half this time declined to coöperate with the Western effort to drop supplies to the Warsaw Resistance. It appeared a calculated Soviet decision to let the Nazis slaughter the anti-Soviet Polish underground; and, indeed, the result was to destroy any substantial alternative to a Soviet solution in Poland. The agony of

Warsaw caused the most deep and genuine shock in Britain and America and provoked dark forebodings about Soviet postwar purposes.

Again history enjoins the imaginative leap in order to see things for a moment from Moscow's viewpoint. The Polish question, Churchill would say at Yalta, was for Britain a question of honor. "It is not only a question of honor for Russia," Stalin replied, "but one of life and death. . . . Throughout history Poland had been the corridor for attack on Russia." A top postwar priority for any Russian régime must be close to that corridor. The Home Army was led by anti-communists. It clearly hoped by its action to forestall the Soviet occupation of Warsaw and, in Russian eyes, to prepare the way for an anti-Russian Poland. In addition, the uprising from a strictly operational viewpoint was premature. The Russians, it is evident in retrospect, had real military problems at the Vistula. The Soviet attempt in September to send Polish units from the Red Army across the river to join forces with the Home Army was a disaster. Heavy German shelling thereafter prevented the ferrying of tanks necessary for an assault on the German position. The Red Army itself did not take Warsaw for another three months. None the less, Stalin's indifference to the human tragedy, his effort to blackmail the London Poles during the ordeal, his sanctimonious opposition during five precious weeks to aerial resupply, the invariable coldness of his explanations ("the Soviet command has come to the conclusion that it must dissociate itself from the Warsaw adventure") and the obvious political benefit to the Soviet Union from the destruction of the Home Army—all these had the effect of suddenly dropping the mask of wartime comradeship and displaying to the West the hard face of Soviet policy. In now pursuing what he grimly regarded as the minimal requirements for the postwar security of his country, Stalin was inadvertently showing the irreconcilability of both his means and his ends with the Anglo-American conception of the peace.

Meanwhile Eastern Europe presented the Alliance with still another crisis that same September. Bulgaria, which was not at war with Russia, decided to surrender to the Western Allies while it still could; and the English and Americans at Cairo began to discuss armistice terms with Bulgarian envoys. Moscow, challenged by what it plainly saw as a western intrusion into its own zone of vital interest, promptly declared war on Bulgaria, took over the surrender negotiations and, invoking the Italian precedent, denied its Western Allies any role in the Bulgarian Control Commission. In a long and thoughtful cable, Ambassador Harriman meditated on the problems of communication with the Soviet Union. "Words," he reflected, "have a different connotation to the Soviets than they have to us. When they speak of insisting on 'friendly governments' in their neighboring countries, they have in mind something quite different from what we would mean." The Russians, he surmised, really believed that Washington accepted "their position that although they would keep us informed they had the right to settle their problems with their western neighbors unilaterally." But the Soviet position was still in flux: "the Soviet Government is not one mind." The problem, as Harriman had earlier told Harry Hopkins, was "to strengthen the hands of those around Stalin who want to play the game along our lines." The way to do this, he now told Hull, was to be understanding of their sensitivity, meet them much more than half way, encourage them and support them wherever we can, and yet oppose them promptly with the greatest of firmness where we see them going wrong. . . . The only way we can eventually come to an understanding with the Soviet Union on the question of non-interference in the internal affairs of other countries is for us to take a definite interest in the solution of the problems of each individual country as they arise.

As against Harriman's sophisticated universalist strategy, however, Churchill, increasingly fearful of the consequences of unrestrained competition in Eastern Europe, decided in early October to carry his sphere-of-influence proposal directly to Moscow. Roosevelt was at first content to have Churchill speak for him too and even prepared a cable to that effect. But Hopkins, a more rigorous universalist, took it upon himself to stop the cable and warn Roosevelt of its possible implications. Eventually Roosevelt sent a message to Harriman in Moscow emphasizing that he expected to "retain complete freedom of action after this conference is over." It was now that Churchill quickly proposed—and Stalin quickly accepted—the celebrated division of southeastern Europe: ending (after further haggling between Eden and Molotov) with 90 percent Soviet predominance in Rumania, 80 percent in Bulgaria and Hungary, fifty-fifty in Jugoslavia, 90 percent British predominance in Greece.

Churchill in discussing this with Harriman used the phrase "spheres of influence." But he insisted that these were only "immediate wartime arrangements" and received a highly general blessing from Roosevelt. Yet, whatever Churchill intended, there is reason to believe that Stalin construed the percentages as an agreement, not a declaration; as practical arithmetic, not algebra. For Stalin, it should be understood, the sphere-of-influence idea did not mean that he would abandon all efforts to spread communism in some other nation's sphere; it did mean that, if he tried this and the other side cracked down, he could not feel he had serious cause for complaint. As Kennan wrote to Harriman at the end of 1944:

> As far as border states are concerned the Soviet government has never ceased to think in terms of spheres of interest. They expect us to support them in whatever action they wish to take in those regions, regardless of whether that action seems to us or to the rest of the world to be right or wrong. . . . I have no doubt that this position is honestly maintained on their part, and that they would be equally prepared to reserve moral judgment on any actions which we might wish to carry out, i.e., in the Caribbean area.

In any case, the matter was already under test a good deal closer to Moscow than the Caribbean. The communist-dominated resistance movement in Greece was in open revolt against the effort of the Papandreou government to disarm and disband the guerrillas (the same Papandreou whom the Greek colonels have recently arrested on the claim that he is a tool of the communists). Churchill now called in British Army units to crush the insurrection. This action produced a storm of criticism in his own country and in the United States; the American Government even publicly dissociated itself from the intervention, thereby emphasizing its detachment from the sphere-of-influence deal. But Stalin, Churchill later claimed, "adhered strictly and faithfully to our agreement of October, and during all the long weeks of fighting the Communists in the streets of Athens not one word of reproach came from *Pravda* or *Izvestia*," though there is no evidence that he tried to call off the Greek communists. Still, when the communist rebellion later broke out again in Greece, Stalin told Kardelj and Djilas of Jugoslavia in 1948, "The uprising in Greece must be stopped, and as quickly as possible."

No one, of course, can know what really was in the minds of the Russian leaders. The Kremlin archives are locked; of the primary actors, only Molotov survives, and he has not yet indicated any desire to collaborate with the Columbia Oral History Project. We do know that Stalin did not wholly surrender to sentimental illusion about his new friends. In June 1944, on the night before the landings in Normandy, he told Djilas that the English "find nothing sweeter than to trick their allies. . . . And Churchill? Churchill is the kind who, if you don't watch him, will slip a kopeck out of your pocket. Yes, a kopeck out of your pocket! . . . Roosevelt is not like that. He dips in his hand only for bigger coins." But whatever his views of his colleagues it is not unreasonable to suppose that Stalin would have been satisfied at the end of the war to secure what Kennan has called "a protective glacis along Russia's western border," and that, in exchange for a free hand in Eastern Europe, he was prepared to give the British and Americans equally free hands in their zones of vital interest, including in nations as close to Russia as Greece (for the British) and, very probably—or at least so the Jugoslavs believe—China (for the United States). In other words, his initial objectives were very probably not world conquest but Russian security.

It is now pertinent to inquire why the United States rejected the idea of stabilizing the world by division into spheres of influence and insisted on an East European strategy. One should warn against rushing to the conclusion that it was all a row between hard-nosed, balance-of-power realists and starry-eyed Wilsonians. Roosevelt, Hopkins, Welles, Harriman, Bohlen, Berle, Dulles and other universalists were tough and serious men. Why then did they rebuff the sphere-of-influence solution?

The first reason is that they regarded this solution as containing within itself the seeds of a third world war. The balance-of-power idea seemed inherently unstable. It had always broken down in the past. It held out to each power the permanent temptation to try to alter the balance in its own favor, and it built this temptation into the international order. It would turn the great powers of 1945 away from the objective of concerting common policies toward competition for postwar advantage. As Hopkins told Molotov at Teheran, "The President feels it essential to world peace that Russia, Great Britain and the United States work out this control question in a manner which will not start each of the three powers arming against the others." "The greatest likelihood of eventual conflict," said the Joint Chiefs of Staff in 1944 (the only conflict which the J.C.S., in its wisdom, could then glimpse "in the foreseeable future" was between Britain and Russia), ". . . would seem to grow out of either nation initiating attempts to build up its strength, by seeking to attach to herself parts of Europe to the disadvantage and possible danger of her potential adversary." The Americans were perfectly ready to acknowledge that Russia was entitled to convincing assurance of her national security—but not this way. "I could sympathize fully with Stalin's desire to protect his western borders from future attack," as Hull put it. "But I felt that this security could best be obtained through a strong postwar peace organization."

Hull's remark suggests the second objection: that the sphere-of-influence approach would, in the words of the State Department in 1945, "militate against the establishment and effective functioning of a broader system of general security in which all countries will have their part." The United Nations, in short, was seen as the alternative to the balance of power. Nor did the universalists see any necessary incompatibility between the Russian desire for "friendly governments" on its frontier and the American desire for self-determination in Eastern Europe. Before Yalta the State Department judged the general mood of Europe as "to the left and strongly in favor of far-reaching economic and social reforms, but not, however, in favor of a left-wing totalitarian regime to achive these reforms." Governments in Eastern Europe could be sufficiently to the left "to allay Soviet suspicions" but sufficiently representative "of the center and *petit bourgeois* elements" not to seem a prelude to communist dictatorship. The American criteria were therefore that the government "should be dedicated to the preservation of civil liberties" and "should favor social and economic reforms." A string of New Deal states—of Finlands and Czechoslovakias—seemed a reasonable compromise solution.

Third, the universalists feared that the sphere-of-interest approach would be what Hull termed "a haven for the isolationists," who would advocate America's participation in Western Hemisphere affairs on condition that it did not participate in European or Asian affairs. Hull also feared that spheres of interest would lead to "closed trade areas or discriminatory systems" and thus defeat his cherished dream of a low-tariff, freely trading world.

Fourth, the sphere-of-interest solution meant the betrayal of the principles for which the Second World War was being fought—the Atlantic Charter, the Four Freedoms, the Declaration of the United Nations. Poland summed up the problem. Britain, having gone to war to defend the independence of Poland from the Germans, could not easily conclude the war by surrendering the independence of Poland to the Russians. Thus, as Hopkins told Stalin after Roosevelt's death in 1945, Poland had "become the symbol of our ability to work out problems with the Soviet Union." Nor could American liberals in general watch with equanimity while the police state spread into countries which, if they had mostly not been real democracies, had mostly not been tyrannies either. The execution in 1943 of Ehrlich and Alter, the Polish socialist trade union leaders, excited deep concern. "I have particularly in mind," Harriman cabled in 1944, "objection to the institution of secret police who may become involved in the persecution of persons of truly democratic convictions who may not be willing to conform to Soviet methods."

Fifth, the sphere-of-influence solution would create difficult domestic problems in American politics. Roosevelt was aware of the six million or more Polish votes in the 1944 election; even more acutely, he was aware of the broader and deeper attack which would follow if, after going to war to stop the Nazi conquest of Europe, he permitted the war to end with the communist conquest of Eastern Europe. As Archibald MacLeish, then Assistant Secretary of State for Public Affairs, warned in January 1945,

> The wave of disillusionment which has distressed us in the last several weeks will be increased if the impression is permitted to get abroad that potentially totalitarian provisional governments are to be set up without adequate safeguards as to the holding of free elections and the realization of the principles of the Atlantic Charter.

Roosevelt believed that no administration could survive which did not try everything short of war to save Eastern Europe, and he was the supreme American politician of the century.

Sixth, if the Russians were allowed to overrun Eastern Europe without argument, would that satisfy them? Even Kennan, in a dispatch of May 1944, admitted that the "urge" had dreadful potentialities: "If initially successful, will it know where to stop? Will it not be inexorably carried forward, by its very nature, in a struggle to reach the whole—to attain complete mastery of the shores of the Atlantic and the Pacific?" His own answer was that there were inherent limits to the Russian capacity to expand—"that Russia will not have an easy time in maintaining the power which it has seized over other people in Eastern and Central Europe, unless it receives both moral and material assistance from the West." Subsequent developments have vindicated Kennan's argument. By the late forties, Jugoslavia and Albania, the two East European states farthest from the Soviet Union and the two in which communism was imposed from within rather than from without, had declared their independence of Moscow. But, given Russia's success in maintaining centralized control over the international communist movement for a quarter of a century, who in 1944 could have had much confidence in the idea of communist revolts against Moscow?

Most of those involved therefore rejected Kennan's answer and stayed with his question. If the West turned its back on Eastern Europe, the higher probability, in their view, was that the Russians would use their security zone, not just for defensive purposes, but as a springboard from which to mount an attack on Western Europe, now shattered by war, a vacuum of power awaiting its master. "If the policy is accepted that the Soviet Union has a right to penetrate her immediate neighbors for security," Harriman said in 1944, "penetration of the next immediate neighbors becomes at a certain time equally logical." If a row with Russia were inevitable, every consideration of prudence dictated that it should take place in Eastern rather than Western Europe.

Thus idealism and realism joined in opposition to the sphere-of-influence solution. The consequence was a determination to assert an American interest in the postwar destiny of all nations, including those of Eastern Europe. In the message which Roosevelt and Hopkins drafted after Hopkins had stopped Roosevelt's initial cable authorizing Churchill to speak for the United States at the Moscow meeting of October 1944, Roosevelt now said, "There is in this global war literally no question, either military or political, in which the United States is not interested." After Roosevelt's death Hopkins repeated the point to Stalin: "The cardinal basis of President Roosevelt's policy which the American people fully supported had been the concept that the interests of the U.S. were worldwide and not confined to North and South America and the Pacific Ocean."

For better or worse, this was the American position. It is now necessary to attempt the imaginative leap and consider the impact of this position on the leaders of the Soviet Union who, also for better or for worse, had reached the bitter conclusion that the survival of their country depended on their unchallenged control of the corridors through which enemies had so often invaded their homeland. They could claim to have been keeping their own side of the sphere-of-influence bargain. Of course, they were working to capture the resistance movements of Western Europe; indeed, with the appointment of Oumansky as Ambassador to Mexico they were even beginning to enlarge underground operations in the Western Hemisphere. But, from their viewpoint, if the West permitted this, the more fools they; and, if the West stopped it, it was within their right to do so. In overt political matters the Russians were scrupulously playing the game. They had watched in silence while the British shot down communists in Greece. In Jugoslavia Stalin was urging Tito (as Djilas later revealed) to keep King Peter. They had not only acknowledged Western preëminence in Italy but had recognized the Badoglio régime; the Italian Communists had even voted (against the Socialists and the Liberals) for the renewal of the Lateran Pacts.

They would not regard anti-communist action in a Western zone as a *casus belli;* and they expected reciprocal license to assert their own authority in the East. But the principle of self-determination was carrying the United States into a deeper entanglement in Eastern Europe than the Soviet Union claimed as a right (whatever it was doing underground) in the affairs of Italy, Greece or China. When the Russians now exercised in Eastern Europe the same brutal control they were prepared to have Washington exercise in the American sphere of influence, the American protests, given the paranoia produced alike by Russian history and Leninist ideology, no doubt seemed not only an act of hypocrisy but a threat to security. To the Russians, a stroll into the neighborhood easily became a plot to burn down the house: when, for example, damaged American planes made emergency landings in Poland and Hungary, Moscow took this as attempts to organize the local resistance. It is not unusual to suspect one's adversary of doing what one is already doing oneself. At the same time, the cruelty with which the Russians executed their idea of spheres of influence—in a sense, perhaps, an unwitting cruelty, since Stalin treated the East Europeans no worse than he had treated the Russians in the thirties—discouraged the West from accepting the equation (for example, Italy = Rumania) which seemed so self-evident to the Kremlin.

So Moscow very probably, and not unnaturally, perceived the emphasis on self-determination as a systematic and deliberate pressure on Russia's western frontiers. Moreover, the restoration of capitalism to countries freed at frightful cost by the Red Army no doubt struck the Russians as the betrayal of the principles for which *they* were fighting. "That they, the victors," Isaac Deutscher has suggested, "should now preserve an order from which they had experienced nothing but hostility, and could expect nothing but hostility . . . would have been the most miserable anti-climax to their great 'war of liberation.' " By 1944 Poland was the critical issue; Harriman later said that "under instructions from President Roosevelt, I talked about Poland with Stalin more frequently than with any other subject." While the West saw the point of Stalin's demand for a "friendly government" in Warsaw, the American insistence on the sovereign virtues of free elections (ironically in the spirit of the 1917 Bolshevik decree of peace, which affirmed "the right" of a nation "to decide the forms of its state existence by a free vote, taken after the complete evacuation of the incorporating or, generally, of the stronger nation") created an insoluble problem in those countries, like Poland (and Rumania) where free elections would almost certainly produce anti-Soviet governments.

The Russians thus may well have estimated the Western pressures as calculated to encourage their enemies in Eastern Europe and to defeat their own minimum objective of a protective glacis. Everything still hung, however, on the course of military operations. The wartime collaboration had been created by one thing, and one thing alone: the threat of Nazi victory. So long as this threat was real, so was the collaboration. In late December 1944, von Rundstedt launched his counter-offensive in the Ardennes. A few weeks later, when Roosevelt, Churchill and Stalin gathered in the Crimea, it was in the shadow of this last considerable explosion of German power. The meeting at Yalta was still dominated by the mood of war.

Yalta remains something of an historical perplexity—less, from the perspective of 1967, because of a mythical American deference to the sphere-of-influence thesis than because of the documentable Russian deference to the universalist thesis. Why should Stalin in 1945 have accepted the Declaration on Liberated Europe and an agreement on Poland pledging that "the three governments will jointly" act to assure "free elections of governments responsive to the will of the people"? There are several probable answers: that the war was not over and the Russians still wanted the Americans to intensify their military effort in the West; that one clause in the Declaration premised action on "the opinion of the three governments" and thus implied a Soviet veto, though the Polish agreement was more definite; most of all that the universalist algebra of the Declaration was plainly in Stalin's mind to be construed in terms of the practical arithmetic of his sphere-of-influence agreement with Churchill the previous October. Stalin's assurance to Churchill at Yalta that a proposed Russian amendment to the Declaration would not apply to Greece makes it clear that Roosevelt's pieties did not, in Stalin's mind, nullify Churchill's percentages. He could well have been strengthened in this supposition by the fact that *after* Yalta, Churchill himself repeatedly asserted the terms of the October agreement as if he regarded it, despite Yalta, as controlling.

Harriman still had the feeling before Yalta that the Kremlin had "two approaches to their postwar policies" and that Stalin himself was "of two minds." One approach emphasized the internal reconstruction and development of Russia; the other its external expansion. But in the meantime the fact which dominated all political decisions—that is, the war against Germany —was moving into its final phase. In the weeks after Yalta, the military situation changed with great rapidity. As the Nazi threat declined, so too did the need for coöperation. The Soviet Union, feeling itself menaced by the American idea of self-determination and the borderlands diplomacy to which it was leading, skeptical whether the United Nations would protect its frontiers as reliably as its own domination in Eastern Europe, began to fulfill its security requirements unilaterally.

In March Stalin expressed his evaluation of the United Nations by rejecting Roosevelt's plea that Molotov come to the San Francisco conference, if only for the opening sessions. In the next weeks the Russians emphatically and crudely worked their will in Eastern Europe, above all in the test country of Poland. They were ignoring the Declaration on Liberated Europe, ignoring the Atlantic Charter, self-determination, human freedom and everything else the Americans considered essential for a stable peace. "We must clearly recognize," Harriman wired Washington a few days before Roosevelt's death, "that the Soviet program is the establishment of totalitarianism, ending personal liberty and democracy as we know and respect it."

At the same time, the Russians also began to mobilize communist resources in the United States itself to block American universalism. In April 1945 Jacques Duclos, who had been the Comintern official responsible for the Western communist parties, launched in *Cahiers du Communisme* an uncompromising attack on the policy of the American Communist Party. Duclos sharply condemned the revisionism of Earl Browder, the American Communist leader, as "expressed in the concept of a long-term class peace in the United States, of the possibility of the suppression of the class struggle in the postwar period and of establishment of harmony between labor and capital." Browder was specifically rebuked for favoring the "self-determination" of Europe "west of the Soviet Union" on a bourgeois-democratic basis. The excommunication of Browderism was plainly the Politburo's considered reaction to the impending defeat of Germany; it was a signal to the communist parties of the West that they should recover their identity; it was Moscow's alert to communists everywhere that they should prepare for new policies in the postwar world.

The Duclos piece obviously could not have been planned and written much later than the Yalta conference—that is, well before a number of events which revisionists now cite in order to demonstrate American responsibility for the Cold War: before Allen Dulles, for example, began to negotiate the surrender of the German armies in Italy (the episode which provoked Stalin to charge Roosevelt with seeking a separate peace and provoked Roosevelt to denounce the "vile misrepresentations" of Stalin's informants); well before Roosevelt died; many months before the testing of the atomic bomb; even more months before Truman ordered that the bomb be dropped on Japan. William Z. Foster, who soon replaced Browder as the leader of the American Communist Party and embodied the new Moscow line, later boasted of having said in January 1944, "A post-war Roosevelt administration would continue to be, as it is now, an imperialist government." With ancient suspicions revived by the American insistence on universalism, this was no doubt the conclusion which the Russians were reaching at the same time. The Soviet canonization of Roosevelt (like their present-day canonization of Kennedy) took place after the American President's death.

The atmosphere of mutual suspicion was beginning to rise. In January 1945 Molotov formally proposed that the United States grant Russia a $6 billion credit for postwar reconstruction. With characteristic tact he explained that he was doing this as a favor to save America from a postwar depression. The proposal seems to have been diffidently made and diffidently received. Roosevelt requested that the matter "not be pressed further" on the American side until he had a chance to talk with Stalin; but the Russians did not follow it up either at Yalta in February (save for a single glancing reference) or during the Stalin-Hopkins talks in May or at Potsdam. Finally the proposal was renewed in the very different political atmosphere of August. This time Washington explicitly mislaid the request during the transfer of the records of the Foreign Economic Administration to the State Department. It did not turn up again until March 1946. Of course this was impossible for the Russians to believe; it is hard enough even for those acquainted with the capacity of the American government for incompetence to believe; and it only strengthened Soviet suspicions of American purposes.

The American credit was one conceivable form of Western contribution to Russian reconstruction. Another was lend-lease, and the possibility of reconstruction aid under the lend-lease protocol had already been discussed in 1944. But in May 1945 Russia, like Britain, suffered from Truman's abrupt termination of lend-lease shipments—"unfortunate and even brutal," Stalin told Hopkins, adding that, if it was "designed as pressure on the Russians in order to soften them up, then it was a fundamental mistake." A third form was German reparations. Here Stalin in demanding $10 billion in reparations for the Soviet Union made his strongest fight at Yalta. Roosevelt, while agreeing essentially with Churchill's opposition, tried to postpone the matter by accepting the Soviet figure as a "basis for discussion"—a formula which led to future misunderstanding. In short, the Russian hope for major Western assistance in postwar reconstruction foundered on three events which the Kremlin could well have interpreted respectively as deliberate sabotage (the loan request), blackmail (lend-lease cancellation) and pro-Germanism (reparations).

Actually the American attempt to settle the fourth lend-lease protocol was generous and the Russians for their own reasons declined to come to an agreement. It is not clear, though, that satisfying Moscow on any of these financial scores would have made much essential difference. It might have persuaded some doves in the Kremlin that the U.S. government was genuinely friendly; it might have persuaded some hawks that the American anxiety for Soviet friendship was such that Moscow could do as it wished without inviting challenge from the United States. It would, in short, merely have reinforced both sides of the Kremlin debate; it would hardly have reversed deeper tendencies toward the deterioration of political relationships. Economic deals were surely subordinate to the quality of mutual political confidence; and here, in the months after Yalta, the decay was steady.

The Cold War had now begun. It was the product not of a decision but of a dilemma. Each side felt compelled to adopt policies which the other could not but regard as a threat to the principles of the peace. Each then felt compelled to undertake defensive measures. Thus the Russians saw no choice but to consolidate their security in Eastern Europe. The Americans, regarding Eastern Europe as the first step toward Western Europe, responded by asserting their interest in the zone the Russians deemed vital to their security. The Russians concluded that the West was resuming its old course of capitalist encirclement; that it was purposefully laying the foundation for anti-Soviet régimes in the area defined by the blood of centuries as crucial to Russian survival. Each side believed with passion that future international stability depended on the success of its own conception of world order. Each side, in pursuing its own clearly indicated and deeply cherished principles, was only confirming the fear of the other that it was bent on aggression.

Very soon the process began to acquire a cumulative momentum. The impending collapse of Germany thus provoked new troubles: the Russians, for example, sincerely feared that the West was planning a separate surrender of the German armies in Italy in a way which would release troops for Hitler's eastern front, as they subsequently feared that the Nazis might succeed in surrendering Berlin to the West. This was the context in which the atomic bomb now appeared. Though the revisionist argument that Truman dropped the bomb less to defeat Japan than to intimidate Russia is not convincing, this thought unquestionably appealed to some in Washington as at least an advantageous side-effect of Hiroshima.

So the machinery of suspicion and counter-suspicion, action and counter-action, was set in motion. But, given relations among traditional national states, there was still no reason, even with all the postwar jostling, why this should not have remained a manageable situation. What made it unmanageable, what caused the rapid escalation of the Cold War and in another two years completed the division of Europe, was a set of considerations which this account has thus far excluded.

Up to this point, the discussion has considered the schism within the wartime coalition as if it were entirely the result of disagreements among national states. Assuming this framework, there was unquestionably a failure of communication between America and Russia, a misperception of signals and, as time went on, a mounting tendency to ascribe ominous motives to the other side. It seems hard, for example, to deny that American postwar policy created genuine difficulties for the Russians and even assumed a threatening aspect for them. All this the revisionists have rightly and usefully emphasized.

But the great omission of the revisionists—and also the fundamental explanation of the speed with which the Cold War escalated—lies precisely in the fact that the Soviet Union was *not* a traditional national state.[4] This is where the "mirror image," invoked by some psychologists, falls down. For the Soviet Union was a phenomenon very different from America or

[4] This is the classical revisionist fallacy—the assumption of the rationality, or at least of the traditionalism, of states where ideology and social organization have created a different range of motives. So the Second World War revisionists omit the totalitarian dynamism of Nazism and the fanaticism of Hitler, as the Civil War revisionists omit the fact that the slavery system was producing a doctrinaire closed society in the American South. For a consideration of some of these issues, see "The Causes of the Civil War: A Note on Historical Sentimentalism" in my *The Politics of Hope* (Boston, 1963).

Britain: it was a totalitarian state, endowed with an all-explanatory, all-consuming ideology, committed to the infallibility of government and party, still in a somewhat messianic mood, equating dissent with treason, and ruled by a dictator who, for all his quite extraordinary abilities, had his paranoid moments.

Marxism-Leninism gave the Russian leaders a view of the world according to which all societies were inexorably destined to proceed along appointed roads by appointed stages until they achieved the classless nirvana. Moreover, given the resistance of the capitalists to this development, the existence of any non-communist state was *by definition* a threat to the Soviet Union. "As long as capitalism and socialism exist," Lenin wrote, "we cannot live in peace: in the end, one or the other will triumph—a funeral dirge will be sung either over the Soviet Republic or over world capitalism."

Stalin and his associates, whatever Roosevelt or Truman did or failed to do, were bound to regard the United States as the enemy; not because of this deed or that, but because of the primordial fact that America was the leading capitalist power and thus, by Leninist syllogism, unappeasably hostile, driven by the logic of its system to oppose, encircle and destroy Soviet Russia. Nothing the United States could have done in 1944–45 would have abolished this mistrust, required and sanctified as it was by Marxist gospel —nothing short of the conversion of the United States into a Stalinist despotism; and even this would not have sufficed, as the experience of Jugoslavia and China soon showed, unless it were accompanied by total subservience to Moscow. So long as the United States remained a capitalist democracy, no American policy, given Moscow's theology, could hope to win basic Soviet confidence, and every American action was poisoned from the source. So long as the Soviet Union remained a messianic state, ideology compelled a steady expansion of communist power.

It is easy, of course, to exaggerate the capacity of ideology to control events. The tension of acting according to revolutionary abstractions is too much for most nations to sustain over a long period: that is why Mao Tse-tung has launched his Cultural Revolution, hoping thereby to create a permanent revolutionary mood and save Chinese communism from the degeneration which, in his view, has overtaken Russian communism. Still, as any revolution grows older, normal human and social motives will increasingly reassert themselves. In due course, we can be sure, Leninism will be about as effective in governing the daily lives of Russians as Christianity is in governing the daily lives of Americans. Like the Ten Commandments and the Sermon on the Mount, the Leninist verities will increasingly become platitudes for ritual observance, not guides to secular decision. There can be no worse fallacy (even if respectable people practiced it diligently for a season in the United States) than that of drawing from a nation's ideology permanent conclusions about its behavior.

A temporary recession of ideology was already taking place during the Second World War when Stalin, to rally his people against the invader, had to replace the appeal of Marxism by that of nationalism. ("We are under no illusions that they are fighting for us," Stalin once said to Harriman. "They are fighting for Mother Russia.") But this was still taking place within the strictest limitations. The Soviet Union remained as much a police state as ever; the régime was as infallible as ever; foreigners and their ideas were as suspect as ever. "Never, except possibly during my later experience as ambassador in Moscow," Kennan has written, "did the insistence of the Soviet authorities on isolation of the diplomatic corps weigh more heavily on me . . . than in these first weeks following my return to Russia in the final months of the war. . . . [We were] treated as though we were the bearers of some species of the plague"—which, of course, from the Soviet viewpoint, they were: the plague of skepticism.

Paradoxically, of the forces capable of bringing about a modification of ideology, the most practical and effective was the Soviet dictatorship itself. If Stalin was an ideologist, he was also a pragmatist. If he saw everything through the lenses of Marxism-Leninism, he also, as the infallible expositor of the faith, could reinterpret Marxism-Leninism to justify anything he wanted to do at any given moment. No doubt Roosevelt's ignorance of Marxism-Leninism was inexcusable and led to grievous miscalculations. But Roosevelt's efforts to work on and through Stalin were not so hopelessly naïve as it used to be fashionable to think. With the extraordinary instinct of a great political leader, Roosevelt intuitively understood that Stalin was the *only* lever available to the West against the Leninist ideology and the Soviet system. If Stalin could be reached, then alone was there a chance of getting the Russians to act contrary to the prescriptions of their faith. The best evidence is that Roosevelt retained a certain capacity to influence Stalin to the end; the nominal Soviet acquiescence in American universalism as late as Yalta was perhaps an indication of that. It is in this way that the death of Roosevelt was crucial—not in the vulgar sense that his policy was then reversed by his successor, which did not happen, but in the sense that no other American could hope to have the restraining impact on Stalin which Roosevelt might for a while have had.

Stalin alone could have made any difference. Yet Stalin, in spite of the impression of sobriety and realism he made on Westerners who saw him during the Second World War, was plainly a man of deep and morbid obsessions and compulsions. When he was still a young man, Lenin had criticized his rude and arbitrary ways. A reasonably authoritative observer (N. S. Khrushchev) later commented, "These negative characteristics of his developed steadily and during the last years acquired an absolutely insufferable character." His paranoia, probably set off by the suicide of his wife in 1932, led to the terrible purges of the mid-thirties and the wanton murder of thousands of his Bolshevik comrades. "Everywhere and in everything," Khrushchev says of this period, "he saw 'enemies,' 'double-dealers' and 'spies.' " The crisis of war evidently steadied him in some way, though Khrushchev speaks of his "nervousness and hysteria . . . even after the war began." The madness, so rigidly controlled for a time, burst out with new and shocking intensity in the postwar years. "After the war," Khrushchev testifies,

> the situation became even more complicated. Stalin became even more capricious, irritable and brutal; in particular, his suspicion grew. His persecution mania reached unbelievable dimensions. . . . He decided everything, without any consideration for anyone or anything.

> Stalin's wilfulness showed itself . . . also in the international relations of the Soviet Union. . . . He had completely lost a sense of reality; he demonstrated his suspicion and haughtiness not only in relation to individuals in the USSR, but in relation to whole parties and nations.

A revisionist fallacy has been to treat Stalin as just another Realpolitik statesman, as Second World War revisionists see Hitler as just another Stresemann or Bismarck. But the record makes it clear that in the end nothing could satisfy Stalin's paranoia. His own associates failed. Why does anyone suppose that any conceivable American policy would have succeeded?

An analysis of the origins of the Cold War which leaves out these factors —the intransigence of Leninist ideology, the sinister dynamics of a totalitarian society and the madness of Stalin—is obviously incomplete. It was these factors which made it hard for the West to accept the thesis that Russia was moved only by a desire to protect its security and would be satisfied by the control of Eastern Europe; it was these factors which charged the debate between universalism and spheres of influence with apocalyptic potentiality.

Leninism and totalitarianism created a structure of thought and behavior which made postwar collaboration between Russia and America—in any normal sense of civilized intercourse between national states—inherently impossible. The Soviet dictatorship of 1945 simply could not have survived such a collaboration. Indeed, nearly a quarter-century later, the Soviet régime, though it has meanwhile moved a good distance, could still hardly survive it without risking the release inside Russia of energies profoundly opposed to communist despotism. As for Stalin, he may have represented the only force in 1945 capable of overcoming Stalinism, but the very traits which enabled him to win absolute power expressed terrifying instabilities of mind and temperament and hardly offered a solid foundation for a peaceful world.

The difference between America and Russia in 1945 was that some Americans fundamentally believed that, over a long run, a modus vivendi with Russia was possible; while the Russians, so far as one can tell, believed in no more than a short-run modus vivendi with the United States.

Harriman and Kennan, this narrative has made clear, took the lead in warning Washington about the difficulties of short-run dealings with the Soviet Union. But both argued that, if the United States developed a rational policy and stuck to it, there would be, after long and rough passages, the prospect of eventual clearing. "I am, as you know," Harriman cabled Washington in early April, "a most earnest advocate of the closest possible understanding with the Soviet Union so that what I am saying relates only to how best to attain such understanding." Kennan has similarly made it clear that the function of his containment policy was "to tide us over a difficult time and bring us to the point where we could discuss effectively with the Russians the dangers and drawbacks this status quo involved, and to arrange with them for its peaceful replacement by a better and sounder one." The subsequent careers of both men attest to the honesty of these statements.

There is no corresponding evidence on the Russian side that anyone seriously sought a modus vivendi in these terms. Stalin's choice was whether his long-term ideological and national interests would be better served by a short-run truce with the West or by an immediate resumption of pressure. In October 1945 Stalin indicated to Harriman at Sochi that he planned to adopt the second course—that the Soviet Union was going isolationist. No doubt the succession of problems with the United States contributed to this decision, but the basic causes most probably lay elsewhere: in the developing situations in Eastern Europe, in Western Europe and in the United States.

In Eastern Europe, Stalin was still for a moment experimenting with techniques of control. But he must by now have begun to conclude that he had underestimated the hostility of the people to Russian dominion. The Hungarian elections in November would finally convince him that the Yalta formula was a road to anti-Soviet governments. At the same time, he was feeling more strongly than ever a sense of his opportunities in Western Europe. The other half of the Continent lay unexpectedly before him, politically demoralized, economically prostrate, militarily defenseless. The hunting would be better and safer than he had anticipated. As for the United States, the alacrity of postwar demobilization must have recalled Roosevelt's offhand remark at Yalta that "two years would be the limit" for keeping American troops in Europe. And, despite Dr. Eugene Varga's doubts about the imminence of American economic breakdown, Marxist theology assured Stalin that the United States was heading into a bitter post-war depression and would be consumed with its own problems. If the condition of Eastern Europe made unilateral action seem essential in the interests of Russian security, the condition of Western Europe and the United States offered new temptations for communist expansion. The Cold War was now in full swing.

It still had its year of modulations and accommodations. Secretary Byrnes conducted his long and fruitless campaign to persuade the Russians that America only sought governments in Eastern Europe "both friendly to the Soviet Union and representative of all the democratic elements of the country." Crises were surmounted in Trieste and Iran. Secretary Marshall evidently did not give up hope of a modus vivendi until the Moscow conference of foreign secretaries of March 1947. Even then, the Soviet Union was invited to participate in the Marshall Plan.

The point of no return came on July 2, 1947, when Molotov, after bringing 89 technical specialists with him to Paris and evincing initial interest in the project for European reconstruction, received the hot flash from the Kremlin, denounced the whole idea and walked out of the conference. For the next fifteen years the Cold War raged unabated, passing out of historical ambiguity into the realm of good versus evil and breeding on both sides simplifications, stereotypes and self-serving absolutes, often couched in interchangeable phrases. Under the pressure even America, for a deplorable decade, forsook its pragmatic and pluralist traditions, posed as God's appointed messenger to ignorant and sinful man and followed the Soviet example in looking to a world remade in its own image.

In retrospect, if it is impossible to see the Cold War as a case of American aggression and Russian response, it is also hard to see it as a pure case of Russian aggression and American response. "In what is truly tragic," wrote Hegel, "there must be valid moral powers on both the sides which come into collision. . . . Both suffer loss and yet both are mutually justified." In this sense, the Cold War had its tragic elements. The question remains whether it was an instance of Greek tragedy—as Auden has called it, "the tragedy of necessity," where the feeling aroused in the spectator is "What a pity it had to be this way"—or of Christian tragedy, "the tragedy of possibility," where the feeling aroused is "What a pity it was this way when it might have been otherwise."

Once something has happened, the historian is tempted to assume that it had to happen; but this may often be a highly unphilosophical assumption. The Cold War could have been avoided only if the Soviet Union had not been possessed by convictions both of the infallibility of the communist word and of the inevitability of a communist world. These convictions transformed an impasse between national states into a religious war, a tragedy of possibility into one of necessity. One might wish that America had preserved the poise and proportion of the first years of the Cold War and had not in time succumbed to its own forms of self-righteousness. But the most rational of American policies could hardly have averted the Cold War. Only today, as Russia begins to recede from its messianic mission and to accept, in practice if not yet in principle, the permanence of the world of diversity, only now can the hope flicker that this long, dreary, costly contest may at last be taking on forms less dramatic, less obsessive and less dangerous to the future of mankind.

Suggested Reading

Among the useful surveys of the Cold War are John Lukacs's *A New History of the Cold War*,* rev. ed. (1962), Paul Hammond's *American Foreign Policy Since 1945** (1969), Norman Graebner's *Cold War Diplomacy, 1945–1960** (1961), an analysis from a realist perspective; John Spanier's *American Foreign Policy Since World War II*, rev. 4th ed. (1971), from the same perspective; Walter LaFeber's *America, Russia, and the Cold War, 1945–1971*,* rev. ed. (1972), a revisionist volume; and Stephen Ambrose's *The Rise to Globalism** (1971), also a revisionist book.

The early intellectual sources for most later Cold War revisionism are William Appleman Williams' *American-Russian Relations, 1781–1947* (1952) and *The Tragedy of American Diplomacy*,* 2nd rev. ed., (1972), which explain the Cold War in terms of the ideology of Open Door expansionism, and D. F. Fleming's *The Cold War and Its Origins*, 2 vols. (1961), which wavers between Wilsonianism and Williams. Three important books by Gabriel Kolko offer a radical analysis of wartime and postwar foreign policy: *The Politics of War, 1943–1945** (1968), *The Roots of American Foreign Policy** (1969), and, with Joyce Kolko, *The Limits of Power: The World and United States Foreign Policy** (1972). Other important revisionist studies include Lloyd Gardner's *Architects of Illusion** (1970); Gar Alperovitz' *Atomic Diplomacy** (1965); Barton J. Bernstein, ed., *Politics and Policies of the Truman Administration** (1970); David Horowitz' *The Free World Colossus** (1965), which largely summarizes Fleming's *Cold War;* and David Horowitz, ed., *Corporations and the Cold War** (1969), a radical analysis. Other useful volumes include Richard Barnet's *Intervention and*

*Revolution** (1969), which explains U.S. expansion in terms of national security managers and not economic or ideological imperatives; Diane Shaver Clemens' *Yalta* (1971); David Green's *The Containment of Latin America* (1971); Isaac Deutscher's *Stalin** (1949), which stresses Stalin's conservatism in the war and postwar years; and Gar Alperovitz' *Cold War Essays** (1970), which in Chapter IV discusses the ideological sources of foreign policy (following Williams).

Adam Ulam in *Expansion and Co-Existence** (1968) discusses the origins of the Cold War, notes that it was rooted in competing state systems, but also contends that Stalin was responsible. In *The Rivals: America and Russia Since World War II* (1971), Ulam extended his analysis to include more on American policy but retained his general conclusions. John Gaddis in *The United States and the Origins of the Cold War, 1941–1947** (1972) suggests that Stalin, because he was more free to maneuver independently of public opinion, might be held primarily responsible for the Cold War, but Gaddis concludes that the Cold War emerged from various factors in Russia (the quest for security, the role of ideology, the personality of Stalin, and so on) and in the United States (the hope of self-determination, illusions of omnipotence, anti-Communism, public opinion, and so forth). Critics of Gaddis contend that he uses public opinion and popular anti-Communism as *deus ex machina*, that he provides considerable evidence that challenges his conclusions and framework, and that he even admits that Roosevelt did grant sections of Eastern Europe to the Soviets and that the Truman Administration sought to reverse that understanding—a reversal that Alperovitz and Bernstein stress in focusing American responsibility for the Cold War.

Critiques of Cold War revisionism include Robert Tucker's *The Radical Left and American Foreign Policy** (1971), which focuses usually on Kolko and Williams; Charles Maier's "Revisionism and the Interpretation of Cold War Origins," *Perspectives in American History*, IV (1970); Henry Pachter's "Revisionist Historians and the Cold War," *Dissent*, XVI (1968); Adam Ulam's "Re-Reading the Cold War," *Interplay*, III (1969); and Hans Morgenthau's "The Cold War as History," *New York Review of Books* (July 10, 1969), a review of Kolko's *Politics of War*. "Origins of the Post-war Crisis" and Paul Seabury and Brian Thomas' "Cold War Origins," both in *Journal of Contemporary History*, III (1968), are critical of revisionism, but focus on Fleming, Horowitz, and Alperovitz, not on Williams or Kolko (whose work appeared later).

Important memoirs and interpretations by former policy-makers include George Kennan's *Memoirs** (1967), Dean Acheson's *Present at the Creation** (1969), W. Averell Harriman's *America and Russia in a Changing World* (1970), Charles Bohlen's *The Transformation of American Foreign Policy* (1969), Louis Halle's *The Cold War as History** (1967), Harry S. Truman's *Memoirs* (2 vols., 1955–56), and James F. Byrnes' *Speaking Frankly* (1947).

* Also published in paperback edition.

The Cold War
in Asia:
Korea and Vietnam

From Korea to Vietnam: The Failure of a Policy Rooted in Fear

Stephen Ambrose

The Korean War, like the Vietnam war in the 1960s, upset America's European allies, disrupted American politics, and contributed to the early retirement of a Democratic president. But in contrast to the 1960s, in the 1950s Americans did not challenge the underlying assumptions of the Cold War. Indeed, the Korean War hardened these assumptions and further weakened the tiny organized left. For most Americans, debate on the war was limited to two issues. Had Secretary of State Dean Acheson invited North Korean aggression and thereby blundered or betrayed America? What were the appropriate tactics and goals in conducting the war? Nearly all Americans agreed on the interpretation of the origins of the war: North Korea had attacked South Korea and the Soviet Union was behind the plot. Challenges to this orthodoxy by the Communist and Progressive parties only confirmed the beliefs of most Americans that the organized left was anti-American and in bondage to the Soviet Union.

The origins of the war still remain unclear, and troubling questions have again risen. But for President Harry S. Truman on June 27, 1950 the issues, as he explained them to the nation, seemed clear: "The attack upon Korea makes it plain beyond all doubt

395

Near Saigon, Vietnam, 1967 (Philip Jones Griffiths from Magnum)

that communism has passed beyond the use of subversion to conquer independent nations and will now use armed invasion and war" (*Public Papers of The Presidents: Truman*, 1950, p. 492). Korea, he said privately, was "the Greece of the Far East. If we are tough enough now, there won't have to be any next step" (Cabell Phillips, *The Truman Presidency* [1966], p. 297). Relying on what was later called the domino theory, he told congressmen, "If we let Korea down, the Soviets will keep right on going and swallow up one piece of Asia after another. If we were to let Asia go, the Near East would collapse and . . . [also perhaps] Europe . . . [We must also aid] Indo-China, the Philippines, and Formosa" (Truman's meeting with Congressional leaders, June 26, 1950, Elsey Papers, Truman Library). The State Department promptly cabled an alert to key American diplomats: "Possible that Korea is only the first of series of coordinated actions on part of Soviets" (Glenn D. Paige, *The Korean Decision, June 24–30, 1950* [1959], p. 134).

In June 1950, as the Progressive Party then noted and some revisionist historians have since maintained, there was strong circumstantial evidence that the Korean War caught Stalin unprepared and there was no evidence that Russia had planned or sponsored the attack. Were American policy-makers simply wrong in their analysis? Or, as I. F. Stone suggested in 1952, had some helped start the war? Or did South Korea start it alone (*The Hidden History of the Korean War* [1952])? Many sources are still closed but the most plausible explanation is that North Korea did attack South Korea without prior approval or knowledge of the Soviets. This is the conclusion of Stephen Ambrose of Louisiana State University at New Orleans, who links the Korean War to the intervention in Vietnam and relates both to the earlier assumptions about the Cold War.

Focusing on the earlier containment doctrine and the Truman Administration's belief in the domino theory, Ambrose loosely explains the analysis of policy-makers in justifying intervention in Europe and Asia: They concluded that "the American economy had become so intimately related to the rest of the world . . . that it could not survive on a hostile globe." Aside from the Truman Doctrine in 1947 and the Marshall Plan in 1948, the

From Korea to Vietnam: The Failure of a Policy Rooted in Fear. From *The Progressive* (November 1970). Reprinted by permission of *The Progressive.*

Administration, according to Ambrose, was thwarted in implementing its anticommunist policies. The Congress would not provide the funds or programs for containment. A major program for rearmament (National Security Council document 68), which would have raised the military budget 200 to 300 per cent, was politically impossible without a crisis in international affairs that would convert recalcitrant legislators. Adding to Truman's problems, his Administration was under attack for the "loss" of China and would have to recast its China policy in order to quell the McCarthyites. The Administration had to prove that it could get tough with the communists.

These "needs were met" by the Korean War, concludes Ambrose. It reversed American policy toward Chiang, saved the Nationalist dictator, "proved" the aggressiveness of communism, and allowed Truman to secure NSC-68, with its huge military budget that included European rearmament. Unfortunately Ambrose remains unclear about whether Truman (1) cynically created the crisis because he believed he needed a crisis, or (2) merely misinterpreted the situation in Korea for ideological reasons and his misinterpretation contributed to the solution of many of his problems. At present there is insufficient evidence to establish the "created crisis" contention, and a careful historian investigating this issue would have to look not simply at Truman's initial commitment to South Korea on June 25 but also at the decisions by Truman and his associates in the next week that led to a full-scale commitment of U.S. ground troops.

Friendly critics of Ambrose might raise other objections. He implies, wrongly, that Truman had indicated before the war that he wanted NSC-68. Actually, as Ambrose briefly acknowledges, Truman was then still practicing fiscal orthodoxy and resisting Acheson's efforts, in June 1950, to expand the defense budget. In examining the Korean War, some revisionists might also extend Ambrose's analysis and stress that this conflict was a civil war, that there had been a long history of border clashes, that there was a guerrilla movement in the South, and that North Korea's cautious military strategy during the first days of the war suggests that she expected that her attack would unleash a revolt in the South ("The North Korean Labor Party's Factions," *Jiyu* [May 1967], translated in *Selected Summaries of Japanese Magazines*, June 26–July 3, 1967).

Unfriendly critics of Ambrose's analysis view the
early containment policy in Europe as wise and
necessary, contend that the Kremlin was eager to
extend its influence abroad, find that the American
intervention in Korea was useful, and believe that it
did for a time establish American credibility: the
willingness to fight to stop communism in Europe or
Asia. These critics would deny Ambrose's assertion
that containment was a "euphemism for the expansion
of American influence and dominance." Finally, they
might challenge Ambrose to be more specific about
precisely what assumptions he believes link Korea
and Vietnam. In addition to the domino theory and
the needs of the American economy, did policy-
makers believe they were acting to keep open the
options in the future to establish democracy in these
embattled areas? Or did they simply put forth that
argument for public consumption?

*O*n June 24, 1950, American foreign policy in the Pacific
was remarkably close to what some of the doves of 1970 want it to be today. At its heart, the policy of 1950 was one of maintaining positions of
strength on Asia's offshore islands, especially Japan, Okinawa, and the
Philippines, avoiding all entanglements on the mainland, and recognizing the
fundamental fact of Asian politics—the emergence of Communist China.

American troops had been withdrawn from South Korea, so there were
no American combat units anywhere on the Asian mainland. Mao Tse-
tung's troops were preparing an amphibious operation against Chiang Kai-
shek's remnants on Formosa, and President Harry Truman and Secretary of
State Dean Acheson had warned American ambassadors around the world to
be prepared for the repercussions stemming from the final fall of the Chinese Nationalist government.

In Indochina, the French were struggling, without much success, to eradi-
cate the Communist Ho Chi Minh and his Vietminh, while in the Philippines
the government faced a serious challenge from the Communist Huks. The
United States was giving tidbits of aid to both counterrevolutionary efforts
but, in view of the budget restraints at home and what was felt to be the
overwhelming need to rearm Europe (not to mention the United States
itself), scarcely enough to effect the outcome in Indochina. America's over-
all policy remained one of holding to its offshore bases, protected by the
world's most powerful navy, staying out of the Chinese civil war, and
avoiding any involvement on the mainland.

There had been two recent statements by Truman Administration spokesmen making this policy clear. On January 12, 1950, at the National Press
Club, Secretary Acheson had drawn a line on a map to indicate the Ameri-

can defensive perimeter—the line excluded South Korea and Formosa. And on May 2, Senator Tom Connally of Texas, chairman of the Senate Foreign Relations Committee, said he was afraid South Korea would have to be abandoned. He thought the Communists were going to overrun Korea when they got ready, just as they "will overrun Formosa." Connally said he did not think Korea was "very greatly important. It has been testified before us that Japan, Okinawa, and the Philippines make the chain of defense which is absolutely necessary."

That remained the American position until June 25, 1950, the day hostilities began in Korea. Then, after only a few hours of meetings with Acheson and a select group of top advisers, without consulting Congress or the United Nations or America's European allies, Mr. Truman announced that he was sending supplies to South Korea, immediately increasing aid to the French in Indochina and to the Philippine government, and ordering the U.S. Seventh Fleet to sail between the Chinese mainland and Formosa to prevent the expected invasion of the island by the Communists. Mr. Truman had, in short, involved the United States in four civil wars at once, and, except in the Philippines, all in areas the Americans had previously regarded as outside their sphere of influence. The United States was *on* the Asian mainland.

These were sweeping policy decisions, among the most important of the entire Cold War, carrying with them enormous long-term implications. They were hardly the kind that a government ordinarily makes without deliberation. Yet Mr. Truman later claimed that he made them solely as a result of the Korean War, the outbreak of which astonished him—as it supposedly did General Douglas MacArthur's headquarters in Tokyo—as much "as if the sun had suddenly gone out." For a man who had been surprised, Mr. Truman had recovered with amazing speed.

Actually, as I. F. Stone has shown in his book, *The Hidden History of the Korean War*, there was no surprise. The Americans had a good general idea of what was coming and had their countermeasures prepared. Intelligence reports on North Korean intentions had been specific enough to allow the U.S. State Department, days before the attack, to prepare a resolution to submit to the Security Council of the United Nations condemning North Korea for aggression.

At the time, the Soviet Union was boycotting the United Nations for its refusal to seat Red China; the State Department was prepared to take its resolution to the General Assembly if the Russians came back to the Security Council and exercised their veto. But the Soviets did not return, for they had been caught off guard. Stalin, in fact, seems to have been the most surprised by the outbreak of hostilities; certainly the Americans were much better prepared to move for U.N. action than the Russians were. The resolution the Americans pushed through the Security Council on the day of the attack branded the North Koreans as aggressors, demanded a cessation of hostilities, and requested a withdrawal behind the thirty-eighth parallel. The resolution was a brilliant stroke, for without any investigation at all it established war guilt and put the United Nations behind the official American version.

The speed and scope of the American response to the Korean War were truly impressive. So were the Cold War advantages that accrued. America eventually established a costly hegemony over non-Communist Asia, gained gigantic (and strategically invaluable) military bases for itself in South Korea, Formosa, Indochina, and Thailand, aroused public support for an enormously increased Department of Defense budget (from $13 billion in 1950 to $50 billion the next year), made possible European, including West German, rearmament, and in general put the United States on a permanent Cold War footing. In addition, the Americans saved the governments of Chiang in Formosa and Syngman Rhee in South Korea from certain extinction. After a thorough examination of these and other pieces of circumstantial evidence, Stone, and historian D. F. Fleming, in his work, *The Cold War and Its Origins*, have charged that the South Koreans—with American support—began the war.

Before that accusation can be examined, however, it is necessary to understand the basis of the Truman policy. How did it come about that the United States became committed to the containment of Communism everywhere, whatever the cost? Which is only another way of asking, "How did we get on the Asian mainland?" and "How did we get to Vietnam?"

The United States fights in Vietnam for many reasons, but the chief reason is a set of assumptions about the nature of the world, assumptions given wide currency by our policy-makers. These views were formed largely by the events preceding the Korean War and by the interpretation of the origins of that war. It is to that conflict we must look if we are to understand American policy today.

When Harry Truman became President of the United States, he led a nation anxious to return to traditional civil-military relations and the historic American foreign policy of noninvolvement. The public, as it demonstrated by electing a Republican Congress in 1946, wanted an up-dated version of Harding's return to normalcy, with the emphasis on a speedy demobilization from World War II, lower taxes, less Government interference in the economy, and a foreign policy that would rely on the atomic bomb and/or the United Nations to keep the peace. There was no general perception of a threat to America's vital interests.

Mr. Truman and his senior advisers were adamantly opposed to the budding isolationism, primarily because they had a different set of assumptions. They did see a threat, one posed by monolithic Communism directed from the Kremlin, that aimed at world conquest and whose tactics—in the words of George Kennan, a State Department planner and one of the authors of the containment of Communism concept—would be "to make sure that it has filled every nook and cranny available to it in the basin of world power." The Truman Administration was convinced that only the United States could prevent the Kremlin from achieving its victory, but to do so it would have to swing American public opinion to a more "realistic" view of the nature of the world.

In March, 1947, Mr. Truman led the way when he called on Congress to provide aid to the Greek government, the rather shabby rightist monarchy which was threatened by an indigenous guerrilla movement. Mr. Truman assumed that the Greek Communists were directed and aided by Stalin (a judgment almost no historian would accept today). As the then Under Secretary of State Dean Acheson put it, if Greece were lost, Turkey would be untenable. Russia would move in and take control of the Dardanelles, with the "clearest implications" for the Middle East. Morale would sink in Italy, Germany, and France. Acheson was describing what would later be called the domino theory, although—as always—he was more colorful in his choice of symbols. One rotten apple, Acheson said, would infect the whole barrel.

The biggest apple of them all, the United States, would not escape, the theory contended. The American economy had become so intimately related to the rest of the world, especially Europe and Latin America, that it could not survive on a hostile globe. "The whole world should adopt the American system," Mr. Truman declared in a speech of March 6, 1947. "The American system can survive in America only if it becomes a world system."

To persuade the American people, and the economy-minded Republican Congress, to pay the cost of containing Communism and spreading the American economic system, Mr. Truman needed a cause more inspiring than one of providing support for the Greek monarchy. He provided it. "We must assist free peoples to work out their destinies in their own way," he declared on March 12, 1947, in asking for aid to Greece, thereby making an unlimited and consequently indiscriminate commitment. "At the present moment in world history every nation must choose between alternative ways of life," he asserted, thereby creating a sense of permanent and universal crisis.

The critics, ranging from Walter Lippmann and publications like *The Progressive* to Senator Robert Taft, warned that such globalism would eventually erode American political institutions, subvert domestic efforts at reform, and ruin the economy, but Mr. Truman ignored them, for he pursued a greater goal. America's mission was "to insure the peaceful development of nations, free from coercion . . . to make possible lasting freedom and independence for all."

The messianic hope of redeeming history drove President Truman. "I believe that it must be the policy of the United States to support free peoples who are resisting attempted subjugation by armed minorities or by outside pressures," he declared, which amounted to a definition of what was to become American policy for the next twenty years. It was a brilliant political speech and it worked, as Congress gave the President the money he wanted.

The following year, 1948, Mr. Truman got the Marshall Plan through the same Republican Congress, thereby starting Western Europe on the road to recovery and insuring that France, Britain, and West Germany would stick to the United States in any confrontation with the Soviet Union. Communism in Europe had been contained, or so it seemed.

The trouble was that, aside from the millions given to Greece and Turkey, and the extensive Marshall Plan aid, Congress was unwilling to provide the funds needed for containment. Mr. Truman could not get Universal Military Training; he could not save the draft; America's armed forces continued to dwindle; the American stockpile of atomic weapons was by no means sufficient to deter the Red Army if it chose to march across the Elbe River; and the Europeans showed no inclination to tamper with their budding prosperity by assuming the cost of rearming. America had a policy in Europe—containment—but it did not have the military muscle to implement it if the 175 Russian divisions marched; nor did the American or Western European peoples show the slightest inclination to pay the heavy costs involved in building that muscle. By June, 1950, the Truman Administration had reached an impasse in Europe.

At home, Truman faced criticism of his earlier foreign policy. The West had lost Czechoslovakia, but Mr. Truman boasted that he had saved Greece, Turkey, Italy, and Western Europe. The use of such concepts as "won" or "lost," however, had serious repercussions. The Republicans had not made an issue of foreign policy in the 1948 elections (only third-party Presidential candidate Henry Wallace did), and by 1950 they tended to believe that their failure to do so was a key factor in their defeat. They began, almost gleefully, to charge the Truman Administration with having "lost" China and with losing the Philippines, Formosa, South Korea, and Indochina. The Republicans, led by Senator Joseph McCarthy, began to insist that the Truman Administration, and most notably Secretary Acheson, was soft on Communism, or worse.

The Democrats were bewildered and angry. With some justice, they wondered what more they could have done to stand up to the Soviets, especially in view of the funds available, funds drastically limited by the very Republicans who now demanded blood for the State Department's shortcomings. Mr. Truman desperately wanted to extend containment to Asia, but he could not even implement it in Europe.

Mr. Truman's frustrations, in the spring of 1950, were great. Foreign and military policy were moving in opposite directions. While Acheson advocated ever greater commitments to the non-Communist world, Louis Johnson, a curious kind of Secretary of Defense, was scuttling the Navy's supercarrier and doing everything he could to keep the Defense Department budget under $13 billion, all in accord with Mr. Truman's own policy of balancing the budget. Mr. Truman had commissioned a major study of America's strategic position; the final result reached his desk in early June, 1950, as National Security Council paper number 68 (thereafter known as NSC 68). Still classified and unpublished twenty years later, it was one of the key historic documents of the Cold War. NSC 68, as Senator Henry Jackson, Washington Democrat, observed, was "the first comprehensive statement of a national strategy."

NSC 68 advocated, in the words of one of its authors, "an immediate and large-scale build-up in our military and general strength and that of our allies with the intention of righting the power balance." It did so on the basis of an analysis of the Soviet Union which held that the Soviets were not only dedicated to preserving their own power and ideology but to extending and consolidating power by absorbing new satellites and weakening their enemies. Implicit in the analysis was the idea that whenever the West lost a position of strength, whether it be a military base or a colony undergoing a war of national liberation, the Kremlin was behind it. This came close to saying that all change was directed by the Communists and should be resisted. The analysis also assumed that if America were willing to try, it could stop change.

The paper was realistic in assessing what it would cost America to become the world policeman. Instead of the $13 billion the Truman Administration was planning on spending annually on defense, NSC 68 wanted to start with $35 billion in fiscal year 1951 and move up to $50 billion a year later. Politically, this was impossible. Truman recognized, as he later wrote, that NSC 68 "meant a great military effort in time of peace. It meant doubling or tripling the budget, increasing taxes heavily, and imposing various kinds of economic controls. It meant a great change in our normal peacetime way of doing things." He refused to allow any publicity about NSC 68 and indicated that he would do nothing about revising the budget until after the Congressional elections in November, 1950. He knew that without a major crisis there was no chance of selling the program to the Congress or to the country.

The contradictory pressures on foreign policy, meanwhile, were almost maddening. While President Truman and Acheson defended themselves from charges of having given China to Mao, they simultaneously had to prepare for even more embarrassments, most notably the expected loss of Formosa and South Korea.

In Korea, all was tension. Postwar Soviet-American efforts to unify the country, where American troops had occupied the area south of the thirty-eighth parallel, and Russia the area to the north, had achieved nothing. In 1947 the United States had submitted the Korean question to the U.N. General Assembly for disposition. Russia, fearful of the implications, had refused to go along. The Soviets reasoned that if the question of Korea could be given to the General Assembly, where the United States controlled a voting majority, nothing would prevent the United States from giving the problem of divided Germany to the Assembly too. The Soviets therefore refused to allow the U.N. Commission on Korea to enter North Korea.

Elections were held in South Korea in May, 1948; Syngman Rhee became president. The Russians set up a government in North Korea. Both the United States and the Soviets withdrew their occupation troops; both continued to give military aid to their respective zones, although the Russians did so on a larger scale.

Rhee was a petty dictator and an embarrassment to the United States. In January, 1950, Philip C. Jessup, U.S. Ambassador-at-large, told the Korean National Assembly that the United States was dissatisfied with the severe restraints on civil liberties which it had imposed. In April, Acheson told Rhee flatly that he either had to hold previously scheduled but consistently delayed elections or lose American aid. Rhee gave in, although on the eve of the elections he arrested thirty of his leading opponents in anti-Communist raids. Still his party collected only forty-eight seats, with 120 going to other parties, mostly on the left. The new Assembly then began to indicate that it wanted to consider unification with the North. Rhee was faced with the total loss of his position.

There was a curious incident shortly after the South Korean elections, one that none of the historians of the Korean War has examined in depth. On June 9 the radio at Pyongyang, North Korea's capital, denounced the recent elections in the South as fraudulent and called for a general election throughout Korea. The North Koreans proposed an election on August 5 of a general legislative organ that would meet in Seoul, capital of South Korea. Rhee, his prime minister, and the U.N. Commission in Korea would all be barred.

Rhee scoffed at the call for elections, dismissing it as "poppycock propaganda" but the U.N. Commission indicated that it was interested, and on June 11, John Gaillard, an American member of the Commission, crossed the thirty-eighth parallel to talk to three North Korean representatives. They gave him copies of the appeal for an election, then crossed the parallel themselves with hundreds of copies of the appeal, which they intended to distribute to the South Koreans. Rhee's police immediately arrested them. There appears to be no evidence that Washington ever explored Pyongyang's suggestion for general elections, and this raises interesting questions about the entire U.S. policy regarding Korea.

Events everywhere in Asia were moving towards a crisis. The British were out of India, revolt was stirring in Malaya, and the Dutch had been forced to leave Indonesia. In Indochina, the French were barely able to hold on. Nearly all the independent Asian governments were hostile to the West. The substitution of native leaders, usually radical, for the white rulers in Asia carried with it terrifying implications for Washington. There was a real possibility that American corporations would lose both their access to the raw materials (especially metals) and to the markets of Southeast Asia. Strategically, none of the new governments would be able to serve as an effective counter to the Chinese, which meant an end to the balance of power in Asia. Only Rhee in South Korea and Chiang in Formosa swam against the powerful tide, and the West did not have the military means available at that time to keep either of its proxies in power. What the Americans liked to call "stability in Asia" was threatened.

The crisis was most acute in China, for if the Chinese Communists drove Chiang off Formosa they would complete their victory and eventually the United States would have to recognize the Communists as the legitimate government of China, which would mean—among other things—giving Chiang's seat on the U.N. Security Council to Mao. The United States would no longer be able to regard Chiang as head of a government or maintain the fiction that he would someday return to his rightful place as ruler of all of China. This in turn would require a new definition of the economic and political relations between China and the United States.

Since late 1949, President Truman had consistently refused to provide aid to Chiang, who had proved to be a poor investment at best. The President insisted—rather late in the game—that the United States would not be drawn into the Chinese civil war. This policy was consistent with the European orientation of the Truman Administration and, in terms of the money Congress had made available for foreign aid, it was realistic. Its only possible outcome, however, was an end to Chiang's pretensions and an American acceptance of the Chinese Communists among the family of nations.

The domestic political results for the Democrats of such a course of events were frightening to contemplate. Already former President Herbert Hoover had joined with Senator Taft in demanding that the U.S. Pacific Fleet be used to prevent an invasion of Formosa, while other Republicans advocated using the fleet to carry Chiang's forces back to the mainland for the reconquest of China. If Mr. Truman wished to quiet the McCarthyites at all, he would have to rethink his China policy.

By June, 1950, a series of desperate needs had come together. Mr. Truman had to have a crisis to sell the NSC 68 program of a huge U.S. military buildup. Chiang could not hold on, nor could Rhee, without an American commitment; the U.S. Air Force and Navy needed a justification to retain their bases in Japan; the Democrats had to prove that they could get tough with the Communists. Most of all, the Americans had to establish themselves on the mainland before the white man was driven out of Asia and its islands forever.

The needs were met on June 25, 1950. The outbreak of the Korean War came as a godsend to Chiang, Rhee, and the Truman Administration. Since it "proved" the aggressiveness of international Communism, the war enabled Mr. Truman to push through the NSC 68 program with its vastly increased military budgets, American aid for European rearmament, and an enormously expanded American military presence in Asia.

When President Truman announced that the Seventh Fleet was going to the Formosan Straits, Peiping immediately charged that the Pentagon was seeking to establish a military base on Chinese territory and asked the United Nations to order the Americans to withdraw. Warren Austin, U.S. Ambassador to the United Nations, refuted the charge indignantly, while Mr. Truman declared that the United States "would not seek any special position or privilege on Formosa." Jakob Malik, the Russian delegate, then accused the United States of lusting for bases in Formosa and supported his charge by quoting General MacArthur's statements to the effect that America intended to establish and hold air fields on the island. Mr. Truman rejoined that MacArthur did not speak for the Administration. Yet, as everyone knows, the United States now has enormous air bases on Formosa. By the same token, the Americans declared throughout the Korean War that they had no intention of maintaining troops there once the conflict ended. Lyndon Johnson was to say the same thing about Vietnam.

For more than a decade and a half after the Korean War began, almost no one seriously questioned the Truman Administration's interpretation of the cause of the war, which held that it began because Stalin told the North Koreans to go ahead and attack South Korea. This interpretation strengthened the notion that there was an international Communist conspiracy, centered in the Kremlin, and that therefore all wars of national liberation were carried out by Russian proxies solely to serve the interests of the Soviet Union. This view in turn allowed the Americans to dash into Lebanon at President Eisenhower's orders, to attempt by force, with President Kennedy's approval, to overthrow Castro, to intervene in the Dominican Republic at President Johnson's command, and most of all to involve this country in Vietnam.

The interpretation of the causes of the Korean War, in short, has helped shape American assumptions about the nature of the world. The interpretation may conceivably be correct, but there are questions concerning it that must be asked, and answered, before it can be fully accepted. The standard explanation, for example, as to why the Russians were not in the United Nations during the critical period when the Korean War began, is that Stalin simply made a mistake. He did not think the Americans would return to the Korean peninsula, nor did he expect the United States to go to the United Nations and ask for a condemnation of aggression by North Korea. But Stalin was ordinarily a cautious man who made few mistakes.

The explanation that he was surprised by the American reaction, even if he was, is clearly unsatisfactory, for it leaves unanswered a further query: why did not Stalin send his ambassador back to the Security Council after the first U.S. resolution went through on June 25, the day war broke out, branding North Korea as the aggressor?

The importance of the second question lies in the fact that not until June 27—two days after the outbreak of hostilities—did the United States introduce the second resolution—passed that day—which recommended to the members of the United Nations that they aid South Korea in restoring peace. It was the June 27 resolution which gave the United States U.N. cover for its essentially unilateral action in Korea. Those who wish to maintain that the Russians started the North Koreans on their way south must explain why the Soviets were not in the United Nations to protect their own interests in that world body.

The second mystery about the Soviets is why they took no action elsewhere. President Truman and Acheson assumed from the start that the Korean War was a feint. They reasoned that Stalin wanted them to put America's strength into the Pacific so that he could then march against a defenseless West Europe. The Americans countered this expected strategy by concentrating their military build-up in Europe, not Korea (much to General MacArthur's disgust; indeed, this was a basic cause of the Truman-MacArthur controversy).

Administration supporters have argued that Stalin did not move in Europe only because the United States beat him to the punch. The trouble with that view is that it took months for the Americans to get any strength into Europe; in the meantime, Stalin did nothing. If he started the Korean War as part of a worldwide offensive, as Mr. Truman argued, where was the rest of the offensive?

Finally, if the Russians started the whole thing, where were they at the critical moment? The North Koreans pushed the South Koreans and the small American contingent steadily south until early August, when MacArthur's forces were pinned into a beachhead around Pusan. But the North Koreans were incapable of delivering the final blow and had to watch, more or less helplessly, as MacArthur built up his strength and made his position invulnerable.

Red Army officers must have watched from afar with anguish, for their experience against the Germans only five years earlier had made them the world's leading experts on knocking out defensive positions. If Russia did indeed urge the North Koreans to attack, and if Stalin's aim was in fact to conquer the peninsula, why were no Red Army advisers sent to the North Koreans at the decisive moment? MacArthur himself testified later that no Russians had ever been seen anywhere in the Korean peninsula during the war. Once the Americans had intervened, but before they arrived in great strength, why did not the Russians send a few "volunteer" units to Korea to insure the final push of MacArthur's forces into the sea?

The idea that Russia and China acted in concert in starting the war has, fortunately, long since disappeared. A 1960 RAND Corporation study, *China Crosses the Yalu*, by Allen S. Whiting, concluded that the Chinese were the most surprised of anyone by the outbreak of hostilities in Korea. Mao's two major priorities in June, 1950, were to use his army to reconstruct China and to invade Formosa. His troop dispositions reflected these priorities, and were about as bad as they possibly could have been to support a war in Korea. Indeed, the big losers in the war—aside from the Korean people—were the Chinese, who lost their chance to grab Formosa and who had to divert desperately needed human and material resources from reconstruction and the building of a new society to keep American troops from the Yalu River at China's southern door. The Russians lost too, for Stalin's worst fears were realized as a direct result of the war—West Germany was rearmed and integrated into an anti-Soviet military alliance, and the United States began a massive rearmament program.

The big winners were Chiang, Rhee, and the Truman Administration, which extended containment to Asia, gained additional military bases in the Far East, unilaterally wrote the Japanese peace treaty, retained American markets and access to the natural resources of Southeast Asia, proved to the public that it was not "soft on Communism," and in general reversed the tide of change—at least for a time—that had been running so strongly against the white man in the Far East.

As noted earlier, I. F. Stone and D. F. Fleming have carefully examined the problem of whose needs were met by the Korean War, and who won and who lost, and concluded that the North Koreans were merely responding to aggression by Rhee, an aggression encouraged by Chiang and the United States. But while the circumstantial evidence is strong, these charges almost certainly go too far. The North Korean offensive was too strong, too well coordinated, and too successful to be simply a counterattack.

But granting that the North Koreans were the aggressors does not automatically make the Truman Administration interpretation of the origins of the war correct. There are too many questions that must be answered before it can be accepted.

The most reasonable tentative conclusion is that the North Koreans took matters into their own hands. They decided they could over-run the peninsula before the Americans could reinforce the South Koreans—an assessment that was not far wrong—and they moved. They probably expected that the United States would not intervene at all. Certainly we have had sufficient evidence in the late 1960s of North Korean independence from the Kremlin to make this judgment reasonable.

For our time, the important point is that Mr. Truman seized the opportunity to extend containment to the Asian mainland, thereby reversing entirely—and evidently permanently—America's Pacific policy, on the basis of a highly dubious interpretation of the causes of the conflict, based in turn on a belief in an international Communist conspiracy that never existed. The irony is that of all Mr. Truman's dramatic actions in the last week of June, 1950, the least noticed turned out to be the most important—the increase in U.S. aid to the French in Indochina that demonstrated his determination to prevent Ho Chi Minh from gaining control of Vietnam.

The seeming inevitability of American foreign policy in the postwar period—the Russians act, we react to preserve freedom—rests, in its essentials, on one basic assumption. President Truman, Acheson, and the other architects of the policy of containment (which was never more than an euphemism for the expansion of American influence and dominance) believed—or at least professed to believe—that the Kremlin had a "strategy" for world conquest.

For those who demanded proof of Stalin's intentions, the Administration pointed above all to the supposed Russian influence and support for the Greek rebels, Ho Chi Minh, and the North Koreans. Historians, however, are finding it extraordinarily difficult to come by any solid evidence of Russian involvement on a significant scale in Greece, Indochina, or even North Korea (after 1948).

The obsessive American fears, in short, not to mention the violent American reaction, were based on assumptions that were almost surely wrong. Taking into account all that flowed from those assumptions—McCarthyism, the Cold War, ABMs, Indochina, and so on—this is the major tragedy of our times.

How Could Vietnam Happen? An Autopsy

James Thomson, Jr.

No foreign war in the nation's history has so torn apart American society as has the Vietnam war. By 1968 already the war had become a major political issue, dividing the Democratic Party and rocking the nation's campuses. Between 1966 and 1972 the war cost the United States well over $130 billion in direct military expenditures. Up to the autumn of 1972 the United States had suffered more than 350,000 casualties, including more than 45,000 fatalities, thereby making this war the fourth bloodiest in American history.

Defenders of the American presence in Vietnam often contend that Communism must be halted there in order, variously, to contain China, to defend freedom, to restore democracy, to prevent the "domino" effect, and to protect American security. The continuing war, according to this analysis, is in America's national interest and South Vietnam must not be "abandoned."

Liberal and conservative opponents, contending that the "free world" is not seriously threatened by events in Vietnam, rebut various portions of the arguments supporting the war. To these critics, the war is a mistake: a blunder or series of blunders flowing (in various combinations) from poor intelligence, bureaucratic inertia and loyalty, excessive military influence, the pride of policy-makers, and out-dated anti-Communism. This general analysis, supple in details, has been used to explain the origins of American military intervention under Kennedy, as well as the later escalation of the war under Johnson and Nixon.

Writing within this loose framework, James Thomson, Jr., a Harvard historian who served on the White House and State Department staffs in the Kennedy and early Johnson years, offers his analysis of "How Could Vietnam Happen?" Part of the explanation, he contends, lies in the "legacy of the fifties"—a belief that China was on the march, a fear of defeats in Asia (like the earlier "loss" of China), and the exclusion of China experts from the councils of government. Linked to this set of reasons, he contends, was the subtle racism among policy-makers, who believed that Asian life was cheap, and the constraining pressure of bureaucracy on dissent within the government. Admitting his own doubts about the war at an early stage, he usefully describes how dissent is "domesticated." The bureaucracy, he suggests, can be powerful, subtle, and overwhelming.

His line of interpretation has been criticized from two perspectives—one liberal and the other radical. From the liberal side, Leslie Gelb, another adviser and an author of the Pentagon Papers, has rebutted the "mistake" theory while acknowledging the influence of portions of what Thomson calls the "legacy of the fifties" ("Vietnam: The System Worked," *Foreign Policy*, I [1971]). Gelb contends that neither the Kennedy nor Johnson Administrations expected to win in Vietnam: they were not significantly misguided by the military or by intelligence reports, but, rather, the Administrations devised policies in order to gain time, in order to stave off the defeat in Vietnam, which they considered politically disastrous abroad and at home. Defeat, according to Gelb, would weaken America's overall position in international affairs. For Gelb, as for Thomson, the Democrats feared another "loss" in Asia and the unleashing of a new wave of McCarthyism. These fears influenced American policy, but it was a policy conceived simply to delay disaster, not to win.

In contrast, radical analysts, critical of both Gelb's

How Could Vietnam Happen? An Autopsy. From *Atlantic Monthly*, CCXXI (April 1968), pp. 47–53. Copyright © 1968 by The Atlantic Monthly Company, Boston, Mass. Reprinted by permission of The Atlantic Monthly Company and the author.

and Thomson's conclusions, contend that intervention in Vietnam is simply the most recent, and most costly, example of the long-run American policy of anti-Communism and opposition to left-wing revolutions abroad. For evidence, they point to the record of postwar interventions: Greece (the Truman Doctrine) in 1947, the Philippines in 1949, Korea (the Korean War) in 1950, Iran in 1953, Guatamala in 1954, Lebanon in 1958, the Bay of Pigs in 1961, and the Dominican Republic in 1965. According to the radical analysis, American leaders have believed that the American political economy depended on stopping the spread of Communism and blocking left-wing revolution: each threatened to remove nations from the international capitalist system, to close markets for goods and investments, to end access to raw materials, to disrupt international trade patterns, to create serious economic and political dislocations, and ultimately to endanger American prosperity and democracy. The belief in the domino theory, the radicals contend, explains American intervention.

Truman, Eisenhower, Kennedy, Johnson, and Nixon, radicals note, have all honestly subscribed to the domino theory in justifying much of their policies. Eisenhower, in 1954, clearly explained this theory in the case of Indo-China:

You have a row of dominoes set up, you knock over the first one and what will happen to the last one is the certainty that it will go over very quickly. So you could have a beginning of a disintegration that would have the most profound influences.

Now, with respect to the first one, two of the items from this particular area that the world uses are tin and tungsten. They are very important. There are others, of course, the rubber plantations and so on.

Then with respect to more people passing under this domination, Asia, after all, has already lost some 450 million of its peoples to the Communist dictatorship, and we simply can't afford greater losses.

But when we come to the possible sequence of events, the loss of Indochina, of Burma, of Thailand, of the Peninsula, and Indonesia following, now you begin to talk about areas that not only multiply the disadvantages that you would suffer through loss of materials, sources of materials, but now you are talking really about millions and millions and millions of people.

Finally, the geographical position achieved thereby does many things. It turns the so-called island

*defensive chain of Japan, Formosa, of the Philippines
and to the southward; it moves in to threaten Australia
and New Zealand.*

*It takes away, in its economic aspects, that region
that Japan must have as a trading area or Japan, in
turn, will have only one place in the world to go—that
is, toward the Communist areas in order to live.*

*So, the possible consequences of the loss are just
incalculable to the free world* (Eisenhower press
conference, April 7, 1954, in Public Papers . . .
Eisenhower, 1954, p. 383).

The domino theory, contrary to some of its critics,
does not assume that military expansion is necessarily
the preeminent threat of Communism. As Eisenhower
explains in the passage above, the domino process can
be more subtle and involves trade.

In his inaugural address, Eisenhower, echoing the
analysis of the Truman Administration, had offered a
larger analysis of the American political economy:

*No free people can for long cling to any privilege or
enjoy any safety in economic solitude. For all our
own material might, even we need markets in the
world for the surpluses of our farms and our factories.
Equally, we need for these same farms and factories
vital materials and products of distant lands. This basic
law of interdependence, so manifest in the commerce
of peace, applies with thousand-fold intensity in the
event of war* (Eisenhower speech of January 20, 1953,
in Public Papers . . . Eisenhower, 1953, p. 4).

The issue for radicals is not whether policy-makers
sincerely believed in the domino theory but whether
the theory is correct. Put simply, was intervention
essential to preserving American capitalism or was
intervention dictated by a dysfuntional ideology? Is
economic expansion abroad essential for American
capitalism? In addition, were American leaders sincere
in wanting to create democracy abroad? On these
issues radicals divide. According to some, hostility to
communism is inevitable and necessary under
capitalism. For others, such hostility is the result of a
flawed, but correctable, ideology. Regardless of their
conclusions on these matters, radicals must go beyond
ideology or theories of economic imperatives to
explain why some policy-makers concluded that
intervention in Vietnam had become too costly while
others continued to support the venture. In addressing
this set of questions, radicals have to look at such

issues as bureaucracy, pride, personality, and political fears and expectations—the very issues on which most conservative and liberal opponents of the war concentrate.

The dialog between radicals and other opponents of the war raises questions that Thomson's essay does not adequately define: What was the basic mistake in Vietnam? Armed intervention? Or not withdrawing when the cost rose dramatically? For most liberal and conservative opponents of the war, the basic error was the continued miscalculation of costs after the early intervention. For radicals, however, the error was not tactical but moral and fundamentally politico-economic: intervention itself.

*A*s a case study in the making of foreign policy, the Vietnam War will fascinate historians and social scientists for many decades to come. One question that will certainly be asked: How did men of superior ability, sound training, and high ideals—American policy-makers of the 1960s—create such costly and divisive policy?

As one who watched the decision-making process in Washington from 1961 to 1966 under Presidents Kennedy and Johnson, I can suggest a preliminary answer. I can do so by briefly listing some of the factors that seemed to me to shape our Vietnam policy during my years as an East Asia specialist at the State Department and the White House. I shall deal largely with Washington as I saw or sensed it, and not with Saigon, where I have spent but a scant three days, in the entourage of the Vice President, or with other decision centers, the capitals of interested parties. Nor will I deal with other important parts of the record: Vietnam's history prior to 1961, for instance, or the overall course of America's relations with Vietnam.

Yet a first and central ingredient in these years of Vietnam decisions does involve history. The ingredient was *the legacy of the 1950s*—by which I mean the so-called "loss of China," the Korean War, and the Far East policy of Secretary of State Dulles.

This legacy had an institution by-product for the Kennedy Administration: in 1961 the U.S. government's East Asian establishment was undoubtedly the most rigid and doctrinaire of Washington's regional divisions in foreign affairs. This was especially true at the Department of State, where the incoming Administration found the Bureau of Far Eastern Affairs the hardest nut to crack. It was a bureau that had been purged of its best China expertise, and of farsighted, dispassionate men, as a result of McCarthyism. Its members were generally committed to one policy line: the close containment and isolation of mainland China, the harassment of "neutralist" nations which sought to avoid alignment with either Washington or Peking, and the maintenance of a network of alliances with anti-Communist client states on China's periphery.

Another aspect of the legacy was the special vulnerability and sensitivity of the new Democratic Administration on Far East policy issues. The memory of the McCarthy era was still very sharp, and Kennedy's margin of victory was too thin. The 1960 Offshore Islands TV debate between Kennedy and Nixon had shown the President-elect the perils of "fresh thinking." The Administration was inherently leery of moving too fast on Asia. As a result, the Far East Bureau (now the Bureau of East Asian and Pacific Affairs) was the last one to be overhauled. Not until Averell Harriman was brought in as Assistant Secretary in December, 1961, were significant personnel changes attempted, and it took Harriman several months to make a deep imprint on the bureau because of his necessary preoccupation with the Laos settlement. Once he did so, there was virtually no effort to bring back the purged or exiled East Asia experts.

There were other important by-products of this "legacy of the fifties":

The new Administration inherited and somewhat shared *a general perception of China-on-the-march*—a sense of China's vastness, its numbers, its belligerence; a revived sense, perhaps, of the Golden Horde. This was a perception fed by Chinese intervention in the Korean War (an intervention actually based on appallingly bad communications and mutual miscalculation on the part of Washington and Peking; but the careful unraveling of that tragedy, which scholars have accomplished, had not yet become part of the conventional wisdom).

The new Administration inherited and briefly accepted *a monolithic conception of the Communist bloc*. Despite much earlier predictions and reports by outside analysts, policy-makers did not begin to accept the reality and possible finality of the Sino-Soviet split until the first weeks of 1962. The inevitably corrosive impact of competing nationalisms on Communism was largely ignored.

The new Administration inherited and to some extent shared the *"domino theory" about Asia*. This theory resulted from profound ignorance of Asian history and hence ignorance of the radical differences among Asian nations and societies. It resulted from a blindness to the power and resilience of Asian nationalisms. (It may also have resulted from a subconscious sense that, since "all Asians look alike," all Asian nations will act alike.) As a theory, the domino fallacy was not merely inaccurate but also insulting to Asian nations; yet it has continued to this day to beguile men who should know better.

Finally, the legacy of the fifties was apparently compounded by an uneasy sense of a worldwide Communist challenge to the new Administration after the Bay of Pigs fiasco. A first manifestation was the President's traumatic Vienna meeting with Khrushchev in June, 1961; then came the Berlin crisis of the summer. All this created an atmosphere in which President Kennedy undoubtedly felt under special pressure to show his nation's mettle in Vietnam—if the Vietnamese, unlike the people of Laos, were willing to fight.

In general, the legacy of the fifties shaped such early moves of the new Administration as the decisions to maintain a high-visibility SEATO (by sending the Secretary of State himself instead of some underling to its first meeting in 1961), to back away from diplomatic recognition of Mongolia in the summer of 1961, and most important, to expand U.S. military assistance to South Vietnam that winter on the basis of the much more tentative Eisenhower commitment. It should be added that the increased commitment to Vietnam was also fueled by a new breed of military strategists and academic social scientists (some of whom had entered the new Administration) who had developed theories of counterguerrilla warfare and were eager to see them put to the test. To some, "counterinsurgency" seemed a new panacea for coping with the world's instability.

So much for the legacy and the history. Any new Administration inherits both complicated problems and simplistic views of the world. But surely among the policy-makers of the Kennedy and Johnson Administrations there were men who would warn of the dangers of an open-ended commitment to the Vietnam quagmire?

This raises a central question, at the heart of the policy process: Where were the experts, the doubters, and the dissenters? Were they there at all, and if so, what happened to them?

The answer is complex but instructive.

In the first place, the American government was sorely *lacking in real Vietnam or Indochina expertise.* Originally treated as an adjunct of Embassy Paris, our Saigon embassy and the Vietnam Desk at State were largely staffed from 1954 onward by French-speaking Foreign Service personnel of narrowly European experience. Such diplomats were even more closely restricted than the normal embassy officer—by cast of mind as well as language —to contacts with Vietnam's French-speaking urban elites. For instance, Foreign Service linguists in Portugal are able to speak with the peasantry if they get out of Lisbon and choose to do so; not so the French speakers of Embassy Saigon.

In addition, the *shadow of the "loss of China"* distorted Vietnam reporting. Career officers in the Department, and especially those in the field, had not forgotten the fate of their World War II colleagues who wrote in frankness from China and were later pilloried by Senate committees for critical comments on the Chinese Nationalists. Candid reporting on the strengths of the Viet Cong and the weaknesses of the Diem government was inhibited by the memory. It was also inhibited by some higher officials, notably Ambassador Nolting in Saigon, who refused to sign off on such cables.

In due course, to be sure, some Vietnam talent was discovered or developed. But a recurrent and increasingly important factor in the decision-making process was *the banishment of real expertise.* Here the underlying cause was the "closed politics" of policy-making as issues become hot: the more sensitive the issue, and the higher it rises in the bureaucracy, the more completely the experts are excluded while the harassed senior generalists take over (that is, the Secretaries, Undersecretaries, and Presidential Assistants). The frantic skimming of briefing papers in the back seats of limousines is no substitute for the presence of specialists; furthermore, in times of crisis such papers are deemed "too sensitive" even for review by the specialists. Another underlying cause of this banishment, as Vietnam became more critical, was the replacement of the experts, who were generally and increasingly pessimistic, by men described as "can-do guys," loyal and energetic fixers unsoured by expertise. In early 1965, when I confided my grow-ing policy doubts to an older colleague on the NSC staff, he assured me that the smartest thing both of us could do was to "steer clear of the whole Viet-nam mess"; the gentleman in question had the misfortune to be a "can-do guy," however, and is now highly placed in Vietnam, under orders to solve the mess.

Despite the banishment of the experts, internal doubters and dissenters did indeed appear and persist. Yet as I watched the process, such men were effectively neutralized by a subtle dynamic: *the domestication of dissenters.* Such "domestication" arose out of a twofold clubbish need: on the one hand, the dissenter's desire to stay aboard; and on the other hand, the non-dissenter's conscience. Simply stated, dissent, when recognized, was made to feel at home. On the lowest possible scale of importance, I must confess my own considerable sense of dignity and acceptance (both vital) when my senior White House employer would refer to me as his "favorite dove." Far more significant was the case of the former Undersecretary of State, George Ball. Once Mr. Ball began to express doubts, he was warmly institutional-ized: he was encouraged to become the inhouse devil's advocate on Vietnam. The upshot was inevitable: the process of escalation allowed for periodic requests to Mr. Ball to speak his piece; Ball felt good, I assume (he had fought for righteousness); the others felt good (they had given a full hear-ing to the dovish option); and there was minimal unpleasantness. The club remained intact; and it is of course possible that matters would have gotten worse faster if Mr. Ball had kept silent, or left before his final departure in the fall of 1966. There was also, of course, the case of the last institutional-ized doubter, Bill Moyers. The President is said to have greeted his arrival at meetings with an affectionate, "Well, here comes Mr. Stop-the-Bombing . . ." Here again the dynamics of domesticated dissent sustained the rela-tionship for a while.

A related point—and crucial, I suppose, to government at all times—was *the "effectiveness" trap*, the trap that keeps men from speaking out, as clearly or often as they might, within the government. And it is the trap that keeps men from resigning in protest and airing their dissent outside the gov-ernment. The most important asset that a man brings to bureaucratic life is his "effectiveness," a mysterious combination of training, style, and connec-tions. The most ominous complaint that can be whispered of a bureaucrat is: "I'm afraid Charlie's beginning to lose his effectiveness." To preserve your effectiveness, you must decide where and when to fight the mainstream of policy; the opportunities range from pillow talk with your wife, to private drinks with your friends, to meetings with the Secretary of State or the President. The inclination to remain silent or to acquiesce in the presence of the great men—to live to fight another day, to give on this issue so that you can be "effective" on later issues—is overwhelming. Nor is it the tendency of youth alone; some of our most senior officials, men of wealth and fame, whose place in history is secure, have remained silent lest their connection with power be terminated. As for the disinclination to resign in protest: while not necessarily a Washington or even American specialty, it seems more true of a government in which ministers have no parliamentary back-bench to which to retreat. In the absence of such a refuge, it is easy to rationalize the decision to stay aboard. By doing so, one may be able to prevent a few bad things from happening and perhaps even make a few good things happen. To exit is to lose even those marginal chances for "effectiveness."

Another factor must be noted: as the Vietnam controversy escalated at home, there developed *a preoccupation with Vietnam public relations as opposed to Vietnam policy-making*. And here, ironically, internal doubters and dissenters were heavily employed. For such men, by virtue of their own doubts, were often deemed best able to "massage" the doubting intelligentsia. My senior East Asia colleague at the White House, a brilliant and humane doubter who had dealt with Indochina since 1954, spent three quarters of his working days on Vietnam public relations: drafting presidential responses to letters from important critics, writing conciliatory language for presidential speeches, and meeting quite interminably with delegations of outraged Quakers, clergymen, academics, and housewives. His regular callers were the late A. J. Muste and Norman Thomas; mine were members of the Women's Strike for Peace. Our orders from above: keep them off the backs of busy policy-makers (who usually happened to be nondoubters). Incidentally, my most discouraging assignment in the realm of public relations was the preparation of a White House pamphlet entitled *Why Vietnam*, in September, 1965; in a gesture toward my conscience, I fought—and lost—a battle to have the title followed by a question mark.

Through a variety of procedures, both institutional and personal, doubt, dissent, and expertise were effectively neutralized in the making of policy. But what can be said of the men "in charge"? It is patently absurd to suggest that they produced such tragedy by intention and calculation. But it is neither absurd nor difficult to discern certain forces at work that caused decent and honorable men to do great harm.

Here I would stress the paramount role of *executive fatigue*. No factor seems to me more crucial and underrated in the making of foreign policy. The physical and emotional toll of executive responsibility in State, the Pentagon, the White House, and other executive agencies is enormous; that toll is of course compounded by extended service. Many of today's Vietnam policy-makers have been on the job for from four to seven years. Complaints may be few, and physical health may remain unimpaired, though emotional health is far harder to gauge. But what is most seriously eroded in the deadening process of fatigue is freshness of thought, imagination, a sense of possibility, a sense of priorities and perspective—those rare assets of a new Administration in its first year or two of office. The tired policy-maker becomes a prisoner of his own narrowed view of the world and his own clichéd rhetoric. He becomes irritable and defensive—short on sleep, short on family ties, short on patience. Such men make bad policy and then compound it. They have neither the time nor the temperament for new ideas or preventive diplomacy.

Below the level of the fatigued executives in the making of Vietnam policy was a widespread phenomenon: *the curator mentality* in the Department of State. By this I mean the collective inertia produced by the bureaucrat's view of his job. At State, the average "desk officer" inherits from his predecessor our policy toward Country X; he regards it as his function to keep that policy intact—under glass, untampered with, and dusted—so that he may pass it on in two to four years to his successor. And such curatorial service generally merits promotion within the system. (Maintain the status quo, and you will stay out of trouble.) In some circumstances, the inertia bred by such an outlook can act as a brake against rash innovation. But on many issues, this inertia sustains the momentum of bad policy and unwise commitments—momentum that might otherwise have been resisted within the ranks. Clearly, Vietnam is such an issue.

To fatigue and inertia must be added the factor of internal confusion. Even among the "architects" of our Vietnam commitment, there has been persistent *confusion as to what type of war we were fighting* and, as a direct consequence, *confusion as to how to end that war.* (The "credibility gap" is, in part, a reflection of such internal confusion.) Was it, for instance, a civil war, in which case counterinsurgency might suffice? Or was it a war of international aggression? (This might invoke SEATO or UN commitment.) Who was the aggressor—and the "real enemy"? The Viet Cong? Hanoi? Peking? Moscow? International Communism? Or maybe "Asian Communism"? Differing enemies dictated differing strategies and tactics. And confused throughout, in like fashion, was the question of American objectives; your objectives depended on whom you were fighting and why. I shall not forget my assignment from an Assistant Secretary of State in March, 1964: to draft a speech for Secretary McNamara which would, *inter alia,* once and for all dispose of the canard that the Vietnam conflict was a civil war. "But in some ways, of course," I mused, "it *is* a civil war." "Don't play word games with me!" snapped the Assistant Secretary.

Similar confusion beset the concept of "negotiations"—anathema to much of official Washington from 1961 to 1965. Not until April, 1965, did "unconditional discussions" become respectable, via a presidential speech; even then the Secretary of State stressed privately to newsmen that nothing had changed, since "discussions" were by no means the same as "negotiations." Months later that issue was resolved. But it took even longer to obtain a fragile internal agreement that negotiations might include the Viet Cong as something other than an appendage to Hanoi's delegation. Given such confusion as to the whos and whys of our Vietnam commitment, it is not surprising, as Theodore Draper has written, that policy-makers find it so difficult to agree on how to end the war.

Of course, one force—a constant in the vortex of commitment—was that of *wishful thinking.* I partook of it myself at many times. I did so especially during Washington's struggle with Diem in the autumn of 1963 when some of us at State believed that for once, in dealing with a difficult client state, the U.S. government could use the leverage of our economic and military assistance to make good things happen, instead of being led around by the nose by men like Chiang Kai-shek and Syngman Rhee (and, in that particular instance, by Diem). If we could prove that point, I thought, and move into a new day, with or without Diem, then Vietnam was well worth the effort. Later came the wishful thinking of the air-strike planners in the late autumn of 1964; there were those who actually thought that after six weeks of air strikes, the North Vietnamese would come crawling to us to ask for peace talks. And what, someone asked in one of the meetings of the time, if they don't? The answer was that we would bomb for another four weeks, and that would do the trick. And a few weeks later came one instance of wishful thinking that was symptomatic of good men misled: in January, 1965, I encountered one of the very highest figures in the Administration at a dinner, drew him aside, and told him of my worries about the air-strike option. He told me that I really shouldn't worry; it was his conviction that before any such plans could be put into effect, a neutralist government would come to power in Saigon that would politely invite us out. And finally, there was the recurrent wishful thinking that sustained many of us through the trying months of 1965–1966 after the air strikes had begun: that surely, somehow, one way or another, we would "be in a conference in six months," and the escalatory spiral would be suspended. The basis of our hope: "It simply can't go on."

As a further influence on policy-makers I would cite the factor of *bureaucratic detachment*. By this I mean what at best might be termed the professional callousness of the surgeon (and indeed, medical lingo—the "surgical strike" for instance—seemed to crop up in the euphemisms of the times). In Washington the semantics of the military muted the reality of war for the civilian policy-makers. In quiet, air-conditioned, thick-carpeted rooms, such terms as "systematic pressure," "armed reconnaissance," "targets of opportunity," and even "body count" seemed to breed a sort of games-theory detachment. Most memorable to me was a moment in the late 1964 target planning when the question under discussion was how heavy our bombing should be, and how extensive our strafing, at some midpoint in the projected pattern of systematic pressure. An Assistant Secretary of State resolved the point in the following words: "It seems to me that our orchestration should be mainly violins, but with periodic touches of brass." Perhaps the biggest shock of my return to Cambridge, Massachusetts, was the realization that the young men, the flesh and blood I taught and saw on these university streets, were potentially some of the numbers on the charts of those faraway planners. In a curious sense, Cambridge is closer to this war than Washington.

There is an unprovable factor that relates to bureaucratic detachment: the ingredient of *cryptoracism*. I do not mean to imply any conscious contempt for Asian loss of life on the part of Washington officials. But I do mean to imply that bureaucratic detachment may well be compounded by a traditional Western sense that there are so many Asians, after all; that Asians have a fatalism about life and a disregard for its loss; that they are cruel and barbaric to their own people; and that they are very different from us (and all look alike?). And I *do* mean to imply that the upshot of such subliminal views is a subliminal question whether Asians, and particularly Asian peasants, and most particularly Asian Communists, are really people— like you and me. To put the matter another way: would we have pursued quite such policies—and quite such military tactics—if the Vietnamese were white?

It is impossible to write of Vietnam decision-making without writing about language. Throughout the conflict, words have been of paramount importance. I refer here to the impact of *rhetorical escalation* and to the *problem of oversell*. In an important sense, Vietnam has become of crucial significance to us *because we have said that it is of crucial significance*. (The issue obviously relates to the public relations preoccupation described earlier.)

The key here is domestic politics: the need to sell the American people, press, and Congress on support for an unpopular and costly war in which the objectives themselves have been in flux. To sell means to persuade, and to persuade means rhetoric. As the difficulties and costs have mounted, so has the definition of the stakes. This is not to say that rhetorical escalation is an orderly process; executive prose is the product of many writers, and some concepts—North Vietnamese infiltration, America's "national honor," Red China as the chief enemy—have entered the rhetoric only gradually and even sporadically. But there is an upward spiral nonetheless. And once you have *said* that the American Experiment itself stands or falls on the Vietnam outcome, you have thereby created a national stake far beyond any earlier stakes.

Crucial throughout the process of Vietnam decision-making was a conviction among many policy-makers: that Vietnam posed a *fundamental test of America's national will*. Time and again I was told by men reared in the tradition of Henry L. Stimson that all we needed was the will, and we would then prevail. Implicit in such a view, it seemed to me, was a curious assumption that Asians lacked will, or at least that in a contest between Asian and Anglo-Saxon wills, the non-Asians must prevail. A corollary to the persistent belief in will was a *fascination with power* and an awe in the face of the power America possessed as no nation or civilization ever before. Those who doubted our role in Vietnam were said to shrink from the burdens of power, the obligations of power, the uses of power, the responsibility of power. By implication, such men were soft-headed and effete.

Finally, no discussion of the factors and forces at work on Vietnam policy-makers can ignore the central fact of *human ego investment*. Men who have participated in a decision develop a stake in that decision. As they participate in further, related decisions, their stake increases. It might have been possible to dissuade a man of strong self-confidence at an early stage of the ladder of decision; but it is infinitely harder at later stages since a change of mind there usually involves implicit or explicit repudiation of a chain of previous decisions.

To put it bluntly: at the heart of the Vietnam calamity is a group of able, dedicated men who have been regularly and repeatedly wrong—and whose standing with their contemporaries, and more important, with history, depends, as they see it, on being proven right. These are not men who can be asked to extricate themselves from error.

The various ingredients I have cited in the making of Vietnam policy have created a variety of results, most of them fairly obvious. Here are some that seem to me most central:

Throughout the conflict, there has been *persistent and repeated miscalculation* by virtually all the actors, in high echelons and low, whether dove, hawk, or something else. To cite one simple example among many: in late 1964 and early 1965, some peace-seeking planners at State who strongly opposed the projected bombing of the North urged that, instead, American ground forces be sent to South Vietnam; this would, they said, increase our bargaining leverage against the North—our "chips"—and would give us something to negotiate about (the withdrawal of our forces) at an early peace conference. Simultaneously, the air-strike option was urged by many in the military who were dead set against American participation in "another land war in Asia"; they were joined by other civilian peace-seekers who wanted to bomb Hanoi into early negotiations. By late 1965, we had ended up with the worst of all worlds: ineffective and costly air strikes against the North, spiraling ground forces in the South, and no negotiations in sight.

Throughout the conflict as well, there has been *a steady give-in to pressures for a military solution* and only minimal and sporadic efforts at a diplomatic and political solution. In part this resulted from the confusion (earlier cited) among the civilians—confusion regarding objectives and strategy. And in part this resulted from the self-enlarging nature of military investment. Once air strikes and particularly ground forces were introduced, our investment itself had transformed the original stakes. More air power was needed to protect the ground forces; and then more ground forces to protect the ground forces. And needless to say, the military mind develops its own momentum in the absence of clear guidelines from the civilians. Once asked to save South Vietnam, rather than to "advise" it, the American military could not but press for escalation. In addition, sad to report, assorted military constituencies, once involved in Vietnam, have had a series of cases to prove: for instance, the utility not only of air power (the Air Force) but of supercarrier-based air power (the Navy). Also, Vietnam policy has suffered from one ironic byproduct of Secretary McNamara's establishment of civilian control at the Pentagon: in the face of such control, interservice rivalry has given way to a united front among the military—reflected in the new but recurrent phenomenon of JCS unanimity. In conjunction with traditional congressional allies (mostly Southern senators and representatives) such a united front would pose a formidable problem for any President.

Throughout the conflict, there have been *missed opportunities, large and small, to disengage ourselves from Vietnam on increasingly unpleasant but still acceptable terms.* Of the many moments from 1961 onward, I shall cite only one, the last and most important opportunity that was lost: in the summer of 1964 the President instructed his chief advisers to prepare for him as wide a range of Vietnam options as possible for postelection consideration and decision. He explicitly asked that all options be laid out. What happened next was, in effect, Lyndon Johnson's slow-motion Bay of Pigs. For the advisers so effectively converged on one single option—juxtaposed against two other, phony options (in effect, blowing up the world, or scuttle-and-run)—that the President was confronted with unanimity for bombing the North from all his trusted counselors. Had he been more confident in foreign affairs, had he been deeply informed on Vietnam and Southeast Asia, and had he raised some hard questions that unanimity had submerged, this President could have used the largest electoral mandate in history to de-escalate in Vietnam, in the clear expectation that at the worst a neutralist government would come to power in Saigon and politely invite us out. Today, many lives and dollars later, such an alternative has become an elusive and infinitely more expensive possibility.

In the course of these years, another result of Vietnam decision-making has been *the abuse and distortion of history*. Vietnamese, Southeast Asian, and Far Eastern history has been rewritten by our policy-makers, and their spokesmen, to conform with the alleged necessity of our presence in Vietnam. Highly dubious analogies from our experience elsewhere—the "Munich" sellout and "containment" from Europe, the Malayan insurgency and the Korean War from Asia—have been imported in order to justify our actions. And more recent events have been fitted to the Procrustean bed of Vietnam. Most notably, the change of power in Indonesia in 1965–1966 has been ascribed to our Vietnam presence; and virtually all progress in the Pacific region—the rise of regionalism, new forms of cooperation, and mounting growth rates—has been similarly explained. The Indonesian allegation is undoubtedly false (I tried to prove it, during six months of careful investigation at the White House, and had to confess failure); the regional allegation is patently unprovable in either direction (except, of course, for the clear fact that the economies of both Japan and Korea have profited enormously from our Vietnam-related procurement in these countries; but that is a costly and highly dubious form of foreign aid).

There is a final result of Vietnam policy I would cite that holds potential danger for the future of American foreign policy: *the rise of a new breed of American ideologues who see Vietnam as the ultimate test of their doctrine.* I have in mind those men in Washington who have given a new life to the missionary impulse in American foreign relations: who believe that this nation, in this era, has received a threefold endowment that can transform the world. As they see it, that endowment is composed of, first, our unsurpassed military might; second, our clear technological supremacy; and third, our allegedly invincible benevolence (our "altruism," our affluence, our lack of territorial aspirations). Together, it is argued, this threefold endowment provides us with the opportunity and the obligation to ease the nations of the earth toward modernization and stability: toward a full-fledged *Pax Americana Technocratica*. In reaching toward this goal, Vietnam is viewed as the last and crucial test. Once we have succeeded there, the road ahead is clear. In a sense, these men are our counterpart to the visionaries of Communism's radical left: they are technocracy's own Maoists. They do not govern Washington today. But their doctrine rides high.

Long before I went into government, I was told a story about Henry L. Stimson that seemed to me pertinent during the years that I watched the Vietnam tragedy unfold—and participated in that tragedy. It seems to me more pertinent than ever as we move toward the election of 1968.

In his waning years Stimson was asked by an anxious questioner, "Mr. Secretary, how on earth can we ever bring peace to the world?" Stimson is said to have answered: "You begin by bringing to Washington a small handful of able men who believe that the achievement of peace is possible.

"You work them to the bone until they no longer believe that it is possible.

"And then you throw them out—and bring in a new bunch who believe that it is possible."

Suggested Reading

In the next few years the Korean War will become the new battleground of Cold War revisionism. As early as 1951, Wilbur Hitchcock was troubled by the orthodox theories of Soviet responsibility for the attack and suggested in "North Korea Jumps the Gun," *Current History*, XX (1951) that the Soviet Union did not initiate the war at that time though it still clung to its hopes of "liberating" the South. In *The Hidden History of the Korean War** (1952), I. F. Stone, reversing his earlier orthodox views, suggested that South Korea attacked North Korea and that Rhee and MacArthur may have planned the attack to serve their own interests. Gabriel and Joyce Kolko, in *The Limits of Power** (1972), building on some of Stone's notions, stress that the war solved many problems for the Truman Administration and constituted the crisis necessary to secure congressional authorization of larger defense budgets and European rearmament. In *America, Russia and the Cold War, 1945–1971*, rev. ed. (1972), Walter LaFeber emphasized also that the war led to rearmament and the extension of alliances. Edward Friedman and Mark Selden's collection *America's Asia** (1971) includes a number of essays sharply critical of American policy in the early 1950s.

The most detailed account of the Administration's decisions to intervene in the Korean War is Glenn D. Paige's *The Korean Decision, June 24–30, 1950** (1968). The related issue of the Administration's strategy in conducting the war is treated in John Spanier's *The Truman-MacArthur Controversy and the Korean War** (1959). Among the important memoirs by policy-makers are Truman's *Memoirs**, Vol. II (1955) and Dean Acheson's *Present at The Creation* (1969), though the latter should be supplemented by Gaddis Smith's *Dean Acheson* (1972), a biography based on his still-closed private papers. Important studies of the pre–Korean War military budgets and strategies are available in Warner Schilling *et al.*, eds., *Strategy, Politics, and National Defense Budgets* (1962).

Ellen Hammer's *The Struggle for Indochina, 1940–1955* (1956) is a valuable study of French policies in the early postwar years. Jean Lacouture in *Vietnam Between Two Truces** (1966) emphasizes the indigenous and independent nature of the guerrilla movement. Douglas Pike's *Viet Cong** (1966), by a USIA employee, stresses the primacy of Hanoi in the rebellion.

Useful surveys critical of American involvement in Vietnam include Theodore Draper's *The Abuse of Power** (1966) and George Kahin and John Lewis' *The United States in Vietnam** (1965). An examination of the Second World War period is Edward Drachman's *United States Policy Toward Vietnam* (1970). Richard Barnet in *Intervention and Revolution** (1968), Gabriel Kolko in *The Roots of American Foreign Policy** (1969), Ralph Stavins *et al.* in *Washington Plans an Aggressive War** (1971), and Noam Chomsky in *At War with Asia** (1969) are sharply critical of American policy. Chomsky, using the Pentagon Papers, extended his analysis in "Vietnam—The Wolves," *New York Review of Books* (June 15, 1972), a fine summary of the radical analysis. Additional criticisms of American policy by Chomsky, Kolko, Howard Zinn *et al.* are in the Senator Gravel edition of *The Pentagon Papers** (Beacon, 1971) vol. V.

Arthur Schlesinger, Jr., in *The Bitter Heritage** (1967) contends (along with many liberals) that the entanglement in Vietnam resulted from "the politics of inadvertance." In "Vietnam and the End of the Age of the Superpowers," *Harper's* (1969), he attributes the "tragedy" partly to a "warrior class" and partly to the "catastrophic extension . . . of valid principles." Another liberal analysis, by Leslie Gelb, "Vietnam: The System Worked," was challenged in "Letters-I," both in *Foreign Policy*, I (1971), and by Schlesinger in *New York Review of Books* (October 21, 1971), which provoked a reply from Gelb in *New York Review of Books* (December 2, 1971). David Halberstam's *The Best and the Brightest* (1972) is a gracefully written study, based on many interviews, of the sources of the "tragedy" and emphasizes the role of personality and bureaucracy.

The government's explanation of American involvement was presented in a publication of the State Department, *Aggression From the North: The Record of North Vietnam's Campaign to Conquer South Vietnam.* The thinking of policy-makers can be examined in the *Department of State Bulletin* (1964–) and in *Vietnam Hearings** (1966), a collection of testimony before the Senate Foreign Relations Committee. President Kennedy's policies are also discussed in Arthur Schlesinger, Jr.'s *A Thousand Days** (1965), Theodore Sorenson's *Kennedy** (1965), and Roger Hilsman's *To Move a Nation** (1967). President Johnson's policies are defended in his *The Vantage Point** (1971), and his reversal in 1968 is explained by Townsend Hoopes in *The Limits of Intervention** (1969), an inside account by the former Under Secretary of the Air Force; and by George Christian in *The President Steps Down** (1970), by the President's former press secretary. W. W. Rostow's *The Diffusion of Power, 1957–1972* (1972), by an architect of the Vietnam policies, is a spirited defense of intervention and escalation.

* Also published in paperback edition.

Contemporary America:
Domestic Affairs

WOMEN of the WORLD UNITE
SISTERS OF THE WORLD UNITE
Sol
Undergr

The Revolt of the Urban Ghettos, 1964-1967

Joseph Boskin

As the civil rights movement declined, many of the
nation's black ghettos erupted into violence during
the mid-1960s. Though some politicians and many
citizens sought to interpret these conflagrations
as planned events, most social analysts have treated
the uprisings as spontaneous protests against ghetto
conditions. Operating within this interpretive
framework, Joseph Boskin of Boston University, the
author of the following essay, stresses that sizable
numbers of blacks were involved, that most members
of the ghetto supported the uprising, and that much of
the violence was directed at the available symbols
of oppressive white power: the police, whose actions
often sparked the conflagrations, and white-owned
businesses. Such social service institutions as libraries
and even schools, in contrast, were usually ignored.
There was, then, Boskin suggests, an underlying
pattern and purpose—perhaps even a rationality—to
the violence that many outsiders viewed as random,
aimless, and even self-defeating.

He concludes that the conflagrations stemmed not
only from white racism but also from differing
attitudes by blacks and whites toward the city and
their differing capacity to escape the urban miasma.
For many whites, long troubled by the city and able
to flee to suburbs and exurbs, the urban core was at

427

best a place to work and sometimes a place to find entertainment. For blacks, however, who were restricted to urban ghettos by prejudice and poverty, the city, once the "promised land," had become a source and symbol of despair, frustration, and resentment. For these entrapped people who constituted an underclass defined by color, the uprisings expressed racial antagonism, class hostility, anger at white affluence, and the frustration of socio-political powerlessness. Boskin, though using the terms *riot* and *revolt* interchangeably, asserts that blacks were not seeking revolution, only the benefits and rights periodically promised by democratic capitalism. Recent civil rights and poverty legislation, he contends, had increased their hopes and made their plight more painful, their resentment more fierce. Underlying these recent developments, he might have added, was the growing belief in sectors of the black community that the American system had an obligation to move toward establishing racial equality. Perhaps, in turn, this belief, rooted in one stream of American values, loosely explains what Boskin notes but cannot adequately explain—why so few policemen and firemen were killed.

Boskin concludes that the uprisings also had another social function: they effectively dramatized the plight of blacks, Puerto Ricans, and Mexican-Americans. The rapid decline of uprisings, he maintains, resulted from activist organizations within the community which have sometimes "cooled" the situation and often channeled energies into other forms of protest. By Boskin's standards, any final assessment of the uprisings, when balanced against the lives (mostly black) and property (mostly white-owned) destroyed, depends on future developments: the resulting community solidarity and racial pride among blacks, as well as the value of white America's efforts to deal with ghetto problems.

The Revolt of the Urban Ghettos: 1964–1967. From *Annals of the American Academy of Political and Social Science,* CCCLXXXII (March 1969), pp. 2–14. Reprinted by permission of the author and the publisher.

*A*lternating extremes of elation and despair have characterized black protest in the 1960's. Vacillating between the studied nonviolent and the spontaneous violent approaches to the entrapments of ghetto life, Negro behavior has mirrored the dilemma of the exploited, dark-skinned person: whether to withstand the rejection of the majority in the hope that ameliorative actions would bring rewards within the system or to lash out and destroy the hated environment, thus bringing abrupt awareness to the majority and release for oneself. Over one hundred major revolts in as many cities in the incredibly short space of three years have demonstrated that for those blacks outside of the civil rights and other allied protest movements of the mid-1950's and early 1960's, the course of protest was to be disruptive and violent. Clearly, the behavior of blacks in the large and small ghettos connoted a consensus of attitude toward their own communities, one another, and the larger society. Their actions signified the most important underclass revolt[1] in recent American history.

The Continuing Conflict of Race

The urban protest riots proved to be the pivotal black response. The riots affected the course of the civil rights movement; they coalesced the young, lower- and middle-class Negroes in the cities; they marked the growing conflict between the generations and the classes in Negro communities throughout the nation. Further, they symbolized the inability of American democracy to cope effectively with the historical-psychological problem of racism. The riots, in fact, split the nation in the 1960's and prompted the period of polarization. The clashes of the summer of 1967, however, marked an end to the spontaneous outbursts of the previous period of urban violence. A new stance was effected, as militant groups fashioned a framework of sociopolitical objectives essentially absent in the earlier period of protest.

As the incidence of riots marked the departure from the civil rights period, this new expression of protest in the 1960's can be differentiated from the more characteristic form of urban racial violence which prevailed in the past. With the exception of the Harlem riots of 1935 and 1943, which seemed more clearly to be the consequence of economic and wartime conditions, the riots of the past two centuries were initiated by Caucasians and were motivated by racist attitudes.

In these racial episodes, Negroes suffered the bulk of personal and property damage, with little restitution offered from civil authorities. Between 1900 and 1949, there were thirty-three major interracial clashes. Of these, eighteen occurred during the period of World War I and its aftermath, whereas five occurred during World War II. Obviously, the majority of these occurrences reflected situations of a critical nature.

---

[1] The terms "riot" and "revolt" are used interchangably in this study. They describe acts of assault on the status quo and its tangible legitimate authorities, in this instance, the police and business establishments.

From the end of World War II until 1964, there were several large-scale urban disturbances which reflected the underlying potential for social violence. None of these conflicts expanded into major urban conflagrations. Rather, most of the clashes were manifestations of what Allen Grimshaw has called "assaults upon the accommodative structure," that is, Negro challenges to the socioeconomic structure of a community. The most intense violence occurred when minority groups attempted to change residential patterns or when a number of Caucasians defined the situation as one in which such an attempt was being made.

The volatility of these situations was constantly reflected in the years following the termination of the war. Resentment against Negroes who moved into all-white neighborhoods resulted in more than a hundred incidents: the Airport Homes violence in Chicago in November 1945; the Fernwood Project violence, also in Chicago, August 1947; the Georgia house-bombings in May 1947; and the highly publicized violence of 1951 in Cicero, Illinois. Some of the weapons employed by white assaulters—bricks, guns, sniping, Molotov cocktails—were those which were utilized by blacks in the 1960's. Racial violence also occurred when Negroes attempted to use public recreational facilities traditionally reserved for Caucasians in northern and midwestern cities. In sum, the race riots which raged in American society from the turn of the century until the mid-1960's reflected extensions of white racism. The rebellions which began in 1964 represented a major response to that racism.

The explosion of the blacks in the urban ghettos from 1964 to 1967 was presaged three decades ago in the lines of poet Langston Hughes:

> Negroes,
> Sweet and docile,
> Meek, humble, and kind:
> Beware the day
> They change their minds! [2]

As late as the year of the first riots came the powerful words of Kenneth Clark, the eminent psychologist, in his work *Dark Ghetto:* "The poor are always alienated from normal society, and when the poor are Negro, as they increasingly are in the American cities, a double trauma exists—rejection on the basis of class and race is a danger to the stability of the society as a whole." [3] And, in 1965, a shocked but largely lethargic suburban society was admonished by Mayor Robert Wagner of New York:

> There are lions in the streets, angry lions, aggrieved lions, lions who have been caged until the cages crumbled. We had better do something about those lions, and when I speak of lions I do not mean individuals. I mean the spirit of the people. Those who have been neglected and oppressed and discriminated against and misunderstood and forgotten. [4]

---

[2] Langston Hughes, "Roland Hayes Beaten," *One-Way Ticket* (New York: Alfred A. Knopf, 1949), p. 86.

[3] Kenneth Clark, *Dark Ghetto* (New York: Harper and Row, 1964), p. 21.

[4] Quoted in Gurston D. Goldin, "Violence: The Integration of Psychiatric and Sociological Concepts," *Notre Dame Lawyer*, Vol. XL, No. 5, 1965, p. 513.

Yet, despite a year of violent urban disruptions and countless admonitions from leaders in the Caucasian and black communities, the disturbances were ascribed to a minority of disgruntled blacks. Few were prepared—even after studies had demonstrated that a sizable proportion of Negroes were actively involved in the rebellions—to accept the fact that Negroes were indeed alienated from American society and angry enough to destroy the environments immediately surrounding them which represented the outside repressive world.

That blacks vented their antagonism on the buildings, streets, and businesses within their immediate reach and avoided these same places in exclusively white areas is crucial to an understanding of their motivations. Central to the development of the *zeitgeist* of the revolts were the attitudes of the Caucasian not only regarding the Negro—which, to understate the situation, is well understood as being antagonistic—but regarding the Negro's environment, that is, the city itself. The experience of the blacks in their mass migration into the core cities was inextricably related to the attitudes of whites toward the cities. For it is not merely the fact of high-density populations living in slum conditions which brought blacks to convulsive actions but, more importantly, the approach which predominates in relation to those enclaves which we call the city. The riot was a response to the interaction of both majority and minority in their respective attitudes toward the ghetto and the city. An essential component of its origin was the majority's rejection of the city as a viable and creative environment within which to live. Thus, an ecological malaise was one of the primary causes of the violent protest.

The City: Never the Promised Land

One of the most poignant and enduring conflicts in our national life, frequently subtle, yet constantly gnawing, has been the antagonism between rural and urban America. This has been far more than a conflict between the political and power interests of divergent human locales; it has been a conflict in the American consciousness, and is implicit in the American value system. Since the early nineteenth century, millions of Americans have yielded to a seemingly fatal attraction to make the great migration from farm and village to the city. Whatever may have been the harsh imperatives which guided them, there was a persistent tendency to look back, with a degree of nostalgia and with a sense of irreparable loss, to an idyllic rural setting. In a nation in which the forces of urbanization were unrelenting, where urban living was clearly the shape of the future, there was a deep conviction, as Walter Lippmann wrote, that the city should not be acknowledged as the American ideal. This mood was not limited merely to those who had strayed from the intended ways, but was shared by those who were born in the city environs. The city has never been conceived as being the preferred place to inhabit permanently, nor has it been romanticized in the arts and mass media. It has rarely been regarded as a focus for creative living.

The burgeoning of industry, and the expansion of the middle class, with its increased financial and physical mobility, enabled the nostalgic rural life to be transplanted into suburbia and exurbia. Thus, for this group of urban dwellers, alternatives of living were possible. The actuality of choice, however, gave rise to an ambivalence in which the best and worst of feelings conjoined: the desire for the idealized rural life-style and a strong desire to partake in the activities of the city.

The movement into the cities in the past two centuries, then, was not accomplished without the creation of a basic paradox. The economic means to achieve a fuller life, though associated with the city, was not fulfilled within the city. The compromise of the suburban community seemed to provide a solution to the uncomfortable dilemma of rural versus urban life. Seemingly, one could have the best of both styles. Several difficulties, however, prevented the suburb from becoming the American middle-class nirvana. The magnitude of the march to the suburbs necessitated mass transportation to and from the central cities. The city administrators' choice, the freeway, soon became a strangulated contact with the city, bringing it not close enough, yet too far away. Yet, many who lived in suburbia were economically dependent upon the city, so that contact with the core city was never physically far removed. Ironically, too, transportation arteries made possible the invisibility of the ghettos.

The development of a sophisticated mass communications system, in the form of television, in the early 1950's reinforced the ambivalent antagonisms towards the city. Throughout the 1950's and 1960's, television portrayed the city as a violent, unhealthy, dirty, corrupt, lonely, unseemly place for people to live, develop, and grow. Survival appeared to be the main component dramatized in series after series. With the exceptions of such productions as were borrowed from earlier successful radio shows, the bulk of television performances were antiurban in substance. In such medical series as "Ben Casey," "The Young Interns," and "The Nurses," psychological maladies or life and death were constant themes. The decade of the 1920's, depicted in such series as "The Roaring Twenties" and "The Untouchables," consistently associated the city with gang violence. In such outstanding series as "Naked City," which dealt with some realistic problems of life in New York, and "East Side, West Side," a series based on the experiences of a social worker, the promise and potential of the city were lacking. Television largely reinforced the image of the city earlier perpetuated by literature and the movies. As Herbert Kosower has correctly noted: "Almost all of Hollywood's films deal with contemporary urban life on a superficial fantasy plane."[5] Even *Street Scene, On the Waterfront, The Naked City, The Pawnbroker,* and *A Thousand Clowns* tended to reflect the harsh aspects of urban life.

Resistance to city living grew from several sources. The organization of the city was felt to be antagonistic to basic American values. It bred impersonality, detachment, and unhealthy conditions. Criticism stemmed from the conception of the city as being anti-individualistic. Groups of people were herded together in living and working conditions which placed a premium on co-operative and collectivistic solutions to social problems.

[5] Herbert Kosower, King Vidor, and Joseph Boshur, "The Arts," *Psychology Today,* Vol. II, No. 3 (August 1968), p. 16.

The city was further indicted for altering the landscape of America, for denying its past and playing havoc with its future. As Anselm Strauss has accurately written, the United States managed to develop an industrial economy without developing a thoroughly urbanized citizenry. Americans, he noted, entered upon the great urbanization of the nineteenth century "protestingly, metaphorically walking backward."[6]

The image of the city was capped in the catch phrase originally ascribed to New York City: "It's a nice place to visit but I wouldn't want to live there." Living was to be done in the suburbs, away from the source of corruptions. The "Promised Land," then, was to be sought outside the city.

Aided by affluence, millions fled from the city into the landscaped suburbs—leaving the core cities to the newer migrant and immigrant groups. Negro-, Puerto Rican-, Mexican-, and Japanese-Americans, and other smaller American minority groups with dark or nonwhite skins, filled the central cities. By the 1960's, all major and most smaller cities had sizable numbers of various ethnic groups in the downtown areas, living in slum ghettos, breathing the increasingly foul urban air, and becoming increasingly alienated. They gradually developed an urban consciousness—a consciousness of the entrapped underclass.

The sense of entrapment stemmed from the inability of the ethnic groups to break out of the urban ghetto and become part of the burgeoning middle classes. Alienation grew out of the anger of betrayal, a betrayal that began when the inner city dwellers were made the inheritors of decaying cities. That they were being deserted, that the promised land in the North and West was drying up, as Langston Hughes caustically expressed it, "like a raisin in the sun," became increasingly clear in the decades of the 1950's and 1960's. Claude Brown, in his *Manchild in the Promised Land*, an affectionate portrayal of Harlem, began his sketch with this denial of the promise:

> I want to talk about the first Northern urban generation of Negroes. I want to talk about the experiences of a misplaced generation, of a misplaced people in an extremely complex, confused society. This is a story of their searching, their dreams, their sorrows, their small and futile rebellions, and their endless battle to establish their own place in America's greatest metropolis—and in America itself.
>
> The characters are sons and daughters of former Southern sharecroppers. These were the poorest people of the South, who poured into New York City during the decade following the Great Depression. These migrants were told that unlimited opportunities for prosperity existed in New York and that there was no "color problem" there. They were told that Negroes lived in houses with bathrooms, electricity, running water, and indoor toilets. To them, this was the "promised land" that Mammy had been singing about in the cotton fields for many years. . . . It seems that Cousin Willie, in his lying haste, had neglected to tell the folks down home about one of the most important aspects of the promised land: it was a slum ghetto. There was a tremendous difference in the way life was lived up North. There were too many people full of hate and bitterness crowded into a dirty, stinky, uncared-for closet-size section of a great city.
>
> Before the soreness of the cotton fields had left Mama's back, her knees

6 Anselm Strauss, *Images of the American City* (New York: Free Press, 1961), p. 123.

were getting sore from scrubbing "Goldberg's" floor. Nevertheless, she was better off; she had gone from the fire into the frying pan.

The children of these disillusioned colored pioneers inherited the total lot of their parents—the disappointments, the anger. To add to their misery, they had little hope of deliverance. For where does one run to when he's already in the promised land?[7]

One runs to one's soul brother.

The significant consequences of the great migration along the hallelujah trail was the development of an urban consciousness in the ghettos of the industrial cities. Alain Locke, in his important book in the 1920's, *The New Negro,* took cognizance of the ecological forces at work in Harlem. Proscription and prejudice, he noted, had thrown dissimilar black elements into a common area of contact and interaction. Prior to the movement into Harlem, the Negro was "a race more in name than in fact, or to be exact, more in sentiment than in experience." The central experience between these groups, he continued, was that of "a common condition rather than a life in common. In Harlem, Negro life is seizing upon its first chances for group expression and self-determination."[8] The fusing of sentiment and experience in Harlem was repeated over and again in ghettos across the country. Indeed, ghetto experience became a common denominator, its life-style and language and conditions a similarity of experiences.

Had the ghetto become a viable environment within a dynamic city existence, the level of grievance-consciousness shared by Negroes would have been muted. But the opposite occurred. Instead, the ghetto became a dead-end to those who lived in it. It became an object of loathing, a mirror of a squalid existence. Feelings of hopelessness and isolation were recurrent themes in the testimony of the slum residents, wrote the United States Commission on Civil Rights in 1967. When asked what she would do if she had sufficient income, one resident declared, "The first thing I would do myself is to move out of the neighborhood. I feel the entire neighborhood is more or less a trap."[9]

Compounding these antagonisms were, of course, the intensifying anti-urban attitudes of whites. "The people in Harlem," wrote James Baldwin in *Nobody Knows My Name,* two years before the first protest riot, "know they are living there because white people do not think they are good enough to live elsewhere. No amount of 'improvement' can sweeten this fact. . . . A ghetto can be improved in one way only: out of existence."[10] These resentments were further exacerbated by the obvious disparity between the Caucasian and black neighborhoods. Said a young man to Budd Schulberg in the Watts Happening Coffee House immediately after the riots:

The contrast: the spectacular growth of central and west L.A. vs. the stagnation of Watts. . . . You've conquered it, baby. You've got it made. Some

[7] Claude Brown, *Manchild in the Promised Land* (New York: New American Library, 1965), pp. vii–viii.

[8] Alain Locke, *The New Negro* (New York: Albert and Charles Boni, 1925), pp. 6–7.

[9] U.S., Commission on Civil Rights, *A Time to Listen . . . A Time to Act* (Washington, D.C.: U.S. Government Printing Office, 1967), p. 6.

[10] James Baldwin, *Nobody Knows My Name* (New York: Delta Books, 1962), p. 65.

nights on the roof of our rotten falling down buildings we can actually see your lights shining in the distance. So near and yet so far. We want to reach out and grab it and punch it on the nose.[11]

The mythical urban melting pot began to simmer and finally boiled over.

The protest riots which occurred in massive profusion were thus the consequence of a myriad of historical and ecological factors which fused in the 1960's. Their outstanding feature was a collective mode of attitude, behavior, and sense of power.

The Cry: Burn, Baby, Burn

The sudden burst of rage which rent Harlem in July 1964 was the third mass outburst in that community in the twentieth century. On two previous occasions, the first time during the Great Depression and the second during World War II, blacks in one of the most highly concentrated, racially, ethnic ghettos in the nation signified their protest in spontaneous rioting. Unlike the earlier uprisings which were confined to Harlem, however, the actions in 1964 proved to be the beginning of an urban black protest throughout the country. In city after city, summer after summer, blacks took vengeance by wrecking the hated symbols within their own ghetto areas.

The violent protest in Harlem was rapidly repeated in seven other urban Negro ghettos in the next two months: Bedford-Stuyvesant (Brooklyn), Rochester, Paterson, Jersey City, Elizabeth, Philadelphia, and Dixmoor (Chicago). In 1965 eruptions occurred in five cities, the major conflagrations taking place in Chicago and especially in Los Angeles. Large-scale rioting increased in intensity in the following year, when blacks took to the streets in twenty cities, including Cleveland, Chicago, Omaha, East Oakland, and San Francisco. The year 1967 began on a volatile note as disturbances occurred in the spring in the Southern cities of Nashville, Jackson, and Houston. As the heat of the summer increased, so did the temper for violence. There were mass assaults in Roxbury (Boston), Tampa, Dayton, Atlanta, Buffalo, and Cincinnati in the month of June. Within the next two months, Negroes swarmed through the ghettos of twenty-two cities in the North, Midwest, and South, with the largest riots taking place in Toledo, Grand Rapids, Plainfield (New Jersey), Milwaukee, and especially in Newark and Detroit. By 1968 the rioting had subsided, suggesting that the anger had been channeled into aggressive community programs.

The toll of the rioting over the four-year period was devastating. Between 1964 and 1967, approximately 130 civilians, mainly Negroes, and 12 civil personnel, mainly Caucasian, were killed. Approximately 4,700 Negroes and civil personnel were injured. Over 20,000 persons were arrested during the melees; property damages mounted into the hundreds of millions of dollars; many cities resembled the hollowed remnants of war-torn cities.[12]

Despite the disparity of distance, there was a consensus of attitudes and a

[11] "Watts—End or Beginning," *Los Angeles Times*, Calendar, May 15, 1966, p. 3, col. 2.

[12] The rioting which occurred following the assassination of Dr. Martin Luther King in April 1968 is not covered in this paper. These actions were not specifically related to the origins and spread of the urban revolt.

similarity of actions among those urban blacks who revolted and those who supported the violent protest.[13] Significantly, the riots were largely unplanned, unorganized, and unscheduled. Ray Lewis, a Cleveland youth worker, explained the origins of the outbreak in that city: "It wasn't that people planned our riot so consciously. But take a Negro ghetto where men sit around for years saying, "we gonna get whitey," and you build up a group knowledge of what to do."[14] Taken together, the riots were the actions of a people, poor and dispossessed and crushed in huge numbers into large slum ghettos, who rose up in wrath against a society committed to democratic ideals. Their outburst was an expression of class antagonism, resentment against racial prejudice, anger at the unreachable affluence around them, and frustration at their sociopolitical powerlessness. "What are these people riotin' about in other cities?" exclaimed Efelka Brown, of the "Sons of Watts," an organization set up to train young males in trade skills. "They want *recognition* and the only way they goin' get it is to riot. We don't want to overthrow the country—we just want what we ain't got."[15]

The sense of betrayal of expectations brought about a focus on the grievances of the past and present. The visibility of an affluent, comfortable, middle-class life, made possible by a powerful mass communications system, was in itself enough to induce dual feelings of resentment and emulation. Pronouncements by the political establishment, however, served only to increase these emotions. Thus, enticed by advertising of the leisure life, excited by legislative programs such as the Civil Rights Acts and the War on Poverty, lured by television programs depicting middle-class life, and hopeful of change in their environment, the poor anticipated an imminent improvement in their socioeconomic position. The failure of society effectively to raise the status of those trapped in the cities contributed immensely to the smoldering resentments.

The urge to retaliate, to return the hurts and injustices, played an integral part of the protest. By itself, the riot was not "a major thing," stated James Richards to the United States Commission on Civil Rights after the Hunter's Point riot in San Francisco in 1966:

> It was just an idea to strike out at something and someone. Even if you don't do anything but break a window or a chair or something like this, you feel that you are hurting a white man or something like this because the white man is the one that is doing everything to you that causes you to have all these problems on you now.[16]

Similar expressions of deep-welled anger were heard from Puerto Ricans in Spanish Harlem. Piri Thomas, author of *Down These Mean Streets*, in

---

[13] For a further analysis of the 'consensus of attitudes and behavior,' see Joseph Boskin, "Violence in the Ghettos: A Consensus of Attitudes," in *Violence in Contemporary Society*, ed. Joseph Frank, *New Mexico Quarterly*, Vol. XXXVII, No. 4 (Winter 1968), pp. 317–334.

[14] John Allan Long, "After the Midwest Riots," *Christian Science Monitor*, November 10, 1966, p. 11.

[15] "The Hard-Core Ghetto Mood," *Newsweek*, Vol. LXX, No. 8, August 21, 1967, p. 21.

[16] *A Time to Listen . . . A Time to Act*, p. 5.

testimony before the National Advisory Commission on Civil Disorders, described the origins of the explosion in that area:

> Did you ever stand on street corners and look the other way, at the world of muchos ricos and think, I ain't got a damn? Did you ever count the garbage that flowed down dirty streets, or dig in the back yards who in their glory were a garbage dumps dream? Did you ever stand on rooftops and watch night time cover the bad below? Did you ever put your hand around your throat and feel your pulse beat say, "I do belong and there's not gonna be nobody can tell me, I'm wrong?" [17]

Intense grievances vis-à-vis their inability to achieve even the basic promises of American life of work, status, and housing combined with other minor factors to make the cities highly combustible. The National Advisory Commission found in almost all the cities surveyed "the same major grievance topic among Negro communities."[18] The Commission ranked three levels of grievances among Negroes:

First Level of Intensity:
1. Police practices
2. Unemployment and underemployment
3. Inadequate housing
Second Level of Intensity:
1. Inadequate education
2. Poor recreational facilities and programs
3. Ineffectiveness of the political structure and grievance mechanisms
Third Level of Intensity:
1. Disrespectful white attitudes
2. Discriminatory administration of justice
3. Inadequacy of federal programs
4. Inadequacy of municipal services
5. Discriminatory consumer and credit practices
6. Inadequate welfare programs [19]

To strike out against the visible symbols of white society became a sign of brotherhood. In more than one instance, rock-throwing blacks placed missiles into the hands of residents of the community, saying, "You're either with us or against us, man." In the Watts riot, Mervin Dymally, a Negro assemblyman, was asked by one of the rioters to prove his loyalty by heaving an object at a police car. Dymally refused, saying, "No, man, I'm for peace." The boy quickly replied, "No, you're with the man."[20] Many residents of ghetto areas who did not participate in the actions shouted their approval to those on the streets.

That a general approval, a collective behavior, pervaded the ghettos can be borne out by analysis of the actions of blacks. The two groups singled

[17] Piri Thomas, in testimony before the National Advisory Commission on Civil Disorders, September 21, 1967.
[18] U.S., Riot Commission, *Report of the National Advisory Commission on Civil Disorders* (New York: Bantam Books, 1968), p. 143.
[19] *Ibid.*, pp. 143–144.
[20] *Report of the Governor's Commission on the Los Angeles Riot*, Vol. II (Sacramento, 1966), pp. 88–89.

out for attack were the police and Caucasian-owned businesses. Relations between the police and the minorities, particularly members of the dark-skinned ethnic groups, have always been volatile. As an institution, the police have reflected the attitudes of the majority. To have expected the police to act as a social agency oriented towards reform or conflict-amelioration is to misconstrue their primary function as they view it: namely, the maintenance of law and order. Thus, the police have practiced physical attacks and verbal harassment on minority-group members without interference. Though the public was generally unaware of the treatment accorded minority-ethnic-group members, a prejudicial attitude on its part sanctioned police actions. The language of the police vis-à-vis Negroes—"nigger," "monkey," "them," "boy"—were terms in general usage in American culture. For many years, blacks have attempted to bring to light the ample evidence of discriminatory beatings and humiliations. One such attempt in 1965, by furious blacks in the South-Central area of Los Angeles, compiled a listing of the discriminatory remarks of the then Los Angeles Chief of Police William H. Parker—which resulted in a fifteen-page report entitled "Police Chief William H. Parker Speaks"—and distributed it in the community.[21]

Yet, the police became a main focal point for attack not only because of their attitude toward and behavior with minority groups, but primarily because they came to symbolize the despised invisible white power structure. Of the institutional contacts with which ghetto-dwellers have intimate contact—schools, social welfare and employment agencies, medical facilities, business owners—the police embody the most crushing authority. For many blacks, the police had come to represent more than enforcement of law; they were viewed as members of an occupying army and as an oppressive force acting on behalf of those who rule their environment but who fled it for the greener pastures. "A policeman is an object of contempt," Ernie W. Chambers of Omaha bitterly stated in testimony given before the National Advisory Committee on Civil Disorders.[22] The system represented by the police has been oppressive, the method of rule has been heavy with force, and the phrase "maintain law and order" has been directed basically towards the control of Negroes. "Like why, man, should I get home?" angrily inquired a young black during the Watts riot. "These cops have been pushin' me 'round all my life. Kickin' my ——— and things like that. Whitey ain't no damn good, he talks 'bout law and order, it's his law and order, it ain't mine [word deleted by the Commission]."[23]

That a collective wrath directed against the police goaded the ghetto residents is evident from an analysis of the early stages of the riots. It is significant that most revolts began as a consequence of an incident in which the police were, in some manner, involved. In several instances, the initiating episode was in the line of routine activity. In the Watts situation, for instance,

[21] William H. Parker, "Police Chief William H. Parker Speaks" (Los Angeles: Community Relations Conference of Southern California, 1965).

[22] Ernie W. Chambers, in testimony before the National Advisory Commission on Civil Disorders, September 23, 1967. The Commission described Chambers as a "grass-roots leader."

[23] *Report of the Governor's Commission on the Los Angeles Riot*, Vol. I (Sacramento, 1966), p. 43.

police stopped two men who were driving in an intoxicated condition. Nevertheless, the significance of the specific event bore no relation to the more serious undercurrent of animosity which had been previously created. In other cases, verbal and physical actions by the police were instrumental in increasing a tense situation by inflaming the ghetto people, as happened in the Newark riot of 1967, which really began when the police charged out of the station house towards a large group of demonstrating and jeering Negroes.

Equally instructive is the fact that snipers, despite their numbers, hit extremely few policemen and firemen during the three years of rioting. The low number of deaths of law officials could hardly be ascribed to poor marksmanship. By 1967, especially in Detroit, the incidence of sniper fire had increased considerably; yet, only four law officers were killed, as compared to thirty-nine civilians. Indeed, of the eighty-three persons who died in seventy-five disorders analyzed by the Permanent Sub-committee on Investigations of the Senate Committee on Government Operations in 1967, approximately ten persons were public officials, primarily law officers and firemen, whereas the remainder were civilians, primarily Negroes.[24]

White businessmen were the second most exposed group singled out for attack. Resentment against the practices of exploitation, in the form of hidden and higher interest rates, shoddy goods and lower quality, higher prices and questionable service, had likewise been building for many years. The communications system in the community had long isolated such business establishments. Consequently, the majority of stores damaged and looted were those against which ill-feelings had developed. Negro stores frequently were protected by identifying signs: "Blood Brother," "Soul Brother," "Negro-owned." Not only were black businesses generally left untouched, but so, too, were libraries, schools, hospitals, clinics, and, surprisingly, governmental agencies. There were instances of bricks and sniper fire hitting these various buildings; however, no concerted attack was conducted. Many places burned down because of the refusal of the rioters to permit fire engines into the area.

Nevertheless, retail businesses suffered a much greater proportion of the damage during the violence than public institutions, industrial properties, or private residences. In Newark in 1967, 1,029 establishments listed damage to buildings or loss of inventory or both.[25] Those businesses which were hardest hit by rioters were those which were felt to be the most exploitative in their business practices: liquor, clothing, food, and furniture stores. Indeed, in at least nine of the riots studied by the President's National Advisory Commission on Civil Disorders, the damage was, in part, the result of "deliberate attacks on white-owned businesses characterized in the Negro community as unfair or disrespectful toward Negroes."[26]

The riot brought a sense of exultation in the community. It served as a release of frustration, anger, and helplessness. Even those participants who afterwards regretted their actions admitted to the joy that they had per-

[24] *Report of the National Advisory Commission on Civil Disorders*, pp. 115–116.
[25] *Ibid.*
[26] *Ibid.*

sonally experienced. In testimony before the McCone Commission, conducted after the riot in central Los Angeles, Winston Slaughter, age twenty, a junior college student, responded to the question: "Do you think the riot helped or hurt the Negro cause?"

> Well, you can say regret and then you can say there are some who are glad it happened. Now, me personally, I feel that I regret it, yes. But, deep down inside I know I was feeling some joy while it was going on, simply because I am a Negro.[27]

Others felt no regret, but a sense of pride. As the riots spread to other ghetto areas, those communities which experienced no turmoil felt the need to emulate their brothers. An exchange between three young blacks after the Detroit riot indicated the fulfilling exuberance of the historical moment:

> "Those buildings goin' up was a pretty sight," a long-legged kid said. "I sat right here and watched them go. And there wasn't nothin' them honkies could do but sweat and strain to put it out."

> "Yeah, man," a pal chimed in, "it's about time those honkies started earnin' their money in this neighborhood."

> "You know," said Long Legs, "we made big news. They called this the country's worst race riot in history."

> "Yeah," said another gangly kid, straddling the railing. "My kids goin' to study about that in school, and they'll know their old man was part of it."

> "We got the record man," exulted another youth. . . . "They can forget all about Watts and Newark and Harlem. This is where the riot to end all riots was held." [28]

Further, the protest riot assumed certain features of conventional warfare. The weapons and tactics employed were those standardized in the past thirty years: Molotov cocktails, selected targets, visible enemies, harassing tactics, sniping, mobility, and a capitulation to a more powerful military force in the form of national guardsmen or federal troops. Parallels between war as a means of confronting an enemy and the protest riot could also be observed in the attitudes of ghetto residents. Although the term "riot" was used by blacks, it became clear that they meant to describe their actions in a larger sense. "We in a war," a black youth told a reporter. "Or hasn't anybody told you that?"[29]

The attitude of immediacy was heard from many persons. "Many Negroes would rather die than live under conditions as they are now," exclaimed a male at a youth symposium. "For these people, riots present the only chance of ever achieving equality."[30] An absence of fear was notable among those who actively participated in the streets. "The cops think we are scared of them because they got guns," stated a male in testimony before the

[27] *Report of Governor's Commission on the Los Angeles Riot,* Vol. XIII (Sacramento, 1966), pp. 28–29.
[28] "The Hard-Core Ghetto Mood," p. 20.
[29] *Ibid.*
[30] California, Alameda County, Human Relations Commission, "Youth Discuss Racial Problems," *Human Relations News,* Vol. I, No. 2 (September 1967), p. 1.

McCone Commission, "but you can only die once: if I get a few of them I don't mind dying."[31] Thus, the riots were emotionally liberating. The joy in retaliating and the fun in looting reinforced the feelings of communal action. The individual acts fused with the collective act. The term "we" was used with frequency among the protesting rioters: "We put ourselves on the map." "We were whole again." During the civil violences, there was a partial suspension of conscience. "This liberation from conscience and from conscientiousness made possible for the rioters an involvement and an extreme commitment usually denied them."[32] Moreover, the pride in action played an integral role in the historical consciousness of the community. Two years after the Watts riot, black and brown high school students, selected to participate in an upward-bound educational project, were asked to complete a form which contained the question: "What kinds of civil rights activities have you participated in?" One student answered: "Watts Riot." Such statements and actions indicate a high degree of participation in the protest disturbances.

Several significant studies have pointedly noted a high degree of community participation in the violence of the small and large riots in the 1960's. The Los Angeles Riot Study (LARS), initiated immediately after the 1965 riot, collated the interviews of 2,070 persons living within the curfew area.[33] The group of Negroes interviewed was a random sample, stratified by age, sex, and income. Interviews were approximately two hours in length; the interview covered questions of attitude toward the riot, activity in the riot, general social and political attitudes, and background information. The LARS survey noted that the majority of Negroes had spent their childhood in the South but that over 60 per cent of the sample had matured in urban areas. Significantly, about the same percentage had lived in Los Angeles ten years or longer at the time of the riot. Contrary to reports about the low educational level of the rioters, the study indicated that over half of the sample had completed high school. Contrary to popular assumptions as well, the study indicated that 72 per cent of the males and 35 per cent of the females were employed in August 1965.

With regard to participation in the riot, the LARS survey demonstrated that up to 15 per cent of the Negro adult population, or about 22,000 persons, were active at some point during the rioting; that an additional 35 or 40 per cent, or 51,000 persons, were active spectators. Support for the violence was greater among the younger persons, was greater among men than women, and was as great among relatively long-time residents of South-Central Los Angeles as it was among the more recent migrants from the South. The latter point is of particular importance, inasmuch as it undercut the notion that the riot was largely the work of the unacculturated and of the recent influx of migrants from the South.

A high percentage of the community supported the violence, in attitude if not in action. Approximately 34 per cent of the sample were favorably

---

[31] *Report of Governor's Commission on the Los Angeles Riot*, Vol. I, p. 16.
[32] Frederick J. Hacker and Aljean Harmetz, "What the McCone Commission Didn't See," *Frontier*, Vol. XVII, No. 5 (March 1966), p. 13.
[33] Institute of Government and Public Affairs, University of California, Los Angeles, 1967.

disposed toward the actions, and 38 per cent of the population in the curfew area felt that the revolt would help in their quest to improve their positions. Only 20 per cent indicated that the riot hurt the community. In sum, a high proportion of persons in the riot area participated in, or gave support to, the action of fellow residents.

Studies undertaken after the LARS report substantially corroborated its conclusions. The National Advisory Commission on Civil Disorders conducted 1,200 interviews in approximately twenty cities, studied arrest records in twenty-two cities, and elicited additional reports from participants. According to the Report of the Commission, the typical rioter was an unmarried male, between the ages of fifteen and twenty-four, born in the state, and a lifelong resident of the city in which the riot occurred. His education was substantially good, having attended high school, and, economically, his position was approximately the same as his counterpart who did not actively participate in the riot. Nonetheless, he was more likely to be working in a menial or low-status job as an unskilled laborer. In special surveys taken after the Newark and Detroit revolts, interviewers noted strong feelings of racial pride, "if not racial superiority."[34] The riot experience was a definite factor in increased self- and communal pride:

> INTERVIEWER: You said you were feeling good when you followed the crowd?
> RESPONDENT: I was feeling proud, man, at the fact that I was a Negro. I felt like I was a first-class citizen. I didn't feel ashamed of my race because of what they did [Detroit, 1967].[35]

The nature of the rioting which marked the mid-1960's appeared to undergo serious change by the end of the decade. Two indications of this change were, firstly, the Detroit riot of 1967 in which a sizable proportion of Caucasians joined with the Negroes in burning and looting, thus indicating a meshing of an economic underclass; and, secondly, the development and intensity of the Black Power movement. The activists have been concerned with developing cultural, economic, and political programs within the community. These activist organizations have, on more than one occasion, prevented violent outbreaks by ghetto residents who were angered by representatives of the power structure, particularly the police. Within the broad Black Power movement, moreover, militant groups have counseled for the termination of non-violence as a technique of bringing about necessary change. "We know that we cannot change violent people by non-violence," read a mimeographed sheet handed out by the Black Student Union at the University of California, San Diego, immediately after the assassination of Dr. Martin Luther King in April 1968. "We must build mass armed self-defense groups. We must unite to get rid of the government and people that oppress and murder Black People." Thus, by the end of the decade, the energies of the younger blacks were oriented toward more specific, militant goals.

In sum, the revolts in the mid-1960's—more than the nonviolent movement of Dr. Martin Luther King and the extraordinarily powerful civil

---

[34] *Report of the National Advisory Commission on Civil Disorders*, p. 133.
[35] *Ibid*.

rights movement of the early 1960's—directed attention to the anguished plights of millions of Negroes, Puerto Ricans, and Mexican-Americans living in the urban centers of the country. The spontaneous outbursts, the collective actions, and the consensual attitudes of blacks and browns highlighted the failure of American society to recognize the problems of the racial minority groups in the cities. The events stemmed not only from the tradition of racist mentality but also from the ambiguous attitudes towards the city itself. The enormity of the failure led to one of the most intense social crises in American society in the twentieth century.

The Changing Base
of the American
Student Movement

Milton Mankoff and Richard Flacks

In the 1950s liberal intellectuals were fond of chiding
college students for their complacency and
conformity, for their quest for security and their lack
of idealism. A generation seared by the Depression
and intimidated by McCarthyism, college students in
the 1950s were politically cautious, suspicious, even
fearful. On many college campuses the major student
concerns were usually social: the important events
were often dances, homecomings, and football games
—with occasional panty raids adding dashes of sexual
titillation. The students were dubbed by their critics
"the silent generation."

The first significant break with this pattern
occurred in early 1960 when black students in the
South began sitting in at Woolworth counters to
protest segregation at the lunch counter, and white
students in the North organized picketing and
boycotts of Woolworth stores in support of this
Southern movement. In the next few years, graduate
students established a few radical journals, white and
black students cooperated to create the Southern
Non-Violent Coordinating Committee (SNCC), and
some students critical of liberalism organized Students
for a Democratic Society (SDS). These developments,

when examined later in the decade, would be interpreted as marking the rise of a New Left, but in 1963 they still seemed only ripples in American college life.

The events of 1964 changed the belief that the earlier developments were only ripples. That summer, hundreds of white students went south to organize schools and to register black voters. In the autumn, the Free Speech Movement burst forth at the University of California at Berkeley, thereby dramatizing the changes in student life and indicating that a marked shift in attitudes had taken place on the campus. FSM, with its demands for political participation of students, quickly broadened its analysis to include a critique of the multiversity and of bureaucracy in American education. Rather than being an isolated phenomenon, FSM was soon followed by a growing antiwar movement on campus, political protests at many schools, and the increasing politicization of students. By 1967, the antiwar movement was attacking ROTC, war research, and recruiting by defense contractors and the military on campus—in short, the involvement of universities and colleges in the war in Vietnam. For many, relying on the developing radical analysis, higher education was viewed as essential to corporate capitalism and was organized and controlled by the dominant class. School, according to these conceptions, was just another institution perpetuating the "system."

With the rise of the civil rights movement in the early 1960s and the eruption of FSM, social analysts began to investigate the psychological and social characteristics of participants in the "movement," as the loose amalgam of protest organizations and activities was known. While some scholars like Lewis Feuer found a conflict of generations with youth revolting against their parents, most scholars, including Richard Flacks ("The Liberated Generation: An Exploration of the Roots of Student Protest," *Journal of Social Issues*, 23 [1967]) and Kenneth Keniston (*Young Radicals: Notes on Committed Youth* [1968]), concluded that the "movement" members of the early and mid-1960s were raised in " 'humanistic,' liberal, middle-class families" where they learned to be "concerned about social problems,

The Changing Base of the American Student Movement. From *Annals of the American Academy of Political Social Science*, CCCXCV (May 1971), pp. 55–56, 59–66. Reprinted by permission of the authors.

skeptical of authority, and to take university ideals seriously." But the growth of the student movement in the *late* 1960s and the spread of student protests raised issues about whether the social base of student activism had changed.

To examine these issues, sociologists Milton Mankoff, of Queens College, and Flacks, of the University of California at Santa Barbara and a founder of SDS, studied radicals at the University of Wisconsin at Madison who were involved in protests to bar Dow Chemical recruiters from campus in late 1967. Mankoff and Flacks divided the radicals into two "generations"—veteran cadre (at least three years of political activity prior to May 1968 when the survey was made) and nonveteran cadre—and found a shift in the background and family relations of the two "generations." The newer radicals were more like nonradicals in background, and the fathers of the newer radicals were far less likely than the fathers of the older radicals to have been liberal or radical. Family socialization, according to the authors, was becoming less important in explaining the political behavior of students. The movement was now drawing from a broader social base.

Moving beyond their case study, the two sociologists contend that, by the late 1960s, there were important changes in the youth movement and new ways of expressing allegiance to that movement. A deepening cultural crisis and the segregation of youth, they argue, created "youth consciousness": "a consciousness in considerable tension with established authority." The early schism between politics of opposition (New Left) and the culture of opposition ("hippie"), they conclude, had broken down with new challenges to the legitimacy of the system, its hostility to the cultural needs and aspirations of youth, and the subsequent repression of youth. Mankoff and Flacks suggest that a "quasi-class consciousness" had developed among youth and they link it to the possibility of a truly "class conscious movement."

Their essay, a mixture of analysis, prophecy, and prescription, might be challenged at a number of points. First, some critics might contend that it is dangerously vague in defining the "movement" and dubiously lumps together political activists and the culturally alienated without fully acknowledging the continuing tensions and divisions. Second, the Mankoff-Flacks analysis, by failing to distinguish more carefully among members of the movement, cannot explain the defections of students to electoral politics in 1968 or 1972 and their belief in the legitimacy of the system. Indeed, the "movement," if defined by its radical political activity, was weakening and even contracting in the year after the American invasion of Cambodia—presumably the period in which Mankoff and Flacks were writing. Despite these criticisms, their essay provides important data on the shifts in the social base of student radicalism, a useful perspective on the student unrest of the past decade, and thoughtful suggestions about future social developments.

Ever since the rebirth of student protest in the early 1960's, social scientists have been almost exclusively interested in studying the social and psychological characteristics of movement participants. Over the past few years, as a result of intensive investigations of the activists in the Berkeley Free Speech Movement, Vietnam Summer, and other protests, a rather clearcut consensus has emerged concerning the social and characterological base of student activism.

Portrait of the Young Activist

The collective portrait of the student protesters provided by the extant literature includes the following elements: First, activists tend to come disproportionately from upper middle-class families living in large urban areas, and particularly those portions of the upper middle class that depend upon high levels of educational achievement. Both parents tend to be involved with "careers"; the fathers are very likely to be successful professionals as opposed to businessmen. Second, parents of movement-oriented youth are likely to be politically liberal. Relatively few activists come from conservative or apolitical backgrounds. Third, children raised in the Jewish tradition or without any formal religious training are significantly more likely to become activists than are Christian youth. Fourth, some studies have shown that activists have experienced relatively permissive early socialization practices, compared to non-activists. Their parents were willing to give them a considerable amount of freedom to develop their own life styles and values.

In addition to social background, research has shown that activists are more likely to be intellectually and academically oriented than non-activists; activists tend to be recruited from among those students who demonstrate relatively high academic achievement. Very few are drawn from the ranks of academic underachievers or persons of low intellectual ability. Moreover, activist students tend to specialize in the social sciences and humanities as compared to non-activists. Thus, their intellectual orientations and academic prowess are directed toward those areas of study which help to understand society and culture. Finally, activist students are particularly likely to eschew conventional instrumental attitudes toward education in favor of a conception which places education in the service of self-development rather than of material success.[1]

Thus, the consensus derived from the pioneering empirical research views the white student movement in the United States as the outcome of an interaction between students drawn from a particular family milieu and embodying particular values and aspirations with regard to the university system and the larger society. The student activist is, according to this body of research, explicitly socialized to be concerned about social problems, to be skeptical of authority, and to take university ideals seriously. Early socialization tended to de-emphasize personal, material success in favor of social consciousness, political participation, and intellectual fulfillment as central life goals.

A major implication of the early research on the socio-psychological underpinnings of student activism was that campus protest was likely to be substantially limited to those students who were raised in the "humanistic," liberal, intellectually oriented, middle-class social environments characteristic of the first waves of campus protesters. Indeed, given the notoriously apolitical upbringing of most Americans and the apparent stability of the political system, it seemed plausible, even as recently as three years ago, to expect that radicalism and protest were destined to remain the property of an important but relatively small minority of American students.

. . .

A Survey at Wisconsin

FAMILY POLITICAL-SOCIAL RELATIONS

When we consider the political and social relationships between parents and their activist offspring, it is clear that veteran students are considerably more likely to have fathers who were either very liberal or radical politically themselves than are the non-veterans. Moreover, while the differences in permissiveness are modest and not statistically significant, non-veteran students are significantly more likely to experience parental disapproval of their current life styles than are veteran cadre. These changes in parental-student relations show a definite convergence between non-veteran and veteran cadre.

[1] The profile of the radical student activist of the 1960's is drawn from several empirical studies. The most widely cited include the following: Richard Flacks, "The Liberated Generation: An Exploration of the Roots of Student Protest," *Journal of Social Issues* 23 (July, 1967), pp. 52–75; William Watts and David Whittaker, "Free Speech Advocates at Berkeley," *Journal of Applied Behavioral Science* 2 (January–March, 1966), pp. 41–62; Kenneth Keniston, *Young Radicals: Notes on Committed Youth* (New York: Harcourt Brace and World, 1968); Paul Heist, "Intellect and Commitment: The Faces of Discontent," in O. W. Knorr and W. J. Minter, eds., *Order and Freedom on the Campus: The Rights and Responsibilities of Faculties and Students* (Boulder, Colo.: Western Interstate Commission for Higher Education, 1965), pp. 61–69; David Westby and Richard G. Braungart, "Class and Politics in the Family Backgrounds of Student Political Activists," *American Sociological Review* 31 (October, 1966), pp. 690–692.

TABLE   Comparison of Veteran and Non-Veteran Cadre and Student Cross Section on Selected Variables Relevant to Student Activism

	DEMOGRAPHIC CHARACTERISTICS (IN PERCENTAGES)		
	City Size Students who lived in city of 100,000 or more for most of their lives	Educational Achievement Fathers with college degree	Religion Students raised in Jewish tradition or without any religious affiliation
Veteran Cadre (N = 137)	51.8	65.1	65.4
Non-Veteran Cadre (N = 94)	36.2	54.2	39.4

	FAMILY POLITICAL-SOCIAL RELATIONS (IN PERCENTAGES)		
	Father's Political Ideology Students who perceive their fathers as being "very liberal" or "radical"	Parental Discipline Students who claim highly permissive child-rearing during adolescence	Parental Approval Students who claim their parents approve of their present life style
Veteran Cadre (N = 137)	32.8	47.4	49.6
Non-Veteran Cadre (N = 94)	15.9	35.1	31.9

	STUDENT POLITICAL-INTELLECTUAL CULTURE (IN PERCENTAGES)			
	Academic Performance Students with B or better average as undergraduates	Major Field Students specializing in general sciences or humanities	Success Ideology Students who consider it important to succeed in career	Informal Political Education Students who read many* political periodicals
Veteran Cadre (N = 137)	58.4	81.0	58.5	32.1
Non-Veteran Cadre (N = 94)	52.1	79.8	51.1	14.9

* Nine or more.

STUDENT POLITICAL-INTELLECTUAL CULTURE

Finally, if we consider what can best be called students' political-intellectual culture, it appears that academic performance and major field of specialization remain largely the same between the different generations of cadre. An interesting finding is that the newer recruits are actually slightly less likely—though, again, statistical significance is lacking—to consider it important to succeed in a career. If the extant literature has always described the "young radicals" as eschewing conventional materialism, one would certainly have expected that the movement, as it grew, would come to encompass those who sought more conventional career patterns but nevertheless could embrace a desire for radical social change. Apparently this has not been the case. Several interpretations of this finding are possible, perhaps the most likely being that to be a radical implies a serious commitment to devote oneself primarily to political activity, activity that is increasingly felt to preclude a normal career development.

The one area in which the political-intellectual culture of the newer movement cadre differs significantly from that of the veterans, and converges with that of the general student body, is in the realm of informal political education. Students were asked to list the political periodicals that they read at least occasionally, and the data show that veteran cadre are much more likely to read many political periodicals (nine or more) than the non-veterans. This finding, we believe, is of great potential import, and its implications for the development of a radical movement in the future will be considered below.

Implications for a Radical Movement

The finding that the radical activist core at the University of Wisconsin involves an increasing proportion of students from conventional backgrounds—that, in fact, it is increasingly difficult to differentiate the activists from the student body as a whole on the basis of family origin—is, we believe, likely to be replicated at other institutions. For instance, a study by Weissberg at the University of Chicago, conducted in 1966, showed that, even at an earlier time, there were similar distinctions between movement "veterans" and those who were participating in their first demonstration—the latter being substantially similar in social background to the student body as a whole, the former fitting closely the classic portrait.[2]

It seems clear, then, that the growth of the student movement in these years is not attributable simply to its appeal to the offspring of the liberal, educated middle class, although of course these young people continue to play a major role within it. Instead, the movement has spread well beyond its initial ranks to include increasing proportions of Roman Catholics and Protestants as well as Jews and "secular" youth, increasing proportions of the offspring of businessmen, white-collar and blue-collar workers as well as the children of professionals and intellectuals, increasingly numbers of youth raised as Republicans in "middle-America" as well as Democrats in big eastern cities.[3] Moreover, together with these changes in the social base of

[2] Charlotte Weissberg, "Students Against the Rank," unpublished master's essay, Department of Sociology, University of Chicago, 1968.

[3] In the Wisconsin study, an analysis of differences between veteran and non-veteran *Declaration* signers, encompassing marginal supporters of the movement as well as radicals and militants, indicates that changes in the social base of the movement are even more pronounced among peripheral participants than among the core activists. By 1971, with the 1968 Democratic convention, the Chicago conspiracy trial, and the Cambodian invasion increasing the radicalization of campuses, it is reasonable to assume that the trends outlined in the Wisconsin data collected in the spring of 1968 have become even more pronounced. Since the mid-sixties, and particularly in the past few years, the

the movement have occurred changes in the definition of activist commitment. It is no longer possible to restrict that definition to those who belong to this or that organization or who have demonstrated some form of systematic commitment to political action. For the movement has developed a rich variety of ways in which allegiance to it can be symbolically and behaviorally expressed, among which the role of the "politico" is decreasingly central.

It is plausible to argue that students and young people generally have the capacity to develop a collective consciousness functionally akin to the "class consciousness" postulated by Marxism. Marx, for instance, argued that proletarian class consciousness would arise in part because workers had been brought together in situations of intense interaction and segregation, as a result of the emergence of the factory system. This circumstance is perhaps even more true for young people in industrializing and developed societies, who are herded together for prolonged periods under conditions of sharp segregation from other strata. In fact, in the United States, the sixties marked the first time in history that the great majority of young people, including those from 16 to 21, were thus agglomerated and segregated—in high schools, colleges and universities, in military camps, and in urban ghettoes. Thus, a critical and necessary condition for the emergence of collective consciousness has been created for young people, irrespective of their social origins.[4]

But, of course, collective consciousness with an oppositional thrust requires a bit more than simply the opportunity for intense interaction. The theory of revolutionary class consciousness roots such opposition in the fact that those who are gathered together have the common experience of exploitation, material deprivation, and permanent political powerlessness. Youth consciousness, however, has not been principally rooted in such material sources of discontent; indeed, youth movements everywhere have generally been started by students who came from economically and socially advantaged and privileged families.

Generational movements may be distinguished from class-based oppositional movements in that the roots of the former are found primarily in cultural crises while the latter are determined by crises in the political economy. To be very brief about it, students and young people are likely to move toward self-conscious rebellion when prevailing official values and symbols appear irrelevant or retrogressive in the face of the need for radical social change. The classic condition for such a cultural crisis has been the situation of rapid modernization of feudal, agrarian societies. Under these conditions, young people experience profound dislocation as they leave their tradition-oriented communities and families; they experience the universities as centers of badly needed new values and ideological perspectives; they experience the regime as unwilling or unable to accept and implement these

---

growth of black and so-called Third World student activism has also contributed to a need for a recasting of theoretical and empirical research on the student movement. This paper is limiting its concerns to the largely white student movement.

[4] For a fuller analysis of the segregation and concentration of American youth in the postwar period, compare Richard Flacks, *Youth and Social Change in American Society* (Chicago: Markham, forthcoming).

new perspectives. The cultural crisis of developing countries is thus experienced as both a national crisis of authority and a personal crisis of identity. Student movements have always represented a primary attempt to solve both the social and the personal problems at once.[5]

The depth and extent of student unrest in the United States and other advanced industrial societies in recent years lends credence to the view that these societies have now entered a period of cultural crisis—one which has no doubt been developing for several decades. This crisis has to do with the impact of general affluence and large-scale bureaucratic organization on allegiance to the "Protestant ethic," on modes of child rearing, on sexual identity, on attitudes toward work, property, competition, and self-expression. As the vitality of traditional values declines, young people, especially, experience cultural incoherence and chaos. Established institutions appear to operate at cross purposes and to lack internal consistency. For example, the media promulgate hedonism and indulgence while the schools continue to uphold self-discipline. Parents promote self-gratification and consumership while at the same time expecting self-control and achievement. Furthermore, in the quest for cultural coherence and stable meanings, young people find few established, authoritative voices or models. Under the circumstances, young people are increasingly disposed to question the official culture and established institutions, and they are increasingly likely to turn to each other in the quest for coherence and identity.[6]

It is our argument, then, that the combination of deepening cultural crisis (rooted in the impact of advanced technology on traditional capitalist values) with a rapidly expanded incorporation of young people into segregated enclaves created the ground for the emergence of widespread generational consciousness—a consciousness in considerable tension with established authority. But the primary expression of that consciousness throughout the sixties was the so-called "youth culture"—a complex of music, drugs, fashion, language, and sentiment, exhibiting considerable alienated content, but also rather explicitly hostile to organized political involvement and action.

In the sixties, students and other young people who sought to express and resolve the cultural crisis through organized political action were very much a special minority. In retrospect, it is not at all surprising that these young people should have been primarily those who were reared with a special interest in politics and a particular emphasis on social concern. The average white child in this country is not raised to seek solutions through political

[5] Compare S. N. Eisenstadt, *From Generation to Generation* (Glencoe, Ill.: Free Press, 1956); Philip Altbach, "Students and Politics," in S. M. Lipset, ed., *Student Politics* (New York: Basic Books, 1967), pp. 74–96; S. M. Lipset, "Students and Politics in Comparative Perspective," *Daedalus* 97 (Winter, 1968), pp. 97–123.

[6] A provocative interpretation of America's cultural crisis which traces its roots to the "disaccumulation" period of capitalism in the twentieth century can be found in Martin Sklar, "On the Proletarian Revolution and the End of Political-Economic Society," *Radical America* 3 (May–June, 1969), pp. 1–41. Sklar's discussion of the alienated young intelligentsia in the 1920's shows parallels with contemporary dissident cultural themes. The collapse of the counter-culture of the 1920's in the face of economic depression suggests that one must eschew any linear theory of societal change. The cultural revolt of the present period presupposes economic stability and affluence, conditions which, given the cyclical behavior of capitalist economies, should not be taken for granted.

means, or to possess any urgent sense of societal responsibility, or to feel any concrete skepticism about the claims of political authority.[7] Accordingly, conventionally reared students and youth who experienced cultural malaise turned predominantly to drugs, youth culture, religious experiment, and other apolitical models of expression.

Throughout much of the past decade, it was commonplace to believe that there was a more or less fundamental schism between the New Left and the "hippies"—that, in fact, political opposition and cultural alienation were mutually exclusive responses to social crisis. Many observers argued further that the narcotic, disaffiliative attractions of the youth culture would undoubtedly undermine impulses toward political activism; for example, a number of early civil rights activists found solace with "acid" after "burning themselves out" in Mississippi.

But the channeling of youthful malaise into "counter cultural" experiment and away from politicized challenges to authority depends first of all on the continued legitimacy of established authority in the eyes of youth and, second, on the existence of an atmosphere in which unconventional and, indeed, extra-legal cultural experiment and innovation are permitted and, in certain respects, sponsored by the authorities. Since many young people were already predisposed to question the claims of authority, and since many persons of all ages in the society were, by the early sixties, already deeply troubled about the racial crisis, the Cold War, and the effects of advanced technology, student activism in favor of basic reform was received with considerable interest and sympathy on the campus from the beginning of the decade. On the other hand, even the early New Left activists tended to accept the basic legitimacy of the political system, and focused their protest on particularly racist and militarist elites rather than on the regime or the system as a whole.

A crucial factor in the delegitimation of the political system, for student activists in particular and for students in general, was the failure of established agencies of reform—such as the labor movement, liberal Democrats, liberal intellectual and religious elements—to mobilize an effective national coalition for fundamental reform.

Had the established liberal/labor/civil rights leadership coalition been able to break early from commitment to the Cold War, and to mount an aggressive grass-roots movement of reform (as SDS advocated in its early days), had the emergent southern movement and the early student activists been recognized and fully supported by the established liberal leadership, had charismatic figures not been eliminated and others not demoralized, then the widespread radicalization of students—and particularly the "deauthorization" of the political system for them—would very likely not have occurred.

Of course, as has been widely observed, the growing mistrust of the political system, arising out of the racial crisis, was profoundly accelerated, deepened, and diffused by the Vietnam War, by the domestic consequences of the war, by the so-called "credibility gap," and by the failure in 1968 of the political parties to recognize popular antiwar feeling in any effective fashion.

[7] David Easton and Jack Dennis, "The Child's Image of Government," THE ANNALS, 361 (September, 1965), pp. 40–57.

In addition to sensing the unresponsiveness of the political system, apolitical young people in this period have come to experience the major institutions of the society as biased against their "cultural" needs, interests, and aspirations. In particular, as increasing numbers of young people have wished for the time, space, resources, and freedom to experiment with new values, life styles, and identities, they have found such opportunities limited or contradicted by the actual operation of the society. Many, especially those most attracted to political activism, hoped, for instance, that the universities would provide the resources and opportunities for the cultural quest. In this, they have been sharply frustrated—hence, the demand for "relevance," or they have experienced considerable repression—as, for instance, in the effort by the Berkeley administration to close the campus to recruitment for off-campus activism (thus precipitating the Free Speech Movement of 1964). Many young men experienced the draft and the associated system of "channeling" as a most concrete barrier to self-fulfillment. As drug use spread in the youth culture, increasing numbers of young people experienced regular harassment at the hands of the police, and the institutionalization of the youth culture was repeatedly undermined by the combined efforts of the police and by commercial exploiters, both legal and illegal. In short, virtually all efforts to sustain a counter-culture, to find time, space, resources, and freedom for experiment, have come up against the necessity of resisting efforts by the authority structure to undermine or frustrate these aspirations.

Data from the Wisconsin study demonstrate rather clearly the radicalizing effects of repression: Of the 125 students who claimed to have experienced some form of "political repression" as a consequence of their political belief or activity, 49 percent reported that they became more radical, and 41 percent reported that they became more politically active as a result. It seems plausible that many of these were among the more moderate, conventional students rather than among those who fit the classical portrait of the activist.

Our argument, then, has been this: Radical student activism has spread to include a much more diverse group of students than those depicted in the well-known research on the social-psychological characteristics of student protesters. Thus, such research, and its underlying premise that the effects of political socialization in the family are permanent and overriding, no longer serves as an adequate guide to understanding the processes of politicalization and radicalization among American youth. Instead, attention must now be focused on the hypothesis that a quasi-class consciousness has emerged among students, facilitated by the enormous concentration of young people in universities and fostered by the general cultural crisis in American society. This generational consciousness has been politicized and radicalized in part as a result of the catalytic efforts of the New Left, but primarily because political authority has been substantially delegitimated and institutional authority has been unable to accommodate the cultural aspirations of many students and young people.

These students and young people do not, however, form a class; their status is by definition transitory; their segregation, although enormously functional in the development of collective consciousness, ultimately walls them off from connection to the majority of the population and from access to decisive resources for power. There are, however, elements of the student situation which suggest the possible emergence of a more truly class-conscious movement in the Marxian sense.

One of the central findings of the classic research on the social base of the student movement was that student activists were the children of men and women who were themselves highly educated and who were involved in occupations for which advanced education was a requisite. These parents were concentrated in the social service professions—in education, medicine, law, social work—and in intellectual work. It is clear that this stratum—the "intelligentsia"—has been, on the one hand, in some degree of tension with the prevailing culture for several generations, and, on the other hand, constitutes the most rapidly growing sector of the labor force.[8]

Other data, provided by Samuel Lubell, suggest that students most likely to move Left and to be attracted to protest, even though socialized in conservative or conventional families, are those oriented to "intelligentsia"-related occupations.[9] Indeed, the Wisconsin data discussed here show that one continuing difference between new and veteran activists versus the student body as a whole is the concentration of the activists in the social sciences.

It is possible, then, that a major source of student radicalism, in addition to the situation of students and the cultural problems experienced by young people, is the emergence of a new type of alienated worker—the "educated" or "new" working class. The general point would be that advanced industrial capitalism requires the rapid growth of a mass intelligentsia, specially trained for technical and cultural innovation, for organizational problem-solving, and for modernization. These new workers experience alienation in their work partly because their training leads them to be critical of the status quo and because they find established authority recalcitrant in making needed reforms, partly because their conditions of work are "over-bureaucratized" and insufficiently autonomous, and partly because, in what they believed to be an imperialist and racist social order, they play roles of domination which are repugnant to their liberally educated sensibilities.[10]

On this analysis, university-style confrontations and related activity should begin to spread to other institutions in which the young intelligentsia are concentrated: hospitals, newspaper offices, publishing houses, government bureaus, and the like. The 1968 Wisconsin data do not indicate that non-veteran radicals were any less likely to be specializing in the social sciences and humanities than were veteran radicals. The failure, thus far, of radical political ideology to make substantial inroads among students in the physical, natural, and engineering sciences would lead one to predict that future confrontations would be limited largely to governmental service bureaucracies. This would leave the productive sector of private industry relatively immune to the radical activity by scientific-technical workers that

8 See Richard Flacks, "The Revolt of the Young Intelligentsia," *Trans-action* 7 (June, 1970), pp. 47–55.

9 Samuel Lubell, "That Generation Gap," *The Public Interest* (Fall, 1968), pp. 52–60.

10 Herbert Gintis, "The New Working Class and Revolutionary Youth," *Socialist Revolution* 1 (June, 1970), pp. 13–43.

played such a crucial role in the massive rebellion in France in May, 1968. Nevertheless, the recent development of "proletarianization" in scientific-technical fields, complete with job insecurity and coupled with a growing awareness of the relationship between capitalist production and ecological catastrophe, may serve to radicalize students in these fields who were previously indifferent or hostile toward radical ideology. Further, if "educated labor" comes to conceive of itself in working-class rather than in "professional" terms, the grounds for linkage between student radicalism and the more traditional sectors of the working class might come into existence.

In addition to becoming rooted in the class consciousness of new occupational groups, generational consciousness can be institutionalized in another way—that is, through what might be called the "territorialization" of the youth revolt. As increasing numbers of diverse young people become attracted to radical politics and counter-cultural life styles, they tend to congregate in neighborhoods near large universities and in major cities. Recently, such locations have begun to be perceived as the places in which the time, space, resources, and freedom for cultural innovation and political mobilization can be at least partially sustained. Increasingly, as such territorial consciousness has taken hold, these locales have been the arenas of severe police-youth confrontations, providing incidents which generally heighten the sense of solidarity and community within these locales. As the youth revolt moves off campus in this way, it is clear that the social base of the movement will become increasingly heterogeneous, spreading beyond the ranks of those who can attend school and attracting increasing numbers of working-class and "drop-out" young people and young adults.

The rising receptivity to violent street fighting and sabotage in the youth movement is perceived as primarily a consequence of the failure of the political system to be an effective instrument of change. But it is also a function of the increasing heterogeneity of the youth movement. The original student activist, raised in a "humanistic" family, was overwhelmingly pacifist in temperament. Indeed, those few "old" New Leftists who have joined such groups as Weathermen have gone through veritable agonies of self-transformation in order to become capable of street combat. Our observations during the recent period of severe physical confrontation in Isla Vista suggest that it is not the organized veteran radicals who are most active but the less politicized, newly radicalized youth, socialized in "mainstream" American homes, who view pacifism as unmasculine and violence as more normal.[11]

. . . .

[11] Richard Flacks and Milton Mankoff, "Revolt in Santa Barbara: Why They Burned the Bank," *The Nation* 210 (March 23, 1970), pp. 337–340.

Why Women's Liberation

Marlene Dixon

In the 1960s Americans presented new definitions and
fresh discoveries of social problems, new challenges
to authority, and new criticisms of sexual and social
roles—for blacks and whites, for men and women.
The last major movement appearing in the decade was
the women's liberation movement, from its inception
a loose coalition of shifting groups with varying,
sometimes competing, analyses and programs.

Its origins can be traced to various sources. An
intellectual influence of considerable importance was
Betty Friedan's *The Feminine Mystique* (1963), a
best-selling volume that examined the plight of the
unhappy housewife trying to find fulfillment through
her home, children, and husband. The book's
emphasis on middle-class white women, its implication
that interesting jobs were awaiting the career-minded,
its contention that shifts in advertising and the
women's magazines created the "mystique"—all this
was optimistic and comforting. It implied that the
problem was defined, that change was easy, and that
remedies only awaited small acts of will. This analysis
comfortably fit into the framework of moderate,
liberal reform.

Other women joined the movement as a result of
their own experiences in the radical and civil rights
organizations of the early and mid-1960s. Committed
to struggles for human equality and against
oppression, these young women slowly became aware

458   MARLENE DIXON

of their own exploitation and oppression. They were
"chicks," sexual objects, helpers, secretaries, never
leaders and seldom even aggressive sexual marauders.
A few might boast of "making it" with male leaders,
but even then the women were defining themselves by
the social position of their men. Becoming aware and
critical of their unequal position, women in the
movement gropingly came to define their problems.
Their bitterness, their rage that had so long been
suppressed, burst forth as they concluded that they
had much in common precisely because they were
women and that meant that they were objects of
oppression. From their discussions various analyses of
"male chauvinism" emerged, and two were especially
popular: it was produced by capitalistic society; and
it was more deeply rooted in men themselves.

For working women the evidence of discrimination
and oppression also became more visible and often
unacceptable. They realized that they were barred
from many positions and pushed into duller,
lower-paying jobs. Often, when performing the same
tasks, women found that they were receiving lower
pay. On the average, women earned about half of
what men did and the gap between their earnings
widened considerably in the 1960s. Even when
allowances are made for differences in education and
experience, the pattern of discrimination still prevails.
In 1969, for example, full-time white men workers
received an average income of about $9,650, while
white women received only $5,339. Nonwhite men
earned an average of $6,021, but nonwhite women
earned only $4,299 (Bureau of the Census, Consumer
Income, P-60, No. 75 (December 14, 1970). Put
bluntly, white women tended to earn less than black
men, and black women were the primary victims of
both racial and sexual prejudice.

In the following essay written in 1969, Marlene
Dixon, a radical sociologist now at McGill University,
sketches the background of the women's liberation
movement and offers a brief analysis of the sources
of women's oppression—"male supremacy, marriage,
and the structure of wage labor." She concludes that
radical social change is essential for substantial
improvement in the position of women, and that
socialism is a minimum requirement. Emphasizing the
commonalty of oppression for women, she contends

Why Women's Liberation. From *Ramparts* (December 1969), pp. 58–63. Copyright ©
1969 by Ramparts Magazine, Inc. Reprinted by permission of the Editors.

that "the intrinsic radicalism of the struggle for women's liberation links women with all other groups."

In a later essay, "A Critique of the Women's Movement" (*Berkeley Journal of Sociology*, XVI [1971–72]), Dixon bitterly criticizes the movement and repudiates part of her own earlier analysis. She charges that the call for "social equality" for all women was superficial and that sexism and racism are not analogous ("racism is a thousand times more virulent"). The emphasis on solidarity had obscured internal class contradictions within the movement, she concludes:

Working class women and middle class women, student women and professional women, black women and white women have more conflicting interests than could ever be overcome by their common experience based on sex discrimination. The illusions of sisterhood lasted as long as they did because Women's Liberation was a white, middle class movement. The voice of poor and working class women was heard only infrequently, while the racism of white, middle class women permitted them to reject the criticism and reservations expressed by black women.

Consciousness-raising groups, for example, she maintains, catered to the middle class and ignored the facts that many women were experiencing "poverty and . . . threats of genocide."

Her analysis of recent history and her contention that sex oppression is an inadequate basis on which to build a movement provoked a sharp response from other women who claimed that she distorted history, misunderstood the movement, and mangled Marxism (Ann Leffler and Dair Gillespie, "A Feminist Reply: We Deny the Allegations and Defy the Alligator," *Berkeley Journal of Sociology* XVI [1971–72]). Dixon's own earlier essay, some of her recent critics assert, is actually an effective rebuttal of her later revisionism.

*T*he 1960's has been a decade of liberation; women have been swept up by that ferment along with blacks, Latins, American Indians and poor whites—the whole soft underbelly of this society. As each oppressed group in turn discovered the nature of its oppression in American society, so women have discovered that they too thirst for free and fully human lives. The result has been the growth of a new women's movement, whose base encompasses poor black and poor white women on relief, working women exploited in the labor force, middle class women incarcerated in the split level dream house, college girls awakening to the fact that sexiness is not the crowning achievement in life, and movement women who have discovered that in a freedom movement they themselves are not free. In less than four years women have created a variety of organizations, from the nationally based middle class National Organization of Women (NOW) to local radical and radical feminist groups in every major city in North America. The new movement includes caucuses within nearly every New Left group and within most professional associations in the social sciences. Ranging in politics from reform to revolution, it has produced critiques of almost every segment of American society and constructed an ideology that rejects every hallowed cultural assumption about the nature and role of women.

As is typical of a young movement, much of its growth has been underground. The papers and manifestos written and circulated would surely comprise two very large volumes if published, but this literature is almost unknown outside of women's liberation. Nevertheless, where even a year ago organizing was slow and painful, with small cells of six or ten women, high turnover, and an uphill struggle against fear and resistance, in 1969 all that has changed. Groups are growing up everywhere with women eager to hear a hard line, to articulate and express their own rage and bitterness. Moving about the country, I have found an electric atmosphere of excitement and responsiveness. Everywhere there are doubts, stirrings, a desire to listen, to find out what it's all about. The extent to which groups have become politically radical is astounding. A year ago the movement stressed male chauvinism and psychological oppression; now the emphasis is on understanding the economic and social roots of women's oppression, and the analyses range from social democracy to Marxism. But the most striking change of all in the last year has been the loss of fear. Women are no longer afraid that their rebellion will threaten their very identity as women. They are not frightened by their own militancy, but liberated by it. Women's Liberation is an idea whose time has come.

The old women's movement burned itself out in the frantic decade of the 1920's. After a hundred years of struggle, women won a battle, only to lose the campaign: the vote was obtained, but the new millennium did not arrive. Women got the vote and achieved a measure of legal emancipation, but the real social and cultural barriers to full equality for women remained untouched.

For over 30 years the movement remained buried in its own ashes. Women were born and grew to maturity virtually ignorant of their own history of rebellion, aware only of a caricature of blue stockings and suffragettes. Even as increasing numbers of women were being driven into the labor force by the brutal conditions of the 1930's and by the massive drain of men into the military in the 1940's, the old ideal remained: a woman's place was in the home and behind her man. As the war ended and men returned to resume their jobs in factories and offices, women were forced back to the kitchen and nursery with a vengeance. This story has been repeated after each war and the reason is clear: women form a flexible, cheap labor pool which is essential to a capitalist system. When labor is scarce, they are forced onto the labor market. When labor is plentiful, they are forced out. Women and blacks have provided a reserve army of unemployed workers, benefiting capitalists and the stable male white working class alike. Yet the system imposes untold suffering on the victims, blacks and women, through low wages and chronic unemployment.

With the end of the war the average age at marriage declined, the average size of families went up, and the suburban migration began in earnest. The political conservatism of the '50's was echoed in a social conservatism which stressed a Victorian ideal of the woman's life: a full womb and selfless devotion to husband and children.

As the bleak decade played itself out, however, three important social developments emerged which were to make a rebirth of the women's struggle inevitable. First, women came to make up more than a third of the labor force, the number of working women being twice the prewar figure. Yet the marked increase in female employment did nothing to better the position of women, who were more occupationally disadvantaged in the 1960's than they had been 25 years earlier. Rather than moving equally into all sectors of the occupational structure, they were being forced into the low-paying service, clerical and semi-skilled categories. In 1940, women had held 45 per cent of all professional and technical positions; in 1967, they held only 37 per cent. The proportion of women in service jobs meanwhile rose from 50 to 55 per cent.

Second, the intoxicating wine of marriage and suburban life was turning sour; a generation of women woke up to find their children grown and a life (roughly 30 more productive years) of housework and bridge parties stretching out before them like a wasteland. For many younger women, the empty drudgery they saw in the suburban life was a sobering contradiction to adolescent dreams of romantic love and the fulfilling role of women as wife and mother.

Third, a growing civil rights movement was sweeping thousands of young men and women into a moral crusade—a crusade which harsh political experience was to transmute into the New Left. The American Dream was riven and tattered in Mississippi and finally napalmed in Viet-Nam. Young Americans were drawn not to Levittown, but to Berkeley, the Haight-Ashbury and the East Village. Traditional political ideologies and cultural myths, sexual mores and sex roles with them, began to disintegrate in an explosion of rebellion and protest.

The three major groups which make up the new women's movement—working women, middle class married women and students—bring very different kinds of interests and objectives to women's liberation. Working women are most concerned with the economic issues of guaranteed employment, fair wages, job discrimination and child care. Their most immediate oppression is rooted in industrial capitalism and felt directly through the vicissitudes of an exploitative labor market.

Middle class women, oppressed by the psychological mutilation and injustice of institutionalized segregation, discrimination and imposed inferiority, are most sensitive to the dehumanizing consequences of severely limited lives. Usually well educated and capable, these women are rebelling against being forced to trivialize their lives, to live vicariously through husbands and children.

Students, as unmarried middle class girls, have been most sensitized to the sexual exploitation of women. They have experienced the frustration of one-way relationships in which the girl is forced into a "wife" and companion role with none of the supposed benefits of marriage. Young women have increasingly rebelled not only against passivity and dependency in their relationships but also against the notion that they must function as sexual objects, being defined in purely sexual rather than human terms, and being forced to package and sell themselves as commodities on the sex market.

Each group represents an independent aspect of the total institutionalized oppression of women. Their differences are those of emphasis and immediate interest rather than of fundamental goals. All women suffer from economic exploitation, from psychological deprivation, and from exploitive sexuality. Within women's liberation there is a growing understanding that the common oppression of women provides the basis for uniting across class and race lines to form a powerful and radical movement.

Racism and Male Supremacy

Clearly, for the liberation of women to become a reality it is necessary to destroy the ideology of male supremacy, which asserts the biological and social inferiority of women in order to justify massive institutionalized oppression. Yet we all know that many women are as loud in their disavowal of this oppression as are the men who chant the litany of "a woman's place is in the home and behind her man." In fact, women are as trapped in their false consciousness as were the mass of blacks 20 years ago, and for much the same reason.

As blacks were defined and limited socially by their color, so women are defined and limited by their sex. While blacks, it was argued, were preordained by God or nature, or both, to be hewers of wood and drawers of water, so women are destined to bear and rear children, and to sustain their husband with obedience and compassion. The Sky-God tramples through the heavens and the Earth Mother–Goddess is always flat on her back with her legs spread, putting out for one and all.

Indeed, the phenomenon of male chauvinism can only be understood when it is perceived as a form of racism, based on stereotypes drawn from a deep belief in the biological inferiority of women. The so-called "black analogy" is no analogy at all; it is the same social process that is at work, a process which both justifies and helps perpetuate the exploitation of one group of human beings by another.

The very stereotypes that express the society's belief in the biological inferiority of women recall the images used to justify the oppression of blacks. The nature of women, like that of slaves, is depicted as dependent, incapable of reasoned thought, childlike in its simplicity and warmth, martyred in the role of mother, and mystical in the role of sexual partner. In its benevolent form, the inferior position of women results in paternalism; in its malevolent form, a domestic tyranny which can be unbelievably brutal.

It has taken over 50 years to discredit the scientific and social "proof" which once gave legitimacy to the myths of black racial inferiority. Today most people can see that the theory of the genetic inferiority of blacks is absurd. Yet few are shocked by the fact that scientists are still busy "proving" the biological inferiority of women.

In recent years, in which blacks have led the struggle for liberation, the emphasis on racism has focused only upon racism against blacks. The fact that "racism" has been practiced against many groups other than blacks has been pushed into the background. Indeed, a less forceful but more accurate term for the phenomenon would be "social Darwinism." It was the opinion of the social Darwinists that in the natural course of things the "fit" succeed (i.e., oppress) and the "unfit" (i.e., the biologically inferior) sink to the bottom. According to this view, the very fact of a group's oppression proves its inferiority and the inevitable correctness of its low position. In this way each successive immigrant group coming to America was decked out in the garments of "racial" or biological inferiority until the group was sufficiently assimilated, whereupon Anglo-Saxon venom would turn on a new group filling up the space at the bottom. Now two groups remain, neither of which has been assimilated according to the classic American pattern: the "visibles"—blacks and women. It is equally true for both: "it won't wear off."

Yet the greatest obstacle facing those who would organize women remains women's belief in their own inferiority. Just as all subject populations are controlled by their acceptance of the rightness of their own status, so women remain subject because they believe in the rightness of their own oppression. This dilemma is not a fortuitous one, for the entire society is geared to socialize women to believe in and adopt as immutable necessity their traditional and inferior role. From earliest training to the grave, women are constrained and propagandized. Spend an evening at the movies or watching television, and you will see a grotesque figure called woman presented in a hundred variations upon the themes of "children, church, kitchen" or "the chick sex-pot."

For those who believe in the "rights of mankind," the "dignity of man," consider that to make a woman a person, a human being in her own right, you would have to change her sex: imagine Stokely Carmichael "prone and silent"; imagine Mark Rudd as a Laugh-In girl; picture Rennie Davis as Miss America. Such contradictions as these show how pervasive and deep-rooted is the cultural contempt for women, how difficult it is to imagine a woman as a serious human being, or conversely, how empty and degrading is the image of woman that floods the culture.

Countless studies have shown that black acceptance of white stereotypes leads to mutilated identity, to alienation, to rage and self-hatred.

Human beings cannot bear in their own hearts the contradictions of those who hold them in contempt. The ideology of male supremacy and its effect upon women merits as serious study as has been given to the effects of prejudice upon Jews, blacks, and immigrant groups.

It is customary to shame those who would draw the parallel between women and blacks by a great show of concern and chest beating over the suffering of black people. Yet this response itself reveals a refined combination of white middle class guilt and male chauvinism, for it overlooks several essential facts. For example, the most oppressed group within the feminine population is made up of black women, many of whom take a dim view of the black male intellectual's adoption of white male attitudes of sexual superiority (an irony too cruel to require comment). Neither are those who make this pious objection to the racial parallel addressing themselves very adequately to the millions of white working class women living at the poverty level, who are not likely to be moved by this middle class guilt-ridden one-upmanship while having to deal with the boss, the factory, or the welfare worker day after day. They are already dangerously resentful of the gains made by blacks, and much of their "racist backlash" stems from the fact that they have been forgotten in the push for social change. Emphasis on the real mechanisms of oppression—on the commonality of the process—is essential lest groups such as these, which should work in alliance, become divided against one another.

White middle class males already struggling with the acknowledgment ment of their own racism do not relish an added burden of recognition: that to white guilt must soon be added "male." It is therefore understandable that they should refuse to see the harshness of the lives of most women—to honestly face the facts of massive institutionalized discrimination against women. Witness the performance to date: "Take her down off the platform and give her a good fuck," "Petty Bourgeois Revisionist Running Dogs," or in the classic words of a Berkeley male "leader," "Let them eat cock."

Among whites, women remain the most oppressed—and the most unorganized—group. Although they constitute a potential mass base for the radical movement, in terms of movement priorities they are ignored; indeed they might as well be invisible. Far from being an accident, this omission is a direct outgrowth of the solid male supremist beliefs of white radical and left-liberal men. Even now, faced with both fact and agitation, leftist men find the idea of placing any serious priority upon women so outrageous, such a degrading notion, that they respond with a virulence far out of proportion to the modest requests of movement women. This only shows that women must stop wasting their time worrying about the chauvinism of men in the movement and focus instead on their real priority: organizing women.

Marriage: Genesis of Women's Rebellion

The institution of marriage is the chief vehicle for the perpetuation of the oppression of women; it is through the role of wife that the subjugation of women is maintained. In a very real way the role of wife has been the genesis of women's rebellion throughout history.

Looking at marriage from a detached point of view one may well ask why anyone gets married, much less women. One answer lies in the economics of women's position, for women are so occupationally limited that drudgery in the home is considered to be infinitely superior to drudgery in the factory. Secondly, women themselves have no independent social status. Indeed, there is no clearer index of the social worth of a woman in this society than the fact that she has none in her own right. A woman is first defined by the man to whom she is attached, but more particularly by the man she marries, and secondly by the children she bears and rears—hence the anxiety over sexual attractiveness, the frantic scramble for boyfriends and husbands. Having obtained and married a man the race is then on to have children, in order that their attractiveness and accomplishments may add more social worth. In a woman, not having children is seen as an incapacity somewhat akin to impotence in a man.

Beneath all of the pressures of the sexual marketplace and the marital status game, however, there is a far more sinister organization of economic exploitation and psychological mutilation. The housewife role, usually defined in terms of the biological duty of a woman to reproduce and her "innate" suitability for a nurturant and companionship role, is actually crucial to industrial capitalism in an advanced state of technological development. In fact, the housewife (some 44 million women of all classes, ethnic groups and races) provides, unpaid, absolutely essential services and labor. In turn, her assumption of all household duties makes it possible for the man to spend the majority of his time at the workplace.

It is important to understand the social and economic exploitation of the married woman, since the real productivity of her labor is denied by the commonly held assumption that she is dependent on her husband, exchanging her keep for emotional and nurturant services. Margaret Benston, a radical women's liberation leader, points out:

> In sheer quantity, household labor, including child care, constitutes a huge amount of socially necessary production. Nevertheless, in a society based on commodity production, it is not usually considered even as "real work" since it is outside of trade and the marketplace. This assignment of household work as the function of a special category "women" means that this group *does* stand in a different relationship to production. . . . The material basis for the inferior status of women is to be found in just this definition of women. In a society in which money determines value, women are a group who work outside the money economy. Their work is not worth money, is therefore valueless, is therefore not even real work. And women themselves, who do this valueless work, can hardly be expected to be worth as much as men, who work for money.

Women are essential to the economy not only as free labor, but also as consumers. The American system of capitalism depends for its survival on the consumption of vast amounts of socially wasteful goods, and a prime target for the unloading of this waste is the housewife. She is the purchasing agent for the family, but beyond that she is eager to buy because her own identity depends on her accomplishments as a consumer and her ability to satisfy the wants of her husband and children. This is not, of course, to say that she has any power in the economy. Although she spends the wealth, she does not own or control it—it simply passes through her hands.

In addition to their role as housewives and consumers, increasing numbers of women are taking outside employment. These women leave the home to join an exploited labor force, only to return at night to assume the double burden of housework on top of wage work—that is, they are forced to work at two full-time jobs. No man is required or expected to take on such a burden. The result: two workers from one household in the labor force with no cutback in essential female functions—three for the price of two, quite a bargain.

Frederick Engels, now widely read in women's liberation, argues that, regardless of her status in the larger society, within the context of the family the woman's relationship to the man is one of proletariat to bourgeoisie. One consequence of this class division in the family is to weaken the capacity of men and women oppressed by the society to struggle together against it.

In all classes and groups, the institution of marriage functions to a greater or lesser degree to oppress women; the unity of women of different classes hinges upon our understanding of that common oppression. The nineteenth century women's movement refused to deal with marriage and sexuality, and chose instead to fight for the vote and elevate the feminine mystique to a political ideology. That decision retarded the movement for decades. But 1969 is not 1889. For one thing, there now exist alternatives to marriage. The most original and creative politics of the women's movement has come from a direct confrontation with the issue of marriage and sexuality. The cultural revolution—experimentation with life-styles, communal living, collective child-rearing—have all come from the rebellion against dehumanized sexual relationships, against the notion of women as sexual commodities, against the constriction and spiritual strangulation inherent in the role of wife.

Lessons have been learned from the failures of the earlier movement as well. The feminine mystique is no longer mistaken for politics, nor gaining the vote for human rights. Women are now all together at the bottom of the work world, and the basis exists for a common focus of struggle for all women in American society. It remains for the movement to understand this, to avoid the mistakes of the past, to respond creatively to the possibilities of the present.

Women's oppression, although rooted in the institution of marriage, does not stop at the kitchen or the bedroom door. Indeed, the economic exploitation of women in the workplace is the most commonly recognized aspect of the oppression of women.

Most women who enter the labor force do not work for "pin money" or "self-fulfillment." Sixty-two per cent of all women working in 1967 were doing so out of economic need (i.e., were either alone or with husbands earning less than $5,000 a year). In 1963, 36 per cent of American families had an income of less than $5,000 a year. Women from these families work because they must; they contribute 35 to 40 per cent of the family's total income when working full-time, and 15 to 20 per cent when working part-time.

Despite their need, however, women have always represented the most exploited sector of the industrial labor force. Child and female labor were introduced during the early stages of industrial capitalism, at a time when most men were gainfully employed in crafts. As industrialization developed and craft jobs were eliminated, men entered the industrial labor force, driving women and children into the lowest categories of work and pay. Indeed, the position of women and children industrial workers was so pitiful, and their wages so small, that the craft unions refused to organize them. Even when women organized themselves and engaged in militant strikes and labor agitation—from the shoemakers of Lynn, Massachusetts, to the International Ladies' Garment Workers and their great strike of 1909—male unionists continued to ignore their needs. As a result of this male supremacy in the unions, women remain essentially unorganized, despite the fact that they are becoming an ever larger part of the labor force.

The trend is clearly toward increasing numbers of women entering the work force: women represented 55 per cent of the growth of the total labor force in 1962, and the number of working women rose from 16.9 million in 1957 to 24 million in 1962. There is every indication that the number of women in the labor force will continue to grow as rapidly in the future.

Job discrimination against women exists in all sectors of work, even in occupations which are predominantly made up of women. This discrimination is reinforced in the field of education, where women are being short-changed at a time when the job market demands higher educational levels. In 1962, for example, while women constituted 53 per cent of the graduating high school class, only 42 per cent of the entering college class were women. Only one in three people who received a B.A. or M.A. in that year was a woman, and only one in ten who received a Ph.D. was a woman. These figures represent a decline in educational achievement for women since the 1930's, when women received two out of five of the B.A. and M.A. degrees given, and one out of seven of the Ph.D's. While there has been a dramatic increase in the number of people, including women, who go to college, women have not kept pace with men in terms of educational achievement. Furthermore, women have lost ground in professional employment. In 1960 only 22 per cent of the faculty and other professional staff at colleges and universities were women—down from 28 per cent in 1949, 27 per cent in 1930, 26 per cent in 1920. 1960 does beat 1919 with only 20 per cent— "you've come a long way, baby"—right back to where you started! In other professional categories: 10 per cent of all scientists were women, 7 per cent of all physicians, 3 per cent of all lawyers, and 1 per cent of all engineers.

Even when women do obtain an education, in many cases it does them little good. Women, whatever their educational level, are concentrated in the lower paying occupations. The figures in Chart A tell a story that most women know and few men will admit: most women are forced to work at clerical jobs, for which they are paid, on the average, $1,600 less per year than men doing the same work. Working class women in the service and

CHART A   Comparative Statistics for Men and Women in the Labor Force, 1960

Occupation	Percentage of Working Women in Each Occupational Category	Income of Year-Round Full-Time Workers		Numbers of Workers in Millions	
		Women	Men	Women	Men
Professional	13%	$4,358	$7,115	3	5
Managers, Officials and Proprietors	5	3,514	7,241	1	5
Clerical	31	3,586	5,247	7	3
Operatives	15	2,970	4,977	4	9
Sales	7	2,389	5,842	2	3
Service	15	2,340	4,089	3	3
Private Household	10	1,156	—	2	—

SOURCES U.S. Department of Commerce, Bureau of the Census "Current Population Reports," P-60, No. 37, and U.S. Department of Labor, Bureau of Labor Statistics, and U.S. Department of Commerce, Bureau of the Census.

operative (semi-skilled) categories, making up 30 per cent of working women, are paid $1,900 less per year on the average than are men. Of all working women, only 13 per cent are professionals (including low-pay and low-status work such as teaching, nursing and social work), and they earn $2,600 less per year than do professional men. Household workers, the lowest category of all, are predominantly women (over 2 million) and predominantly black and third world, earning for their labor barely over $1,000 per year.

Not only are women forced onto the lowest rungs of the occupational ladder, they are in the lowest income levels as well. The most constant and bitter injustice experienced by all women is the income differential. While women might passively accept low-status jobs, limited opportunities for advancement, and discrimination in the factory, office and university, they choke finally on the daily fact that the male worker next to them earns more, and usually does less. In 1965 the median wage or salary income of year-round full-time women workers was only 60 per cent that of men, a 4 per cent loss since 1955. Twenty-nine per cent of working women earned less than $3,000 a year as compared with 11 per cent of the men; 43 per cent of the women earned from $3,000 to $5,000 a year as compared with 19 per cent of the men; and 9 per cent of the women earned $7,000 or more as compared with 43 per cent of the men.

What most people do not know is that in certain respects, women suffer more than do non-white men, and that black and third world women suffer most of all.

CHART B   Median Annual Wages for Men and Women by Race, 1960

Workers	Median Annual Wage
Males, White	$5,137
Males, Non-White	$3,075
Females, White	$2,537
Females, Non-White	$1,276

SOURCE   U.S. Department of Commerce, Bureau of the Census. Also see: President's Commission on the Status of Women, 1963.

Women, regardless of race, are more disadvantaged than are men, including non-white men [Chart B]. White women earn $2,600 less than white men and $500 less than non-white men. The brunt of the inequality is carried by 2.5 million non-white women, 94 per cent of whom are black. They earn $3,800 less than white men, $1,800 less than non-white men, and $1,200 less than white women.

There is no more bitter paradox in the racism of this country than that the white man, articulating the male supremacy of the white male middle class, should provide the rationale for the oppression of black women by black men. Black women constitute the largest minority in the United States, and they are the most disadvantaged group in the labor force. The further oppression of black women will not liberate black men, for black women were never the oppressors of their men—that is a myth of the liberal white man. The oppression of black men comes from institutionalized racism and economic exploitation: from the world of the white man. Consider the following facts and figures.

The percentage of black working women has always been proportionately greater than that of white women. In 1900, 41 per cent of black women were employed, as compared to 17 per cent for white women. In 1963, the proportion of black women employed was still a fourth greater than that of whites. In 1960, 44 per cent of black married women with children under six years were in the labor force, in contrast to 29 per cent for white women. While job competition requires ever higher levels of education, the bulk of illiterate women are black. On the whole, black women—who often have the greatest need for employment—are the most discriminated against in terms of opportunity. Forced by an oppressive and racist society to carry unbelievably heavy economic and social burdens, black women stand at the bottom of that society, doubly marked by the caste signs of color and sex.

The rise of new agitation for the occupational equality of women also coincided with the re-entry of the "lost generation"—the housewives of the 1950's—into the job market. Women from middle class backgrounds, faced with an "empty nest" (children grown or in school) and a widowed or divorced rate of one-fourth to one-third of all marriages, returned to the workplace in large numbers. But once there they discovered that women, middle class or otherwise, are the last hired, the lowest paid, the least often promoted, and the first fired. Furthermore, women are more likely to suffer job discrimination on the basis of age, so the widowed and divorced suffer particularly, even though their economic need to work is often urgent. Age discrimination also means that the option of work after child-rearing is limited. Even highly qualified older women find themselves forced into low-paid, unskilled, or semi-skilled work—if they are lucky enough to find a job in the first place.

The realities of the work world for most middle class women—that they become members of the working class, like it or not—are understandably distant to many young men and women in college who have never had to work, and who tend to think of the industrial "proletariat" as a revolutionary force, to the exclusion of "bourgeois" working women. Their image of the "pampered middle class woman" is factually incorrect and politically naive. It is middle class women forced into working class life who are often the first to become conscious of the contradiction between the "American Dream" and their daily experience.

Faced with discrimination on the job—after being forced into the lower levels of the occupational structure—millions of women are inescapably presented with the fundamental contradictions in their unequal treatment and their massive exploitation. The rapid growth of women's liberation as a movement is related in part to the exploitation of working women in all occupational categories.

Male supremacy, marriage, and the structure of wage labor—each of these aspects of women's oppression has been crucial to the resurgence of the women's struggle. It must be abundantly clear that radical social change must occur before there can be significant improvement in the social position of women. Some form of socialism is a minimum requirement, considering the changes that must come in the institutions of marriage and the family alone. The intrinsic radicalism of the struggle for women's liberation necessarily links women with all other oppressed groups.

The heart of the movement, as in all freedom movements, rests in women's knowledge, whether articulated or still only an illness without a name, that they are not inferior—not chicks, nor bunnies, nor quail, nor cows, nor bitches, nor ass, nor meat. Women hear the litany of their own dehumanization each day. Yet all the same, women know that male supremacy is a lie. They know they are not animals or sexual objects or commodities. They know their lives are mutilated, because they see within themselves a promise of creativity and personal integration. Feeling the contradiction between the essentially creative and self-actualizing human being within her, and the cruel and degrading less-than-human role she is compelled to play, a woman begins to perceive the falseness of what her society has forced her to be. And once she perceives this, she knows that she must fight.

Women must learn the meaning of rage, the violence that liberates the human spirit. The rhetoric of invective is an equally essential stage, for in discovering and venting their rage against the enemy—and the enemy in everyday life is men—women also experience the justice of their own violence. They learn the first lessons in their own latent strength. Women must learn to know themselves as revolutionaries. They must become hard and strong in their determination, while retaining their humanity and tenderness.

There is a rage that impels women into a total commitment to women's liberation. That ferocity stems from a denial of mutilation; it is a cry for life, a cry for the liberation of the spirit. Roxanne Dunbar, surely one of the most impressive women in the movement, conveys the feelings of many:

> We are damaged—we women, we oppressed, we disinherited. There are very few who are not damaged, and they rule. . . . The oppressed trust those who rule more than they trust themselves, because self-contempt emerges from powerlessness. Anyway, few oppressed people believe that life could be much different. . . . We are damaged and we have the right to hate and have contempt and to kill and to scream. But for what? . . . Do we want the oppressor to admit he is wrong, to withdraw his misuse of us? He is only too happy to admit guilt—then do nothing but try to absorb and exorcise the new thought. . . . That does not make up for what I have lost, what I never had, and what all those others who are worse off than I never had. . . . Nothing will compensate for the irreparable harm it has done to my sisters. . . . How could we possibly settle for anything remotely less, even take a crumb in the meantime less, than total annihilation of a system which systematically destroys half its people. . . .

Suggested Reading

Civil rights, black history, and violence were largely neglected areas of study until the events of the 1960s attracted scholars and journalists who focused on these subjects. Arthur Waskow in *From Race Riot to Sit-In** (1966) briefly surveys events from 1919, and Anthony Lewis in *Portrait of a Decade** (1964) examines the struggle against segregation from 1954 to 1964. Valuable studies of changes in the civil rights movement include Vincent Harding's "Black Radicalism: The Road from Montgomery," in Alfred Young, ed., *Dissent: Explorations in the History of American Radicalism** (1968), and Allen J. Matusow's "From Civil Rights to Black Power: The Case of SNCC, 1960–1966," in Barton J. Bernstein and Matusow, eds., *Twentieth-Century America*,* 2nd ed. (1972).

Violence in the past is analyzed in Hugh D. Graham and Ted Gurr, eds., *Violence in America: Historical and Comparative Perspective** (1969). An important study of recent unrest is the *Report of the National Advisory Commission on Civil Disorders** (1968). Other useful studies include Robert Fogelson's *Violence as Protest* (1971) and Robert Connery, ed., Urban Riots* (1969). Jerry Cohen and William Murphy's *Burn, Baby, Burn!** (1966) and Robert Conot's *Rivers of Blood, Years of Darkness** (1968) are journalistic accounts of the Watts riot.

Kenneth Keniston has analyzed youth in three important volumes: *The Uncommitted** (1965), a study of alienated students; *Young Radicals** (1968), an examination of participants in "Vietnam Summer"; and *Youth and Dissent* (1971), a collection of previously published essays. Defenses of the counterculture include Philip Slater's *The Pursuit of Loneliness** (1970), Theodore Roszak's *The Making of the Counter Culture** (1969), Abbie Hoffman's *Woodstock Nation** (1969), and Charles Reich's *The Greening of America** (1970). Volumes critical of the youth culture include Lewis Feuer's *The Conflict of Genera-

*tions** (1969), Raymond Aron's *The Elusive Revolution: Anatomy of a Student Revolt* (1970), and John Aldridge's *In the Country of the Young* (1970).

The history of the New Left is examined in the introduction to Massimo Teodori, ed., *The New Left: A Documentary History** (1969), the best of the anthologies on the subject. Other useful collections include Mitchell Cohen and Dennis Hale, eds., *The New Student Left** (1967); Priscilla Long, ed., *The New Left** (1969), and Paul Jacobs and Saul Landau, eds., *The New Radicals** (1966). A useful collection of critiques is Irving Howe, ed., *Beyond the New Left** (1970), drawn from *Dissent* magazine, an independent socialist, anti-Stalinist journal founded in the early 1950s.

Historians, with a few notable exceptions, long neglected the subject of women in American (and western) society, and the historical literature on the postwar years is quite scanty. The rise of women's liberation has recently inspired scholars to examine women's history, and a notable recent volume is William Chafe's *The American Woman: Her Changing Social, Economic, and Political Roles, 1920–1970* (1972), a sympathetic survey that stresses the economic role and the impact of the Depression and war, and includes a section on "The Revival of Feminism." The postwar revival, he contends, can be explained partly by the improving conditions of women: they had already departed in great numbers from their more restricted spheres of activity and belief.

The best introduction to the women's liberation movement is still through its literature. Cellestine Ware's *Woman Power** (1970) is an effective guide to the movement and its various groups up to the period 1969–70. Two valuable collections from the movement are Robin Morgan, ed., *Sisterhood is Powerful** (1970) and Leslie B. Tanner, ed., *Voices From Women's Liberation** (1970). Three books published in 1970 and 1971 were especially influential: Kate Millet's *Sexual Politics** (1970), which focused on creative literature and employed blunt categories; Germaine Greer's *The Female Eunuch** (1971), a powerful, intentionally impressionistic, analysis of modern woman; and Shulamith Firestone's *Dialectic of Sex** (1970), which views a biologically derived class system as the source of all forms of oppression (including race) and offers a new radical analysis while rejecting the then-current leftist analysis as insufficiently radical. There are numerous small journals from the movement as well as a magazine with wide-circulation, *Ms.* (1972–   ), which manages to be quite eclectic.

Two criticisms of many of the assumptions of the movement are Norman Mailer's *The Prisoner of Sex** (1971) and Midge Decter's *The New Chastity and Other Arguments Against Women's Liberation* (1972)—with the latter provoking a harsh review by Adrienne Rich, "The Anti-Feminist Woman," *New York Review of Books*, XIX (November 30, 1972).

* Also published in paperback edition.

A 3
B 4
C 5
D 6
E 7
F 8
G 9
H 0
I 1
J